IMAGE SEGMENTATION

Edited by **Pei-Gee Peter Ho**

Image Segmentation
Edited by Pei-Gee Peter Ho

Published by InTech
Janeza Trdine 9, 51000 Rijeka, Croatia

Publishing Process Manager Ivana Lorkovic

Technical Editor Teodora Smiljanic

Cover Designer InTech Design Team

Additional hard copies can be obtained from orders@intechopen.com

Image Segmentation, Edited by Pei-Gee Peter Ho
p. cm.
ISBN 978-953-307-228-9

For EU product safety concerns:
IN TECH d.o.o., Prolaz Marije Krucifikse Kozulić 3, 51000 Rijeka, Croatia,
info@intechopen.com or visit our website at intechopen.com.

Meet the editor

Dr. Pei-Gee Peter Ho was born in Hsinchu, Taiwan. He received his BSEE from National Cheng Kung University, Tainan, Taiwan in 1976. After two years military service, he worked two years in On-Line Power System Dispatch group of Taiwan Power Company. In 1981, he was awarded a research assistantship and obtained the MSEE degree from UMass Dartmouth. During the following 20 plus years he has worked in various electrical and computer engineering companies such as Wang Lab., Brooktrout Technology, Compugraphics, SystemSoft, Ennovate Networks, Quarry Technology, Lockheed Martin Inc. and was primarily associated with embedded computing systems, networking, and device driver developments. He received his Ph.D. degree in Electrical and Computer Engineering from UMass Dartmouth in January 2008. He is now working in the Digital Signal Processing Algorithm and Software Design group in Range and Engineering department of NUWC at Newport, Rhode Island USA.

Contents

Preface

It was estimated that 80% of the information received by human being is visual. Image processing is evolving fast and continually. During the past 10 years, there has been a significant increase in knowledge-based image analysis, image recognition as well as image segmentation. To study a specific object in an image, its boundary can be highlighted by an image segmentation procedure.

The objective of the image segmentation is to simplify the representation of pictures into meaningful information by partitioning into image regions. Image segmentation is a technique to locate certain objects or boundaries within an image. There are many algorithms and techniques have been developed to solve image segmentation problems, though, none of the method is a general solution. Among the best, these are neural networks segmentation, one-dimensional signal segmentation, multi-scale segmentation, model based segmentation, graphic partitioning, region growing and K-mean clustering segmentation methods.

This book brings together many different aspects of the current research on several fields associated to digital image segmentation. Four main parts have been defined and allowed gathering the 27 chapters around the following topics: Survey of Image Segmentation Algorithms, Image Segmentation methods, Image Segmentation Applications and Hardware Implementation of Image Segmentation.

The book starts with a first set of chapters which addresses most recent general approaches in the image segmentation fields. One can find discussion about various new trends on image segmentation techniques. The evolutionary image segmentation algorithms and methods are presented next. Recently the most used approach in segmentation of medical images is the level set which is based on optimization mathematics. A segmentation of the image plane is computed by locally minimizing an appropriate energy functional $E(C)$ by evolving the contour C of the region to be segmented starting from an initial contour. In general, this method may use either an explicit (parametric) or implicit representation of the contours. The active contour (also called snakes) image segmentation scheme is very popular in medical surgery these days. The basic idea of the dual snakes is to reject local minima by using two contours: one which contracts from outside the target and one which expands from inside. Such proposal makes possible to reduce the sensitivity to initialization through the comparison between the two contours energy and positions. The newly developed combined Autoregressive time series imaging modeling with either region growing or Support Vector Machine as classifiers are detailed in one of the book chapter. In order to solve the image segmentation thresholding problem , a new way of using an optimization algorithm based on learning automata for multilevel thresholding is proposed in one chapter of this book. The pixon concept based on a set of disjoint regions with constant shapes and variable sizes was introduced in 1993 to decreases the computational time on image segmentation. A few innovative methods to improve the efficiency are also included. Nevertheless, the image segmentation applications that demand constrained response times, the specific hardware implementation is required. In this book, the chapter title "Hardware Implementation of a Real-Time Image Segmentation Circuit based on Fuzzy Logic for Edge Detection Application" provides the hardware approach for image segmentation.

Last, but not the least, we would like to thank all contributors to this book for their research, Intech publisher CEO Dr. Aleksandar Lazinica and Ms. Ivana Lorkovic for their publishing effort. I am sure that you will enjoy reading this book and get many helpful ideas and overviews on your own study.

Pei-Gee Peter Ho, Ph.D.
DSP Algorithm development group
Naval Undersea Warfare Center at Newport RI,
USA

Part 1

Survey of Image Segmentation Algorithms

1

A Survey of Image Segmentation by the Classical Method and Resonance Algorithm

Fengzhi Dai[1], Masanori Sugisaka[2] and Baolong Zhang[3]
[1]*Tianjin University of Science and Technology*
[2]*Nippon Bunri University, ALife Robotics Co., Ltd*
[3]*Tianjin University of Science and Technology, GianTOPtics Technology Co., Ltd*
[1,3]*China*
[2]*Japan*

1. Introduction

Computer vision and recognition plays more important role on intelligent control (Chen & Hwang, 1998). For an intelligent system, it is necessary to acquire the information of the external world by sensors, to recognize its position and the surrounding situation. Camera is one of the most important sensors for computer vision. That is to say, the intelligent system endeavours to find out what is in an image taken by the camera: traffic signs, obstacles or guidelines.

For image analysis, image segmentation is needed, which means to partition an image into several regions that have homogeneous texture feature. This process is usually realized by the region-based, boundary- based or edge-based method (Castleman, 1998). And from the viewpoint of clustering, it is divided into supervised and unsupervised texture segmentation.

Since before segmentation, the intelligent control system seldom knows the feature of the image, e.g. which type and how many types of textures exist in an image, thus the unsupervised segmentation algorithm is always needed, although it is more difficult than the supervised method (Dai, Zhao & Zhao, 2007).

In this chapter, the classical method (Agui & Nagao, 2000) and the resonance theory (Heins & Tauritz, 1995; He & Chen, 2000) are proposed respectively for image segmentation. The classical method is simple but practicable, which will be introduced in section 2. But for some situations, it is not suitable for complex image segmentation (e.g., the gradient variations of intensity in an image).

We know that human vision can recognize the same texture that has gradient variations of intensity. And many image segmentation methods are proposed based on the change of intensity (Nakamura & Ogasawara, 1999; Deguchi & Takahashi, 1999). But they always fail to handle the wide-ranged gradations in intensity (Jähne, 1995). It is usually difficult to give a suitable threshold for pixel-based image processing methods to deal with this gradation.

Resonance algorithm is an unsupervised method to generate the region (or feature space) from similar pixels (or feature vectors) in an image. It tolerates gradual changes of texture to some extent for image segmentation. The purpose of section 3 is to propose the resonance-theory-based method for image segmentation, which means that the same texture in an image will be resonated into one region by seed pixels. This method assumes that the

differences of feature between adjacent pixels of the same texture must be within a tolerable range. Thus the selection of feature distance to segment them is important.
In this chapter, Section 2 introduces the classical method. Section 3 gives the resonance theory and the algorithm for image segmentation. Section 4 is the conclusion.

2. The classical method

2.1 The principle

This section introduces the classical method for image segmentation, and the example is to recognize the simple characters (the digit and letter). Recognizing the whole word needs to segment it into the characters 0 to 9, a to z, or A to Z firstly. The principle (Agui, Nakajima & Kimi, 1990; Tanaka, 1989) and a result of segmentation is shown in Fig. 1. This section is simple but is the original meaning of image segmentation, which is useful when the reader wants to understand image segmentation clearly.

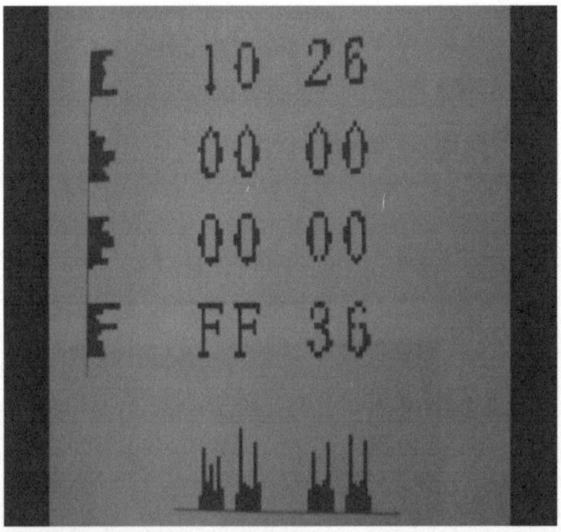

Fig. 1. The principle of segmentation

Fig. 1. gives the example of the digit segmentation. In the image there are some digits but as the image style, not the character. If the computer or intelligent system wants to recognize these digits autonomously, first image segmentation is needed to search and locate each digit, and then recognize them.
The method is that it calculates the values of the pixels by searching the X-axis and Y-axis to find the neighboring distribution of the digits (looking for the break of the character).
For each line (row and column) where there is a character, it appears that the values of pixels is not 0. If there are blanks, it means that they are the space between one character and another. Thus it gives the position of the break of the characters. In Fig. 1, there are four rows and four columns of digits.

2.2 Image segmentation

If there are several targets in an image, image segmentation is necessary: locating and isolating the targets in an image and then identifying them. Once isolated, the targets can be measured and classified. The general image segmentation algorithm (Agui, Nakajima & Kimi, 1990) is shown in Fig. 2a. And Fig. 2b is the result of segmentation for the word 'R05'. Table 1 gives the segmented result. The steps for character segmentation are divided into 2 steps:

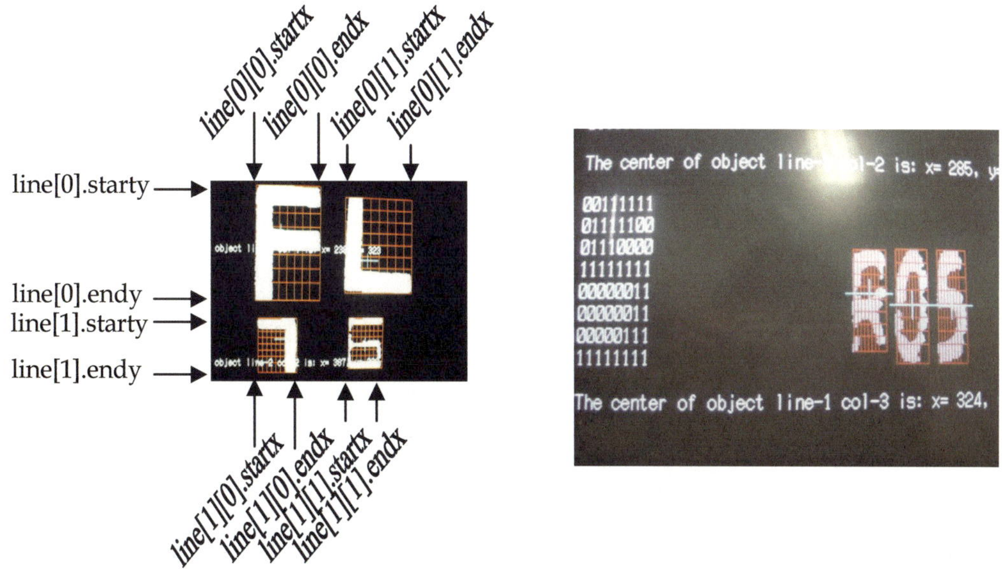

(a) Principle (b) Segmentation result

Fig. 2. The classical image segmentation algorithm

<table>
<tr><td colspan="2">Result for Fig. 2a</td><td colspan="3">Result for Fig. 2b</td></tr>
<tr><td colspan="2">There are two rows.
row-0 has two targets,
row-1 has two targets.</td><td colspan="3">There is One row.
row-0 has three target.</td></tr>
<tr><td colspan="2">(top, bottom, left, right) is</td><td colspan="3">(top, bottom, left, right) is</td></tr>
<tr><td>row-0, col-0: F
(line[0].starty,
line[0].endy,
line[0][0].startx,
line[0][0].endx)</td><td>row-0, col-1: L
(line[0].starty,
line[0].endy,
line[0][1].startx,
line[0][1].endx)</td><td rowspan="2">row-0, col-0: R
(line[0].starty,
line[0].endy,
line[0][0].startx,
line[0][0].endx)</td><td rowspan="2">row-0, col-1: 0
(line[0].starty,
line[0].endy,
line[0][1].startx,
line[0][1].endx)</td><td rowspan="2">row-0, col-2: 5
(line[0].starty,
line[0].endy,
line[0][2].startx,
line[0][2].endx)</td></tr>
<tr><td>row-1, col-0: 7
(line[1].starty,
line[1].endy,
line[1][0].startx,
line[1][0].endx)</td><td>row-1, col-1: 6
(line[1].starty,
line[1].endy,
line[1][1].startx,
line[1][1].endx)</td></tr>
</table>

Table 1. Segmented result of Fig. 2a, b

1. Search the screen from top to bottom line-by-line horizontally to find the start and the end line that contains how many rows of characters: the variables are line[0].starty, line[0].endy, line[1].starty and line[1].endy in Fig. 2a, which means that the image contains two rows of characters. The horizontal location of the first row of characters is from line[0].starty to line[0].endy, the second is from line[1].starty to line[1].endy, respectively.
2. For each row of characters, search the image from left to right vertically to locate and calculate how many characters in each row. For example, in Fig. 2a for characters within

line[0].starty and line[0].endy, there are two letters in this row. They are the letter 'F' from line[0][0].startx to line[0][0].endx, and 'L' from line[0][1].startx to line[0][1].endx. Thus each character (letter or digit) can be segmented.

2.3 An experimental result

Fig. 3 shows an experiment (including the image sampling, processing, segmentation and recognition), which is to segment the image and then recognize each character one by one.

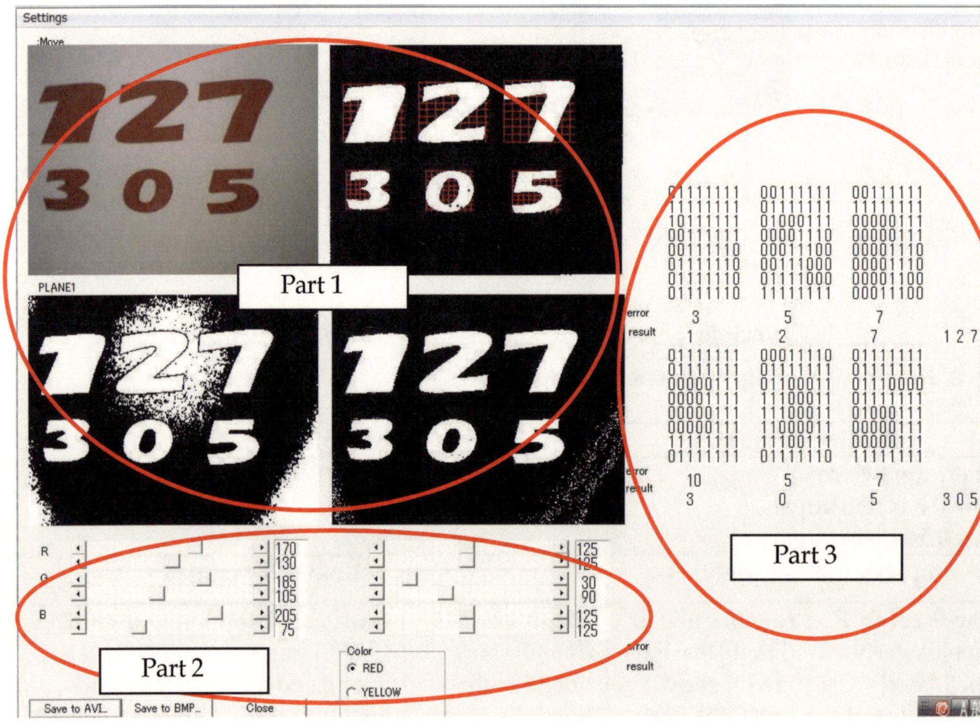

Fig. 3. An example of the classical image segmentation

In Fig. 3, part 1 is the image sampling and segmentation. The top-left window in part 1 gives the image sampled directly from the camera. After image processing, the segmented result is shown in the top-right window (Dai, Shimogaki & Fujihara, 2008).

Part 2 in Fig. 3 shows some parameters for image processing. These parameters can be adjusted based on environment in real time, so that the result of image processing is good enough to segmentation.

Part 3 is the process for character recognition. The feature vector of each segmented character is extracted and then matches it to the templates. By the template matching method (Snyder & Qi, 2004), each digit or letter can be recognized respectively, and then the whole meaning of the word can be understood by combination of the meaning of each character.

2.4 Problem of the classical method

From the above explanation, we see that the classical method is really simple but practicable. It can segment the characters in an image by locating and calculating how many rows of characters, and how many characters in each row.

But this method cannot segment the characters in Fig. 4 correctly. Since the classical method cannot correctly divide the image into two rows of character (the numbers "127" and "305") by any horizontal line (the dashed lines), the wrong result is appeared: all the characters in the image are recognized into one row. Of cause the correct number cannot be gotten.

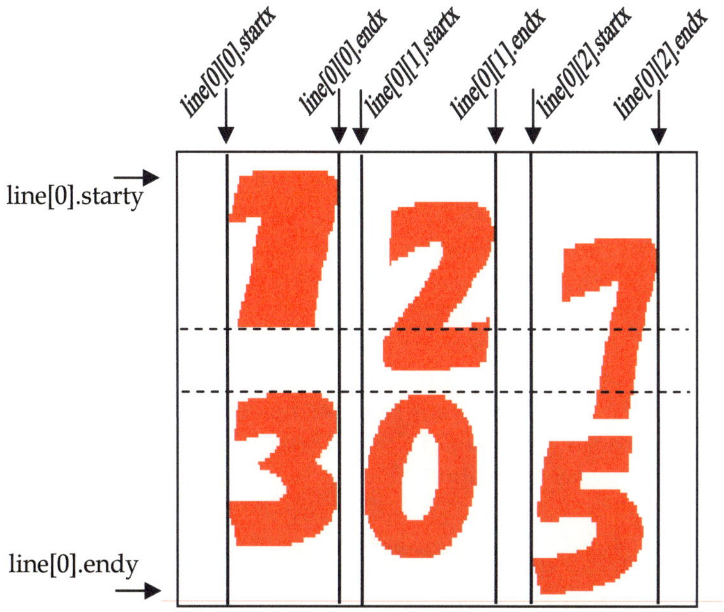

Fig. 4. An example for wrong segmentation by the classical method

3. Resonance theory and algorithm

3.1 Resonance theory

The resonance theory (He & Chen, 2000) can be expressed in Fig. 5. Assumes that in a scene of space, each point has a mass *m*. These points are not isolated from each other but inter-connected by inter-force. In Fig. 5, two points (a) and (b) are given and the distance between them is *d*.

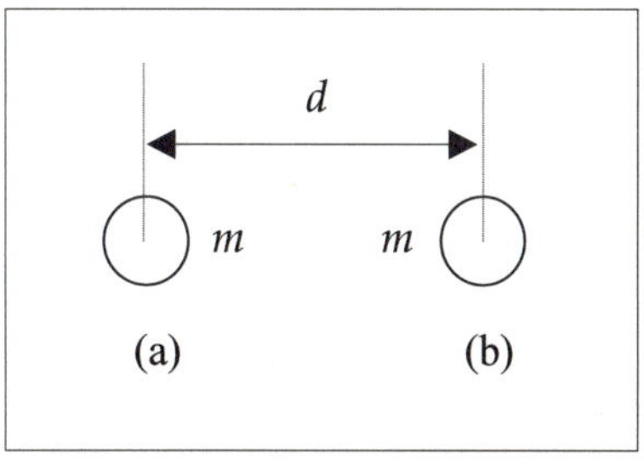

Fig. 5. Resonance theory

If an externally sinusoidal force *F* adds to the point (a), the movement of the point (a) can be expressed by

$$m\ddot{y} + b\dot{y} + ky = F\cos wt \tag{1}$$

b, k are the parameters of the system and point, the values of which are not important to the following explanation. $\dot{y}$ and $\ddot{y}$ means the first and second-order derivatives with respect to the time t for the motive distance y. The frequency of force F is w. Its stable solution is

$$y(t) = A\sin(wt + \theta) \tag{2}$$

where

$$A = F / \sqrt{m^2(w^2 - w_0^2)^2 + b^2w^2} \tag{3}$$

is the oscillating amplitude. θ is the initial phase, $w_0 = \sqrt{k / m}$ is called the natural frequency. From Eq. (3), if the frequency of the external force F (to the point (a)) is equal to the natural frequency w_0, the amplitude A has the maximal value, and this case is called the resonance between the external force and the point (a).

Since we have assumed that the points are not isolated, the motion of the point (a) will result in the spreading of its effect to other points that are around it. This is the resonance among the points, which is the theory for image segmentation proposed in section 3.2 to 3.4. From the analysis of the resonance mechanics (He & Chen, 2000), the amplitude of point (b) with the distance of d from (a) has the feature of

$$A_{(\text{distance}=d)} \propto A_{(\text{point a})} / \sqrt{d} \tag{4}$$

From the above analysis, if we assume that point (a) is the source to resonate and another point (b) can be largely affected, then the difference between the external frequency and the natural frequency, and the distance d between those two points should be small sufficiently. These two conditions can be satisfied by:

1. A threshold is set to ensure the difference of external frequency from the natural frequency is small enough.
2. The resonance algorithm is used within the adjacent points (in image segmentation) to ensure the distance between them is small enough.

3.2 Resonance algorithm

By the spreading of the resonance, the adjacent points that have the same or similar feature (e.g. texture in an image) are clustered into one region. It seems like the general region growing algorithm (Castleman, 1998; Jähne, 1995), but they are essentially different.

Region growing method partitions an image by the threshold directly: in an image, defining the maximum and minimum thresholds for each region to segment them. If an image contains complex color (or gray level) gradation, the selection of threshold is difficult.

Differently, the resonance algorithm emphasizes the similarity between the adjacent points, not the threshold for global usage. And the resonance can be spread from point to point. Thus the problem caused by gradation in intensity can be solved. Only the sudden change of features between adjacent points can be regarded as the boundary of different regions.

Define $P_\delta(a,b)$ as the path between the point a and b (a and b need not to be adjacent) under the threshold δ (the value to estimate the difference of features between two adjacent points). If there are sequences of adjacent points connecting between a and b, all of which

have the same features or have different features between the adjacent points but below δ, they form the connected path by the determination of the path between point a and b.
And if s is a point in an image, all points x_i that satisfies $P_\delta(s,x_i)$ will form the region $R_\delta(s)$. The point s is always called as seed (Dai, Zhao & Zhao, 2007; He & Chen, 2000). Remember that the region $R_\delta(s)$ is not centered by the point s, but refers to a region that all points in which have the same features to s, or the difference of features between adjacent points below δ.
Now the principle of the resonance algorithm for image segmentation is clear (in image processing, the point is called pixel): From one or some seed pixels, the adjacent pixels that belong to the same region under δ are clustered until all the pixels are searched.
From the above definitions and the transfer of resonance, we see that the selection of seeds does not influence the segmentation result in an image.
Fig. 6 gives the expression of the resonant process. In Fig. 6, a is the seed pixel, from which to resonate all the space in the image.

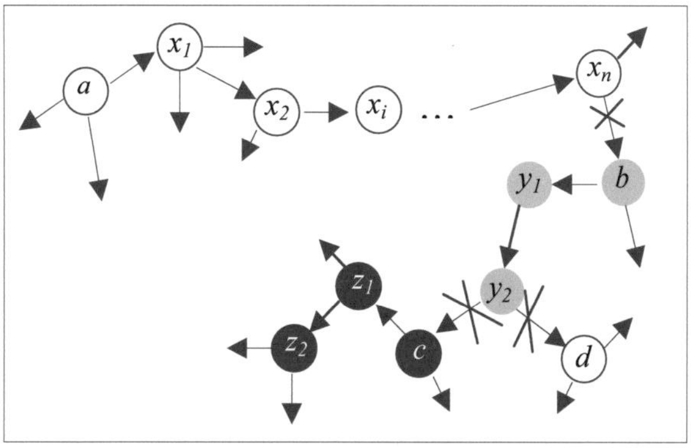

Fig. 6. Resonance process

By comparing with the difference of feature values between the point a and the adjacent pixels, all the pixels in $P_\delta(a,x_i)$ are labeled to belong to one region, e.g. $R_\delta(a)$ (Regin-1) = {a, x_i (i = 1,…,n)}. Next, from x_n to the pixel b, the difference between them is larger than δ, b is defined as a pixel belonging to a new region, e.g. $R_\delta(b)$ (Region-2) = {b, y_j (j = 1,…,m)}, all the pixels in which are $P_\delta(b,y_j)$. The same is to $R_\delta(c)$ (Region-3) = {c, z_k (k = 1,…,l)} that are $P_\delta(c,z_k)$ until all the pixels are labeled. The selection of seeds will not affect the result of segmentation.
From Fig. 6, although the pixel d has the same feature to Region-1, since it is far from Region-1 and is segmented by other regions, by the resonance theory, the pixel d cannot be resonated by any pixel in Region-1. Thus a new region creates from the point d. That is to say, the number of the segmented regions in an image does not absolutely equal to the number of real different texture types. In fact, this is not the weakness of the algorithm. Just as this case, it clearly shows that between Region-1 and the pixel d, there must exist some other textures.
Thus by the resonance theory, the resonance algorithm is determined by three important elements:

1. One or several seed points,
2. The features to determine the difference between points,
3. The parameter of the threshold δ.

And the steps of the resonance algorithm for image segmentation are:

1. Initialization. $R_\delta(0)$.
2. Segmentation. Find new region $R_\delta(i)$.
3. Termination after having searched all pixels.
4. Result. $R = \bigcup_{i=0}^{M} R_\delta(i)$.

Thus we see that this method is to find a harmonious threshold within adjacent points, not to estimate a global value. Fig. 7 gives the flow chart of the resonance algorithm for image segmentation.

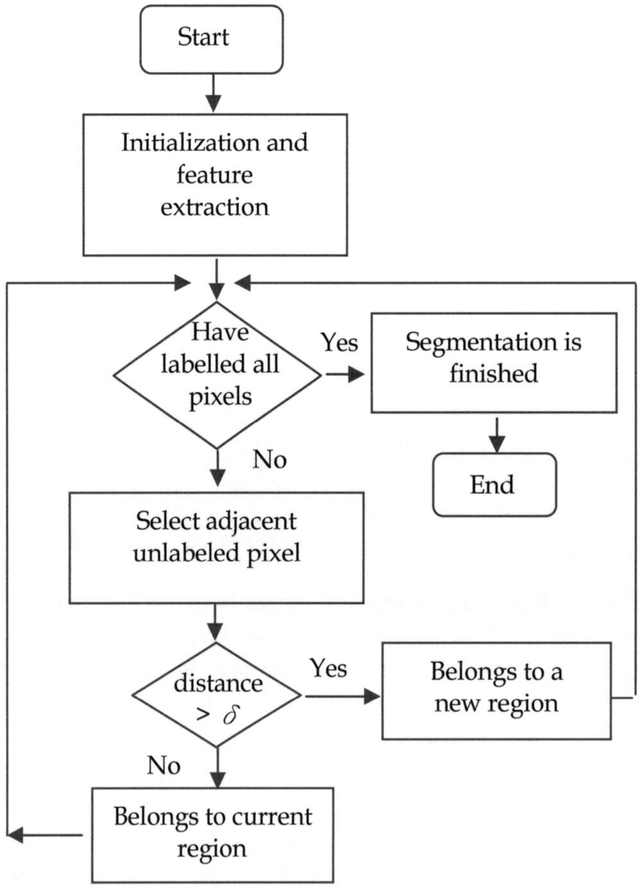

Fig. 7. Resonance algorithm

3.3 Selection of elements

Selection of the three elements of the resonance algorithm will be considered in this section. First, we see that from the resonance theory and the transfer of resonance, the initial place of the seed does not influence the segmentation result in an image. Thus the seed can be selected randomly.

The threshold δ is important in the resonance algorithm. Too large will include surplus regions into one while too small reject some points that belong to the same region. δ should be larger than the distance in one region and less than the difference between two different regions. But different images, or different regions in one image, may have different thresholds. We propose an automatic selection method for δ.

Since δ is used to partition the different regions in an image, it is rather a range of values (determine the maximum and minimum values) than a fixed value to ensure the points have the same or similar features in one region.

If δ for different regions in an image are selected well, then all the regions are segmented stably. That is to say, when the correct δ varies by a small value, the change of regions in an image is not distinct. Other word is that if the selection of δ is incorrect, a small change of it may vary the area of region greatly. This is the influence of δ for the region segmentation, and comparatively, it can be used as criterion to estimate δ.

Since the suitable threshold should be selected to ensure greater than the intra-region feature difference and less than the inter-region feature differences (Castleman, 1998; He & Chen, 2000), from the initial seeds, the resonance begins from the current region to extend to other regions with the rise of δ.

Fig. 8 is an example. In a unit square, three different regions are in it: the black, the gray and white region. The area of black is $S_{\text{black}} = \frac{1}{2}\times\frac{1}{2}=\frac{1}{4}=0.25$, the area of gray is $S_{\text{gray}} = \frac{3}{4}\times\frac{3}{4}-S_{\text{black}}=\frac{5}{16}=0.3125$, and the white $S_{\text{white}} = 1-\frac{3}{4}\times\frac{3}{4}=\frac{7}{16}=0.4375$.

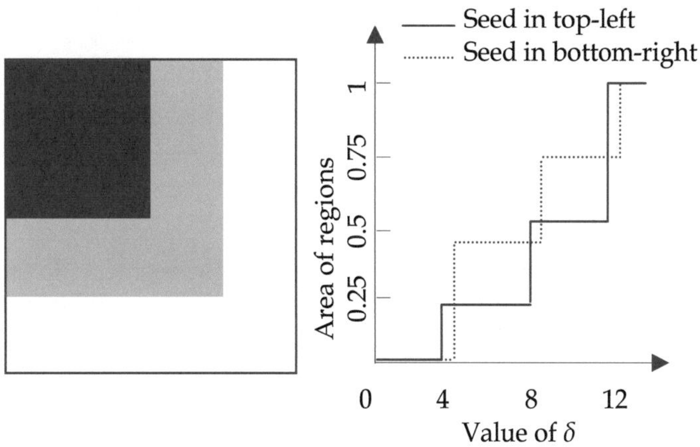

(a) (b)

Fig. 8. δ - area curve

Fig.8b gives the δ-area curves of Fig.8a for the seed point selected in the top-left and bottom-right corner respectively, from which we see that the selection of seeds will affect the parameter δ, but not affect the segmentation result (He & Chen, 2000).

Another element for resonance is the selection of features to estimate whether the distance between two adjacent points is below δ or not. In fact, it can be chosen by any features of the image, and the different selection of features results to different threshold δ. In this chapter, the eight-connectivity is used to connect the pixels of the object.

3.4 Image segmentation

When there are multi-objects in an image, image segmentation is necessary: locating and isolating the objects from the image and then identifying them. Once isolated, the objects can be measured and classified. The correct segmentation should be that it divides the image S into several independent regions $\{S_1, S_2, \ldots, S_n\}$, each region represents one kind of textures (Tanaka, 1989).

$$\begin{aligned} &(1)\quad S = \bigcup_{i=1}^{n} S_i \\ &(2)\quad S_i \cap S_j = \Phi \qquad \text{for all } i \neq j \\ &(3)\quad P_r(S_i) = 1 \qquad \text{for all } i \end{aligned} \tag{5}$$

$P_r(x)$ is the probability of the existence of x and Φ is the null set.

Fig. 9a (a strong light is given behind the right hand of the black rectangle) is always used to compare the results among different image processing algorithms, which is the scene of setting the experiment. Fig. 9b is the original experimental image extracted from Fig. 9a.

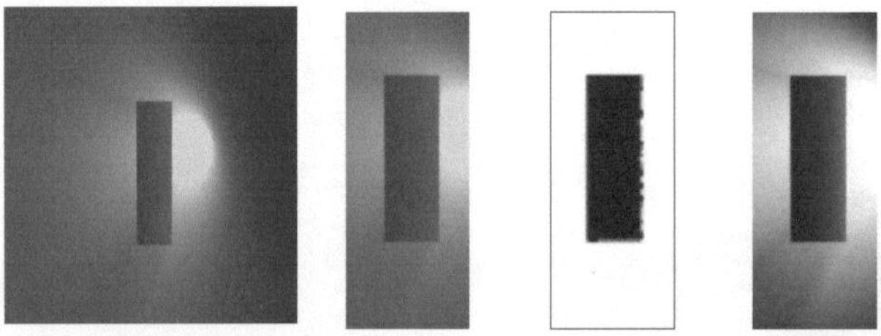

(a) (b) (c) (d)

Fig. 9. Compared experiment

By using the resonance algorithm proposed in the chapter, the segmentation result is given in Fig. 9c, in which the effect of light is removed, so that the background is in one region. A compared result is given in Fig. 9d by the reinforcement histogram algorithm (Castleman, 1998), which shows that the background is difficult to be clustered into one region.

3.5 The experiment

In this section, compared to the conventional method, the natural image in real environment will be applied to analyze the resonance algorithm for image segmentation.

Fig. 10 shows the source image and the segmentation result (Dai, Fujihara & Sugisaka, 2008). In the original image of Fig. 10a, sky and trees are two main regions, while the color of the sky is varied gradually by clouds.

Fig. 10b is the result after segmented by the proposed resonance algorithm. We adopt the gray level as the feature and the seed pixel is selected from the top-left corner of the image. The image is divided into three parts. The sky is separated into part-1 and 3 by a trunk of tree in the image. Part-2 is the region of trees. The influence of clouds is greatly eliminated because the resonance algorithm can handle gradual changes of intensity.

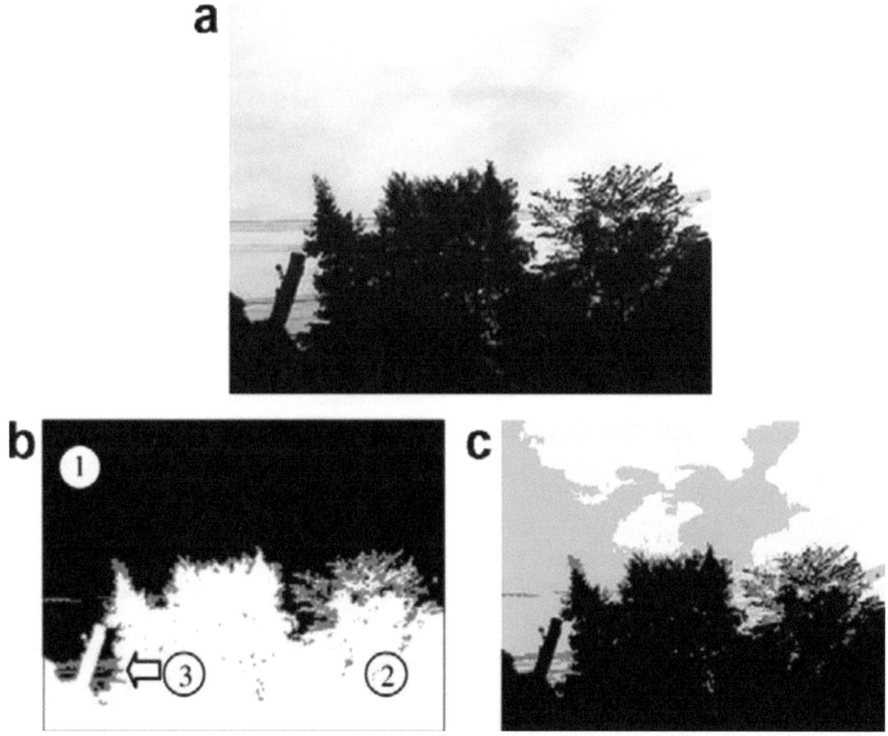

Fig. 10. Image segmentation: (a) color image, (b) by the resonance algorithm, (c) by the histogram analysis

Also if we do not satisfy that the sky is separated, the part-1 and 3 can be combined by the later processing easily, because the features of them are the same. The compared result is given by Fig. 10c, which is produced by the general histogram analysis method. It shows that the influence of the clouds cannot be ignored.

4. Conclusion

In this chapter, first the classical method for image segmentation is introduced. It is suitable for digit or letter segmentation and the program to realize the method is easy to be composed. But it still has some limitations.

In the second part of the chapter, the resonance theory and algorithm, and the three important elements of resonance are introduced.

The unsupervised resonance algorithm is proposed for complex image segmentation, which has the feature to eliminate the influence of gradual changes of texture in intensity to some extent.

The resonance algorithm for image segmentation is to search the same or similar texture pixels (among the adjacent pixels) so as to cluster them into one region: the resonance is spread among all the pixels within the image.

The compared result is also given and shows that the resonance algorithm emphasizes the similarity among the adjacent pixels rather than the global threshold values, and the segmentation result is satisfied. But there are some problems still existed to be solved:

1. How to select the parameter δ more correctly,
2. How to improve the program to fasten the algorithm.

5. Acknowledgment

This work is sponsored in part by the Scientific Research Foundation of Tianjin University of Science and Technology (China) for the Introduced Talented Scholars, No. 20100408.

6. References

Agui, T.; Nakajima, M. & Kimi, J. (1990). *Image Processing with C: PC9801 Series MS-DOS* (in Japanese). Shoko-do press, ISBN 4-7856-3076-0, Japan

Agui, T. & Nagao, T. (2000). *Introduction to image processing using programming language C.* Shoko-do press (in Japanese), ISBN 4-7856-3124-4, Japan

Castleman, K. (1998). *Digital Image Processing,* Original edition published by Prentice Hall, Inc., a Simon & Schuster Company, Press of Tsinghua University, ISBN 7-302-02828-1/TN.88, China

Chen, P. & Hwang Y. (1998). SANDROS: A dynamic graph search algorithm for motion planning, *IEEE Transactions on Robotics and Automation,* Vol. 14, No. 3, pp. 390-403, ISSN 1042-296X, NEW YORK

Dai, F.; Fujihara, Y. & Sugisaka, M. (2008). Image Segmentation by Resonance Algorithm, *Proceedings of the International Conference on Instrumentation, Control and Information Technology,* pp. 2018-2022, ISBN 978-4-907764-29-6, Tokyo, Japan, August 2008, SICE, Tokyo

Dai, F.; Shimogaki, D. & Fujihara, Y. (2008). Research on Digit Recognition by Image Processing for Autonomous Mobile Robot. *Proceedings of the Thirteenth International Symposium on Artificial Life and Robotics,* pp. 827-830, ISBN 978-4-9902880-2-0, Oita, Japan, January 31 - February 2, 2008, Shubundo Insatsu Co. Ltd., Japan

Dai, F.; Zhao, J. & Zhao, H. (2007). The Application of Resonance Algorithm for Image Segmentation, *Journal of Applied Mathematics and Computation,* Vol. 194/2, pp. 453-459, December 2007, ISSN 0096-3003

Deguchi, K. & Takahashi, I. (1999). Image-based simultaneous control of robot and target object motion by direct-image-interpretation, *Proceedings of the 1999 IEEE/RSJ International Conference of Intelligent Robot and System,* Vol. 1, pp. 375-380, 99CH36289, Kyongju, Korea, October 1999

He, H. & Chen, Y. (2000). Unsupervised texture segmentation using resonance algorithm for natural scenes, *Pattern Recognition Letters,* Vol. 21, 2000, pp. 741-757

Heins, L. & Tauritz, D. (1995). *Adaptive Resonance Theory (ART): An Introduction,* Department of Computer Science, Leiden University, IR-95-35, May/June, 1995. "http://www.wi.leidenuniv.nl/art"

Jähne, B. (1995). *Digital Image Processing - Concepts, Algorithms, and Scientific Applications.* The Third Edition, Springer-Verlag, ISBN 3-540-59298-9, Germany

Nakamura, T. & Ogasawara, T. (1999). On-line visual learning method for color image segmentation and object tracking, *Proceedings of the 1999 IEEE/RSJ International Conference on Intelligent Robots and Systems,* Vol. 1, pp. 222-228, 99CH36289, Kyongju, Korea, October 1999

Snyder, W. & Qi, H. (2004). *Machine Vision,* the Press of Syndicate of the University of Cambridge, ISBN 0-521-83046-X, UK

Tanaka, H. (1989). *Image Processing and Application Technology* (in Japanese), Kogyo Chosakai Publishing Co., Ltd., ISBN 4-7693-1072-2, Japan

2

A Review of Algorithms for Segmentation of Retinal Image Data Using Optical Coherence Tomography

Delia Cabrera DeBuc, PhD
Bascom Palmer Eye Institute, University of Miami Miller School of Medicine
United States of America

1. Introduction

In the context of biomedical imaging analysis and computer-assisted diagnosis, segmentation analysis is an intense field of research and development. The most difficult part of medical image analysis is the automated localization and delineation of structures of interest. Automated data evaluation is one way of enhancing the clinical utility of measurements. In particular, medical image segmentation extracts meaningful information and facilitate the display of this information in a clinically relevant way. A crucial role for automated information extraction in medical imaging usually involves the segmentation of regions of the image in order to quantify volumes and areas of interest of biological tissues for further diagnosis and localization of pathologies.

Optical coherence tomography (OCT) is a powerful imaging modality used to image various aspects of biological tissues, such as structural information, blood flow, elastic parameters, change of polarization states and molecular content (Huang et al., 1991). OCT uses the principle of low coherence interferometry to generate two or three dimensional imaging of biological samples by obtaining high-resolution cross-sectional backscattering profiles. A variety of successful algorithms for computer-aided diagnosis by means of OCT image analysis are presented in the literature, but robust use in clinical practice is still a major challenge for ongoing research in OCT image analysis. There are, therefore, efforts being made to improve clinical decision making based on automated analysis of OCT data. Particularly, in ophthalmology, efforts have been made to characterize clinically important features, such as damage to the fovea and optic nerve, automatically.

The transfer of image analysis models from algorithmic development into clinical application is currently the major bottleneck due to the complexity of the overall process. For example, the process to establish an application for OCT medical image analysis requires difficult and complex tasks that should considers the following actions: 1) to define the OCT image data structures representing relevant biomedical features and the algorithms determining a valid example for given image values, 2) to select meaningful values for all technical parameters of the image data structures and algorithms and, as a result, to configure such a method to operate on specific OCT clinical data, 3) to run the algorithm with the selected parameters to find the individual model instance that best explains the input image and 4) to validate the procedure to ensure a trustworthy result from an automated segmentation algorithm even if a gold standard is unavailable.

This chapter is intended to give a broad, but by no means complete, overview over common segmentation methods encountered in OCT retinal image processing. To do this, some algorithms that are representative for each class in some detail are described. In addition an understanding of the original derivation and motivation of each algorithm is provided, instead of merely stating how each method functions. This is of high importance in order to get an idea where and under what circumstances a method can function and when one can expect an algorithm to fail. To briefly motivate why one should consider different segmentation algorithms, consider the example of a 2D OCT image in Fig. 1. Simple thresholding can be used to mark the locations of the inner and outer boundaries of the retina in this OCT image. But some boundary sections are not properly identified due to poor contrast or low resolution, making it impossible to identify the exact extent of the retina in this image (see Fig.1A). Since these boundaries are found by a threshold procedure, their estimated locations could be sensitive to relative differences in reflectance between the outer and deeper retinal structures. By choosing a different segmentation algorithm (see Fig. 1B), identification of the retinal boundaries can be improved (Cabrera Fernández et al., 2005b). All segmentation methods that have been proposed in the literature aim at improving retinal image segmentation in this or other aspects. The causes for problems such as the ones in Fig. 1 can by manifold, many times being inherent to the respective image acquisition method itself.

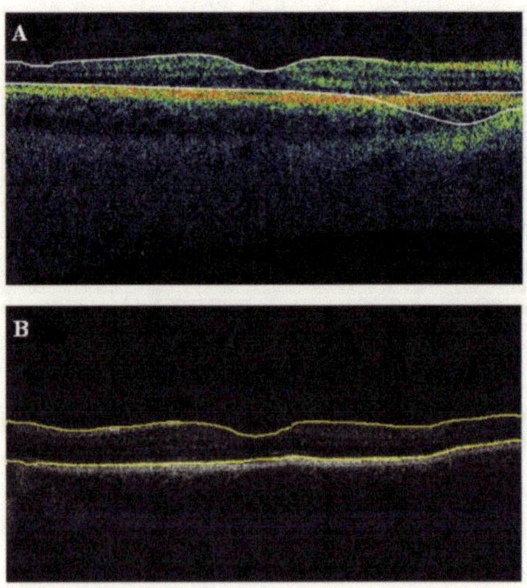

Fig. 1. Segmentation results showing the performance of the Stratus OCT custom built-in algorithm compared to the results using a custom algorithm. A) Macular scan obtained from a healthy eye. Note the misidentification of the outer boundary of the retina outlined in white. B) Results obtained for the same eye using a custom algorithm. Note that the custom algorithm was able to correctly detect the outer boundary of the retina.

The chapter is organized as follows. The next section continues with an outline of current retinal imaging modalities. Section 3 explains the physical principles and technical details of how OCT works. The interpretation of the OCT image along with the current and future technology development of OCT systems is also presented in this section. Section 4 provides the necessary background about medical image segmentation approaches. A review of algorithms for segmentation of retinal image data using OCT is presented in Section 5. All published (within the author's awareness) papers related to retinal image segmentation are gathered into this single compilation. Section 6 offers some concluding remarks.

2. Current retinal imaging modalities

Millions of people worldwide live with retinal disease and the accompanying threat of severe vision loss or blindness. During the last few years, the retinal research field has undergone a dramatic change in terms of diagnostic tools and therapies that have resulted in substantial benefits for patients suffering from retinal disease. Traditionally the retina has been observed either directly via an ophthalmoscope or similar optical devices such as the fundus camera. The field of ophthalmology was revolutionized in 1851 with the invention of the ophthalmoscope by Hermann von Helmholtz (von Helmholtz, 1851) as for the first time detailed examinations of the interior of the eye could be made in living patients. The ophthalmoscope and later the fundus camera remained the primary methods of ocular examination into the 1960's, and they are standard tools still effective and in use today, although they are not without limitations, and both require trained users to operate and make diagnoses.

With advances in medical technology, more powerful techniques were introduced. In 1961 fluorescein angiography was developed by Novotny and Alvis, a procedure in which sodium fluorescein is injected into a vein, and under filtered light the sodium fluorescein within the blood fluoresces, glowing brightly and providing easily observed patterns of blood flow within the eye (Novotny & Alvis, 1961). This allows the arteries, capillaries and veins to be easily identified and photographed, and from this, large amounts of information concerning the health or otherwise of the circulatory system can be determined.

During the 1990's the indocyanine green dye angiography technique was developed; similarly to the flourescein angiography a dye is injected into the bloodstream, however the indocyanine green dye glows in the infra-red section of the spectrum. The indocyanine green dye approach only came into widespread use when digital cameras sensitive into the infra-red became commonly available, and it complements fluorescein angiography by highlighting different aspects of the vasculature of the eye. In particular it enhances the structure of the choroid, which is the layer of blood vessels beneath the retina. These two techniques can be used together to gain a more thorough understanding of the structure and pathologies affecting an eye. They can illustrate patterns of blood flow, haemorraging and obstructions within the vascular system, but, like the ophthalmoscope, both require trained medical staff to perform the procedure, and a clinical environment where the images can be taken and analyzed. In addition to these methods for observing the vasculature of the eye there are a range of other, more advanced, methods of mapping structures and changes within the eye, including ultrasound, OCT and laser-based blood flowmeters in development and in use. All of these can be used to scan the eye and make observations and diagnoses on the eye and circulatory system. Specifically, the introduction of OCT imaging in daily routine have resulted in some of the central changes to retinal disease understanding and management. Figure 2 shows the operational range of the OCT technology compared to standard imaging.

OCT is a rapidly emerging medical imaging technology that has applications in many clinical specialties. OCT uses retroreflected light to provide micron-resolution, cross-sectional scans of biological tissues (Hee et al., 1995; Huang et al., 1991; Izatt et al., 1994a).

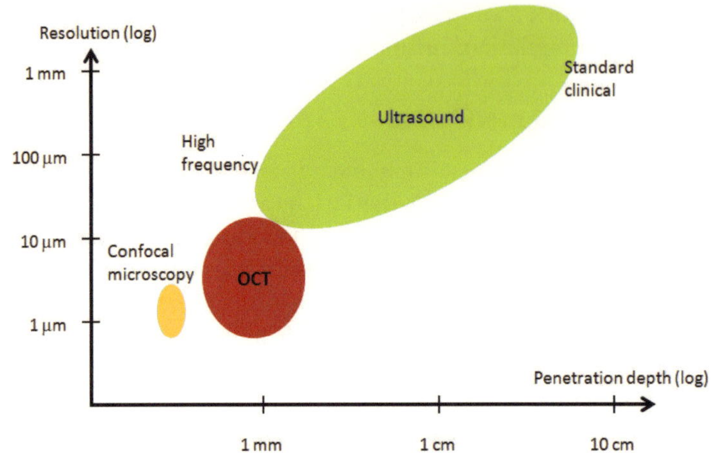

Fig. 2. OCT vs. standard imaging.

The first micron-resolution OCT system for imaging human retina *in vivo* was introduced in 1991 (Huang et al., 1991). In ophthalmology; OCT is a powerful medical imaging technology because it enables visualization of the cross- sectional structure of the retina and anterior eye with higher resolutions than any other non-invasive imaging modality (Huang et al., 1991). The depth resolution of OCT is extremely fine, typically on the order of 0.01mm or 0.4 thousandth of an inch. An OCT image represents a cross-sectional, micron scale picture of the optical reflectance properties of the tissue (Huang et al., 1991). This image can either be used to qualitatively assess tissue features and pathologies or to objectively make quantitative measurements.

While this is just a brief introduction to some of the diagnostic tools available to obtain retinal images, to draw diagnoses from these images requires specialist training, and to adequately extract and track the retinal damage from the images often takes extensive image processing and analysis. Once automatic image analysis is possible, those at risk of numerous diseases and problems of the retinal tissue can be rapidly identified and referred for further treatment. The development of this methodology would also allow automated tracking of the progress of such health problems as diabetic retinopathy, and track changes in the eyes as the subject ages. This would have numerous health benefits, including providing an early prediction of retinal diseases.

3. Optical coherence tomography background

The clinical potential of OCT technology in ophthalmology was originally recognized in the early 1990s. OCT is an extension of optical coherence domain reflectometry to imaging in two or three dimensions (Brezinski et al., 1996). This imaging technique generates a cross-sectional image by recording axial reflectance profiles while the transverse position of the optical beam on the sample is scanned. Thus, the longitudinal location of tissue structures are determined by measuring the time-of-flight delays of light backscattered from these structures. The optical delays are measured by low coherence interferometry. Light reflected from deeper layers has a longer propagation delay than light reflected from more superficial layers.

Conventional or time domain OCT (TDOCT) is based on the principle of low coherence interferometry which is a powerful tool to section a transparent object. Low coherence means that the system employs a wide range of wavelengths. The most straightforward and currently the most common interferometer for OCT is a simple Michelson interferometer (see Fig 3) (Michelson & Morley, 1887). A low-coherence source illuminates the interferometer. The light is split by a 50/50 beamsplitter into a sample and a reference path. Light retroreflected from the reference and the sample is recombined at the beamsplitter and half is collected by a photodetector in the detection arm of the interferometer. Half of the light is returned towards the source, where it is lost. In addition, the reference arm light is typically attenuated by orders of magnitude in order to improve signal to noise ratio.

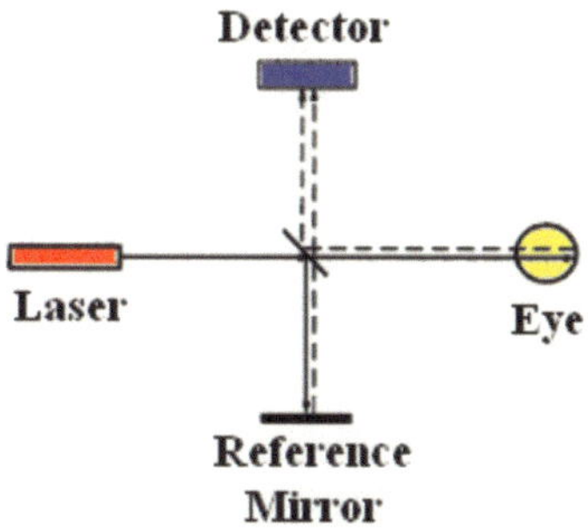

Fig. 3. Schematic drawing of the principle of OCT emphasizing how it is essentially a Michelson intereferometer. The outgoing light paths are solid lines, while reflected light is drawn as dashes lines.

The axial resolution of an OCT image depends on the coherence length which is a fundamental property of the light source, whereas transverse resolution for OCT imaging is determined by focused spot size, as in microscopy. By rapidly varying the reference arm mirror and synchronously recording the magnitude of the resulting interference signal, a single axial profile or A-scan is obtained which is a graph of the optical reflectivity versus distance in the eye. A sequence of such A-scans is obtained by scanning the probe beam across the entire retina which forms a B-scan tomogram. As a result, a cross-sectional view of the structure similar to a histology section is obtained.

OCT can be used for retinal imaging and anterior segment imaging. The OCT for ophthalmic examination is similar to a slit lamp for anterior segment imaging and a fundus camera for retinal imaging. The instrumentation includes a video display for operator viewing of the anterior segment or fundus while obtaining the OCT images and a simultaneous computer display of the tomograms. Images are stored via computer for the diagnostic record (Puliafito, 1996).

3.1 Interpreting OCT images

The OCT signal from a particular tissue layer is a combination of its reflectivity and the absorption and scattering properties of the overlying tissue layers. Strong reflections occur at the boundaries between two materials of different refractive indices and from a tissue that has a high scattering coefficient along with a disposition to scatter light in the perfectly backward direction (Huang et al., 1991; Puliafito, 1996). Thus, an OCT image is a map of the reflectivity of the sample. In most tissues, main sources of reflection are collagen fiber bundles, cell walls, and cell nuclei. Dark areas on the image represent homogeneous material with low reflectivity, such as air or clear fluids. The imaging light is attenuated in the sample, so there is an exponential decrease in the intensity of the image with depth. Blood attenuates the signal faster than collagenous tissues, fat and fluids attenuate the signal the least.

In OCT images, the signal strength is represented in false color. High backscatter appears red-orange and low backscatter appears blue-black (see Fig. 4). Thus, tissues with different reflectivity are displayed in different colors. It is important to note that OCT image contrast arises from intrinsic differences in tissue optical properties. Thus, coloring of different structures represents different optical properties in false color image and it is not necessarily different tissue pathology (see Fig. 4). The exact relationship between the histology of the tissue and the OCT map is still under investigation. Relative high reflectivity layers correspond to areas of horizontal retinal elements such as the nerve fiber layer at the retinal surface or deeper plexiform layers and a single layer of retinal pigment epithelium (RPE) and choroid. Relative low reflectivity layers correspond to the nuclear layers and a single layer of photoreceptor inner and outer segments. Warm colors (red to white) represent areas of relative high reflectivity, while cold colors (blue to black) represent areas of relative low reflectivity.

In the retina, the vitreoretinal interface is demarcated by the reflections from the surface of the retina. The retinal pigment epithelium (RPE) and choriocapillaris layer (ChCap) is visualized as a highly reflective red layer and represents the posterior boundary of the retina. Below the choriocapillaris weakly scattered light returns from the choroid and sclera because of attenuation of the signal after passing through the neurosensory retina, RPE, and ChCap. The outer segments of the rods and cones appear as a dark layer of minimal reflectivity anterior to the RPE and ChCap. The intermediate layers of the retina exhibit moderate backscattering (see Fig. 4). The fovea appears as a characteristic thinning of the retina. The lateral displacement of the retina anterior to the photoreceptors is evident (see Fig. 4).

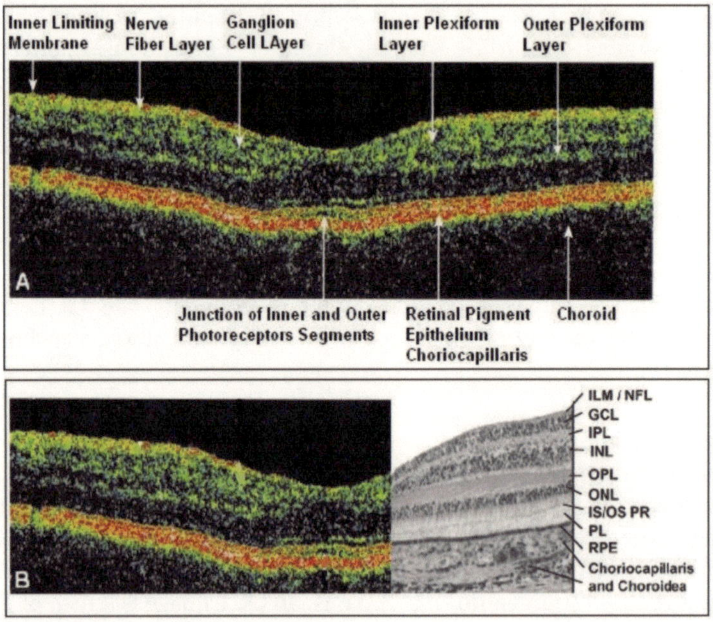

Fig. 4. OCT image of the normal human macula. (A) Stratus OCT image showing the various cellular layers of the retina. (B) Comparison of the OCT image (same as shown in A) to a histologic micrograph of the normal human macula.

3.2 Quantitative measurements of retinal morphology

OCT can aid in identifying, monitoring and quantitatively assessing various posterior segment conditions including macular edema, age-and-non-age related macular degeneration, full and partial-thickness macular hole, epiretinal membrane, intaretinal exudate, idiopathic central serous chorioretinopathy, RPE detachment, detachment of the neurosensory retina, and macular lesions associated with optic nerve head pits or glaucoma Figure 5 shows exemplary images of two of the above cited pathological cases obtained with a RTVue FD-OCT system (Optovue Inc., Freemonth, CA).

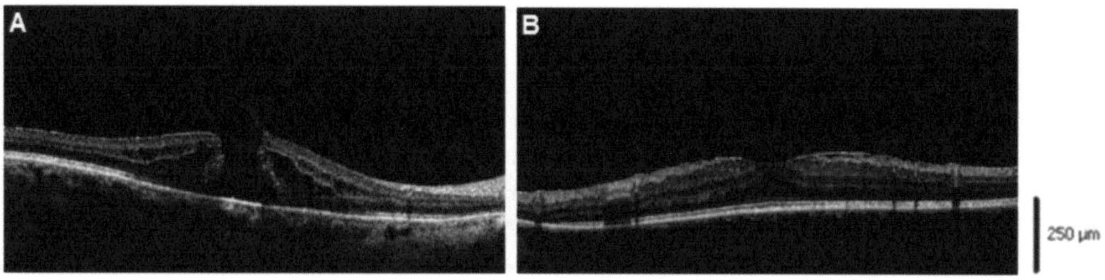

Fig. 5. OCT images showing two OCT B-scans (6 mm length) from pathological retinas. A) Macular hole, B) Epiretinal membrane.

As a matter of fact, OCT can demonstrate the presence of edema where it is not seen on biomicroscopy or angiographically. A very important feature of the OCT system is that it provides information on the retinal structures. For example, the location of fluid accumulation in relation to the different retinal layers may be determined and the response to treatment without the need to perform invasive studies such as fluorescein angiography may be objectively monitored. At the same time it may be possible to explain why some patients respond to treatment while others do not. OCT has significant potential both as a diagnostic tool and particularly as a way to monitor objectively subtle retinal changes induced by therapeutic interventions. Thus, OCT may become a valuable tool in determining the minimum maintenance dose of a certain drug in the treatment of retinal diseases, and may demonstrate retinal changes that explain the recovery in some patients without angiographically demonstrable improvement and lack of recovery in others.

In the clinical routine, measurement of retinal thickness by the OCT software depends on the identification of the internal limiting membrane and the hyper-reflective band believed to correspond to the retinal pigment epithelium - choriocapillaris interface (or, more precisely, the photoreceptor inner-outer segment border in the case of third generation OCTs). The OCT software algorithms calculates the distance between these 2 boundaries across all of the sampled points and interpolates the retinal thickness in the unsampled areas between these lines. However, once the various layers can be identified and correlated with the histological structure of the retina, it may seem relevant to measure not only the entire thickness of the retina, but the thickness of the various cellular layers. Moreover, measuring the reflectance of the various retinal layers on OCT images may also be of interest. Drexler et al. have shown in *in vitro* and *in vivo* (Bizheva et al., 2006; Hermann et al., 2006) studies that physiological processes of the retina lead to optical density changes that can be observed by a special M-mode OCT imaging, known as optophysiology. Thus, it also seems rational that quantitative analysis of reflectance changes may provide clinically relevant information in retinal patophysiology.

3.3 Recent developments in OCT technology

The emergence of ultrabroad bandwidth femtosecond laser technology has allowed the development of an ultra-high resolution OCT, which has been demonstrated to achieve axial resolutions of 3 μm during *in vivo* imaging of the human retina, which is two orders of magnitude higher than what can be achieved by conventional ultrasound imaging. Figure 6 shows the ultrahigh resolution OCT cross section of a normal human macula showing all of the major layers and internal structures of the retina. The ultrahigh resolution OCT will in effect be a microscope capable of revealing certain histopathological aspects of macular disease in the living eye.

As it was previously explained, in the conventional or time domain OCT (TDOCT) system the length of the reference arm in an interferometer is rapidly scanned over a distance corresponding to the imaging depth range. The mechanism of scanning largely limits the acquisition speed and makes real-time imaging impossible. In recent years a new model OCT based on Fourier domain interferometry has emerged, and it has been called spectral domain OCT (SDOCT) or Fourier domain OCT (FDOCT) (Fercher et al., 1995; Fercher et al., 2003; Hausler & Lindner, 1998). SDOCT can avoid scanning of the reference, thus it can reach very high acquisition speed. As a matter of fact, in time domain OCT the location of scatters in the sample is observed by generation of interferometric fringes at the detector as the reference reflector position is axially translated. In contrast, Fourier domain OCT required the reference arm to be held fixed, and the optical path length difference between sample and reference reflections is encoded by the frequency of the interferometric fringes as a function of the source spectrum. Two configurations have prevailed in Fourier domain systems: spectral domain (SD) OCT uses a grating to spatially disperse the spectrum across an array-type detector, and in swept source (SS) OCT a narrow band laser is swept across a broad spectrum, encoding the spectrum as a function of time. SDOCT offers a significant sensitivity advantage over TDOCT (Choma et al., 2003; de Boer et al., 2003, Leitgeb et al., 2003; Mitsui, 1999).

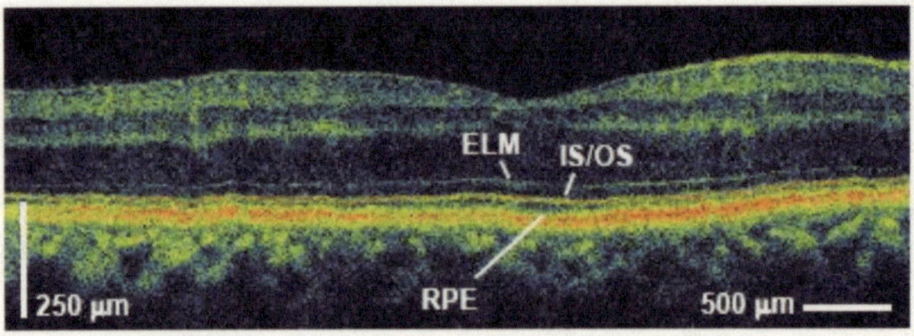

Fig. 6. Ultrahigh resolution OCT cross section of a normal human macula with 3 microns resolution (Courtesy "James Fujimoto," (Fujimoto et al., 2003)).

New technology has also been developed to improve resolution in the transverse dimension. In the current commercial application of OCT, the transverse resolution is limited by the intrinsic ocular aberrations of the eye. The transverse resolution can be significantly improved by correcting the aberrations across a large pupil using adaptive optics (AO). A high axial (3 μm) and improved transverse (5–10 μm) resolution AO-OCT system was demonstrated for the first time in *in vivo* retinal imaging (Hermann et al., 2004).

The instrument uses a wavefront sensor that measures the aberrations in patient's eyes and then adjusts the surface of an adaptive mirror to correct the visual flaws. An improvement of the transverse resolution of two to three times, compared with ultrahigh resolution OCT systems used so far, was obtained by using adaptive optics A significant signal-to-noise ratio improvement of up to 9 dB in corrected compared with uncorrected OCT tomograms was also achieved. Zawadzki et al. also demonstrated the ability to image microscopic blood vessels and the cone photoreceptor mosaic using an AO-OCT instrument with high 3D resolution(4x4x6 µm) (Zawadzki et al., 2005). AO-OCT is currently the only option for studying living retinal tissue at the cellular level and clinical trials of the instrument are still being performed.

Another limitation of OCT technology has been the difficulty in accurately localizing the cross-sectional images and correlating them with a conventional en face view of the fundus. One way to localize and visually interpret the images would be to integrate a scanning laser ophthalmoscope (SLO) into the OCT, thereby mapping OCT pixels to the conventional en face view of the SLO. This rationale was used by Ophthalmic Technologies Inc (Toronto, Canada) to develop the Spectral OCT-SLO in 2004 (Podoleaunu et al., 2004). The system simultaneously produces SLO and OCT images that are created through the same optical path, and therefore correspond pixel to pixel. OCT-SLO, offers multiple views from a single scan with perfect registration of images. OCT-SLO imaging offers very accurate localisation of pathology with enhancement of the vitreoretinal interface. Its ability to align serial topographies and to fuse other modalities, with real-time, ultrahigh resolution capability and multi-planar anterior segment imaging should make it an invaluable addition to the diagnostic arsenal of the vitreoretinal surgeon.

A number of other instruments have also been built based on variations of the basic OCT system. For instance, polarization-sensitive optical coherence tomography (PS-OCT) uses polarization-altering optics in the arms of the interferometer to determine the sample birefringence from the magnitude of the back-reflected light (de Boer et al., 1997; de Boer et al., 2003). This instrument can be used to assess effects such as retinal nerve fiber layer thickness (Cense et al., 2002), early osteoarthritic changes in cartilage (Hermann et al., 1999) or burn depth in thermally damaged tissue (de Boer et al., 1998). Optical coherence microscopy (OCM) is a hybrid instrument that uses a system of high numerical aperture to achieve resolutions comparable to confocal microscopy but with increased depth of penetration (Izatt et al., 1994b). This instrument has been applied to gastrointestinal tissues and promises to enable endoscopically based cellular imaging (Izatt et al., 1996; Aguirre et al., 2003). Doppler optical coherence tomography (Doppler OCT) is an augmentation capable of simultaneous blood flow mapping and spatially resolved imaging (Chen et al., 1997; Izatt et al., 1997; Westphal et al., 2002; Wong et al., 2002; Yazdanfar et al., 2003; Zhao et al., 2000; Ding et al., 2002; Ren et al., 2002). Doppler flow measurements can be performed by measuring the Doppler shift of light scattered from blood. Doppler OCT has been used to explore the human retinal flow dynamics (Yazdanfar et al., 2003); and it is a promising imaging technology for quantitatively assessing capillarity density and angiogenesis (Fujimoto et al., 2003).

Functional OCT imaging is another emerging modality that facilitates the assessment of functional or biochemical properties of the investigated tissue. Spectroscopic OCT imaging using broadband light sources enables the spectrum of the backscattered light from each pixel to be measured (Morgner et al., 2000). This extension of OCT is closely related to classical Fourier transform infrared spectroscopy and has the advantage that the

spectroscopic information can be acquired at multiple wavelengths across the available bandwidth of the light source in a single measurement (Boppart et al., 1999). The potential of Spectroscopic OCT in developmental and cellular biology is really promising.
As it can be seen, a wide range of OCT imaging platforms with rapidly emerging applications spanning a range of fields has been developed. The rapid advances in OCT imaging are likely to alter the practice of ophthalmology dramatically in the next several years. Increased resolution and imaging speeds, wavefront correction, improved multiple functionality of the OCT systems; and the possibility of quantitative 3D modeling are just a few of the features to look for in the future. Further advances may transform the OCT from an ancillary procedure to a common and necessary "optical biopsy". Indeed, future ophthalmologists will use the next generation of OCT devices as a broad based tool for comprehensive ophthalmic examinations; and may even diagnose macular disorders exclusively by digital imaging, without a funduscopic examination.

4. Medical image segmentation approaches

Imaging operations may be broadly classified according to four categories: preprocessing, visualization, manipulation and analysis. Segmentation is a common used operation in preprocessing approaches and an essential operation for most visualization, manipulation and analysis tasks in image processing (see Fig. 7). Segmentation is, therefore, the most critical among all imaging procedures, and also the most challenging.
Segmentation purpose is to identify and delineate objects. Here, an object refers to any physical object such as an anatomical organ or a pathological entity such as a tumor or cyst (see Fig. 8). Segmentation is defined as the partitioning of an image into non-overlapping, component regions which are homogeneous with respect to some characteristic such as intensity or texture (Haralick et al., 1985; Gonzalez & Woods, 1992; Pal & Pal, 1993). Typically, image segmentation consist of two related tasks: recognition and delineation. Recognition consists of determining approximately the objects' location in the image. For example, in Figure 9, this task involves determining the location of the RNFL, GCL, IPL, etc. This does not involve the precise specification of the region occupied by the object. Delineation involves determining the objects' precise spatial extent and composition including gradation of intensities. In Figure 9 again, if retinal tissue is the object structure of interest, then delineation consists of the spatial extent of the RNFL and GCL separately, and for each element (i.e. pixels for 2D and voxels for 3D) in each object, specifying a characteristic value of the object (for example, RNFL thickness or volume). Once the objects are defined separately, the RNFL and GCL can be individually visualized, manipulated and analyzed. While automatic and human-assisted are the only two approaches for recognition tasks, numerous methods are available for delineation. Approaches to delineation can be classified as: 1) boundary-based and 2) region-based (Kim & Hori, 2000).
Numerous approaches regarding image segmentation techniques are available in the literature. Some of these techniques use only the gray level histogram, some use spatial details while others use fuzzy set theoretic approaches. Most of these techniques are not suitable for noisy environments. In particular, segmentation approaches can be classified according to the methodology used in the segmentation strategy (see Fig. 10):

1. *Classical segmentation methods*: These approaches classically partition an image into non-overlapping segments which are homogeneous with respect to some characteristic such as intensity or texture (Haralick et al., 1985; Gonzalez & Woods, 1992; Pal & Pal, 1993).

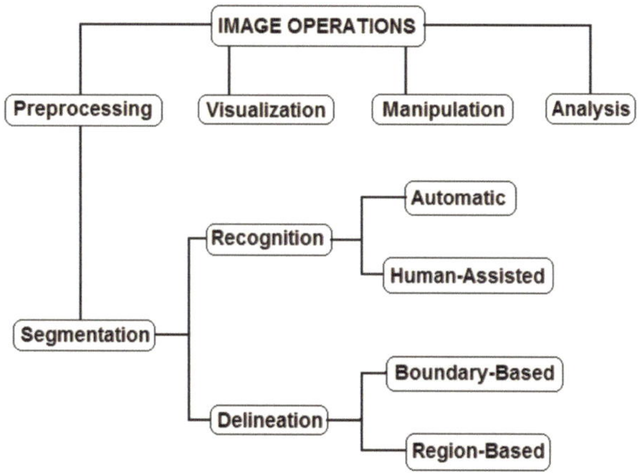

Fig. 7. Classification of image operations.

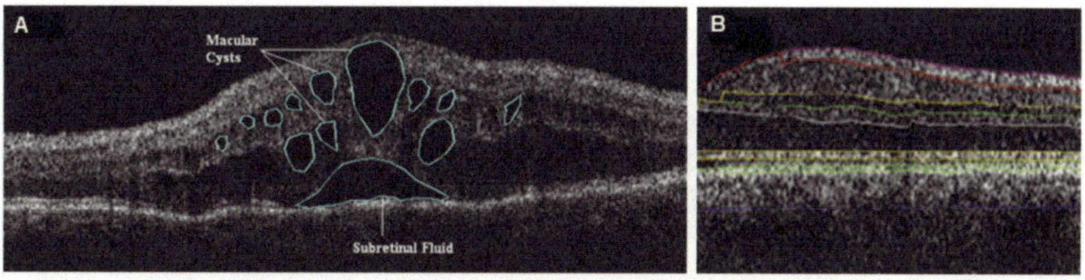

Fig. 8. OCT image segmentation results showing isolated retinal features of interest. A) OCT B-scan showing multiple lesions in the central retinal area of a patient with age related macular degeneration. Macular cysts and the subretinal fluid area were segmented using a deformable model (Cabrera Fernández et al., 2005a). B) Segmentation result showing the intraretinal layers outlined on an OCT B-scan section obtained from a healthy subject.

2. *Pixel classification methods*: These methods basically do not require the constraint that regions be connected. Thresholding, classifier, clustering, and Markov random field (MRF) approaches can be considered pixel classification methods. Thresholding is the most intuitive approach to segmentation (Sahoo et al., 1988). Specifically, algorithms based on threshold create a partitioning of the image based on quantifiable features, like image intensity or gradient magnitude. These algorithms map and cluster pixels in a feature space called a histogram. Thresholds are chosen at valleys between pixel clusters so that each pair represents a region of similar pixels in the image. The segmentation is then achieved by searching for pixels that satisfy the rules defined by the thresholds. Thresholds in these algorithms can be selected manually according to a priori knowledge or automatically through image information. Thresholding algorithms can be divided into edge-based ones (e.g. Canny edge detector and Laplacian edge detector), region-based ones (e.g. region growing algorithms) and hybrid ones (e.g. watershed algorithms). Edge-based algorithms attempt to find edge pixels while eliminate the noise influence. Thresholds in the edge-based algorithms are related with the edge information. Region-based algorithms exploit the fact that pixels

inside a structure tend to have similar intensities. Region growing algorithms, once initial seeds are selected, search for the neighboring pixels whose intensities are inside the intervals defined by the thresholds and then merge them to expand the regions. Hybrid algorithms fuse region information with a boundary detector to complete the segmentation. Typical hybrid algorithms are the level set method with regularizers and the watershed algorithm. Particularly, the watershed algorithms (Yezi et al., 1999) combine the image intensity with the gradient information. In addition, the methodology of using MRF based methods to the problem of segmentation has received a great deal of attention in the past decade (Tamás et al., 2000). MRF modeling itself is not a segmentation method but a statistical model which can be used within segmentation methods. As shown in Fig. 10, MRF is a region-based approach. MRF models spatial interactions between neighboring or nearby pixels. Hence, the classification of a particular pixel is based, not only on the intensity of that pixel, but

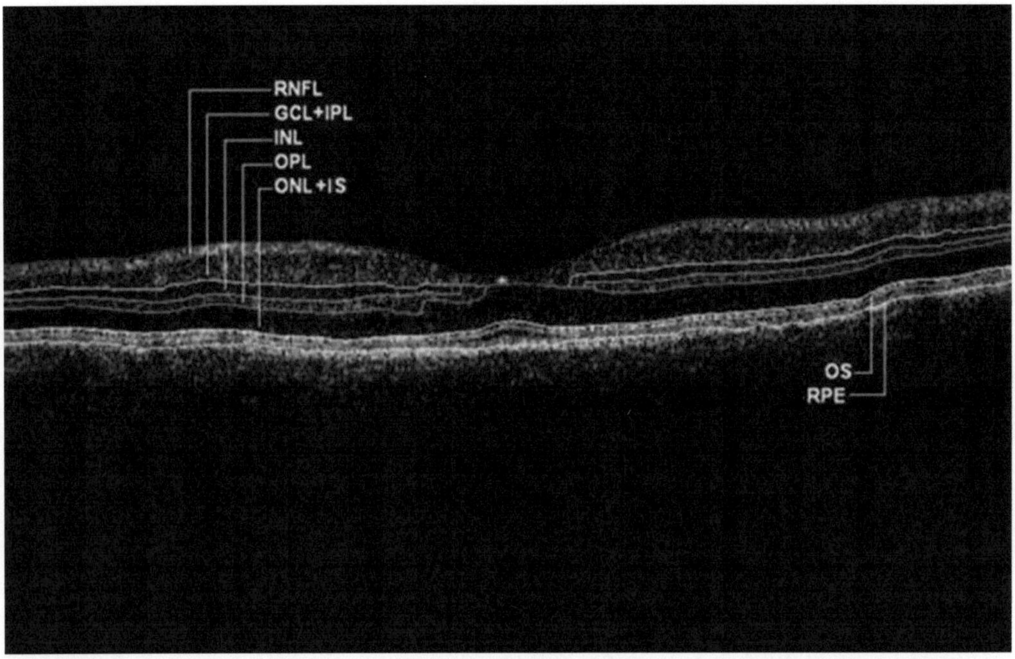

Fig. 9. Segmentation results for an OCT B-scan obtained from a healthy normal eye. The layers have been labeled as: ILM: inner limiting membrane, RNFL: retinal nerve fiber layer, GCL+IPL complex: ganglion cell layer and inner plexiform layer, INL: inner nuclear layer, OPL: outer plexiform layer, ONL: outer nuclear layer, OS: outer segment of photoreceptors, and retinal pigment epithelial layer (RPE). We note that the sublayer labeled as ONL is actually enclosing the external limiting membrane (ELM) and IS, but in the standard 10 μm resolution OCT image this thin membrane cannot be visualized clearly, making the segmentation of the IS difficult. Therefore, this layer classification is our assumption and does not reflect the actual anatomic structure. Also, observe that since there is no significant luminance transition between GCL and IPL, the outer boundary of the GCL layer is difficult to visualize in the Stratus OCT image shown. Thus, a combined GCL+IPL layer is preferable.

also on the classification of neighbouring pixels. These local correlations provide a mechanism for modeling a variety of image properties (Li, 1995). MRF is often incorporated into clustering segmentations such as *K*-means under a Bayesian prior model (Held et al., 1997; Pappas et al., 1992; Rajapakse et al. 1997).

3. *Pattern recognition methods*: Since structures in medical images can be considered as patterns, pattern recognition techniques can be used in segmentation procedures. There are supervised and unsupervised classification methods used to perform segmentation. Supervised classification algorithms are pattern recognition techniques that require training data that are manually segmented and then used as references for automatically segmenting new data. Typical supervised algorithms include artificial neural network (ANN), support vector machine (SVM) and active appearance models (AAM) (Alirezaie et al., 1997; Cootes et al., 2001; Wang et al., 2001). Unsupervised classification algorithms, also known as clustering algorithms, do not require a training set but they do require initial parameters to perform segmentation. Commonly used unsupervised classification algorithms include Fuzzy C-means algorithm (FCM), iterative self-organizing data analysis technique algorithm (ISODATA) and unsupervised neural network (Cheng et al., 1996; Mohamed et al., 1998; Wong et al., 2002).
4. *Deformable model methods*: These are model-based techniques for delineating region boundaries using closed parametric curves or surfaces that deform under the influence of internal and external forces. Deformable models can be classified into parametric and geometric models depending on the contour representation. These algorithms are usually interpreted as a modeling of curve evolution because they delineate an object boundary in an image by placing a closed curve or surface near the desired boundary and then allowing to undergo an iterative relaxation process. The parametric deformable models sample contours as discrete points and track them according to their respective moving equations. The moving equation for the parametric deformable models can be derived through either energy functional or dynamic forces. A priori knowledge can be easily incorporated to the procedures of parametric models. The geometric deformable models are based on the level set method (Osher & Sethian, 1988), which embed the moving contour into a higher dimensional level set function and view the contour as its zero level set. Then, instead of tracking the contour points, the zero level set of the level set function are tracked. The advantage of doing so is that topological changes can be naturally handled and the geometric properties of the contour such as normal vector and curvature can be calculated implicitly. Consequently, the computational complexity is decreased.
5. *Global optimization methods*: A growing number of image segmentation approaches use energy minimization techniques (Boykov & Funka-Lea, 2006; Kolmogorov & Zabih, 2004). Among all the various energy minimization techniques for segmentation, graph cuts are based on partitioning a graph by a minimum cut / maximum flow optimization algorithm (Greg et al., 1986; Ford & Fulkerson, 1956). The image is represented using an adjacency graph. Each vertex of the graph represents an image pixel, while the edge weight between two vertices represents the similarity between two corresponding pixels. Usually, the cost function to be minimized is the summation of the weights of the edges that are cut.
6. *Registration Methods*: The standard method used is the atlas-guided approach which treats segmentation as a registration problem (Maintz & Viergever, 1998). Typically, the atlas is generated by compiling information on the anatomy that requires segmentation

and then used as a reference frame for segmenting new images. This approach is theoretically similar to classifier methods but it is implemented in the spatial domain of the image rather than in a feature space. This approach uses a procedure known as atlas warping which first finds a one-to-one transformation that maps a pre-segmented atlas image to the target image that requires segmenting. The warping can be performed using linear transformations (Andreasen et al., 1996; Lancaster et al., 1997; Talairach and P. Tournoux, 1988).

7. *Model-fitting methods*: These approaches usually fits a simple geometric shape such as an ellipse or parabola to the locations of extracted image features in an image (Pathak et al., 1998). It is a technique which is specialized to the structure being segmented but is easily implemented and can provide good results when the model is appropriate. A more general approach is to fit spline curves or surfaces to the features (Kim & Hori, 2000).
8. *LEGION based*: These approaches are a biologically plausible computational framework for image analysis based on a biologically inspired oscillator network, called the locally excitatory globally inhibitory oscillator network (LEGION) (von der Malsburg, 1981;

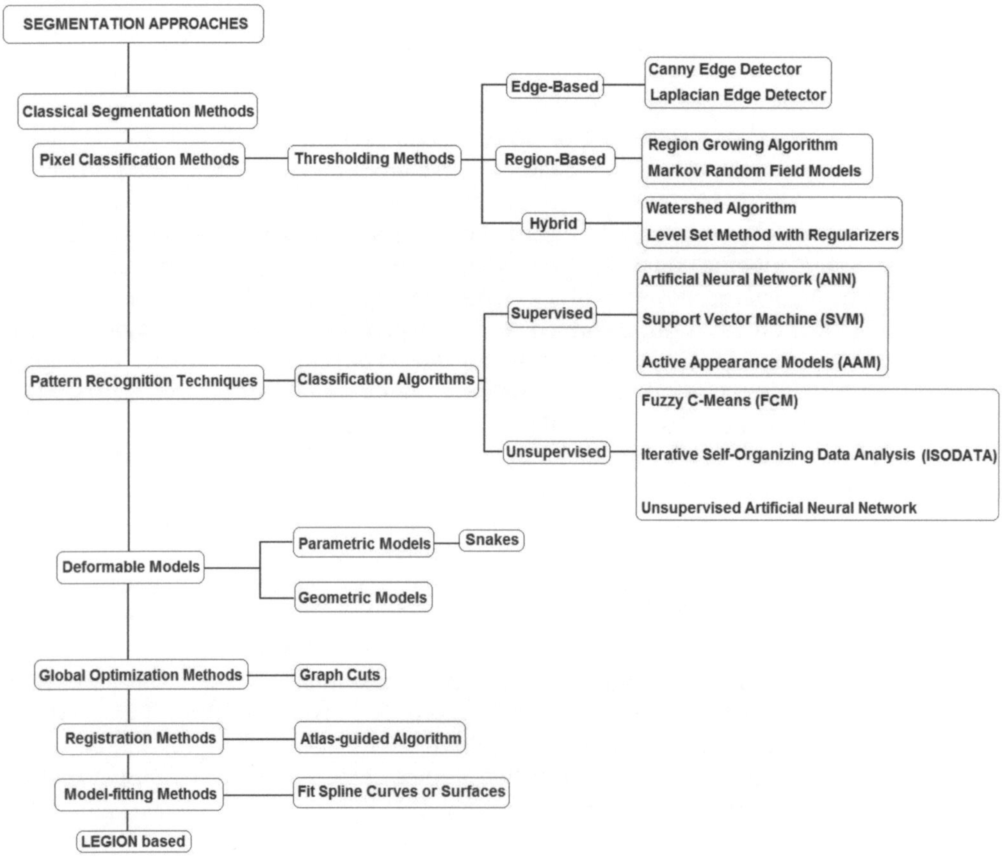

Fig. 10. Classification of segmentation approaches.

Wang & Terman, 1995; Wang & Terman, 1997). The network was proposed based on theoretical and experimental considerations that point to oscillatory correlation as a representational scheme for the working of the brain. The oscillatory correlation theory assumes that the brain groups and segregates visual features on the basis of correlation between neural oscillations (von der Malsburg, 1981; Wang & Terman, 1995).

As a final point, it is noteworthy to mention that years of research in segmentation have demonstrated that significant improvements on the final segmentation results may be achieved by using notably more sophisticated feature selection procedures, more elaborate segmentation techniques, taking into account prior distribution on the labels, region processes, or the number of classes, finally, involving (e.g. in the case of energy-based segmentation models) more costly optimization techniques.

5. Review of algorithms for segmentation of retinal image data using OCT

In opthalmology, a number of segmentation approaches of retinal image data using OCT have been proposed to enhance the clinical benefit of the OCT technology in the process of clinical decision making. The success of OCT in the investigation and treatment of retinal diseases might be best illustrated by the progress in automated analysis and the recent advancement of this technology from time domain to spectral domain (Cense et al., 2004; Drexler & Fujimoto, 2008; Fercher et al., 1995; Huang et al., 1991; Wojtkowski et al., 2003). The segmentation of the retinal structure is a challenging topic that faces major problems. First, OCT images suffer from the intrinsic speckle noise, which decreases the image quality and complicates the image analysis. This particular noise is the foundation of existing problems in the precise identification of the boundaries of the various cellular layers of the retina and other specific retinal features present in the OCT tomograms. Second, since the intensity pattern in OCT images results from absorption and scattering of light in the retinal tissue, intensity of a homogeneous area decreases with increasing imaging depth deterministically. This complicates segmentation algorithms which are commonly based on the assumption that intensity variations of homogeneous regions are only due to noise and not intrinsic to the imaging modality. The third problem is the low optical contrast in some regions of the OCT images due to the optical shadows of the retinal blood vessels resulting from the high haemoglobin absorption of light. Finally, motion artifacts and sub-optimal imaging conditions affecting the quality of the OCT tomograms also cause failure in the segmentation approaches or reduce their accuracy.

In this section, a number of approaches that have appeared in the literature on OCT image segmentation are described. This review concentrates on automated and semi-automated algorithms developed to segment the various cellular layers of the retina, structural irregularities associated to retinal disease (e.g. drusen and fluid-filled regions), and particular features of the optic nerve head in OCT images. Specifically, automation in OCT image analyses requires the establishment of parameters and features obtained from quantitative measurements of OCT data such as optical and structural parameters, scattering properties and refractive index of biological tissues. Thus, Table 1 gives an overview of the approaches discussed in this section based on the details of the above quantitative parameters and features. Although retinal blood vessel segmentation methods often consist of applying segmentation algorithms to fundus images, and more recently to advanced OCT images (e.g. SDOCT and UHR OCT) using the vessel shadows (Wehbe et al., 2007), I consider this application of segmentation to be a separate branch of research and do not included it in this review. The segmentation methods that will be reviewed can be classified into three groups based on the dimension (D) of the image analyzed. In particular, a number of different methods have been reported under the 1D, 2D and 3D categories (see Table 1). Segmentation approaches of OCT retinal images differ depending on the number of retinal features (e.g. number of intraretinal layers and fluid-filled regions) to be segmented, and on their robustness in the presence of inherent speckle noise, retinal blood vessel shadows and structural irregularities at the fovea, macula and optic nerve in pathological retinal tissue. Most of the initial segmentation algorithms are based on information retrieved from either gradient or conventional intensity data. However, some recent segmentation methods are based on more complex models, such as active contours and optimal graph search methods. It is worthy of mention that all existing published segmentation approaches have been basically introduced to overcome the limitation of the commercial OCT softwares and most of them have provided additional quantitative information of the retinal structure.

As it can be seen in Table 1, a number of segmentation approaches have been proposed to segment the retinal structure. The initial segmentation method proposed by Hee *et al.* was based on intensity variation and demonstrated the potential of OCT as a quantitative tool to measure total retina and RNFL thickness (Hee et al., 1995a, 1995b; Hee, 1997). This very first method used a 1D edge detection kernel approach, which is independent of the absolute signal level in the image, to compute the derivative of reflectivity versus axial distance for each A-scan in the OCT image. Thus, it is more effective than threshold identification. Specifically, the detection kernel identified the strongest two edges in each A-scan using peak-detection in more than 90% of the A-scans. Huang *et al.* used a similar approach to characterize the retina and outer retina choroid complex in hereditary retinal degenerations in experimental animals and humans (Huang et al., 1998). This early work, to the knowledge of the author, represents the first study to characterize and quantify OCT signals in relation to the optical properties of retinal layers. In contrast, George *et al.* used a dual threshold to segment the retina and choriocapillaries structure from OCT images (George et al., 2000). Unfortunately, very little information is available about this work. However, simple thresholding is sensitive to noise and intensity inhomogeneities in OCT images because it does not take into account the spatial characteristics of the image. Koozekanani, *et al.* introduced a Markov random field (MRF) model for extracting the inner and outer retinal boundaries from radial scans of the macula (Koozekanani et al., 2001). This autoregressive model showed to be more robust on the macular region of normal retinas than standard column-wise thresholding methods. Particularly, retinal thickness was calculated with an error comparable to the 10μm resolution of the OCT system used, representing a substantial improvement over clinical measurements provided by the Humphrey 2000 OCT built-in algorithm. Although a difficulty associated with MRF models is the proper selection of parameters controlling the strength of spatial interactions, Koozekanani's model is entirely independent and involves no critically tuned parameters. However, the main problem of this model is to find reliable "seed" points for OCT images of retinal pathologies. On the other hand, since this model relies on simply connecting 1D points, makes it sensitive to noise. Thus, it demands to apply special rules to correct for errors in the extracted layer borders because the model per se is sensitive to noise.

Since the problem with thresholding lies in the selection of the threshold, Herzog *et al.* proposed a method based on edge maximization and smoothness constraints to choose an optimal threshold to utomatically extract the optic nerve and retinal boundaries from axial OCT scans through the optic nerve head (ONH) (Herzog et al., 2004). A method to automatically segment the curve to extract the nerve head profile was also proposed. An interesting aspect is that in this approach the boundaries are obtained by maximizing the number of edges that lie on the boundary while minimizing the boundary's average rate of change. The algorithm generally identified the correct vitreal-retinal boundary in the images except in regions where the OCT signal was severely attenuated due to shadowing. This study is the first published work on ONH segmentation using TDOCT data. Two years later, a more efficient methodology to segment OCT nerve head images and extract the necessary parameters for clinical measurements such as the cup-to-disk ratio and RNFL thickness was proposed by Boyer *et al.* (Boyer et al., 2006) The improved methodology is esentially a parabolic model of the cup geometry and an extension of the Markov model introduced by Koozekanani *et al.* This study is the first published work on clinical parameter extraction taking advantage of the optic nerve head cross-sectional geometry in TDOCT images. Recently, Shrinivasan *et al.* also used a modification of the Koozekanini algorithm to perform quantitative measurements of the outer retinal morphology using UHR OCT (Shrinivasan et al., 2008). In this study the thick scattering region of the outer retina previously attributed to the RPE is shown to consist of distinct scattering bands corresponding to the photoreceptor outer segment tips, RPE, and Bruch's membrane.

Gregori *et al.* presented the first algorithm that was able to locate automatically and/or interactively the complex geometry and topology typical of many macular pathologies in TDOCT images (Stratus OCT system), and lately in SDOCT images (Cirrus HD-OCT unit) (Gregori et al., 2004; Gregori et al., 2005; Gregori et al., 2008). Unfurtunately, this is a proprietary algorithm that has not been described in detail because has been licensed to Carl Zeiss Meditec, and it is currently part of the commercial Cirrus HD-OCT instrument. However, it is a robust algorithm able to locate the boundaries of the major anatomical layers internal to the retina with great accuracy not only in eyes presenting abnormal and unusual anatomy but also in poor quality images. Table 1 includes a summary of all the results that have been presented in the ARVO meetings since 2004.

In 2005, algorithms based only on intensity variation were also presented (Shahidi et al., 2005; Ishikawa et al., 2005; Cabrera Fernández et al., 2005b). In general, these algorithms overcame the limitations of the commercial OCT3/Stratus OCT software and also provided additional quantitative information. For example, Shahidi *et al.* segmented three retinal segments by using a simple search of peaks corresponding to high- and low-intensity bands, and an improved edge detection approach using the correlation between axial A-scans was presented in a more recent study (Bagci et al., 2007). Ishikawa *et al.* used a modified median filter and an adaptive thresholding method based on the reflectivity histogram of each A-scan line to segment four layer structures within the retina (Ishikawa et al., 2005). A similar adaptive thresholding approach along with an intensity peak detection procedure was also employed by Ahlers *et al.* to segment data from patients with RPE detachments (Ahlers et al., 2008). This study was also based on the work by Gregori *et al.* (Gregori et al., 2005). It is worthy of mentioning that the work of Ishikawa *et al.* was the first report demonstrating that the thickness of the innermost layers in the macula had diagnostic power comparable with that of circumpapillary nerve fib er layer (cpNFL) in glaucoma studies (Ishikawa et al., 2005). Later on, Tan *et al. using* a 2D gradient approach in a dynamic programming framework also confirmed that glaucoma primarily affects the thickness of the inner retinal layers (RNFL, GCL, IPL) in the macula (Tan et al., 2008). Cabrera Fernández *et al.* used complex diffusion filtering to reduce speckle noise without blurring retinal structures and a peak finding algorithm based on local coherence information of the retinal structure to determine seven intraretinal layers in a automatic/semi-automatic framework (Cabrera Fernández et al., 2005b). This algorithm searches for edges in a map obtained by calculating the first derivative of the structure coherence matrix using the denoised image. Although, good results were obtained for some pathological Stratus OCT images, the algorithm in its original development was prone to failure and allowed detected boundaries to overlap. This algorithm worked reliably for data from 72 OCT B-scans from healthy normal subjects. The automatic/semi-automatic framework developed by Cabrera Fernández *et al.* was used to demonstrate for the first time the potential of OCT quantification for early DR damage (Cabrera Fernández et al., 2008; Cabrera DeBuc et al., 2010). The early segmentation work of Gregori *et al.*, Ishikawa *et al.* and Cabrera Fernández *et al.* allowed the automated generation of 2D thickness maps of individual retinal layers and, therefore, also a more local analysis of the retinal morphology using Stratus OCT data before the introduction of advanced OCT systems (Gregori et al.,2005; Ishikawa et al., 2005; Cabrera Fernández et al., 2005b).

A different approach using active contour algorithms has been used to quantify structural irregularities in OCT retinal images. For example, Cabrera Fernández *et al.* applied for the first time a deformable model to TDOCT images of retinas demonstrating cystoids and subretinal fluid spaces using a semi-automatic framework (Cabrera Fernández et al., 2004; Cabrera Fernández et al., 2005a). Specifically, this method used a nonlinear anisotropic diffusion filter to remove strong speckle noise and a gradient vector flow (GVF) snake model to extract fluid-filled regions in the retinal structure of AMD patients. Extension of this deformable model framework to a daily routine image analysis might prove to be difficult and unpractical since the algorithm requires manual interaction to place an initial model and choose appropriate parameters. Mujat *et al.* used deformable splines to assess the thickness of the RNFL in SDOCT images. (Mujat et al., 2005). Although all the model parameters were set based on a large number of OCT scans in different retinal areas, contour initialization is still a major problem because it must be close to the true boundary locations. In addition, though sensitivity to initialization was not reported in this study, the approach was highly vulnerable to the existence of blood vessels and other morphological retinal features. However, the advantage of this automated snake methodology is that it is able to provide larger area maps of the RNFL thickness facilitating the correct registration of ROIs with visual field defects which could allow better longitudinal evaluation of RNFL thinning in glaucoma studies. In 2009, Yazdanpanah *et al.* presented a modified Chan-Vese's energy-minimizing active contour algorithm in a multi-phase framework to segment SDOCT data from rodent models. This approach incorporated a circular shape prior based on expert anatomical knowledge of the retinal layers, avoiding the need for training

(Yazdanpanah, et al., 2009). Although the sensitivity of the algorithm with respect to model parameters and initialization was not tested, the experimental results showed that this approach was able to detect with good accuracy the desired retinal layers in OCT retinal images from rats compared to the ground truth segmentation used in the evaluations performed. Moreover, the algorithm was not evaluated for images including the foveal pit. Later on, Mishra *et al.* also presented a modified active contour algorithm based on a sparse dynamic programming method and a two-step kernel based optimization scheme (Mishra et al., 2009). Although this effective algorithm achieves accurate intra-retinal segmentation on rodent OCT images under low image contrast and in the presence of irregularly shaped structural features, results on images including the foveal pit region were not given and no quantitative evaluation using a large data set was provided.

Baroni *et al.* used a multi-step approach to extract the boundaries of the vitreo-retinal interface and the inner and outer retina by maximizing an edge likelihood function (Baroni et al., 2007). Interestingly, the effect of intravitreal injection of triamcinolone acetonide for the treatment of vitreo-retinal interface syndrome was evaluated using a set of measures such as thickness measurement, densitometry, texture and curvature extracted from the identified retinal layers. This study was the first report, to the knowledge of the author, that demonstrated the potential of texture information in TDOCT retinal images as a complimentary information of retinal features to aid diagnosis. Another intensity variation based approach to segment the posterior retinal layers, which is resistant to discontinuities in the OCT tomogram, was presented by Szulmowski *et al* (Szulmowski et al., 2007). Furthermore, the quantitative analysis has been largely limited to total retinal thickness and/or inner and outer retinal thickness in early studies exploring the correlation between histology and OCT in rodents (e.g. see Kocaoglu et al., 2007 & Ruggeri et al., 2007). Recently, more intensity variation based approaches have also been presented (see Table 1 for details) (Fabritius et al., 2009; Tumlinson et al., 2009; Koprowski et al., 2009 ; Lu et al., 2010 and Yang et al., 2010) Among them, it is worthy to mention that Fabritius *et al.* incorporated 3D intensity information to improve the intensity based segmentation and segmented the ILM and RPE directly from the OCT data without massive pre-processing in a very faster manner. (Fabritius et al., 2009). Likewise, Yang *et al.* presented a fast, efficient algorithm that simultaneously utilized both local and global gradient information (Yang et al., 2010). This approach skillfully used an A-scan reduction technique to reduce the execution time to 16 seconds per volume (480x512x128 voxels) without remarkably degrading the accuracy or reproducibility of the results. In addition, an alternative promising method was introduced by Mayer *et al.*, who used a fuzzy C-means clustering technique to automatically segment RNFL thickness in circular OCT B-scans without the need of parameter adaptation for pathological data (Mayer et al., 2008).

In contrast to the edge detection approaches mentioned above, a multi-resolution hierarchical support vector machine (SVM) was used in a semi-automatic approach to calculate the thickness of the retina and the photoreceptor layer along with the volume of pockets of fluid in 3D OCT data (Fuller et al., 2007). In this approach, the SVM included scalar intensity, gradient, spatial location, mean of the neighbors, and variance. Although this SVM method performed well on both healthy and diseased OCT data, a major drawback was that some voxels were mis-classified resulting in scattered noise in the thickness maps. In addition, this method requires that the user paints the areas of interest in

any slice of the volume. Thus, the training data set grows through painting increasing the complexity of the SVM, and as a result more time is required to complete the segmentation task. A different approach was presented by Tolliver *et al.*, who used a graph partitioning algorithm that assumes that different regions of the OCT image correspond to different modes of oscillation. The oscillation steps that represent the retinal edges are then determined by an eigenvector calculation (Tolliver et al., 2008). By using the eigenvector from the prior step as a starting point, for finding the new eigenvector, the approach works in only a small number of steps. In this study, the accuracy range for the detected boundaries was good and the algorithm performed well in the presence of retinal pathology. On the contrary to the vast majority of the studies cited so far, Götzinger *et al.* used PS-OCT to segment the RPE layer employing polarization scramble features. Even though the two algorithms presented facilitated a better visualization and quantification of RPE thickening and RPE atrophies when compared to algorithms based on intensity images, a PS-OCT system is needed to acquire polarization data (Götzinger et al., 2008).
A more complex approach to OCT retinal layer segmentation using gradient and/or intensity information in a 3D context was presented by Haecker *et. al.*, who generated a composite 3D image from radial linear TDOCT 2D scans and performed a 3D graph-search (Haecker et al., 2006). The basic idea of this graph approach is to break a graph into paths or fragments, which are utilized as filtering features in graph search. The early development of Haecker *et al.*'s algorithm extracted only 2 intratretinal layers and was evaluated on data from 18 controls and 9 subjects with papilledema (Haecker et al., 2006). This approach was further developed into a multilayer segmentation (Garvin et al., 2008) showing superior results for high quality OCT data. This graph-search approach potentially increased the accuracy of segmentation by using weights describing both edge and regional information to segment the volume. However, assumptions on the layers, as Garvin *et. al.* made, may be violated in pathological cases, or parameters have to be adapted for either normal subjects or pathological patients. Even though this elegant method can guarantee to find the global minimums when compared to deformable models, its computational complexity can really increase the computation time if more complex constraints are required to segment diseased retinal images showing common structural irregularities and a less ideal foveal pit. In 2009, Abramoff *et al.* combined a multiscale 3D graph search algorithm and a voxel column classification algorithm using a k-NN classifier to segment the ONH cup and rim (Abramoff, et al., 2009). This preliminary study showed for the first time a high correlation between segmentation results of the ONH cup and rim from SDOCT images and planimetry results obtained by glaucoma experts on the same eye. Later on, Lee *et al.* presented an improved and fully automatic method based on a similar methodology using graph search combined with a k-NN classifier that employed contextual information combined with a convex hull-based fitting procedure to segment the ONH cup and rim (Lee et al., 2010). In general, the methodology showed good performance but additional processing steps to compensate for the presence of vessels in and around the ONH would be required to reduced misclassified A-scans on the vessels and increase the accuracy of the ONH rim or cup contour segmentation. Similarly, Hu *et al.* used a graph-theoretic approach to segment the neural canal opening (NCO) and cup at the level of RPE/Bruch's membrane complex (Hu et al., 2010). Qellec et al. presented a promising method for detecting footprints of fluid-filled regions in SDOCT images from AMD patients (Quellec et al., 2010). This approach also used

a multiscale 3D graph search method to identify automatically a total of 10 intraretinal layers. The segmented layers were characterized by their thickness and 3D textural features. As in the Baroni et al. study, this report confirmed that useful 3D textural information can be also extracted from SDOCT scans to aid local retinal abnormality detection. In addition, Chiu *et al.* reported a skillful approach based on graph-based theory and dynamic programming that significantly reduced the processing time required for image segmentation and feature extraction (Chiu et al., 2010). This methodology is able to address sources of instability such as the merging of layers at the fovea, uneven tissue reflectivity, vessel hypo-reflectivity and the presence of pathology. Interestingly, the approach incorporates an automatic initialization that bypasses the need for manual endpoint selection.

The development of SDOCT systems has also made possible a better visualization and identification of the RPE-Bruch's membrane providing the ability to image drusen. As a result, segmentation algorithms have been recently presented to quantify drusen area and volume in AMD patients. For example, Farsiu *et al.* presented the DOCTRAP algorithm that is based on a modified implementation of the GVF snake model to accurately segment drusen in SDOCT images of AMD eyes (Farsiu et al., 2008). This methodology also included a semi-supervised approach to correct for segmentation errors such as false regions marked as drusen in images showing RPE elevation unrelated to drusen. The approach presented by Fuller *et al.* and described above also facilitates the semi-automatic segmentation of drusen in SDOCT images (Fuller et al., 2007). Gregrori *et al.* has also measured drusen area and volume using quantitative descriptors of drusen geometry in three dimensional space (Gregori et al., 2008). In addition, Yi *et al.* characterized ONH drusen using a commercial available software (see Table 1 for details) (Yi et al., 2009).

Kajić *et al.* presented a promising novel statistical model based on texture and shape able to capture the variance of the training data used to segment unseen data (Kajic et al., 2007). As the authors themselves stated, this guarantees that the segmentation will be close to the ground truth and less sensitive to noise. This algorithm successfully segments 8 intraretinal layers on 3D OCT data even under conditions which prove extremely difficult for some pre-existing segmentation approaches cited in the literature. It also has the potential of segmenting choroid layers and the ONH. In this study, for the first time, an error measure is computed from a large manually segmented data set which was certainly segmented twice by different operators.

6. Concluding remarks

In contrast to OCT technology development which has been a field of active research since 1991, OCT image segmentation has only being fully active explored during the last decade. However, it continues to be one of the more difficult and at the same time most commonly required steps in OCT image analysis, therefore, there does not and can not exist a typical segmentation method that can be expected to work equally well for all tasks. The works cited in this review spread from the 1997's until September 2010. Of course, the citation in this review is by no means complete. For example, an early active research topic such as manual tools for image segmentation has not been covered. It is also worthy the mentioning that it was difficult to assess the robustness of the various segmentation approaches because of many authors have used different OCT imaging setups and reported limited quantitative validation. Accordingly, a careful evaluation of different available academic and commercial segmentation methods using common test datasets is required to choose the one that best solves the given image processing task.

Current research in the segmentation of OCT images is striving towards improving the accuracy, precision, and computational speed of segmentation methods, as well as reducing the amount of manual interaction. On the other hand, most of the reported computation times of segmentation methods on 2D and 3D OCT datasets (see Table 1) are not really practical for general clinical use. However, segmentation methods will be particularly valuable in areas such as computer assisted surgery, where real-time visualization of the anatomy is a crucial component. For increasing computational efficiency, multiscale processing and parallelizable methods appear to be promising approaches (Sylwestrzak et al., 2010). As a matter of fact, the current expanding use of 3D OCT systems along with the advances in volume rendering techniques, is now shifting slowly the focus of segmentation to volume segmentation. In addition, the potential of OCT image segmentation to evaluate therapeutic or adverse effects of experimental interventions in time-course experiments might prove to be even more important to translate insights from bench to bedside in a proficient and timely manner.

Since OCT allows real-time data acquisition, future research will strive towards improving automation and data evaluation in near real time to support retinal disease screening and diagnosis. Automated segmentation still remains one of the most difficult problems in the world of OCT retinal image segmentation. This dificulty mainly arises due to the sheer size of the datasets coupled with the complexity and variability of the pathological retinal anatomy. The situation is worsened by the shortcomings of OCT imaging systems, such as sampling artifacts, noise, low contrast etc. which may cause the boundaries of retinal structures to be indistinct and disconnected. Recently, Liu *et al.* introduced a very effective approach for automated macular pathology identification in retinal OCT images (Liu et al., 2010). This method uses a machine learning approach that has the potential to provide unsupervised objective classifications for automated OCT data analysis in real time. Computational efficiency is particularly important in real-time processing applications for computer aided diagnosis and surgical planning. As a matter of fact, segmentation algorithms do have the capability to run in parallel with the OCT scanning method and to provide a concrete support for clinical decision making in real time.

Finally, it is worthy of mention that automated segmentation methods will never replace physicians but they will likely become crucial elements of medical image interpretation. Thus, there are numerous challenges to improve clinical decision making based on automated processing of OCT data, as outlined throught this chapter, for engineers, mathematicians, physicists and physicians working to advance the field of OCT image analysis.

7. Acknowledgement

I would like to acknowledge my amazing husband, Arthur, who was infinitely supportive and always poised to provide external motivation when I needed it most writing this chapter with our new baby boy around. Recognition is also due to my beautiful baby boy, Arthur Anthony, who provides me with joy and a healthy perspective on life that inspires me to work.

First Author/Year/ OCT system	Feature Studied	Sample Size	Preprocessing	Segmentation Method	Automation	Error Correction/ Refinement Method	Validation (key points)	Remark	Computation Time
Hee, MR., 1997/ TDOCT (Humphrey 2000 OCT)	Retinal and RNFL thickness	Imaging data from various pathological retina	Low-pass filtering: 2D center-weighted kernel	1D edge-detection kernel/peak-detection approach	Automated	Interpolation and local edge-detection	Reproducibility of the RNFL thickness in 10 glaucomatous eyes	First report of image processing techniques and methods of extracting quantitative information from OCT images	Not reported
Huang, Y., 1998, TDOCT (Humphrey 2000 OCT)	Thickness of the retina and outer retina choroid complex (ORCC=photoreceptor layer+RPE+anterior choroid); and the reflectivity posterior to ORCC	OCT data from human subjects (normal & with hereditary retinal degenerations) and degenerative avian and swine retinas	2D lineal smoothing (3x3 center-weighted Gaussian smoothing filter applied 5 times)	Algorithm based on signal amplitude and slope calculated using a 1st-derivative weighted filter	Automated	None	Not reported	First report of quantitative OCT results in hereditary retinal degenerations in experimental animals and humans	Not reported
George, A., 2000/ TDOCT (Humphrey 2000 OCT)	Thickness and volume of the retina and choriocapillaries	Information not available(I/N/A)	Median filter and image homogenization using Nagao filter	Dual threshold to segment the retina and choriocapillaries structures	Automated	(I/N/A)	(I/N/A)	(I/N/A)	(I/N/A)
Koozekanani, D., TDOCT (2001, Humphrey 2000 OCT)	Inner and outer borders of the retina	1450 images (B-scans)	4x4 median filter (applied twice)	1D edge detection kernel/Markov Boundary Model	Automated	Manual correction for evaluation purposes and linear interpolation to correct segmentation errors	Automatic and manual measurements differed by less than 25 µm, and in 89% of the tests the difference was less than 10 µm (near the resolution limit)	Algorithm offered performance significantly superior to the Humphrey 2000 OCT's built-in algorithm	Not reported
Herzog, A., 2004, TDOCT (Humphrey 3000 OCT)	ONH and retinal boundaries from axial OCT scans through the ONH	Exemplary OCT B-scans taken at the ONH	Median filter (4x4 applied twice)	Adaptive threshold algorithm based on edge maximization and smoothness constraints	Automated	None	None	First published results on ONH segmentation and geometric characterization from OCT data	Not reported
Gregori, G., 2004-, TDOCT (Stratus OCT) and SDOCT	Global boundaries (ILM, RPE),	Stratus OCT: 40 OCT B-scans	Non-linear anisotropic filter	Iterative boundary detection	Automated /Semi-Automated	None	Agreement with boundaries determined by	First segmentation algorithm that was able to locate	Not reported

(Cirrus HD-OCT)	NFL, GCL+IPL, boundaries of epiretinal membranes and other vitreous structures, the boundaries of cystic spaces, drusen, and RPE detachment	SDOCT: 150 eyes (full range of retinal diseases), 30 glaucomatous eyes and 30 normal eyes	(Structural Correlation Algorithm for Speckle Removal (SCASR))	algorithm			visual inspection agreed on at least 99% of the pixels and never diverges by more than 10% of the correct local retinal thickness. Automated detected boundaries were within 20 microns from manually drawn boundaries on well over 90% of pixels	automatically and/or interactively the complex geometry/topology typical of many macular pathologies.	
Shahidi, M., 2005, TDOCT (OCT3 Carl-Zeiss Meditec)	Thickness of the total retina and 3 retinal segments	OCT data from 10 healthy subjects	Median filter	Peak search algorithm (simple search of peaks corresponding to high- and low-intensity bands)	Automated	None	Reproducibility of thickness measurements showed that changes of 28 to 36 µm can be detected with 95% confidence	Algorithm averaged thickness profiles in the transversal direction producing less refined thickness profiles	Not reported
Ishikawa, H., 2005, TDOCT (Stratus OCT)	Various retinal layers/segments (4)	Forty-seven subjects (23 normal and 24 with glaucoma)	Modified mean filter (kernel size 7x5)	Adaptive thresholding technique (cutoff threshold was calculated based on reflectivity histogram of each A-scan line)	Automated	None	Algorithm failure of at least one detected border in approximately 10% of the good-quality images.	First segmentation algorithm that demonstrated the thickness of the innermost layers in the macula had diagnostic power comparable with that of cpNFL.	Not reported
Cabrera Fernández, D., 2005, TDOCT (Stratus OCT)	Cystoids and subretinal fluid-filled regions	OCT images from 7 patients with AMD	Nonlinear anisotropic diffusion filter	Gradient vector flow snake model	Semi-Automated	Manual correction for evaluation purposes	Mean distance between all extracted contours using the snake algorithm and the expert's contours was below 3 pixels.	First deformable model applied to OCT images of AMD patients demonstrating cystoids and subretinal fluid spaces.	84-92 seconds (on average) for a set of six radial OCT B-scans in a Pentium 4 CPU, 2.26 GHz
Mujat, M., 2005, experimental SDOCT	RNFL thickness	Two volumetric data sets of the same eye from a single subject	Anisotropic filtering	Deformable splines (snake algorithm)	Automated	None	Algorithm performed well in 350 frames with only few and isolated boundary detection errors	Provided large area maps of the RNFL thickness facilitating the correct registration of ROIs in glaucoma longitudinal studies	62 seconds for a single image (1000 A-scans) on a 3.2 GHz Pentium 4 processor

Cabrera Fernández, D., 2005, TDOCT (Stratus OCT)	Various retinal layers/segments (7)	72 OCT B-scans from normal subjects and 4 B-scans from pathological eyes	Complex diffusion filter	OCTRIMA software which uses a peak search algorithm based on local coherence information of the retinal structure.	Automated /Semi-Automated	Manual correction to eliminate segmentation pitfalls (if any) during the automatic procedure	All instances of algorithm failure were in regions which had extremely low reflectivity or almost no structural information.	First segmentation algorithm that demonstrated the potential of OCT's quantification for early DR damage.	24 seconds for filtering-segmenting each OCT B-scan (1024x512-pixel) on a personal computer (Pentium 4 CPU, 2.26 GHz).
Boyer, K., 2006, TDOCT (OCT 3000 Zees-Humphrey)	ONH (cup-to-disk ratio) and RNFL thickness	OCT data from 59 axial OCT nerve head scans	2D median filter (4x4 applied twice) along with a Palladian of Gaussian (1D) edge detector	Parabolic model of cup geometry and an extension of the Markov model introduced by Koozekanani, *et al.* to segment the retinal-nerve head surface, identify the choroid-nerve head boundary, and the extent of the optic cup	Automated	A glaucoma specialist marked the cup end points in 59 images in order to compare cup endpoints selected by the ophthalmologist to those selected automatically by the algorithm.	A correlation coefficient for cup diameter above 0.8 and above 0.9 for the disk diameter	First published results on clinical parameter extraction taken advantage of the ONH cross-sectional geometry in OCT images	Total processing time of 9.42 seconds (7.62 seconds for extracting the retinal-vitreal boundary requires, 0.793 seconds segmenting the cup limits, and 1.004 seconds for segmenting the disk limits) on a Pentium M, 1.8 GHz processor with 1 GByte of RAM
Baroni,M., 2007, TDOCT (OCT2 Carl-Zeiss Meditec)	ILM, RNFL, inner retina (IR), including GCL and IPL; and outer retina (OR), including OPL and inner photoreceptor layers (IPL)	16 pathologic OCT images from patients with crinkled cellophane maculopathy	Two 1D filters were used: 1) median filtering (5 pixels) along the A-scans; 2) Gaussian kernel in the longitudinally direction	2D dynamic programming where edge detection uses a Gaussian gradient applied cross-sectionally, as a 1D filter (detection of peaks using cumulative horizontal histograms and boundaries obtained by	Automated	None	None	First multi-step segmentation approach that demonstrated the potential of texture information in TDOCT images as a complimentary information of retinal features to aid diagnosis	Not reported

				maximizing an edge likelihood function)					
Szkulmowski, M., 2007, experimental SDOCT	Posterior retinal layers	OCT data from normal eyes and eyes with a selection of retinal pathologies	None	Variation of a multiple thresholding algorithm that identifies regions in the tomogram that have similar intensity and variance	Semi-Automated	Evaluation of the quality of segmentation requires operator intervention.	Not reported	Segmentation method is resistant to discontinuities in the tomogram	About 5 minutes for full processing of a data volume containing 200 images with 600 A-scans/image on a personal computer with a Pentium 4, 2 GHz processor
Ruggeri, M., 2007, experimental SDOCT	ILM, RPE layers along with tumor volume in small animals	OCT data from normal and diseased rodent eyes	Not reported	3D segmentation algorithm that detects the ILM and RPE boundaries by means of an iterative procedure by which an initial guess is repeatedly evaluated and improved	Automated for extracting the inner and outer borders of the retina. Manual segmentation was performed on each cross-sectional OCT image to obtain the boundaries of the tumor in the retinoblastoma model.	None	None	Algorithm facilitates the thickness map of the rodent retina	Not reported
Fuller, AR., 2007, experimental 3D OCT	Thickness of the retina and the photoreceptor layer along with the volume of pockets of fluid	Data from patients with AMD and retinal detachment	Noise is handled by considering voxel's mean value and variance across multiple resolutions in the SVM approach	Multi-resolution Hierarchical Support vector machine (SVM)	Semi-Automated	Manual segmentation tool for evaluation purposes	68% of the thickness differences between the SVM segmentation and the manual segmentation fell below 6 voxel units	SVM approach with global awareness by considering statistical characteristics at multiple levels of resolution	Less than two minutes (on average) for the full thickness segmentation performed on a computer with 3GB of RAM (dual processor 3GHz Intel Xeon)

Tan, O., 2008, TDOCT (Stratus OCT)	Various retinal layers/ segments	149 glaucomatous patients and 47 normal patients	Gaussian smoothing filtering	Gradient approach using dynamic programming (2D approach)	Automated	Progressive segmentation	Repeatability of thickness measurements showed the potential of using the thickness of both retina and inner retinal layers for tracking glaucoma progression.	Segmentation results confirmed that glaucoma primarily affects the thickness of the inner retinal layers (RNFL, GCL, IPL) in the macula.	Not reported
Garvin, M., 2008, TDOCT (Stratus OCT)	Various retinal layers/ segments (5)	OCT data from 12 patients (24- 3D image datasets) with unilateral anterior ischemic optic neuropathy (AION).	2D spectral reducing anisotropic diffusion filter	Optimal 3D graph search (graphs are constructed from edge/regional image information and a priori surface smoothness and interaction constraints)	Automated	Average of three experts' tracings as a reference standard was used for evaluation purposes	Overall mean unsigned border positioning error was 6.1 ± 2.9 μm, a result comparable to the interobserver variability (6.9 ± 3.3 μm)	First reported approach for the automated 3D segmentation of intraretinal layers.	Mean segmentation time (after alignment/registration) was 4.1 ± 0.9 min (using a Windows XP workstation with a 3.2-GHz Intel Xeon CPU).
Shrinivasan, VJ., 2008, UHR-OCT	Various retinal layers/ segments (6) but main focus on the outer retina segmentation	OCT data from 43 healthy subjects	Median filter (3 pixels) in the transverse direction	Modification of Koozekanani algorithm	Automated	Linear interpolation to correct for segmentation errors	Segmentation accuracy of the outer retinal layers was assessed by comparing automated vs. manually assisted measurements	Quantitative measurements of the outer retinal morphology were used to aid interpretation of the scattering bands posterior to IS/OS juntion visualized on UHR OCT images	Not reported
Ahlers, C., 2008, SDOCT (Cirrus HD-OCT)	Inner and outer borders of the retina along with the volume and area of fPEDs	OCT data from 22 patients with fPED	Morphological filtering to eliminate thin vitreous membranes from the thresholded image	Adaptive thresholding technique and intensity peak detection	Automated	None	Quality control of the automatic segmentation revealed reasonable results in over 90% of examinations	Automatic segmentation facilitated a thickness map showing the configuration of intraretinal fluid in much higher detail. Algorithm is able to track retinal- and subretinal changes in patients with RPE detachments	Not reported

Mayer, M., 2008, SDOCT (Spectralis HRA+OCT, Heidelberg Engineering)	RNFL thickness	OCT data from 5 normal and 7 glaucoma eyes	2D mean filter (kernel size 7x5) for speckle denoising along with complex diffusion filtering to aid segmentation.	Fuzzy C-means clustering technique	Automated	None	97% of the upper and 74% of the lower RNFL layer boundary points lied within a 2 pixel range from the manual segmentation of the evaluation data set	NFL segmentation method of circular OCT scans that is applicable to normal as well as pathological data, different patients and varying scanner settings without parameter adaptation	45 seconds on a 2Ghz Pentium IV for a 512x496 circular B-scan
Bagci, AM., 2008/TDOCT (Stratus OCT) & SDOCT (RTVue 100 OCT, Optovue, Freemont, CA)	Various retinal layers/ segments (6)	Data from healthy subjects: TDOCT (15) and SDOCT (10)	Directional filtering (2D filter with a wedge-shaped pass band)	2D edge detection algorithm based on the first derivative of Gaussian in the vertical direction	Automated	None	Difference between automated and manual segmentation was ≤ 4.2 µm, and almost identical to the difference between manual measurements by three observers (≤4.4 µm)	Edge detection uses: 1) the correlation between adjacent A-scans, 2) gray-level mapping technique to overcome uneven tissue reflectivity and variance across subjects	Not reported
Tolliver, D., 2008, SDOCT (3D OCT Cirrus)	Difficult boundary contours (4)	OCT data from 9 pathological subjects and 2 normative subjects	N/A	Spectral rounding	Automated	For evaluation purposes, manual segmentation was performed for 4 randomly selected scans per subject	The aggregate accuracy range for the detected boundaries was [85-99]%	Algorithm is able to track complex boundary contours in the presence of retinal pathology	Not reported
Farsiu, S., 2008, SDOCT (Bioptigen Inc., Durham, NC)	Drusen area, RPE and RNFL inner border	OCT data from 6 AMD eyes (a total of 228 SDOCT B-scans)	Low-pass filtering	DOCTRAP algorithm based on a modified implementation of the GVF based deformable snake method	Automated /Semi-Automated	Manual correction tool to modify the automated segmentation results. AMD images were also manually segmented by 2 experts for evaluation purposes.	Not reported	Algorithm takes advantage of differences of drusen substructures revealed by SDOCT facilitating drusen area and volume measurements	About 6.5 seconds to automatically segment, display and record drusen locations (image size: 512x1000 pixels) on a Intel Centrino-Duo 2.4 GHz CPU
Gotzinger, E., 2008, PS-OCT	RPE	OCT data from healthy volunteers (1) and patients with AMD (1) and pseudovitellif	Fixed pattern noise removal	Two algorithms: 1) Based on retardation data 2)Based on local variations of the polarization	Automated	None	Not reported	Algorithms facilitated a better visualization and quantification of RPE thickening and RPE atrophies when compared to	Algorithm 1: 8.3 minutes (without preprocessing and cornea compensation) for volumes

		orm dystrophy (1)		state calculated using Stokes vector analysis				algorithms based on intensity images.	with 60 B-scans (100 A-scans each) Algorithm 2: 31 minutes using an AMD Athlon 64X2 Dual Core Processor 4800+, 2.41 GHz, 2 GB RAM
Mishra, A., 2009, experimental HR-OCT (high speed)	Various retinal layers	OCT data from healthy and diseased rodent retina	Speckle noise and other typical artifacts in OCT images are handled by using an adaptive vector-valued kernel function in the precise layer boundary optimization step	Modified active contour algorithm by using 1) sparse dynamic programming method and 2) two-step kernel based optimization scheme	Automated	None	Not reported	Algorithm achieves accurate intra-retinal segmentation on retinal OCT images under low image contrast and in the presence of irregularly shaped structural features	5 seconds per image on an Intel Pentium 4 2.4 GHz machine with 1 GB of RAM.
Yazdanpanah, A., 2009, experimental FD-OCT	Various retinal layers (5)	20 OCT images from rodent models (4) of retinal degeneration	None	Modified Chan–Vese's energy-minimizing active contour algorithm (augmented with shape prior and weight terms)	Automated / Semi-Automated (user initialization prior to segmentation)	Manual segmentation for evaluation purposes	An average dice similarity coefficient of 0.85 was obtained when measuring the area similarity between the manual and automated segmentation	First multi-phase framework to segment OCT data that incorporates a circular shape prior based on expert anatomical knowledge of the retinal layers, avoiding the need for training	Not reported
Fabritius, T., 2009, experimental SDOCT	Inner and outer borders of the retina	Data from a healthy volunteer and from patients with ARMD (1) and PCV(1)	No denoising required	Intensity signal-based thresholding segmentation	Automated	Manual segmentation for evaluation purposes	Error smaller than 5 pixels in 99.7 (99.2) % of scans for the RPE (ILM) segmentation	Incorporated 3D intensity information to improve the intensity based segmentation. ILM and RPE can be segmented directly from the OCT data without massive pre-processing in a very faster manner.	About 17-21 seconds for 140 frames with 1022 depth scans

Yi, K., 2009, experimental SDOCT	ONH drusen	OCT data from one exenteration patient and 4 glaucoma patients	Anisotropic diffusion filter	Commercially available software from Amira interfaced with ITK's open source C++ algorithms	Automated	None	Not reported	First segmentation approach that is able to facilitate 3D imaging of the shape, size and location of ONH drusen	Not reported
Abramoff, 2009, SDOCT (Cirrus-OCT)	ONH cup and rim	OCT data (200x200x1024 voxels) from 34 glaucoma patients	None	Multiscale 3-D graph search algorithm to segment three retinal surfaces and a voxel column classification algorithm using a k-NN classifier	Automated	A nine k-NN classifier is used to refine/smooth the appearance of segmentation results. In addition, the correlation between algorithm-determined cup to-disc (c/d) ratio and planimetry-derived c/d by 3 experts was calculated for evaluation purposes	The correlation of algorithm c/d ratio to experts 1, 2, and 3 was 0.90, 0.87, and 0.93, respectively.	First algorithm that shows a high correlation between segmentation results of the ONH cup and rim from SDOCT images and planimetry results obtained by glaucoma experts on the same eye	Not reported
Tumlinson, 2009, experimental FD-OCT	Various retinal layers/segments (8)	OCT data from a dark-adapted human subject	Median filter	Thresholded edge-finding algorithm that first applies directionally biased filtering, finds positive and negative edges using derivative filters, and assigns those edges to layer boundaries based on a set of rules.	Automated	None	None	Algorithm exploited information in adjacent B-scans making simpler the segmentation task used to investigate for the first time depth-resolved slow retinal intrinsic optical signals	Comparable to the calculation of the fast Fourier transform (FFT) for translation of raw spectral data into structural tomograms (volume data: 512x 512x1024 on a Condor computer cluster)
Koprowski, R., 2009, SDOCT (Copernicus)	Retinal contours (inner, outer and others)	Various artificial images and one OCT scan	Median filter	Random Contour detection algorithm based on area analysis	Automated	None	Error analysis only reported for artificial images	Contours extraction depend on parameter selection	Not reported. But authors mentioned computation time is a major drawback of the algorithm

Kajic, V. , 2010, 3DOCT	Various retinal layers (8)	466 B-scans from 17 eyes	Dual-tree complex wavelet (DTCW) denoising	Statistical model based on texture and shape that captures the variance of the training data used to segment unseen data.	Automated	None	Evaluation against a large set of manual segmentations (a difference of only 2.6% against the inter-observer variability)	First time, an error measure is computed from a large manually segmented data set (segmented twice by different operators)	Not reported
Zhihong, H., 2010, SDOCT (Cirrus HD-OCT)	neural canal opening (NCO) and cup at the level of RPE/Bruch□s membrane complex	OCT data from 34 patients (68 eyes) with glaucoma or glaucoma suspicion	None	graph-theoretic approach	Automated	B-spline used to smooth/refine the NCO and cup boundaries. In addition, computer-aided planimetry was performed by 3 experts to create a reference standard	Mean unsigned and signed border differences of 2.81 ± 1.48 pixels (0.084 ± 0.044 mm) and -0.99 ± 2.02 pixels (-0.030 ± 0.061 mm) respectively for NCO segmentation	Algorithm is able to detect natural ONH anatomic structures of and optic cup	Not reported
Chiu, SJ., 2010/SDOCT (Bioptigen Inc., Durham, NC)	Various retinal layers (7)	Data from 10 healthy subjects	Gaussian filter along with rectangular averaging filter (3 × 19 pixels)	Graph-based algorithm and dynamic programming	Automated	Manual segmentation for evaluation purposes	Fully automatic algorithm differed from one of the manual graders by an average of 0.95 pixels.	Automatic initialization that bypasses the need for manual endpoint selection	9.74 seconds per image (on average) for 108 B-scans (64-bit OS, Intel Core2 Duo CPU at 2.53 GHz, and 4 GB RAM).
Lee, K., 2010, SDOCT (Cirrus HDOCT)	ONH cup and rim	27 SDOCT scans (200x200x1024 voxels) from 14 glaucoma patients	Median filtering and averaging Based smoothing	Multiscale 3-D graph search algorithm to segment four retinal surfaces and a	Automated	Local fitting method using the convex hulls of the segmentation to refine/smooth the contours of the ONH rim and cup. In addition, two glaucoma experts annotated the cup and rim area in stero- color photographs using planimetry to create the reference standard for evaluation	Unsigned error for the optic disc cup was 2.52+/-0.87 pixels (0.076+/-0.026 mm) and for the neuroretinal rim was 2.04+/-0.86 pixels (0.061+/-0.026 mm).	Fast and fully automatic method to segment the optic disc cup and rim in 3-D SD-OCT volumes	About 132 S (80 seconds to segment 4 intraretinal surfaces using the multiscale 3-D graph search approach, and 52 seconds for the feature extraction and classification) on a PC (Microsoft Windows XP Professional x64 edition,

						purposes			Intel Core 2 Duo CPU at 3.00 GHz, 4GB RAM)
Lu, S., 02010, SDOCT (Spectralis OCT, Heidelberg Engineering)	Various retinal layers (5)	OCT data from 4 normal healthy eyes	Bilateral filter and median filter	Algorithm based on the Canny's edge detector for the non-vessel sections. Linear interpolation is used for the layer boundaries in the vessel sections	Automated	Manual segmentation for evaluation purposes (16 OCT images)	Segmentation errors for the RNFL were less than 5 μm on average	Algorithm first detects the retinal blood vessels and then split the OCT image into multiple vessel and non-vessel sections.	Not reported
Yang, Q., 2010, SDOCT (Topcon 3D OCT-1000)	Various retinal layers (9)	OCT data (38 Scans) from 38 individuals, 19 glaucoma patients and 19 controls	None	Algorithm based on a dual-scale gradient information and a shortest path Search using dynamic programming	Automated	Manual segmentation for evaluation purposes	Overall the ICC of each boundary was above 0.94, the mean coefficient of variation was less than 7.4%, and the mean standard deviation was less than 2.8μm.	Algorithm is able to segment low-intensity and low-contrast OCT images in a very short time without degrading the accuracy In addition, pre-extraction of vessel locations, which is not a trivial operation, is unnecessary	About 45 seconds for each 3D volume (480x512x128 voxels) in normal segmentation processing mode and 16 seconds in fast segmentation mode using A-scan reduction technique
Quellec , G., 2010, SDOCT (Cirrus, HD-OCT)	Various retinal layers (10) along with fluid-filled regions	OCT data from 13 normal eyes and from 23 eyes with CNV, intra-, and sub-retinal fluid and pigment epithelial detachment	Wavelets	Multiscale 3-D graph search approach	Automated	Manual segmentation for evaluation purposes	Mean unsigned surface positioning errors were less than 6 μm.	Confirmed that useful 3-D textural information can be also extracted from SD-OCT scans to aid local retinal abnormality detection.	70 seconds per eye for 10 layer detection on a 200x1024x200 voxel volume using a standard PC at 2.4 GHz; (800 MB of RAM)

Table 1. Overview of OCT segmentation approaches.

8. References

Abràmoff, MD., Lee, K., Niemeijer, Wallace, L., Alward, M., Greenlee, EC., Garvin, MK., Sonka, M. & Kwon, YH. (2009). Automated Segmentation of the Cup and Rim from Spectral Domain OCT of the Optic Nerve Head. *Invest. Ophthalmol. Vis. Sci.* 2009 50: 5778-5784

Ahlers, C., Simader, C., Geitzenauer, W., Stock, G., Stetson, P., Dastmalchi, S & Schmidt-Erfurth, U. (2008). Automatic segmentation in three-dimensional analysis of fibrovascular pigmentepithelial detachment using high-definition optical coherence tomography. *Br. J. Ophthalmol.* 92, 197-203

Aguirre AD., Hsiung, P., Ko, P., Hartl, TH.& Fujomoto JG. (2003) High-resolution optical coherence microscopy for high-speed in vivo cellular imaging. *Optics Lett.* 2064-2066 28

Alirezaie, J., Jernigan, M E., Nahmias, C., (1997). Neural Network-Based Segmentation of Magnetic Resonance Images of the Brain, *IEEE Trans. on Nuclear Science*, 44:194-8

Andreasen, NC., Rajarethinam, J., Cizadlo, T. Arndt, S., Swayze, VW., Flashman, LA., O'Leary. DS, Ehrhardt, JC. & Yuh, WT. (1996) Automatic atlas-based volume estimation of human brain regions from MR images. *J. Comp. Assist. Tom.*, 20:98–106

Bagci, AM., Shahidi, M., Ansari, R., Blair, M., Blair, NP & Zelkha, R. (2008). Thickness profiles of retinal layers by optical coherence tomography image segmentation. *Amer. J. Ophthalmol.*, vol. 146, no. 5, pp. 679–687

Baroni, M., Fortunato, P. & Torre, AL. (2007). Towards quantitative analysis of retinal features in optical coherence tomography. *Medical Engineering and Physics* 29(4), 432–441

Bizheva, K., Pflug, R., Hermann, B., Povazay, B., Sattmann, H., Qiu, P., Anger, E., Reitsamer, H., Popov, S., Taylor, JR., Unterhuber, A., Ahnelt, P. & Drexler, W. (2006). Optophysiology: depth-resolved probing of retinal physiology with functional ultrahigh-resolution optical coherence tomography. *Proc. Natl. Acad. Sci. USA* 28, 103, 5066-71

Boppart, SA., Drexler, W., Morgner, U., Kirtner, FX. & Fujimoto, JG. (1999). Ultrahigh Resolution and Spectroscopic OCT Imaging of Cellular Morphology and Function, *Proceedings of Inter-Institute Workshop on In Vivo Optical Imaging at the National Institutes of Health*, A. H. Gandjbakhche, Ed., pp. 56–61

Boykov, Y., & Funka-Lea, G. (2006). Graph cuts and efficient N-D image segmentation. *Int. J. Comput. Vision*, vol. 70, pp. 109–131

Boyer, KL., Herzog, A., Roberts, C. (2006). Automatic recovery of the optic nervehead geometry in optical coherence tomography. *IEEE Trans Med Imaging.* May; 25(5):553-70. PubMed PMID: 16689260.

Brezinski, ME., Tearney, GJ., Bouma, BE., Izatt, JA., Hee, MR., Swanson, EA., Southern, JF., & Fujimoto, JG. (1996). Optical coherence tomography for optical biopsy: properties and demonstration of vascular pathology. *Circulation, 93 (6)*: pp. 1206-1213.

Cabrera Fernández, D., Villate, N., Puliafito, CA. & Rosenfeld, PJ. (2004). Comparing total macular volume changes measured by Optical Coherence Tomography with retinal lesion volume estimated by active contours. *Invest. Ophthalmol. Vis. Sci.* 45: E-Abstract 3072.

Cabrera Fernández, D. (2005a). Delineating fluid-filled region boundaries in optical coherence tomography images of the retina," *IEEE Trans. Med. Imag.,*vol. 24, no. 8, pp. 929–945

Cabrera Fernández, D. Salinas, HM & Puliafito, CA. (2005b). Automated detection of retinal layer structures on optical coherence tomography images. *Optics Express* 13(25), 10,200–10,216

Cabrera Fernández, Somfai, GM., Tátrai, E., Ranganathan, S., Yee, DC., Ferencz, M. & Smiddy, WE. (2008) Potentiality of Intraretinal Layer Segmentation to Locally Detect Early Retinal Changes in Patients With Diabetes Mellitus Using Optical Coherence Tomography *Invest. Ophthalmol. Vis. Sci.* 49: E-Abstract 2751.

Cabrera DeBuc, D. & Somfai, GM. (2010). Early detection of retinal thickness changes in diabetes using Optical Coherence Tomography," Med. Sci. Monit. 16(3), MT15–MT21

Cense, B., Chen, TC., Hyle, P.B, Pierce,MC &de Boer, JF. (2002). In vivo depth-resolved birefringence measurements of the human RNFL by PS-OCT. *Optics Lett.* 27, 1610-1612

Cense, B., Nassif, N., Chen, T., Pierce, M., Yun, SH., Park, B., Bouma, B., Tearney, B. & de Boer, JF (2004). Ultrahigh resolutionhigh-speed retinal imaging using spectral-domain optical coherence tomography, *Opt. Express*. 12(11), 2435–2447 (2004).

Chen, Z., Milner, TE., Dave, D. & Nelson JS. (1997). Optical Doppler tomographic imaging of fluid flow velocity in highly scattering media. Optics Lett. 22, 64-66

Cheng, K S., Lin, J S. & Mao, CW. (1996). The Application of Competitive Hopfield Neural Network to Medical Image Segmentation. *IEEE Trans. on Med. Img.*, 15:560-7

Chiu, SJ.,Li, CT., Nicholas, P.,Toth, CA., Izatt, JA, & Sina Farsiu. (2010). Automatic segmentation of seven retinal layers in SDOCT images congruent with expert manual segmentation. *Optic Express*. Vol. 18, No. 18. pp. 19413-19428

Choma, MA., Sarunic, MV., Yang, C., Izatt, JA. (2003). Sensitivity advantage of swept source and Fourier domain optical coherence tomography. *Optics Express.* 11: 2183-2189

Cootes, T F., Edwards, G J., Taylor, C J. (2001). Active Appearance Models. *IEEE Trans. Pattern Analysis and Machine Intelligence,* 23: 681-85

deBoer, JF., Milner, TE., vanGemert, MJC. & Nelson, JS. (1997). Two-dimensional birefringence imaging in biological tissue by polarization-sensitive optical coherence tomography. *Optics Letters, 22*(12), 934-936

deBoer, JF., Shrinivas, SM., Malekafzali, A., Chen, Z. & Nelson, JS. (1998). Imaging thermally damaged tissue by polarization sensitive OCT. *Optics Express*. 3, 212-218

de Boer, JF., Cense, B., Park, BH., Pierce, MC., Tearney, GJ., & Bouma, BE. (2003). Improved signal-to-noise ratio in spectral-domain compared with time-domain optical coherence tomography. *Optics Letters, 28* (21), 2067-2069

Ding, Z., Zhao, Y.,Ren, H., Nelson, JS. & Chen, Z. (2002). real-time phase-resolved OCT and optical Doppler tomography. Optic Express. 10, 236-245

Drexler, W. & Fujimoto, JG. (2008). State-of-the-art retinal optical coherence tomography, *Prog. Retin. Eye Res.* 27(1), 45–88

Fabritius, T., Makita, S., Miura, M., Myllyla, R. & Yasuno, Y. (2009). Automated segmentation of the macula by optical coherence tomography. *Opt. Express* 17(18), 15659-15669

Farsiu, S., Chiu, SJ., Izatt, JA., Toth, CA. (2008). Fast detection and segmentation of drusen in retinal optical coherence tomography images. *Photonics West, Ophthalmic Technologies.* San Jose, CA; 68440D-68441-68412

Fercher, AF., Hitzenberger, CK., Kamp, G. & Elzaizt, SY. (1995). Measurement of intraocular distances by backscattering spectral interferometry. *Opt. Commun.* 117(1-2), 43–48

Fercher, AF., Drexler, W., Hitzenberger, C.K. (2003). Optical coherence tomography. Principles and applications. *Rep Prog Phys.* 66: 239-303

Ford, L. & Fulkerson, D. (1956). Maximal flow through a network. *Canadian Journal of Mathematics.* 8. 399-404

Fuller, AR., Zawadzki, RJ., Choi, S., Wiley, DF., Werner, JS. & Hamann, B. (2007). Segmentation of Threedimensional Retinal Image Data. *IEEE Transactions on Visualization and Computer Graphics* 13(6), 1719–1726

Fujimoto, JG. (2003). Optical coherence tomography for ultrahigh resolution in vivo imaging. *Nature Biotechnology*, Vol. 21, No. 11, pp 1361-67

Garvin, MK., Abramoff, MD., Kardon, R., Russell, SR., Wu, X. & Sonka, S. (2008). Intraretinal Layer Segmentation of Macular Optical Coherence Tomography Images Using Optimal 3-D Graph Search. *IEEE Transactions on Medical Imaging* 27(10), 1495 - 1505

George, A., Dillenseger, JA., Weber, A. & Pechereau, A. (2000). Optical coherence tomography image processing. *Investigat. Ophthalmol. Vis.Sci.*, vol. 41, pp. S173–S173

Gonzalez, RC. & Woods, RE. (1992) *Digital Image Processing*. Addison-Wesley

Götzinger, E., Pircher, M., Geitzenauer, W., Ahlers, C., Baumann, B., Michels, S., Schmidt-Erfurth, U. & Hitzenberger, CK. (2008). Retinal pigment epithelium segmentation by polarization sensitive optical coherence tomography. Opt. Express 16(21), 16410–16422

Greig, D., Porteous, B. & Seheult, A. (1989). Exact maximum a posteriori estimation for binary images. *Journal of the Royal Statistical Society* 51(2) (1989) 271-279

Gregori, G. & Knighton, RW. (2004). A Robust Algorithm for Retinal Thickness Measurements using Optical Coherence Tomography (Stratus OCT). *Invest. Ophthalmol. Vis.Sci.*45:E-Abstract-3007

Gregori, G., Knighton, RW., Jiao, S., Huang, X., Rosenfeld, PJ. & Puliafito, CA. 3-D OCT Maps of Retinal Pathologies. (2005) *Invest. Ophthalmol. Vis. Sci.* 2005 46: E-Abstract 1055.

Gregori, G., Gregori, NZ., Knighton, RW., Lujan, BJ. Puliafito, CA. & Rosenfeld, PJ. (2008). Imaging Drusen With Spectral Domain Optical Coherence Tomography. *Invest. Ophthalmol. Vis.Sci.*49:E-Abstract-4234

Greig, D., Porteous, B., Seheult, A. (1989). Exact maximum a posteriori estimation for binary images. *Journal of the Royal Statistical Society.* 51(2), 271-279

Haeker, M., Abràmoff, M., Kardon, R., Sonka, M. (2006). Segmentation of the surfaces of the retinal layer from OCT images. *Med Image Comput Comput Assist Interv.* 9 (Pt 1):800-7. PubMed PMID: 17354964.

Haralick, RM. & Shapiro, LG. (1985). Image segmentation techniques. *Comput. Vis. Graph. Im. Proc.*, 29:100–132

Hausler, G. & Lindner, MW. (1998). Coherence Radar and Spectral Radar. New tools for dermatological diagnosis. *J Biomed Opt* 1998; 3: 21-31

Hee, MR., Izatt, JA., Swanson, EA., Huang, D., Schuman, JS., Lin, CP., Puliafito, CA. & Fujimoto, JG. (1995a). Optical coherence tomography of the human retina. *Arch. Ophthalmol.* 113, 325-32

Hee, MR., Izatt, JA., Swanson EA., Huang, D., Schuman, JS., Puliafito, CA. & J. G. Fujimoto. (1995b). Optical coherence tomography for micron-resolution ophthalmic imaging. *IEEE Eng. Med. Biol.*, vol. 14, pp. 67–76

Hee, MR. (1997). Optical Coherence Tomography of the eye. Thesis (PhD). Massachusetts Institute of Technology, Source DAI-B 58/04, p. 1952.

Held, K., Kops, ER., Krause, BJ., Wells, WM. Kikinis, R., & Muller-Gartner, HW. (1997). Markov random field segmentation of brain MRI images. *IEEE T. Med. Imag.*, 16(6)

Hermann JM., Pitris, C., Bouma, BE., Boppart, SA., Jesser, CA., Stamper, DL., Fujimoto, JG., Brezinski, ME. (1999). High-resolution imaging of normal and osteoarthritic cartilage with OCT. J. Rheumatol. 26, 627-635

Hermann, B., Fernandez, EJ., Unterhubner, A. Sattmann,H., Fercher, AF., Drexler, Prieto, WPM., & Artal, P. (2004). Adaptive-optics ultrahigh-resolution optical coherence tomography. *Opt. Lett.* 29, 2142-2144

Hermann, B., Považay, B., Unterhuber, A. Lessel, M., Sattmann, H., Schmidt-Erfurth, U. & Drexler, W. (2006). Optophysiology of the Human RetinaWith Functional Ultrahigh Resolution Optical Coherence Tomography. Invest. Ophthalmol. Vis. Sci. 2006 47: E-Abstract 1672

Herzog, A., Boyer, KL. & Roberts, C. (2004). Robust Extraction of the Optic Nerve Head in Optical Coherence Tomography. *CVAMIA-MMBIA*, LNCS 3117, pp. 395–407

Hu, Z., Abramoff, MD., Kwon, YH., Lee, K., Garvin, M. (2010). Automated Segmentation of Neural Canal Opening and Optic Cup in 3-D Spectral Optical Coherence Tomography Volumes of the Optic Nerve Head. *Invest Ophthalmol Vis Sci.* Jun 16. [Epub ahead of print] PubMed PMID: 20554616

Huang, D., Swanson, EA., Lin, CP., Schuman, JS., Stinson, GW., Chang, W., Hee, MR., Flotte,T., Gregory, K., Puliafito, CA. & Fujimoto JG. (1991). Optical coherence tomography. *Science* 254, 1178–81

Huang, Y., Cideciyan, AV., Papastergiou, GI., Banin, E., Semple-Rowland, SL., Milam, AH., Jacobson, SG. (1998). Relation of optical coherence tomography to microanatomy in normal and rd chickens. *Invest. Ophthalmol. Vis. Sci.* 39: 2405-2416.

Ishikawa, H., Piette, S., Liebmann, JM. & Ritch, R. Detecting the inner and outer borders of the retinal nerve fiber layer using optical coherence tomography. (2002). *Graefe's Archive for Clinical and Experimental Ophthalmology.* May;240(5):362-71

Ishikawa, I., Stein, DM., Wollstein, G., Beaton, S., Fujimoto, JG. & Schuman, JS. (2005). Macular Segmentation with Optical Coherence Tomography. *Investigative Ophthalmology and Visual Science (IOVS)* 46(6), 2012–2017

Izatt, JA., Hee, MR., Swanson, EA., Lin,CP., Huang, D., Schuman, JS., Puliafito, CA. & Fujimoto, JG. (1994a). Micrometer-scale resolution imaging of the anterior eye in vivo with optical coherence tomography. *Arch. Ophthalmol.* 112, 1584-9

Izatt, JA., Hee, MR., Owen, GM.,Swanson, EA. & Fujimoto, JG. (1994b). Optical coherence microscopy in scattering media. *Optics Lett.* 19. 590-592

Izatt, JA., Kulkami, MD., Wang, H-W., Kobayashi, K., & Sivak MV. (1996). Optical coherence tomography and microscopy in gastrointestinal tissues. *IEEE J. Selected Topics Quantum Electron.* 2, 1017-1028

Izatt, JA., Kulkami, MD.,Yazdanfar, S., Barto, JK. & Welch, AJ. (1997). In vivo bidirectional color Doppler flow imaging of picoliter blood volumes using OCT. *Optics Lett.* 22, 1439-1441

Kajić, V., Považay, B., Hermann, B., Hofer, B., Marshall, D., Rosin, PL. & Drexler, (2010). W. Robust segmentation of intraretinal layers in the normal human fovea using a novel statistical model based on texture and shape analysis. *Opt. Express* 18(14), 14730–14744

Kocaoglu, OP., Uhlhorn, SR., Hernandez, E., Juarez, RA., Will, R Parel, J-M., & Manns, F. (2007). Simultaneous Fundus Imaging and Optical Coherence Tomography of the Mouse Retina.*Invest. Ophthalmol. Vis. Sci.* 48: 1283-1289.

Kolmogorov, V. & Zabih, R. (2004). What energy functions can be minimized via graph cuts?, *IEEE PAMI*, vol. 26, pp. 147–159

Koozekanani, D., Boyer, KL.,Roberts, C. (2001). Retinal Thickness Measurements in Optical Coherence Tomography Using a Markov Boundary Model. *Medical Imaging, IEEE Transactions on* 20(9), 900–916

Koprowski, R. & Wrobel, Z. (2009). Layers recognition in tomographic eye image based on random contour analysis. *Computer recognition Syst. 3, AISC 57,* Kurzynski, M. & Wozniak, M. (Eds), pp. 471-478, Springer-Verlag, Berlin Heidelberg

Lancaster, JL., Rainey, LH., Summerlin, JL., Freitas, CS., Fox, PT., Evans, AC., & Mazziotta, JC. (1997). Automated labeling of the human brain: A preliminary report on the development and evaluation of a forward-transform method. Human Brain Mapping., 5:238-242

Lee, K., Abramoff, MD., Niemeijer, M., Garvin, MK., Sonka, M. (2010). 3-D segmentation of retinal blood vessels in spectral-domain OCT volumes of the optic nerve head. *Proc. of SPIE Medical Imaging: Biomedical Applications in Molecular, Structural, and Functional Imaging*, vol. 7626, p. 76260V, 2010

Leitgeb, RA., Schmetterer, I., Drexler, W., Fercher, AF., Zawadzki, RJ. & Bajraszewskit, J. (2003). Real-time assessment of retinal blood flow with ultrafast acquisition by color Doppler Fourier domain optical coherence tomography. *Optics Express*; 11: 3116-3121

Li, SZ. (1995) *Markov random field modeling in computer vision*. Springer-Verlag, ISBN:4-431-70145-1, London, UK

Liu,Y., Chen, M., Ishikawa, H., Wollstein, G., Schuman, JS. & Rehg, JM. (2010). In: *Automated Macular Pathology Diagnosis in Retinal OCT Images Using Multi-Scale Spatial Pyramid with Local Binary Patterns.*T. Jiang et al. (Eds.), pp. 1–9, MICCAI 2010, Part I, LNCS 6361, Springer-Verlag, Berlin, Heidelberg

Lu, S., Cheung, C., Liu, J., Lim, S., Leung, C. & Wong, T. (2010). Automated Layer Segmentation of Optical Coherence Tomography Images. *IEEE Trans Biomed Eng.*; 57(10), 2605-8

Maintz, JBA. & Viergever., MA. (1998). A survey of medical image registration. *Med. Im. Anal.*, 2:1–36

Mayer, MA., Tornow, RP., Bock, R., Hornegger, J. & Kruse, FE. (2008). Automatic Nerve Fiber Layer Segmentation and Geometry Correction on Spectral Domain OCT Images Using Fuzzy C-Means Clustering. *Invest. Ophthalmol. Vis. Sci.* 49: E-Abstract 1880

Michelson AA. & Morley EW. (1887). Philos. Mag. S.5, 24 (151), 449-463

Mishra, A., Wong, A., Bizheva, K. & Clausi, DA. (2009). Intra-retinal layer segmentation in optical coherence tomography images. *Opt. Express* 17(26), 23719–23728

Mitsui, T. (1999). Dynamic range of optical reflectometry with spectral interferometry. *Jap J Appl Phys* (Part 1 Regular Papers Short Notes & Review Papers); 38: 6133-6137

Mohamed, NA., Ahmed, MN., Farag A. (1998). Modified Fuzzy C-mean in Medical Image Segmentation. *Proceedings of the 20th Annual International Conference of the IEEE,* 3:1377-80.

Morgner, U., Drexler, W., Kartner, FX., Li, XD., Pitris, C., Ippen, EP., Fujimoto, JG. (2000). Spectroscopic optical coherence tomography. *Optics Lett.* 25, 111-113

Mujat, M., Chan, R., Cense, B., Park, B., Joo, C., Akkin, T., Chen, T. & de Boer, J. (2005). Retinal nerve fiber layer thickness map determined from optical coherence tomography images. *Optics Express* 13(23). 9480–9491

Novotny, HR & Alvis, DL. (1961). A method of photographing fluorescence in circulating blood in the human retina. *Circulation.* 24(1):82–86

Osher, S. & Sethian, J. (1988). Fronts Propagating with curvature-dependent speed: algorithms based on Hamilton-Jacobi formulations. *J. Comp. Phys.*, 79: 12-49

Pal, NR. & Pal., SK. (1993). A review on image segmentation techniques. *Patt. Rec.*, 26:1277–1294

Pappas, TN. (1992). An adaptive clustering algorithm for image segmentation. *IEEE Trans. Signal Processing.* 40(4):901-914

Pathak, SD., Grimm, PD., Chalana, V. & Kim, Y. (1998). Pubic arch detection in transrectal ultrasound guided prostate cancer therapy. *IEEE T. Med. Imag.*, 17:762–771

Podoleanu, AG., Dobre, GM., Cucu, RG., Rosen, R., Garcia, P., Nieto, J., Will, D., Gentile, R., Muldoon, T., Walsh, J., Yannuzzi, L.A., Fisher, Y., Orlock, D., Weitz, R., Rogers, J.A., Dunne, S., Boxer, A. (2004). Combined multiplanar optical coherence tomography and confocal scanning ophthalmoscopy. *J. Biomed. Opt. 9, 86–93*

Puliafito CA. (1996). *Optical Coherence Tomography of Ocular Diseases*. Thorofare, NJ: SLACK Inc

Quellec, G., Lee, K., Dolejsi, M., Garvin, MK., Abràmoff, MD. & Sonka, M. (2010). Three-dimensional analysis of retinal layer texture: identification of fluid-filled regions in SD-OCT of the macula. *IEEE Trans. Med. Imaging* 29(6), 1321–1330

Rajapakse, C., Giedd, JN. & Rapoport, JL. (1997). Statistical approach to segmentation of single-channel cerebral mr images. *IEEE T.Med. Imag.*, 16:176-186

Ren, H. (2002). Phase-resolved functional Optical Coherence Tomography: simultaneous imaging of in situ tissue structure, blood flow velocity, standard deviation, birefringence, and Stokes vectors in human skin. *Optics Lett.*27, 1702-1704

Ruggeri, M., Wehbe, H., Jiao, S., Gregori, G., Jockovich, ME., Hackam, A., Duan, Y. & Puliafito, CA. (2007) In Vivo Three-Dimensional High-Resolution Imaging of Rodent Retina with Spectral-Domain Optical Coherence Tomography. *Invest. Ophthalmol. Vis. Sci.* 48: 1808-1814

Sahoo, PK., Soltani, S.,Wong, AKC. (1988). A survey of thresholding techniques. *Comput Vision Graphics Image Process* 41:233–260

Sarkar, S., Boyer, K. (1991). Optimal impulse response zero crossing based edge detectors. *Computer Vision Graphics Image Process: Image Understanding* 54, 224–243

Shahidi, M., Wang, Z. & Zelkha, R. (2005). Quantitative Thickness Measurement of Retinal Layers Imaged by Optical Coherence Tomography. *American Journal of Ophthalmology* 139(6), 1056 - 1061

Smith RT, Chan JK, Nagasaki T, Sparrow JR, Barbazetto I. (2005). Automated detection of macular drusen using geometric background leveling and threshold selection. *Arch Ophthalmol* 2005;123:200-206

Sylwestrzak, M., Szkulmowski, M., Szlag, D. & Targowski, P. (2010). Real-time imaging for SDOCT with massively parallel data processing. *Photonics Letter of Poland.* vol. 2(3), 137-139.

Sziranyi, T., Zerubia, J., Czuni, L., Geldreich, D. & Kato, Z. (2000). Image Segmentation Using Markov Random Field Model in Fully Parallel Cellular Network Architectures. *Real-Time Imaging.* 6, 195-211

Szulmowski, M., Wojtkowski, M., Sikorski, B., Bajraszewski, B., Srinivasan, VJ., Szkulmowska, A., Kaluzny, JJ., Fujimoto, JG & Kowalczyk, A. (2007). Analysis of posterior retinal layers in spectral optical coherence tomography images of the normal retina and retinal pathologies. *Journal of Biomedical Optics* 12(4)

Talairach, J. & Tournoux, P. (1988). *Co-Planar Stereotaxic Atlas of the Human Brain. 3-Dimensional Proportional System: An Approach to cerebral Imaging.* Thieme Medical Publisher, Inc., Stuttgart, NY

Tan, O., Li,. G., Lu, AT., Varma, R., Huang, D. (2008). Advanced Imaging for Glaucoma Study Group. Mapping of macular substructures with optical coherence tomography for glaucoma diagnosis. *Ophthalmology.* Jun;115(6):949-56

Tolliver, DA., Koutis, Y., Ishikawa, H., Schuman, JS., & Miller, GL. (2008). Automatic Multiple Retinal Layer Segmentation in Spectral Domain OCT Scans via Spectral Rounding. *Invest. Ophthalmol. Vis. Sci.* 49: E-Abstract 1878

von der Malsburg, C. (1981). The correlation theory of brain function. *Technical report.* Max-Planck-Institute Biophysical Chemestry

von Helmholtz, H. (1851) In World Encyclopedia. Oxford University Press, 2005.

Wang, DL. & Terman. D. (1995). Locally excitatory globally inhibitory oscillator networks. *IEEE Transactions on Neural Networks.* 6(1):283-286

Wang, DL. & Terman, D. (1997). Image segmentation based on oscillatory correlation. Neural Computing.9:805-836.

Wang, S., Zhu, W Y., Liang, Z P. (2001). ShapeDeformation: SVM Regression and Application to Medical Image Segmentation. *Eight International Conference on Computer Vision,* 2:209-16

Westphal, V., Yazdanfar, S, Rollins, AM., Izatt, JA. (2002) Real time, high-velocity resolution color Doppler Optical Coherence Tomography. *Optics Lett.* 27, 34-36

Wojtkowski M., Bajraszewski T., Targowski P., Kowalczyk A. (2003). Real-time in vivo imaging by high-speed spectral optical coherence tomography. *Opt Lett.* 2003 Oct 1;28(19):1745-7

Wong, RC. (2002). Visualization of subsurface blood vessels by color Doppler Optical Coherence Tomography in rats: before and after hemostatic therapy. *Gastrointest. Endosc.* 55, 88-95

Yang, Q., Reisman, CA., Wang, z., Fukuma, Y., Hangai, m., Yoshimura, N., Tomidokoro, A., Araie, M., Raza, AR., Hood, DC. & Chan, K. (2010). Automated layer segmentation of macular OCT images using dual-scale gradient information. *Optics Express*. Vol. 18, No. 20, pp. 21294-21307

Yazdanfar, S., Rollins, AM., Izatt, JA. (2003). In vivo imaging of human retinal flow dynamics by color Doppler Optical Coherence Tomography. *Arch. Ophthalmol.* 121, 235-239

Yazdanpanah, A., Hamarneh, G., Smith, B., Sarunic, M. (2009). Intra-retinal layer segmentation in optical coherence tomography using an active contour approach. *Med Image Comput Comput Assist Interv.* 12(Pt 2):649-56

Yezzi ,A., Tsai, A., Willsky, A. (1999). A statistical approach to snakes for bimodal and trimodal imagery. *Proceedings of the seventh IEEE international conference on computer vision*, pp. 898–903.Washington, DC: IEEE Computer Society

Yi, K., Mujat, M., Park, BH., Sun, W., Miller, JW., Seddon, JM., Young, LH., de Boer, JF. & Chen, TC. (2009). Spectral domain optical coherence tomography degeneration for quantitative evaluation of drusen and associated structural changes in non-neovascular age-related macular. *Br J Ophthalmol.* 93: 176-181

Zawadzki, RJ., Jones, SM., Olivier, SS., Zhao, M., Bower, BA., Izatt, JA., Choi, S., Laut, S. & Werner, JS. (2005). Adaptive-optics optical coherence tomography for high-resolution and high-speed 3D retinal in vivo imaging. Optics Express. Vol. 13, No. 21, pp. 8533-8546

Zhao, Y. (2000) Phase-resolved Optical Coherence Tomography and Optical Doppel Tomography for imaging blood flow in human skin with fast scanning speed and high velocity sensitivity. *Optics Lett.* 25, 114-116

Part 2

Image Segmentation Methods

3

Image Segmentation through Clustering Based on Natural Computing Techniques

Jose Alfredo F. Costa and Jackson G. de Souza
Federal University of Rio Grande do Norte
Brazil

1. Introduction

Natural Computing (NC) is a novel approach to solve real life problems inspired in the life itself. A diversity of algorithms had been proposed such as evolutionary techniques, Genetic Algorithms and Particle Swarm Optimization (PSO). These approaches, together with fuzzy and neural networks, give powerful tools for researchers in a diversity of problems of optimization, classification, data analysis and clustering.

Clustering methods are usually stated as methods for finding the hidden structure of data. A partition of a set of N patterns in a p-dimensional feature space must be found in a way that those patterns in a given cluster are more similar to each other than the rest. Applications to clustering algorithms range from engineering to biology (Xu & Wunsch II, 2005; Xu & Wunsch, 2008; Jain et al., 1999).

Image segmentation techniques are based on Pattern Recognition concepts and such a task aims to identify behavior in a data set. In the context of image segmentation, the data set represents image data, coded as follows: the light intensity value (the pixel data) represents a pattern, an item in the data set, and the color information is represented by columns (the feature vectors). Clustering techniques represent the non-supervised pattern classification in groups (Jain et al., 1999). Considering the image context, the clusters correspond to some semantic meaning in the image, which is, objects. More than simple image characteristics, these grouped semantic regions represent information; and image segmentation is applicable in an endless list of areas and applications, for example: computer-aided diagnosis (CAD) being used in the detection of breast cancer on mammograms (Doi, 2007), outdoor object recognition, robot vision, content-based image, and marketplace decision support.

Among the many methods for data analysis through clustering and unsupervised image segmentation is: Nearest Neighbor Clustering, Fuzzy Clustering, and Artificial Neural Networks for Clustering (Jain et al., 1999). Such bio and social-inspired methods try to solve the related problems using knowledge found in the way nature solves problems. Social inspired approaches intend to solve problems considering that an initial and previously defined weak solution can lead the whole population to find a better or a best so far solution.

This chapter presents concepts and experimental results of approaches to data clustering and image segmentation using (NC) approaches. The main focus are on Evolutionary Computing, which is based on the concepts of the evolutionary biology and individual-to-population adaptation, and Swarm Intelligence, which is inspired in the behavior of individuals, together, try to achieve better results for a complex optimization problem.

Genetic and PSO based K-means and fuzzy K-means algorithms are described. Results are shown for data clustering using UCI datasets such as Ruspini, Iris and Wine and for image texture and intensity segmentation using images from BrainWeb system.
The remainder of the chapter is organized in the following form: section 2 describes Data Clustering and Image Segmentation; section 3 presents the state-of-the-art in Image Segmentation techniques; section 4 presents Natural Computing; section 5 focuses on clustering using Natural Computing methods. Section 6 presents experimental results and discussion and section 8 gives the conclusions and final considerations.

2. Image segmentation and data clustering

Digital Image Processing is an extremely important and fundamental task to image analysis, whose main task is the separation or isolation of image regions, reducing the data space to be analyzed. On monochromatic images, image segmentation algorithms are based on the following image gray level properties (Gonzalez & Woods, 2003):

a. **Discontinuity**: the objective is to find hard changes on gray level, using this information as the method to edge detection; and
b. **Similarity**: closest pixels are very similar.

Some of the main challenges to the scientific community are related to the development of techniques that realize the automatic or unsupervised image segmentation. In controlled environment the image segmentation process is easily achieved than in a non-controlled environment, where light and other circumstances affect physical process of image acquisition.
Image segmentation applications contemplate many areas of Computer Graphics. In the case of Computer Vision, one of the objectives is make robots move in a semi or non-controlled environment, and realize tasks like find and interact with specific objects. Another area of interest is the automatic vehicle guiding. On Image Understanding and Analysis there is Content Based Image Retrieval, that aims to develop efficient search engines that can find items on an image database by using a reference image, detecting similarities.
The mathematical formulation of segmentation is defined as follows (Raut et al., 2009):
Let I be the set of all image pixels, then by applying segmentation we obtain different unique non-overlapping regions $\{S_1, S_2, S_3, ..., S_n\}$ which, when combined, form I:

$$\bigcup_{i=1,n}^{n} S_i = I \quad \text{where } S_i \cap S_j = \varnothing \tag{1}$$

where:

a. S_i is a connected region, $i = 1, 2, \ldots, n$
b. $P(S_i)$ = TRUE for $i = 1, 2, \ldots, n$
c. $P(S_i \cup S_j)$=FALSE for $i \neq j$
d. $P(S_i)$ is a logical predicate defined over points in set S_i.

Eq. 1 is a condition that indicates that segmentation must be complete: every pixel in the image must be covered by segmented regions, which must by disjoint.

2.1 Data clustering

In a very simple level of abstraction, the image segmentation process is very close to the clustering problem. To find clusters in a data set is to find relations amongst unlabeled data. The "relation" means that some data are in some way next to another that they can be grouped. It is found in (Jain et al., 1999) that the components of a clustering task are:

1. **Pattern representation includes**: feature selection, which identifies the most effective subset of the original features to use in clustering; and feature extraction, which is the preprocessing of the input features.
2. A **Distance measure** is used to determine pattern proximity. A simple, and, perhaps, the most used, distance function is the Euclidean Distance.
3. **Clustering** relates to finding the groups (or, labeling the data) and it can be hard (an element belongs to one group only) or fuzzy (an element belongs to one group following a degree of membership).
4. **Data abstraction** is an optional phase and extracts a simple and compact representation of a data set and, in the case of data clustering, some very representative patterns are chosen: the centroids.
5. **Assessment of output** is the process of evaluating the clustering result. Cluster validation techniques are, also, a traditional approach to dynamic clustering (Omram et al., 2006).

Two classical clustering algorithms are used in this work: K-means (Forgy, 1965) and Fuzzy C-Means (Zadeh, 1994).

2.1.1 K-means

K-means objective if minimize the J function, which represents the minimization of the distance between objects (patterns) and clusters:

$$J_{\text{K-means}} = \sum_{k=1}^{K} \sum_{j \in S_k} d^2(x_j, c_k) \tag{2}$$

where:

a. k is the number of clusters evaluated (in a space defined by S_k)
b. x_j is the pattern j evaluated in relation to the centroid c_k
c. $d^2(x_j, c_k)$ is the distance between pattern x_j and centroid c_k

The algorithm performs as follows:

a. Initialize K centroids (for example, randomly)
b. Until a stop criterion is not satisfied
   a. Calculate the distances between all elements in the dataset and the K centroids. Elements closer to centroids form clusters
   b. Centroids are updated (assume the clusters values)

The main advantages of this algorithm are (Turi, 2001):

a. Is easy to implement
b. The complexity is $O(N_p)$, which makes it very applicable to large datasets.

The main disadvantages are (Davies, 1997):

a. It is dependent on the dataset
b. It is a greedy algorithm, which depends upon initial conditions that can lead to sub-optimal solutions
c. The number of clusters (K) must be informed by the user.

2.1.2 Fuzzy C-means

The Fuzzy C-means (FCM) algorithm is defined by (Bezdek et al., 1987) as follows: let $c \geq 2$ be an integer; let $X = \{x_1,...,x_n\}$ be a finite dataset which contains at least $c < n$ distinct points; and let R^{cn} be the set of all real matrices $c \times n$. A partition of the X set is represented by a matrix $U = [u_{ik}] \in R^{cn}$ whose elements satisfy the following equations:

$$u_{ik} \in [0,1], \qquad 1 \leq i \leq c; 1 \leq k \leq n \tag{3}$$

$$\sum_{i=1}^{c} u_{ik} = 1, \qquad 1 \leq k \leq n \tag{4}$$

$$\sum_{k=1}^{n} u_{ik} > 0, \qquad 1 \leq i \leq c \tag{5}$$

where v_i is the centroid of cluster i (most representative element). Partitions and centroids are chosen from the minimization of the functional J:

$$J_{\mathrm{m}}(U,v) = \sum_{k=1}^{n}\sum_{i=1}^{c}(\mu_{ik})^m |x_k - v_i|^2 \tag{6}$$

where $1 \leq m' < \infty$ is the *fuzzyficator parameter* and $|.|$ is a distance measure. Yet, the following condition is necessary for every i:

$$v_i = \frac{\sum_{i=1}^{n}(u_{ik})^m x_k}{\sum_{k=1}^{n}(u_{ik})^m} \tag{7}$$

and, for every k, in such a way that if $d_{ik} = |x_k - v_i|^2 > 0$ for every i, then the following is true for every i:

$$u_{ik} = \frac{1}{\sum_{i=1}^{c}\left(\frac{d_{ik}}{d_{jk}}\right)^{\frac{1}{m-1}}} \tag{8}$$

This chapter understands Clustering and Image Segmentation as a similar task. We make no distinction between them, in the view of the experiments. For a review on clustering techniques, please refer to (Jain et al., 1999; Xu & Wunsch, 2005; Hruschka et al., 2009).

3. The state-of-the-art

Some image segmentation techniques are presented by (Raut et al., 2009) and they can be classified in:

a. **Threshold-based techniques**: are generally used for gray level images. A threshold value T is defined to split the image in two parts: foreground and background based on pixel value

b. **Histogram-based techniques**: the histogram of all the pixels is calculated, and according to peaks and valleys different clusters are formed
c. **Edge detection techniques**: first and second order derivatives are used for detection of edges. Edges are divided in two categories: intensity edges and texture edges
d. **Region-based techniques**: uses region growing and region splitting-merging procedures. Region growing procedure groups pixels or sub regions into large regions based on predefined criteria. Region split-merge divides image into disjoint regions and then either merge and/or split to satisfy prerequisite constraints
e. **Watershed Transformation techniques**: considered to be more stable than the previous techniques, it considers the gradient magnitude of an image (GMI) as a topographic surface. Pixels having the highest GMI correspond to watershed lines, which represent region boundaries. Water placed on any pixel enclosed by a common watershed line flows downhill to a common local intensity minima (LMI). Pixels draining to a common minimum form a catchments basin, which represent the regions.

Clustering can be formally considered as a particular kind of NP-hard grouping problem (Hruschka et al., 2009). This assumption has stimulated much research and use of efficient approximation algorithms.

Many variations of approaches have been introduced over last 30 years, and image segmentation remains an open-solution problem. Recently there has been an increase in the presence of optimization-based techniques. (Angus, 2007) proposed a technique for a Population-based Ant Colony Optimization (PACO) to Multi-objective Function Optimization (MOFO). (Raut et al., 2009) proposed an approach used for prediction using segmentation. They use a Graph-Partitioning technique which has some bases on Ontology. In summary, image features may contain concepts (definitions of things) and relations between concepts. This makes up a knowledge database used for object prediction.

Important to note about the almost obvious result in the use of optimization techniques and how much it differs from, for example, the much well known K-means algorithm: the optimization technique will, theoretically, always find a better solution. Let *single* be an algorithm that finds one solution; let *multi* be an algorithm based on *single* that executes it about 100 times; from the 100 times, *multi* finds the better solution. It is possible that the *single's* solution is the same found by *multi*, but optimization techniques tend to actually see the problem by the worst side, i.e. if there is a *local best* maybe there is a *global best*. This behavior demonstrates the *expectation-exploitation* dilemma. As we will see in Section 4, most of the Natural Computing techniques are based on some common facts:

a. A population can achieve better results than one individual [of that population];
b. Every population needs some sort of change in its life. It is called progress or evolution;
c. The evolution can obey a random process, sometimes called mutation, and it can occur when a population tend to remain unchanged for a long period of time;
d. Every population has an individual that knows a very good solution. Sometimes, this individual can be crossed over another individual (that knows a good solution too) to generate another, eve better individual;
e. It is also a good approach to select the most capable individuals from one population (parents), cross over them, and create the next generation of individuals (descendants). It is assumed that every generation is better than the previous one;
f. There is a method to calculate how good an individual is, to measure it. It is often called *fitness function*.

This chapter is located in this context of optimization techniques. We present some techniques to solve clustering and image segmentation problems and discussion about experiments and results.

4. Natural computing

According to (Castro, 2007) Natural Computing is the computational version of the process of extracting ideas from nature to develop computational systems, or using natural materials to perform computation. It can be classified in (Castro, 2007):

a. **Computing inspired by nature**: algorithms take inspiration from nature to solve complex problems;
b. **The simulation and emulation of nature by means of computing**: a synthetic whose product mimics natural phenomena;
c. **Computing with natural materials**: the use of novel materials to perform computation to substitute or complement silicon-based computers.
d. Next section presents some of the most representative approaches.

4.1 Artificial Neural Networks (ANN)

An Artificial Neural Network, as found in (Haykin, 1998), is a massively distributed parallel built-in processor composed of simple processing units (the neurons) that act, naturally, to store useful knowledge which is acquired through a learning process that yields better results when the processing units work in a network interconnected form (the neural network).

The learning process, realized through a learning algorithm, resembles brain in two aspects:

a. Knowledge is obtained by the network from its environment through a learning process, which means the network does not acts in an unknown environment. ANN fits in a class of algorithms that need an instructor, a professor, who identifies and models the domain, presents data to the network and evaluate obtained results;
b. Forces connecting neurons, the synapse, are used to store achieved knowledge.

Some useful properties of ANN are:

1. Non-linearity
2. Mapping between Input-Output
3. Adaptability
4. Fault-tolerance
5. Uniformity of analysis and project

4.2 Evolutionary computing

The ideas of evolutionary biology and how descendants carry on knowledge from their parents to be adaptive and better survive are the main inspiration to develop search and optimization techniques for solving complex problems.

Evolutionary Algorithms have their bases on biology and, specifically, Evolutionary Theory and adapting organisms. (Castro, 2007) says that this category of techniques are based on the existence of a population of individuals that are capable of reproduction and are subject to genetic variation, followed by selection of new more adapted individuals in its environment.

There are many variations in the concept of Evolutionary Algorithms:

a. Genetic Algorithms
b. Evolutionary Strategies
c. Evolutionary Programming and
d. Genetic Programming

Although, they are all based on the following principles:

a. A population of individuals reproduces and transmits characteristics to other generations (inheritance). This concept determines that every individual, called *chromosome* carries a potential solution to the optimization problem in question. The solution represents the *genetic trace* of the individual, the chromosomes' components, the *alleles*, and it's encoded and structured in some way. These individuals are capable of reproduction, which is, a combination between two individuals and, after this process, future generation carry characteristics of previous ones.
b. Genetic variation: the individual reproduction mechanism generates modifications in the genetic trace of the next population's individuals. A process known as *mutation* allows the exploration of new solutions inside the search space.
c. Natural selection: the living environment for individuals is competitive, for only one of them will give a most adequate and useful solution to a given problem. So, it's necessary to define some way to verify how much an individual is able to participate in the process of generation of new individuals. The evaluation is realized through a performance evaluation function, known as *fitness function*.

It is important to remember that some characteristics of living organisms are not present in the formulation of evolutionary methods. (Bar-Cohen, 2006) presents some of them:

a. In nature, the occurrence of climate variations and environmental situations changes the characteristics of species through time and are fundamental to the verification of how much skilled an organism is. Evolutionary algorithms, otherwise, consider that the fitness function is constant in time.
b. In natural evolution, individuals of different species can battle and only one will survive. In evolutionary algorithms there is only one species.

In summary, with bases in (Krishna & Murty, 1999) an evolutionary algorithm is composed of the following steps:

1. Initialization of Population or Initial Generation: is often a random process to generate individuals for the initial population.
2. Selection: chromosomes of a previous population are selected to be part of the reproduction process. In general, a probabilistic distribution is used and the selection is based in the value of the fitness function for every individual.
3. Mutation: the individual's encoded solution, the allele, generated in the reproduction process, is exchanged in some way to make the algorithm don't stay stuck on *local optima*, but, through an exploration process, stay next to the *global optima*.

This process of generation of new individuals and population modification or update is repeated several times, until a stop criterion is satisfied.

Some applications of evolutionary algorithms are:

- Planning (i.e.: routing and scheduling)
- Design (i.e.: signal processing)
- Simulation and identification
- Control
- Classification (i.e.: machine learning, pattern recognition)

4.3 Swarm intelligence

Optimization based on swarm intelligence corresponds to methods that have become target of recent scientific researches. (Brabazon & O'Neill, 2006) indicates that there are two variations of this swarm model:

a. The first is inspired in bird flock social behavior
b. The second is based on behavior of insects, like ants.

The term "swarm intelligence" can have many definitions. (Castro, 2007) quotes some of them:

- Swarm intelligence is a property of non-intelligent agent systems with limited individual capabilities that exhibit collective intelligent behavior (White & Parurek, 1998).
- Swarm intelligence includes every effort to design algorithms or distributed devices to solve problems inspired in collective behavior or social insects and other animal societies (Bonabeau et al., 1999).

Ant Colony Optimization (ACO) was designed in 1997 by Dorigo and collaborators. They showed how the behavior of ants following pheromone could be used to optimize Travelling Salesman Problem (TSP) (Kennedy & Eberhart, 2001). For a detailed presentation of this method, please refer to (Brabazon & O'Neill, 2006).

Particle Swarm Optimization (PSO) (Kennedy & Eberhart, 2001) is a population based stochastic algorithm, modeled after the observation and bird flock behavior simulation. Even being very similar to other evolutionary approaches, PSO defines that each individual (called *particle*) benefits from its own previous solutions (a notion of history) (Omram, 2004). The theory that delineates PSO design is under the Adaptive Culture Model and three fundamental principles are taken into account:

a. **To evaluate**: learning is based on the analysis that every individual make of its own responses to external stimuli.
b. **To compare**: individuals are stimulated to compare themselves to other individuals, mainly that ones who have better performance and success.
c. **To imitate**: the logical consequence of the previous principles, it directs the individuals on their learning process.

4.3.1 The algorithm

The classical PSO design is that each particle, amongst the multitude of individuals (the swarm), flies through the search space (Omram, 2004) and carries on a potential solution to the optimization problem (Omram et al., 2006). The movement of each particle, which is, the changing of position, is determined by an equation that considers he current position of the particle and a velocity vector (Omram, 2004; Omram et al., 2006):

$$\mathbf{x}_i = \mathbf{x}_i(t) + \mathbf{v}_i(t+1) \tag{9}$$

$$\mathbf{v}_i(t+1) = \varpi \mathbf{v}_i(t) + c1r1\left(\mathbf{p}_i(t) - \mathbf{x}_i(t)\right) + c2r2\left(\mathbf{p}_g(t) - \mathbf{x}_i(t)\right) \tag{10}$$

where, according to (Omram et al., 2006):

a. ω is the inertia weight, which controls the impact of the previous velocity
b. *c1* and *c2* are acceleration constants
c. r*1*~U(*0,1*) and r*2*~U(*0,1*)
d. U(*0,1*) is a uniform distribution between 0 and 1

e. $\mathbf{p}_i(t)$ is the *cognitive component*, which represents the experience of particle i about where is the best solution. It considers the memory of particle's previous solutions
f. $\mathbf{p}_g(t)$ is the *social component*, which represents the experience of the whole swarm about where is the best solution

A user defined maximum velocity can be used to constraint the velocity update (Kennedy & Eberhart, 2001). The performance of the particle is measured using a fitness function which depends on the optimization problem.

The PSO algorithm is summarized as follows:
1. For each particle, randomly position it in the search space and randomly initialize its velocity vector
2. Repeat while until a stop criterion is satisfied
   a. For each particle
      i. Evaluate its quality (using the fitness function)
      ii. Update its best position
      iii. Update swarm's best position
      iv. Update its velocity (Eq. 10)
      v. Update its position (Eq. 9)

4.4 Artificial Immune Systems

Artificial Immune Systems (AIS) is a term to adaptive systems, emerging in 1980's, that extract ideas and metaphors from the biologic immune system to solve computer problems (Castro, 2007).

The main idea is inspired in following understanding (Castro, 2007):
a. that every living organism have the ability to resist over illness caused by pathogenic agents (virus or bacteria)
b. the first rule of the immune system is to protect the body or structure of the living organism; the cells of the immune system are capable to recognize molecular patterns (some sort of molecular signature) that is present within pathogens
c. once the pathogen is recognized, cells send each other signals that indicates the need for fight against the illness

This framework of immunologic engineering is composed by (Castro, 2007):
a. a representation of the system's components
b. a set of mechanisms to evaluate the interaction between individuals and their environment. The environment is simulated by a series of stimuli (input patterns), one or more evaluation functions (fitness)
c. adaptive procedures rule the system dynamics, which is, how its behavior changes over the time.

As can be seen, there is a very large set of naturally inspired approaches, each one needing its own chapter to be clearly detailed. This chapter will focus on Genetic Algorithms and Particle Swarm Optimization.

5. Clustering and image segmentation based on natural computing

This section presents two clustering methods based on GA and PSO, both used in clustering and image segmentation.

5.1 Genetic K-means algorithm

Genetic Algorithms have been applied to many function optimization problems and are shown to be good in finding optimal and near optimal solutions (Krishna & Murty, 1999). Aiming to solve the partitional clustering algorithm problem of finding a partition in a given data, with a number of centroids (or clusters), Genetic K-Means Algorithm (GKA) is introduced by (Krishna & Murty, 1999); it establishes an evaluation criterion based on the minimization of the *Total Within Cluster Variation* (TWCV), an objective function that is defined as follows (Doi, 2007; Lu et al., 2004): given **X**, the set of N patterns, and X_{nd} the dth feature of a pattern Xn, G_k the kth cluster and Z_k the number of patterns in G_k, the TWCV is defined as:

$$TWCV = \sum_{n=1}^{N}\sum_{d=1}^{D} X_{nd}^{\;2} - \sum_{k=1}^{K}\frac{1}{Z_k}\sum_{d=1}^{D} SF_{kd}^{\;2} \tag{11}$$

where SF_{kd} is the sum of the dth features of all patterns in G_k. The TWCV is also known as *square-error measure* (Krishna & Murty, 1999). The objective function, thus, tries to minimize the TWCV, finding the clustering that has centroids attending concepts of (Omram et al., 2006) *compactness* (patterns from on cluster are similar to each other and different from patterns in other clusters) and *separation* (the clusters' centroids are well-separated, considering a distance measure as the Euclidean Distance). It is found in (Bandyopadhyay & Maulik, 2002) another method for genetic algorithm based clustering that uses another fitness function, the Davies-Boudin index, which is a function of the ration of the sum of within-cluster scatter to between-cluster separation. As will be seen later, other validation indexes may be used and despites the objective function, GKA main aspects are:

1. **Coding**. Refers to how to encode the solution (the chromosome); one way of doing this is the *string-of-group-numbers encoding* where for Z coded solutions (partitions), represented by strings of length N, each element of each string (an allele) contains a cluster number.
2. **Initialization**. The initial population P_0 is defined randomly: each allele is initialized to a cluster number. The next population P_{i+1} is defined in terms of the selection, mutation and the K-means operator.
3. **Selection**. Chromosomes from a previous population are chosen randomly according to a distribution.
4. **Mutation**. The mutation operator changes an allele value depending on the distances of the cluster centroids from the corresponding pattern.
5. **K-Means Operator (KMO)**. This operator is used to speed up the convergence process and is related to one step of the classical K-means algorithm. Given a chromosome, each allele is replaced in order to be closer to its centroid.

Another approach, K-Means Genetic Algorithm (KGA), is presented in (Bandyopadhyay & Maulik, 2002) and shows a slight modification to the definitions presented before: the crossover operator is added to the algorithm and it is a probabilistic process that exchanges information between two parent chromosomes for generating two new (descendant) chromosomes.

5.2 Clustering using Particle Swarm Optimization

Different approaches are found that implement clustering based PSO algorithms, such as (Omram et al., 2006) and (Omram, 2004). A PSO-based Clustering Algorithm (PSOCA) can be defined as follows (Omram, 2004; Omram et al., 2006): in the context of data clustering, a single particle represents de set of K cluster centroids, in other words, each particle represents a solution to the clustering problem and, thus, a swarm represents a set of candidate data clusterings. The main steps are:

a. Initialize particle position and velocity (for each particle);
b. While a stop criterion is not found, for each particle:
    a. Calculates particle's quality
    b. Finds particle's best and global best
    c. Updates particle's velocity.

6. Experiments and results

The experiments rely on evaluate numerical results of clustering algorithms based on Genetic Algorithms and PSO. As previously seen, both methods are modeled to allow a switch of the traditional and basic clustering algorithm. Thus, this allows us to define the following algorithms variations:

a. Genetic K-means Algorithm (GKA)
b. Genetic Fuzzy C-means Algorithm (GFCMA)
c. PSO-based K-means Algorithm (PSOKA)
d. PSO-based Fuzzy C-means Algorithm (PSOFCMA)

The datasets used in data clustering experiments are the following:

a. **Ruspini**: two-dimensional dataset with 75 patterns. Has four classes easily separable
b. **Wine**: thirteen dimensions and 178 patterns. Has three classes
c. **Iris**: four-dimensional dataset with 150 patterns. Has three classes

Implementation was made in Matlab and used the Fuzzy Clustering and Data Analysis Toolbox (Balasko et al., 2005).

To best evaluate the results, considering classification error, in each dataset was added another dimension, corresponding to the cluster number associated to the pattern. Cluster Validation Indexes (CVI) was used to obtain numerical results and guide the possible best solution found by the algorithms: Davies-Bouldin (DB), SC (separation and compactness), S (separation), and Xie-Beni (XB). For a review on CVI please refer to (El-Melegy et al., 2007).

To compare the effectiveness of GA and PSO-based approaches, Table 1 presents K-means and FCM clustering results for Ruspini, Wine and Iris datasets. It can be seen that FCM performs better than K-means considering the CVI and Error of classification.

Table 2 presents GKA and GFCMA clustering results for Ruspini, Wine and Iris datasets. It can be seen that, in general, GKA got better results than K-means, FCM and GFCMA.

CVI	K-Means			FCM
	Min	Mean	Max	-
DB	0.61212	0.69081	0.77991	0.62613
SC	0.46308	0.48372	0.51758	0.62798
S	0.00446	0.00465	0.00497	0.00638
XB	3.41458	4.47178	4.93836	3.97634
Error (%)	11.33	19.60	42.67	10.67

(a)

CVI	K-Means			FCM
	Min	Mean	Max	-
DB	0.29046	0.44717	0.87690	0.33632
SC	0.27625	0.35350	0.51807	0.36330
S	0.00407	0.00665	0.01296	0.00541
XB	2.88926	7.18313	8.57401	6.04515
Error (%)	0.00	30.43	100.00	0.00

(b)

CVI	K-Means			FCM
	Min	Mean	Max	-
DB	1.10551	1.26082	1.57878	1.30418
SC	0.95495	0.97880	1.25538	1.62948
S	0.00664	0.00682	0.00859	0.01197
XB	1.90714	1.96253	2.17519	0.97245
Error (%)	2.81	6.19	47.75	5.06

(c)

Table 1. Clustering results for K-means and FCM: (a) Iris; (b) Ruspini; (c) Wine

CVI	GKA			GFCMA		
	Min.	Mean	Max.	Min.	Mean	Max.
DB	0.58931	0.61651	0.66188	0.45831	0.62613	0.64908
SC	0.43933	0.45049	0.45839	0.62725	0.62947	0.63466
S	0.00389	0.00416	0.00458	0.00630	0.00638	0.00644
XB	2.50475	2.58308	2.68649	1.35521	1.63055	1.85673
Error (%)	10.67	32.39	68.00	10.00	15.42	55.33

(a)

CVI	GKA			GFCMA		
	Min.	Mean	Max.	Min.	Mean	Max.
DB	0.29046	0.29046	0.29046	0.29046	0.32035	0.32237
SC	0.27625	0.27625	0.27625	0.36330	0.36332	0.36339
S	0.00407	0.00407	0.00407	0.00540	0.00541	0.00542
XB	2.81341	2.90996	3.04789	0.77498	1.28165	1.95288
Error (%)	0.00	11.56	100.00	0.00	7.19	76.00

(b)

CVI	GKA			GFCMA		
	Min.	Mean	Max.	Min.	Mean	Max.
DB	1.10055	1.10605	1.29697	0.84352	1.11319	1.30337
SC	0.96569	0.96961	0.97382	1.62937	2.41962	5.31974
S	0.00670	0.00674	0.00680	0.01197	0.01913	0.04760
XB	1.52923	1.58911	1.63309	0.60118	0.60694	5.31974
Error (%)	3.37	9.11	23.03	5.06	17.10	53.37

(c)

Table 2. Clustering results for GKA and GFCMA: (a) Iris; (b) Ruspini; (c) Wine

Fig. 1 shows clustering results for Wine dataset using GFCMA and GKA methods (PCA is used to reduce dimensions) obtaining error rate of 5.05% and 4.5%, respectively.

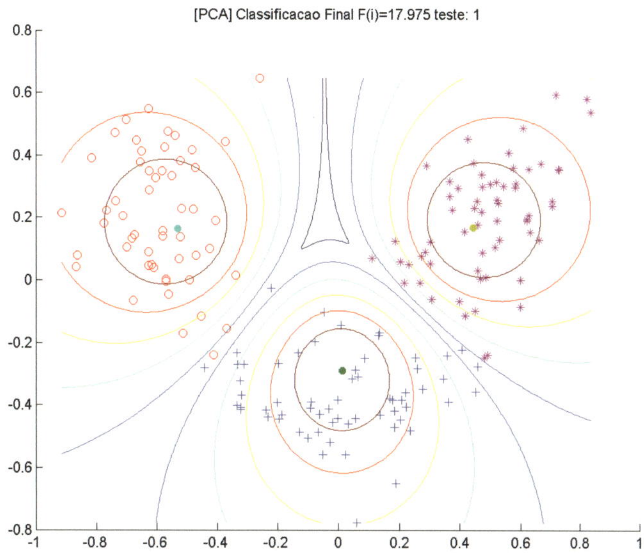

(a)

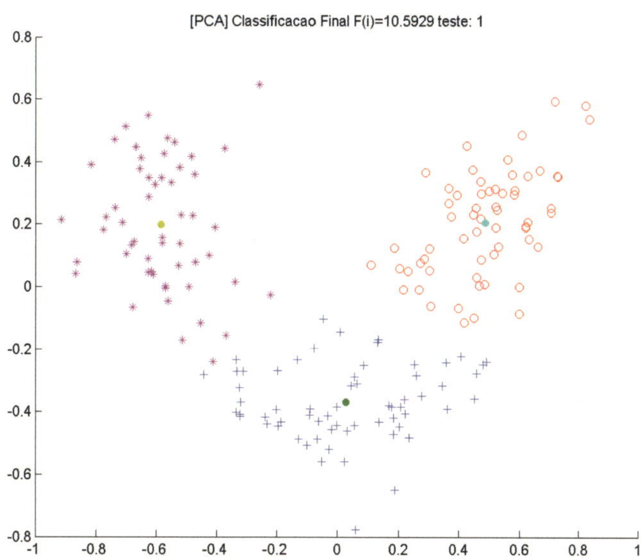

(b)

Fig. 1. GA clustering results for Wine dataset: (a) GFCMA; (b) GKA

CVI	PSOKA			PSOFCMA		
	Min.	Mean	Max.	Min.	Mean	Max.
DB	0.27045	0.36780	0.52796	0.57841	0.62335	0.62613
SC	0.39613	0.47915	0.54635	0.62484	0.62749	0.62796
S	0.00365	0.00421	0.00516	0.00637	0.00637	0.00638
XB	1.19575	1.52560	2.06278	1.21399	1.37726	1.68562
Error (%)	6.00	65.97	100.00	10.67	15.75	35.33

(a)

CVI	PSOKA			PSOFCMA		
	Min.	Mean	Max.	Min.	Mean	Max.
DB	0.00471	0.00489	0.29046	0.00538	0.00540	0.00541
SC	0.29046	0.30640	0.33533	0.29046	0.30042	0.32035
S	0.00832	0.71131	1.68594	0.36314	0.36328	0.36330
XB	0.18273	1.01053	1.75728	0.80723	1.44156	3.27777
Error (%)	0.00	22.25	100.00	0.00	9.81	92.00

(b)

CVI	PSOKA			PSOFCMA		
	Min.	Mean	Max.	Min.	Mean	Max.
DB	0.23707	0.69798	1.02811	0.86679	1.10988	1.30337
SC	0.79707	0.95203	1.22435	1.62937	1.62937	1.62937
S	0.00479	0.00672	0.00870	0.01197	0.01197	0.01197
XB	1.19477	1.36998	1.54367	0.59022	0.60331	0.61588
Error (%)	5.06	31.25	72.47	5.06	13.80	49.44

(c)

Table 3. Clustering results for PSOKA and PSOFCMA: (a) Iris; (b) Ruspini; (c) Wine

Table 3 summarizes clustering results for PSOKA and PSOFCMA. It can be seen that PSOKA performs better than PSOFCMA considering CVI and PSOFCMA is better than PSOKA considering Error (error of classification). Fig. 2 presents PSOFCMA and PSOKA clustering for Wine.

The dataset used in image segmentation experiments was obtained from the BrainWeb system (BrainWeb, 2010; Cocosco et al., 1997; Kwan et al., 1996; Kwan et al., 1999; Collins et al., 1998), it corresponds to simulated MR images of T1 modality, 0% noise, and 0% intensity. BrainWeb dataset contains 10 classes that range from background to connective material. For ground truth and classification error evaluation is used the "crisp" dataset. Fig. 3 presents a slice from the MRI Volume in BrainWeb that is used as dataset for experiments. Fig. 3a represents the input to algorithms. Fig. 3b represents the ground truth. Image segmentation approaches of current work are unsupervised, so the ground truth is used only as a final evaluation step, to quantify image segmentation results.

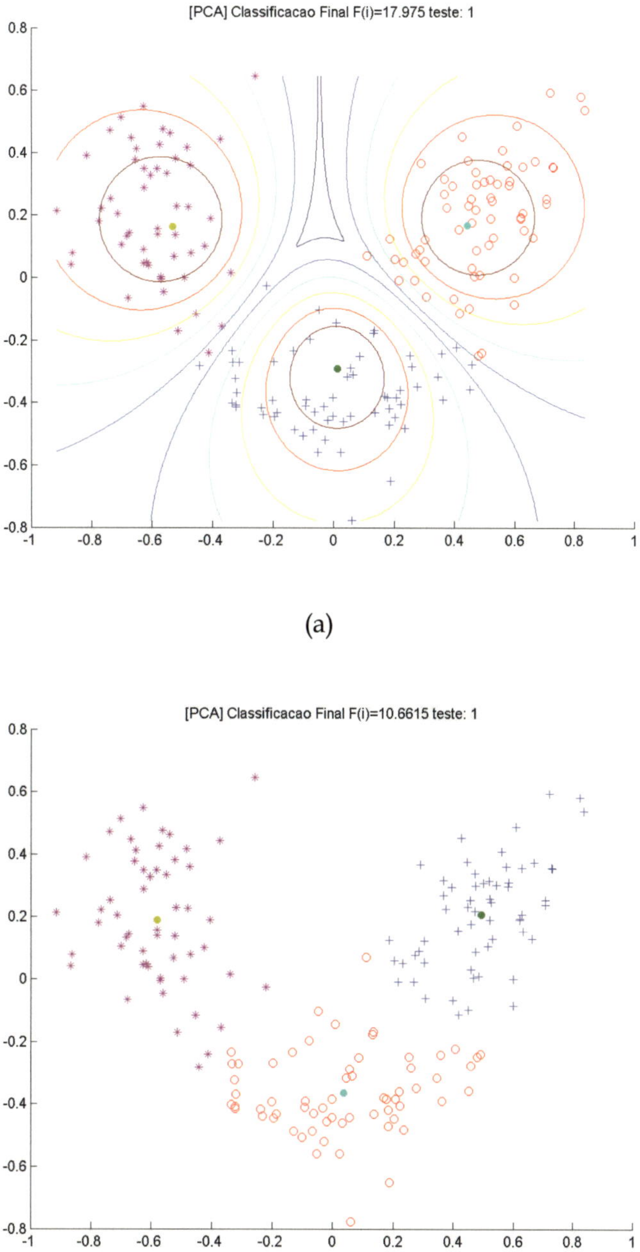

(a)

(b)

Fig. 2. PSO clustering results for Wine dataset: (a) PSOFCMA; (b) PSOKA

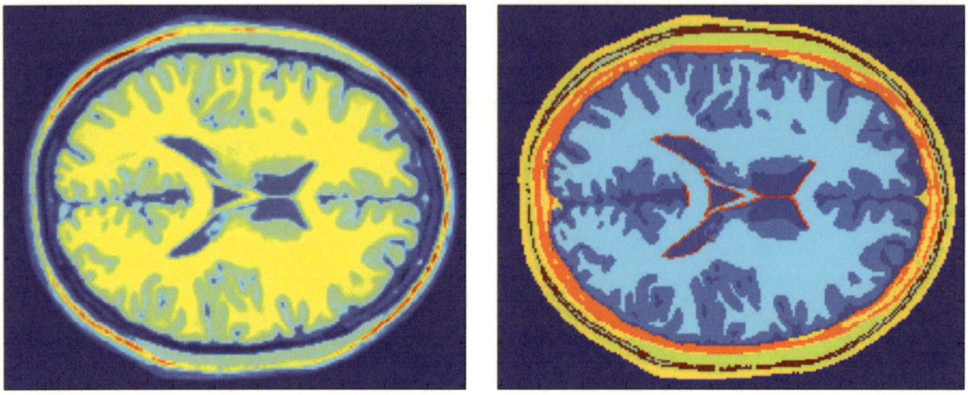

(a) (b)

Fig. 3. Slice from volume in BrainWeb dataset: a) fuzzy dataset; b) crisp dataset

Final objective is to find the correct classes that represent brain regions. Fig. 4 shows crisp dataset in detail and with every class individually.

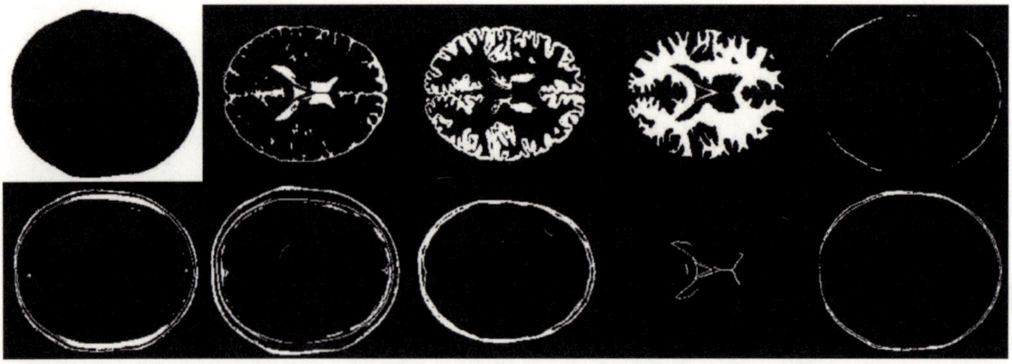

Fig. 4. Crisp dataset in detail: every class corresponding to one brain region in BrainWeb

Cluster Validation Indexes are commonly used to evaluate image segmentation, but results did show that classification error was not acceptable - experiments did show it was around 90%. From this assumption, another study has begun in the direction of finding a better way to evaluate image segmentation. (Chabrier et al., 2006) work on unsupervised image segmentation evaluation methods present several approaches. Amongst them we use the Rosenberger's evaluation criterion, which is defined by following equation (Chabrier et al., 2006):

$$ROS(I_R) = \frac{1 + \frac{1}{C_{N_R}^2} \sum_{i,j=1,i\neq j}^{N_R} \left(\left| \overline{g}_I(R_i) - \overline{g}_I(R_j) \right| / 512 - 4 / 255^2 N_R \right) \sum_{i=1}^{N_R} \sigma^2(R_i)}{2} \tag{12}$$

where:

a. I_R corresponds to the segmentation result of image I in a set of regions $R = \{R_1, ..., R_{N_R}\}$ having N_R regions

b. $\overline{g}_I(R_i)$ can be generalized to a feature vector computed on the pixels values of the region R_i . The same occurs for $\overline{g}_I(R_j)$

c. $C^2_{N_R}$ is the number of combinations of 2 regions among N_R

According to (Chabrier et al., 2006) this criterion combines intra and interregions disparities: intraregion is computed by the normalized standard deviation of gray levels in each region; interregions disparity computes the dissimilarity of the average gray level of two regions in the segmentation result.

For comparison purposes experiments were taken for classical K-means and Fuzzy C-means (FCM) algorithms, considering 100 rounds - with maximum 100 iterations each. Table 4 presents best results considering lower classification error.

Measure	K-means			FCM
	Min.	*Mean.*	*Max.*	--
DB	**0.33098**	0.39152	0.47994	0.38630
MSE	**39.47764**	181.26347	749.88781	86.35377
SC	0.15269	0.20480	**0.27183**	0.29905
S	1.00000	4.32406	**10.00000**	0.00001
XB	**141.13651**	997.30277	26302.67634	145.14488
ROS	**0.50030**	0.50036	0.50042	0.50039
Error (%)	**50.21514**	65.40306	84.72134	68.78071

Table 4. Image Segmentation results for K-means and FCM

Important to note is that there were no heuristics for experiments with K-means and FCM: values from Table 4 are obtained may be different every time the experiment runs, unless for FCM, for it has the same results have always been found.

Fig. 5 and Fig. 6 show qualitative results for K-means and FCM, respectively.

Both image segmentations using K-means and FCM shows that all classes have many classification errors and many of them are indistinguishable from each other. In other words, most classes are very similar.

Current work's objective is that approaches under investigation (GKA, GFCMA, PSOKA and PSOFCMA) achieve better values for all measures and classification error. Each method runs in a set of experiments, which evaluate the effect of some parameters:

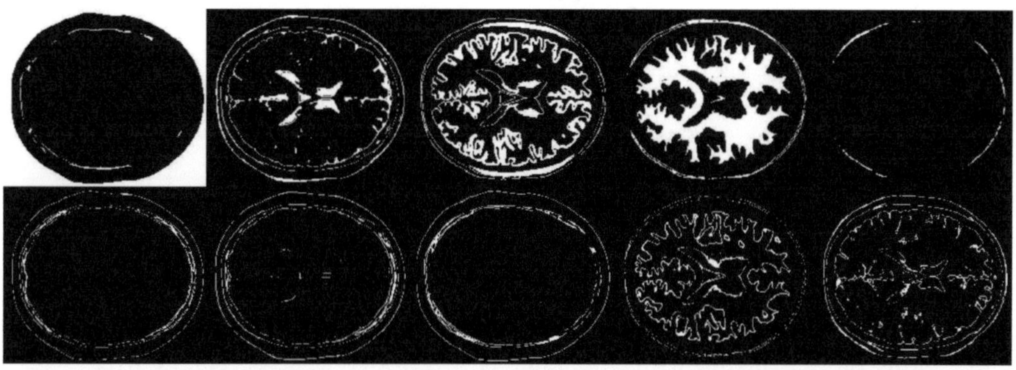

Fig. 5. Crisp dataset in detail: every class corresponding to one brain region in BrainWeb

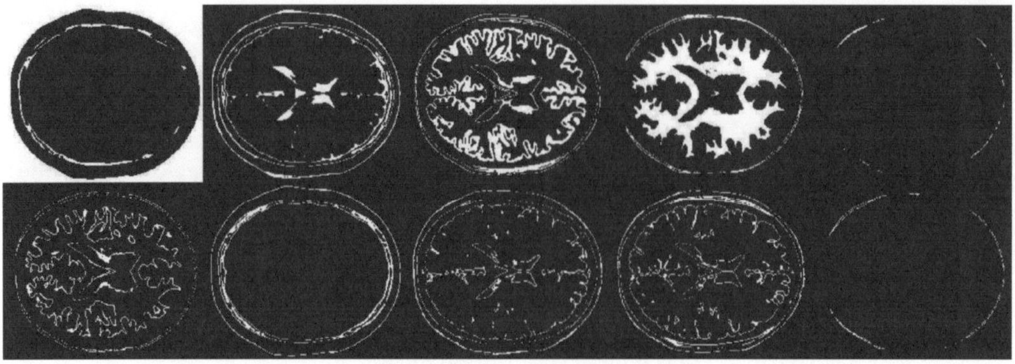

Fig. 6. Crisp dataset in detail: every class corresponding to one brain region in BrainWeb

a. Parameters for GKA and GFCMA
- Crossover rate
- Mutation rate
- Number of generations
- Population size

b. Parameters for PSOKA and PSOFCMA
- Maximum velocity
- Number of individuals in swarm

For each approach the fitness function is based on one of measures: Cluster Validation Indexes, MSE or ROS. This can be considered a parameter to the algorithm as well. Some measures need to be minimized (DB, MSE, XB, ROS) and others need to be maximized (SC, S). It is important to note that current approaches are unsupervised. This means that obtaining classification error has no influence on approaches' behavior and is used only as a way to evaluate its performance in a controlled scenario.

Based on observations from experiments, GKA and GFCMA experiments evaluate best when they use crossover rate of 70%, mutation rate of 0.5% and number of generations around 100. Higher numbers of generation values have no influence. Population size is of 10 individuals. Numerical results for GKA and GFCMA are shown by Table 5.

Measure\Algorithm	GKA		GFCMA	
	Value	Error	Value	Error
DB	**0.30636**	63.53082	0.34955	66.07175
MSE	**12.40774**	66.08193	74.99295	72.4037
SC	0.42729	68.42427	**0.90113**	48.82756
S	0.00002	72.61756	**0.00007**	51.29974
XB	124.14228	66.22705	**84.06929**	72.45716
ROS	0.50026	63.51045	**0.50025**	**40.63447**

Table 5. Image Segmentation results for GKA and GFCMA

According to results from Table 5 it is noted that GFCMA experiment with ROS measure outperforms other experiment's configurations - considering classification error. Fig. 7 shows classes for GFCMA's experiment that achieved best results.

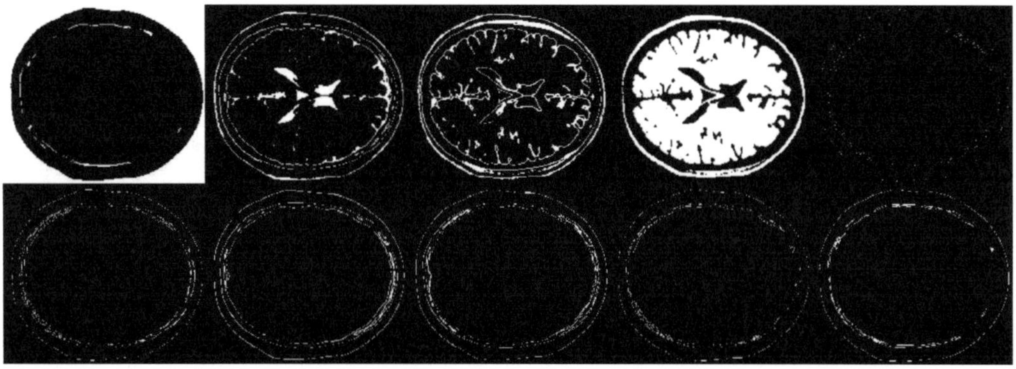

Fig. 7. Crisp dataset in detail: every class corresponding to one brain region in BrainWeb

PSOKA and PFOFCMA experiments use a maximum velocity parameter equals to 0.2 and stops when stabilization is found (value of objective function does not change across 10 iterations). Table 6 shows numerical results for PSOKA and PSOFCMA.

Measure\Algorithm	PSOKA		PSOFCMA	
	Value	Error	Value	Error
DB	0.34345	71.69336	**0.33365**	65.24938
MSE	**14.26504**	72.21529	74.46232	69.18044
SC	0.77279	66.34926	**0.99548**	71.43621
S	**0.00007**	68.00163	0.00004	71.37001
XB	260.60458	**60.57489**	**94.1416**	68.5312
ROS	**0.50018**	66.03356	0.50030	68.31479

Table 6. Image Segmentation results for PSOKA and PSOFCMA

Table 6 shows that PSOKA experiment with XB measure got lower classification error. Fig. 8 shows brain regions for PSOKA's experiment that achieved best results.

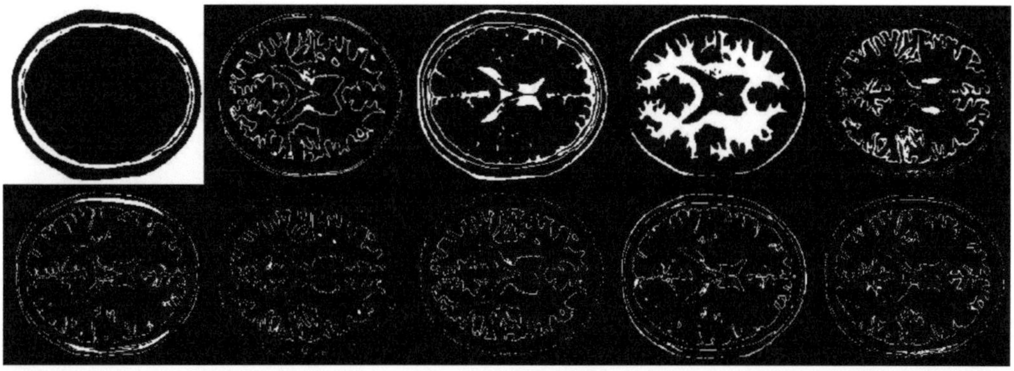

Fig. 8. Crisp dataset in detail: every class corresponding to one brain region in BrainWeb

Experiments with BrainWeb dataset had the ground truth to evaluate the approaches and used gray scale images. To show the performance of approaches with general purpose images, we will segment color images: Lena, Peppers and Duck.

(a) (b) (c)

Fig. 9. Color images: a) Lena; b) Peppers; and c) Duck

Results will show segmentation results considering each approach and all quality measures. The number of clusters proceeds as follows: Lena - 6 classes; Peppers - 5 classes; and Duck - 3 classes. Image has been resized to 96 x 96 pixels, RGB color. Tables 7 to 9 and Figures 10 to 12 present quantitative and qualitative image segmentation results, respectively. For these datasets there is no ground truth (no true labels). Thus, the evaluation about how measure/approach has the best result need to be made through quantitative and qualitative results. Best quantitative results are bolded in tables. Best qualitative results are harder to analyze, so the methodology is to consider:

a. For Peppers image: well defined frontiers and region homogeneity
b. For Lena image: well defined frontiers between skin, hat and hair and region homogeneity
c. For Duck image: well defined frontiers between duck body, mouth and glasses/ background

This criterion is used to qualitatively evaluate image segmentation results. Considerations about the results are presented in next section.

Measure\Algorithm	**GKA**	**GFCMA**	**PSOKA**	**PSOFCMA**
DB	0.56110	0.56504	**0.54677**	0.6147
MSE	**211.10835**	651.25003	239.515	640.409
SC	1.47962	**8.50041**	1.4389	8.09223
S	0.00017	**0.00140**	0.00032	0.00087
XB	8.67126	**3.70102**	5.69572	4.11349
ROS	0.49947	0.51484	**0.48019**	0.51205

Table 7. Image Segmentation results for Peppers image

Fig. 10. Qualitative image segmentation results for Peppers image. Rows: 1 - GFCMA, 2 - GKA, 3 - PSOFCMA, 4 - PSOKA. Columns: 1 - DB, 2 - MSE, 3 - SC, 4 - S, 5 - XB, 6 - ROS.

Measure\Algorithm	GKA	GFCMA	PSOKA	PSOFCMA
DB	0,63599	0,67499	**0,44408**	0,62798
MSE	**105,67107**	373,08084	114,80000	369,99500
SC	0,89346	**10,49051**	1,21201	4,71058
S	0,00012	**0,00112**	0,00023	0,00052
XB	11,58644	6,47175	7,62521	**5,82961**
ROS	0,54312	0,54141	**0,53541**	0,54345

Table 8. Image Segmentation results for Lena image

Fig. 11. Qualitative image segmentation results for Lena image. Rows: 1 - GFCMA, 2 - GKA, 3 - PSOFCMA, 4 - PSOKA. Columns: 1 - DB, 2 - MSE, 3 - SC, 4 - S, 5 - XB, 6 - ROS.

Measure\Algorithm	GKA	GFCMA	PSOKA	PSOFCMA
DB	0,43669	0,44730	**0,30422**	0,44495
MSE	**260,16469**	542,49030	347,33520	536,90780
SC	1,05008	**4,85890**	1,08519	29,61981
S	0,00021	**0,00243**	0,00019	0,00081
XB	9,32596	6,74430	**1,83358**	7,99377
ROS	**0,46663**	0,56625	0,50669	0,58084

Table 9. Image Segmentation results for Duck image

Fig. 12. Qualitative image segmentation results for Duck image. Rows: 1 - GFCMA, 2 - GKA, 3 - PSOFCMA, 4 - PSOKA. Columns: 1 - DB, 2 - MSE, 3 - SC, 4 - S, 5 - XB, 6 - ROS.

7. Conclusion and future research

The present work presents two natural computing methods for data clustering and image segmentation, their implementation and some results, one based on Genetic Algorithms and the other based on Particle Swarm Optimization. The task of image segmentation is not a trivial process. Considering the medical imaging context it is highly important the specialist's opinion about the results found. As the MRI dataset is simulated the experiments were guided by this situation. Thus, it is necessary to make experiments with real MRI imagery. Color images were used as well to analyze the performance of approaches on general purpose image segmentation.

The methodology used in this work was based on the following:

1. To implement the algorithms
2. To evaluate clustering results on known databases
3. To use the obtained results to guide tests with image segmentation. Image segmentation tests must consider image characteristics.

As the present methods are based on Evolutionary Computation and all have a performance (fitness) function, there must be some way to guide this evolution, so tests were made considering several Clustering Validation Indexes (DB, SC, S and XB), a commonly used

error measure (MSE) and an image segmentation specific measure (ROS). Also, when available, a measure of classification error was used to identify the method's final and overall performance. CVI, MSE and ROS can be used as a function of quality of a solution (population/generation for GKA or particle for PSO).
Considering classical clustering, K-means outperforms FCM considering classification error. Qualitative analysis shows that both algorithms did not identify correctly any of the classes and it is dificult to evaluate the quality of solution because, according to ground truth, most classes are merged or part of one class is in other class. Class 1, which may be background is the most correctly identified, even having some elements from other class in its interior. Classes 2 and 4 are almost correct also.
Considering GA, the lower classification error was obtained by GFCMA (around 40%), with ROS index. GFCMA also got best results considering SC, S, XB and ROS measures. Qualitative result shows that the same considerations for K-means and FCM apply to GFCMA, but most classes are almost identical, which results in weak qualitative evaluation. The quantitative measures were also enhanced. Only index S was better with K-means.
Considering PSO, the lower classification error was obtained by PSOKA (around 60%), with XB index. PSOKA was better considering MSE, S and ROS, while PSOFCMA was better considering DB, SC and XB. Curiously, better value of XB was not the one that obtained lower classification error. PSO also enhanced quantitative measures.
MRI dataset evaluation has considered the ground truth, so it was possible to evaluate experiment's results considering classification error. Experiments were made to evaluate the performance of GA and PSO considering general purpose color images. For Peppers image, GFCMA got best quantitative results (indexes SC, S and XB), followed by PSOKA (indexes DB and ROS). Qualitative analysis shows that GFCMA with index DB got best results, considering that red and green peppers where correctly separated and GFCMA also identify some background (between peppers). For Lena image, GFCMA (indexes SC and S) and PSOKA (indexes DB and ROS) got best results. Qualitative analysis shows that all approaches had problems with regions of hat and skin. Considering skin and hair, GFCMA with ROS index and PSOKA with ROS index got best results. For Duck image, GKA (indexes MSE and ROS), GFCMA (indexes SC and S) and PSOKA (indexes DB and XB) got best quantitative results. Qualitative analysis shows that GKA with index SC and S, PSOFCM with index SC and S got best results.
Most experiments using classical K-means and FCM run to 100 iterations - and more iteration could lead to lower error values. It's necessary to remember that GA and PSO both use only one iteration of K-means and FCM, and the convergence is fast (about 5 to 10 iterations). The problem of possible premature convergence of PSO is investigated by (Yong-gang, et al., 2005), which proposed the Improved PSO (IPSO) algorithm. This is a problem to take into account as a try to improve image segmentation results for PSO and GA also.
In summary, considering the results obtained from the experiments, it can be said that methods based on FCM performed better. As the present work does not evolves to image registration and classification more evaluation is necessary to argue about Fuzzy C-means superiority over K-means, in terms of the implemented algorithms. The use of image segmentation benchmarks to compare to obtained results is also a task for future research, together with studies about newer approaches and definitions for GA and PSO, mainly considering image characteristics, like texture, region and borders (frontiers).

One problem with these evolutionary algorithms is that the only concern is the quality of the solution, with little attention given to computational efficiency (Hruschka et al., 2009). The authors also analyze that the literature on clustering and image segmentation techniques based on evolutionary or natural computing does not provide detailed theoretical analyses in terms of time complexity. As we agree with this argumentation, one future work is the correct understanding of these algorithms in terms of computational efficiency and complexity.

8. References

Angus, D. (2007). Population-based ant colony optimization for multi-objective function optimization, *Proceedings of the 3rd Australian Conference on Progress in Artificial Life 2007*, pp. 232-244, Eds. Lecture Notes In Computer Science. Springer-Verlag, Berlin, Heidelberg

Balasko, B.; Abonyi, J; and Feil, B. (2005). Fuzzy Clustering and Data Analysis Toolbox. Online: http://www.mathworks.com/matlabcentral/fileexchange/7486

Bandyopadhyay, S. & Maulik, U. (2002). Genetic clustering for automatic evolution of clusters and application to image classification. *Pat. Recog*. Vol. 35. pp. 1197-1208. Elsevier

Bar-Cohen, Y. (2006). *Biomimetics: biologically inspired technologies.* Taylor & Francis, California

Brabazon, A. & O'Neill, M. (2006). *Biologically inspired algorithms for financial modeling.* Springer Natural Computing Series. Springer-Verlag, Berlin

BrainWeb (2010). BrainWeb: Simulated Brain Database. Online: http://mouldy.bic.mni.mcgill.ca/brainweb/

Castro, L. N. (2007), Fundamentals of natural computing: an overview, *Physics of Life Reviews*, Vol. 4, Issue 1, pp. 1-36, March 2007, ISSN 1571-0645

Chabrier, S.; Emile, B.; Rosenberger, C.; and Laurent, H. (2006). Unsupervised Performance Evaluation of Image Segmentation. *EURASIP Journal on Applied Signal Processing*, Vol. 2006, pp 1-12

Cocosco, C.A.; Kollokian, V.; Kwan, R.K.-S. & Evans, A.C. (1997). BrainWeb: Online Interface to a 3D MRI Simulated Brain Database. NeuroImage -- Proceedings of 3-rd International Conference on Functional Mapping of the Human Brain. Vol. 5. No. 4. part 2/4, S425, Copenhagen, May 1997

Collins, D.L.; Zijdenbos, A.P.; Kollokian, V.; Sled, J.G.; Kabani, N.J.; Holmes, C.J. & Evans, A.C. (1998). Design and Construction of a Realistic Digital Brain Phantom. IEEE Transactions on Medical Imaging. Vol. 17. No. 3. pp. 463-468, June 1998

Davies, E. (1997). *Machine Vision: Theory, Algorithms, Practialities.* Academic Press, 2nd ed.

Doi, K. (2007). Computer-aided diagnosis in medical imaging: Historical review, current status and future potential. *Comp. Medical Imaging and Graphics.* Vol. 31, pp. 198-211. Elsevier

El-Melegy, M.; Zanaty, E.A.; Abd-Elhafiez, W.M. & Farag, A. (2007). On Cluster Validity Indexes in Fuzzy and Hard Clustering Algorithms for Image Segmentation. *IEEE International Conference on Image Processing, 2007 (ICIP 2007).* Vol. 6, pp.VI-5-VI-8, ISBN 978-1-4244-1437-6, Sept. 16 2007-Oct. 19 2007, San Antonio, TX

Forgy, E. (1965). Cluster Analysis of Multivariate Data: Efficiency versus Interoperability of Classification. *Biometrics (21)*, pp. 768-769

Gonzalez, R. C. & Woods, R. E. (2003). *Digital Image Processing*. 3rd ed., Prentice Hall, Inc., New Jersey

Halkidi, M.; Batistakis, Y. & Vazirgiannis, M. (2001). Clustering algorithms and validity measures, *Proceedings Thirteenth International Conference on Scientific and Statistical Database Management*, pp. 3-22, 0-7695-1218-6, Jul. 2001, Fairfax, VA

Haykin, S. (1998). *Neural Networks: a comprehensive foundation*, 2nd ed. Prentice Hall

Hruschka, E.R.; Campello, R.J.G.B.; Freitas, A.A. & de Carvalho, A.C.P.L.F. (2009). A Survey of Evolutionary Algorithms for Clustering. *IEEE Transactions on Systems, Man, and Cybernetics, Part C: Applications and Reviews*. Vol. 39. No. 2, pp.133-155, March 2009, ISSN 1094-6977

Jain, A. K.; Murty, M. N. & Flynn, P. J. (1999). Data clustering: a review. *ACM Computer Surveys*. Vol. 31, pp. 264-323

Kennedy, J. & Eberhart, R. C. (2001). *Swarm intelligence: collective, adaptive*. The Morgan Kaufmann Series in Evolutionary Computation. Morgan Kaufmann, New York

Krishna, K. & Murty, N. (1999). Genetic K-Means Algorithm. *IEEE Trans. Systems, Man and Cybernetics - Part B: Cybernetics*. Vol. 29. No. 3. pp. 433-439

Kwan, R.K.-S.; Evans, A.C. & Pike, G.B. (1996). An Extensible MRI Simulator for Post-Processing Evaluation. *Visualization in Biomedical Computing (VBC'96). Lecture Notes in Computer Science*. Vol. 1131. pp. 135-140. Springer-Verlag

Kwan, R.K.-S.; Evans, A.C. & Pike, G.B. (1999). MRI simulation-based evaluation of image-processing and classification methods. *IEEE Transactions on Medical Imaging. 18(11):1085-97*, Nov 1999.

Mathworks (2010). MATLAB - The Language Of Technical Computing. Online: http://www.mathworks.com/products/matlab/. Last access: 11/11/2010.

Omram, M. G. H. (2004) *Particle Swarm Optimization Methods for Pattern Recognition and Image Processing*, Ph.D. Thesis, University of Pretoria, Pretoria

Omram, M. G.; Salman, A. & Engelbrecht, A. P. (2006). Dynamic clustering using particle swarm optimization with application in image segmentation. *Pattern Anal. Applic.* (8), pp. 332-344, Springer-Verlag, London

Raut, S.; Raghuvanshi, M.; Dharaskar, R. & Raut, A. (2009). Image Segmentation - A State-Of-Art Survey for Prediction, *Proceedings of International Conference on Advanced Computer Control 2009*, pp. 420-424, ISBN 978-1-4244-3330-8, Singapore, Jan. 2009, IEEE Computer Society

Turi, R. H. (2001). *Clustering-based Colour Image Segmentation*. Ph.D. Thesis. Monash University, Australia

Xu, R. & Wunsch II, D. (2005). Survey of clustering algorithms, *IEEE Transactions on Neural Networks*. Vol. 16. No. 3, pp. 645-678, May 2005, ISSN 1045-9227

Yong-gang, L.; Wei-hua, G.; Chun-hua, Y. & Jie, L. (2005). Improved PSO algorithm and its application. *Journal of Central South University of Technology*. Vol. 12. No. 1. pp. 222-226

Zadeh, L. A. (1994). Fuzzy logic, neural networks, and soft computing. *Communications of the ACM (37)*, pp. 77-84

4

Segmentation with Learning Automata

Erik Cuevas, Daniel Zaldivar and Marco Pérez-Cisneros
Departamento de Electrónica, Universidad de Guadalajara
México

1. Introduction

Several image processing applications aim to detect and mark remarkable features which in turn might be used to perform high-level tasks. In particular, image segmentation seeks to group pixels within meaningful regions. Commonly, gray levels belonging to the object are substantially different from the gray levels featuring the background. Thresholding is thus a simple but effective tool to isolate objects of interest from the background. Its applications include several classics such as document image analysis, whose goal is to extract printed characters (Abak et al., 1997; Kamel & Zhao, 1993) logos, graphical content, or musical scores; also it is used for map processing which aims to locate lines, legends, and characters (Trier & Jain, 1995). It is also used for scene processing, aiming for object detection and marking (Bhanu, 1986); Similarly, it has been employed to quality inspection for materials (Sezgin & Sankur, 2001; Sezgin & Tasaltin, 2000), discarding defective parts.

Thresholding selection techniques can be classified into two categories: bi-level and multi-level. In bi-level thresholding, one limit value is chosen to segment an image into two classes: one represents the object and the other represents the background. When an image is composed of several distinct objects, multiple threshold values have to be selected for proper segmentation. This is called multilevel thresholding.

A variety of thresholding approaches have been proposed for image segmentation, including conventional methods (Guo & Pandit, 1998; Pal & Pal, 1993; Shaoo et al., 1988; Snyder et al., 1990) and intelligent techniques such as in (Chen & Wang, 2005; Chih-Chih, 2006). Extending the algorithm to a multilevel approach may arise some inconveniences: (i) they may have no systematic and analytic solution when the number of classes to be detected increases and (ii) the number of classes is either difficult to be predicted or must be pre-defined. However, this parameter is unknown for many real applications.

In order to solve these problems, an alternative approach using an optimization algorithm based on learning automata for multilevel thresholding is proposed in this paper. In the traditional multilevel optimal thresholding, the intensity distributions belonging to the object or to the background pixels are assumed to follow some Gaussian probability function; therefore a combination of probability density functions is usually adopted to model these functions. The parameters in the combination function are unknown and the parameter estimation is typically assumed to be a nonlinear optimization problem (Gonzalez & Woods, 1990). The unknown parameters that give the best fit to the processed histogram are determined by using a LA algorithm (Thathachar & Sastry, 2002).

The main motivation behind the use of LA as an optimization algorithm for parameter adaptation is to use its capabilities of global optimization when dealing to multimodal surfaces. Using LA, the search for the optimum is done within a probability space rather than seeking within a parameter space as done by other optimization algorithms (Najim &Poznyak, 1994). Learning automata is referred to as an automaton, acting embedded into an unknown random environment. Such automaton improves its performance to obtain an optimal action. On the other hand, an action is applied to a random environment and gives a fitness value to the selected action of the automata. The response of the environment is used by automata to select its next action. This procedure is continued to reach the optimal action.

LA has been used for solve different sorts of engineering problems. For instance, pattern recognition (Seyed-Hamid, 2008), adaptive control (Zeng et al., 2000) signal processing (Howell & Gordon, 2000) and power systems (Wu, 1995). Recently, some effective algorithms have been proposed for multimodal complex function optimization based on the LA (see (Howell & Gordon, 2000; Thathachar & Sastry, 2002; Zeng & Liu, 2005; Beygi & Meybodi, 2006)). Furthermore, it was shown experimentally that the performance of these optimization algorithms is comparable to or better than the genetic algorithm (GA) in [22]. This work employs the algorithm proposed in (Zeng & Liu, 2005), which is called continuous action reinforcement learning automata (CARLA).

In this chapter, an automatic image multi-threshold approach based on Learning Automata is presented. Hereby the segmentation process is considered to be similar to an optimization problem. First, the algorithm approximates the 1-D histogram of the image using a mix of Gaussian functions whose parameters are calculated using the Learning automata method. Each Gaussian function approximating the histogram represents a pixel class and therefore the threshold points.

This chapter is organized as follows. Section 2 presents the Gaussian approximation to the histogram. Section 3 presents the LA algorithm, while Section 4 shows the determination of the threshold points. In section 5 the implementation details are shown. Experimental results for the proposed approach are presented in Section 6, finally the conclusion are presented in Section 7.normal)

2. Gaussian approximation

Assuming an image has L gray levels $[0,\ldots,L-1]$, following a gray level distribution which can be displayed in the form of the histogram $h(g)$. In order to simplify the description, the histogram is normalized and is considered as a probability distribution function:

$$h(g)=\frac{n_g}{N},\ h(g)\geq 0,$$
$$N=\sum_{g=0}^{L-1} n_g,\ \text{and} \sum_{g=0}^{L-1} h(g)=1, \tag{1}$$

Assuming that n_g denotes the number of pixels with gray level g while N is the total number of pixels in the image. The histogram function can be contained into a mix of Gaussian probability functions, yielding:

$$p(x)=\sum_{i=1}^{K} P_i \cdot p_i(x)=\sum_{i=1}^{K} \frac{P_i}{\sqrt{2\pi\sigma_i}} \exp\left[\frac{-(x-\mu_i)^2}{2\sigma_i^2}\right] \tag{2}$$

considering that P_i is the a priori probability of class i, $p_i(x)$ is the probability distribution function of gray-level random variable x in class i, μ_i and σ_i are the mean and standard deviation of the i-th probability distribution function, and K is the number of classes within the image. In addition, the constraint $\sum_{i=1}^{K} P_i = 1$ must be satisfied.

The typical mean square error consideration is used to estimate the $3K$ parameters P_i, μ_i and σ_i, $i = 1, \ldots, K$. For example, the mean square error between the composite Gaussian function $p(x_i)$ and the experimental histogram function $h(x_i)$ is defined as follows:

$$J = \frac{1}{n}\sum_{j=1}^{n}\left[p(x_j) - h(x_j)\right]^2 + \omega \cdot \left| \left(\sum_{i=1}^{K} P_i \right) - 1 \right| \qquad (3)$$

Assuming an n-point histogram as in [13] and ω being the penalty associated with the constrain $\sum_{i=1}^{K} P_i = 1$. In general, the determination of parameters that minimize the square error is not a simple problem. A straightforward method to decrease the partial derivatives of the error function to zero considers a set of simultaneous transcendental equations (Gonzalez & Woods, 1992). An analytical solution is not available due to the non-linear nature of the equations. The algorithm therefore makes use of a numerical procedure following an iterative approach based on the gradient information. However, considering that the gradient descent method may easily get stuck within local minima. In the standard gradient method, the new operation point lies within a neighbourhood distance of the previous point. This is not the case for adaptation algorithm based on stochastic principles such as LA, as the new operating point is determined by probability function and is therefore not considered to be near the previous operating point. This gives the algorithm a higher ability to locate the global minima.

Some previous experiences have shown that the intelligent approaches actually provide a satisfactory performance in case of image processing problems (Chen & Wang, 2005; Chih-Chih, 2006; Baştürk & Günay, 2009; Lai & Tseng, 2001; Tseng & Lai, 1999). The LA algorithm is therefore adopted in order to find the parameters and their corresponding threshold values.

3. Learning automata

LA operates by selecting actions via a stochastic process. Such actions operate within an environment while being assessed according to a measure of the system performance. Figure 1a shows the typical learning system architecture. The automaton selects an action (**X**) probabilistically. Such actions are applied to the environment, and the performance evaluation function provides a reinforcement signal β. This is used to update the automaton's internal probability distribution whereby actions that achieve desirable performance are reinforced via an increased probability, while those not-performing actions are penalised or left unchanged depending on the particular learning rule which has been employed. Over time, the average performance of the system will improve while a given limit is reached. In terms of optimization problems, the action with the highest probability would correspond to the global minimum as demonstrated by rigorous proofs of convergence available in (Narendra & Thathachar, 1989) and (Najim & Poznyak, 1994).

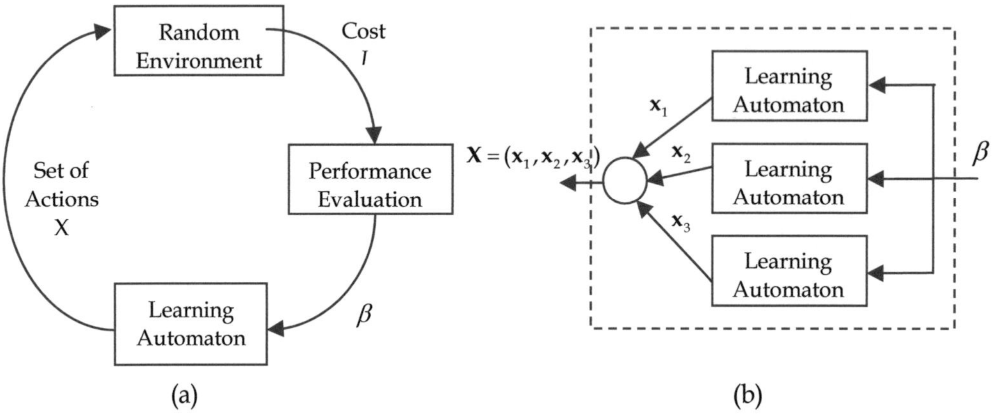

Fig. 1. (a) Reinforcement learning system and (b) Interconnected automata.

A wide variety of learning rules have been reported in the literature. One of the most widely used algorithms is the linear reward/inaction (L_{RI}) scheme, which has been shown to guaranteed convergence properties (see [1008]). In response to action $\mathbf{x}_i$, being selected at time step k, the probabilities are updated as follows:

$$\begin{aligned} p_i(n+1) &= p_i(n) + \theta \cdot \beta(n) \cdot (1 - p_i(n)) \\ p_j(n+1) &= p_j(n) - \theta \cdot \beta(n) \cdot p_j(n) \text{ if } i \neq j \end{aligned} \tag{4}$$

being θ a learning rate parameter and $0 < \theta < 1$ and $\beta \in [0,1]$ the reinforcement signal; $\beta = 1$ indicates the maximum reward and $\beta = 0$ is a null reward. Eventually, the probability of successful actions will increase to become close to unity. In case that a single and foremost successful action prevails, the automaton is deemed to have converged.

With a large number of discrete actions, the probability of selecting any particular action becomes low and the convergence time can become excessive. To avoid this, learning automata can be connected in a parallel setup as shown by Figure 1b. Each automaton operates a smaller number of actions and the 'team' works together in a co-operative manner. This scheme can also be used where multiple actions are required.

Discrete stochastic learning automata can be used to determine global optimal states for control applications with multi-modal mean square error surfaces. However, the discrete nature of the automata requires the discretization of a continuous parameter space, and the level of quantization tends to reduce the convergence rate. A sequential approach may be adopted (Howell & Gordon, 2000) to overcome such problem by means of an initial coarse quantization. It may be later refined using a re-quantization around the most successful action. In this paper, an inherently continuous form of the learning automaton is used to speed the learning process and to avoid this additional complexity.

3.1 CARLA algorithm

The continuous action reinforcement learning automata (CARLA) was developed as an extension of the discrete stochastic learning automata for applications involving searching of continuous action space in a random environment (Howell & Gordon, 2000). Several CARLA can be connected in parallel, in a similar manner to discrete automata (Figure 1b), to search multidimensional action spaces. The interconnection of the automata is through the

environment however, no direct inter-automata communication exist. The automaton's discrete probability distribution is replaced by a continuous probability density function which is used as the basis for action selection. It operates a reward/inaction learning rule similar to the discrete learning automata. Successful actions receive and increase on the probability of future selection via a Gaussian neighborhood function which increases the probability density in the vicinity of such successful action. Table 1 shows the generic pseudo-code for the CARLA algorithm. The initial probability distribution can be chosen as being uniform over a desired range. After a considerable number of iterations, it converges to a probability distribution with a global maximum around the best action value.
If action x is defined over the range $(x_{\min}, x_{\max})$, the probability density function $f(x,n)$ at iteration n is updated according to the following rule:

$$f(x,n+1) = \begin{cases} \alpha \cdot [f(x,n) + \beta(n) \cdot H(x,r)] & \text{if } x \in (x_{\min}, x_{\min}) \\ 0 & \text{otherwise} \end{cases} \tag{5}$$

With α being chosen to re-normalize the distribution according to the following condition

$$\int_{x_{\min}}^{x_{\max}} f(x,n+1)dx = 1 \tag{6}$$

with $\beta(n)$ being again the reinforcement signal from the performance evaluation and $H(x,r)$ a symmetric Gaussian neighbourhood function centered on $r = x(n)$. It yields

$$H(x,r) = \lambda \cdot \exp\left(-\frac{(x-r)^2}{2\sigma^2}\right) \tag{7}$$

CARLA Algorithm
Initialize the probability density function to a uniform distribution
Repeat
Select an action using its probability density function
Execute action on the environment
Receive cost/reward for previous action
Update performance evaluation function β
Update probability density function
Until stopping condition

Table 1. Generic pseudo-code for the CARLA algorithm

with λ and σ being parameters that determine the height and width of the neighborhood function. They are defined in terms of the range of actions as follows:

$$\sigma = g_w \cdot (x_{\max} - x_{\min}) \tag{8}$$

$$\lambda = \frac{g_h}{(x_{\max} - x_{\min})} \tag{9}$$

The speed and resolution of learning are thus controlled by free parameters g_w and g_h. Let action $x(n)$ be applied to the environment at iteration n, returning a cost or performance index $J(n)$. Current and previous costs are stored as a reference set $R(n)$. The median and minimum values J_{med} and J_{min} may thus be calculated, by means of $\beta(n)$ being defined as:

$$\beta(n) = \max\left\{0, \frac{J_{\text{med}} - J(n)}{J_{\text{med}} - J_{\text{min}}}\right\} \tag{10}$$

To avoid problems with infinite storage, and to allow the system to adapt to changing environments, only the last m values of the cost functions are stored in $R(n)$. Equation (10) limits $\beta(n)$ to values between 0 and 1 and only returns nonzero values for costs that are below the median value. It is easy to understand how $\beta(n)$ affects the learning process informally as follows: during the learning, the performance and the number of selecting actions can be wildly variable, generating extremely high computing costs. However, $\beta(n)$ is insensitive to these extremes and to the very high values of $J(n)$ resulting from a poor choice of actions. As learning continues, the automaton converges towards more worthy regions of the parameter space and these actions within such regions are chosen for evaluation increasingly often. While more of such responses are being received, J_{med} gets reduced. Decreasing J_{med} in the performance index effectively enables the automaton to refine its reference around the better responses previously received, and hence resulting in a better discrimination between the competing selected actions.
To define an action value $x(n)$ which has been associated to this probability density function, an uniformly distributed pseudo-random number $z(n)$ is generated within the range of [0,1]. Simple interpolation is then employed to equate this value to the cumulative distribution function:

$$\int_{x_{\text{min}}}^{x(n)} f(x,n)dx = z(n) \tag{11}$$

For implementation purposes, the distribution is stored at discrete points with an equal inter-sample probability. Linear interpolation is used to determine values at intermediate positions (see full details in [19]).

4. Determination of threshold values

The next step is to determine the optimal threshold values. Considering that the data classes are organized such that $\mu_1 < \mu_2 < \ldots < \mu_K$, the threshold values are obtained by computing the overall probability error for two adjacent Gaussian functions, following:

$$E(T_i) = P_{i+1} \cdot E_1(T_i) + P_i \cdot E_2(T_i), \quad i = 1,2,\ldots,K-1 \tag{12}$$

considering

$$E_1(T_i) = \int_{-\infty}^{T_i} p_{i+1}(x)dx, \tag{13}$$

and

$$E_2(T_i) = \int_{T_i}^{\infty} p_i(x)dx, \tag{14}$$

$E_1(T_i)$ is the probability of mistakenly classifying the pixels in the $(i + 1)$-th class to the i-th class, while $E_2(T_i)$ is the probability of erroneously classifying the pixels in the i-th class to the $(i + 1)$-th class. P_j's are the a priori probabilities within the combined probability density function, and T_i is the threshold value between the i-th and the $(i + 1)$-th classes. One T_i value is chosen such as the error $E(T_i)$ is minimized. By differentiating $E(T_i)$ with respect to T_i and equating the result to zero, it is possible to use the following equation to define the optimum threshold value T_i:

$$AT_i^2 + BT_i + C = 0 \tag{15}$$

considering

$$A = \sigma_i^2 - \sigma_{i+1}^2$$

$$B = 2 \cdot (\mu_i \sigma_{i+1}^2 - \mu_{i+1} \sigma_i^2) \tag{16}$$

$$C = (\sigma_i \mu_{i+1})^2 - (\sigma_{i+1} \mu_i)^2 + 2 \cdot (\sigma_i \sigma_{i+1})^2 \cdot \ln\left(\frac{\sigma_{i+1} P_i}{\sigma_i P_{i+1}}\right)$$

Although the above quadratic equation has two possible solutions, only one of them is feasible (positive and inside the interval). The figure 2 shows the determination process of the threshold points.

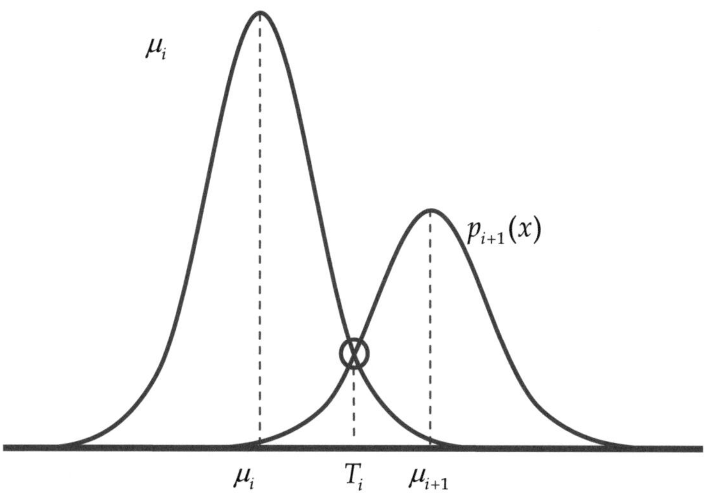

Fig. 2. Determination process of the threshold points

5. Implementation

In the implementation four different pixel classes are used to segment the images. The idea is to show the effectiveness of the algorithm and the little information required for the localization of the threshold points, the implementation could be effortlessly carried out for a bigger number of pixel classes.
To approach the histogram of an image by 4 Gaussian functions (one for each pixel class), it is necessary first, calculate the optimum values of the 3 parameters (P_i, μ_i and σ_i) for each Gaussian function (in this case, 12 values according to equation 2). This problem can be resolved optimizing equation 3, considering that function $p(x)$ is formed by 4 Gaussian functions.
The parameters to be optimized are summarized in table 2. Where k_P^i is the parameter that represents the a priori probability (*P*), k_σ^i represents the variance (σ) and k_μ^i represents the expected value (μ) of the Gaussian function *i*.

Parameters			Gaussian
k_P^1	k_σ^1	k_μ^1	1
k_P^2	k_σ^2	k_μ^2	2
k_P^3	k_σ^3	k_μ^3	3
k_P^4	k_σ^4	k_μ^4	4

Table 2. Parameters to be optimized

In LA optimization, each parameter is considered like an Automaton which chooses actions. The actions correspond to values assigned to the parameter, by a probability distribution inside of an interval. The intervals used in this work for the parameters are defined as $k_P^i \in [0,0.5]$, $k_\sigma^i \in [0,60]$, and $k_\mu^i \in [0,255]$.
For this 12-dimensional problem will be 12 different Automatons which represent the parameters to approach the corresponding histogram. One of the main advantages of the LA is that in a multi-dimensional problem the Automatons are coupled only through the enviorement, thus each Automaton operated independently, during the optimization.
Thus, in each instant n each Automaton chooses an action according to their probability distribution, which can be represented in a vector $A(n)$={ k_P^1, k_σ^1, k_μ^1 ..., k_P^4, k_σ^4, k_μ^4 }. This vector represents a certain approach of the histogram. Then, the quality of the approach is evaluated (according to equation 3) and converted to a reinforcement signal $\beta(n)$ (through equation 10). Having obtained the reinforcement value $\beta(n)$ as product of the elected approach *A(n)*, the distribution of probability is update for n+1 of each Automaton (according to the equation 5). To simplify parameters of equation 8 and 9 are the same for the 12 Automatons, such that $g_w = 0.02$ and g_h =0.3. In this work is considers to limit to 2000 the iterations on the optimization process.
Next, the optimization algorithm is described:

i	Set iteration n=0.	
ii	Define the action set $A(n)$={ k_P^1, k_σ^1, k_μ^1 ..., k_P^4, k_σ^4, k_μ^4 } such that $k_P^i \in [0,0.5]$, $k_\sigma^i \in [0,60]$ and $k_\mu^i \in [0,255]$.	
iii	Define probability density functions at iteration n: $f(k_P^i,n)$, $f(k_\sigma^i,n)$ and $f(k_\mu^i,n)$	
iv	Initialize $f(k_P^i,n)$, $f(k_\sigma^i,n)$ and $f(k_\mu^i,n)$ as an uniform distribution between the defined limits.	
v	Repeat while $n \le 2000$	
	(a)	Using a pseudo-random number generator for each Automaton, select $z_P^i(n)$, $z_\sigma^i(n)$ and $z_\mu^i(n)$ uniformly between 0 and 1.
	(b)	Select $k_P^i \in [0,0.5]$, $k_\sigma^i \in [0,60]$ and $k_\mu^i \in [0,255]$ where the area under the probability density function is $\int_0^{k_P^i(n)} f(k_P^i,n) = z_P^i(n)$, $\int_0^{k_\sigma^i(n)} f(k_\sigma^i,n) = z_\sigma^i(n)$ and $\int_0^{k_\mu^i(n)} f(k_\mu^i,n) = z_\mu^i(n)$.
	(c)	Evaluate the performance using Eq. (3).
	(d)	Obtain the minimum, $J_{\min}$, and median, J_{med} of $J(n)$.
	(e)	Evaluate $\beta(n)$ via Eq. (10).
	(f)	Update the probability density functions $f(k_P^i,n)$, $f(k_\sigma^i,n)$ and $f(k_\mu^i,n)$ using Eq. (5).
	(g)	Increment iteration number n.

The learning system search in the 12-dimensional parameter space with the aim of reducing the values for J in Eq. (3).

6. Experimental results

In this section the performance of the algorithm is tested by two experiments. In both experiments a 4 pixel class segmentation is consider and an approaching of the original histogram of the image by LA. To test the consistency of the algorithm, 10 independent repetitions were made for each experiment.

In the first experiment the image represented in figure 3a was used, whose original histogram is shown in figure 3b. Considering the proposed LA algorithm (detailed in the previous section) a global minimum was obtained (equation 3), the point defined as k_P^1=0.0210, k_σ^1=6, k_μ^1=15, k_P^2=0.0404, k_σ^2=29, k_μ^2=63, k_P^3=0.0608, k_σ^3=10, k_μ^3=93, k_P^4=0.1002, k_σ^4=30, and k_μ^4=163. The values of these parameters define 4 different Gaussian functions, which are represented in figure 4. From the mix of these 4 Gaussian functions, an approach to the original histogram is obtained as shown in figure 5.

The evolution of the probability densities parameters, whose represent the expected values $f(k_\mu^1,n)$, $f(k_\mu^2,n)$, $f(k_\mu^3,n)$ and $f(k_\mu^4,n)$ of the Gaussian functions are shown in figure 6. It can be seen that most of the convergence is achieved at the first 1500 iterations, after that a gradual sharpening of the distribution occurs. The final probability densities (n=2000) can be taken as the final parameter value.

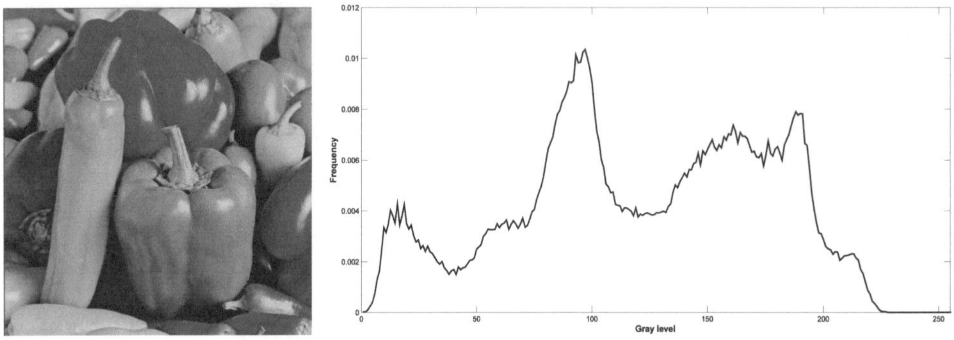

(a) (b)

Fig. 3. (a) Original image used on the first experiment, (b) and its histogram

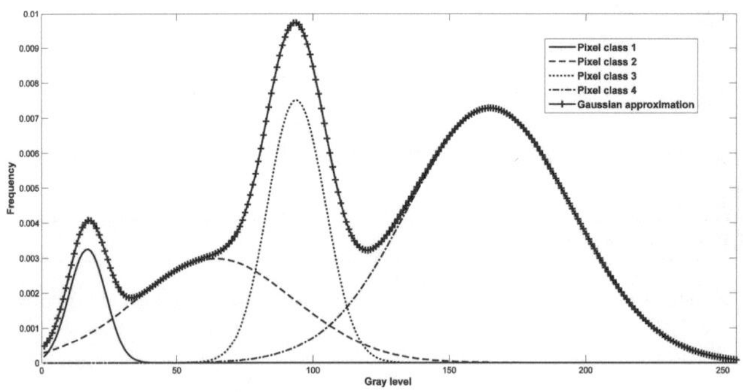

Fig. 4. Gaussian functions obtained by LA

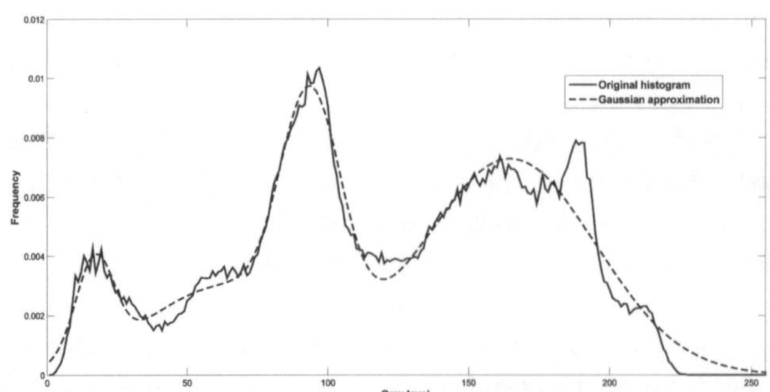

Fig. 5. Comparison between the original histogram and its approach

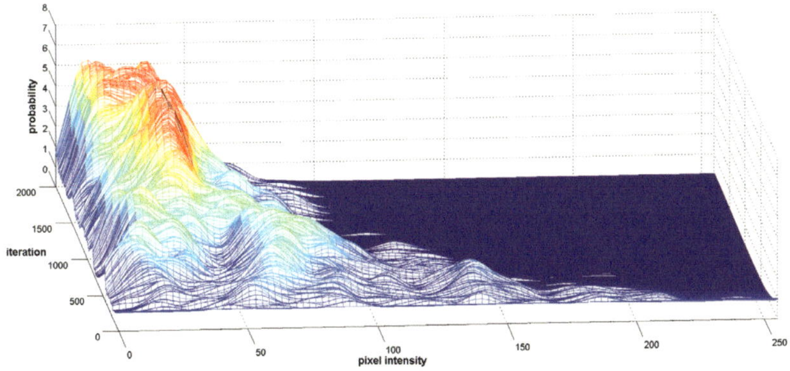
probability
iteration
pixel intensity

(a)

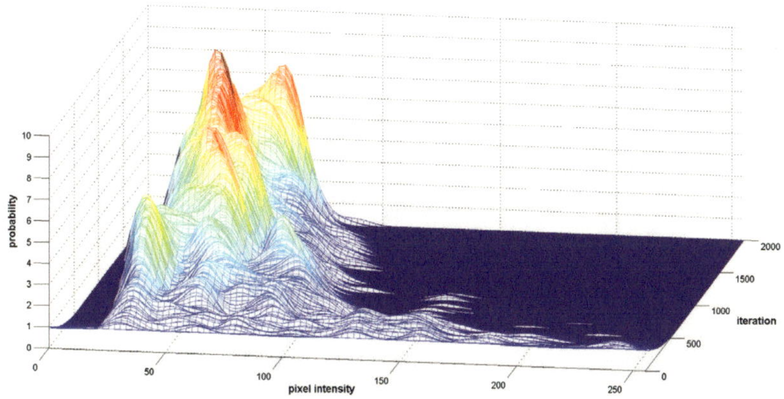
probability
iteration
pixel intensity

(b)

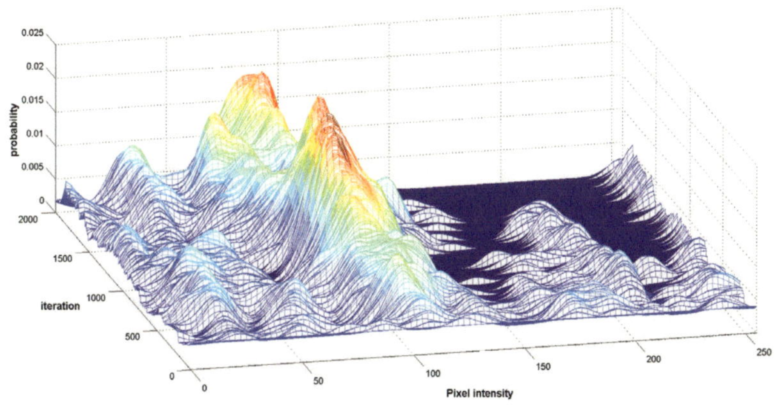
probability
iteration
Pixel intensity

(c)

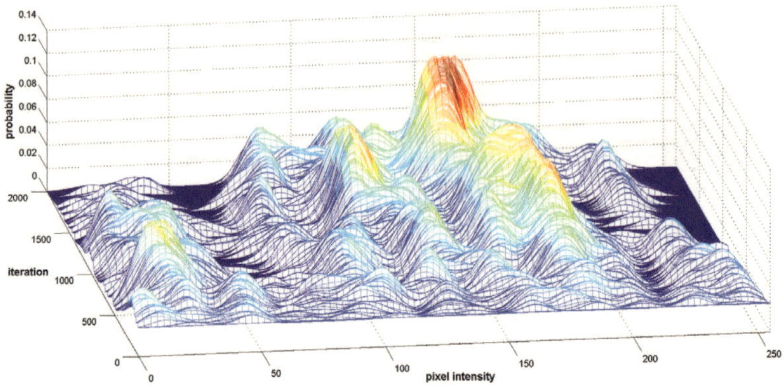

(d)

Fig. 6. Evolution of the probability densities parameters, whose represent the expected values (a) $f(k_{\mu}^{1},n)$, (b) $f(k_{\mu}^{2},n)$, (c) $f(k_{\mu}^{3},n)$ and (d) $f(k_{\mu}^{4},n)$, of the Gaussian functions

From the Gaussian functions obtained by LA (figure 4), the threshold values T_i are calculated considering equations 15-16. From these values the image segmented in 4 classes shown in figure 7 is obtained.

Fig. 7. Image segmented in 4 classes by LA

In the second experiment, the image shown in figure 8 was used. The idea is again, to segment it in 4 different pixel classes using the LA approach proposed in this work. After execute the algorithm with the parameters detailed in the previous sections the Gaussian functions obtained are shown in figure 9a.
The mix of Gaussian functions obtained by the LA algorithm approach to the original histogram, as can be seen in figure 9b. From figure 9b is clear that the algorithm approaches each one of the pixel concentrations, distributed in the histogram, except to the first one (presented approximately around the intensity value 7). This effect shows that the algorithm discards the smallest accumulation of pixels and prefer to cover those classes that contribute to generate a smaller error during optimization of the equation 3. The results can be improved if 5 pixel classes were used (instead of segmenting the image by 4 pixel classes).

Fig. 8. Image used on the second experiment

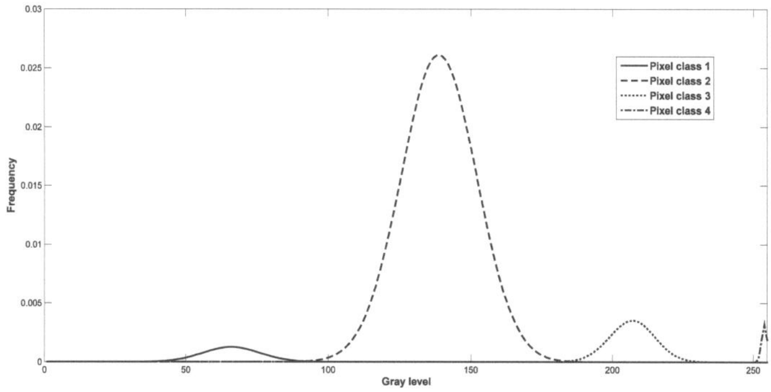

(a)

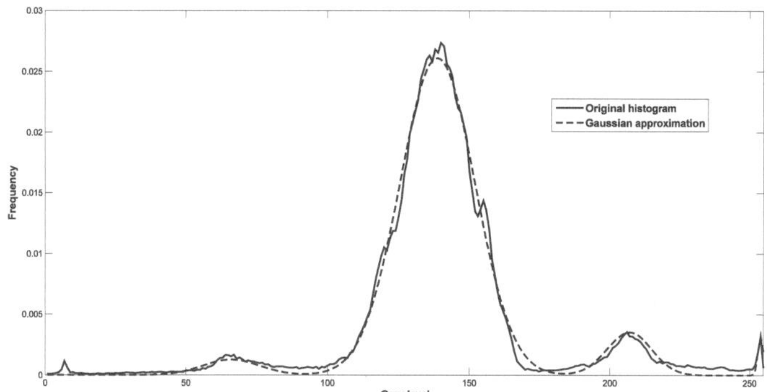

(b)

Fig. 9. (a) Gaussian functions obtained by LA, and (b) its comparison to the original histogram

From the Gaussian functions obtained by LA (figure 9a), the threshold values T_i are calculated considering equations 15-16. From these values the image segmented in 4 classes shown in figure 10 is obtained. Figure 11 shows the separation of each class obtained by the algorithm.

Fig. 10. Segmentation obtained by LA

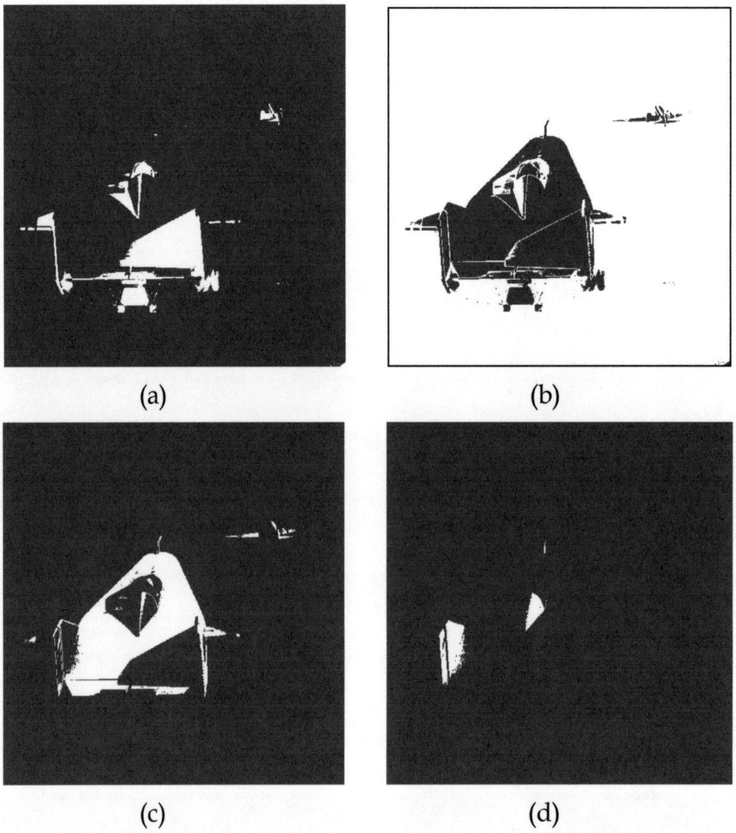

Fig. 11. Separation of each class obtained by the LA algorithm. (a) Pixel class 1, (b) Pixel class 2, (c) Pixel class 3, and (d) Pixel class 3.

6. Conclusions

This works presents a novel segmentation algorithm which includes an automatic threshold determination approach. The overall method can be considered as a Learning automata optimization algorithm. Following the intensity distributions for each object. The intensity distributions of objects and background in an image are assumed to obey Gaussian distributions with distinct variances and means. The histogram of a given image is approach by a mix of Gaussian probability functions. The LA algorithm is used to estimate the parameters in the mix density function obtaining a minimum square error between the density function and the original histogram. The experimental results reveal that the proposed approach can produce satisfactory results. Further work of extending the proposed approach with other techniques and comparing the results with state of the art image segmentation techniques are in progress.

7. Acknowledgments

The first author would like to thank SEP (Mexico) and DAAD (Germany) for its economical support.

8. References

Abak, T.; Baris, U. & Sankur, B. (1997). The performance of thresholding algorithms for optical character recognition, *Proceedings of International Conference on Document Analytical Recognition*, 697–700.

Baştürk, A. & Günay, E. (2009). Efficient edge detection in digital images using a cellular neural network optimized by differential evolution algorithm, *Expert System with Applications*, 36(8), 2645-2650.

Beygi, H. & Meybodi, M. (2006). A new action-set learning automaton for function optimization. *Int. J. Franklin Inst.* 343, 27–47.

Bhanu, B. (1986). Automatic target recognition: state of the art survey, *IEEE Trans. Aerosp. Electron. Syst.* 22, 364–379.

Chen, S. & Wang, M. (2005). Seeking multi-thresholds directly from support vectors for image segmentation, *Neurocomputing*, 67(4), 335-344.

Chih-Chih, L. (2006). A Novel Image Segmentation Approach Based on Particle Swarm Optimization, *IEICE Trans. Fundamentals*, 89(1), 324-327.

Gonzalez, R. & Woods, R. (1992). Digital Image Processing, Addison Wesley, Reading, MA.

Guo, R. & Pandit, S. (1998). Automatic threshold selection based on histogram modes and discriminant criterion, *Mach. Vis. Appl.*, vol.10, pp.331–338.

Howell, M. & Gordon T. (2000). Continuous action reinforcement learning automata and their application to adaptive digital filter design. *Engineering Applications of Artificial Intelligence.* 14, 549–561.

Kamel, M. & Zhao, A. (1993). Extraction of binary character/graphics images from grayscale document images, *Graph. Models Image Process.* 55 (3) 203–217.

Lai, C. & Tseng, D. (2001). An optimal L-filter for reducing blocking artifacts using genetic algorithms, *Signal Process.*, vol.81, no.7, pp.1525-1535.

Najim, K. & Poznyak, A. (1994). Learning Automata - Theory and Applications. Pergamon Press, Oxford.

Narendra, K. & Thathachar, M. (1989). Learning Automata: an Introduction. Prentice-Hall, London.

Pal, N. & Pal, S. (1993). A review on image segmentation techniques, *Pattern Recognit.*, vol.26, pp.1277–1294.

Seyed-Hamid, Z. (2008). Learning automata based classifier, *Pattern Recognition Letters*. 29, 40-48.

Sezgin, M. & Sankur, B. (2001). Comparison of thresholding methods for non-destructive testing applications, *IEEE International Conference on Image Processing*, 764–767.

Sezgin, M. & Tasaltin, R. (2000). A new dichotomization technique to multilevel thresholding devoted to inspection applications, *Pattern Recognition Lett.* 21 (2) 151–161.

Shaoo, P. ; Soltani, S. ; Wong, A. & Chen, Y. (1988). Survey: A survey of thresholding techniques, *Comput. Vis. Graph. Image Process.*, vol.41, pp.233–260.

Snyder, W. ; Bilbro, G. ; Logenthiran, A. & Rajala, S. (1990). Optimal thresholding: A new approach, *Pattern Recognit. Lett.*, vol.11, pp.803–810.

Thathachar, M. & Sastry, P. (2002). Varieties of learning automata: An overview. *IEEE Trans. Systems. Man Cybernet. Part B: Cybernet.* 32, 711–722.

Trier, O. & Jain, A. (1995). Goal-directed evaluation of binarization methods, IEEE Trans. *Pattern Anal. Mach. Intel.* 17 (12) 1191–1201.

Tseng, D. & Lai, C. (1999). A genetic algorithm for MRF-based segmentation of multispectral textured images, *Pattern Recognit. Lett.*, vol.20, no.14, pp.1499–1510.

Wu, Q. (1995). Learning coordinated control of power systems using inter-connected learning automata. *Int. J. Electr. Power Energy Syst.* 17, 91–99.

Zeng, X. & Liu, Z. (2005). A learning automaton based algorithm for optimization of continuous complex function. *Information Sciences*. 174, 165–175.

Zeng, X. ; Zhou, J. & Vasseur, C. (2000). A strategy for controlling non-linear systems using a learning automaton. *Automatica*. 36, 1517–1524.

5

Surround Suppression and Recurrent Interactions V1-V2 for Natural Scene Boundary Detection

Francisco J. Díaz-Pernas, Míriam Antón-Rodríguez, Isabel de la Torre-Díez, Mario Martínez-Zarzuela, David González-Ortega, Daniel Boto-Giralda, and J. Fernando Díez-Higuera

Department of Signal Theory, Communications and Telematics Engineering Telecommunications Engineering School, Valladolid University, Valladolid Spain

1. Introduction

Understanding the brain functioning in visual process is one of the more active areas within neuroscience, modeling and computation. This great interest is due to the fact that vision provides us with the more important information about the surroundings. Oriented early filtering processes, perceptual clustering through emerging features, form and depth perception, figure-ground separation, and object recognition are all involved in the brain visual activity. Important researches have been undertaken to develop models simulating this brain behavior. So, neural models of visual perception biologically motivated in early vision tasks have been arisen versus others not biologically motivated computer vision algorithms. The knowledge about the early vision is notable and, accordingly, the neural modeling of the early vision tasks has been very scientifically productive. There are numerous visual models of the early visual perception (Kokkinos et al., 2007) (Neumann et al., 2007). One of the more significant is the BCS/FCS model of Grossberg and Mingolla (Grossberg & Mingolla, 1985). This model is composed of two systems, boundary contour system (BCS) and feature contour system (FCS), modeling processes given in the interactions among V1, V2 and V4 visual areas. Features so important in the human vision like illusory perception, emergent segmentations, diffusive filling-in are integrated in a coherent way in the BCS/FCS network. This system has experiment an important evolution in its modeling, integrating spatial and orientational competitive processes in a same stage (Mingolla et al., 1999). This model has been the framework of many other researchers in the development of their approaches. Kokkinos et al. (Kokkinos et al., 2008) have recently developed a computational simplification of the BCS/FCS model. They propound a three-stage structure incorporating feature extraction with contrast normalization, boundary formation through a competitive stage of information of feature extraction, cooperative signal, anisotropic image smoothing and large scale signal. In their proposal, they include a comparison to Canny's detector, a classical computer vision algorithm. Kokkinos' architecture shows better results than Canny's algorithm. Main contribution of Kokkinos' is its simplification of the BCS/FCS model more than its evolution as it is somewhat complex.

Several neurophysiological studies show that the response modulation by stimuli beyond the receptive field is a common phenomenon in the V1 area (Petkov & Westenberg, 2003). There are evidences that 80% of the orientation selective cells perform a response suppression over a bar texture surround beyond its receptive field. Based on these studies Petkov and Westenberg (Petkov & Westenberg, 2003) proposed a surround suppression model for the complex cells and they also analyzed this effect by psychophysical experiments. This interesting inhibitory effect has been considered in the development of our proposal of boundary detection neural network. This surround suppression mechanism is not considered in the BCS. Nevertheless, Petrov and Westenberg's network is limited to the simple and complex cells for evaluating the surround suppression effect. Competitive and cooperative processes generated by the V2 hypercomplex cells, are not considered in their proposal. Another important biological evidence is the existence of feedback interactions in the visual cortex (Hubel, 1995). BCS includes a competitive-cooperative loop where the completion boundary and the illusory contour extraction are performed. Neumann and Sepp (Neumann & Sepp, 1999) presented a V1-V2 recurrent process through the integration of the V1 activations from V2 receptive field elongated lobes.

In the work presented in this paper, trying to obtain a model as simple as possible, we propose an architecture considering the more significant mechanisms of the human visual system early processing for color scene stimuli: chromatic and achromatic opponent channels, orientational filtering, surround suppression, V1-V2 recurrent interactions through competitive and cooperative fields. Additionally, we propose an inter-scale information fusion stage in order to obtain the boundary output with all the information gathered from the scene. In (Antón-Rodríguez et al., 2009) we proposed a visual feature extraction architecture for color-texture identification corresponding to the color extension of the BCS/FCS system. In this work we presented a BCS system for processing signals from three channels, two opponent chromatic channels and a luminance one, and two FCS for diffusing the two chromatic channels.

In the present work, we propose a new model with six opponent channels, four chromatic and two achromatic, emerged from the transformation of the RGB image. It also includes new mechanisms, like surround suppression and inter-scale fusion, to achieve the natural scene boundaries.

2. Perceptual boundary recurrent detection neural architecture

The Perceptual boundaRy rEcurrent dEtection Neural (PREEN) proposed model (see Fig. 1) comprises five main components, respectively designated as Colour Opponent stage (CO), Chromatic Contour stage (CC), Competitive Fusion stage (CF), Contour Saliency stage (CS), and Inter-scale Competition (IC). The neural model processing is achieved through multiple spatial scales.

The CO stage transforms the chromatic components of the input signals (RGB) into a bio-inspired codification system, made up of various opponent chromatic channels and an achromatic channel. In order to do this, the CO stage firstly calculates the activations of the long- (L), middle- (M), and short- (S) wavelength retinal cones, and then, it generates the opponent processes, corresponding to the ON-OFF achromatic channel and the L^+M^-, M^+L^-, $S^+(L+M)^-$ and $(L+M)^+S^-$ chromatic opponencies. Studies of the human visual system have found that visual stimuli take part in the color opponent and enhancement processes located in retina and Lateral Geniculate Nucleus (LGN) cells of the mammalian visual system (Hubel, 1995; Wilson et al., 1990).

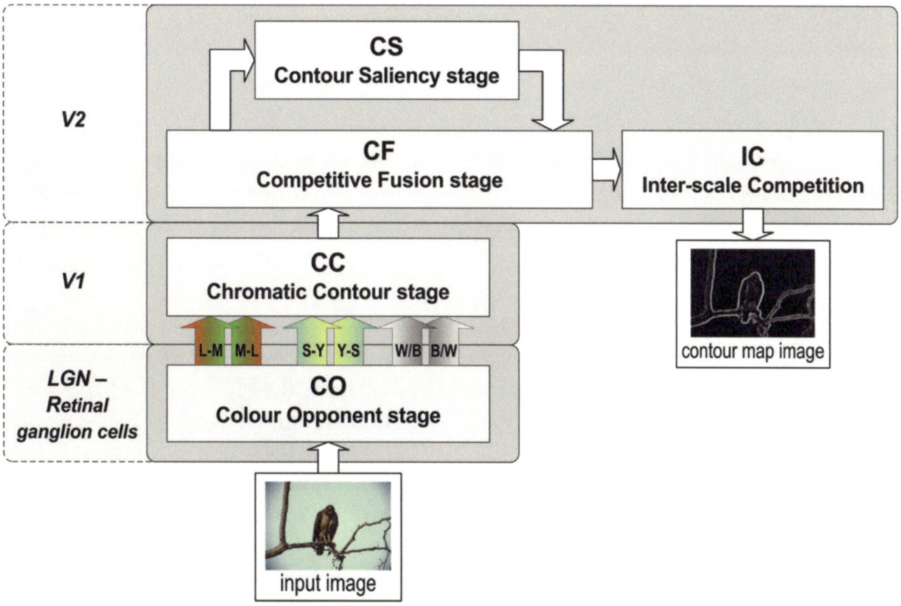

Fig. 1. Proposed model architecture

CC stage is composed of simple and complex cells which filter and perform a surround suppression through multiple scales and orientations in order to extract the real boundaries of the scene. Simple cell multi-scale filtering extracts textural features from both the color opponent and the achromatic signals.

Complex cells use a competition network with surround suppression, which attenuates the contour activities from inner texture areas where it appears a high concentration of false boundaries. Complex cells coherently fuse the color and texture activities, generated by the simple cells, with a behavior inspired in cells from the V1 visual area of the human visual system (Petrov & Westenberg, 2003).

Biologically inspired V1-V2 recurrent interactions take place in the PREEN architecture. CF stage competitively fuses top-down and bottom-up signals, complex-CF-CS, defining and shaping the natural boundaries. CF and CS stages model competitive and cooperative behaviors exhibited in the V2 area of the human visual system (Hubel, 1995).

Final output is constituted by a contour map image corresponding to the natural boundaries with perceptual significance.

The PREEN model architecture includes competitive networks. We model these networks using the membrane potential network (Hodgkin & Huxley, 1990), whose simplified behavior can be expressed according to equation (1).

$$C_M \frac{dV}{dt} = -AV + \left(V^+ - V\right)g^+ + \left(V^- - V\right)g^- \tag{1}$$

where V is the membrane potential, A is a decay constant, V^+ and V^- are the excitatory and inhibitory reversal potentials, and g^+ and g^- are the excitatory and inhibitory total input, respectively.

In a stationary situation, the potential, V, would be defined by equation (2). This is the situation we consider in our model.

$$V = \frac{V^+ g^+ + V^- g^-}{A + g^+ + g^-} \tag{2}$$

where $V^+ \geq 0$ and $V^- \leq 0$.

Equation (2) expresses the membrane potential as the normalization between the net input (difference between excitation and inhibition) and the total input (excitation plus inhibition). So, this normalization computes the ratio contrast and solves the noise-saturation dilemma.

2.1 Colour opponent stage

The CO stage performs chromatic and achromatic opponent competitive processes based on opponent mechanisms and luminance channel competitive enhancement to generate four chromatic signals shaping opponent pairs, L^+M^-, M^+L^-, $S^+(L+M)^-$ and $(L+M)^+S^-$, and two achromatic signals, ON and OFF. This is observed as the generation of three channels of opponent pairs. In hierarchical levels of the human system there are evidences of manifold cases of opponent pairs, both in the motor and visual systems (Zrenner, 1990).

The CO processing contains a previous stage in which luminance (I signal), activations of the long (L signal), middle (M signal), short (S signal) wavelength cones and (L+M) channel activation (Y signal) are generated from R, G and B input signals.

Equations (3), (4) and (5) define the calculations of those activities (Antón-Rodríguez et al., 2009). The luminance signal (I) is computed as a weighted sum; the L, M and S signals are obtained as the transformation matrix of the three chromatic components R, G and B.

$$I = 0.299R + 0.587G + 0.114B \tag{3}$$

$$\begin{bmatrix} L \\ M \\ S \end{bmatrix} = \begin{bmatrix} 0.293 & 0.603 & 0.104 \\ 0.134 & 0.704 & 0.162 \\ 0.046 & 0.099 & 0.854 \end{bmatrix} \begin{bmatrix} R \\ G \\ B \end{bmatrix} \tag{4}$$

$$Y = L + M \tag{5}$$

The CO stage models the behavior of the opponent cells whose main characteristics are their high sensibility and precision to contrasts contours. These attributes recommend their use as a previous step for image contour, shapes, and texture detection (Hubel, 1995). The opponent model for L^+M^- chromatic channels, following membrane competitive network is defined by equation (6).

$$c_{ij}^{lm(s)} = \frac{\sum\left[D_{pq}^{(s)}\right]^+ L_{ij} - \sum\left[-D_{pq}^{(s)}\right]^+ M_{ij}}{A + \sum\left[D_{pq}^{(s)}\right]^+ L_{ij} + \sum\left[-D_{pq}^{(s)}\right]^+ M_{ij}} \tag{6}$$

where $c_{ij}^{lm(s)}$ is the L^+M^- channel cell activity for position *(i,j)*, $[c]^+ = \max(0,c)$, A is a decay constant, and $D_{pq}^{(s)}$ is a difference of Gaussians (see Fig. 2) following equation (7).

$$D_{pq}^{(s)} = D_A\left[\exp\left(\frac{-\left(p^2+q^2\right)}{2\sigma_e^{(s)2}}\right) - \exp\left(\frac{-\left(p^2+q^2\right)}{2\sigma_i^{(s)2}}\right)\right] \tag{7}$$

where σ_e and σ_i are the excitation and inhibition deviations and D_A is the amplitude constant.

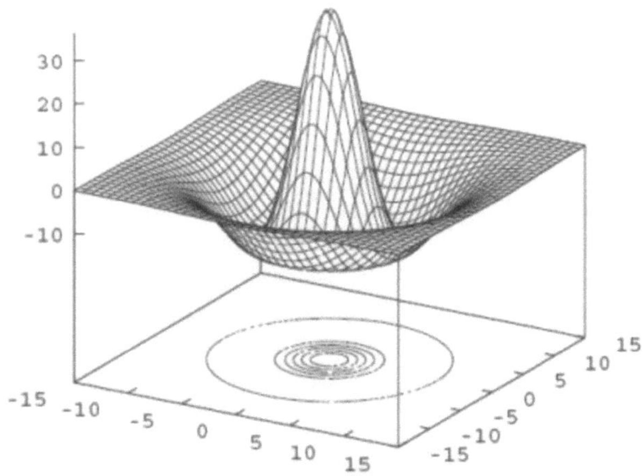

Fig. 2. Difference of Gaussians (dog)

The remainder opponencies, M^+L^-, S^+Y^- and Y^+S^-, are calculated using equation (6) substituting L_{ij} and M_{ij} signals for the corresponding opponency signals.

Analogously to the achromatic process accomplished in the LGN of the human visual system (Hubel, 1995), the neural architecture enhances the luminance signal, I_{ij}, in a competitive network generating two opponent channels ON-center and OFF-center under equation (6), similarly to the chromatic channels, replacing the chromatic signals by the luminance signal. ON channel processing is in charge of enhancing the information of regions with higher luminance intensity in relation to their surroundings, while OFF channel enhances regions with lower luminance intensity than their surroundings.

These competitive processes, derived from equation (6), establish a gain control network over the inputs from chromatic and luminance channels, maintaining the sensibility of cells to contrasts, compensating variable illumination, and normalizing image intensity.

These competitive networks are parallelly applied over three different spatial scales, with suitable values of σ_e and σ_i for the small, medium and large scales (s=0,1,2).

Correlation studies about color codification systems based on trichromatic theory have proven the suitability of using the red-green and blue-yellow opponent signals (Ohta et al., 1980), in all, opponencies of long-middle and short-long-middle wavelength. In like manner, the ganglionar opponent cells with higher presence rate in the retina correspond to L-M opponency, next higher rate is S-(L+M) (Zrenner et al., 1990), so we consider appropriate using the opponencies chosen.

Biologically motivated models for boundary detection, as BCS/FCS (Grossberg et al., 1995) or Kokkinos' model (Kokkinos et al., 2008) do not use chromatic channels for detecting boundaries. They only work with the luminance component. Nevertheless, they use images of natural scenes for validation. It is clearly that the human visual system operating has an essential chromatic component, based on the color opponencies.

2.2 Chromatic Contour (CC)

The Chromatic Contour stage models V1 simple and complex cells. It undertakes the contour extraction and the merging with surround suppression of the simple cell signals, as it can be seen in Fig. 1. CC stage models behaviors of cells located in V1 visual area, orientation and spatial frequency selective cells and information fusion cells (Hubel, 1995).
Simple cells extract contours from chromatic and achromatic CO channels through a Gabor filter bank, using even ($E_{ijk}^{(s)}$) and odd ($O_{ijk}^{(s)}$) components for position (*i,j*), deviation for multiple scales (*s*=0, 1, 2) and orientation (*k*=0, 1, 2, 3, 4, 5 corresponding to θ= 30°, 60°, 90°, 120°, 150°). These cells respond to variations on the textural and color features. Complex Gabor filters have sensibility to orientation, spatial frequency and position (Daugman, 1980). Grossberg, Mingolla et al. (Grossberg et al., 1995) (Mingolla et al., 1999) modeled simple cells with an odd-type filtering in their BCS model. The inclusion of even fields is justified due to the importance of these profiles in texture detection (Landy & Bergen, 1991).
Following the behavior indicated by the membrane potential shown in equation (2), simple cell activities are given by equations (8), (9), (10) and (11).

$$a_{ijk}^{(s)} = \frac{\sum E_{pqk}^{(s)}\left(\left[c_{ij}^{on(s)}\right]^{+} - \left[c_{ij}^{off(s)}\right]^{+}\right)}{A + \sum \left|E_{pqk}^{(s)}\right|\left(\left[c_{ij}^{on(s)}\right]^{+} + \left[c_{ij}^{off(s)}\right]^{+}\right)} \quad (8)$$

$$b_{ijk}^{(s)} = \frac{\sum O_{pqk}^{(s)}\left(\left[c_{ij}^{on(s)}\right]^{+} - \left[c_{ij}^{off(s)}\right]^{+}\right)}{A + \sum \left|O_{pqk}^{(s)}\right|\left(\left[c_{ij}^{on(s)}\right]^{+} + \left[c_{ij}^{off(s)}\right]^{+}\right)} \quad (9)$$

$$e_{ijk}^{lm(s)} = \frac{\sum E_{pqk}^{(s)} c_{ij}^{lm(s)}}{A + \sum | E_{pqk}^{(s)} | c_{ij}^{lm(s)}} \quad (10)$$

$$f_{ijk}^{lm(s)} = \frac{\sum O_{pqk}^{(s)} c_{ij}^{lm(s)}}{A + \sum | O_{pqk}^{(s)} | c_{ij}^{lm(s)}} \quad (11)$$

where $a_{ijk}^{(s)}$, $b_{ijk}^{(s)}$ are the even and odd simple cell activities for the luminance channel, and $e_{ijk}^{lm(s)}$, $f_{ijk}^{lm(s)}$ are the simple cell activities for chromatic channel L^+M^-, position (*i,j*) and orientation k for even and odd filters respectively, $|.|$ represents the absolute value, $[c]^{+} = \max(0,c)$, and A is a decay constant.
For the remainder chromatic channels, the activity equations to use are equations (10) and (11) replacing L^+M^- channel signal by the appropriate channel signal (M^+L^-, S^+Y^-, Y^+S^-).
For each perceptual position (*i,j*) a hyper column of simple cells varying in filter type (filter profile) and orientation *k* is applied to each channel.
The complex cell stage, using two cellular layers, fuses information from simple cells giving rise to a map which contains real contours for each of the three scales used (see Fig. 1).

The first layer of cells is in charge of combining responses from different Gabor filters at each opponent and luminance channel at their three scales (s=0,1,2), as shown in equation (12).

$$h_{ijk}^{(s)} = \left[a_{ijk}^{(s)}\right]^+ + \left[b_{ijk}^{(s)}\right]^+ + \left[e_{ijk}^{lm(s)}\right]^+ + \left[f_{ijk}^{lm(s)}\right]^+ + \\ + \left[e_{ijk}^{slm(s)}\right]^+ + \left[f_{ijk}^{slm(s)}\right]^+ + \left[e_{ijk}^{ml(s)}\right]^+ + \left[f_{ijk}^{ml(s)}\right]^+ + \left[e_{ijk}^{lms(s)}\right]^+ + \left[f_{ijk}^{lms(s)}\right]^+ \tag{12}$$

where $[c]^+ = \max(0,c)$ is a half-wave rectifier.

The second complex cell layer models a competition network with surround suppression (see Fig. 3).

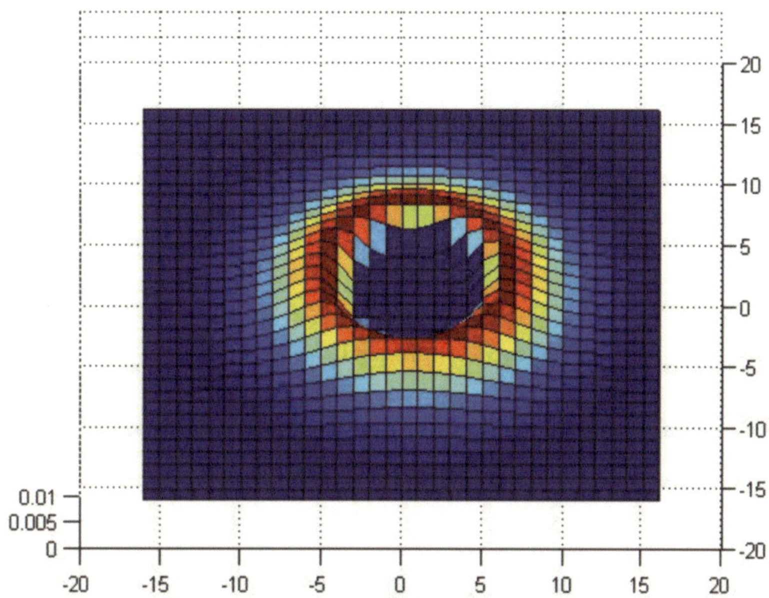

Fig. 3. Surround suppression receptive field of CC complex cells ($S_{ijk}^{(s)}$).

The behavior of layer 2 complex cells is modeled by equation (13):

$$H_{ijk}^{(s)} = \left[\frac{h_{ijk}^{(s)} - \lambda \sum S_{pqk}^{(s)} h_{ij}^{(s)}}{A + h_{ijk}^{(s)} + \sum S_{pqk}^{(s)} h_{ij}^{lm(s)}} \right]^+ \tag{13}$$

being $H_{ijk}^{(s)}$ the CC complex cells output; $h_{ijk}^{(s)}$ is the first layer activity, $S_{ijk}^{(s)} = [-D_{ij}^{(s)}]^+$ is the surround suppression receptive field with $D_{ij}^{(s)}$ a dog following equation (7), as it is shown in Fig. 3, for each of the scales defined by s=0,1,2; A is a decay constant, $\lambda > 0$ is the suppression constant and $[c]^+ = \max(0,c)$. Equation (13) determines the anisotropic surround suppression, as the removal is performed according to the orientations.

In their work, Petrov and Westenberg (Petrov & Westenberg, 2003) observed various manifestations of perceptual modulation by the context. They used image sets of letters and bars, and objects icons (of different sizes and orientations) with superimposed band-spectrum noise. They observed the effects of the surround in contrast for different noise frequencies. The inhibitory effect was modeled designing a non-classical receptive field (non-CRF) defined by a weighting function with a normalized difference of Gaussians profile. This idea is taken in the present paper but with an important difference.
Model proposed of CC complex cells exhibits a positional competition between a position (*i,j*) and its surroundings. These competitive processes establish a gain control network over the fusion channel input, maintaining the sensibility of cells to contrasts, compensating variable illumination, and normalizing image intensity.
In order to obtain a complex non-CRF field external to the CRF field of CC simple cells, we choose same values for σ_e deviations of $S_{ijk}^{(s)}$ and for $\sigma^{(s)}$ deviations of CC simple cells and we fix σ_i deviations of $S_{ijk}^{(s)}$ as twice the value of $\sigma^{(s)}$.
In Fig. 4 it can be observed the effect produced by the surround suppression depending on the inhibition strength (λ=1.0 and λ=2.0). Using a high suppression constant, it is possible to remove areas with a high concentration of weak contour caused by inner texture features (see left column). It can be noticed that the surround suppression model makes the boundaries to have less noisy activities near them, thus achieving a better definition and so a better precision. However, as the surround suppression model cleans up the area around the boundaries, sometimes the recall value diminishes.
In a later work, Grigorescu, Petrov and Westenberg (Grigorescu et al., 2004) proposed a computational step, called surround suppression for detecting boundaries in natural scenes. This step was incorporated to the Canny edge detector. A comparison was performed using 40 natural images, achieving better results with the step included.
To strengthen the analysis about the positive effect of the surround suppression modeling, we took 20 images from the Berkeley Segmentation DataSet (BSDS) and compared the results obtained with and without suppression. In Fig. 4, we can see some processing examples. Fig. 4 (e) includes the F-value curve of the processing with (right) and without suppression (left). We achieved a mean F-value of 0.64 (0.62, 0.66) when processing with suppression versus a mean value of 0.63 (0.69, 0.57) when processing without suppression. It can be observed a slightly better result counting the suppression. A remarkable feature is the significant difference in the precision value, in favor of the model with suppression, and in the recall value, in favor of the model without suppression, which corroborates the previous point.
Using cooperation processes, it is more interesting obtaining high precision than high recall, since these processes generate more boundaries, but also more noise. Accordingly, the model of complex cells showing surround suppression advantages the cooperative processes from V2, which PREEN model includes in the CS stage.
The explained complex cell stage modeling has significant differences with other processing models. The complex cell stage of the BCS model (Grossberg et al., 1995) is in charge of summing simple cell signals. This sum produces an independence of the contrast direction, so as the entire real boundary map is obtained in this stage.

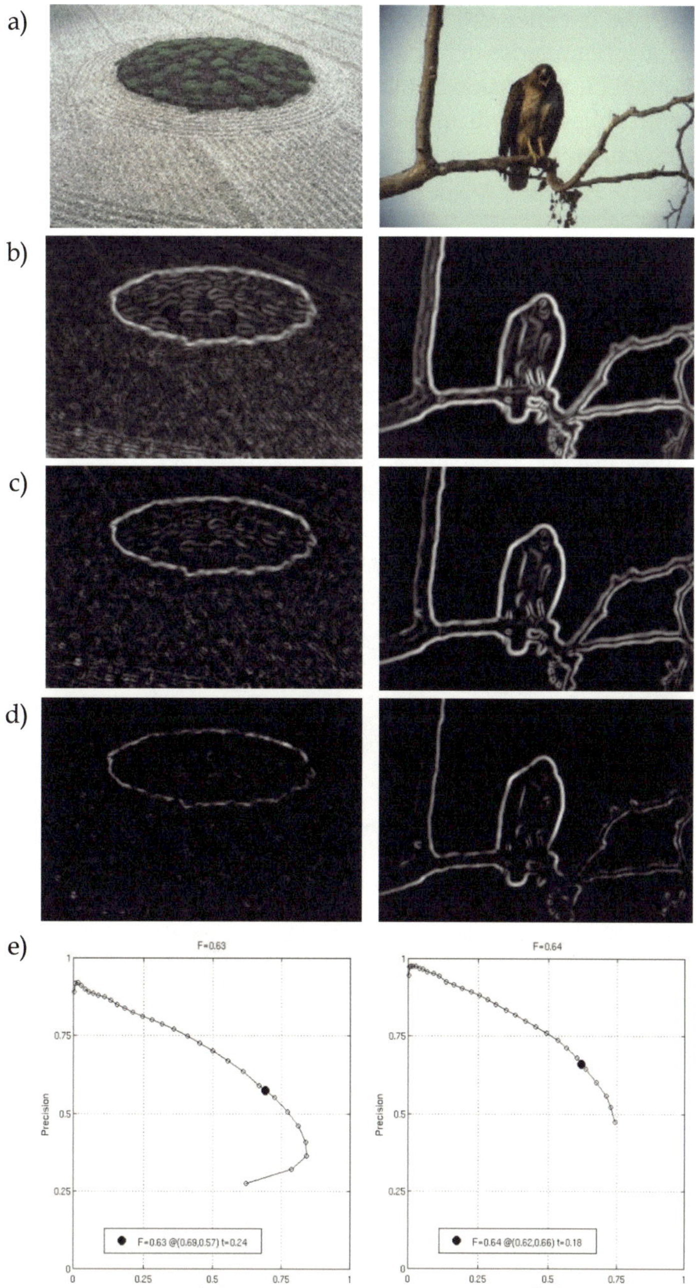

Fig. 4. Effect of complex cell surround suppression. Image on the left: image 86016. Image on the right: image 42049. Row a): original image. Row b): output from first stage (fusion) of complex stage (without surround suppression). Row c): output from CC complex stage for λ=1.0. Row d): output from CC complex for λ=2.0. Row e): F-measure curves (precision and recall) for 20 test images of the Berkeley database, (e)-left without surround suppression and (e)-right with surround suppression.

In PREEN model, the complex cell stage fuses simple cell signals and also removes the surroundings making boundaries to be contrast-independent and more accurate.
Kokkinos et al.'s model uses a shunting inhibition for surround suppression which implies a recurrent stage with obliged stabilization (Kokkinos et al., 2008). PREEN model uses a non-recurrent competition, as the recurrent process is located in upper stages, where V1-V2 interaction occurs.

2.3 Competitive Fusion stage (CF)

CF stage competitively fuses information from CC complex bottom-up and CS cooperation top-down. This stage models the V1-V2 recurrent interactions produced in the PREEN model. This recurrent interaction detects, regulates, and completes boundaries into globally consistent contrast positions and orientations, while it suppresses activations from redundant and less important contours, thus eliminating image noise. There are numerous evidences about the existence of hyper-complex cells in the human visual system, where V1-V2 recurrent interactions occurs (Hubel, 1995). We use a shunting network to model this behavior, where lateral inhibitions occur within cells of the same competitive stage. Equation (14) describes these CF hyper-complex cells functioning. It includes two inhibitions, orientationally and spatially.

$$U_{ijk}^{(s)} = \left[\frac{u_{ijk}^{(s)} - C_i \sum_{r \neq k} \sum_{pq} S_{pqr}^{(s)} U_{pqr}^{(s)} - C_c \sum G_{pq}^{(s)} U_{pqk}^{(s)}}{A + u_{ijk}^{(s)} + \sum G_{pq}^{(s)} U_{pqk}^{(s)}} \right]^+ \tag{14}$$

being $U_{ijk}^{(s)}$ the CF hyper-complex cells output, $u_{ijk}^{(s)} = K_h H_{ijk}^{(s)} + K_f F_{ijk}^{(s)}$ the input to the competition stage: $H_{ijk}^{(s)}$ is the CC complex cells output, $F_{ijk}^{(s)}$ is the CS top-down signal, K_h and K_f are gain constants; the orientational inhibitory receptive field, $S_{pqr}^{(s)}$, is a Gaussian kernel with τ (τ>1) aspect ratio, rotated r grades, and with $\sigma_i^{(s)}$ deviation for each of the scales defined by s=0,1,2; $G_{pq}^{(s)}$ is a Gaussian kernel with $\sigma_u^{(s)}$ deviation for each of the scales, A is a decay constant, C_c and C_i are inhibition constants and $[c]^+ = \max(0,c)$.
Recurrent interaction is solved by an iterative process, where actual state of the $U_{ijk}^{(s)}$ activity depends on the previous state activity and the CS stage feedback activity, $F_{ijk}^{(s)}$.
The inhibitory receptive field in the competition among orientations, $S_{pqr}^{(s)}$, corresponds to a Gaussian rotated r grades, with a very high aspect ratio so that all the points in the line of orientation r passing through (i,j) have a maximum inhibition (see Fig. 5).
The point of difference between competitive stages of PREEN model and BCS system is the competitive model with shunting inhibition used in PREEN model versus a contrast normalization network from BCS system. Shunting inhibition allows higher boundary enhancement and thinning yielding higher precision and deletion of noise activities, which work against cooperative mechanisms, advantaging the recurrent process.

Kokkinos' architecture also uses a shunting inhibition model, including in the competition a gradient signal from the smooth stage through a diffusion process, similar to the FCS stage of the BCS/FCS system. Kokkinos' model does not perform a competition among orientations within this stage. PREEN architecture, similarly to BCS system, proposes a competition among orientations to better define the boundary orientation in each position. In this competition, PREEN uses the inhibition signal from competitive stage neighbor instead of the input signal to the competitive stage taken in the BCS model. That is to say PREEN model heightens the shunting mechanism in the inhibition.

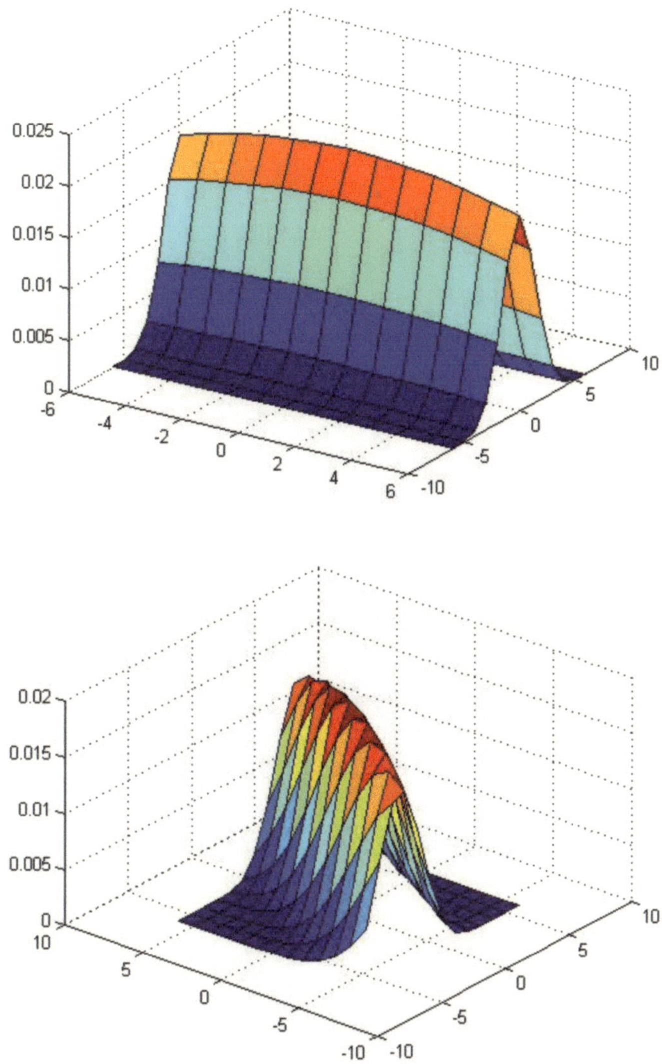

Fig. 5. Orientational inhibition receptive field, $S_{pqr}^{(s)}$.

2.4 Contour saliency stage (CS)

CS stage models the cooperative process for the saliency detection of the contour activity interpolation. In visual cortex, it has been detected cooperative completion or grouping processes by realizing a "bipole property" (Mingolla et al., 1999). This property refers to the disposition of certain cells in visual cortical areas V1 and V2 to fire in the presence of approximately aligned, but spatially separated, image gradients. Salient contours are detected determining existent contour activity in both sides of each position *(i,j)* through a bipole receptive field. The behavior of CS cells is modeled by equation (15).

$$F_{ijk}^{(s)} = \frac{z\left(\sum P_{pqk}^{(s)} U_{pqk}^{(s)}\right) z\left(\sum N_{pqk}^{(s)} U_{pqk}^{(s)}\right)}{A + \left(\sum P_{pqk}^{(s)} U_{pqk}^{(s)}\right)\left(\sum N_{pqk}^{(s)} U_{pqk}^{(s)}\right)} \tag{15}$$

where $U_{ijk}^{(s)}$ is the CF hyper-complex activity, $P_{ijk}^{(s)}$ and $N_{ijk}^{(s)}$ are the lobes of the bipole receptive field of CS cells (see Fig. 6), A is a decay constant, and $z(s)$ is a lineal function with a positive cooperative threshold, α:

$$z(s) = \begin{cases} 0 & \text{si} \quad s \leq \alpha \\ s & \text{si} \quad s > \alpha \end{cases}$$

Each lobe is generated as a Gaussian with an aspect ratio of τ and a profile relation of $K_l^{(s)}$ for each scale s, with a coordinate translation D_c and a rotation k, following equation (16). Fig. 6 shows a dipole example.

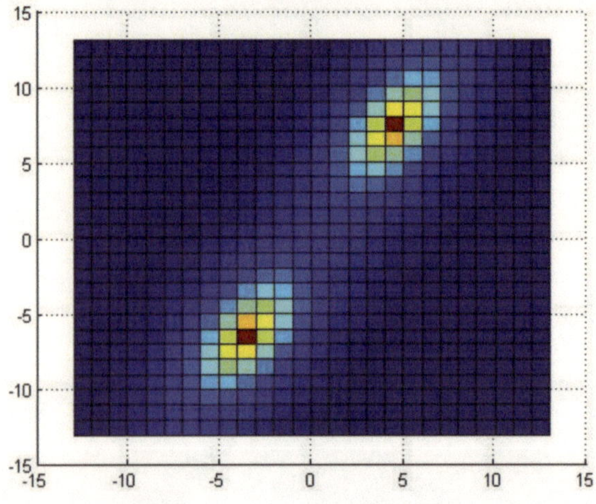

Fig. 6. Oriented bipole receptive field.

$$\begin{aligned} BIP_{ijk}^{(s)} &= \exp\left(-K_l^{(s)} \sqrt{\left(\frac{x'}{\tau}\right)^2 + (y')^2}\right) \\ P_{ijk}^{(s)} &= \frac{1}{\left\| BIP_{ijk}^{(s)} \right\|} BIP_{ijk}^{(s)} \end{aligned} \tag{16}$$

where $\|.\|$ is the L1 norm, the coordinates of the spatial transformation:

$$x' = (x - x_c)\cos(k) + (y - y_c)\sin(k)$$
$$y' = -(x - x_c)\sin(k) + (y - y_c)\cos(k)$$

and the translation origin coordinates are:

$$x_c = D_c \cos(k)$$
$$y_c = D_c \sin(k)$$

Equations for computing $N_{ijk}^{(s)}$ are similar but with a coordinate translation of $-D_c$. Each lobe measures one unit of area, and it is essential to be no activity in the dipole center. Competitive stage output $U_{ijk}^{(s)}$ is normalized, bounded between 0 and 1. Hence, maximum activity in each lobule will be 1. Thereby, we can appropriately choose the value of α.
Thanks to this contour cooperative saliency, illusory boundaries of perceptual figures are extracted as it can be observed in Fig. 7, where it appears the PREEN model processing result of the Kanizsa's square image.

Fig. 7. PREEN processing of Kanizsa's square image.

In BCS system, Kokkinos' model, and PREEN architecture cooperation is performed in a similar way. All uses bipole receptive field cells to generate the cooperative activity produced when both lobes of the receptive field are active. Difference between both models lie in the way of determining when such excitatory situation is produced. As it is expressed in equation (15), PREEN uses the product of the lobe activities to obtain the cooperation activity. Each lobe contributes to excite the dipole cell is its activity exceeds the threshold α. Hence, the product demands the contribution of both lobes and, so, a normalized bipole cell output near 1 will be guaranteed. In remainder cases, the output will be 0.
Kokkinos utilizes the product of the lobule activities but without activation threshold. And BCS uses a pseudo-logic function of decision AND, with a fast saturation function to a value near to 1, and with a threshold of 2 (Mingolla et al., 1999). By doing so, it is guaranteed that the bipole cell exceed 2 only if there are inputs to both lobules.

2.5 Inter-scale Competition stage (IC)

PREEN model proposes an output stage where signals from the three scales are merged in order to obtain the best possible output combining all the information gathered in each scale. While scale increases, noise is better filtered and so boundary signals improve, though precision and thinning become reduced. Noise does not appear in larger scales, but only contours with higher gradient are detected; those are high quality contours but not all existing. Boundaries from the small scale are accurate and thin; the boundary map includes all perceptual boundaries of the natural scene images, therefore achieving a high recall value. It appears evident that better boundary qualities will be found in the small scale signal. However, its small receptive fields cause extracting a significant level of noisy contours. So, precision, recall and thinning are provided by the small scale, and noise shortage is given by larger scales, mainly by the large scale. This analysis leads us to propose next assumptions to model the output stage of the PREEN architecture:

- Small scale signal provides all interesting boundaries for segmenting natural scenes.
- Medium and large scale signals enclose a reduced level of contour noise.
- An accurate boundary of a natural scene generates activity in all the scales.
- Output will be composed of thin and accurate boundaries, with a correct level of recall and generating activity in all the scales.

Basing upon these assumptions, PREEN model proposes a single boundary output signal resulting from the inter-scales competition for detecting boundaries with higher quality. Equation (17) shows the integration of the three scales through an inter-scale competition with major scale context dependent inhibition, ρ_{ijk}.

$$O_{ijk} = \left[\frac{U_{ijk}^{small} - \rho_{ijk} Co \sum G_{pq}^{small} U_{pqk}^{small}}{A + U_{ijk}^{small} + \rho_{ijk} \sum G_{pq}^{small} U_{pqk}^{small}} \right]^{+} \tag{17}$$

where U_{ijk}^{small} is the small scale CF hyper-complex activity, G_{pq}^{small} is a Gaussian kernel with a small scale deviation of σ_{small}, A is a decay constant, C_o is an inhibitory constant, and $[c]^{+} = \max(0,c)$ and ρ_{ij} is the major scale context dependent inhibition gain, defined by equation (18).

$$\begin{aligned} \rho_{ijk} &= \exp\left(-K_o \left(1 - \frac{1}{1 + \eta v_{ijk}} \right) \right) \\ v_{ijk} &= \sum_{8-neightbor} U_{pqk}^{\mathrm{medium}} + \sum_{8-neightbor} U_{pqk}^{\mathrm{large}} \end{aligned} \tag{18}$$

with K_0 and η positive constants; v_{ijk} is the sum of the activities of scales medium and large in the 8-connected neighborhood of the consider position.

Equation (18) shows that ρ_{ijk} has a Gaussian profile, comprised between 0 and 1, with a shape dependent of K_0, and close to 0 when higher contour activity from larger scales. Equation (17) displays strong inhibition when the 8-connected neighborhood from larger scales has a high boundary activity and the boundary activity from the small scale will not be affected if the neighborhood does not include contours. Image areas without contours in larger scales will sharply attenuate the boundary activity from the small scale.

3. Experimental results

We quantitatively compare our method against the Kokkinos et al.'s model (Kokkinos et al., 2008), that has been made available publicly. This model proposes a significant simplification of the BCS/FCS model proposed by Grossberg, Mingolla et al. (Grossberg et al., 1995) (Mingolla et al., 1999). The comparison to the Kokkinos et al.'s proposal (and to the BCS/FCS model by extension) is performed according to a common philosophy about propounding biologically inspired models. Differences among these models lie in the modeling of each stage and substantially in the color contribution of the PREEN model in the boundary detection processes in natural scenes. We will try to demonstrate that natural scenes have a chromatic component essential for defining and processing them. The comparison is accomplished with the boundary-based error, F-measure, which are the measure used in Kokkinos et al.'s paper. The measure computation has been made using the Matlab code supplied in next web page: http://www.eecs.berkeley.edu/Research/Projects/CS/vision/grouping/segbench/. We have used all the 100 test images from the Berkeley Segmentation Dataset (Martin et al., 2001) and their human segmented images were taken as the ground truth to accomplish the F-measure values. Fig. 8-bottom shows a precision-recall curve (PR curve) with the average F-measure value of the boundaries detected in the all 100 test images. In Fig. 9 it can be observed processing examples for the PREEN architecture, including the F-measure values with their precision and recall as well as the position that would achieve in the ranking published in the Berkeley Segmentation Benchmark web page (BSDS, 2001).

Kokkinos et al. (Kokkinos et al., 2008) compared its model to the Canny edge detection algorithm using the images from the Berkeley dataset achieving better results in different scenarios. In their paper, they show the PR curves and the F-measure of the comparisons. Their better setting match with their BCS learned fine scale proposal, achieving an F-measure of 0.573 versus the 0.568 obtained by the Canny's algorithm. PREEN model achieves an F-measure with PR coordinates of 0.59 (0.68, 0.52), as it is shown in Fig. 8. So, it obtains better average result when detecting boundaries. Hence, PREEN boundary detection process achieves higher precision and recall values.

There are three notable differences between Kokkinos et al.' model and PREEN model. As previously said, the more significant one is the color contribution in the PREEN model. Another modeling difference is that PREEN model includes orientational competition, so PREEN obtains more accurate contours. A third significant difference is the output of the model. PREEN includes an inter-scale competitive stage as architecture output. This fusion provides us with an output enclosing all the better features of each scale. The substantial effect of color in the boundary detection process can be analyzed in the boundary detection algorithm ranking published in the Berkeley Segmentation Benchmark web page (http://www.eecs.berkeley.edu/Research/Projects/CS/vision/grouping/segbench/bench/html/algorithms.html). The summary table shows different algorithms for grayscale and color processing. There are versions of algorithms for processing both grayscale and color images and it can be observed that color version obtains better results. Considering the average F-value achieved, PREEN architecture would gain the eighth position in the ranking

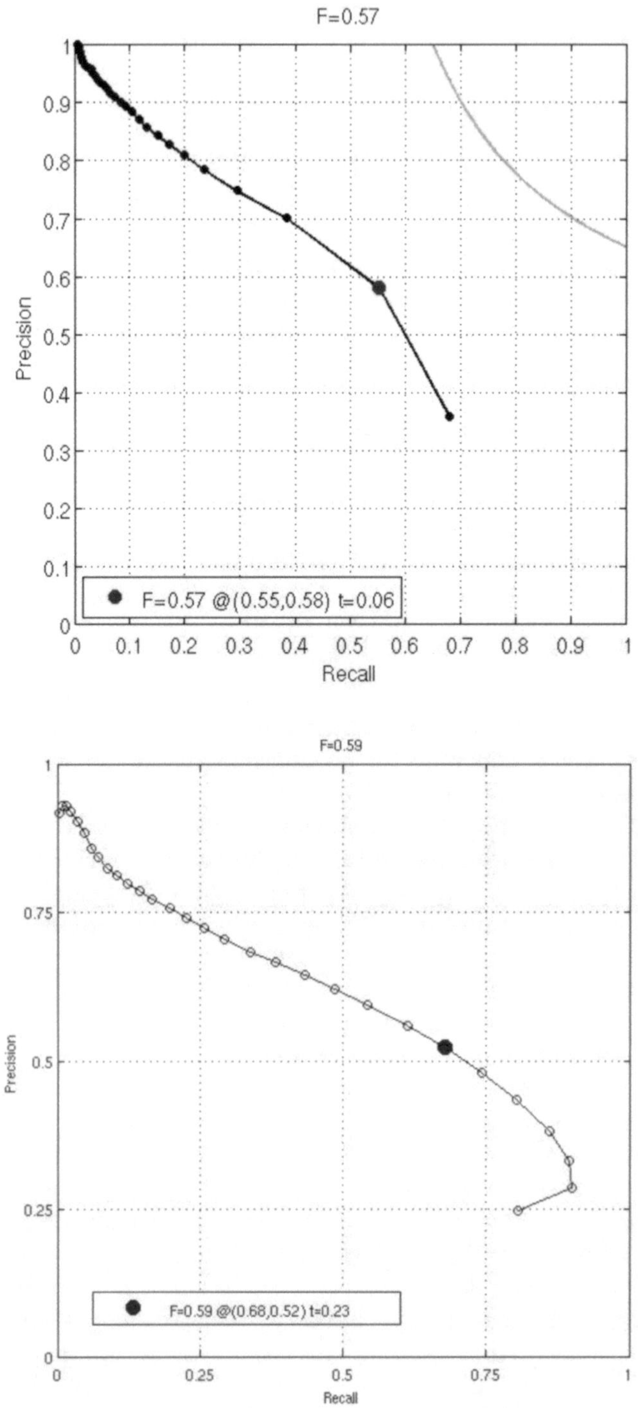

Fig. 8. Comparative results when processing all the 100 images from the test set of the Berkeley database. Top: Color gradient algorithm. Bottom: PREEN architecture.

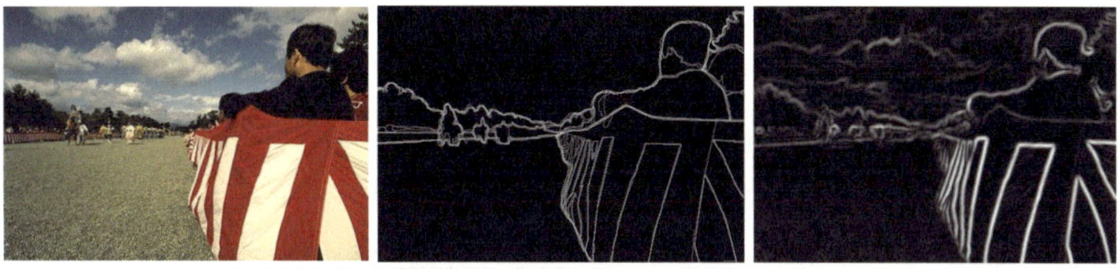

145086, F=0.85 (0.85, 0.84), F_{human}=0.85, ranking=1

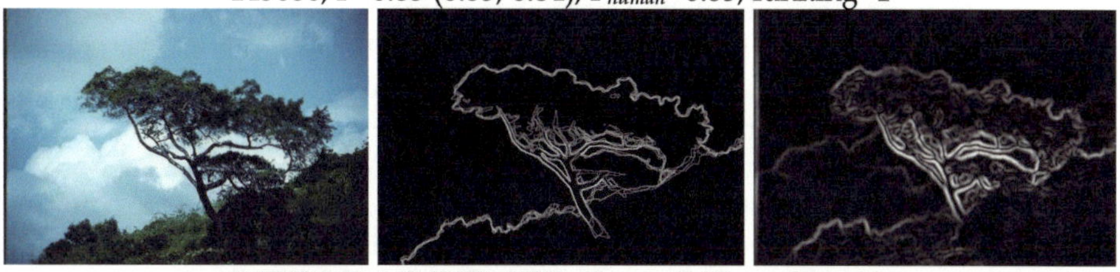

147091, F=0.8 (0.79, 0.82), F_{human}=0.87, ranking=1

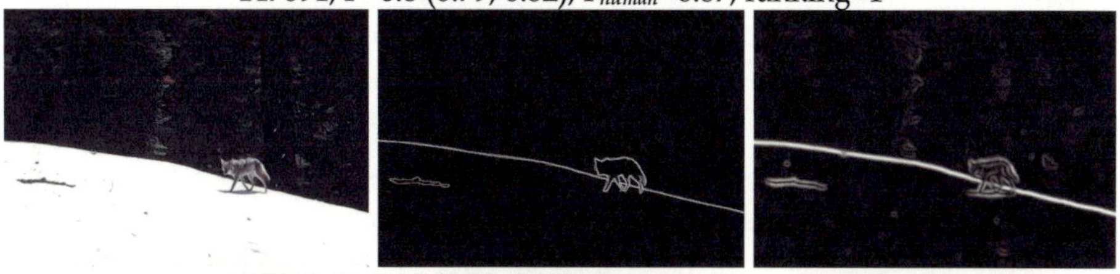

167062, F=0.92 (0.98, 0.87), F_{human}=0.95, ranking=1

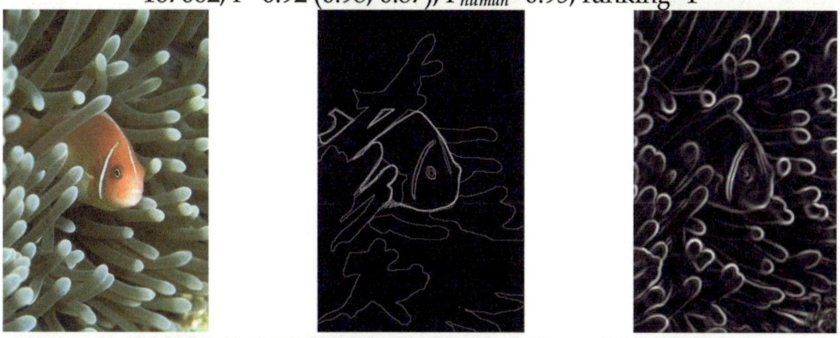

210088, F=0.56 (0.69,0.47), F_{human}=0.54, ranking=3-4

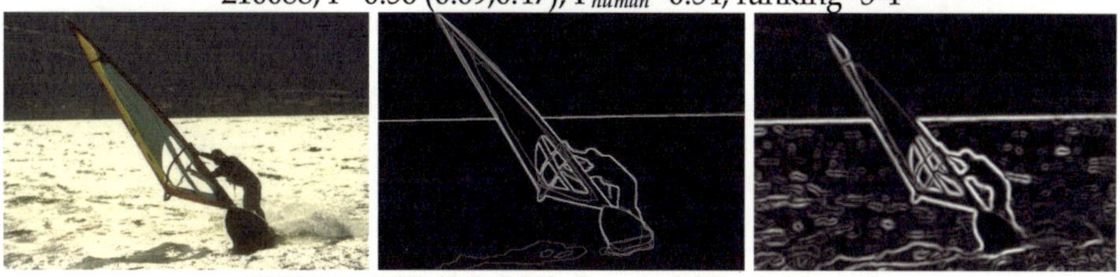

62096, F=0.78 (0.7, 0.87), F_{human}=0.90, ranking=6

Fig. 9. Processing examples of PREEN architecture. Each example includes the image name in the Berkeley Segmentation Dataset, the F-measure value, the recall and precision coordinates, and the position that would achieve in the ranking published in the Berkeley Segmentation Benchmark web-site.

published in the BSDS web page, outperforming the Color Gradient algorithm. The PR curve of this method can be seen in Fig. 8-left (extracted from the aforementioned web page) comparing it to that of the PREEN model. Fig. 8 shows PREEN model achieves outstanding results in some benchmark images, overcoming in some cases the first algorithm in ranking. However, global result is not so excellent, locating the eighth position. This contradiction can be accurately analyzed considering the results shown in Fig. 4 c)-left. The surround effect determines the suppression of weak contours sited near other stronger. When processing image 86016 by the surround suppression PREEN model, we can observed lineal contours are drastically attenuated while round contour is reactivated. Apparently, this can be observed as a positive effect, since it affords the possibility to segment the scene into two regions with perceptual significance: the furrows area and the vegetation round area. However, segmentation performed by humans in the Berkeley database includes lineal contours as significant perceptual boundaries, which makes F-measure achieved by the PREEN architecture under these circumstances will lean to be lower, considerably diminishing the average F-measure value. Fig. 4 c)-right shows the opposite case, PREEN model causes the elimination of weak contours from inside tree branch, which makes boundaries to be finer considering the human segmentation.

4. Conclusion

In this paper we propose a model bio-inspired in the recurrent interactions of the early visual areas for detecting boundaries in color natural scenes, called PREEN model. To perform the comparative analysis, we have chosen BCS/FCS model (Grossberg et al., 1995) (Mingolla et al., 1999) and Kokkinos et al.'s model (Kokkinos et al., 2008) on the grounds of the similar aims. Images used are taken from the Berkeley Segmentation Dataset (BSDS, 2001). Important features of the proposed model are providing a simple and effective modeling, using even and odd oriented filtering, participation of surround suppression mechanisms in the complex cell stage, oriented and positional shunting competition, contour cooperative saliency extraction through bipole interactions, and a new output stage with inhibition among stages.

Test simulations over al the 100 test images from the Berkeley dataset and a comparative analysis have been included. Results achieved outperform those obtained by Kokkinos et al.'s model.

Furthermore, PREEN model has displayed outstanding results, overcoming the best algorithms published in the BSDS web page when processing some images of the database. In the analysis performed we have observed PREEN model favors boundaries with high perceptual significance attenuating the remainder boundaries. Thereby, PREEN model obtains low values in such images with human segmentations including boundaries of secondary importance, more germane to attentive mechanisms. We think if the database would have human segmentations with higher participation, the proposed model would achieve more favorable results. This higher participation, in our view, would mean remove or strongly attenuate secondary boundaries in human segmentations.

5. References

Antón-Rodríguez, M.; Díaz-Pernas, F. J.; Díez-Higuera, J. F.; Martínez-Zarzuela, M.; González-Ortega, D. & Boto-Giralda, D. (2009). Recognition of coloured and textured images through a multi-scale neural architecture with orientational filtering and chromatic diffusion. *Neurocomputing*, Vol. 72 (3713–3725). ISSN: 0925-2312.

Berkeley segmentation dataset and benchmark (2001). http://www.cs.berkeley.edu/projects/vision/grouping/segbench/. Last visited: September 2010.

Daugman, J.G. (1980) Two-dimensional spectral analysis of cortical receptive field profiles. *Vision Research*, Vol. 20 (pp. 847-856). ISSN: 0042-6989.

Grigorescu, C.; Petkov, N. & Westenberg, M.A. (2004). Contour and boundary detection improved by surround suppression of texture edges, *Image and Vision Computing*, Vol. 22, No. 8 (pp. 609-622). ISSN: 0262-8856.

Grossberg, S. & Mingolla, E. (1985). Neural dynamics of form perception: Boundary completion, illusory figures and neon color spreading. *Psychological Review*, Vol. 92 (pp. 173-211). ISSN: 1939-1471.

Grossberg, S., Mingolla, E. and Williamson, J. (1995). Synthethic aperture radar processing by a multiple scale neural system for boundary and surface representation. *Neural Networks*, Vol. 8 (pp. 1005-1028). ISSN: 0893-6080.

Hodgkin, A.L. & Huxley, A.F. (1990). A quantitative description of membrane current and its application to conduction and excitation in nerve, *Bulletin of Mathematical Biology*, Vol. 52, No. 1-2 (pp. 25-71). ISSN: 0092-8240.

Hubel, D. H. (1995). *Eye, Brain, and Vision*. Scientific American Library. W. H. Freeman, New York. ISBN: 978-0-7167-6009-2.

Kokkinos, I.; Deriche, R.; Faugeras, O. & Maragos, P. (2008). Computational analysis and learning for a biologically motivated model of boundary detection. *Neurocomputing*, Vol. 71, No. 10-12 (Jun. 2008) (pp. 1798-1812). ISSN: 0925-2312.

Kokkinos, I.; Deriche, R.; Papadopoulo, T.; Faugeras, O. & Maragos, P. (2007). Towards bridging the gap between biological and computational image segmentation. *INRIA Research Report: Thème BIO- Systèmes biologiques*, Vol. 6317. ISSN: 0249-6399.

Landy, M.S. & Bergen, J.R. (1991). Texture segregation and orientation gradient. *Vision Research*, Vol. 31, No. 4 (pp. 679-693). ISSN: 0042-6989.

Martin, D.; Fowlkes, C.; Tal, D. & Malik, J. (2001). A database of human segmented natural images and its application to evaluating segmentation algorithms and measuring ecological statistics, *Proceedings of the 8th International Conference on Computer Vision*, vol. 2, pp. 416-423, ISBN: 0-7695-1143-0, Vancouver, Canada, July 2001.

Mingolla, E.; Ross, W. & Grossberg, S. (1999). A neural network for enhancing boundaries and surfaces in synthetic aperture radar images. *Neural Networks*, Vol. 12 (499-511). ISSN: 0893-6080.

Neumann, H. & Sepp, W. (1999). Recurrent V1–V2 interaction in early visual boundary processing, *Biological Cybernetics*, Vol. 91 (pp. 425–444). ISSN: 0340-1200.

Neumann, H.; Yazdanbakhsh, A. & Mingolla, E. (2007). Seeing surfaces: The brain's vision of the world. *Physics of Life Reviews*, Vol. 4 (pp. 189-222). ISSN: 1571-0645.

Ohta, Y.I.; Kanade, T. & Sakai, T. (1980). Color information for region segmentation. *Computer graphics and image processing*, Vol. 13 (222-241).

Petkov, N. & Westenberg, M.A. (2003). Suppression of contour perception by band-limited noise and its relation to non-classical receptive field inhibition, *Biological Cybernetics*, Vol. 88 (pp. 236-246). ISSN: 1432-0770.

Wilson, H. R.; Levi, D.; Maffei, L.; Rovamo, J. & De Valois, R. (1990). The perception of form: Retina to striate cortex. In: *Visual perception: The neurophysiological foundations*, L. Spillmann & J. S. Werner (Eds.), (pp. 231–272). San Diego: Academic Press, Inc. ISBN: 0-1265-7675-0.

Zrenner, E.; Abramov, I.; Akita, M.; Cowey, A.; Livingstone, M. & Valberg, A. (1990). Color Perception: Retina to Cortex. In *Visual perception: The neurophysiological foundations*, L. Spillmann & J. S. Werner (Eds.), (Chap. 8). San Diego: Academic Press, ISBN: 0-1265-7675-0.

6

Using Emergence Phenomenon in Meaningful Image Segmentation for Content-based Image Retrieval

Sagarmay Deb
Central Queensland University, 400 Kent Street, Sydney 2000, NSW Australia

1. Introduction

Research on multimedia systems and content-based image retrieval has gained momentum during the last decade. Content-based image retrieval (CBIR) is a very difficult area in the access of multimedia databases simply because there still exist vast differences in the perception capacity between a human and a computer. There are two basic problems that still remain unresolved in the area although some progresses have been made [13]. The first one is the problem of efficient and meaningful image segmentation where we break-up a particular image into meaningful parts based on low-level features like color, texture, shape and spatial locations. Developing a segmentation algorithm which will meaningfully segment all images is yet an open problem in image analysis [8]. The second one is the vast gap existing for an image between low-level features mentioned earlier and high-level or semantic expressions contained in the image like the image of a car, a house, a table and so on [11]. To develop efficient indexing techniques for the retrieval of enormous volumes of images being generated these days, we need to achieve reasonable solutions to these above-mentioned two problems. But only in very limited and selected cases, some kinds of solutions have been achieved with apparently promising experimental results. In this paper we focus our attention on the first problem. The research identifies few issues causing this gap, for example, failure to capture local image details with low level features, unavailability of semantic representation of images, inadequate human involvement in the retrieval, and ambiguity in query formulation [9]. We offer future directions of research in solving this difficult problem using emergence phenomena.

Section one gives an introduction of the area. Section two provides a definition of emergence phenomenon. Section three talks about the use of emergence phenomenon in extracting meanings in image segmentation. Section four suggests future directions of research. We put our concluding remarks in section five.

2. Emergence phenomenon

2.1 Definition of emergence phenomenon

A feature of an image which is not explicit would be emergent feature if it can be made explicit. There are three types of emergence: computational emergence, thermodynamic emergence and emergence relative to a model [1]. In computational emergence, it is assumed computational interactions can generate different features or behaviors [3],[7]. This is one of the approaches in the field of artificial life. Thermodynamic emergence is of the view that new stable features or behaviors can arise from equilibrium through the use of thermodynamic theory. In emergence relative to a model, deviation of the behavior from the original model gives rise to emergence. We will use this latter view in our work.

In computational emergence, new shapes or images develop but within certain limit as programmed by the computer programmers. No new shape can emerge beyond the logic of the program.

In thermodynamic emergence, emergence can be defined as emergence of order from noise. Stochastic processes at micro-level form discrete macro-level structures or behaviors. The example of this type of emergence is gas where stochastic movements of atoms or molecules within the gas create the ordered properties of temperature, pressure and volume at a higher level.

Example of emergence relative to a model is where changes in internal structure and consequently in its behavior occur and we as observers will need to change our model to track the device's behavior in order to successfully continue to predict actions. The example of a square having two triangles hidden in it as given below is of this type.

Whenever we shift our focus on an existing shape in other words an image, new shape emerges. The representation of the new shape is based upon view of the original shape. The new shape emerges as we change our view of the original shape. This is the fundamentally most important idea of emergence.

Two classes of shape emergence have been identified: embedded shape emergence and illusory shape emergence. In embedded shape emergence all the emergent shapes can be identified by set theory kind of procedures on the original shape under consideration. For example, in a set *S = {a, b, c, d, e}*, we can find subsets like *S1 = {a, b, c}*, *S2 = {c, d, e}*, *S3 = {a, c, e}* and so on. But in illusory shape emergence, where contours defining a shape are perceived even though no contours are physically present, this kind of set theory procedures are not enough and more effective procedures have to be applied to find these hidden shapes [4],[5]. These procedures could be based on geometrical, topological or dimensional studies of the original shape.

2.2 Structure, behavior and function of emergence

Structure of a shape is the physical definition of the shape. For example, a box could be rectangular in shape, its length, width and height as well as color, substance like wood, metal or hard paper would define the structure of the shape. Behavior of the box could be to contain certain stuffs in it and the function could be to carry stuff from one place to another using the box as a container, which is the purpose for which the box is used. Emergence of new structure, behavior or function takes place when these descriptions are interpreted in ways not anticipated in the original description [4].

2.3 Examples of emergence

Shape emergence is associated with emergence of individual or multiple shapes. The following figures are examples of shape emergence.

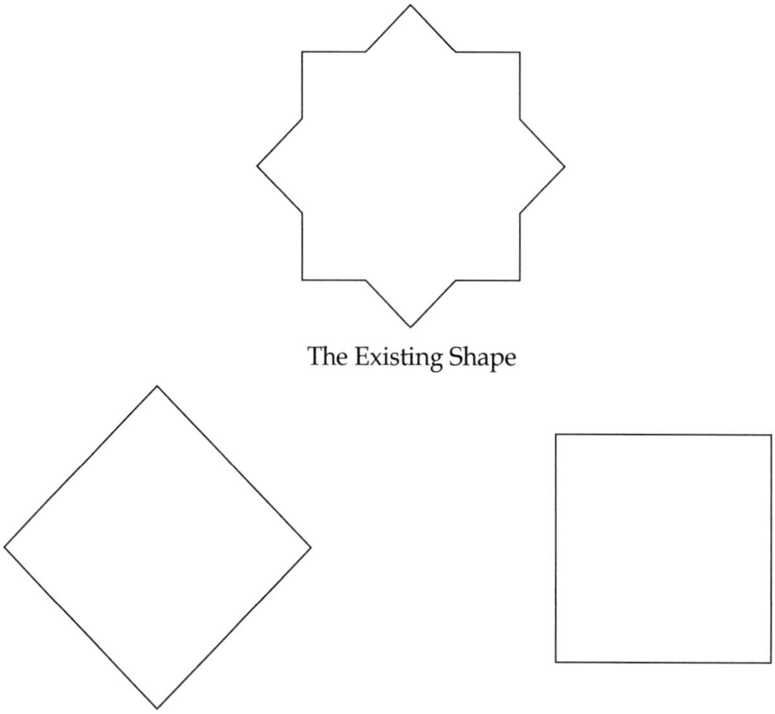

Fig. 1.1. Two emergent shapes derived from the existing one [5]

2.4 Definition of emergence index

Image retrieval where the hidden or emergence meanings of the images are studied and based on those hidden meanings as well as explicit meanings, an index of search is defined to retrieve images is called emergence index.

When images are retrieved based on textual information, various parameters and descriptions might define the input and the images of the database. Whenever there would be symmetry of parameters and descriptions, the image could be retrieved. In CBIR, color, texture and shape are widely used as index to retrieve images. But in our studies, we can find the hidden meanings of the images and whenever those hidden meanings match with the input given, although the original image may not match at all with the input, we can retrieve that image.

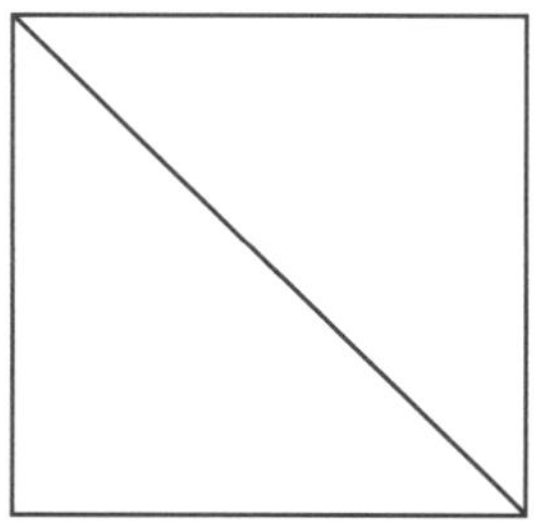

Fig. 1.2. Example of emergence where diagonal generates two triangles

To describe in detail, as we have mentioned, emergence is a phenomenon where we bring out the shapes, which are not explicit but implicit. The above figure shows a simple example of emergence where an apparently square shape has two triangles hidden in it as we discussed earlier.
When an input would come in the form of an image, the image could be studied based on features, constraints, variables, domains and emergence and converted into parametric form. Then the image database would be accessed and each image would be interpreted considering the items mentioned above and converted into parametric form like the input image. Whenever there would be a match between parameters of the input and the images of the database, those records would be selected. In other words, indexing would be decided by the outcome of emergence which means more meaningful images could be found hidden in an image which would otherwise not be understood.
As we have mentioned earlier, many images of the database may not have any apparent similarities with the input, but emergence could bring out the hidden meaning of the image and could establish similarities with the input image. So emergence outcomes of the images would form the index structure of the search.

2.5 Structure of emergence index

2.5.1 Parameter definitions

To make an effective query, the images in the query or database must be analysed so that we know what we are looking for and where to look for. Features, domains, variables, constraints, similarities, indexing are the parameters, which play very important role in similarity searching. Hence they constitute the structure of the emergence index.

Features

Input, as we mentioned earlier, could come in the form of text. For example, the text may indicate we have to pick up all the images of a database that contains the image of a particular person or an object. In this case, nothing much could be done on input side in the sense that we cannot study the input's features etc. We have to go through the images and pick up the image records. But if the query comes in the form of an image of a person then we have to analyse it before accessing the database images. Features would tell us about a few important characteristics of the input image. To start up, our query could be an image where a particular person is sitting on a chair. Then obviously there are two important features in the query image - the particular person and the chair. We have to locate these two features in the database image while searching for similarities.
We know color plays a very important role in the definition of features. Quite often a query might mention an object with certain specified color to be picked up from the databases. Besides, color is being used extensively in various models as a tool in finding symmetry with the input image.
Sometimes the input may be in the form of a sketch. In that case, a similar kind of image should be selected from the image database. The selection should be made on the basis of few dominant characteristics of the input and image and finding similarities in those characteristics.
Texture is another part of the feature where the general alignment of the image like the background part of the image is considered where the image of a person or an object could be the dominant part.

There would be some global features of an image like area, perimeters and a set of rectangles or triangles that cover the entire shape and there would be some local features, which can be obtained from the image's local region.

When we retrieve images by browsing, then in most cases the user does not have clear idea about what he or she is looking for. In this case, there would not be input image and the search through browsing would be manual. The user would have vague idea about the features of the images to be retrieved like the picture of a particular person with certain specified background. In the objective features based queries, the retrieval is performed on an exact match of attribute values whereas in the subjective features, query is specified by features, which could be interpreted differently by different users.

Retrieval by motion facilitates retrieving spatio-temporal image sequence depicting a domain phenomenon that varies in time or geographic space.

Again, sometimes images are retrieved, as we mentioned earlier, by text. In other words, text defines the features of the images to be selected. Then the database is searched based on those features defined in the input [6].

Domain

We now proceed to discuss the domain. Domain is a sort of classification of the images into certain categories. Domain is a way for a class of objects to present knowledge representing a certain concept held by objects [10].

We can make use of the various properties of the features of an image to define the domain in which the image concerned would lie. For example, from an image we can understand whether the image is that of a geographical location of a certain area of the earth or the image is that of a person or object with certain background like a screen or a landscape behind. This kind of classification at the initial stage of search should enable us to access the image database rapidly and more efficiently.

Also in a multimedia database, the database might contain various kinds of records like the images, the data in figures, the documents, audios, videos and so on. The concept of domain would classify them according to their categories.

The domain could also be formulated based on the length of the certain features of the image like finding the images of a particular person or object where the length is of certain range value. Color could also define a domain where the images having a particular color or a combination of colors lie in one domain. Domain could be defined on the basis of objects only. For example, we can pick up image where the images of a triangle and square would be present. We can make it more specific by mentioning color and length or size of the triangle and the rectangle to pick up images like where the triangle is red colored and sides of length, say, *(3, 3, 3)* and rectangle of color white and sides of length, say, *(4, 2).*

Variables

Since in our research we are considering a multimedia database where a particular record in the database could be an image or a data record or a document and so on, the definition of variables would vary depending upon the type of records we are considering.

In an image database, where we would consider two-dimensional pictures, the image of an object or a person have to be measured. If we try to measure it graphically, then the size could be measured in terms of x and y coordinates. Therefore, size would be a very important variable in our research.

Color could be another very important variable. There are, as we know, many colors available and for specific definition of the image, the color would play a very vital role. It is possible to define colors digitally in the sense that each color could be given a digital number like red =*1*, blue = *2* and so on.
Location would point towards where a particular object of interest is situated. If we were interested in finding the image of a person with a certain background at a particular point of the image, then location would tell us about where it is present. In a graphically defined image, the coordinate of the center of the image would give information about the location of the object.
Distance between two particular objects of interest is a variable to be considered. Sometime in an image depicting a geographic picture, the distance between two points is very important. Here also we should be able to measure the distance between two objects by applying graphical methods.
Motion of objects, like storm or cloud moving in a satellite picture, is also an important variable. We have to measure the distance travelled by the object in the picture and then convert it into kilometers and notice the time difference. From these we can measure the speed, velocity and so on of the object.

Constraints

It could be a very good idea to define an image in terms of various constraints in the sense that constraints help define the image more specifically.
In our case of multimedia database, where various kinds of data could be there, the concept of constraints is very important. For example, if the image is that of a rectangle, we know one of the constraints would be that the number of sides of the object is *4*. Then the second constraint would be opposite sides are parallel. The third one would be opposite sides are equal. If we include the emergence phenomenon, then if there is a diagonal drawn on it, this would give rise to two triangles. These constraints together could define the image successfully.
In an image of a geographical map of any part of the world, the concept of constraint would be effective in finding the location. If we are interested in finding a place, for example, an island with triangular shape, then obviously the constraint would be number of sides is *3*. If we have more information about sides like whether any two sides are same or all sides are same or all sides are of different size, then this kind of information should help us identify the object more accurately.

Similarities

In a database containing only data, the input may be a query with certain constraints like to pick up records from a SALARY database where salary is greater than, say, *30000*. In relational database, as we know, this can be accomplished by a SQL command with the following kind of statement:

SEL * FROM SALARY_DB WHERE SALARY > *30000*.

This would pick up all the records with salary > *30000*.
In our multimedia database system, this kind of queries could also be made and we can handle them with this kind of or more complicated SQL statements.
But when the input is in the form of image, then we have to find the similarities of the input in the image part of the database. The basic approach to the problem of similarity is to find

certain parametric values as well as some coordinates of the input image. Then we find the same for various image of the image database and pick up records where some matching occurs. Of course, we study the emergence phenomenon in both input and images of an image database while calculating parameters. For example, if we want to find similarities involving a triangular figure as input, then some of the parametric values could be defined like, number of sides which is 3, length of each sides, color of the triangle. Based on these values and constraints, we can find out similarities in the image database. But in the image database, there could be figures like squares or rectangles with a diagonal drawn on them. Then obviously this diagonal gives rise to two triangles according to emergence. So we have to study these cases too, find out the parameters of these triangles to see whether they match our parameters from the input.

Indexing

In the early stage of data processing, there was no established conception of indexing. Most of the data files were accessed sequentially. This was pretty slow and inefficient particularly when the data file is big enough. To get rid of this problem, the concept of indexing came to the picture. At the initial stage, a number is used to be given against each record by the system in a file created on disk. We could specify these numbers to access any record randomly. Then came the concept of Indexed Sequential Access Method where instead of assigning separate number against each record, a field or a combination of fields were started being used as key. There could be two kinds of indexing, one where the key value in a particular file is unique and the other where the key value could be duplicate. The search method is called Binary Search where to find a particular key value, the whole file is divided into two halves and the part, which contains the particular key value we are searching, is taken and then divided into two halves again. The part here which contains the key value is again taken and divided into two halves. This process continues until it finds the match against the key value.

Nowadays an old file system is hardly used in maintaining computer records. Instead, a database system has been developed. The latest development in this field is Relational Database System, which contains tables to store data.

In our problem of dealing with multimedia databases, which would contain images, the concept of indexing is very important. We are trying to develop a more sophisticated method of indexing where there won't be any clear-cut definition of index against the images, but indexes would be defined based on our study of emergence phenomenon of each of the image. Sometime to locate a particular spot in the geographic map of a part of the world, an input image would point to a particular part and that particular part in one or more than one image could be the outcome of emergence or it could be straight away present in the map without any emergence. In either case, input image refers to an index, which is nothing but that particular spot of the map.

2.5.2 Model of the emergence index

Emergence indexes can be defined out of five factors as discussed in section 2.5.1.

$$EI = f(D, F, V, C, E) \tag{1}$$

Where *EI* stands for emergence index, *D* for domain where the image belongs, *F* for features, *V* for variables which can define the feature's constraints under which the features are defined, *C* for constraints and *E* for emergence characteristics of images.

We believe any image, static or in motion, could be expressed semantically in terms of the above mentioned five parameters.

Construction

We take the case of a square with a diagonal, as mentioned earlier, to build up an emergence index. If this is an image in the database, then firstly we have to put it under certain domain *D* for the ease of accessing. Since images are generated in enormous volume, we have to put them in various separate entities or tables according to certain classification rather than in one table which could be extremely time consuming to access. The table that would contain this square image record would define the domain of the image. We can term it as *TAB1*.
To define the second factor *F*, we find the number of maximum sides present would be *5*, where there are *4* regular sides and *1* diagonal.
The variables are *a, b, c, d, e* where first four define the perimeter of the square and *e* the diagonal.
The constraints *c* are $a = b = c = d$ since it is a square.
The emergence *E* is composed of two triangles with sides *a ,b, e* and c, d, e.
Hence Emergence Index

$$EI = \{TAB1;\ 5;\ a, b, c, d, e;\ a = b = c = d;\ (a, b, e \text{ and } c, d, e)\}$$

3. Use of emergence phenomenon

We provide a very simple example of how emergence phenomenon can give rise to meanings for a segmented image where apparently no meaning exists.

Fig. 1.3. The image of a tiger in a picture before segmentation [12]

Fig. 1.4. The image of the tiger after segmentation [12]

Here we see in Figure 1.3 the image is very clearly of a tiger. We segment the while picture and get the image of the tiger in Figure 1.4. But we note that the figure does not clearly point to the image of the tiger but indicates an animal. So we can interpret the image of the tiger in Figure 1.4 as that of an animal instead of a tiger. This is the outcome of emergence phenomenon where we are able to interpret the segmented image in a different way than original picture shows or in other words we extract different meaning of the segmented image. This would enable us to ascribe some meanings to segmented image which otherwise after segmentation may not deliver any meaning. This way through emergence phenomenon we interpret segmented image in a meaningful way.

4. Suggested future directions of research

There are various attempts made to extract semantic meanings from an image to fill-in the semantic gap between low-level features and high-level semantic meanings which can arise from image segmentation. These include Latent Semantic Indexing (LSI), contextual search, user feedback, data clustering in the extraction of perceptual concepts, content-based soft annotation (CBSA), image classifications, ontology, top-down, ontologically driven approaches and bottom-up, automatic-annotation approaches, using machine learning methods to associate low-level features with query concepts, using relevance feedback to learn users' intention, generating semantic template to support high-level image retrieval, fusing the evidences from HTML text and the visual content of images for WWW image retrieval , use of ontology which represent task-specific attributes, objects, and relations, and relate these to the processing modules available for their detection and recognition, use of context-awareness for identifying image semantics and relationships to contribute to closing the semantic gap between user information requests and the shortcomings of current content-based image retrieval techniques , enhanced ICBIR system which allows users to input partial relevance which includes not only relevance extent but also relevance reason for a multi-phase retrieval where partial relevance can adapt to the user's searching intention in a from-coarse-to-fine manner [2].

Although these are good, constructive progresses in solving the problem of semantic gap in CBIR, they cannot define the semantic meanings of an image specifically. They can contribute to some broad classification of the image in certain groups.

To solve this problem we have to develop devices to define the semantic meanings of an image very specifically from low-level features and that should be done automatically without users' interaction. We seem to be still far away from this objectivity.

As we have shown in Section 3 emergence phenomenon can bring meanings out of a segmented image where apparently no meaning could be found. We plan to work on the theory of emergence index as described in Section 2 in future to generate softwares to provide the assistance in identifying the images from a segmentation.

5. Conclusion

In this paper we studied the problem of extracting meaningful image segmentation using emergence phenomenon. We plan to continue our work in this area to extract meanings from a more complex image segmentation where it is really difficult to find any meaning from the segmented image. Since this is a very important area of research with major implications in all spheres of life beginning with medical images, the necessity of this study cannot be overestimated.

6. References

[1] Cariani, P. (1992). Emergence and Artificial life, in Langton, C., Taylor, C., Farmer, J.D. and Rasmussen, S. (eds), *Artificial Life II,* Addision-Wesley, Reading, pp. 775-797

[2] Deb, S. (2010). Using Relevance Feedback in Bridging Semantic Gaps in Content-based Image Retrieval, The Second International Conference on Advances in Future Internet (AFIN2010) , Venice/Mestre, Italy, July 18 - 25, 2010

[3] Forrest, S. (ed.) (1991). *Emergent Computation,* Elsevier, New York

[4] Gero, J. S. and Maher, M. L. (1994). Computational Support for Emergence in Design, *Information Technology in Design Conference,* Moscow, September 1994

[5] Gero, J. S. (Year Unknown). Visual emergence in design collaboration, Key Center of Design Computing, University of Sydney

[6] Gudivada, V. N. and Raghavan, V. V. (1995). Content-Based Image Retrieval Systems. *IEEE,* September 1995

[7] Langton, G .L. (1989). *Artificial Life,* Addision-Wesley, Reading

[8] Mehta, D., Diwakar, E.S.V.N.L.S., Jawahar, C.V. (2003). A Rule-based Approach to Image Retrieval, www.iiit.net/techreports/2003_8.pdf

[9] Reducing semantic gap in content based image retrieval using region based relevance feedback techniques, (2006), http://www.gscit.monash.edu.au/gscitweb/seminar.php?id=41

[10] Yoshitaka, A., Kishida, S., Hirakawa, M. (1994). Knowledge-Assisted Content-Based Retrieval for Multimedia Databases, *IEEE Multimedi,*Winter 1994, pp.12-21

[11] Zhau, R., Grosky, W.I. (2002). Bridging the semantic gap in image retrieval, http://citeseer.ist.psu.edu/497446.html

[12] Image Segmentation, www.cs.toronto.edu/~jepson/csc2503/segmentation.pdf

[13] Bridging the Semantic Gap in Image Retrieval http://citeseer.ist.psu.edu/497446.html

7

Dual Active Contour Models for Medical Image Segmentation

Gilson Giraldi[1], Paulo Rodrigues[2], Jasjit Suri[3,4] and Sameer Singh[5]
[1]*National Laboratory for Scientific Computing (LNCC)*
[2]*FEI University*
[3]*Biomedical Technologies, Inc. Denver,*
[4]*Idaho State University,*
[5]*Loughborough University,*
[1,2]*Brazil*
[3,4]*USA*
[5]*UK*

1. Introduction

Deformable Models, which includes the popular snake models (Kass et al., 1988) and deformable surfaces (McInerney & Terzopoulos, 1996; Suri & Editors, 2006), are well known techniques for boundary extraction and tracking in 2D/3D images. Basically, these models can be classified into three categories: parametric, geodesic snakes and implicit models. The relationships between these models have been demonstrated in several works in the literature (Sapiro, 1997).

Parametric Deformable Models consist of a curve (or surface) which can dynamically conform to object shapes in response to internal (elastic) forces and external forces (image and constraint ones) (Suri & Editors, 2006). Snake models, also called active contour models, are *2D* deformable models proposed by Kass at al. (Kass et al., 1988) which have been successfully applied in a variety of problems in computer vision and image analysis. Its mathematical formulation makes easier to integrate image data, an initial estimated, desired contour properties and knowledge-based constraints, in a single extraction process (Suri & Editors, 2006).

In fact, despite of the mentioned capabilities, parametric models in general can not deal with topological changes. Among the approaches to deal with the topological limitations of the traditional snake model (Bischoff & Kobbeit, 2004; Oliveira et al., 2004), the T-Snakes has the advantage of being a general one (McInerney & Terzopoulos, 1999). Besides, parametric models are too sensitive to their initial conditions due to nonconvexity problems (see (Davatzikos & Prince, 1999) and references therein). To address this limitation some authors have proposed multiscale techniques (Leymarie & Levine, 1993), dynamic program (DP) (Amini et al., 1990)and dual methods, also called dual snakes (Gunn & Nixon, 1997). The non-invariance under affine transformations is another limitation of the traditional snake models. As a consequence, the internal energy is sensitive to distortions due to changes in viewing geometry. From a dynamical point of view, it means that the elastic forces may affect the efficiency of the energy minimization process (Ip & Shen, 1998). Some methods have been proposed to address this problem (Giraldi & Oliveira, 2004; Ip & Shen, 1998), even in the context of dual active contour models (Gunn & Nixon, 1997).

The basic idea of the dual snakes is to reject local minima by using two contours: one which contracts from outside the target and one which expands from inside. Such proposal makes possible to reduce the sensitivity to initialization through the comparison between the two contours energy and positions. The two contours are interlinked to provide a driving force to carry the contours out of local minima, which makes the solution less sensitive to the initial position (Gunn & Nixon, 1997).

In (Giraldi et al., 2000b), it is presented an extension of the dual method through the T-Snakes. The dual approach was embedded in the T-Snakes framework to propose a generalized dual method: one T-snake contracts and splits from outside the target(s) and the other one(s) expand(s) from inside in the process of seeking for the objects boundaries in an image. Such generalization, called the Dual-T-Snakes model, allows to address some limitations of the dual approach proposed in (Gunn & Nixon, 1997) and offers an efficient framework for dual surface models.

In (Suri & Editors, 2006) some of us present an implicit formulation for dual snakes, based on the level set approach. The key idea of that work is to view the inner/outer contours as a level set of a suitable embedding function. The mathematical background of the method is explained and its utility for segmentation of cell images discussed. Besides, a fast dual front implementation of active contours has been proposed in (Li & Yezzi, 2005) and applied for segmentation of *2D* images. The method is motivated by minimal path technique (Cohen, 2001; Cohen & Kimmel, 1996) and uses fast marching methods (Sethian, 1999) to compute the minimal partition curve that represents the object boundary. The same formulation can be used for both *2D* and *3D* and it was applied for segmentation of the brain cortex (Li & Yezzi, 2005).

Dual active contour models have been applied for feature and geometric measures extraction (Gunn, 1996), boundary extraction on ultrasound images (Chen et al., 2001; 2002), brain surface extraction from PET images (Tohka et al., 2004) and cell image segmentation based on a two stage approach (Bamford & Lovell, 1997; Giraldi et al., 2000b) : (1) the region of interest is reduced; (2) a search based technique, like dynamic programming, is used to find the object boundaries.

In this chapter we review parametric and implicit dual snake models. Following, in section 2, we offer some background for the material. Section 3 gives a review of parametric dual models. The Dual-T-Snakes algorithm and the cell-based dual snake model are discussed in this section. Following, in section 4 we describe the implicit formulations for dual snakes: the Dual-Level-Set and Dual-Front methods. During the presentation of these methods, we show results in medical image segmentation. We offer a discussion on section 5 by comparing the presented methods and by pointing out drawbacks of dual approaches. In section 6 we present the conclusions and future developments in dual approaches.

2. Background review

The original snake model (Kass et al., 1988) is formulated as a functional energy minimization process that consists of an initial model which is carried to the desired object boundary by forces described by the Euler-Lagrange equations. In a different way, the snake evolution can be formulated by local deformations to dynamically reshape the initial model in a process which do not apply minimization techniques explicitly. This approach is used in the T-Snakes model which is revised in section 2.1. On the other hand, implicit formulations based on the level set method can be used, as we shall see in section 2.2.

2.1 T-Snakes model

The classical snake model proposed in (Kass et al., 1988) do not incorporate topological changes. Among the proposals for incorporating topological capabilities to parametric snake models (Bischoff & Kobbeit, 2004; Oliveira et al., 2004), the T-Snakes approach (McInerney & Terzopoulos, 1999) has the advantage of been a general one, in the sense that the same formulation can be used for 2D and 3D, for both splits and merges.

The T-Snakes approach is composed basically by four components (McInerney & Terzopoulos, 1999): (1) a simple CF-triangulation of the image domain; (2) projection of each snake over the grid; (3) a binary function called characteristic function χ, defined on the grid nodes, which distinguishes the interior from the exterior of a snake; (4) a discrete snake model.

To clear the ideas, consider the characteristic functions (χ_1 and χ_2) relative to the two contours pictured in Figure 1. The vertices marked are those where $\max\{\chi_1, \chi_2\} = 1$. Observe that the merge of the curves belongs to the triangles in which the characteristic function changes value.

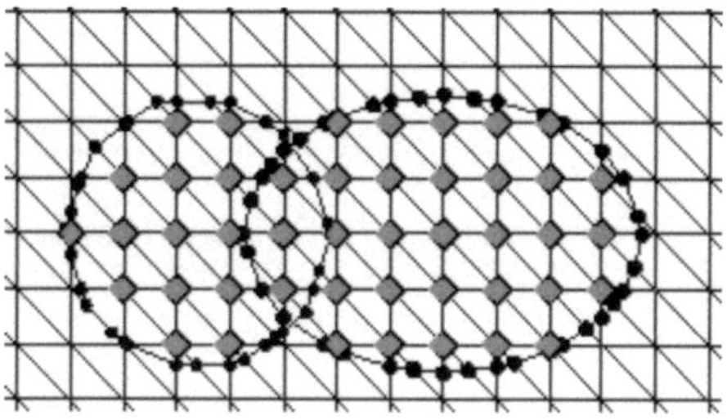

Fig. 1. Two snakes colliding with the inside grid nodes and snake points (snaxels) marked.

Thus, from the points obtained in the step (2), we can choose a set of N points $\{v_i = (x_i, y_i), i = 0, \ldots, N-1\}$ to be connected to form a closed contour (T-Snake). In (Giraldi et al., 2003)we evolve a T-Snake based on a tensile force (B_i), an external (image) force (f_i), and a normal (balloon-like) force (F_i), defined as follows:

$$B_i = w_1 \left(\frac{v_{i-1}^t - 2v_i^t + v_{i+1}^t}{(\Delta s_i)^2} \right), \tag{1}$$

$$f_i = \gamma \nabla P(v_i), \tag{2}$$

$$F_i = k(sign_i)\vec{n}_i, \tag{3}$$

where $\vec{n}_i$ is the normal at the snaxel v_i and w_1, γ, k are force scale factors, $sign_i = 1$ if $I(v_i) \geq T$ and $sign_i = 0$ otherwise (T is a threshold for the image I) and $P = -\|\nabla I\|^2$. The

utility of the balloon-like force given by expression (3) is two-fold. Firstly, it avoids the unwanted contraction effect of the tensile force due to the inflation (see
(Cohen, 1991) for details). Secondly, this force pushes the model towards the object(s) of interest, characterized by the threshold T. The external force f_i given by expression (2) attracts the snake to object boundaries in the image. We update the T-Snake position according to the evolution equation:

$$v_i^{(t+\Delta t)} = v_i^t + \Delta t\left(B_i^t + F_i^t + f_i^t\right), \tag{4}$$

where Δt is a time step. The T-Snakes model incorporates also an entropy condition: "once a node is burnt (passed over by the snake) it stays burnt " (McInerney & Terzopoulos, 1999). A specific termination condition is defined based on the number of deformations steps (temperature) that a triangle was cut by a T-Snake. A T-Snake is considered to have reached its equilibrium state when the temperature of all the snaxels fall bellow a preset value (called "freezing point" in the T-Snakes literature (McInerney & Terzopoulos, 1999)).

2.2 Level set

In this section we review some details of the level set formulation (Malladi et al., 1995). The main idea of this method is to represent the deformable surface (or curve) as a level set $\left\{x \in \Re^3 \middle| G(x) = 0\right\}$ of an embedding function:

$$G : \Re^3 \times \Re^+ \rightarrow \Re, \tag{5}$$

such that the deformable surface (also called front in this formulation), at *t=0*, is given by a surface S:

$$S(t=0) = \left\{x \in \Re^3 \middle| G(x, t=0) = 0\right\}, \tag{6}$$

The next step is to find an Eulerian formulation for the front evolution. Following Sethian (Malladi et al., 1995), let us suppose that the front evolves in the normal direction with velocity $\vec{F}$ that may be a function of the curvature, normal direction, etc.
We need an equation for the evolution of $G(x,t)$, considering that the surface S is the level set given by:

$$S(t) = \left\{x \in \Re^3 \middle| G(x,t) = 0\right\}, \tag{7}$$

Let us take a point $x(t)$, $t \in \Re^+$ of the propagating front S. From its implicit definition given above we have:

$$G(x(t),t) = 0, \tag{8}$$

Now, we can use the Chain Rule to compute the time derivative of this expression:

$$G_t + F\left|\nabla G\right| = 0, \tag{9}$$

where $F = \|dx / dt\|$ is called the speed function and ∇ is the gradient operator, with respect to x. An initial condition $G(x, t = 0)$ is required. A straightforward technique to define this function is to compute a signed-distance function as follows:

$$G(x, t = 0) = \pm d, \tag{10}$$

where d is the distance from x to the surface $S(t = 0)$ and the sign indicates if the point is interior (-) or exterior (+) to the initial front. The "fast marching method" (FMM) can be used to efficiently compute this function (Sethian, 1996).
Finite difference schemes, based on an uniform grid, can be used to solve equation (9). The same entropy condition of T-Surfaces (once a grid node is burnt it stays burnt) is incorporated in order to drive the model to the desired solution (in fact, T-Surfaces was inspired on the level set model (McInerney & Terzopoulos, 1999)).
In this higher dimensional formulation, topological changes can be efficiently implemented. Numerical schemes are stable, and the model is general in the sense that the same formulation holds for 2D and 3D, as well as for merge and splits. Besides, the surface geometry is easily computed. For example, the front normal ($\vec{n}$) and curvature (K) are given, respectively, by:

$$\vec{n} = \nabla G(x, t), \qquad K = \nabla \cdot \left(\frac{\nabla G(x, t)}{\|\nabla G(x, t)\|} \right), \tag{11}$$

where the gradient (∇) and the divergent ($\nabla .$) are computed with respect to x.
The update of the embedding function through expression (9) can be made cheaper if the narrow-band technique is applied. The key idea of this method comes from the observation that the front can be moved by updating the level set function at a small set of points in the neighbourhood of the zero set instead of updating it at all the points on the domain (see (Malladi et al., 1995; Sethian, 1996) for details).

3. Parametric dual models

Parametric dual active contour models have been applied for cell image segmentation (Chen et al., 2002; 2001; Giraldi et al., 2003), features and geometric measures extraction (Gunn, 1996; Gunn & Nixon, 1997). The main advantage of these methods against usual snake models is their capability to reject local minima by using two contours: one which contracts from outside the target and one which expands from inside. Such proposal makes possible to reduce the sensitivity to initialization, by enabling a comparison between the two contours energy, which is used to reject local minima. In what follows, we firstly present the original dual snake model, proposed by Gunn and Nixon (Gunn, 1996; Gunn & Nixon, 1997). Next, we review more recent approaches that incorporate topological abilities (the Dual-T-Snakes) and improve the efficiency for ultrasound images (Dual-Cell)

3.1 Original dual model

The dual snake methodology was firstly proposed in (Gunn & Nixon, 1997). To obtain the conventional continuity and smoothness constraints, but removes the unwanted contraction force, a scale invariant internal energy function (shape model) is developed. In (Gunn &

Nixon, 1997) a snake is considered as a particle system $\{v_i = (x_i, y_i), i = 0,...,N-1\}$ whose particles are linked by internal constraints. The shape model is accomplished by the following internal energy:

$$E_R = \frac{1}{N}\sum_{i=0}^{N-1} E_{\text{int}}(v_i); \qquad E_{\text{int}} = \frac{1}{2}\left(\frac{\|e_i\|^2}{h}\right), \tag{12}$$

where:

$$e_i = \frac{1}{2}(v_{i-1} + v_{i+1}) - v_i + \frac{1}{2}\theta_i R(v_{i-1} + v_{i+1}), \tag{13}$$

h is the average space step, R is a 90° rotation matrix and θ_i is related to the internal angle ϕ_i in the vertex v_i by:

$$\theta_i = \cot\left(\frac{\varphi_i}{2}\right). \tag{14}$$

The Figure 2 helps to understand the geometric meaning of these elements. In this figure, the vector e_i is such that the triangle with vertices $v_{i+1}, v_i + e_i, v_{i-1}$ is isosceles.

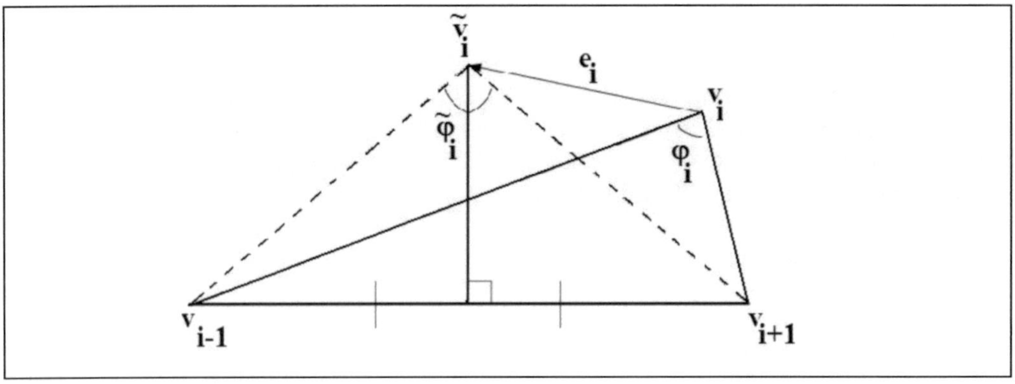

Fig. 2. Geometric elements of the local shape model. Reprinted from (Gunn & Nixon, 1997)

It is clear that E_R has a global minimum when $e_i = 0, \quad i = 0,1,2,...,N-1$. From (13)-(14) it can be shown that this happens when:

$$\varphi_i = \pi(N-2)/(2N), \quad i = 0,1,...,N-1,$$

which are the internal angles of a regular polygon with vertices given by the points v_i (Gunn & Nixon, 1997). The energy (12) can be also shown to be rotation, translation and scale invariant (Gunn & Nixon, 1997). Therefore there is no tendency to contraction as already pointed out for the original snake model (see (Cohen, 1991) for details). With the internal energy given by expression (12), the curve is biased towards a regular polygon (Gunn & Nixon, 1997). As before, the external energy is defined by:

$$E_{ext}(v_i) = -\left\|\nabla I(v_i)\right\|^2. \tag{16}$$

The total energy of the model is given by:

$$E = \frac{1}{N}\sum_{i=0}^{N-1}\left(\lambda E_{\text{int}}(v_i) + (1-\lambda)E_{ext}(v_i)\right). \tag{17}$$

where λ is a smoothing parameter which lies between 0 and 1 (Gunn & Nixon, 1997). This expression guarantees that during the optimization process, the snake will seek for strong object boundaries, due to E_{ext}, whose shape resembles a regular polygon, due to shape model given by expression (12). This fact makes easier to establish the correspondence (matching) between the points of the two contours because the form of the snake during the evolution is limited by the energy (12). The methodology takes advantage of this correspondence by proposing the driving force:

$$F_{driving} = g(t)\frac{u_i - v_i^t}{\left\|u_i - v_i^t\right\|}, \tag{18}$$

where v_i^t is the contour being processed at time t, u_i^t is the contour remaining at rest and $g(t)$ is the strength of the force. The termination condition adopted in (Gunn & Nixon, 1997) is the following one, based on low velocity criterion:

$$\max_i \left\|v_i^{t+1} - v_i^t\right\| < \delta, \tag{19}$$

where δ is a termination parameter.

The dual approach consists in making the inner and outer contours evolve according the following algorithm: The contour with the highest energy is selected. If its motion remains below some termination condition then the driving force (18) is increased until it moves at a rate greater than the chosen threshold δ. When the energy begins to decrease, the added driving force is removed and the contour is allowed to come into equilibrium. The procedure is then repeated until both contours have found the same equilibrium position.

3.2 Dual-T-Snakes algorithm

The key idea behind this method is to explore the T-Snakes framework to propose a generalized dual active contour model: one T-Snake contracts and splits from outside the targets and another one expand from inside the targets (Giraldi et al., 2003; 2000b).

To make the outer snake to contract and the inner ones to expand we assign an inward normal force to the first and an outward normal force to the others according to expressions (3). Also, to turn the T-Snakes evolution interdependent we use the image energy and an affinity restriction.

We use two different definitions for image energy: one for the outer contour (E_{outer}) and another one for the set of inner contours enclosed by it (E_{inner}):

$$E_{outer} = \sum_{i=0}^{N-1}\left(-\left\|\nabla I(v_i)\right\|^2\right)/N. \tag{20}$$

$$E_{inner} = \frac{1}{m}\left(\sum_{k=0}^{m-1}\left(\sum_{i=0}^{N_k-1}\left(-\left\|\nabla I(v_i)\right\|^2\right)/N_k\right)\right). \tag{21}$$

where m is the number of inner curves, N , N_k are the number of snaxels of the outer snake and of the inner snake k, respectively. The normalization is necessary in order to be compared. Otherwise, the snake energy would be a decreasing function of the number of snaxels and comparisons would not make sense.

Following the dual approach methodology (Gunn & Nixon, 1997), if $E_{inner} > E_{outer}$ an inner curve must be chosen. To accomplish this, we use an affinity operator which estimates the pixels of the image most likely to lie on the boundaries of the objects. Based on this operator, we can assign to a snaxel the likelihood that it is close to a boundary. That likelihood is thresholded to obtain an affinity function that assigns to the snaxel a 0-1 value: "0" for the snaxels most likely to lie away from the target boundaries and "1" otherwise.

Then, the inner curve with highest number of snaxels with affinity function value null is chosen. If $E_{inner} < E_{outer}$ the outer snake is evolved if the corresponding affinity function has null entries.

Also, the balance between the energy/affinity of the outer and inner snakes allows to avoid local minima. For instance, if a T-Snake has been frozen, we can increase the normal force at the snaxels where the affinity function is zero, that is, we add a driving force only to the snaxels most like to lie far from the boundary. The self-intersections that may happen during the evolution of a snake when increasing the normal force are naturally resolved by the T-Snakes model. This is way we can use that added normal force to play the role of the driving force used by Gunn and Nixon (avoiding the matching problem required in (Gunn & Nixon, 1997)).

To evaluate similarity between two contours, we use the difference between the characteristic function of the outer snake and the characteristic functions of the inner ones ($Characteristic\_Diff$). For example, in the case of the CF triangulation of the Figure 1 we can stop the motion of all snaxels of an inner snake inside a triangle σ if any of its vertex $v \in \sigma$ has the two following properties: (a). All the six triangles adjacent to v have a vertex where $Characteristic\_Diff = 0$; (b). One of these triangles is crossed by the outer contour

The freezing point (section 2.1) is used to indicate that a T-Snake has found an equilibrium position. In what follows, we call Dual Snake a list of T-Snakes where the first one is an outer contour and the other ones are inner contours. The algorithm can be summarized as follows:

Algorithm 1: Dual-T-Snakes

Put all the dual snakes into a queue.
repeat
  Pop out a dual snake from the queue;
  Use the energies (equations (20) and (21)) and the affinity function to decide the snake to be processed;
if all snaxels of that snake are frozen
  repeat
    increase the normal force at those with affinity zero
  until the snake energy starts decreasing

Remove that added normal force;
repeat
Evolve the snake
until the temperature of all snaxels falls bellow the freezing point; }
Analyze the Characteristic_Diff of the current snake;
if the snake being processed is close to a snake of the other type (inner/outer)
then remove the dual snake from the queue.}
else
mount the resulting dual snake(s) and go to the beginning.
until the queue is empty

The experience with this method shows that it is very useful to reduce the search space. So, we proposed in (Giraldi et al., 2000b) a two stage segmentation approach: (1) the region of interest is reduced by the Dual-T-Snakes; (2) a global minimization technique is used to find the object boundaries. In (Giraldi et al., 2000b) we apply the Viterbi algorithm, which is a dynamic program technique. The search space is constructed by discretizing each curve in N points and establishing a matching between them. Each pair of points is then connected by a segment which is subdivided in M points. This process provides a discrete search space, with NM points, that is pictured in the Figure 3:

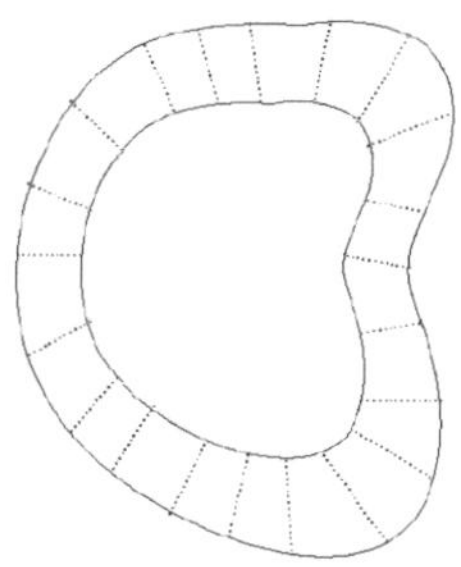

Fig. 3. Search space obtained through a matching between inner and outer snakes.

The target boundary is then determined by minimizing the following energy functional (Gunn, 1996):

$$E_{snake} = \sum_{i=0}^{N-1} E_i. \tag{22}$$

$$E_i = \alpha E_{\text{int}}\left(v_{i-1}, v_i, v_{i+1}\right) + \beta E_{ext}\left(v_i\right) + \lambda E_{line}\left(v_i\right). \tag{23}$$

with E_{int}, E_{ext} and E_{line} defined as follows:

$$E_{\text{int}}\left(v_{i-1}, v_i, v_{i+1}\right) = \left(\frac{v_{i-1} - 2v_i + v_{i+1}}{\left\| v_{i-1} - v_{i+1} \right\|} \right)^2. \tag{24}$$

$$E_{ext}\left(v_i\right) = -\left\| \nabla I\left(v_i\right) \right\|, \qquad E_{line} = \pm I\left(v_i\right), \tag{25}$$

where the real parameters α, β and λ must be chosen in advance. The Viterbi algorithm was also used in (Bamford & Lovell, 1997) and sometimes it is called non-evolutionary dual model, in the sense that it is not based on a curve evolution.
The following example shows the application of the segmentation framework that combines the Dual-T-Snakes and the Viterbi algorithm (Giraldi et al., 2000b; 2003) for a cell image. The Figure 4.a shows a blood cell obtained by an electronic microscope technique. When pass-band filter is applied, we get an edge map resembling a ribbon whose thickness depends on the kernel size of the used filter (Figure 4.b). That is an ideal situation for applying Dual-T-Snakes plus Viterbi because, firstly, the former extracts the ribbon (Figure 4.c). Then, the later is applied to the original image to give the final result (Figure 4.d).

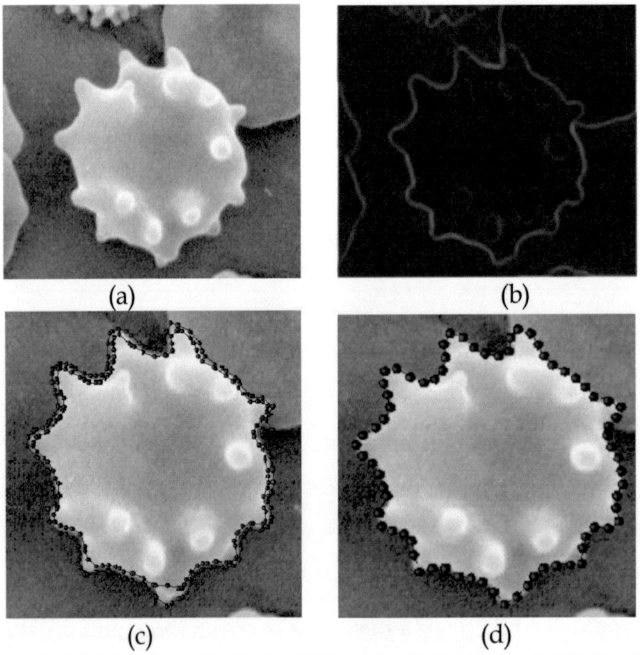

Fig. 4. Search space obtained through a matching between inner and outer snakes. (a)Image to be processed. (b)Band-Pass filtered image. (c)Dual-T-Snakes solution. (d)Viterbi solution.

3.3 Cell-Based dual snake model

In (Chen et al., 2002) it is proposed a cell-based dual snake model for ultrasound image. Boundary extraction and segmentation for this kind of image are a much harder problem than for other image modalities, due to the speckle, the tissue-related textures, and the artifacts resulting from the ultrasonic imaging process. To address such difficulties it is proposed in (Chen et al., 2002) a model which is devised into three main stages, namely, cell generation, cell-based deformation and contour smoothing. In the cell-generation stage, the immersion watershed algorithm (Vincent & Soille, 1991) is used to generate the nonoverlapped cells. To alleviate the interference of speckle in cell generation, the speckle is reduced by using the multiscale Gaussian filters before computing the gradient map. The cell boundaries are defined as the watersheds formed in the gradient map of the speckle-reduced ultrasound images.

Once the cell decomposition of the image domain is performed, we must define the dual snakes and the evolution model. Thus, given an initial contour enclosing the region of interest (ROI), a set of minimum covering cells, $C_1, C_2, ..., C_N$ containing the ROI is found, based on the cells generated in the previous stage (Figure 5). Let Γ_0 and Γ_i be the initial outer and inner snakes, respectively, which are pictured on Figure 5. The outer snake is defined as the outermost boundary of $\bigcup_{i=1}^{N} C_i$. Suppose that the center of the ROI is the cell C_1. Then, its boundary is the initial inner snake Γ_i, also represented on Figure 5.
Let $\Gamma_1{}^t$ and $\Gamma_2{}^t$ be the inner and outer snakes, respectively, at the deformation step *t*. Then, the model energy $E\left(\Gamma_1{}^t \cup \Gamma_2{}^t\right) = E\left(\Gamma_1{}^t\right) + E\left(\Gamma_2{}^t\right)$ is defined by (Chen et al., 2002):

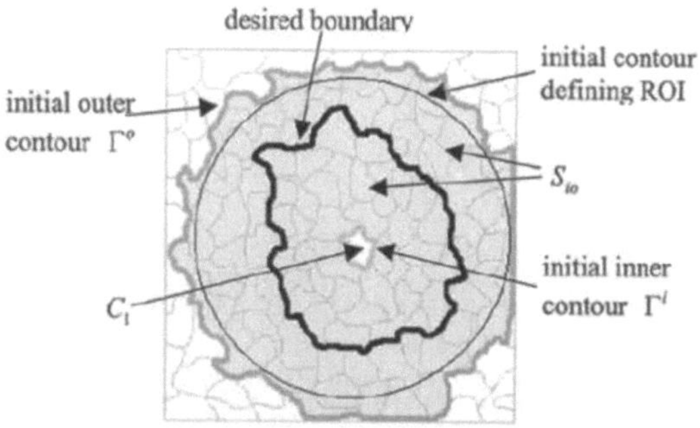

Fig. 5. Region of interest (ROI) and initial snakes. Reprinted from (Chen et al., 2002)

$$E\left(\Gamma_i^t\right) = \alpha_i E_{len}\left(\Gamma_i^t\right) + \beta_i E_\theta\left(\Gamma_i^t\right) + \gamma_i E_{ext}\left(\Gamma_i^t\right) + \delta_i E_{Area}\left(\Gamma_i^t\right). \tag{26}$$

where:

$$E_{len}\left(\Gamma_i^t\right) = \sum_{j=0}^{N-1} \left\| v_{i,j}^t - v_{i+1,j}^t \right\|, \tag{27}$$

$$E_\theta\left(\Gamma_i^t\right) = \sum_{j=0}^{N-1} \cos^{-1}\left(\frac{u_{i,j}^t - u_{i,j+3}^t}{\left\|u_{i,j}^t\right\| \left\|u_{i,j+3}^t\right\|} \right), \tag{28}$$

$$E_{ext}\left(\Gamma_i^t\right) = \sum_{j=0}^{N-1} \left\| \nabla I\left(v_{i,j}^t\right) \right\|, \tag{29}$$

$$E_{Area}\left(\Gamma_i^t\right) = Area\left(S_{io}^t\right), \tag{30}$$

where $v_{i,j}^t$ means the *jth* snaxel of the *ith* snake at time *t*, $u_{i,j}^t = v_{i,j}^t - v_{i,j-3}^t$, S_{io}^t denote the set of cells enclosed by the inner and outer snakes at the deformation step *t*, and $\alpha_i, \beta_i, \gamma_i, \delta_i$, $i = 0,1,...,N-1$ are real parameters that controls the influence of each term in the expression (26).

The first energy term E_{len} gives the perimeter of the contour Γ_j^t. If we take $\alpha_1 < 0$ and $\alpha_2 > 0$, then, minimizing this energy would force the inner snake into expanding outward and the outer snake into contracting. The term E_θ approximates the curvature along the snake and aims to control the smoothness of the contour.
The third energy E_{ext} is the external energy defined based on edge features. The last energy, E_{Area}, is the area covered by the cells in S_{io}^t. When minimizing energy (26) this term will provide the attraction force to pull the inner and the outer snakes to each other.
The energies (27)-(30) may have different ranges. Therefore, the target function to be minimized is the normalized energy variation $\Delta E\left(\Gamma_i^t\right)$ rather than the $E\left(\Gamma_i^t\right)$ itself, that is:

$$\Delta E\left(\Gamma_1^t,\Gamma_2^t;\Gamma_1^{t+1},\Gamma_2^{t+1}\right)= \tag{31}$$

$$\alpha_i \Delta E_{len}\left(\Gamma_i^t\right)+\beta_i \Delta E_\theta\left(\Gamma_i^t\right)+\gamma_i \Delta E_{ext}\left(\Gamma_i^t\right)+\delta_i \Delta E_{Area}\left(\Gamma_i^t\right). \tag{32}$$

where $\Delta E_{len}\left(\Gamma_i^t\right),\Delta E_\theta\left(\Gamma_i^t\right),\Delta E_{ext}\left(\Gamma_i^t\right),\Delta E_{Area}\left(\Gamma_i^t\right)$ have the general form:

$$\Delta E\left(\Gamma_1^t,\Gamma_2^t;\Gamma_1^{t+1},\Gamma_2^{t+1}\right)=$$

$$\frac{\left[E_\rho\left(\Gamma_1^{t+1}\right)+E_\rho\left(\Gamma_2^{t+1}\right)\right]-\left[E_\rho\left(\Gamma_1^t\right)+E_\rho\left(\Gamma_2^t\right)\right]}{\left[E_\rho\left(\Gamma_1^t\right)+E_\rho\left(\Gamma_2^t\right)\right]}$$

with $\rho \in \{len,\theta,ext,Area\}$ and $\alpha_i,\beta_i,\gamma_i,\delta_i$ are the same of expression (26).
Before to proceed, we need other definitions. Let S_1^t be the set of cells inside the ROI that intersect the curve Γ_1^t (similarly for S_2^t). Besides, it is defined in (Chen et al., 2002) the operators Φ and Ψ such that:

$$\Phi\left(S_{io}^t\right)=\Gamma_2^t \qquad and \qquad \Psi\left(S_{io}^t\right)=\Gamma_1^t. \tag{35}$$

The deformation of the model is based on the two operators called cell-erosion and the cell-dilation. These operators are described on Figure 6. The former, denoted by *CE*, is defined as:

$$CE\left(S_{io}^t,C_p\right)=S_{io}^t-\{C_p\},\quad C_p\in\left(S_1^t\cup S_2^t\right)\cap S_{io}^t. \tag{36}$$

The cell-dilation, denoted by *CD*, is defined by:

$$CD\left(S_{io}^t,C_p\right)=S_{io}^t\cup\{C_p\},\quad C_p\in\left(S_1^t\cup S_2^t\right)-S_{io}^t. \tag{37}$$

The cell-based dual snakes evolution is the greedy procedure that aims to minimize the normalized energy variation defined in expression (32). It is based on the following algorithm to find the minimum of the energy variation given by expression (32).

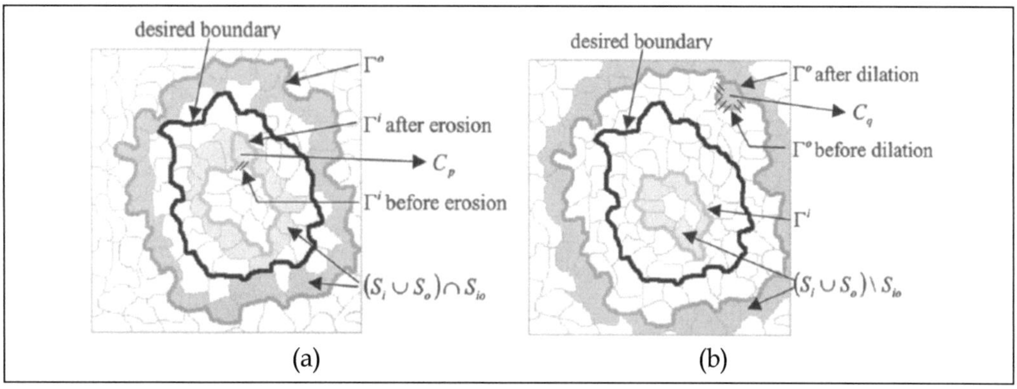

Fig. 6. (a)Erosion operator. (b) Dilation operation. Reprinted from (Chen et al., 2002)

1. Initialization: define S_{io}^0, $\Phi\left(S_{io}^0\right)=\Gamma_2^0$, $\Psi\left(S_{io}^0\right)=\Gamma_1^0$ and and set $t=0$.
2. While $S_{io}^0 \neq \varnothing$,

$$C_e = \arg\min_{C_p \in \left(S_1^t \cup S_2^t\right) \cap S_{io}^t} \left\{ \Delta E_{erode} = \Delta E\left(\Gamma_1^t, \Gamma_2^t; \Phi\left(CE\left(S_{io}^t, C_p\right)\right), \Psi\left(CE\left(S_{io}^t, C_p\right)\right)\right)\right\}, \tag{38}$$

$$C_d = \arg\min_{C_p \in \left(S_1^t \cup S_2^t\right) - S_{io}^t} \left\{ \Delta E_{dilate} = \Delta E\left(\Gamma_1^t, \Gamma_2^t; \Phi\left(CD\left(S_{io}^t, C_p\right)\right) \cup \Psi\left(CD\left(S_{io}^t, C_p\right)\right)\right)\right\}, \tag{39}$$

2.1. If $\Delta E_{erode} < \Delta E_{dilate}$, $S_{io}^{t+1} = CE\left(S_{io}^t, C_e\right)$. Else, $S_{io}^{t+1} = CD\left(S_{io}^t, C_d\right)$.

2.2. $\Gamma_2^{t+1} = \Phi\left(S_{io}^{t+1}\right)$ and $\Gamma_1^{t+1} = \Psi\left(S_{io}^{t+1}\right)$.

Once the boundary is extracted based on this algorithm, some kind of smoothing process may be applied in order to improve it. This stage can be performed by an usual snake model, that is, the dual result is used to initialize a parametric (single) snake model. Other possibility, also discussed in (Chen et al., 2002), would be spline interpolation.
The Figure 7 pictures the stages of the method for breast ultrasound segmentation. Figure 7.a pictures the original image with a benign lesion. This input image is then filtered by a gaussian kernel followed by a Sobel edge detector. The cells generated by the watershed algorithm are pictured on Figure 7.b. The initialization of the method and the obtained result (white contour) are shown on Figures 7.c and 7.d, respectively.

4. Implicit models

In this section we review the implicit formulation for dual models: the Dual-Level-Set and the Dual-Front methods. The former maintains the philosophy of Dual-T-Snakes: one snake contracts and splits from outside the targets and another ones expand from inside the targets (section 3.2). However, the snake model will be the level set described on section 2.2. The later, the Dual-Front method, uses fast marching methods (Sethian, 1999) to propagate two action maps until they met each other generating an interface that represents the boundary. These action maps are derived from potentials that take lower values near the

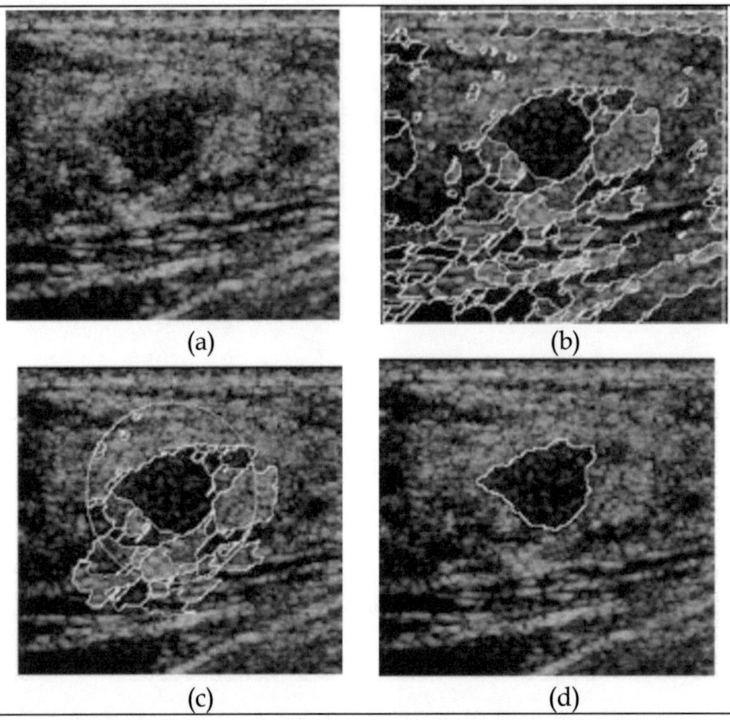

Fig. 7. (a)Original breast ultrasound image. (b) Cells generated by the watershed algorithm. (c)Initial snakes (white contours). (d) Final result. Reprinted from (Chen et al., 2002)

desired boundaries. So, both the Dual-Level-Set and the Dual-Front methods keep the idea of using two linked processes to seek for the global minimum.

4.1 Dual-Level-Set approach

In this section we maintain the philosophy of Dual-T-Snakes: one snake contracts and splits from outside the targets and another ones expand from inside the targets (section 3.2). However, the snake model will be an implicit one. To set ideas, let us consider the Figure 8.a, which shows two contours bounding the search space and Figure 8.b that pictures a surface which zero level set is the union of the two contours just presented.

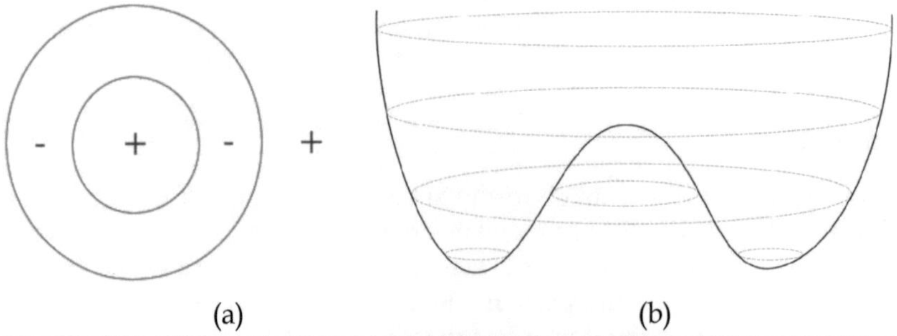

Fig. 8. (a)Dual snakes bounding the search space. (b) Initial function which zero level set is the two contours presented.

If the surface evolves such that the two contours get closer, we can obtain the same behavior of Dual-T-Snakes. That is the key idea of the method proposed by some of us in (Suri & Editors, 2006). In order to accomplish this goal we must define a suitable speed function and an efficient numerical approach. For simplicity, we consider the one dimensional version of the problem pictured on Figure 9. In this case, the level set equation given by expression (9) can be written as:

$$G_t + \frac{\partial G}{\partial x} F = 0. \tag{40}$$

The main point is to design the speed function F such that $G_t > 0$. Therefore, if we set the sign of F opposite to the one of G_x we get this goal, once:

$$G_t = -\frac{\partial G}{\partial x} F = 0. \tag{41}$$

Hence, the desired behavior can be obtained by the sign distribution of F, shown in Figure 9.

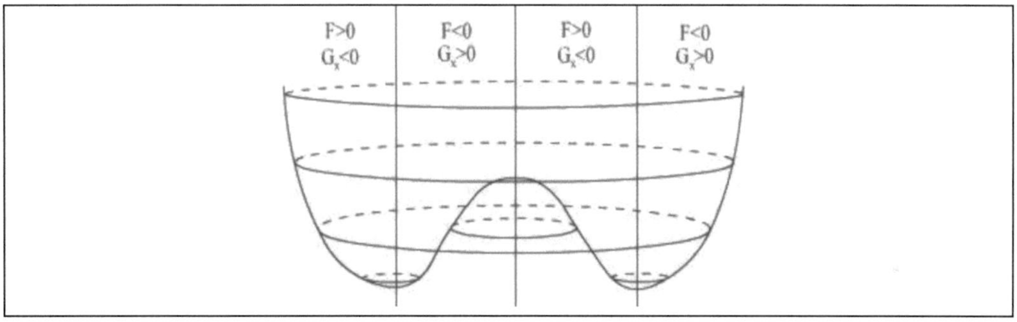

Fig. 9. Sign of speed function.

However, we should notice that $G_x = 0$ for singular points. So, the values of G remain constant over these points because G_t becomes null. Thus, we should be careful about the surface evolution nearby the singular points because anomalies may happen. One possibility to avoid this problem is to stop front evolution before getting close to this point. Another possibility could be to change the evolution equation in order to allow the $G_t \neq 0$ over singular points. Such proposal implies that the isolines may be not preserved, that is, they become a function of time also. Thus:

$$G(x(t), t) = y(t), \tag{42}$$

consequently, by applying Chain rule:

$$G_t + \frac{\partial G}{\partial x}\frac{dx}{dt} = \frac{dy}{dt}, \tag{43}$$

Therefore, we should provide an speed function in y direction.

$$G_t + \left(\frac{\partial G}{\partial x}, -1\right) \cdot \left(\frac{dx}{dt}, \frac{dy}{dt}\right) = 0, \tag{43}$$

We can write this expression as:

$$G_t + F\|\nabla G,-1\| = 0, \tag{45}$$

where F is the speed function. For fronts in $3D$we get:

$$G_t + \frac{\partial G}{\partial x}\frac{dx}{dt} + \frac{\partial G}{\partial y}\frac{dy}{dt} = \frac{dz}{dt}, \tag{46}$$

therefore:

$$G_t + \left(\frac{\partial G}{\partial x}, \frac{\partial G}{\partial y}, -1\right) \cdot \left(\frac{dx}{dt}, \frac{dy}{dt}, \frac{dz}{dt}\right) = 0, \tag{47}$$

One way to deal with these models is through viscous conservation laws (Sethian, 1996). For example, expression (43) becomes:

$$G_t + \frac{\partial G}{\partial x}\frac{dx}{dt} = \varepsilon \frac{\partial^2 G}{\partial x^2}, \tag{48}$$

If dy / dt is replaced by εG_{xx} where ε is a new parameter. For $2D$ we will have:

$$G_t + \left(\frac{\partial G}{\partial x}, \frac{\partial G}{\partial y}\right) \cdot \left(\frac{dx}{dt}, \frac{dy}{dt}\right) = \varepsilon \nabla^2 G, \tag{49}$$

where ∇^2 means the Laplace operator defined by:

$$\nabla^2 G = \frac{\partial^2 G}{\partial x^2} + \frac{\partial^2 G}{\partial y^2}. \tag{50}$$

In our model we will maintain the idea that the front evolves in the normal direction. Thus, expression (49) can be rewritten as:

$$G_t + F\|\nabla G\| = \varepsilon \nabla^2 G, \tag{51}$$

following the same development to derive expression (9). Such model has been studied in the context of front propagation in (Malladi et al., 1995; Sethian, 1996).

Once our application focus is shape recovery in a image I, we must choose a suitable speed function F as well as a convenient stopping term S to be added to the right-hand side of equation (51). Among the possibilities (Suri et al., 2002), the following ones have been suitable for our Dual-Level-Set:

$$F = \frac{1 + \alpha k}{1 + \|\nabla I\|^2}, \tag{52}$$

$$S = \beta \nabla P \cdot \nabla G, \tag{53}$$

where k is the curvature, defined by expression (11), α, β are scale parameters and $P = -\|\nabla I\|^2$. Therefore, we are going to deal with the following level set model:

$$G_t = \left(\frac{1+\alpha k}{1+\|\nabla I\|^2} \right) \|\nabla G\| + \varepsilon \nabla^2 G + \beta \nabla P \cdot \nabla G, \tag{54}$$

The evolution of the fronts follows this governing equation and are interdependent due to the embedding function. However, once the evolution stops, we must evaluate the similarity between the two contours and apply a driving velocity instead of the driving force of section 3.1. The numerical method is a first order one already known in the level set literature (Sethian, 1996). We have also simplified the initialization of the method through smoothed versions of step functions (see (Suri & Editors, 2006), for details).

As usual in level set approaches, we use the narrow band method; that is, only the values of G within a tube placed around the front are updated. When the front moves near to the edge of the tube boundary, the computation is stopped and a new tube is built with the zero level set at the center. For our dual approach, the narrow band is attractive not only for computational aspects but also because it allows an efficient way to evaluate similarity between two contours. In fact, instead of using the criterion of section 3.2, we take the procedure pictured on Figure 10: Firstly, the intersection point is computed (Figure 10.a); then, we take a neighborhood of this point (Figure 10.b) and stop to update the function G in all the grid points inside it or we can set to zero the speed function for these points. We say that those grid points are frozen ones.

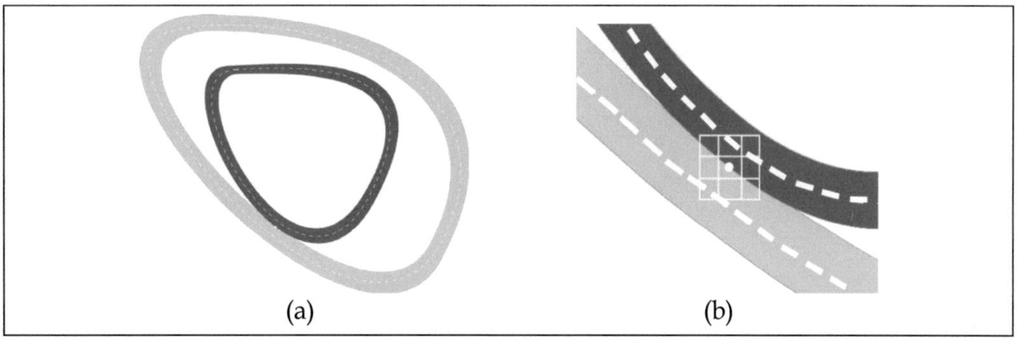

Fig. 10. (a)Narrow bands touching each other. (b) Neighborhood to define similarity between fronts.

Once the fronts stop moving, we must decide in which grid points we add a driving velocity. It is an extra velocity term which goal is the same of the driving force in section 3.2; that is, to keep fronts moving again. Therefore, we get a less sensitive model to the initial position of the fronts. To accomplish this task we can add an extra velocity term to equation (54), called V_{drive}.

We must be careful when choosing the grid points to apply this term. As in the case of Dual-T-Snakes, the fronts may be nearby the boundary somewhere, but far away from the target in another place. We should automatically realize this fact when the fronts stop moving. To accomplish this, we can use the affinity operator explained on section 3.2. Based on this operator, we can define an affinity function that assigns to a grid point inside the narrow band a $0-1$ value: 0 for the grid points most likely to lie away from the target boundaries and 1 otherwise. Like in the Dual-T-Snakes, such affinity operator can be defined through fuzzy segmentation methods (Giraldi et al., 2003), image transforms (Falcão et al., 2001), region statistics, etc. The whole Dual-Level-Set algorithm can be summarized as follows: (1) Initialization through Step Functions; (2) Evolution until fronts stop. (3) Evaluate similarity. If frozen, stop. (4) Add V_{drive} for some time steps. (5) After that, turn-off V_{drive}. Go to step 2.

Likewise in the Dual-T-Snakes model, when all the grid points inside the narrow bands are frozen, we stop the Dual-Level-Set evolution and apply a search based algorithm to get the final result.

Figure 11 shows the application of the Dual-Level-Set to segment the cell image of Figure 11.a. However, instead of taking a band-pass version of it, like in Figure 4.b, we just apply a low pass filter to smooth the image. The Dual-Level-Set parameters are: $\alpha = 0.1$, $\varepsilon = 2.0$, $\beta = 0.1$, $T = 150$, $\Delta t = 0.05$.

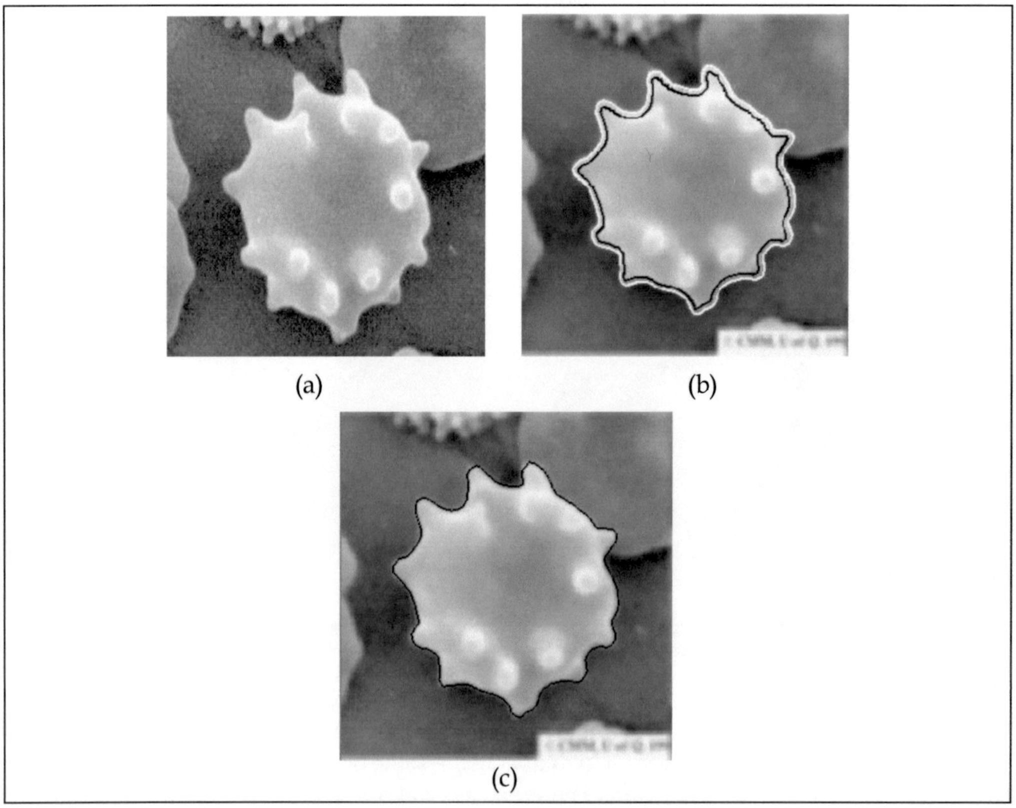

Fig. 11. (a) Original image. (b) Dual-Level-Set result. (c) Final result.

Once the two snakes in Figure 3 are very close to each other, a search method based on a greedy algorithm can be efficient and less expensive then the Viterbi (section 3.2). Firstly, we compute a curve located in-between the two fronts by taking the midpoint of each segment of the search space in Figure 3. The obtained curve can be used to initialize a snake model based on a greedy algorithm that works as follows (Suri & Editors, 2006). For each snaxel v_i we take a 3×3 neighborhood V, and for each pixel $p \in V$ we compute:

$$E(p) = \alpha E_{\text{int}}(v_{i-1}, p, v_{i+1}) + \beta E_{ext}(p) + \lambda E_{line}(p). \tag{55}$$

where E_{int}, E_{ext} and E_{line} are defined in equations (24) and (25), respectively. Then, we solve the problem:

$$p_0 = \arg\min\{E(p);\quad p \in V\}. \tag{56}$$

If $E(p_0) < E(v_i)$ then $v_i \leftarrow p_0$. The Figure 11.c pictures the obtained result.

4.2 Dual-Front approach

In (Li & Yezzi, 2005), a fast and flexible dual-front implementation of active contours is proposed by iteratively dilating an initial curve to form a narrow region and then finding the new closest potential weighted minimal partition curve inside. The method is motivated by minimal path technique (Cohen & Kimmel, 1996; Cohen, 2001). In this method, given a potential $P > 0$ and a point p in the domain Ω, the minimal action map $U_0(p)$ is defined as:

$$U_0(p) = \min_{A_{p_0,p}} \int_{\Omega} \overline{P}(c(s))ds, \tag{57}$$

where $\overline{P} = P + w$, with w been a constant, and $A_{p_0,p}$ is the set of paths connecting p_0 and p. Expression (57) gives the minimal energy integrated along the paths between the starting point p_0 and any point p inside the domain Ω. Because the action map U_0 has only one minimum value at the starting point p_0 and is a convex function in Ω, it can be easily determined by solving the equation (Cohen & Kimmel, 1996):

$$\|\nabla U_0\| = \tilde{P},\quad and\quad U_0 = 0. \tag{58}$$

If we set $\tilde{P} = 1/V$ then this expression becomes the so called Eikonal equation which can be efficiently solved by using fast marching methods (Sethian, 1999). Equations (57)-(58) are the starting point for the dual-front technique (Li & Yezzi, 2005). So, given two points $p_0, p_1 \in \Omega$, the method computes the action maps $U_0(p)$ and $U_1(p)$, respectively, through the solution of expression (58), seeking for the points $p \in \Omega$ such that:

$$U_0(p) = U_1(p). \tag{59}$$

At these points, the level set of the minimal action map U_0 meets the level set of the minimal action map U_1 generating the Voronoi diagram that decomposes the whole image into two regions containing the points p_0 and p_1. We can generalize definition (57) for a set $X \subset \Omega$ through the expression:

$$U_X(q) = \min_{p \in X} U_p(q), \tag{60}$$

that mens, $U_X(q)$ is the minimal energy along the paths of the set $A_{p,q}$ where $p \in X$. Therefore, given two curves c_{in} and c_{out} bounding the search space called R_n in the Figure 12, and two potentials $\tilde{P}_{in}$ and $\tilde{P}_{out}$ that takes lower values near desired boundaries, the dual-front algorithm firstly computes the minimal action maps U_{in} and U_{out} until these two action maps meet each other. Then, the evolutions of the level sets of both the action maps stops and a minimal partition boundary is formed in the region R_n of the Figure 12. Mathematically, this boundary is the solution of the following equations:

$$\|\nabla U_{in}\| = \tilde{P}_{in}, \quad with \quad U_{in}(c_{in}) = 0, \tag{61}$$

$$\|\nabla U_{out}\| = \tilde{P}_{out}, \quad with \quad U_{out}(c_{out}) = 0, \tag{62}$$

$$U_{in}(p) = U_{out}(p). \tag{63}$$

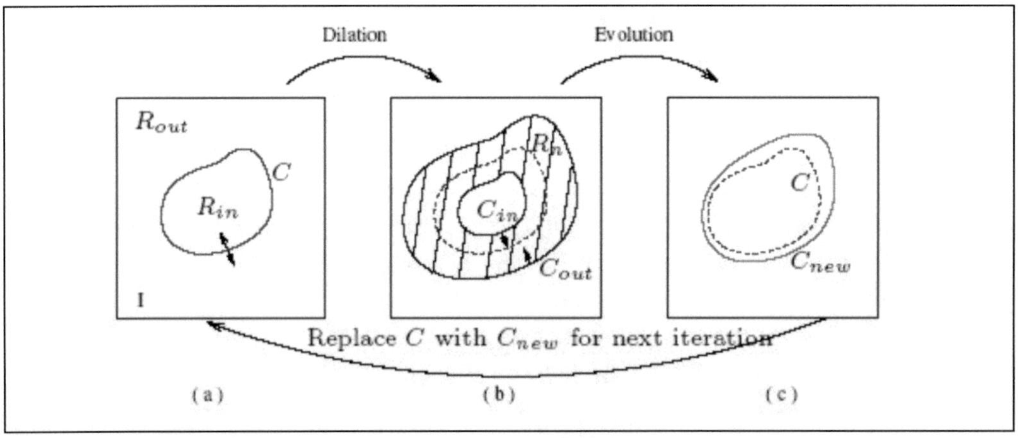

Fig. 12. One interaction of the Dual-Front algorithm. (a) Initial curve $C = c_n$ of the iteration n. (b) Search space defined through dilation of the initial curve c_n with bounds c_{in} and c_{out}. (c) Obtained solution C_{new}, the minimal partition curve. The curve C is replaced by the curve C_{new} to initialize the next iteration. Reprinted from (Li & Yezzi, 2005)

The dual-front approach is an iterative method which is picture on Figure 12. Firstly, the curves c_{in} and c_{out} are placed by user interaction or obtained by dilation of an initial curve, named by C in Figure 12. Then, the minimal partition boundary is computed by solving equations (61)-(63). To perform this task, the actions U_{in} and U_{out} are computed inside the region R_n, through expressions (61) and (62), respectively, until condition (63) is achieved. The obtained result, named by c_{n+1} will replace C for processing the next iteration. The method proceed until the distance between consecutive minimal partition curves is less than a pre-defined threshold δ, that means $d(c_n, c_{n+1}) < \delta$ (like in expressions (19)). The potentials $\tilde{P}_{in}$ and $\tilde{P}_{out}$ are defined in (Li & Yezzi, 2005) using the following general expressions which integrates region based and the edge-based information.

$$\tilde{P}_{in} = w_{in}^r \cdot f\left(\left|I(x,y) - \mu_{in}\right|, \sigma_{in}^2\right) + w_{in}^b \cdot g(\nabla I) + w_{in}, \tag{64}$$

$$\tilde{P}_{out} = w_{out}^r \cdot f\left(\left|I(x,y) - \mu_{out}\right|, \sigma_{out}^2\right) + w_{out}^b \cdot g(\nabla I) + w_{out}, \tag{65}$$

where μ_{in}, σ_{in}^2 are the mean and variance of the image intensity inside region $(R_{in} - R_{in} \cap R_n)$, $\mu_{out}, \sigma_{out}^2$ are the mean and variance of the image intensity inside region $(R_{out} - R_{out} \cap R_{in})$, and $w_{in}^r, w_{in}^b, w_{in}$ are parameters to be set in advance (the same for $w_{out}^r, w_{out}^b, w_{out}$).

The Figure 13 shows an example of the application of the dual-front method for 2D human brain MRI image where the segmentation objective is to find the interface between the gray matter and the white matter. This example is interesting to observe the sensitivity of the method against the width of the search space, called active region in (Li & Yezzi, 2005). We observe that the obtained result was much better for the narrower search space than for the other ones. In this test, the potentials in expressions (64)-(65) are defined by setting $w_{in}^r = w_{out}^r = 1$, $w_{in}^b = w_{out}^b = 0.1$, $w_{in} = w_{out} = 0.1$, and f, g given by:

$$f(x,y) = \left| I(x,y) - \mu_{in} \right|, \tag{66}$$

$$g(x,y) = \left| 1 + (\nabla I)^2 \right|, \tag{67}$$

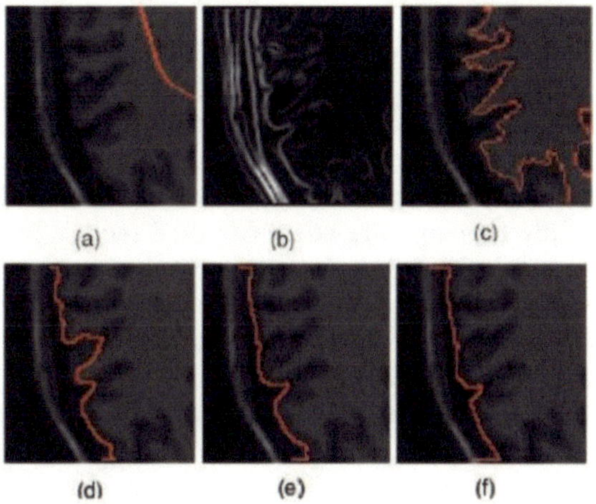

Fig. 13. Sensitivity of the of the Dual-Front against different sizes of the active region (search space): (a) The original *2D* human brain MRI image and the initial curve; (b) The corresponding edge map obtained through the gradient information; (c)-(f) Segmentation results obtained for a search space defined through morphological dilation of the initial curve with 5×5, 7×7, 11×11, 15×15 pixels circle structuring elements, after 15 iterations, respectively. Reprinted from (Li & Yezzi, 2005)

5. Discussion

An important point for dual snakes is how to proceed the evolution after both snakes comes at rest but are far from each other. The affinity operator in the Dual-T-Snakes and Dual-Level-Set models is used in this step, in order to avoid that some snaxels pass over the desired boundary, due to the driving term. Such procedure is bypassed in the original dual model (section 3.1) due to the shape model used. The corresponding energy term may prevents that a snake pass over a global minimum. However, the shape model given by expression (12) limits the application of the method for general shapes and topologies.

On the other hand, in the cell-based dual model, the cell decomposition of the image domain provided by the watershed strongly reduces the search space. Therefore, the energy minimization method may be less sensitive to local minima. That is way authors do not take care about the possibility of snakes reach equilibrium position far from the target. However, it does not seems to be possible to prove that such situation never happens.

In the Dual-Front, actually the level sets of the action map U give the evolution of the front. The velocity of the evolving front is decided by the potential. Therefore, both the potentials in expressions (64)-(65) must be defined such that the velocity is much lower when the evolving fronts arrive the boundary. If the constant $w > 0$, the front velocity will be never null, and so, fronts only stop when the two action maps meet each other. Such policy is interesting to pass over local minima but once there is no an energy balance between fronts the global minimum may be also lost.

Dual-Level-Set as well as Dual-T-Snakes are topologically adaptable deformable models which increases their range of applications. However, such generality has also a price: the care with local minima should be higher than in the original model, for example, because there is no a shape model to bias the solution to the desired shape.

Also, the characteristic function in the Dual-T-Snakes plays a similar role of the embedding function for the Dual-Level-Set in the sense that they provide the framework for topological changes. However, the update of the former is based on exhaustive tests (McInerney & Terzopoulos, 1999) while the later is just a consequence of the model evolution based on the equation (54). As a practical consequence, we observed that it is easier to implement the Dual-Level-Set than the Dual-T-Snakes. Also, we observe in our experiments that sometimes it is more efficient to apply topologically adaptable dual models just to reduce the search space, and, then to apply a search based technique to get the final result. This procedure was exemplified in sections 3.2 and 4.1. It is attractive because it simplifies the choice of parameters for the dual method and makes the computational cost of the application of a global optimization technique smaller.

Despite of the capabilities to reject local minima, dual models have also some disadvantages. Firstly, the method is at least two times more expensive than single approaches. Secondly, the initialization may be a tedious task because the user should set two curves at the beginning of the process. The choice of parameter values is also another point to be careful because in this case there are two snakes to be set.

A fundamental and more difficult point for dual snakes is how to proceed the evolution after both snakes comes at rest but they are far from each other. The snake with higher energy must be evolved, but the method should automatically realize the snaxels most likely to lie away from the boundary. The affinity operator (section 3.2) was proposals to address this problem without imposing restrictions to the snake evolution.

6. Conclusions and the future of dual methods

The original dual approach is an interesting technique to address the sensitivity to local minima of usual snake models. The idea of using two snakes to seek for the global minimum, originally proposed in (Gunn & Nixon, 1997), have been used and extended in recent works. Topological capabilities were incorporated, implicity formulations were developed and a cell-based approach were designed in order to improve the efficiency. This chapter offered a review of these state-of-the-art techniques as well as the background behind dual approaches.

Dual methods can avoid local minima through the comparison between the two contours energy and positions but they are at least two times more expensive than single approaches. Therefore, the ultrasound images seems to be the main target for the application of dual snakes because the difficulties inherent to the segmentation of these images force the application of a more robust approach against local minima.

The application of GPU techniques (Lefohn et al., 2003) must be considered in further works in order to improve the performance of the dual methods. The development of *3D* dual approaches is another point. For example, Dual-Level-Set as well as Dual-T-Snakes can be easily extended to *3D* without any extra machinery. Both the Dual-T-Snakes and the Dual-Level-Set methods are suitable for a parallel implementation in shared memory machines because, in the implicit formulation we must distribute the narrow band evolution while in the parametric case we should focus in the distribution of the T-Snakes processing. Multigrid techniques can be also implemented in both methods through Adaptive Mesh Refinement schemes (Giraldi et al., 2000a; Sethian, 1996).

7. Acknowledgment

Authors would like to thank the support provided by CNPq, CAPES (grant 094/2007) and FAPERJ (grant E-26/170.030/2008)

8. References

Amini, A. A., Weymouth, T. E. & Jain, R. C. (1990). Using dynamic programming for solving variational problems in vision, IEEE Trans. on Pattern Analysis and Machine Intel. 12(9): 855–867.

Bamford, P. & Lovell, B. (1997). A two-stage scene segmentation scheme for the automatic collection of cervical cell images, Proceedings of TENCON '97, Brisbane, Australia. Bischoff, S. & Kobbeit, L. (2004). Snakes with topology control, The Visual Computer 20: 217–228.

Chen, C.-M., LU, H. H.-S. & HSIAO, A.-T. (2001). A dual-snake model of high penetrability for ultrasound image boundary extraction, Ultrasound in Med. Biol. 27(12): 16511665.

Chen, C.-M., LU, H. H.-S. & HUANG, Y.-S. (2002). Cell-based dual snake model: A new approach to extracting highly winding boundaries in the ultrasound images, Ultrasound in Med. Biol. 28(8): 10611073.

Cohen, L. (2001). Multiple contour finding and perceptual grouping using minimal paths, Journal of Mathematical Imaging and Vision 14: 225–236.

Cohen, L. D. (1991). On active contour models and balloons, CVGIP:Image Understanding 53(2): 211–218.

Cohen, L. & Kimmel, R. (1996). Global minimum for active contour models: A minimal path approach, IEEE International Conference on CVPR (CVPR'96), pp. 666–673. Davatzikos, C. & Prince, J. (1999). Convexity analysis of active contour algorithms, Image and Vision Computing 17(1): 27–36.

Falco, A., da Cunha, B. & Lotufo, R. (2001). Design of connected operators using the image foresting transform, SPIE on Medical Imaging, Vol. 4322, pp. 468–479.

Giraldi, G. A. & Oliveira, A. A. F. (2004). Invariant snakes and initialization of deformable models, Int. J. Image Graphics 4(3): 363–384.

Giraldi, G. A., Strauss, E. & Oliveira, A. F. (2000a). A boundary extraction approach based on multi-resolution methods and the T-snakes framework, International Symposium on Computer Graphics, Image Processing and Vision (SIBGRAPI'2000).

Giraldi, G. A., Strauss, E. & Oliveira, A. F. (2000b). A boundary extraction method based on Dual-T-Snakes and dynamic programming, IEEE Computer Society Conference on Computer Vision and Pattern Recognition (CVPR'2000).

Giraldi, G. A., Strauss, E. & Oliveira, A. F. (2003). Dual-T-Snakes model for medical imaging segmentation, Pattern Recognition Letters 24(7): 993–1003.

Gunn, S. R. (1996). Dual Active Contour Models for Image Feature Extraction, PhD thesis, Faculty of Engineering and Applied Science, Department of Eletronics and Computer Science.

Gunn, S. R. & Nixon, M. S. (1997). A robust snake implementation; a dual active contour, IEEE Trans. Pattern Anal. Mach. Intell 19(1): 63–68.

Ip, H. H. S. & Shen, D. (1998). An affine-invariant active contour model (ai-snake) for modelbased segmentation, Image and Vision Computing 16(2): 135–146.

Kass, M., Witkin, A. & Terzopoulos, D. (1988). Snakes: Active contour models, International Journal of Computer Vision 1(4): 321–331.

Lefohn, A., Cates, J. E. & Whitaker, R. T. (2003). Interactive, gpu-based level sets for 3d segmentation, In: Medical Image Computing and Computer Assisted Intervention (MICCAI), pp. 564-572.

Leymarie, F. & Levine, M. D. (1993). Tracking deformable objects in the plane using and active contour model, IEEE Trans. Pattern Anal. Mach. Intell. 15(6): 617–634.

Li, H. & Yezzi, A. (2005). Local or global minima: flexible dual front active contours, Proc. Of Workshop-Comp. Vis. for Biom. Image App. (CVBIA 05, pp. 356–366.

Malladi, R., Sethian, J. A. & Vemuri, B. C. (1995). Shape modeling with front propagation: A level set approach, IEEE Trans. Pattern Anal. Mach. Intell. 17(2): 158–175.

McInerney, T. & Terzopoulos, D. (1996). Deformable models in medical image analysis: A survey, Medical Image Analysis 1(2).

McInerney, T. & Terzopoulos, D. (1999). Topology adaptive deformable surfaces for medical image volume segmentation, IEEE Trans. on Medical Imaging 18(10): 840–850.

Oliveira, A., Ribeiro, S., Farias, R., Esperanca, C. & Giraldi, G. (2004). Loop snakes: Snakes with enhanced topology control, SIBGRAPI '04, pp. 364–371.

Sapiro, G. (1997). Color snakes, Computer Vision and Image Understanding 68(2): 247–253.

Sethian, J. A. (1996). Level Set Methods: Evolving Interfaces in Geometry, Fluid Mechanics, Computer Vision and Materials Sciences, Cambridge University Press.

Sethian, J. A. (1999). Fast marching methods, SIAM Review 41: 199–235.

Suri, J. & (Editors), A. F. (eds) (2006). deformable models: clinical and biological applications, Springer, NY.

Image Segmentation Using Maximum Spanning Tree on Affinity Matrix

Qiang He[1] and Chee-Hung Henry Chu[2]
[1]*Department of Mathematics, Computer and Information Sciences*
Mississippi Valley State University
Itta Bena, MS 38941
[2]*The Center for Advanced Computer Studies*
University of Louisiana at Lafayette
Lafayette, LA 70504-4330
USA

1. Introduction

The objective of image segmentation and clustering is to extract meaningful regions out of an image. A graph theoretic approach, as an alternative to the gradient-based methods, is usually based on the eigenvectors of an affinity matrix [3,4,5,6,7]. The theoretical foundation of this development is the Spectral Graph Theory [1], through which the combinatorial features of a graph can be revealed by its spectra. This characteristic can be applied into graph partitioning and preconditioning. The typical eigendecompostion based segmentation work is called the normalized cuts [6]. The normalized cut measure incorporates the local similarity within cluster and total dissimilarity between clusters. The minimization of this measure is to solve the Rayleigh quotient, a generalized eigenvalue solving problem. However, solving a standard eigenvalue problem for all eigenvectors has exponential complexity and is very time consuming. Shi [6] made use of the sparsity of the affinity matrix and introduced the Lanczos method to simplify the computation of eigenvalues.

In this paper, we give a new image segmentation algorithm using the maximum spanning tree [2]. Our method works on affinity matrix and addresses the physical meanings of an affinity matrix. Instead of computations of eigenvalues and eigenvectors, we proved that the image segmentation could be transformed into an optimization problem: finding the maximum spanning tree of the graph with image pixels as vertices and pairwise similarities as weights. Section 2 describes the related theory and Section 3 gives the experimental results on synthetic and real data to illustrate the performance of this algorithm. Finally, we draw a conclusion and discuss future work in Section 4.

2. Method descriptions

In this section, we first discuss the characteristics of affinity matrix and then define an optimization measure based on the weighted graph associated with an image. The solution to the optimization problem satisfies the clustering standard with maximal within-class similarity and minimum between-class similarity.

2.1 Affinity matrix

The affinity matrix is a symmetric matrix and describes the pairwise pixel similarity. Every element $W_{i,j}$ of an affinity matrix $\mathbf{W}$ represents the similarity between pixels i and j. There are various definitions for the similarity measures. In general, $W_{i,j}$ can be defined as

$$W_{i,j} = e^{-||x_i - x_j||^2/2\sigma^2} \tag{1}$$

where $||.||$ is Euclidean distance and σ is a free parameter. This is somewhat similar to the definition to Gaussian distribution.

The characteristics of an affinity matrix (or similarity measures) are listed as follows.

- Symmetric property
  The affinity matrix is symmetric, that is, $W_{i,j} = W_{j,i}$. So it can be diagonalized.
- Unit normalization
  That is, $0 \le W_{i,j} \le 1$. The similarity $W_{i,j}$ between pixels i and j increases as $W_{i,j}$ goes from 0 to 1 while the dissimilarity decreases.
- Transitive property
  If pixels i and j are similar and pixels j and k are similar, then pixels i and k are similar.
- Coherence property
  That is, $W_{i,j} \ge W_{l,k}$ holds for $\forall i,j,l,k$ if pixels i and j are in the same cluster while pixels l and k are in different clusters.
- If similarity $W_{i,j}$ is greater than some threshold, then we say that pixels i and j are similar.

2.2 Similarity measure for cluster and whole image

Now, we define a similarity measure for one cluster and the whole image. If we consider the affinity matrix represents a weight matrix of a complete graph with all pixels as vertices. Then, there is a maximum spanning tree for this complete graph. Obviously, there is a subaffinity matrix for every cluster. We define the cluster similarity measure as the product of those weights in its maximum spanning tree. That is,

$$S_h = \prod_{i=1}^{N_h - 1} P_i^h \tag{2}$$

where h represents cluster number, N_h is the number of entities (pixels) in cluster h, and P_i^h are weights in the maximum spanning tree of cluster h. Because of the symmetric, transitive, and coherence properties of affinity matrix, we can understand this as follows. Given a pixel p in cluster h, in order to find all pixels in cluster h, we first find the pixel q with maximum similarity to pixel p. Then we find another pixel not in set $\{p,q\}$, but with maximum similarity either with p or with q. Repeatedly, until all pixels of cluster h are found. We can see that this measure is reasonable to represent the maximum within-cluster similarity for cluster h.

After we define cluster similarity measure, we further define a similarity $\mathbf{S}$ for the whole image, as follows

$$\mathbf{S} = \prod_{h=1}^{c} S_h = \prod_{h=1}^{c} \prod_{i=1}^{N_h - 1} P_i^h \tag{3}$$

where c is the number of clusters of image or number of segmentation components.
For convenience, sometimes, we use log on $\mathbf{S}$. We have

$$\log \mathbf{S} = \sum_{h=1}^{c} \log S_h = \sum_{h=1}^{c} \sum_{i=1}^{N_h - 1} \log P_i^h \tag{4}$$

Next, we will show that to maximize the similarity measure $\mathbf{S}$ is to maximize the within-cluster similarity and minimize the between-cluster similarity, which is preferred by the clustering and image segmentation.
Proposition 1. The following optimization problem

$$\underset{h,i}{\operatorname{argmax}} \mathbf{S} = \underset{h,i}{\operatorname{argmax}} \prod_{h=1}^{c} \prod_{i=1}^{N_h - 1} P_i^h \tag{5}$$

guarantees that the within-cluster similarity is maximum and the between-cluster similarity is minimal.
Proof. By contradiction.
Assume that there is a pixel p in cluster m is misclassified into cluster n. In the maximum spanning tree of cluster m, pixel p either connects two edges in the middle of the tree or connects one edge as a leaf node. Consider that the pixel p is removed from the cluster m. If p is a leaf node, then one its associated edge (also the weight) is removed from the maximum spanning tree. If p is in the middle of the tree, then two its associated edges (also the weights) are removed from the maximum spanning tree. But a new edge must be added to connect the two separate parts into a new maximum spanning tree. When pixel p is added into cluster n, it is either in the middle of the tree or exists as a leaf node. However, because of the coherence property of affinity matrix, the pairwise similarity between p and any pixel in cluster n is the smallest in the maximum spanning tree of cluster n, then p can not be added in the middle of the maximum spanning tree of cluster n. So p is added as a leaf node and one more edge (also the weight) is added onto the new maximum spanning tree of cluster n.
If p is removed as a leaf node from the cluster m, its cluster similarity measure S_m becomes

$$S'_m = \frac{S_m}{w_r} \tag{6}$$

where w_r is the removed weight.
If p is removed as a node in the middle of the maximum spanning tree of cluster m, its cluster similarity measure S_m becomes

$$S'_m = \frac{w_a S_m}{w_b w_c} \tag{7}$$

where w_b and w_c are the removed weights from the maximum spanning tree and w_a is the added new weight. From Prim's algorithm [2] (for minimal spanning tree, but inverse weights of maximum spanning tree, we can use it), $w_a \le w_b$ or $w_a \le w_c$. Or else, $w_a > w_b$ and $w_a > w_c$, w_a will be in the maximum spanning tree.

After p is added as a leaf node into the cluster n, its cluster similarity measure S_n becomes

$$S'_n = w_d S_n \tag{8}$$

where w_d is the added weight. Because of coherence property, $w_d < w_r, w_a, w_b, w_c$.

Then either,

$$S'_m \times S'_n = \frac{S_m}{w_r} \times w_d S_n = \frac{w_d}{w_r} S_m S_n < S_m S_n \tag{9}$$

or

$$S'_m \times S'_n = \frac{w_a S_m}{w_b w_c} \times w_d S_n = \frac{w_a w_d}{w_b w_c} S_m S_n < S_m S_n \tag{10}$$

Therefore, the maximum within-cluster similarity and the minimal between-cluster similarity are guaranteed under the above similarity measure.

2.3 Maximum spanning tree

After we define the above optimization problem, we want to solve it. We show that the above optimization problem can be solved by finding a maximum spanning tree for the complete weighted graph of an image. First, we give a brief introduction to Prim's algorithm, which, in graph theory, is used to find a minimum spanning tree for a connected weighted graph. If we inverse all weights of affinity matrix, to find a maximum spanning tree of the original graph is equavalent to finding the minimum spanning tree of the graph with new weights. So Prim's algorithm can be used to find a maximum spanning tree.

Prim's algorithm is an algorithm that finds a minimum spanning tree for a connected weighted graph, where the sum of weights of all the edges in the tree is minimized. If the graph is not connected, then it only finds a minimum spanning tree for one of the connected components.

The time complexity of the Prim's algorithm is $O(|E| \log |V|)$, where $|E|$ is the number of edges in the graph and $|V|$ is the number of nodes. For a complete graph, the number of edges is $|E| = \binom{|V|}{2} = \frac{|V|(|V|-1)}{2}$. This is also the maximum number of edges that a graph can have. So the time complexity of the Prim's algorithm is also $O(|V|^2 \log |V|)$. If we only use the transitive property of affinity matrix and compute the local similarity for a pixel, then there are only eight similarities for a pixel between it and its eight neighboring pixels. The number of edges becomes $|E|=8|V|$ and the complexity becomes $O(|V|\log|V|)$. This will reduce the complexity considerably. On the other hand, the complexity to a standard eigenfunction problems takes $O(|V|^3)$, where $|V|$ is the number of nodes in the graph.

Next, we show that the optimization problem can be solved by finding the maximum spanning tree and then removing the $c-1$ minimal weights.

Proposition 2. The following optimization problem

$$\underset{h,i}{\operatorname{argmax}} \mathbf{S} = \underset{h,i}{\operatorname{argmax}} \prod_{h=1}^{c} \prod_{i=1}^{N_h-1} P_i^h$$

can be solved by finding the maximum spanning tree of the graph associated with the image and then removing the $c-1$ minimal weights.

Proof. Prim's algorithm is used to find the maximum spanning tree.

Searching the maximum spanning tree of the whole image starts from a pixel x in some cluster m. According to coherence property of affinity matrix, the maximum spanning tree of cluster m must be put into the maximum spanning tree of the image first. Then the maximum spanning tree of cluster m will connect some pixel y in another cluster n through a between-cluster edge. From pixel y, the maximum spanning tree of cluster n is put into the maximum spanning tree of the image next. Repeatedly, all maximum spanning trees of clusters will be put in the maximum spanning tree of the image. The $c-1$ minimal weights connect those maximum spanning trees of c clusters into the maximum spanning tree of the whole image. Therefore, we obtain the solution

$$\max \mathbf{S} = \frac{T}{\prod_{l=1}^{c-1} w_l} = \frac{\prod_{k=1}^{N-1} T_k}{\prod_{l=1}^{c-1} w_l} \tag{11}$$

where

$T = \prod_{k=1}^{N-1} T_k$ is the product of all weights in the maximum spanning tree of the whole image.

w_l are the $c-1$ minimal weights.

3. Experimental results

We test our algorithm using synthetic data and real data. The synthetic data are binary data, generated by drawing white squares on the black background. The real data is a kid picture. The number of clusters (components) is give as prior here. The selection of number of clusters is a model selection problem that depends on the application, and is beyond the scope of our discussion here.

Test on synthetic data

The synthetic data are a picture with two white squares on the black background. The similarity is computed using Equation 1 based on intensity values. We chose $\sigma = 0.1$. Then the within-class similarity is

$$e^{-\| x_i - x_j \|^2 / 2\sigma^2} = e^{-\| 0-0 \|^2 / 2 \cdot 0.1^2} = e^{-\| 1-1 \|^2 / 2 \cdot 0.1^2} = e^{0} = 1 \quad (12)$$

and the between-class similarity is

$$e^{-\| x_i - x_j \|^2 / 2\sigma^2} = e^{-\| 1-0 \|^2 / 2 \cdot 0.1^2} = e^{-50} \approx 0 \quad (13)$$

For the data with two white squares, the maximum spanning tree of the image has two edges with zero weights. All other edges have weight one. The zero weight edges are two minimal weights and separate the maximum spanning tree of the image into three spanning trees. One of the new spanning trees represents the background and the other two represent two foreground squares.
The segmentation results are shown in Figure 1. We can see that we obtain perfect results.

(a) (b) (c) (d)

Fig. 1. Image segmentation on synthetic data. (a). the original image (b). the segmented background (white part) (c). the first segmented square (white part) (d). the second segmented square (white part)

Test on real data

The real data is a kid picture. The similarity is computed using Equation 1 based on average values of three channel values. We still chose $\sigma = 0.1$. The segmentation results are shown in Figure 2. The results are reasonable. Since boundary contours of kid face and shirt are not consistent with the background and foreground (kid face or shirt), they can be clearly separated as we chose 5 components.
In real images, because of noise and outliers in cluster, some within-cluster similarities are very small. Correspondingly, some very small weights do not represent the between-cluster separation weights. In practice, we follow the order of edges from the Prim's algorithm and pick those edge weights with considerable differences from (viz. smaller than) its previous and afterwards edge weights as the between-cluster separation edges. This method works robustly for real images. In practice, the χ^2-statistic [4] for histograms may give a better similarity measure for color and texture.

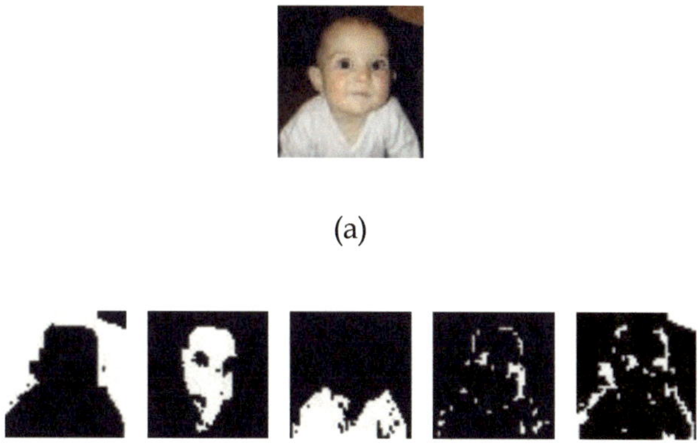

(a)

(b) (c) (d) (e) (f)

Fig. 2. Image segmentation on kid picture. (a). original image (b). the segmented background (white part) (c). the segmented kid face (white part) (d). the segmented shirt (white part) (e,f). the segmented contours (white part)

4. Conclusions

In this paper, we presented a new graph-based image segmentation algorithm. This algorithm finds the maximum spanning tree of the graph associated with the image affinity matrix. Instead of solving eigenvalues and eigenvector, we proved that the image segmentation could be transformed into an optimization problem: finding the maximum spanning tree of a graph with image pixels as vertices and pairwise similarities as weights. In our future work, we will explore different similarity measures and test the segmentation algorithm on more data.

5. References

[1] Chung, F.R.K.: *Spectral Graph Theory*. American Mathematical Society, 1997.

[2] Cormen, T.H., Leiserson, C.E., Rivest, R. L., and Stein, C.: *Introduction to Algorithms*, Second Edition. MIT Press and McGraw-Hill, 2001.

[3] Perona, P. and Freeman, W. T.: A factorization approach to grouping. In *Proc ECCV*, H. Burkardt and B. Neumann, editors, 1998, 655--670.

[4] Puzicha, J., Rubner, Y., Tomasi, C., and Buhmann, J. M.: Empirical evaluation of dissimilarity measures for color and texture. In *Proceedings of the IEEE International Conference on Computer Vision*, 1999, 1165--1173.

[5] Scott, G.L. and Longuet-Higgins, H. C.: Feature grouping by relocalisation of eigenvectors of the proximity matrix. In *Proc. British Machine Vision Conference*, 1990, 103-108.

[6] Shi, J. and Malik, J.: Normalized cuts and image segmentation. In *Proc. IEEE Conf. Computer Vision and Pattern Recognition*, 1997, 731-737.

[7] Weiss, Y.: Segmentation using eigenvectors: a unifying view. In *Proceedings IEEE International Conference on Computer Vision*, 1999, 975-982.

9

Image Segmentation by Autoregressive Time Series Model

Pei-Gee Peter Ho
Naval Undersea Warfare Center, Newport Rhode Island
USA

1. Introduction

The objective of the image segmentation is to simplify the representation of pictures into meaningful information by partitioning into image regions. Image segmentation is a software technique to locate certain objects or boundaries within an image. There are many algorithms and techniques have been developed to solve image segmentation problems for the past 20 years, though, none of the method is a general solution. Among the best, they are neural networks segmentation, one-dimensional signal segmentation, multi-scale segmentation, model based segmentation, graphic partitioning, region growing and K-mean clustering segmentation methods. In this chapter, the newly developed Autoregressive (AR) time series model will be introduced for image segmentation.

Time series statistical models such as Autoregressive Moving Average (ARMA) were considered useful in describing the texture and contextual information of an image. To simplify the computation, a two-dimensional (2-D) Autoregressive (AR) model was used instead. The 2-D AR time series model is particularly suitable to capture the rich image pixel contextual information. This model has been applied for both rough and smooth target surfaces and performed very well for image segmentation.

In the typical statistical approach of image segmentation, there are two broad classes of segmentation procedures: The supervised and the unsupervised segmentation methods. The unsupervised segmentation procedure is the means by which pixels in the image are assigned to classes without prior knowledge of the existence or labeling of the classes. Whereas, in the supervised learning process, a teacher provides a label and cost function for each pattern in a training set and tries to minimize the sum of cost function for all patterns. Each method finds its own applications in the areas of the image analysis. The Support Vector Machine, a close cousin of classical multilayer perceptron neural networks and a newer supervised segmentation procedure, was adopted after feature extraction for single AR model image or pixel features vector extraction from multi-spectral image stack. On the other hand, the unsupervised region growing segmentation method was applied after univariate time series model was built.

For the experimental results by applying the proposed AR time series segmentation model, the USC texture data set as well as satellite digital remote sensing image data are used. The algorithms performance comparisons with other existing contextual models such as Markov Random Field model, K-means, PCA, ICA …etc can be found in reference (Ho, 2008).

2. 2-D Univariate time series image segmentation model and estimation

Time series analysis (Shumway 2000) (Wei, 1990) has been used in many applications, specifically the weather forecast, atmosphere-ocean model for global climate changes and the Dow Jones economics analysis. Interesting enough, at the University of Massachusetts ,Dartmouth School of Marine Science and Technology (SMAST) professor Joachim Gröger (Gröger 2007) can successfully trace a group of cod fishes' approximate swimming routes by time series model analysis on tidal data. In this section, we make use of time series concepts for image data mathematical formulation which is very new. To understand how, we introduce time series theory briefly. The primary objective of time series is to develop certain mathematical models that provide descriptions for sample data. We assume any image can be defined as a collection of random variables indexed according to the order they are obtained in time-space. For example, we consider a sequence of random variables $x_1, x_2, x_3, ...,$ in general, $\{x_t\}$ indexed by t is the stochastic process. The adjacent points in time are correlated. Therefore, the value of series x_t at time t depends in some fashion on the past values $x_{t-1}, x_{t-2}, ...$ Suppose that we let the value of the time series at some point of time t to be denoted by x_t. A stationary time series is the one for which the probabilistic behavior of $x_{t_1}, x_{t_2}, ...x_{t_k}$ is identical to that of the shifted set $x_{t_1+h}, x_{t_2+h}, ..., x_{t_k+h}$. In an image segmentation application, the 2-D image was scanned from left upper corner to right bottom as a sequence of time series pixel values. Further, to simplify the numerical calculations, we model each class of surface textures by 1st order and 2nd order Autoregressive stationary time series models. In another way of thinking, the two-dimensional Markov model is a similar mathematical model to describe. By using time series model, when the within-object interpixel correlation varies significantly from object to object, we can build effective imaging region segementation. The unsupervised Region Growing is a powerful image segmentation method for use in shape classification and analysis. Take one satellite remote sensing example to show, we present the LANDSAT 5 database in the area of Italy's Lake Mulargias image data acquired in July 1996 to be used for the computing experiments with satisfactory preliminary results (figure 1, figure 2 and figure 3). The advanced statistical techniques, such as Gaussian distributed white noise error confidence interval calculations, sampling statistics based on mean and variance properties are adopted for automatic threshold finding during Region Growing iterations. The linear regression analysis with least mean squares error estimation is implemented as a time series system optimization scheme.

2.1 Image modeling and estimation theory

The raw image data are statistically random and can be modeled with some basic ideas of time series analysis and stochastic processes. It is based on a model which treats the pixels (picture elements) of a digitized textural scene as a two-way seasonal time series. A time series is a set of observations, each one is recorded at a specific time t. The target image is well treated as a time series in which the observations are made at the fixed time intervals. Therefore, for a two dimensional image, each pixel gray tone information G(x,y) is equivalent to G(t) in the time series analysis. In the multi-spectral scanner images, the texture information is one of the important characteristics for machine vision analysis. The texture classification techniques include determination of a number of classes to which the texture region belongs. It estimates texture model parameters for a region and constructs the boundaries between different texture regions. The standard probability and the statistics concepts, such as autocovariance and sample covariance functions are considered. The techniques in parameter estimation theory to extract texture typed trend and seasonality from the observed time series are adapted for image segmentation analysis. Due to the fact that rarely is there an exact priori knowledge about the image data, a mathematical model is often used. The time series stationary Autoregressive (AR) models on both the first-order and the second-order with Region Growing algorithm are studied and the results are presented below.

2.2 First-order autoregressive image modeling and parameter estimation

In the first-order AR analysis, each gray tone pixel value of the image is estimated through its neighboring pixels. This is based on the assumption of a causal, linear time invariant remote sensing system. The gray level of the (i,j) th pixel of the remote sensing image is expressed by the equation:

$$x(i,j) = a + b * [x(i-1,j) + x(i,j-1)] + n(i,j) \tag{1}$$

where $n(i,j)$ is modeled as a Gaussian white noise random process. Let $\hat{x}(i,j)$ be an estimate of $x(i,j)$. Note that for an 100 by 100 image array, $i = 1:100$ is the row index, $j = 1:100$ is the column index of the two dimensional image example. Starting with a set of region seeds, the weighted coefficients are determined through unsupervised region growing iterative procedure to group pixels of a subregion into larger regions. The ground truth data were provided as "seeds" for initial processing. The criterion is to minimize the mean square error MSE formulated as (Seber 1977), (Papoulis 2002):

$$MSE = \sum_{i=1}^{100}\sum_{j=1}^{100} E\{[x(i,j) - \hat{x}(i,j)]^2\}$$

which will be a minimum if setting

$$\frac{\partial(MSE)}{\partial a} = 0 \qquad \frac{\partial(MSE)}{\partial b} = 0 \tag{2}$$

By ordinary linear regression calculation, we get the following optimal least squares estimator of the first order AR parameters:

Let

$$z(i,j) = x(i-1,j) + x(i,j-1)$$

Numerator $$= \sum_{i=1}^{M}\sum_{j=1}^{N} z(i,j) * x(i,j) - M * N * E[z(i,j)] * E[x(i,j)] \tag{3}$$

Denominator $$= \sum_{i=1}^{M}\sum_{j=1}^{N} [z(i,j)]^2 - M * N * [E(z(i,j))]^2 \tag{4}$$

M = Total region growing sample row pixels number
N = Total region growing sample column pixels number

$$\hat{b} = \frac{\text{Numerator}}{\text{Denominator}} \tag{5}$$

$$\hat{a} = E(x(i,j)) - \hat{b} * E(z(i,j)) \tag{6}$$

Note that $E(x(i,j))$ denotes the expectation value.

2.3 Second-order autoregressive image modeling and parameter estimation

In the following analysis, each gray tone pixel value of the image is estimated through weighted summation of its neighborhood pixels. This is based on an assumption that a causal, linear time invariant remote sensing system can be modeled mathematically. The gray level of the (i,j) th pixel of the remote sensing image is expressed by the following formula:

$$x(i,j) = a + bx(i-1,j) + cx(i,j-1) + dx(i-1,j-1) + n(i,j) \tag{7}$$

where $n(i,j)$ is assumed a Gaussian white noise random process. Let $\hat{x}(i,j)$ be an estimate of $x(i,j)$ Note that $i = 1$ to M is the row index, $j =$ 1 to N is the column index of the two dimensional image. Starting with a set of region seeds, the weighted coefficients are determined through unsupervised region growing iterative procedure to group pixels of a subregion into larger regions. The ground truth "seeds" data were used for initialization. Again, the same as the 1st order, the criterion is to minimize the mean square error MSE (Haykin 2003) that is formulated as:

$$MSE = \sum_{i=1}^{M}\sum_{j=1}^{N} E\{[x(i,j) - \hat{x}(i,j)]^2\} \tag{8}$$

which will be a minimum if setting

$$\frac{\partial(MSE)}{\partial a} = 0; \quad \frac{\partial(MSE)}{\partial b} = 0; \quad \frac{\partial(MSE)}{\partial c} = 0; \quad \frac{\partial(MSE)}{\partial d} = 0; \tag{9}$$

By centering and scaling of the linear regression data, we can easily find the following matrix operation which relates estimated parameter matrix with covariance matrix of the sample of one image class region.

$$P * \hat{T} = Q \tag{10}$$

Let $\sum x(i,j)$ be the abbreviation of $\sum_{i=1,j=1}^{M,N} x(i,j)$ due to limited mathematical symbol spacing.

M = Total region growing sample row pixels number
N = Total region growing sample column pixels number
Then,

$$Q = \begin{bmatrix} \sum x(i,j) \\ \sum x(i-1,j)x(i,j) \\ \sum x(i,j-1)x(i,j) \\ \sum x(i-1,j-1)x(i,j) \end{bmatrix} \quad (11)$$

$$\hat{T} = \begin{bmatrix} \hat{a} \\ \hat{b} \\ \hat{c} \\ \hat{d} \end{bmatrix} = \text{The optimized parameter matrix} \quad (12)$$

$$P = \begin{bmatrix} M*N & \sum x(i-1,j) & \sum x(i,j-1) & \sum x(i-1,j-1) \\ \sum x(i-1,j) & \sum x(i-1,j)^2 & \sum x(i-1,j)x(i,j-1) & \sum x(i-1,j)x(i-1,j-1) \\ \sum x(i,j-1) & \sum x(i-1,j)x(i,j-1) & \sum x(i,j-1)^2 & \sum x(i,j-1)x(i-1,j-1) \\ \sum x(i-1,j-1) & \sum x(i-1,j-1)x(i-1,j) & \sum x(i-1,j-1)x(i,j-1) & \sum x(i-1,j-1)^2 \end{bmatrix} \quad (13)$$

In which, the estimated parameters $\hat{a}$, $\hat{b}$, $\hat{c}$, $\hat{d}$ can be found from $\hat{T}$ matrix. Also the optimal estimated pixel gray level can be calculated as

$$\hat{x}(i,j) = \hat{a} + \hat{b}x(i-1,j) + \hat{c}x(i,j-1) + \hat{d}x(i-1,j-1) \quad (14)$$

The more iterations performed to grow the region, the more accurate the estimated parameters.

Now, let $$e(i,j) = \hat{x}(i,j) - x(i,j) \quad (15)$$

Decision making for region growing:

A two class discrimination decision can be made by:

$$\text{Set class\_label} = 1 \text{ if } e(i,j) < \text{Threshold} * \sqrt{MSE(optimal)} \quad (16)$$

$$\text{Set class\_label} = 0 \quad \text{otherwise}$$

Where $MSE(optimal)$ is the mean square error calculation of the growing region.

Based on statistical hypotheses and significance property of the sampling theory plus the Gaussian distribution nature of the pixel error populations, the 95% confidence interval threshold can be found as:

$$\text{Threshold} = \sqrt{2/\pi} + \sqrt{1-2/\pi} \quad (17)$$

To prove (17) for the threshold:

$$\text{Threshold} = \sqrt{2/\pi} + \sqrt{1-2/\pi}\,; \quad \text{let } SD = MSE(optimal) \quad (18)$$

The error Gaussian distribution function can be expressed as

$$f(e(I,J))=\frac{1}{\sqrt{2\pi}SD}\exp\left[-1/2(e(I,J)/SD)^2\right] \tag{19}$$

$$E(|e(I,J)|)= 2\int_0^{\infty} e(I,J)(\frac{1}{\sqrt{2\pi}SD}\exp\left[-1/2(e(I,J)/SD)^2\right])\,d(e(I,J)) \tag{20}$$

$$= (\sqrt{2/\pi})*SD \tag{21}$$

$$M_{e(I,J)} = E[|\ e(I,J)\ |] \tag{22}$$

$$(\sigma_{e(I,J)})^2 = E\{(e(I,J) - M_{e(I,J)})^2\} \tag{23}$$

$$= (SD^2) - ((\sqrt{\frac{2}{\pi}})*SD)^2 \tag{24}$$

$$= (1-\frac{2}{\pi})(SD^2) \tag{25}$$

$$\sigma_{e(I,J)} = \sqrt{(1-\frac{2}{\pi})}*SD \tag{26}$$

For 95% confidence of 1-sigma interval value

$$e(I,J) < E[|\ e(I,J)\ |] + \sqrt{(1-\frac{2}{\pi})}*(SD)= \sqrt{\frac{2}{\pi}}*(SD) + \sqrt{(1-\frac{2}{\pi})}*(SD) \tag{27}$$

$$= (\sqrt{2/\pi} + \sqrt{1-2/\pi})*(SD) \tag{28}$$

An example of experiment for explanation:

As shown in figure 1, figure 2 and figure 3, after certain iterations of Lake Mulargias (water) region growing (when we are assured that no more water pixel can be found), we stop processing. By unsupervised region growing the optimized parameter matrix $\hat{T}$ can be determined to classify the entire image.

2.4 Region growing algorithm

Region Growing, as implied by its name, is an algorithm that groups pixel subregions into bigger areas. It starts with a set of known seeds (ground truth information, for example, in figure 2) to grow regions by merging to each seed point those neighborhood pixels that have similar statistical features.

In remote sensing image analysis and segmentation application, there are just a few researchers who proposed or attempted to use region growing. As a matter of fact, its practical implementations have proven that in general, it does work well in most circumstances as far as region segmentation is concerned. In the IEEE IGARSS 2000 paper, Dr. Tilton and Lawrence (Tilton 2000) presented the interactive hierarchical segmentation to

grow a region. But, this method has some limitations and can only apply to certain scenes only. The Region Growing method we proposed is a different approach and can deal with the shortfall they have. Other useful references on the subject can be found in Reference (Haralick 1992).
A basic region growing procedure is Outlined in Table 1.

```
ITERATION_COUNT = 1; MAX_ITERATION = 100;
Border of R = lake seed (water);
Start with lake seed, calculate and estimate A, B, C, D parameters
DO  until ITERATION_COUNT > MAX_ITERATION or NOT LAKE CLASS
  Increment border of R by one pixel up, down, left, right to R'
  for each pixel p at the border of R'-R do
          if ( | e(I,J) | < Threshold * SD ), set CLASS of p = LAKE;
          else
                    CLASS of p = OTHER;       /* CLASSIFICATION */
          Updated calculation of A,B,C,D parameters for R' region with new CLASS LABEL
  End
  ITERATION_COUNT ++ ;
End
```

Table 1. AR Model Based Region Growing Algorithm

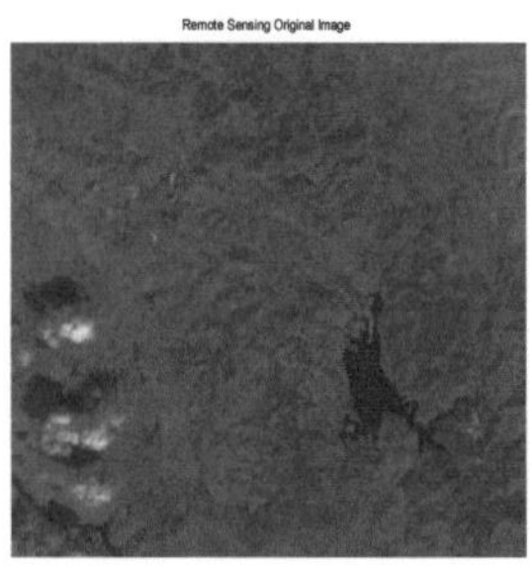

Fig. 1. Original Lake Region Remote Sensing band 5 Image

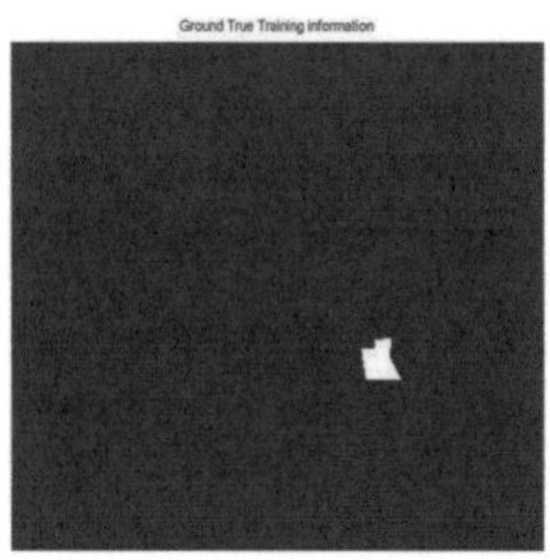

Fig. 2. Ground Truth Information

Fig. 3. Segmentation Result After Region Growing Based On AR Model

In this chapter, we have introduced a new univariate time series AR model based region growing algorithm, which attempts to extract a special property region such as water at Lake Mulagias. As a matter of fact, this new algorithm can be further used to apply to other remote sensing imagery area, such as corn field, city block, grassland, pasture … etc for scene classifications. The computer experiments show that the Time series Region Growing algorithm is efficient for the remote sensing image region segmentation problems.

A Region growing is a procedure that group pixels or subregions into larger regions based on predefined criteria (Ho 2004). By starting with a set of seed points, it forms the growing regions by appending to each seed of the neighboring pixels that have similar properties to the seed points. The process is in the iteration mode as depicted in figure 4, where (a) is the region

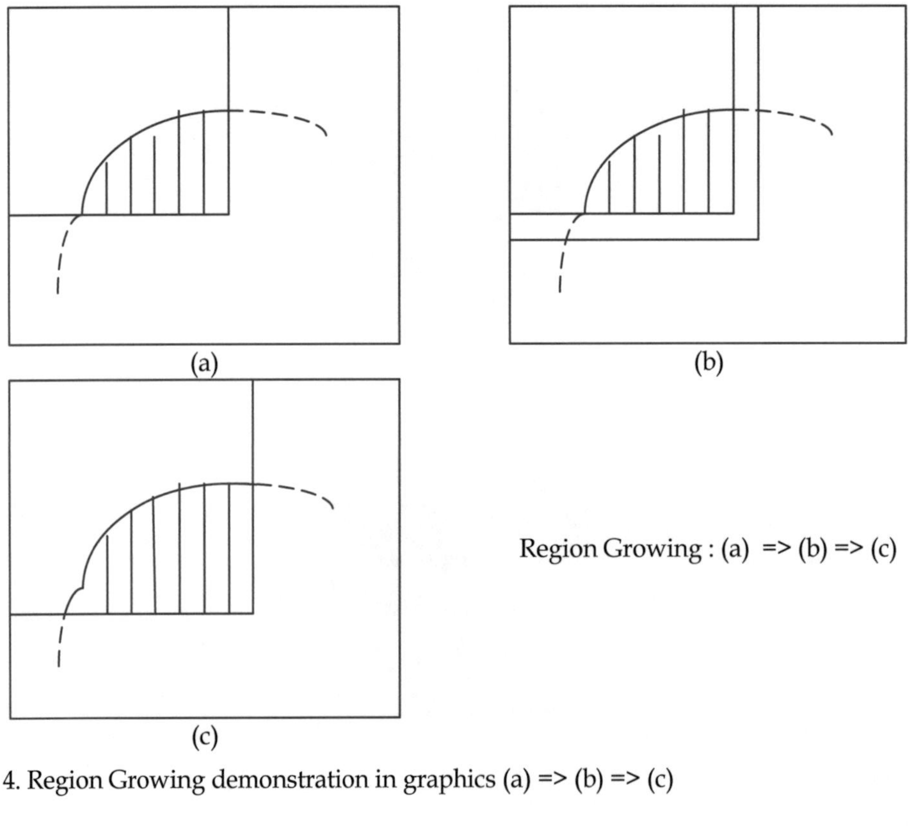

Fig. 4. Region Growing demonstration in graphics (a) => (b) => (c)

before growing, (b) is in the process of growing one pixel layer to the right and one pixel layer toward bottom. After certain decision making, the new region was formed as in (c).
There are many different ways of region growing depends on programmer's preferences. Usually, the first step of image analysis is to partition an input image that is more than one uniform region into several homogeneous subimages (Gonzalez 2004). The region of homogeneity can be determined by many different properties. In region growing method, the image segmentation is implemented by extending some starting pixels or internal small area inside regions to boundaries between texture areas. Pixels in a homogeneous region are expected to be assigned by an identical class. The boundaries will be drawn by the difference in the adjacent class regions. We also need to make sure that regions with the same texture but in different parts of an image are labeled by the same class. In the remote sensing and USC texture type data examples, the texture property for each observed window is extracted from time series 2-D AR model. Under each iteration, the unknown regions were segmented into blocks. Each internal region is expanded by comparing the properties of its surrounding blocks. As texture boundaries are reached, the size of blocks is reduced, each block might contains only one pixel at the end.
Figure 5 shows an example result on USC data set for the effectiveness of the AR time series image segementation.

(a) (b) (c)

Fig. 5. (a) Orginal 3-classes real texture image from USC data base (brickwall, grass and pigskin) (b) The segmentation result after 2-D time series multiclass SVM in black and white display (c) The Segmentation result after 2-D time series multiclass SVM in color display

2.5 Higher order AR model

The 3rd order of AR image model is described as:

$$x(i,j) = a + bx(i-1,j) + cx(i,j-1) + dx(i-1,j-1) + ex(i-2,j) + fx(i,j-2) + n(i,j) \qquad (29)$$

We have done some experiments on the same Lake Mulagias remote sensing data set as well as USC texture data set by 3rd order AR model, but the region segmentation results did not improve further. This told us that the term higher than 2nd order had no impact. The AR model order selection criteria is based on sample estimated error or residuals.

2.6 Experimental results

The following figures from Figure 6 to Figure 13 are the texture and remote sensing segmentation results:

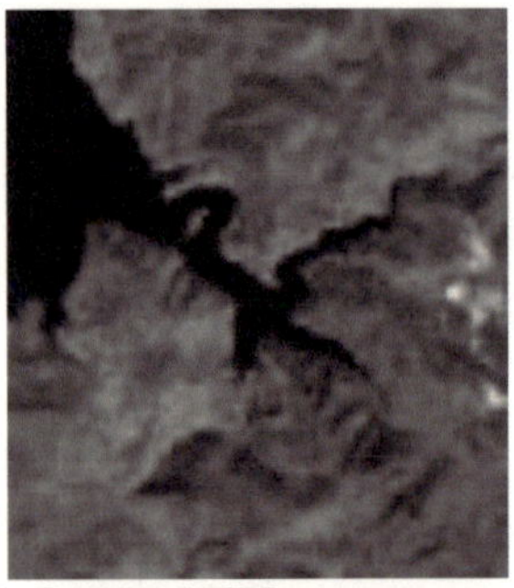

Fig. 6. Original TM remote sensing image of Italy Lake Mulagias

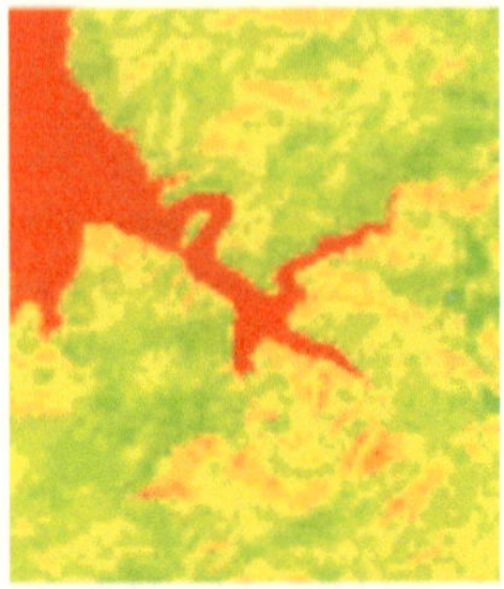

Fig. 7. Original Italy Lake Mulagias displayed in color format

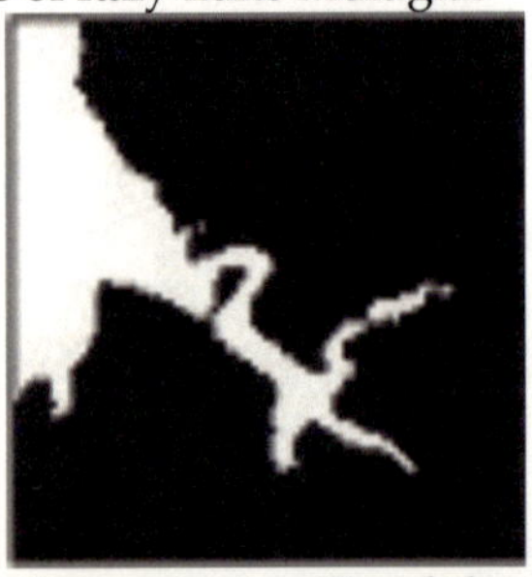

Fig. 8. Segmentation Result by 2nd Order AR in black and white

Fig. 9. Segmentation Result by 2nd Order ARMA in color format

Fig. 10. Original USC brick and grass two classes natural scene

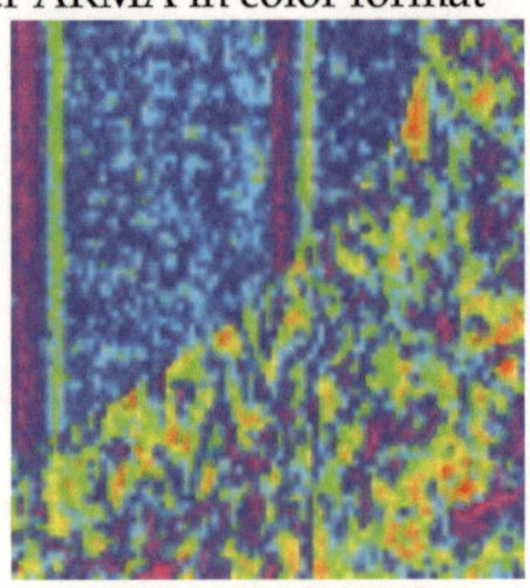

Fig. 11. Original USC brick and grass displayed in color format

Fig. 12. Texture Segmentation Result by 2nd Order AR in black and white

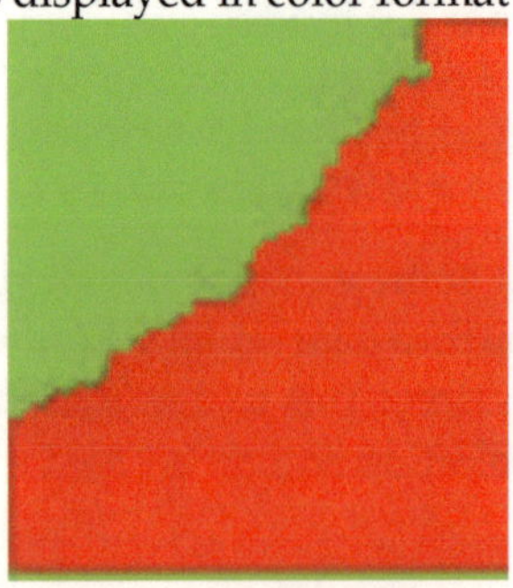

Fig. 13. Texture Segmentation Result by 2nd Order AR in color format

The 2-D time series model based support vector machine (Ho, 2007) was tested with real remote sensing images from satellite and the results in figure 14 shows that this method can perform well in separating lake region from city building with the accuracy of 96.9%.

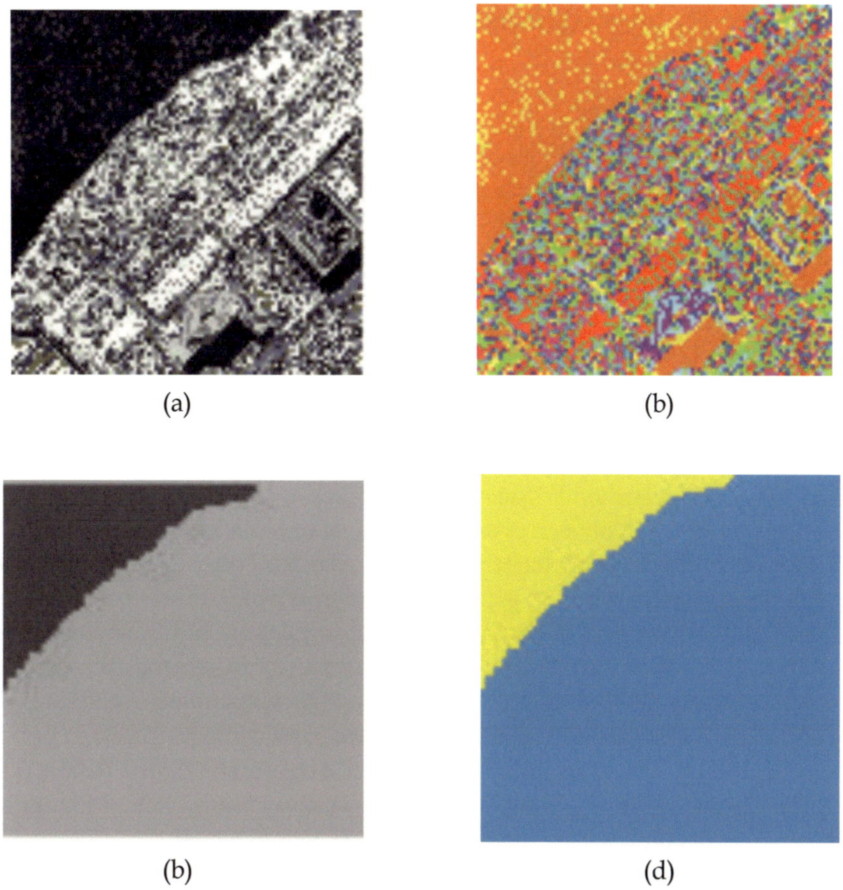

Fig. 14. (a) Original 2 Classes Remote Sensing Image in black and white mode
(b) Original 2 Classes Remote Sensing Image in color mode
(c) The Segmentation Result 2 classes SVM Method
(d) The Segmentation Result after 2 classes SVM Method in color display

3. Contexture image models

A problem of particular importance in remote sensing image classification is the use of contextual information. All experiments indicate that classification performance improves with proper use of contextual information. Because of interest with texture analysis, and the fact that remote sensing data is rich in texture, this problem has been studied by pattern recognition researchers for some time with a number of approaches presented.

Markov random field provides a rigorous mathematical characterization of contextual information of textures from neighboring pixels on an image. Basically the often rich textural information in remote sensing image makes Markov random field a very powerful image model. Another image model is the 2-D multivariate autoregressive time series analysis. The Markov random field model is for a single image while the 2-D multivariate autoregeessive model is for the entire stack of images under consideration and treated as a vector time series. The two image models will be briefly presented in this section.

3.1 Markov random field

Markov random field (MRF) contextual image model assumes that the texture is stochastic and stationary with conditional independence. MRF theory provides a basis for modeling contextual constraints in image processing, analysis, and interpretation (Geman, 1984). Several methods are introduced and published about 2-D image restoration or reconstruction with MRF model. Very recently a comprehensive treatment of Markov random field in remote sensing is given by Serpico and Moser. The neighborhood system of a pixel x, in an MxN image, which contains the contextual information under consideration, consists of adjacent pixels with a Euclidean distance of say r. and r takes an integer value that is denoted as the order of neighborhood system. The neighborhood system with a definitive order is shown in Figure 15 (a), where 1, 2, ······ denote the order of neighborhood system. The second order neighborhood system has eight neighboring pixels. Therefore, it is also called the 8-neighborhood system. In a Markov random field the conditional probability density function of each pixel is dependent only on its neighborhood system So the MRF represents the local characteristics of x. The MRF can be causal or noncausal. Assume that the pixels are scanned sequentially top to down and left to right. The causal MRF depends only on the past while the noncausal or bilateral MRF depends not only on the past but also on the future as shown in Figure 15 (b). In general, the neighborhood system used in image modeling is symmetrical and sequentially ordered. Also, the noncausal Markov chain is usually selected as 2-D image model in practice.

Each observed data $\mathbf{y}$ can be regarded as the noisy version of original data $\mathbf{x}$. In other words, $\mathbf{y} = \mathbf{x} + \mathbf{n}$, where $\mathbf{n}$ is a sample of a white Gaussian noise field with variance σ_n^2. The conditional probability density function of $\mathbf{x}$ given $\mathbf{y}$ is given by:

$$p(\mathbf{x} \mid \mathbf{y}) = \frac{1}{(2\pi\sigma_n^2)^{-MN/2}} \exp\{-\frac{1}{2\sigma_n^2}(\mathbf{y}-\mathbf{x})^T(\mathbf{y}-\mathbf{x})\} \tag{30}$$

The estimation problem is to obtain the original data $\mathbf{x}$ from the observed data $\mathbf{y}$.

As proposed by Jeng and Woods (Jeng 1991), the relationship of a pixel in a compound Gaussian Markov random field (CGMRF) and its neighborhood system is presented by the collection of binary variables $C_o = \{c^k_{m,n} : k = 1, 2, \cdots, 8; m = 1, 2, \cdots, M; n = 1, 2, \cdots, N\}$, where k is the same as the Figure 15 (b). If the neighbor pixels are independent, the associated $c^k_{m,}$ is set to be one and otherwise $c^k_{m,n}$ is equal to zero. Let $A(C_0)$ be the covariance matrix of $\mathbf{x}$, which depends on C_0. The estimation of original image $\mathbf{x}$ is obtained with observed $\mathbf{y}$ and the matrix $A(C_0)$, which should be estimated from the observed $\mathbf{y}$. In general, we have

$$p(\mathbf{x} \mid C_0, \mathbf{y}) \propto \frac{1}{\left(2\pi\sigma_n^2\right)^{-MN/2} * Z(C_0)} \exp\left\{-\frac{1}{2\sigma_x^2}\mathbf{x}^T A(C_0)\mathbf{x} - \frac{1}{2\sigma_n^2}(\mathbf{y}-\mathbf{x})^T I(\mathbf{y}-\mathbf{x})\right\} \tag{31}$$

where I is the identity matrix and $Z(C_0)$ is a normalizing constant called partition function (Jeng 1991). Maximizing the equation gives us the MAP estimate of $\mathbf{x}$

$$\hat{\mathbf{x}}_{MAP} = \left(\frac{\sigma_n^2}{\sigma_x^2} A(C_0) + I \right)^{-1} \mathbf{y} = \left(kA(C_0) + I \right)^{-1} \mathbf{y} \tag{32}$$

To apply this estimation of observed image, the matrix C_0 and the variance ratio k should be estimated with the observed data.

5	4	3	4	5
4	2	1	2	4
3	1	X	1	3
4	2	1	2	4
5	4	3	4	5

(a)

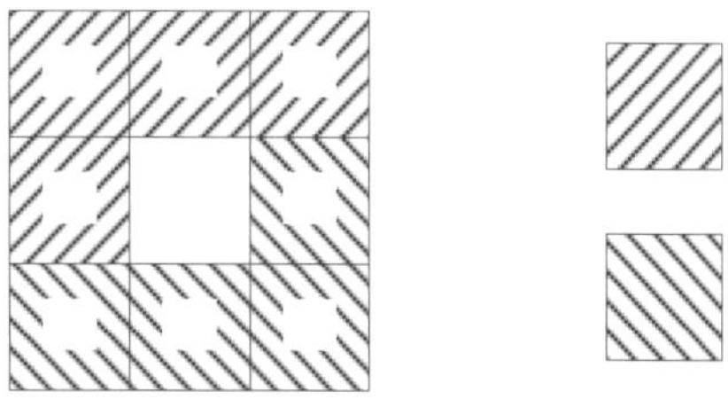

(b)

Fig. 15. The neighborhood system and its order (a) Ordered neighborhood system for MRF. The order of the model relative to x is indicated by numbers; (b) The second order neighborhood system

3.2 2-D Multivariate time series analysis

The remote sensing image data from SAR (Synthetic Aperture Radar), TM (Thermal Mapper) or other sensors can be described by time series image models. To analyze and segment the images, we need to consider the correlation between neighborhood image pixels rather than independent random variables as considered by many pattern recognition researchers. The SAR and TM remote sensing data are in multi-spectral format which consists of a stack of images. There are correlations between pixels in a single image as well as correlations among image slices. The univariate Autoregressive (AR) model is not enough to describe information extracted from multi-spectral satellite sensors. The 2-D Multivariate Vector AR time series model described in this section is aimed to solve this problem.

The multivariate time series data analysis model is a generalized form of univariate models. It is also called ARV (AutoRegressive Vector) model. Each time series observation is a vector containing multiple components.

$$\text{Let } X_i = [x_{1i}, x_{2i}, x_{3i}, ...x_{mi}]^T \qquad -\infty \le i \le \infty \tag{33}$$

$$X_i = W + \phi_1 X_{i-1} + \phi_2 X_{i-2} + ... + \phi_p X_{i-p} + \varepsilon_i \tag{34}$$

X_i : m-by-1 column vector, time series observation variable

ε_i : m-by-1 column vector, multivariate white noise

$\phi_k : k = 1,2,3,.....p$ m-by-m autoregressive parameter matrix

W : m-by-1 Constant Vector (deterministic DC term)

To estimate the Multivariate AR model Parameter Matrix, we need to adopt the least squares method.

Consider an m-dimensional time series and let the Parameter Matrix be

$$B = \begin{bmatrix} W \phi_1 & \phi_2 & .... & \phi_p \end{bmatrix} \tag{35}$$

$$\text{Define } U_v = \begin{bmatrix} 1 \\ X_{v-1} \\ X_{v-2} \\ \cdot \\ \cdot \\ X_{v-p} \end{bmatrix} \tag{36}$$

An AR(p) time series model can be expressed as the following regression model:

$$X_v = BU_v + \varepsilon_v \tag{37}$$

where $\varepsilon_v = noise$ vector with covariance matrix C $v = 1,2,.....n$ and n is the total number of samples.

Let

$$T = \sum_{v=1}^{n} U_v U_v^T \tag{38}$$

$$X = \sum_{v=1}^{n} X_v X_v^T \tag{39}$$

$$S = \sum_{v=1}^{n} X_v U_v^T \tag{40}$$

$$C = E(\varepsilon_v \varepsilon_v^T) \tag{41}$$

The Parameter Matrix $B = \begin{bmatrix} W \phi_1 & \phi_2 & .... & \phi_p \end{bmatrix}$ can be estimated as

$$\hat{B} = ST^{-1} \tag{42}$$

The error covariance matrix can be calculated as:

$$\hat{C} = \frac{1}{n - nf}(X - ST^{-1}S^T) \tag{43}$$

The matrix $\hat{C}$ can be factorized by Cholesky decomposition. The diagonal terms of this factorized Cholesky matrix are used as feature vector inputs to the pattern classifiers such as Support Vector Machine (SVM) or others.

$$\hat{C} = E^T E \tag{44}$$

where E is the upper triangular matrix.

Suppose E is an m-by-m upper triangular, lower triangular or diagonal matrix , the eigenvalues of E are the entries on the main diagonal of E. The eigenvalues of E matrix are the characteristics that E contains. The E matrix contains the major information of the estimated error covariance matrix $\hat{C}$.

The optimal estimated error covariance matrix $\hat{C}$ can be adopted to our remote sensing image classifier. When this optimal parameter matrix $\hat{B}$ is applied to the class that the data belongs, the total estimation errors are small, whereas when it is applied to any other class, the total estimation error would be much larger. Therefore, the differences in total estimation errors can be used in the classification process to distinguish among different remote sensing image classes.

4. Time series model segmentation adopted by international researchers

In this section, we like to present some evidences from international academic researchers to prove the effectiveness and efficiency out of time series models. Research scholars P. Steetal and N. Natarajan of IITM, Chennai-36 (Seetal 2010) was looking at rock fracture mapping problems that has applied to many issues related to rock mechanics. The difficult task was on fracture extraction from rock images. They found one interesting time series algorithm mathematically derived by P. Ho (Ho 2004). By using the first order autoregressive time series image segmentation model, they were able to apply and extract features on both rough and smooth fractures successfully as shown in figure 16 and figure 17. In Steetal and Natarajan computer experiments, three examples of rock fracture image segmentation results were processed by traditional edge detection methods such as Canny, Sobel and Prewitt as well as the newer time series models as described in this book chapter. The Seetal's proposed method is a minor modified version from Ho and Chen (Ho 2004). For the detailed image segmentation result comparisons, please refer to International Journal of Engineering Science and Technology Vol. 2(5), 2010 (Seetal 2010).

5. Conclusion

Image segmentation is one of the difficult tasks in image processing problems. The accuracy of the segmentation will determine a success or failure of the analysis. Therefore, decision making in the segmentation algorithm is very important. In this chapter we have established the innovative autoregressive time series model theory and presented many experimental results to support its image segmentation use. This image model indeed the effectively statistical approach to extract different properties for different objects.

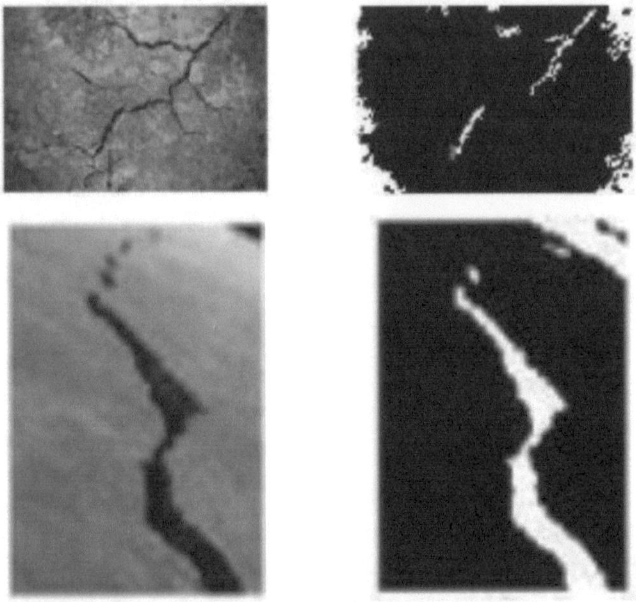

Fig. 16. Two sets of Rock fracture mapping image segmentation by AR time series model, original rock fractures are on the left column, processing results are on the right column ((Seetal 2010)

Fig. 17. Cameraman image segmentation results by AR time series methods, original Image is on the left, AR processing result is on the right (Seetal 2010)

6. References

Box, G. and Jenkins, G. *Time Series Analysis: Forecast and Control*, San Francisco, Holden-Day, 1970.

Bruzzone, L. and Prieto, D. *A Technique for The Selection Of Kernel Function Parameters in RBF neural Networks for Classification of Remote Sensing Images, IEEE Trans. Geosci. Remote Sensing,* Vol. 37, No.2, pp. 1179-1184, March 1999.

Bruzzone, L. *Advanced Methods for the Analysis of Multisensor and Multitemporal Remote-Sensing Images,* PhD dissertation 1998, Electronics and Computer Science, Univeristy of Genova, Italy.

Chapra, S. Canale, R. *Numerical Methods for Engineers with Software and Programming Applications,* 4th edition, McGraw Hill 2002.

Chen, C. editor, *Information Processing for Remote Sensing,* World Scientific 1999, pp. 12-13

Chen, C. and Ho, P. *On the ARMA model based Region Growing method for extracting lake region in a Remote Sensing image,* on *Proceedings of SPIE,* Vol. 5238, Paper No. 5238-13, September 8-12, 2003, Barcelona, Spain.

Chen, H. *Remote Sensing Data Unsupervised Classification Using Gauss-Markov Random Fields and PCA,* MS thesis 2002 ECE University of Massachusetts at Dartmouth.

Cheney W. and Kincaid, D. *Numerical Mathematics and Computing,* 4th edition, Publisher: Gary W. Ostedt Book 1999.

Geman S., Geman D., *Stochastic relaxation, Gibbs distribution, and the Bayesian restoration of images,* IEEE Trans. Pattern Anal. Machine Intell., 6 (6) (1984) 721- 741.

Glantz S. *Primer of Biostatistics,* 5th edition, McGraw-Hill 2002.

Gonzalez Rafael C., Woods Richard E. and Eddins Steven L. *Digital Image Processing using Matlab,* Pearson Prentice Hall, 2004.

Gröger J. P., R. A. Rountree, U. H. Thygesen, D. Jones, D. Martins, Q. Xu and B. Rothschild. *Geolocation of Atlantic cod, Gadus morhua, movements in the Gulf of Maine using tidal information.* Fisheries Oceanography, 2007.

Haykin Simon and Widrow Bernard, *Least-Mean-Square Adaptive Filters,* Wiley and Sons, 2003.

Haralick R.M. and Shapiro L.G. *Computer and Robot Vision* Vol.1 1992.

Ho, P. *Multivariate time series model based support vector machine for multiclass remote sensing image classification and region segmentation,* Ph.D dissertation, Univ. of Massachusetts Dartmouth, Jan. 2008.

Ho, Pei-Gee Peter and Chen C. H., *Time Series Model Based Region Growing Method for Image Segmentation in Remote Sensing Images,* IEEE 2004 International Geoscience and Remote Sensing Symposium, Alaska.

Ho, Pei-Gee Peter, Chen C.H., *2-D Time Series Model Based Support Vector Machine for Remote Sensing Image Segmentation.* Proceedings of International Joint Conference on Neural Networks (IJCNN) paper No.1095, Aug. 12-17, 2007.

Jeng F. C., Woods J. W., *Compound Gauss-Markov random fields for image estimation,* IEEE Trans. on Signal Processing, 39 (.3) (1991) 683-697.

Moler, C. *Numerical Computating with Matlab,* Chapter 10, SIAM 2004 .

Papoulis A. and Pillai S.U., *Probability, Random Variables and Stochastic Processes,* 4th edition, McGraw-Hill 2002.

Prieto, D. *Automatic Analysis of Multisource and Multitemporal Remote-Sensing Data for Land-Cover Monitoring Application,* Ph.D Thesis, University of Genova, 2000.

Serpico S. and Roli, F. *Classification of Multisensor Remote Sensing Images by Structured Neural Netorks,* IEEE Transactions on Geoscience and Remote Sensing, Vol 33, No.3, pp. 562-578, May 1995.

Seetal, P. and Natarajan, N. *Image Segmentation for rock fractures based on ARMA Model*, International Journal of Engineering Science and Technology Vol. 2(5), 2010, pp. 1155-1159.

Seber, G., *Linear Regression Analysis*, PP. 330-334, John Wiley & Sons, 1977.

Shumway Robert H., Stoffer David S., *Time Series Analysis and Its Application*, Springer-Verlag, 2000.

Tilton J.C. and Lawrence W.T., *Interactive Analysis of hierarchical image segmentation*, Proceesings of the IEEE IGARSS 2000.

Wei William W. S., *Time Series Analysis, Univariate and Multivariate Method*, Addison-Wesley, 1990.

10

Evolutionary-based Image Segmentation Methods

Licheng Jiao
Xidian University, Xi'an,
China

1. Introduction

Nearly 72 years ago, Wertheimer [1] pointed out the importance of perceptual grouping and organization in vision and listed several key factors, such as similarity, proximity, and good continuation, which lead to visual grouping. However, even to this day, many of the computational issues of perceptual grouping have remained unresolved. Since there are many possible partitions of an image into subsets, how do you know which one is right? There are two aspects to be considered here. The first is that there may not be a single correct answer. The second aspect is that the partitioning is inherently hierarchical. Prior literature on the related problems of clustering, grouping and image segmentation is huge. Unfortunately, there is not a general method existing to solve the problem.[2]

Image segmentation is one of the central problems in computer vision and pattern recognition. It refers to the process of assigning a label to every pixel in an image such that pixels with the same label share certain visual characteristics. The result of image segmentation is a set of segments (sets of pixels) that collectively cover the entire image. Pixels in the same region are similar with respect to some characteristics or computed properties, such as color, intensity, and texture. Adjacent regions are significantly different with respect to the same characteristics. The goal of segmentation is to simplify and/or change the representation of an image into something that is more meaningful and easier to analyze.[3]

There are many general-purpose approaches available for image segmentation such as threshold methods[4], edge-based methods[5], region-based methods[6], and graph-based methods[7]. Threshold techniques make decisions based on local pixel information. Edge-based methods are based on connecting together broken contour lines. It is prone to failure in the presence of blurring. A region-based method usually partitions an image into connected regions by grouping neighboring pixels of similar intensity levels. Adjacent regions are then merged under some characteristics. Graph-based techniques generally represent the problem in terms of a graph where each node corresponds to a pixel in the image, and an edge connects each pair of vertices. A weight is associated with each edge based on some property of the pixels that it connects, such as their image intensities. Hybrid techniques using a mix of the methods above are also popular.

What listed above also exposed two basic questions:

- What is the precise criterion for a good segmentation?
- How can such a segmentation be computed efficiently?

In contrast to the heuristic nature of the methods above, one would formalize an objective criterion for evaluating a given segmentation. This would allow us to formulate the segmentation problem as an optimization problem. The objective function that one would seek to optimize is the interclass variance that is used in cluster analysis. An optimizer can lead to efficient solutions for optimal segmentation. But the objective function is usually not a monotone chain, therefore the problem is general NP-hard. Following this way, some clustering methods have been applied to solve image segmentation problems. Among them, K-means algorithm [8] is the most popular and simplest one. It can partition an image into K clusters by using an iterative technique. Although it can be proven that the procedure will always terminate, the K-means algorithm does not necessarily find the most optimal configuration, corresponding to the minimum global objective function. The algorithm is also significantly sensitive to the initial randomly-selected cluster centers. As global optimization techniques, evolutionary algorithms (EAs) are likely to be good tools for image segmentation task. In the past two decades, EAs have been applied to image segmentation with promising results [9-16]. These algorithms exploited the metaphor of natural evolution in the context of image segmentation.

In this chapter, in order to solve the image segmentation problem more efficiently, we propose two evolutionary-bsed image segmentation algorithms with different objective functions.The first is a novel approach based on memetic algorithm (MISA). Watershed segmentation is applied to segment original images into non-overlap small regions before performing the portioning process by MISA. MISA adopts a straightforward representation method to find the optimal combination of watershed regions under the criteria of interclass variance in feature space. After implementing cluster-based crossover and mutation, an individual learning procedure moves exocentric regions in current cluster to the one they should belong to according to the distance between these regions and cluster centers in feature space. In order to evaluate the new algorithm, six texture images, three remote sensing images and three natural images are employed in experiments. The experimental results show that MISA outperforms its genetic version, the Fuzzy c-means algorithm, and K-means algorithm in partitioning most of the test problems, and is an effective approach when compared with two state-of-the-art image segmentation algorithms including an efficient graph-based algorithm and a spectral clustering ensemble-based algorithm. The second is manifold evolutionary clustering (MEC). In MEC, the clustering problem is considered from a combinatorial optimization viewpoint. Each individual is a sequence of real integer numbers representing the cluster representatives. Each data item is assigned to a cluster representative according to a novel manifold distance-based dissimilarity measure which can measure the geodesic distance along the manifold. After extracting texture features from an image, MEC determines partitioning of the feature vectors using evolutionary search. We apply MEC to solve seven benchmark clustering problems of artificial data sets, three artificial texture image classification problems and two Synthetic Aperture Radar image classification problems. The experimental results show that in terms of cluster quality and robustness, MEC outperforms the K-Means algorithm, a modified K-Means algorithm using the manifold distance-based dissimilarity measure, and a genetic algorithm-based clustering technique in partitioning most of the test problems.

In the following sections, we will give the descriptions for the two algorithms in detail. Finally, concluding remarks are presented.

2. Natural and remote sensing image segmentation using memetic computing

2.1 Introduction

This work focuses on image segmentation based on memetic computation. Memetic algorithms (MAs) are one of the recent growing areas in evolutionary computation [17]. They are now widely considered as population-based metaheuristic search approaches which may be regarded as a marriage between an evolutionary or any population-based global search and local improvement procedures. Recently, MAs have been well used across a wide range of problem domains. A lot of studies have demonstrated that MAs converge to high-quality solutions more efficiently than their conventional counterparts in many real-world applications [17-32]. MAs have also been applied in the image processing field [33-38]. For example, Fernandez, Garana and Cabello [33] proposed a MA-based method for the correction of illumination inhomogeneities in images. Batenburg [34] designed an EA with hillclimb operator for finding a binary image that satisfies prescribed horizontal and vertical projections. Tirronen, Neri et al. [35] studied the defect detection in paper production by means of image-processing techniques based on memetic differential evolution frameworks. Gesù, Bosco et al. [36,37] introduced a new memetic approach for the reconstruction of binary images. Zhang, Wang and Zhang [38] proposed a novel image watermarking scheme using a MA and wavelet transform.

In this method, in order to solve the image segmentation problem more efficiently, we propose a MA-based approach, Memetic Image Segmentation Algorithm (MISA), and compare the new method with its genetic version (MISA without learning), the K-means algorithm [8], fuzzy c-means algorithm [39], and two state-of-the-art image segmentation algorithms including an efficient graph-based algorithm [7] and a spectral clustering ensemble-based algorithm [40] in segmenting artificial texture images, remote sensing images and natural images.

The rest of this section is organized as follows: Section 1.2 describes some related background including the technologies used in preprocessing the original image and the brief background of MAs. Section 1.3 describes the proposed MA-based image segmentation algorithm. In Section 1.4, we summarize and evaluate the experimental results.

2.2 Related background

Before performing the portioning process by the proposed MISA, some preprocessing should be done on original images, including feature extraction based on the gray-level co-occurrence matrix (GLCM) [41] and wavelet decomposition [42], and over segmenting object images into small regions by watershed segmentation algorithm [6]. In this section, we will introduce these techniques briefly. The MAs will also be introduced in this section.

2.2.1 GLCM based statistic features

GLCM was frequently used in texture analysis and extraction for images [41,43,44]. Texture features are demonstrated by the statistics over the GLCM. Four usually used statistics are angular second moment (also called energy), correlation, entropy, and inverse difference moment (also called inertia). In this method, the 14 statistics, including the previous four suggested by Haralick, Shanmugam and Dinstein [41] are exploited. There are four parameters that must be indicated to generate a GLCM, i.e., the interpixel orientation, distance, grey level quantization, and window size. Here we set the interpixel orientation to $0°$ for convenient calculation. Short interpixel distances typically generate the preferred texture features in image analysis, so we set interpixel distance to 1. The role of different values for gray levels and windows size with respect to statistics from GLCM has been investigated in many literatures [43, 44]. According to their analysis and fine-tuned experiments, in this study, we set the image quantization to 16 and the window size to 9×9 .

2.2.2 Wavelet energy features

Wavelet transform has the ability to examine a signal at different scales [42]. In this section, the undecimated wavelet-based feature vector composed by the energies of the subband coefficients is used. Here we implement three-level wavelet decomposition on each square local area with size of 16×16 . The features of each pixel can be represented as a 10-dimension vector $(e_{LL-1}, e_{LH-1}, e_{HL-1}, e_{HH-1}, e_{LH-2}, e_{HL-2}, e_{HH-2}, e_{LH-3}, e_{HL-3}, e_{HH-3})$, in which, for example e_{LL-1} denotes the energy of the LL subimage in the first level. Wavelet transform generates localized spatial and spectral information simultaneously. The energy of the low-pass subimage e_{LL-1} describes the spectral information. The other features except e_{LL-1} characterize the textural properties. Incorporating all the features will enhance the performance.

2.2.3 Watershed segmentation

We use watershed segmentation [6] to over segment object image into small regions. Each region is almost homogeneous in feature space, while neighboring-regions possess different characters. We operate these regions as a basic unit during most of MISA unless it is necessary to come back to pixels for precise evaluation. The basic concept of watershed segmentation is described as follows.

In an image, ideal step edges do not often exist since every edge is blurred to some contents. A blurred edge can be modeled by a ramp. For a ramp edge, a usual gradient operator will generate a slope of the edge. Thus, the ramp edge cannot be separated from noise if the slope of the edge is small. Wang proposed a multi-scale gradient operator to solve the above problem [45]:

$$MG(f) = \frac{1}{n}\sum_{i=1}^{n}\left[\left((f \oplus B_i) - (f \Theta B_i)\Theta B_{i-1}\right)\right] \tag{1}$$

where $\oplus$ and Θ denote dilation and erosion respectively, and B_i is called structural element of size $(2i-1)\times(2i-1)$, and f is the original image.

If watershed regions are too large, big ones may contain more than one focused subject in image, so that the texture feature in that region may not be homogeneous. If the watershed regions are too small, the computational complexity will increase. This is because there will be more basic units to operate during most of MISA. In order to control the number of watershed regions, we use the watershed segmentation algorithm with markers [6]. In this method, a threshold can be adjusted to get an expected number of regions. In this method, the number of regions is about 1500 in a 256×256 image.

2.2.4 Memetic algorithms

Evolutionary algorithms perform well for global searching because they are capable of quickly finding and exploiting promising regions of search space, but they take a relatively long time to converge to a local optimum. Local improvement procedures quickly find the local optimum of a small region of the search space, but are typically poor global searchers. Thus, several researchers proposed hybrid algorithms combining excellent global exploration characteristics of EAs and efficient refinement capabilities of local search algorithms [46,47]. These hybrid algorithms are known as memetic algorithms (MAs).

MAs assume that combining the features of different methods in a complementary fashion may result in more robust and effective optimization tools. They are population-based meta-heuristic search approaches that have been receiving increasing attention in recent years. They are inspired by Darwinian's principles of natural evolution and Dawkins' notion of a meme defined as the basic unit of cultural transmission. In MAs, a meme is generally considered as an individual learning procedure capable of performing local refinements. Over the past 15 years, MAs have been a hot topic in the fields of both computer science and operational research [17-38]. The typical issues pertinent to MA design [17] include (i) how often individual learning should be applied, (ii) on which solutions individual learning should be used, (iii) how long individual learning should be run, (iv) what maximum computational budget to allocate for individual learning, and (v) what individual learning method or meme should be used for a particular problem, sub-problem or individual.

2.3 The proposed memetic algorithm for image segmentation

2.3.1 Preprocessing and representation

Preprocessing is the first step of our method. In this procedure, we use gray-level co-occurrence matrix and wavelet decomposition for feature extraction of object images. This is done for every pixel in the object image. Some algorithms (such as [15]) operate pixels directly as basic units, which will lead to high computational cost, especially for large images. To reduce the computational complexity, we employ watershed segmentation to segment images into non-overlap small regions. MISA operates these regions instead of every pixel as the basic unit during most of its evolution unless it is necessary to return back to pixels for more precise computation in fitness calculation, learning and crossover operations. Fig.1 illustrates the watershed segmentation process.

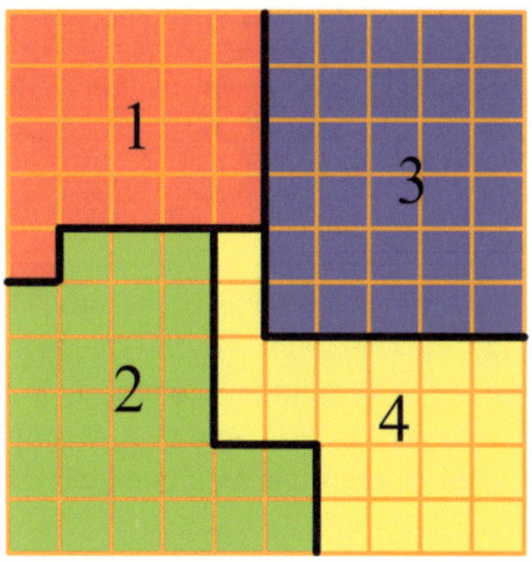

Fig. 1. Illustration of watershed segmentation

In Fig.1, there is an example of an image of 10×10 pixels with each small square divided by the orange lines representing a pixel. We can see that this image contains 4 regions marked by different colors as red, blue, yellow, and green. The watershed segmentation will segment the image into four regions divided by the black boldface lines. Then, these four regions are the basic unit that we operate during most of MISA.

After preprocessing, we get the following data from the object image: (i) feature matrix, which stores the features of each pixel and is used in initialization with minimum spanning tree, learning and fitness calculation; (ii) coordinate of pixels, which are used in fitness calculation; (iii) pixel number of each region, which is used in learning; (iv) dissimilarity matrix, which is used in initialization with minimum spanning tree.

Many EC-based clustering algorithms [48-51] have used an indirect representation approach that borrows from the K-Means algorithm - the representation codes are for cluster center only, and each data item is subsequently assigned to a cluster representative according to an appointed dissimilarity measure. The most popular dissimilarity measure is the Euclidean distance. By using Euclidean distance as a measure of dissimilarity, these evolutionary clustering methods as well as the K-Means algorithm have good performance on the data set with compact super-sphere distribution, but tend to fail on the data set organized in more complex and unknown shapes. This indirect representation approach can not overcome the main drawback of the K-means algorithm unless a more flexible dissimilarity measure is adopted [15]. Furthermore, this indirect representation approach is not suitable for individual evolutionary and learning operation. In this study, a straightforward encoding method is used here for image segmentation problem. In this coding, every locus represents the corresponding region in the image, and the gene on each locus is the cluster label of the corresponding region.

In our method, coding length (CL) in MISA is the number of regions obtained from watershed segmentation of the object image. The serial labels of locus present the corresponding regions in image, that means the i-th locus represents the i-th regions. The segmentation of an image is expressed by encoding individual with cluster labels of regions. Cluster label of each region is put on its corresponding locus as the gene. Fig. 2 illustrates this code structure.

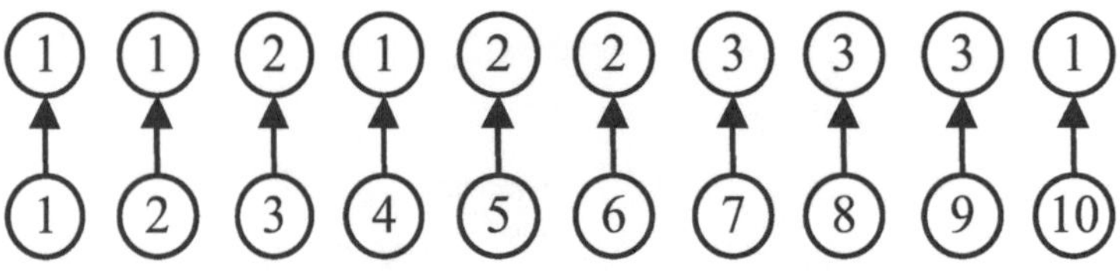

Fig. 2. Illustration of coding structure

Here we exhibit the code of an image which owns 10 regions. The lower numbers denote the region labels. They are arranged in order from 1 to 10. The upper numbers are cluster labels corresponding to each region. In this individual, regions 1, 2, 4 and 10 belong to cluster 1, regions 3, 5 and 6 belong to cluster 2, and regions 7, 8 and 9 belong to cluster 3. This straightforward representation method is very convenient for evolutionary and learning operation as shown in Section 3.2.

In order to guide the evolution to a meaningful direction related to optimal segmentation, Euclid distances in feature space between every pixel and the centroids of the cluster it belongs to are calculated. Then, we sum up all these distances and use the reciprocal of this summation as the fitness of MISA. This segmentation fitness is defined in Equation (2).

$$fitness = \frac{1}{\sum_{i=1}^{CN}\sum_{j=1}^{RN_i}\sum_{k=1}^{PN_j} dis(p_{ijk}, m_i)} \tag{2}$$

where RN_i is the number of regions in the i-th cluster, PN_j is the number of pixels in the j-th region, p_{ijk} denotes the k-th pixel in the j-th region of the i-th cluster, and m_i is the centroid of all pixels of the i-th cluster in feature space. Although we operate watershed regions of image during most of the evolution, it is necessary to return to every pixel, so that we can get a more precise segmentation evaluation. In Equation (2),

$$dis(p_{ijk}, m_i) = \sqrt{\sum_{g=1}^{FN}\left(p_{ijk_g} - m_{i_g}\right)^2} \tag{3}$$

FN is the number of features and p_{ijk_g} and m_{i_g} denote the g-th feature of the current pixel and cluster centroid respectively. Therefore, the aim of MISA is to find an individual with maximum fitness.

2.3.2 Memetic image segmentation algorithm

The main loop of MISA is as follows.

Algorithm 1.1. Memetic Image Segmentation Algorithm (MISA)

Step 1. Preprocessing. Feature extraction based on GLCM and wavelet decomposition, and over segmenting object image into non-overlapping small regions by watershed segmentation.

Step 2. Initialization. Giving the termination criterion, setting the initial parameters, generating a diverse population.

Step 3. Crossover and Mutation. A cluster-based crossover operator and random mutation operator are implemented in this step.

Step 4. Learning. A supervised local searching strategy is used to improve some individuals with probability.

Step 5. Evaluation and Selection. Tournament selection with elitism strategy is used after fitness calculation.

Step 6. Termination Test: If termination criterion is satisfied, export the individual with the highest fitness and return the corresponding image segmentation result, stop the algorithm; otherwise, go to **Step 3**.

2.3.2.1 Initialization

The following parameters have to be set in this step: population size (*PS*), the proportion of initial individuals generated using minimum spanning tree (*MSTP*), crossover probability (*CP*), mutation probability (*MP*), learning intensity (*LI*), and cluster number (*CN*). The termination criterion is to run until the number of generations reaches the maximum value (*Gmax*).

The initial population is generated by two different methods to get a diverse population. Some initial individuals are generated based on minimum spanning tree (MST), and the others are generated randomly. The details are as follows:

$\lceil MSTP \times PS \rceil$ individuals are generated based on minimum spanning tree (MST). The idea of MST is introduced to find a meaningful distribution of all regions. Dissimilarity matrix from preprocessing is used to build a complete MST by Prim's algorithm. In dissimilarity matrix, the number of the *i*-th row and the *j*-th column represents the dissimilarity degree of the *i*-th region to the *j*-th region. The smaller of the number is, the closer between the *i*-th region and the *j*-th region. Here the dissimilarity degree between the *i*-th region r_i and the *j*-th region r_j is calculated in Equation (4).

$$Dissimilarity\left(r_i,r_j\right)=\sqrt{\sum_{k=1}^{FN}\left(r_{i_k}-r_{i_k}\right)^2} \tag{4}$$

Here FN is the number of features and r_{i_k} and r_{i_k} are the value of the *k*-th feature of r_i and r_j.

Based on MST, we break up links selected randomly to produce individuals. The whole MST represents one cluster which includes all the regions in the image; and removing n links leads to n more clusters. Breaking up different links will produce different distribution among clusters. Fig. 3 and 4 show this procedure with dissimilarity matrix given in Table 1.

Region No.	1	2	3	4	5	6	7	8	9	10
1	Inf	0.7	4.67	0.69	4.73	4.72	4.63	2.56	2.44	2.46
2	0.7	Inf	4.42	0.58	4.53	4.52	4.33	2.28	2.25	2.21
3	4.67	4.42	Inf	4.63	0.53	0.67	6.27	4.79	5.29	4.99
4	0.69	0.58	4.63	Inf	4.75	4.77	4.58	2.5	2.45	2.31
5	4.73	4.53	0.53	4.75	Inf	0.29	6.17	4.76	5.25	4.98
6	4.72	4.52	0.67	4.77	0.29	Inf	6.19	4.78	5.26	5.03
7	4.63	4.33	6.27	4.58	6.17	6.19	Inf	2.16	2.22	2.41
8	2.56	2.28	4.79	2.5	4.76	4.78	2.16	Inf	0.64	0.52
9	2.44	2.25	5.29	2.45	5.25	5.26	2.22	0.64	Inf	0.73
10	2.46	2.21	4.99	2.31	4.98	5.03	2.41	0.52	0.73	Inf

Table 1. An example of dissimilarity matrix

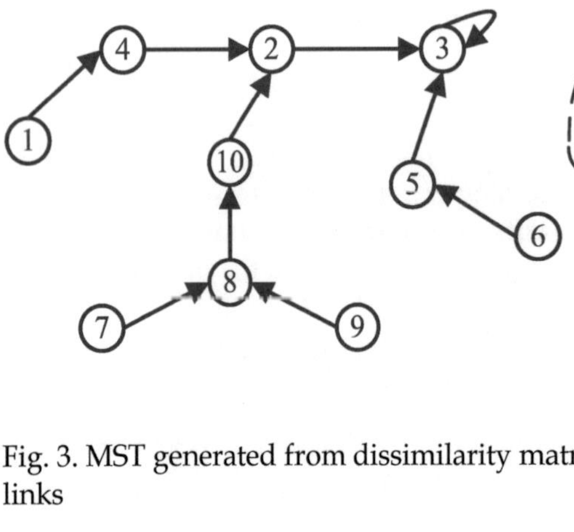

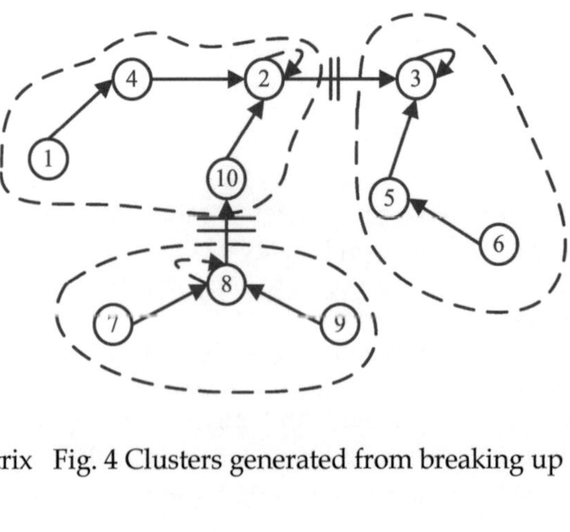

Fig. 3. MST generated from dissimilarity matrix Fig. 4 Clusters generated from breaking up links

Based on dissimilarity matrix shown in Table 1, we can get a Prim MST starting from region 3, which is illustrated in Fig. 3. If we break up the links between 2 and 3, 8 and 10, we can get a cluster distribution as $\{1,2,4,10\}$, $\{3,5,6\}$ and $\{7,8,9\}$, as shown in Fig. 4.

The rest $PS - \lceil MSTP \times PS \rceil$ individuals are generated randomly, namely, for each locus and we put a random cluster label ranges from 1 to CN as its gene.

2.3.2.2 Crossover and Mutation

Based on the meaning of crossover that children should get part of the information from parents, we create a novel crossover operator, called cluster-based crossover (CC). In this algorithm, the role of crossover is to change the cluster distribution of one parent individual by the cluster distribution information of the other parent individual. To make the crossover meaningful for segmentation, we try to cross corresponding clusters of two parents, individuals A and B. For example, we divide an image into three clusters, where A is composed of clusters α_1, α_2, α_3 and B is composed of clusters β_1, β_2, β_3. Here $\alpha_1 = \{a_x \mid a_x \in \text{cluster 1}\}$, $\alpha_2 = \{a_y \mid a_y \in \text{cluster 2}\}$, $\alpha_3 = \{a_z \mid a_z \in \text{cluster 3}\}$, $\beta_1 = \{b_x \mid b_x \in \text{cluster 1}\}$, $\beta_2 = \{b_y \mid b_y \in \text{cluster 2}\}$, $\beta_3 = \{b_z \mid b_z \in \text{cluster 3}\}$, ($x \in (1,CL)$, $y \in (1,CL)$, $z \in (1,CL), x \neq y \neq z$). First, mean values of every feature of each pixel in each cluster are calculated. Then, the modulus values of these mean values for each cluster are sorted from small to large. This calculation is similar to Equation (4) in section 3.2.1. For example, if the orders of clusters in A and B are $\alpha_2\alpha_1\alpha_3$ and $\beta_3\beta_2\beta_1$ respectively, then, α_2 will be crossed with β_3, α_1 with β_2, and α_3 with β_1. This idea is similar to multi-point crossover. The number of 'points' equals to the number of clusters. For convenient operation, we re-label $\alpha_2\alpha_1\alpha_3$ and $\beta_3\beta_2\beta_1$ as $\alpha_1\alpha_2\alpha_3$ and $\beta_1\beta_2\beta_3$ respectively, without removing regions of any cluster.

Two individuals are chosen from the population randomly, and then the corresponding clusters between them are fixed and then crossed as mentioned above. The detailed steps are described as follows, where nc is the number of regions to be "crossed" in current cluster and α_{i_j} denotes the *j*-th region in cluster α_i and *CN* denotes the cluster number.

Algorithm 1.2. Cluster-based Crossover (CC)

Crossover: A **cross** B

Step 1. Set $i = 1$

Step 2. If $i \leq CN$, go to **Step 3**, otherwise, **stop**

Step 3. Set $nc =$ random number from 1 to the size of the i -th cluster in A.

Step 4. Select nc regions randomly from the i -th cluster of A, set $j = 1$.

Step 5. If α_{i_j} does not exist in β_i, then put i on the a_{i_j} -th gene of B

Step 6. $j = j + 1$, if $j \leq nc$ go to **Step 5**, otherwise, $i = i + 1$, go to **Step 2**.

In CC, A crosses B and B crosses A, producing two children. Both of them inherit parts of the information from the two parents. We illustrate CC in Fig. 5.

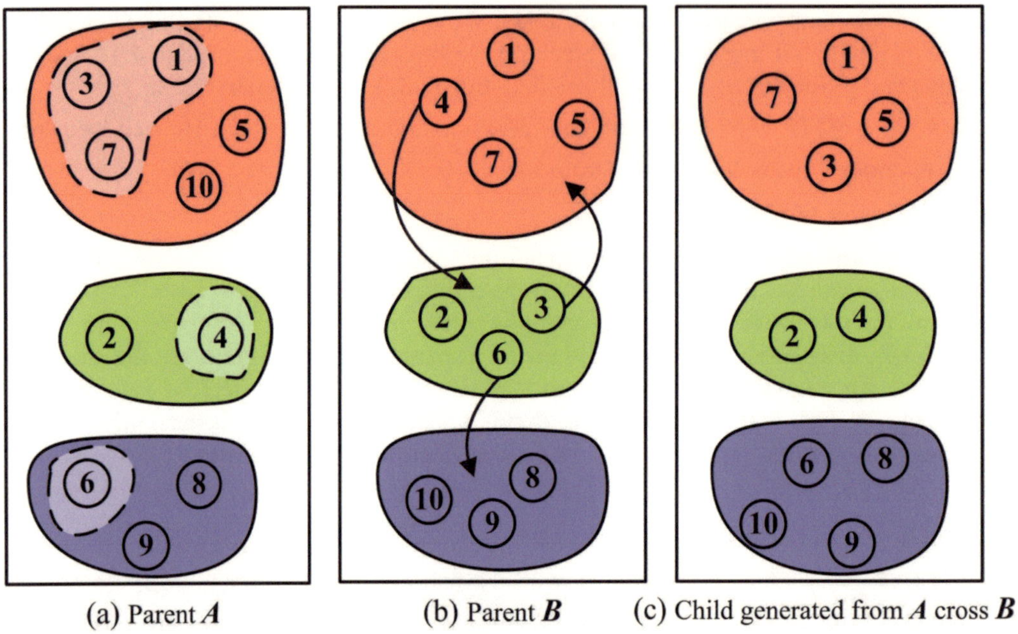

Fig. 5. An illustration of cluster-based crossover

Fig. 5 shows that in individual *A*, the cluster 1 to 3 are $\{1,3,7,5,10\}$, $\{2,4\}$, and $\{6,8,9\}$, respectively. In individual *B*, the cluster distribution is $\{1,4,5,7\}$, $\{2,3,6\}$ and $\{8,9,10\}$. For example, we begin by selecting 3 regions in cluster 1 of *A*, which is $\{1,3,7\}$ with light red shadow. In individual *B*, region 1 and 7 are in cluster 1, but region 3 exists in cluster 2, so we move region 3 from cluster 2 to cluster 1. In the same way, after all the same procedures are applied on the rest clusters, we get the child individual illustrated in Fig.5(c).

In the mutation phase, we change the cluster distribution randomly as follows, where *A* denotes an individual, A_j is the *j*-th gene of *A*. *MP* denotes mutation probability, *CN* denotes the cluster number, and *CL* denotes coding length.

Algorithm 1.3. Mutation

Step 1. Set $j = 1$

Step 2. If $j \le CL$, set r = a random number range from 0 to 1, $i = A_j$, go to **Step 3**; Otherwise, **stop**

Step 3. If $r < MP$, set l = a random number range from 1 to $CN \wedge l \ne i$.

Step 4. $A_j = l$, $j = j + 1$, go to **Step 2**.

In mutation, if a gene should be mutated due to probability, it will change into another cluster number generated randomly. This means the region corresponding to this locus will be moved into another cluster.

2.3.2.3 Individual Learning Method

Within the computational intelligence community, research on MA has since grown significantly and the term has come to be associated with the pairing of meta-heuristics or population-based methodologies with a separate lifetime learning process that materializes in various forms of individual learning methods or memes, which are generally regarded as lifetime learning procedures capable of generating refinement on given individual(s). [32] In MISA, we introduce an individual learning method based on cluster distribution as is described in Algorithm 1.4. The basic idea is firstly, identify the most distinct region in each cluster. Then, for each of these regions, we find the cluster with the most similar average feature values, and assign the region to this cluster. In Algorithm 1.4, AG_i is the average feature values of the *i*-th cluster and AG_{im_i} is the average feature values of the m_i -th region in the *i*-th cluster where *PS* denotes population size, *CN* denotes the cluster number, *LI* denotes learning intensity, and *CL* denotes coding length.

Algorithm 1.4. Individual Learning

Step 1. Set $a = 1$

Step 2. If $a \le PS$, go to **Step3**, otherwise **stop.**

Step 3. For the a-th individual in population, r is a random number from 0 to 1, if $r > 0.5$, go to **Step4**, otherwise, $a = a + 1$, go to **Step3**.

Step 4. Set $c = 1$.

Step 5. For $1 \le i \le CN$, find m_i =arg max $\left\| AG_i - AG_{im_i} \right\|_2$.

Step 6. For $1 \le i \le CN$, move the m_i -th region to cluster j = arg min $\left\| AG_j - AG_{im_i} \right\|_2$. If $i = j$, that means the m_i -th region doesn't need to be moved.

Step 7. $c = c + 1$. If $c \le \lfloor LI \times CL \rfloor$, go to **Step 5**, otherwise, $a = a + 1$, go to **Step 2**.

For more precise evaluation, we return back to pixels to calculate AG_i instead of using the average feature values of each region in cluster i directly, which is shown in Equation (5). As described above, AG_i is a vector that comprises *FN* features.

$$AG_i = \frac{\sum_{j=1}^{RN_i} \sum_{k=1}^{PN_j} p_{ijk}}{\sum_{j=1}^{RN_i} PN_j} \tag{5}$$

where RN_i is the number of regions in the *i*-th cluster, PN_j is the number of pixels in the *j*-th region, p_{ijk} denotes the feature vector of the *k*-th pixel in the *j*-th region of the *i*-th cluster, defined as Equation (6).

$$p_{ijk} = \left(p_{ijk_1}, p_{ijk_2}, \ldots, p_{ijk_{FN}} \right) \tag{6}$$

Fig. 6 illustrates an example of the individual learning procedure.

In Fig. 6, $\{1,2,3,4,5\}$, $\{6,7,8,9,10,11\}$ and $\{12,13,14,15,16\}$ demonstrate the three clusters before learning, we label them as cluster1, cluster2 and cluster3, respectively. After the calculation shown in Step 5 and Step 6 of Algorithm 1.4, region 4, 8 and 12 are shown to be the most distinct regions of each cluster. And cluster3, cluster1, and cluster2 are the ones with most similar features for region 4, 8 and 12 respectively. Therefore, the learning processing will remove region 4, 8 and 12 to cluster3, cluster1 and cluster2 respectively.

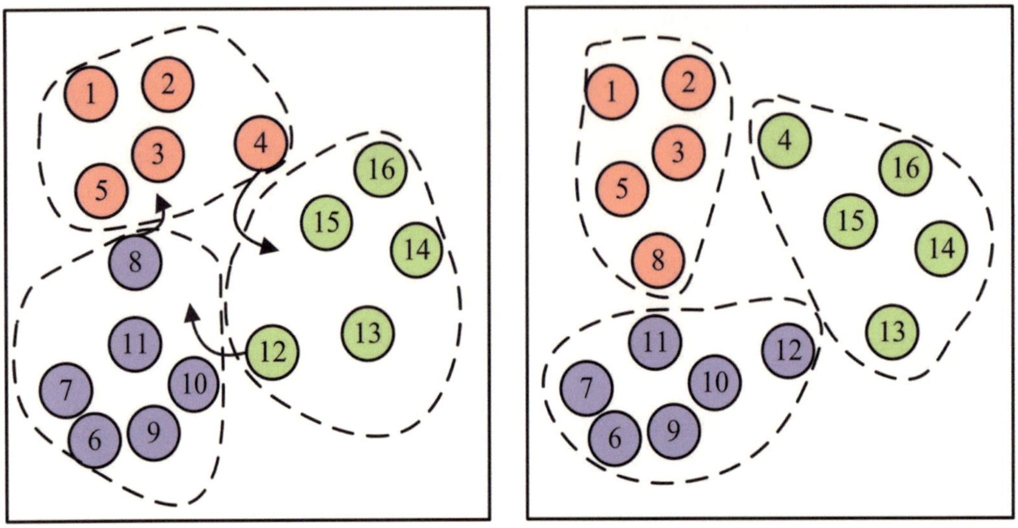

(a) Before learning (b) After learning

Fig. 6. Illustration of an example of the individual learning procedure

From the description above, we can see that half of the whole population is selected randomly each time to learn. For each individual in learning, $\lfloor LI \times CL \rfloor$ regions are detected. LI should be adjusted properly as if it is too small, the learning's effect is not enough. However, it is also unnecessary to set the LI too big. This is because learning is a local searching strategy so when it comes to the local optimum, the following learning will not change any cluster, which makes it meaningless and a waste of the computation.

2.4 Experimental study

2.4.1 Experimental setup

In order to validate the performance of MISA, we apply it to twelve image segmentation problems including six artificial texture images, three remote sensing images and three natural images. The results will be compared with the K-means algorithm (KM) [8], Fuzzy c-means algorithm (FCM) [39], the genetic image segmentation algorithm (GISA, MISA without learning), and two state-of-the-art image segmentation algorithms including an efficient graph-based image segmentation algorithm (EGSA) [7] and the spectral clustering ensemble algorithm (SCEA) [40].

Based on the parameter sensitivity analysis (as described in Section 1.4.5), for MISA, the parameters are set as follows: The maximum number of generations is 50, population size is 30, MST initialization proportion is 0.6, crossover probability is 0.8, mutation probability is 0.005, and learning intensity is 0.5. For GISA, the parameters are set as follows: The maximum number of generations is 200, population size is 30, MST initialization proportion is 0.6, crossover probability is 0.8, and mutation probability is 0.005. Under these parameter settings, the computational costs of MISA and GISA are about equivalent. For KM and FCM, the maximum iterative number is set to 500, and the stop threshold is 10^{-10}. The software of EGSA is downloaded directly from the author's homepage (http://people.cs.uchicago.edu/~pff/segment/). SCEA was proposed by us in 2008. We will perform it under the tuned parameters. Here 30 component spectral clustering with Nyström method are combined, and 100 regions are sampled in each component spectral clustering algorithm. The scaling parameter for each component is randomly selected from the interval [3, 12].

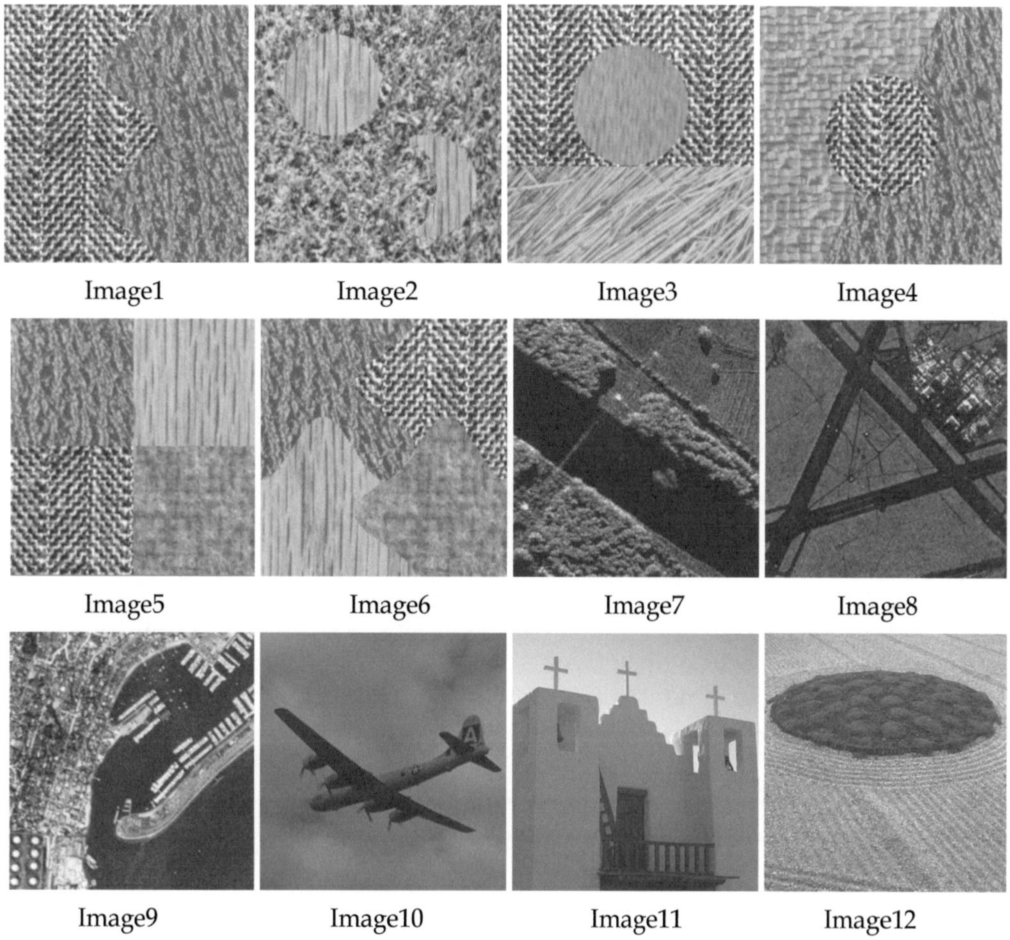

Fig. 7. The original images used in this study

The original images are shown in Fig. 7. Image1 to Image6 are artificial texture images with the size of 256×256 from the Brodatz texture images [52]. Their standard classification images are shown in Fig. 8. Image7 to Image9 are remote sensing images. Image7 is a Ku-band SAR image of the Rio Grande River nearby Albuquerue, New Mexico, USA. Image8 is a Ku-band image of the China Lake Airport, California, USA. Image9 is an optical remote sensing image of Shelter Island, San Diego. The sizes of these images are all 256×256, too. Image10 to Image12 are natural images. The sizes of them are 256×256, 320×320, and 330×320, respectively.

The watershed segmentation results of the twelve test images are shown in Fig. 9.

Fig. 8. The true partitioning of the artificial texture images

2.4.2 Results on artificial texture images

Image1 and Image2 contain two textures, Image3 and Image4 contain three textures and Image5 and Image6 contain four textures. Gray level, GLCM and wavelet features are used. In these experiments, the true partitioning is known. Thus we can calculate the clustering correct ratio directly by contrasting a segmentation result to the corresponding true

Problem	Correct Ratio (Standard Deviation)					
	MISA	GISA	EGSA	SCE	FCM	KM
Image1	**0.9844** (0.0069)	0.9837 (0.0021)	0.9705 (0)	0.9842 (0.0005)	0.9841 (0)	0.9835 (0)
Image2	**0.9770** (0.0012)	0.9746 (0.0015)	0.9341 (0)	0.8630 (0.0158)	0.9745 (0)	0.9719 (0)
Image3	0.9475 (0.0018)	0.9442 (0.0026)	**0.9517** (0)	0.8983 (0.0950)	0.7863 (0.2938)	0.7807 (0.2883)
Image4	0.9539 (0.0010)	0.9505 (0.0418)	0.9421 (0)	**0.9614** (0.0014)	0.9502 (0)	0.9505 (0.0001)
Image5	**0.9622** (0.0008)	0.9588 (0.0014)	0.8326 (0)	0.9114 (0.0783)	0.7400 (0.2718)	0.7711 (0.2608)
Image6	**0.9493** (0.0004)	0.9485 (0.0006)	0.8871 (0)	0.9319 (0.0408)	0.8243 (0.2737)	0.8243 (0.2642)

Table 2. Statistic results obtained from MISA, GISA, EGSA, SCEA, FCM and KM on the artificial texture images

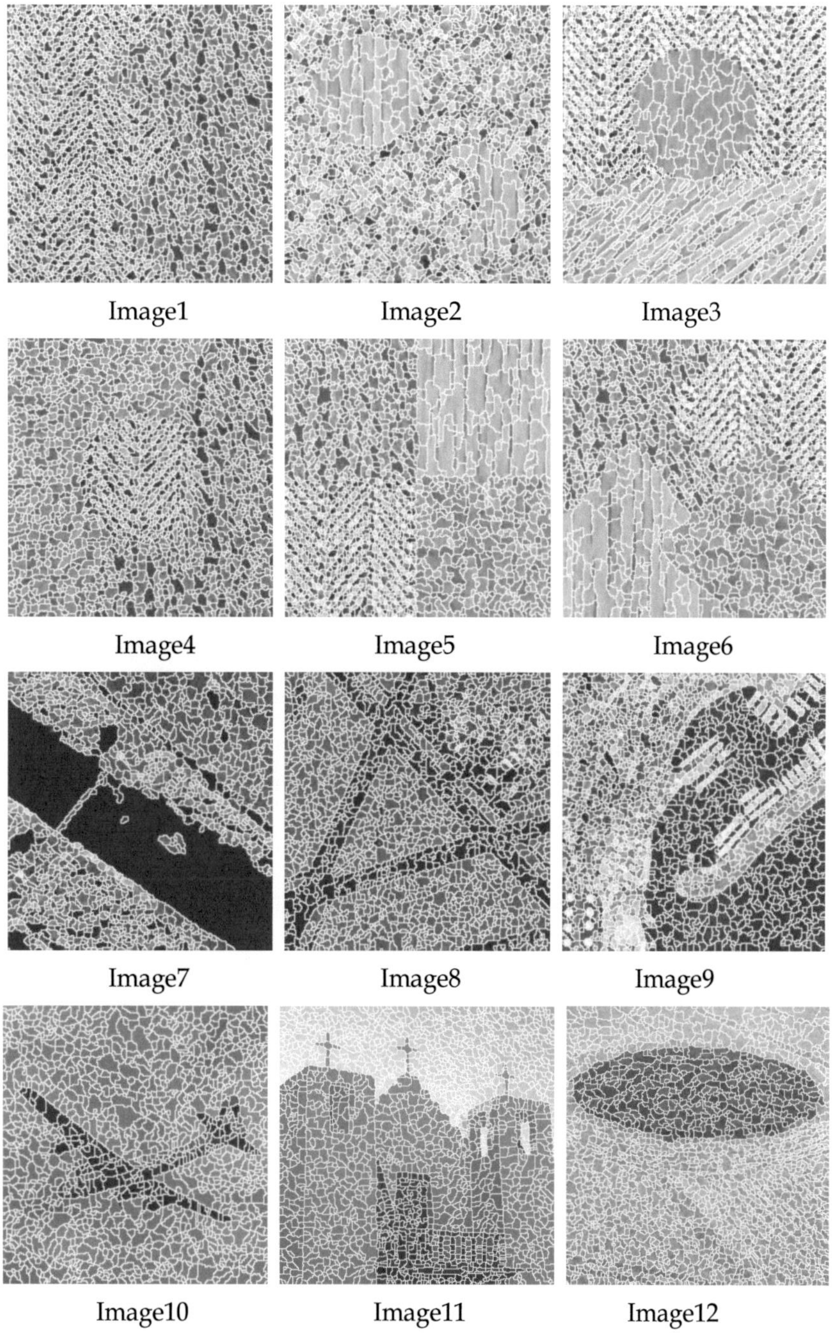

Fig. 9. The watershed segmentation results of Image 1 to Image 12.

partitioning. The average results of clustering correct ratios and standard deviations based on 30 independent runs are shown in Table 2. Fig. 10 shows the typical results of them obtained from the six algorithms. For each test image, the six segmentation images arranged from upper left to lower right are typical results of MISA, GISA, EGSA, SCEA, FCM and KM, respectively. Table 2 shows that MISA obtains higher correct ratio than GISA, FCM and KM do for all these six images, and gets the best correct ratio among all the six algorithms on Image1, Image2, Image5 and Image6. EGSA and SCEA get better correct ratios than MISA does on Image3 and Image4, respectively. EGSA is not a random algorithm, so all the standard deviations of its results are 0. MISA exceeds EGSA greatly on Image5 and Image6 and surpasses SCEA apparently on Image2 and Image3 in correct ratios. MISA exceeds KM and FCM greatly on Image3, Image5 and Image6 in both the correct ratios and standard deviation. Fig. 10 illustrates the above numerical comparisons visually.

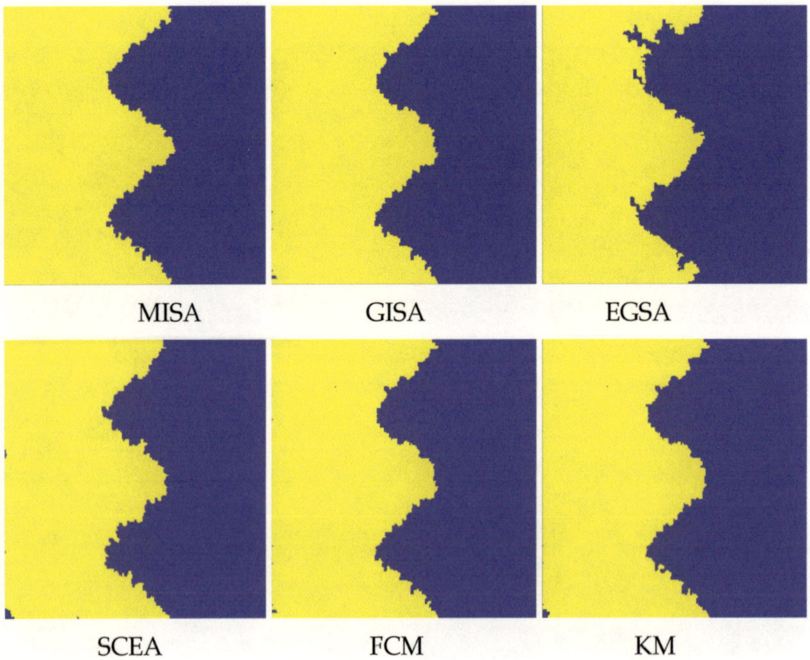

(a) Segmentation results of Image1

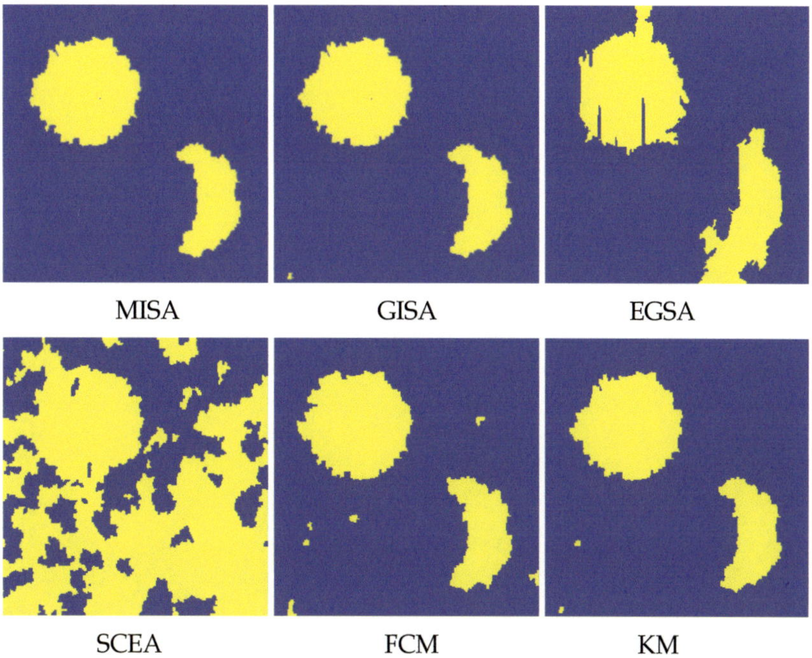

(b) Segmentation results of Image2

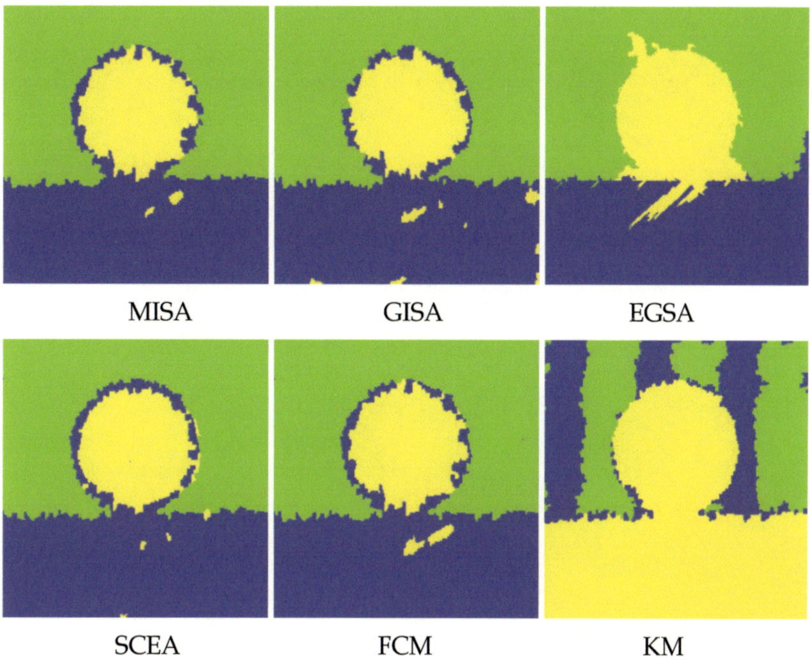

(c) Segmentation results of Image3

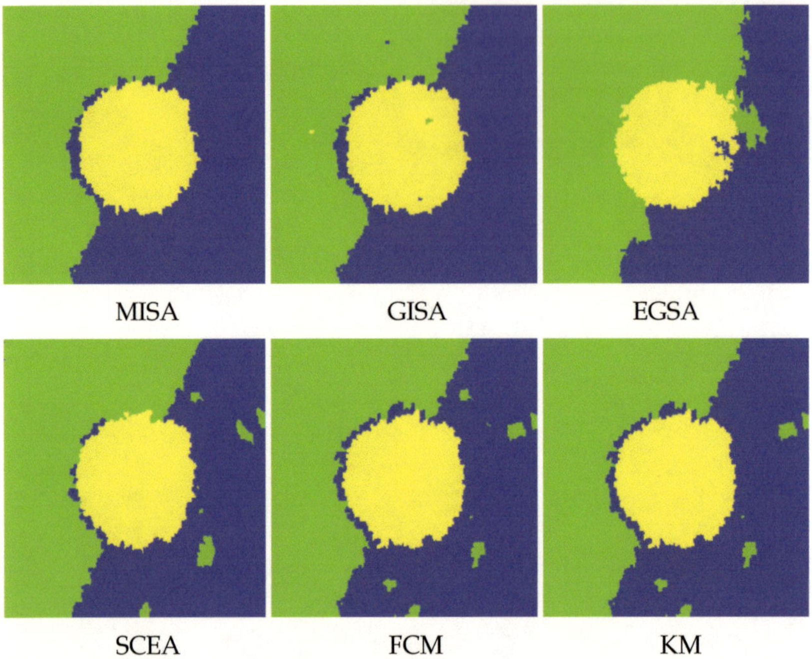

(d) Segmentation results of Image4

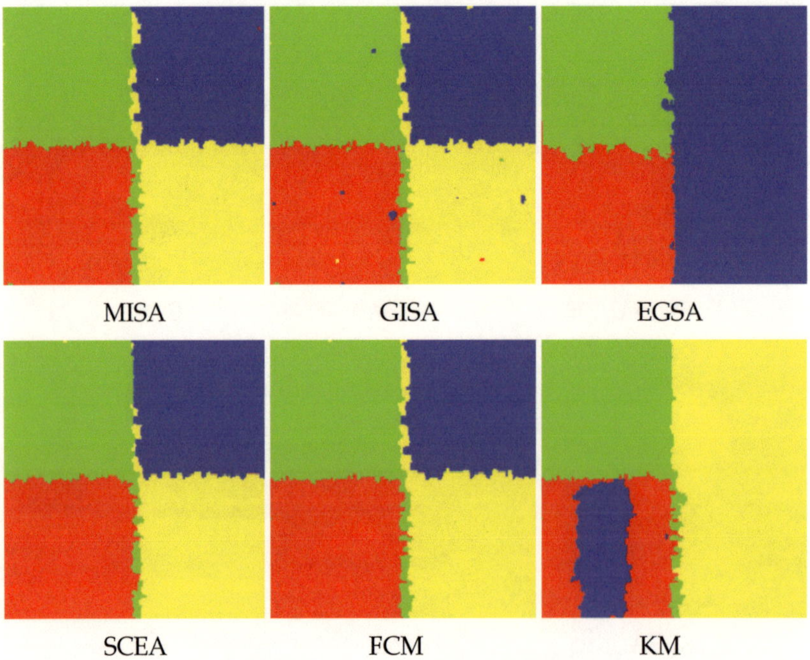

(e) Segmentation results of Image5

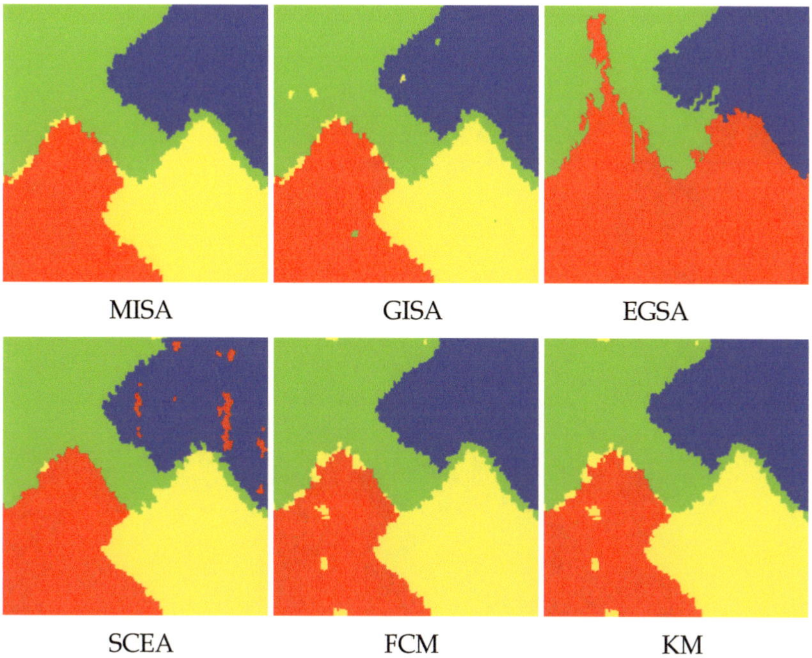

(f) Segmentation results of Image6

Fig. 10. Typical results obtained from the compared algorithms on the artificial texture images

2.4.3 Results on remote sensing Images

Fig. 11 shows the typical results on remote sensing images. For each test image, the six segmentation images arranged from upper left to lower right are typical results of MISA, GISA, EGSA, SCEA, FCM and KM respectively. Gray level and wavelet features are used. For these remote sensing images, there is no true partitioning for reference, thus numerical results could not be obtained here.

For Image7, MISA makes the river bank clearer, and generates more homogeneous lower crops part than GISA does. But both MISA and GISA lose the crop line on the upper left corner. EGSA lose the crop part in the lower left part and the island in the river, but generates a clear bridge. SCEA and FCM might confuse the vegetations with the river. KM loses most of the bridge and other detailed information.

For Image8, MISA gets very clear edges and integrates the building area, leaving some speckles in the center which are the trails of thin roads there. In the GISA results, some buildings are lost in the background. GISA produces some speckles because 200 generations are not enough for it to converge. EGSA and SCEA produce unacceptable results which mix up major cluster information. Both FCM and KM generate coarse edges of the main roads and lose detailed information of other narrow roads in the center and upper right.

For Image9, MISA and GISA can distinguish details on the port area but generate some speckles on the land area. EGSA doesn't confuse the land area on the left with water, but misses detailed information on the port area. SCEA, FCM and KM have worse results when compared with MISA on the port area and compared with EGSA on the land area.

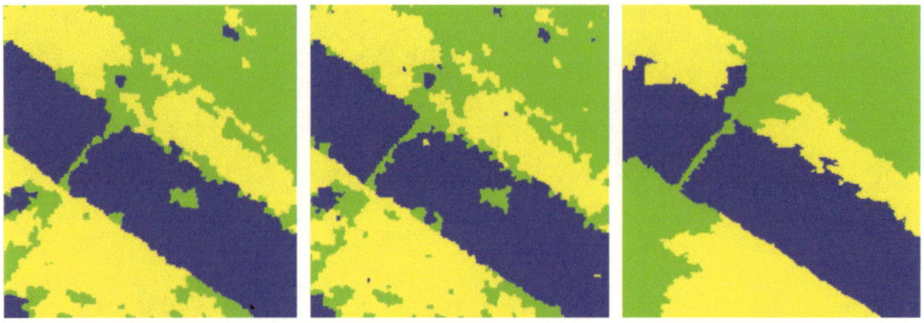

MISA GISA EGSA

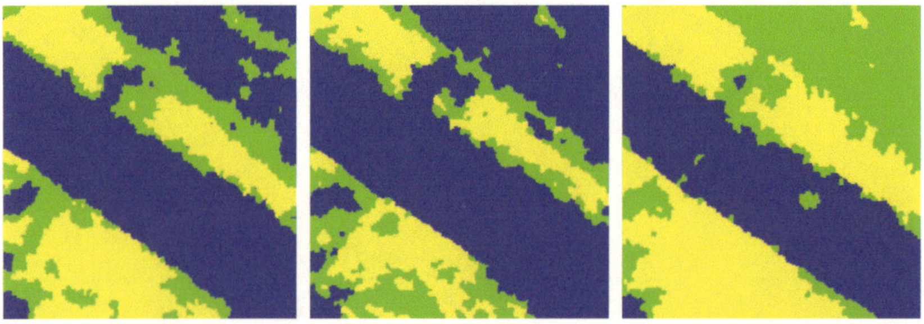

SCEA FCM KM

(a) Segmentation results of Image7

MISA GISA EGSA

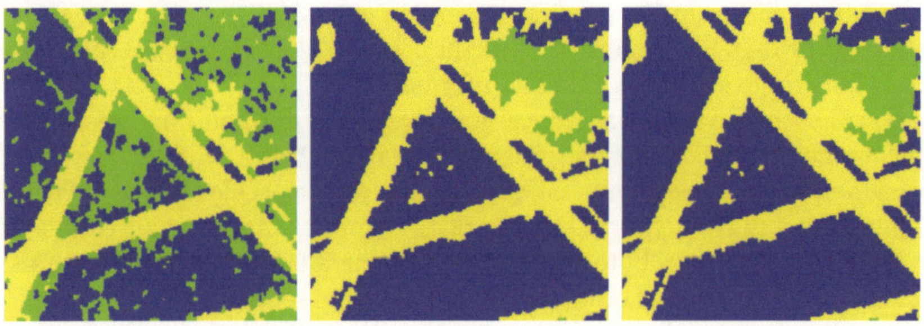

SCEA FCM KM

(b) Segmentation results of Image8

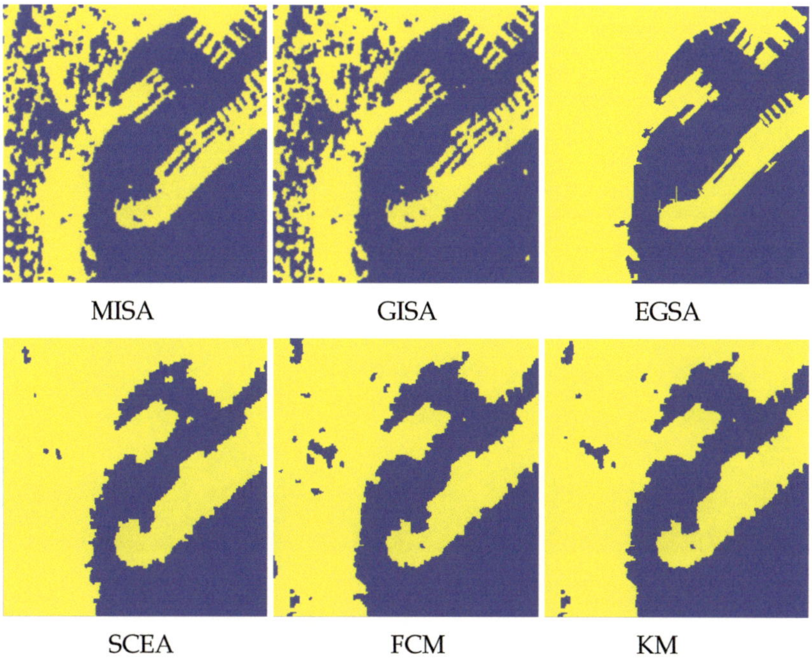

(c) Segmentation results of Image9

Fig. 11. Typical results obtained from the compared algorithms on the remote sensing images

2.4.4 Results on natural images

Fig. 12 shows the typical results on natural images. For each image, the six segmentation images arranged from upper left to lower right are typical results of MISA, GISA, EGSA, SCEA, FCM and KM respectively. Gray level and wavelet features are used for experiments here.

Image10 is segmented into three clusters; Image11 and Image12 are segmented into two clusters. Apparently, MISA produces the best results. GISA also gets better results than FCM and KM. EGSA, SCEA, FCM and KM lose a lot of details and even confuse very large parts in segmenting Image12.

2.4.5 Sensitivity in relation to parameters

Fig.13 shows the convergence curves of MISA and GISA got from experiments on the artificial texture Image4, the remote sensing Image9, and the natural Image12. Each experiment is repeated 30 times for statistical evaluation, and the points in those figures are the average values. We can see that MISA converges within no more than 50 generations on all the experiments, while GISA can not converge within 100 generations.

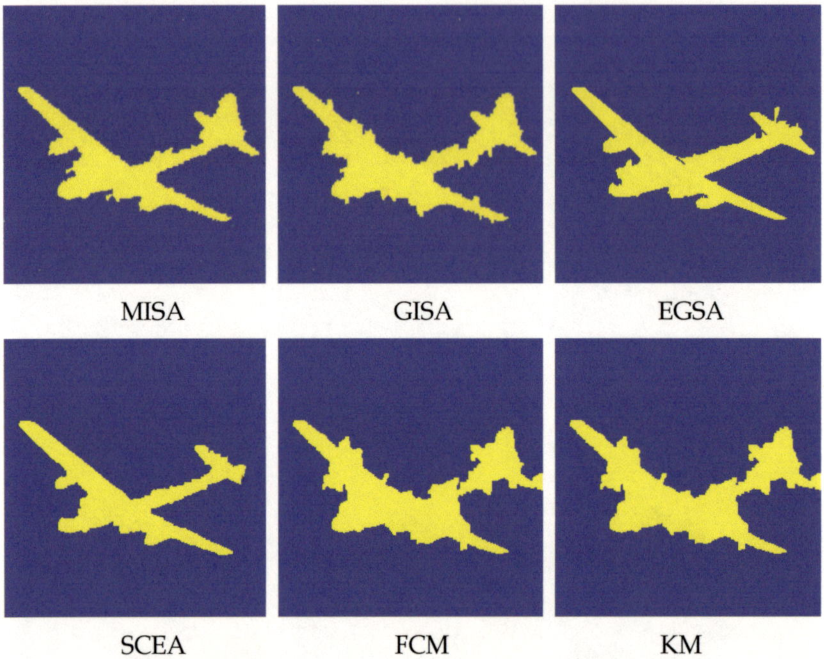

(a) Segmentation results of Image10

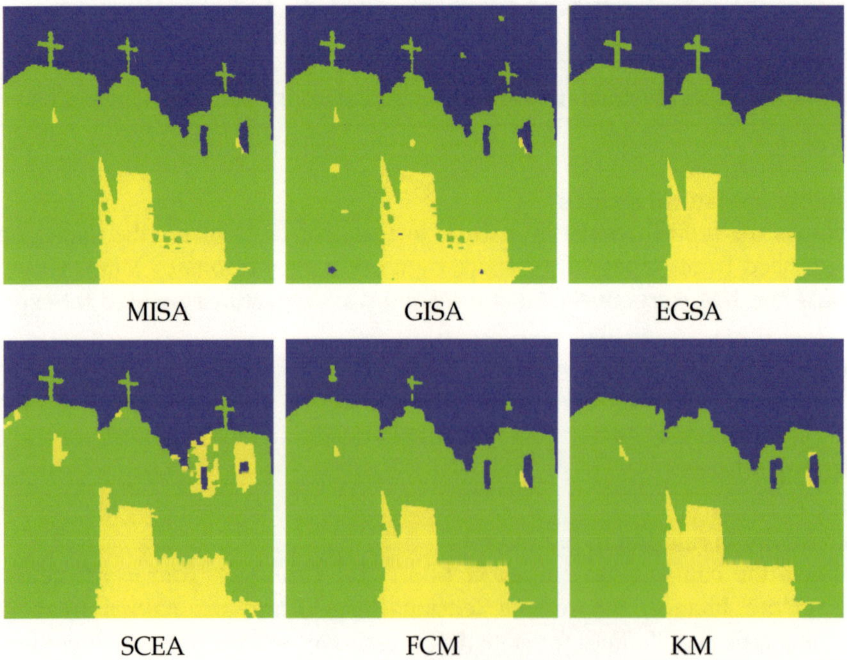

(b) Segmentation results of Image11

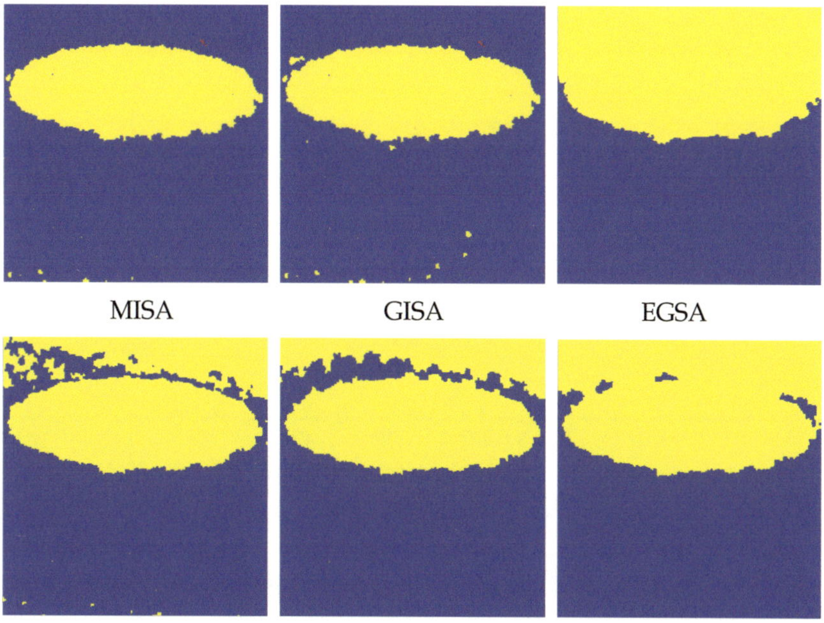

(c) Segmentation results of Image12

Fig. 12. Typical results obtained from the compared algorithms on the natural images

Fig. 14 shows the curves which show the influence of learning intensity. We make use of correct ratios of the six artificial texture images to exhibit the effect of learning intensity. The experiments are repeated 30 times, and we plot their statistical average values. Based on Fig. 14, we can see that the correct ratio increases as the learning intensity is reinforced before at about 0.2. After that , the curves fluctuate but do not increase apparently. This demonstrates that learning intensity should be adjusted properly as a small value is not enough for good convergency while a big one will lead to wasting of computation.

3. Image texture classification using a manifold distance based evolutionary clustering cethod

3.1 Introduction

Image classification or segmentation based on texture features using unsupervised approaches has been a challenge topic. Texture is an important property of some images. A lot of texture feature extraction methods have been developed over the past three decades. These texture features can be categorized into four major categories [53, 54]: statistical, geometrical, model-based, and signal processing. Among them, gray-level co-occurrence features, first proposed by Haralick, Shanmugam and Dinstein [55], are one of the most common features used in literature. In some images, the same object region may vary in appearance from image to image as well as within the same image. Thus, the selected training samples in a supervised algorithm may not be sufficient to include all the class variability throughout the image. Under these conditions, unsupervised classification, i.e. clustering, may be more effective. There are a variety of clustering approaches that could be

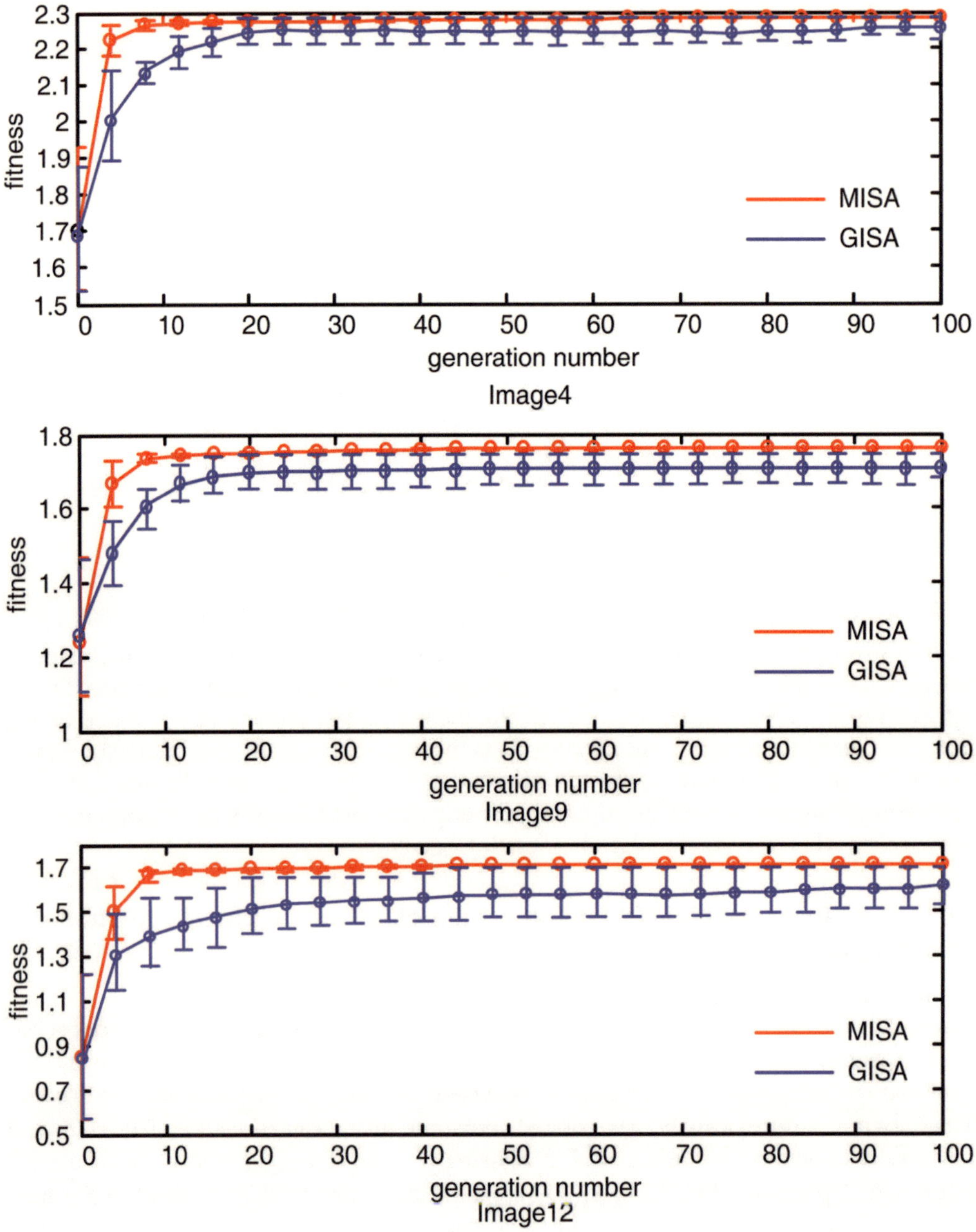

Fig. 13. The convergence curves of MISA and GISA

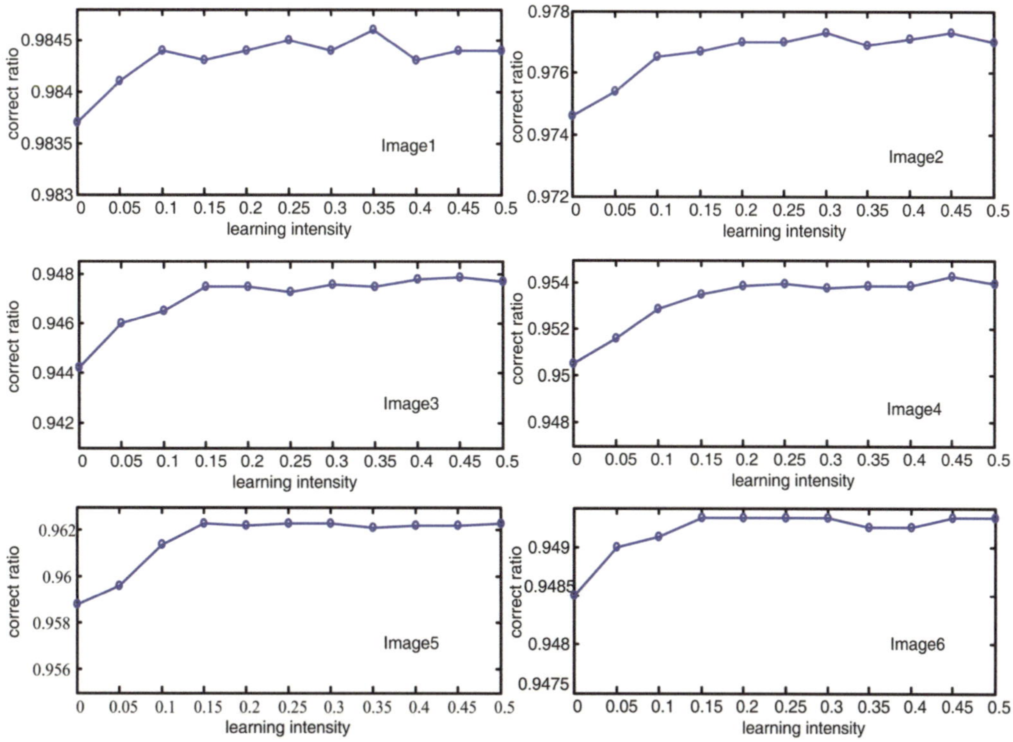

Fig. 14. The influence of learning intensity versus correct ratio

used to assign class labels to the feature vectors. These approaches can be categorized into two groups [56, 57]: hierarchical clustering and partitional clustering, where partitional clustering approaches, such as K-Means Algorithm [58], partition the data set into a specified number of clusters by minimizing certain criteria. Therefore, they can be treated as an optimization problem. As global optimization techniques, Evolutionary Algorithms (EAs) are likely to be a good choice for this task.

EAs, including Genetic Algorithm (GA), Evolutionary Strategy (ES), Evolutionary Programming (EP), etc., have been used for clustering tasks commonly in literature [59~62]. A variety of EA representations for clustering solutions have been explored, such as the straightforward encoding with each gene coding for the cluster membership of the corresponding data item, and the locus-based adjacency representation [62]. Many researchers [59~61] have chosen to use a more indirect approach that borrows from the K-Means algorithm: the representation codes for cluster center only, and each data item is subsequently assigned to a cluster representative according to an appointed dissimilarity measure. The most popular dissimilarity measure is the Euclidean distance. By using Euclidean distance as a measure of dissimilarity, these evolutionary clustering methods as well as the K-Means algorithm have a good performance on the data set with compact super-sphere distributions, but tends to fail in the data set organized in more complex and unknown shapes, which indicates that this dissimilarity measure is undesirable when clusters have random distributions. As a result, it is necessary to design a more flexible dissimilarity measure for clustering. Su and Chou [63] proposed a nonmetric measure based on the concept of point symmetry, according to which a symmetry-based version of the K-

Means algorithm is given. This algorithm assigns data points to a cluster center if they present a symmetrical structure with respect to the cluster center. Therefore, it is suitable to clustering data sets with clear symmetrical structure. Charalampidis [64] recently developed a dissimilarity measure for directional patterns represented by rotation-variant vectors and further introduced a circular K-Means algorithm to cluster vectors containing directional information.

In order to solve the texture classification task effectively, in this study, we design a novel evolutionary clustering method, named manifold evolutionary clustering (MEC). In MEC, we adopt an indirect encoding approach, namely, each individual is a sequence of real integer numbers representing the cluster representatives. Each data item is assigned to a cluster representative according to a novel dissimilarity measure which can measure the geodesic distance along the manifold. After extracting texture features from an image, MEC determines a partitioning of the feature vectors using evolutionary search. The effectiveness of MEC will be validated by comparing with the K-Means algorithm, a modified K-Means algorithm using the manifold distance-based dissimilarity measure [65], and the genetic algorithm-based clustering technique proposed by Maulik and Bandyopadhyay [60] in solving seven benchmark clustering problems of artificial data sets, three artificial texture image classification problems and two Synthetic Aperture Radar (SAR) images classification problems.

The remainder of this section is organized as follows: Section 2.2 describes the novel manifold distance-based dissimilarity measure. Section 2.3 describes the evolutionary clustering algorithm based on the novel dissimilarity measure. In Section 2.4, we summary and evaluate the experimental results.

3.2 A novel manifold distance-based dissimilarity measure

A meaningful measure of distance or proximity between pairs of data points plays an important role in partitional clustering approaches. Most of the clusters can be identified by their location or global characteristics. Through a large mount of observation, we have found the following two consistency characteristics of data clustering.

a. Local consistency refers that data points close in location will have a high affinity.
b. Global consistency refers that data points locating in the same manifold structure will have a high affinity.

For real-world problems, the distribution of data points takes on a complex manifold structure, which results in the classical Euclidian distance metric can only reflect the local consistency, but fail to describe the global consistency. We can illustrate this problem by the following example. As shown in Fig. 15, we expect that the affinity between point *a* and point *e* is higher than the affinity between point *a* and point *f*. In other words, we are looking for a measure of dissimilarity according to which point *a* is closer to point *e* than to point *f*. In terms of Euclidian distance metric, however, point *a* is much closer to point *f* than to *e*, thus without reflecting the global consistency. Hence for complicated real world problems, simply using Euclidean distance metric as a dissimilarity measure can not fully reflect the characteristics of data clustering.

Here, we want to design a novel dissimilarity measure with the ability of reflecting both the local and global consistency. As an example, we can observe from the data distribution in Fig. 15 that data points in the same cluster tend to lie in the same manifold.

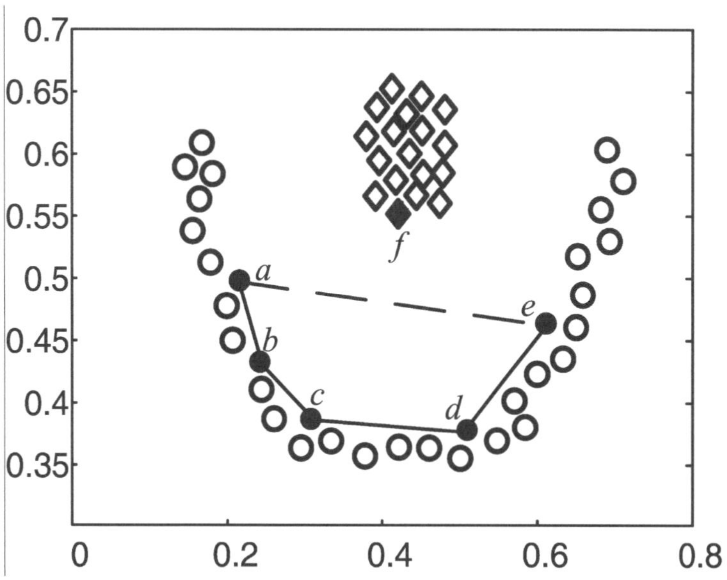

Fig. 15. An illustration of that the Euclidian distance metric can not reflect the global consistency.

At first, data points are taken as the nodes V of a weighted undirected graph $G=(V,E)$. Edges $E=\{W_{ij}\}$ reflect the affinity between each pair of data points. We expect to design a dissimilarity measure that assigns high affinity to two points if they can be linked by a path running along a manifold, and a low affinity if they cannot. This concept of dissimilarity measure has been shown in experiments to lead to significant improvement in classification accuracy when applied to semi-supervised learning [66, 67]. The aim of using this kind of measure is to elongate the paths that cross different manifolds, and simultaneously shorten those that not cross.

To formalize this intuitive notion of dissimilarity, we need first define a so-called manifold length of line segment. We have found a property that a distance measure describing the global consistency of clustering does not always satisfy the triangle inequality under the Euclidean metric. As shown in Fig. 15, to describe the global consistency, it is required that the length of the path connected by shorter edges is smaller than that of the direct connected path, i.e. $\overline{ab}+\overline{bc}+\overline{cd}+\overline{de}<\overline{ae}$. In other words, a direct connected path between two points is not always the shortest one.

Enlightened by this property, we define a manifold length of line segment as follows.

Definition 1. The manifold length of line segment (x_i,x_j) is defined as

$$L(x_i,x_j)\triangleq \rho^{dist(x_i,x_j)}-1 \tag{7}$$

where $dist(x_i,x_j)$ is the Euclidean distance between x_i and x_j; $\rho>1$ is the flexing factor. Obviously, the manifold length of line segment possesses the property mentioned above, thus can be utilized to describe the global consistency. In addition, the manifold length between two points can be elongated or shortened by adjusting the flexing factor ρ.

According to the manifold length of line segment, we define a new distance metric, called manifold distance metric, which measures the distance between a pair of points by searching for the shortest path in the graph.

***Definition* 2.** Let data points be the nodes of graph $G=(V,E)$, and $p\in V^l$ be a path of length $l=|p|-1$ connecting the nodes p_1 and $p_{|p|}$, in which $(p_k,p_{k+1})\in E$, $1\le k<|p|$. Let $\mathbf{P}_{i,j}$ denote the set of all paths connecting data points x_i and x_j. The manifold distance between x_i and x_j is defined as

$$D(x_i,x_j)\triangleq \min_{p\in \mathbf{P}_{i,j}} \sum_{k=1}^{|p|-1} L(p_k,p_{k+1}). \tag{8}$$

The manifold distance satisfies the four conditions for a distance metric, i.e. $D(x_i,x_j)=D(x_j,x_i)$; $D(x_i,x_j)\ge 0$; $D(x_i,x_j)\le D(x_i,x_k)+D(x_k,x_j)$ for all x_i,x_j,x_k; and $D(x_i,x_j)=0$ if and only if $x_i=x_j$.

As a result, the manifold distance metric can measure the geodesic distance along the manifold, which results in any two points in the same manifold being connected by a lot of shorter edges within the manifold while any two points in different manifolds are connected by a longer edge between manifolds, thus achieving the aim of elongating the distance among data points in different manifolds and simultaneously shortening the distance among data points in the same manifold.

3.3 Evolutionary clustering based on the manifold distance

By using EAs to solving clustering tasks, it is necessary to design the individual representation method and the heuristic search operators, and formulate the objective function for optimization.

3.3.1 Representation and operators

In this study, we consider the clustering problem from a combinatorial optimization viewpoint. Each individual is a sequence of real integer numbers representing the sequence number of K cluster representatives. The length of a chromosome is K words, where the first gene represents the first cluster, the second gene represents the second cluster, and so on. As an illustration, let us consider the following example.

***Example* 1.** Let the size of the data set is 100 and the number of clusters being considered is 5. Then the individual (6, 19, 91, 38, 64) represents that the 6-th, 19-th, 91-st, 38-th, and 64-th points are chosen to represent the five clusters, respectively.

This representation method does not mention the data dimension. If the size of the data set is N and the number of clusters is K, then the search space is N^K.

Crossover is a probabilistic process that exchanges information between two parent individuals for generating offspring. In this study, we use the uniform crossover [68] because it is unbiased with respect to the ordering of genes and can generate any combination of alleles from the two parents [62, 69]. An example of the operation of uniform crossover on the encoding employed is shown in example 2.

***Example* 2.** Let the two parent individuals are (6, 19, 91, 38, 64) and (3, 29, 17, 61, 6), randomly generate the mask (1, 0, 0, 1, 0), then the two offspring after crossover are (6, 29,

17, 38, **64**) and (3, 19, 91, 61, 64). In this case, the first offspring is not (6, 29, 17, 38, **6**) because the 6 in bold is repeat, we keep it unchanged.
Each individual undergoes mutation with probability p_m as example 3.
Example 3. Let the size of the data set is 100 and the number of clusters being considered is 5. Then the individual (6, 19, 91, 38, 64) can mutate to (6, $19+\lfloor(100\text{-}19)\times random\text{+}1\rfloor$, 91, 38, 64) or (6, $19\text{-}\lfloor(19\text{-}1)\times random\text{+}1\rfloor$, 91, 38, 64) equiprobably when the second gene is chosen to mutate, *random* denotes a uniformly distributed random number in the range [0,1).

3.3.2 Objective function

Each data item is assigned to a cluster representative according to its manifold distance to the cluster representatives. As an illustration, let us consider the following example.
Example 4. Let the 6-th, 19-th, 91-st, 38-th, and 64-th points represent the five clusters, respectively. For the first point, we compute the manifold distance between it and the 6-th, 19-th, 91-st, 38-th, and 64-th points, respectively. If the manifold distance between the first point and the 38-th point is the minimum one, then the first point is assigned to the cluster represented by the 38-th point. All the points are assigned in this way.
Subsequently, the objective function is computed as follows:

$$Dev(C) = \sum_{C_k \in C} \sum_{i \in C_k} D(i, \mu_k) \tag{9}$$

where C is the set of all clusters, μ_k is the representative of cluster C_k, and $D(i,\mu_k)$ is the manifold distance between the i-th data item of cluster C_k and μ_k.

3.3.3 Manifold evolutionary clustering algorithm

In MEC, the processes of fitness computation, roulette wheel selection with elitism [70], crossover and mutation are executed for a maximum number of generations Gmax. The best individual in the last generation provides the solution to the clustering problem. The main loop of MEC is as follows.

Algorithm 2.1. Manifold Evolutionary Clustering (MEC)

Begin
1. t=0
2. randomly initialize population $\boldsymbol{P}(t)$
3. assign all points to clusters as the manifold distance and compute the objective function values of $\boldsymbol{P}(t)$
4. if $t< G_{max}$
5. t=t+1
6. select $\boldsymbol{P}(t)$ from $\boldsymbol{P}(t\text{-}1)$ using roulette wheel selection with elitism
7. crossover $\boldsymbol{P}(t)$
8. mutate $\boldsymbol{P}(t)$
9. go to step 3
10. end if
11. output the best and stop

End

The initial population in step 2 is initialized to K randomly generated real integer number in $[1, N]$, where N is the size of the data set. This process is repeated for each of the P chromosomes in the population, where P is the size of the population.

3.4 Experimental study

3.4.1 Experimental setup

In order to validate the performance of MEC, we first apply MEC to seven benchmark clustering problems of artificial data sets. The results will be compared with the K-Means algorithm (KM) [58], a modified K-Means algorithm using the manifold distance-based dissimilarity measure (DSKM) [65], and the genetic algorithm-based clustering technique (GAC) proposed by Maulik and Bandyopadhyay [60]. In all the algorithms, the desired number of clusters is set to be known in advance.

In the second experiment, we will solve three artificial texture image classification problems using MEC, GAC, DSKM and KM, respectively.

In the third experiment, we will solve the classification problems of one X-band SAR image and one Ku-band SAR image by using MEC, GAC, DSKM and KM, respectively.

In the image classification experiments (the second and third experiments), we will use the gray-level co-occurrence matrix (GLCM) [55] method to extract texture features from images. There are many statistics that can be determined from each GLCM, such as angular second moment, contrast, correlation, sum of squares, entropy, and so on. Following [54], in this study, we chose three statistics, dissimilarity, entropy and correlation which indicate the degree of smoothness of the texture, the homogeneity and the correlation between the gray level pair, respectively. There are four parameters that must be indicated in order to generate co-occurrence data, namely, interpixel orientation, interpixel distance, the number of gray levels and window size. Typically, interpixel orientation is set to $0^{\circ}, 45^{\circ}, 90^{\circ}, 135^{\circ}$ since this is easiest to implement. Short interpixel distances have typically achieved the best success, so interpixel distance is 1 will be used. This combination of offset and orientation has characterized SAR texture well [54]. The role of varying the values of the number of gray levels and windows size with respect to GLCM statistics has been presented in many references [54, 71]. After their analysis and fine-tune experiments, in this study, we set the number of gray levels is 16 and the window size is 13×13.

The parameter settings used for MEC and GAC in our experimental study are given in Table 3. For DSKM and KM, the maximum iterative number is set to 500, and the stop threshold is 10^{-10}.

Parameter	MEC	GAC
Maximum Number of generations	100	100
population size	50	50
Crossover probability	0.8	0.8
Mutation probability	0.1	0.1

Table 3. Parameter settings for MEC and GAC

In the first two experiments, the true partitioning is known, we will evaluate the performance using two external measures, the Adjusted Rand Index [62, 72, 73] and the Clustering Error [65].

The Adjusted Rand Index [72] is a generalization of the Rand Index [74] which takes two partitioning as the input and count the number of pair-wise co-assignments of data items between the two partitioning. Given a set of N points $S=\{p_1,p_2,\cdots,p_N\}$, suppose $U=\{u_1,u_2,\cdots,u_K\}$ and $V=\{v_1,v_2,\cdots,v_K\}$ represent two different partitions of the points in S such that $\bigcup_{i=1}^{K} u_i = \bigcup_{j=1}^{K} v_j = S$ and $u_i \cap u_{i'} = v_j \cap v_{j'} = \varnothing$ for $1 \le i \ne i' \le K, 1 \le j \ne j' \le K$. Suppose that U is the known true partition, and V is a clustering result. Let a be the number of pairs of points in the same class in U and in the same class in V, b be the number of pairs of points in the same class in U but not in the same class in V, c be the number of pairs of points in the same class in V but not in the same class in U, and d be the number of pairs of points in different classes in both partitions. The quantities a and d can be interpreted as agreements, and b and c as disagreements. Then the Rand Index is $\frac{a+d}{a+b+c+d}$. The Rand Index lies between 0 and 1, when the two partitions agree perfectly, the Rand Index is 1. A problem with the Rand Index is that the expected value of the Rand index of two random partitions does not take a constant value (say zero). The Adjusted Rand Index proposed by Hubert and Arabie [72] assumes the generalized hypergeometric distribution as the model of randomness, i.e. the U and V partitions are picked at random such that the numbers of points in the classes are fixed. Let n_{ij} be the number of points that are in both class u_i and class v_j. Let $n_{i\bullet}$ and $n_{\bullet j}$ be the number of points in class u_i and class v_j respectively. Under the generalized hypergeometric model, it can be shown that:

$$E\left[\sum_{i,j}\binom{n_{ij}}{2}\right]=\left[\sum_i\binom{n_{i\bullet}}{2}\cdot\sum_j\binom{n_{\bullet j}}{2}\right]/\binom{n}{2} \tag{10}$$

Then the Adjusted Rand Index is given as

$$R(U,V)=\frac{\sum_{i,j}\binom{n_{ij}}{2}-\left[\sum_i\binom{n_{i\bullet}}{2}\cdot\sum_j\binom{n_{\bullet j}}{2}\right]/\binom{n}{2}}{\frac{1}{2}[\sum_i\binom{n_{i\bullet}}{2}+\sum_j\binom{n_{\bullet j}}{2}]-[\sum_i\binom{n_{i\bullet}}{2}\cdot\sum_j\binom{n_{\bullet j}}{2}]/\binom{n}{2}} \tag{11}$$

The Adjusted Rand Index return values in the interval [0, 1] and is to be maximized.
Let the known true partition be $U=\{u_1,u_2,\cdots,u_K\}$ and the clustering result be $V=\{v_1,v_2,\cdots,v_K\}$. $\forall i,j \in \{1,2,\cdots,K\}$, *Confusion*$(i,j)$ denotes the number of same data points both in the true cluster u_i and in the cluster v_j produced. Then, the Clustering Error is defined as

$$CE(U,V)=\frac{1}{N}\sum_{i=1}^{K}\sum_{\substack{j=1\\ i\ne j}}^{K} Confusion(i,j), \tag{12}$$

where N is the size of data set. Note that there exists a renumbering problem, so the Clustering Error is computed for all possible renumbering of V, and the minimum one is taken. The Clustering Error also returns values in the interval [0, 1] and is to be minimized.

3.4.2 Implementation results on benchmark clustering problems

We first select seven artificial data sets, named Line-blobs, Long1, Size5, Spiral, Square4, Sticks, and Three-circles to study a range of different interesting data properties. The distribution of data points in these data sets can be seen in Fig. 16. We perform 30 independent runs on each problem. The average results of the two metrics, Clustering Error and Adjusted Rand Index, are shown in Table 4.

Problem	Clustering Error				Adjusted Rand Index			
	MEC	GAC	DSKM	KM	MEC	GAC	DSKM	KM
line-blobs	**0**	0.263	0.132	0.256	**1**	0.399	0.866	0.409
Long1	**0**	0.445	**0**	0.486	**1**	0.011	**1**	0.012
Size5	**0.010**	0.023	0.015	0.024	**0.970**	0.924	0.955	0.920
Spiral	**0**	0.406	**0**	0.408	**1**	0.034	**1**	0.033
Square4	0.065	**0.062**	0.073	0.073	0.835	**0.937**	0.816	0.816
Sticks	**0**	0.277	**0**	0.279	**1**	0.440	**1**	0.504
three-circles	**0**	0.569	0.055	0.545	**1**	0.033	0.921	0.044

Table 4. Results of MEC, GAC, DSKM and KM on artificial data sets where the results in bold are the best ones

From Table 4, we can see clearly that MEC did best on six out of the seven problems, while GAC did best only on the Square4 data set. DSKM also obtained the true clustering on three problems. KM and GAC only obtained desired clustering for the two spheroid data sets, i.e. Size5 and Square4. This is due to that the structure of the other five data sets does not satisfy convex distribution. On the other hand, MEC and DSKM can successfully recognize these complex clusters, which indicate the manifold distance metric are very suitable to measure complicated clustering structure. When comparisons are made between MEC and DSKM, MEC obtained the true clustering on the Long1, Spiral, Sticks, Line-blobs and Three-circles in all the 30 runs, but DSKM can not do it on the Line-blobs and Three-circles. Further more, for the Size5 and Square4 problems, MEC did a little better than DSKM in both the Clustering Error and the Adjusted Rand Index. The main drawback of DSKM is that it has to recalculate the geometrical center of each cluster as the K-Means algorithm after cluster assignment which reducing the ability of reflecting the global consistency. MEC made up this drawback by evolutionary searching the cluster representatives from a combinatorial optimization viewpoint. In order to show the performance visually, the typical simulation results on the eight data sets obtained from MEC are shown in Fig. 16.

3.4.3 Implementation results on artificial texture image classification

Image1 is a simple 256×256 bipartite image (Fig. 17(a)). The original image contains two textures, cork and cotton, selected from the Brodatz texture images [75]. Fig. 17(b) represents the true partitioning of Image1. Image2 also contains two textures as shown in Fig. 17(c), and Fig. 17(d) represents its true partitioning. Image3 is a more complicated texture synthesized image with 4 classes, and Fig. 17(e) and (f) represent the original image and the true partitioning, respectively.

We perform 30 independent runs on each problem. The average results of the two metrics, Clustering Error and Adjusted Rand Index, are shown in Table 5. Fig. 18 to Fig. 20 are the typical implementation results obtained from the four algorithms, MEC, GAC, DSKM and KM, in clustering the three texture images, respectively.

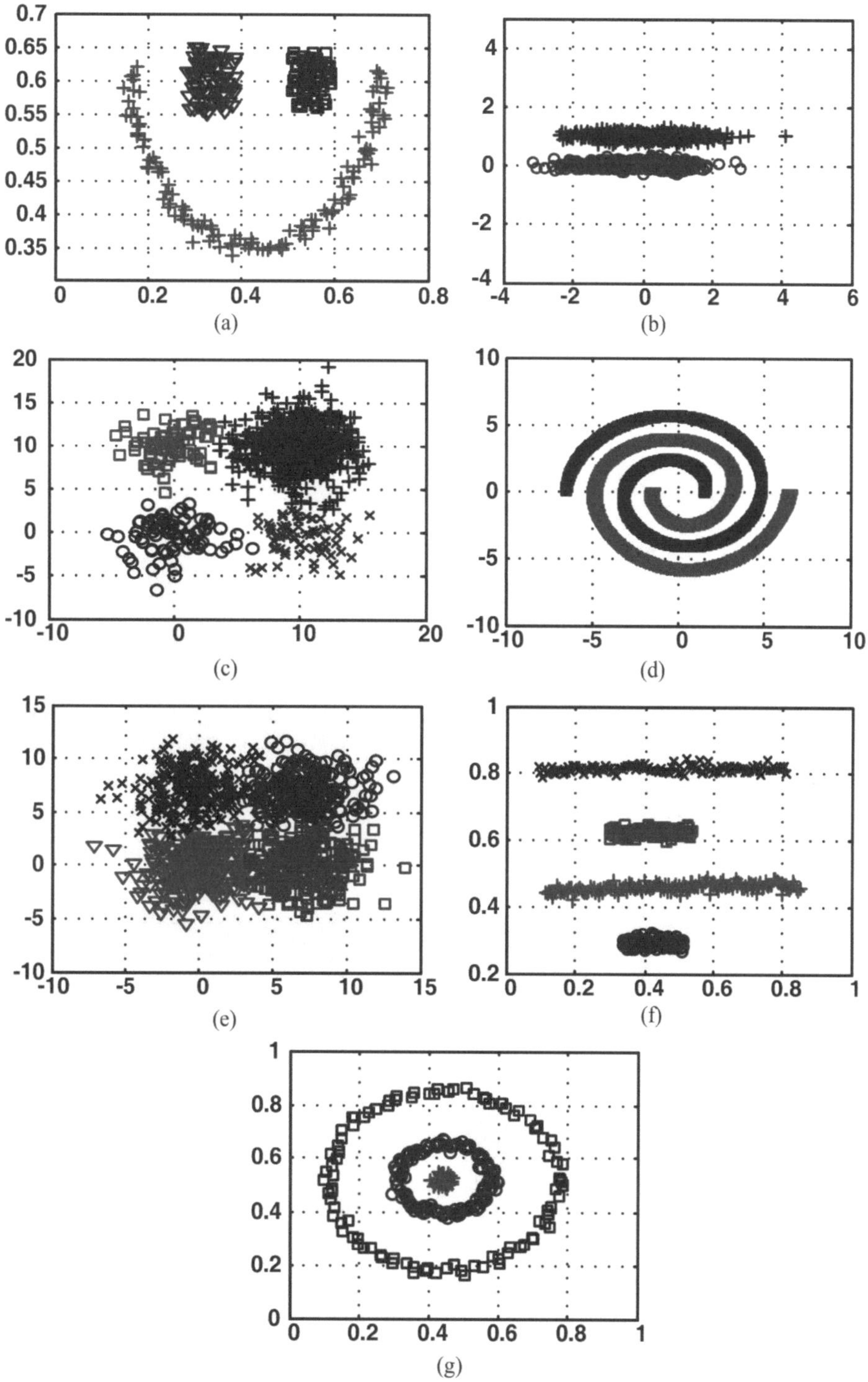

Fig. 16. The typical implementation results on the artificial data sets obtained from MEC. (a) Line- blobs; (b) Long1; (c) Size5; (d) Spiral; (e) Square4; (f) Sticks; (G) Three-circles.

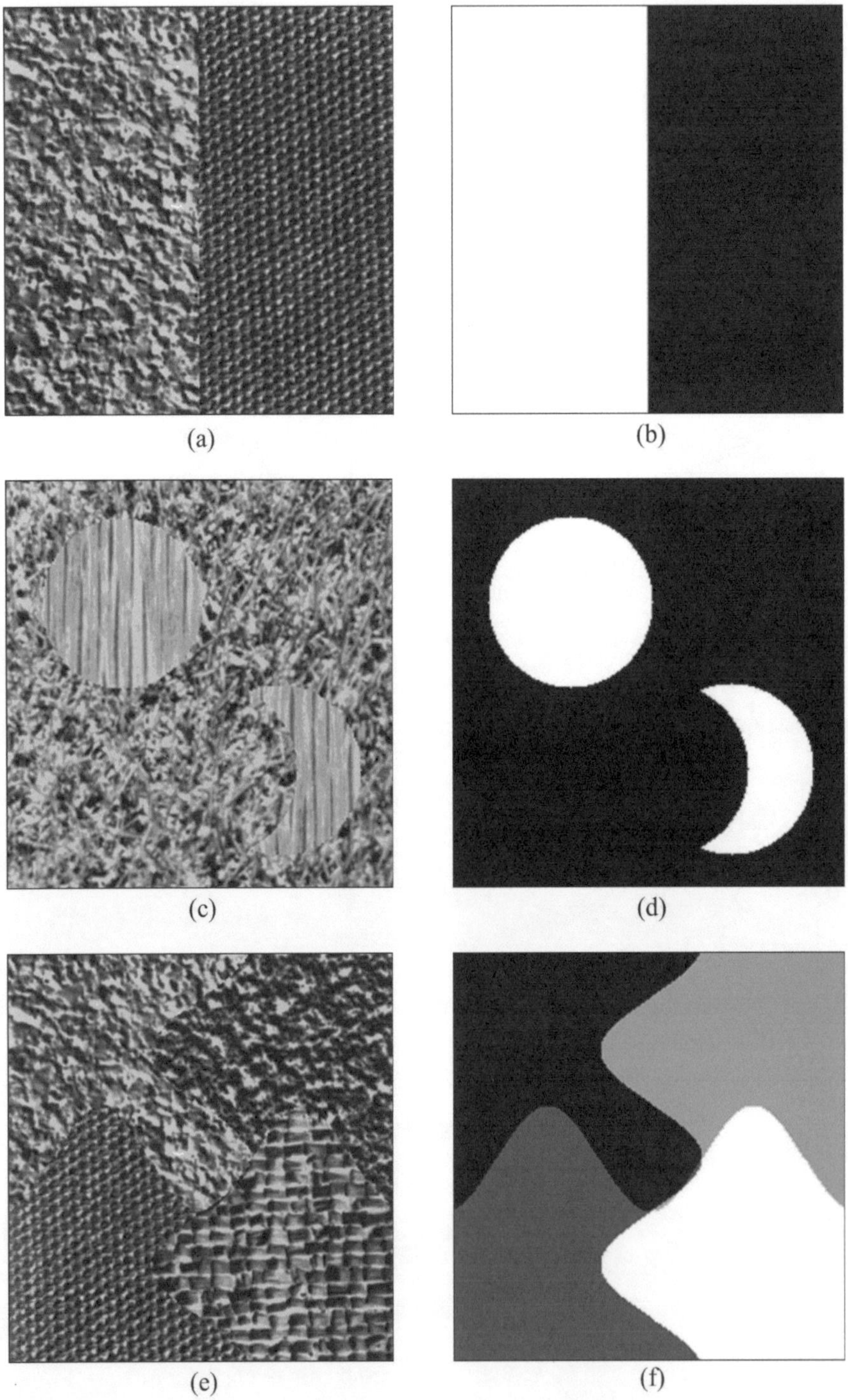

Fig. 17. Artificial texture images and their true partitioning. (a) Original Image1; (b) True partitioning of Image1; (c) Original Image2; (d) True partitioning of Image2; (e) Original Image3; (f) True partitioning of Image3.

Problem	Clustering Error				Adjusted Rand Index			
	MEC	GAC	DSKM	KM	MEC	GAC	DSKM	KM
Image1	**0.0030**	0.0069	0.0035	0.0071	**0.9462**	0.9115	0.9437	0.9113
Image2	**0.0037**	0.1594	0.0072	0.2017	**0.9376**	0.9057	0.9109	0.8869
Image3	**0.1212**	0.2554	0.1858	0.2899	**0.8638**	0.8012	0.8117	0.8094

Table 5. Results of MEC, GAC, DSKM and KM on artificial texture image classification where the results in bold are the best ones

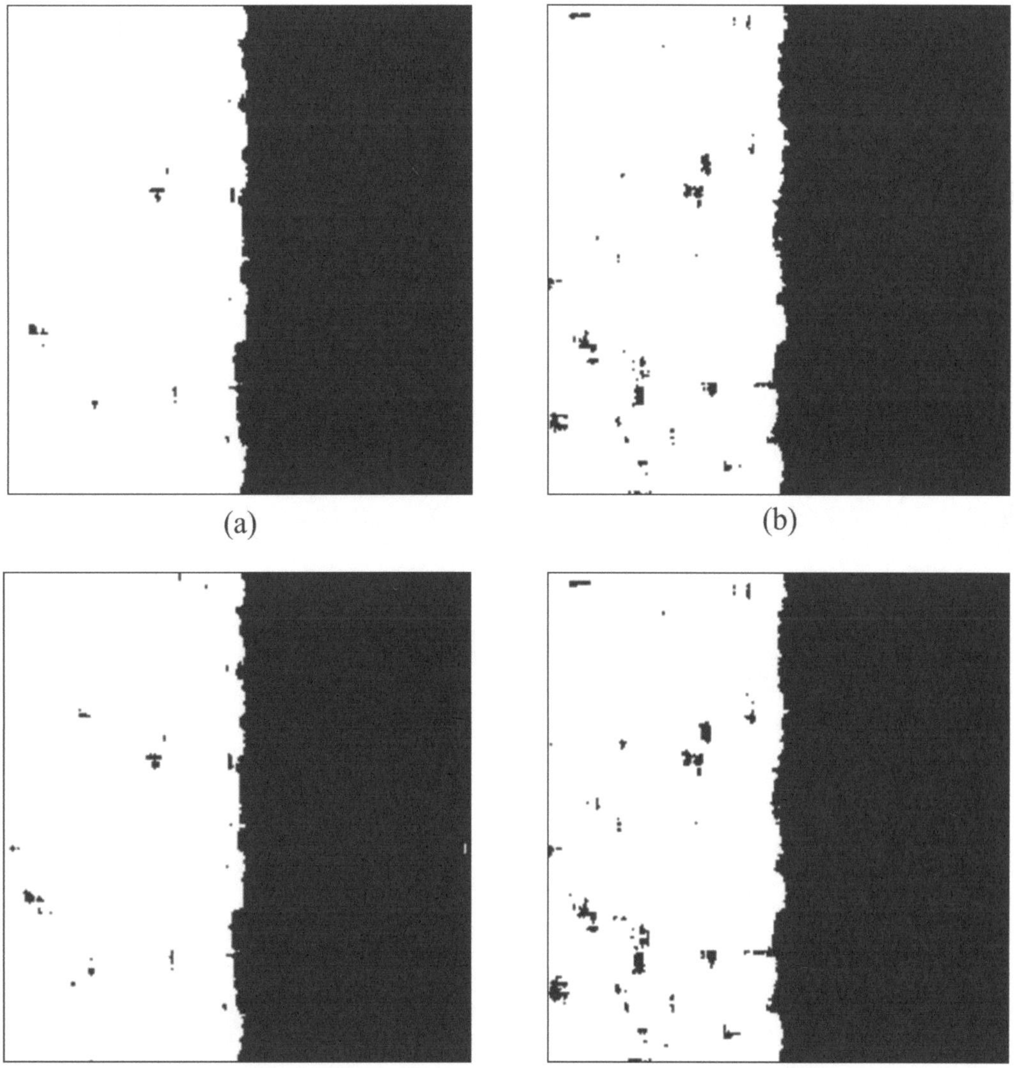

(a) (b) (c) (d)

Fig. 18. The typical implementation results obtained from (a) MEC, (b) GAC, (c) DSKM and (d) KM in clustering Image1.

As shown in Table 5, all the average values of Cluster Error obtained from MEC, GAC, DSKM and KM in clustering Image1 are less than 1%, so all the four algorithms are easily able to segment the Image1. The values of Cluster Error and Adjusted Rand Index and Fig. 18 also show that the results obtained from MEC and DSKM are much better than the results of GAC and KM because both MEC and DSKM assign data items according to the manifold distance while GAC and KM assign data items according to Euclidian distance. However, the computational cost of the manifold distance is much larger than that of Euclidian distance. MEC and DSKM have similar results in clustering Image1.

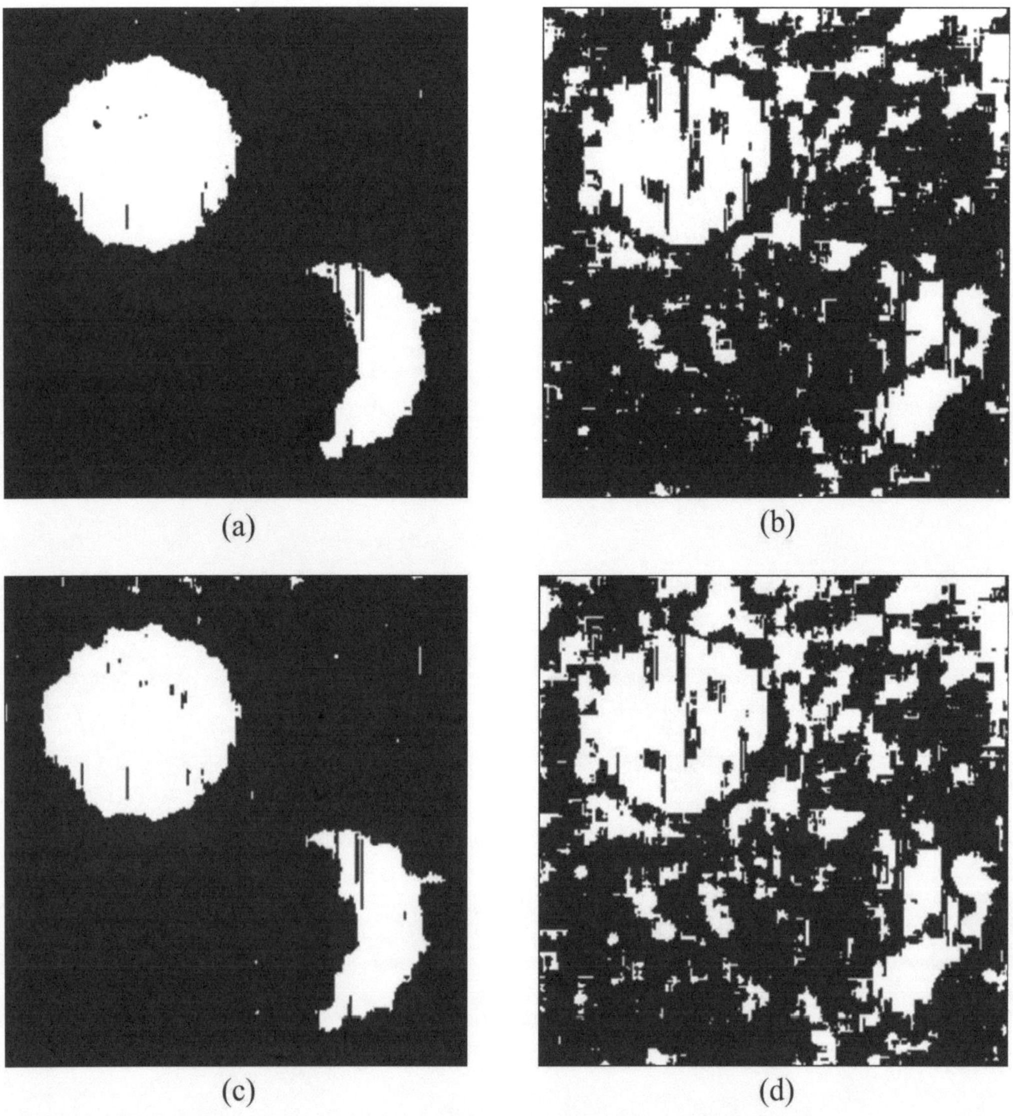

Fig. 19. The typical implementation results obtained from (a) MEC, (b) GAC, (c) DSKM and (d) KM in clustering Image2.

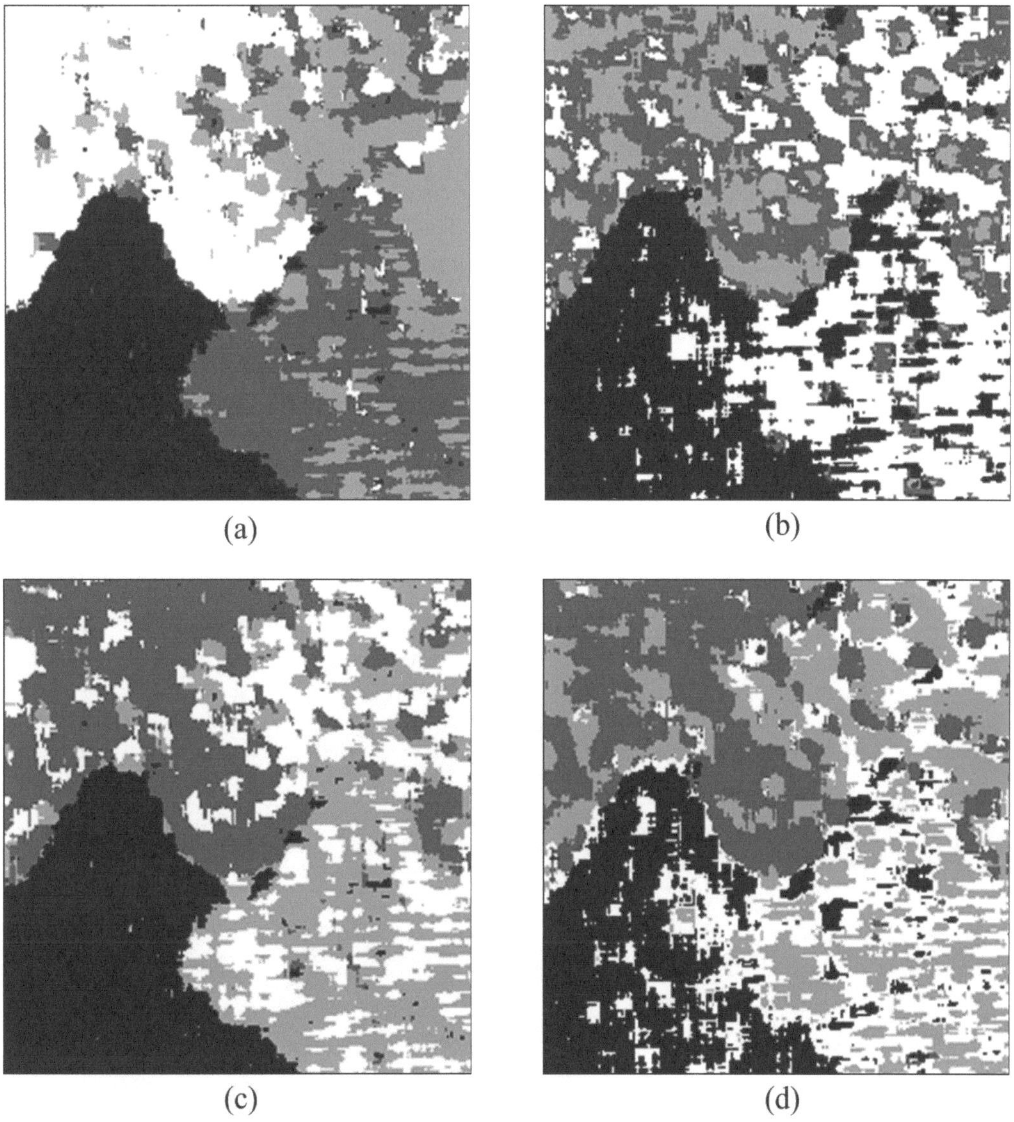

Fig. 20. The typical implementation results obtained from (a) MEC, (b) GAC, (c) DSKM and (d) KM in clustering Image3.

In clustering Image2, the average value of Cluster Error obtained from MEC is much smaller than the results obtained from GAC, DSKM and KM, and the average value of Adjusted Rand Index of MEC is obviously greater than the results obtained from GAC, DSKM and KM. So MEC does best in this problem. Fig. 19 also shows that the MEC result and DSKM result are obviously better than the GAC result and KM result, and the MEC result is better than the DSKM result. MEC segment the two textures better than DSKM may be due to MEC search the two cluster representatives using evolutionary searching but DSKM has to recalculate the geometrical center of each cluster after cluster assignment in each iteration which reduces the ability of reflecting the global consistency.

In clustering the more complicated texture image Image3, all the average values of Cluster Error are greater than 12%, so none of the four algorithms can segment the image very well based on GLCM features. However, Table 5 and Fig. 20 show that MEC does much better than the other three algorithms.

3.4.4 Implementation results on remote sensing image classification

The first image, as shown in Fig. 21(a), is an X-band SAR image of a lakeside in Switzerland. The size of the image is 140×155 pixels. We want to classify the image into three clusters, namely, the lake, the city, and the mountainous region. The second image, as shown in Fig. 21(b), is a Ku-band SAR image of the Rio Grande River nearby Albuquerque, New Mexico, USA. The size of the image is 256×256 pixels. We want to classify the image into three clusters, namely, the river, the vegetation, and the crop. Fig. 22 and Fig. 23 shows the clustering results obtained from the MEC, DSKM, GAC and KM in clustering these two SAR image respectively.

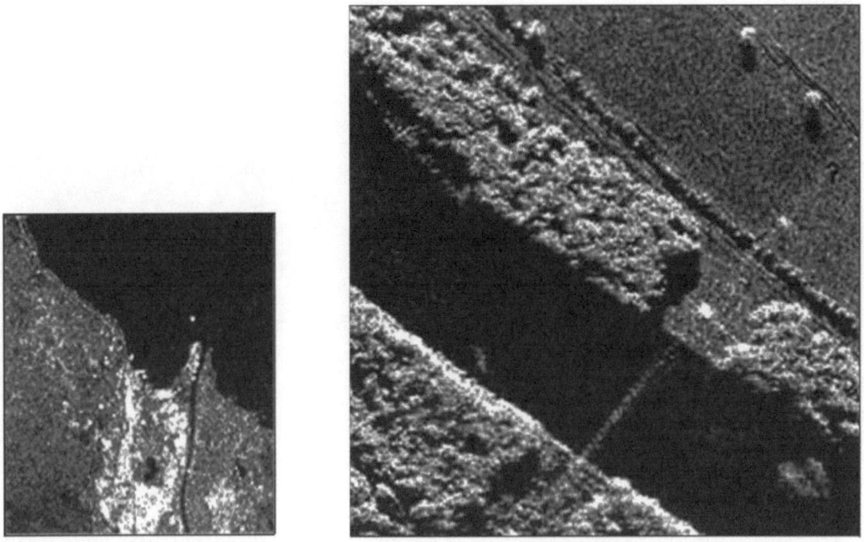

(a) (b)

Fig. 21. Original SAR images. (a) X-band SAR image; (b) Ku-band SAR image.

Fig. 22 shows that all methods are readily able to perform the classification of the X-band SAR image. Fig. 22(b) and (d) show that many mountainous regions in the bottom left are recognized as lake by KM and GAC. Fig.22 (a) and (c) show that MEC can recognize these regions and DSKM can obviously reduce these error recognitions. Meanwhile, KM confuses many mountainous regions in the top left with city seriously. MEC reduce these errors mostly. Generally speaking, the MEC method outputs relatively better partitioning.

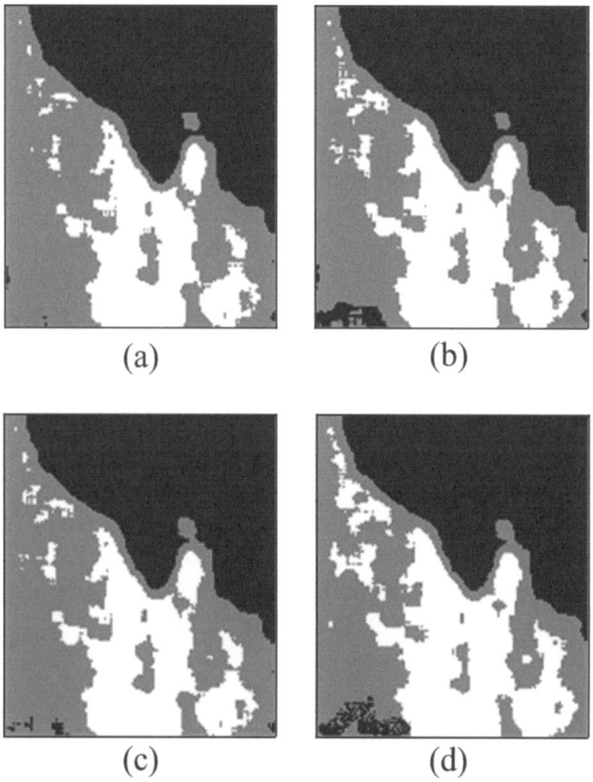

Fig. 22. Implementation results obtained from (a) MEC, (b) GAC, (c) DSKM and (d) KM in clustering the X-band SAR image.

Fig. 23 shows that the MEC, GAC, DSKM and KM generate different results, and all the methods do not perform as well as the first SAR image. Generally speaking, the two methods based on the manifold distance generate better partitioning than GAC and KM. The dissimilarity measure based on Euclidean distance tends to confuse the crop with river. Relatively, MEC and DSKM generate better partitioning of the river region. In distinguishing the vegetation and crop, the partitioning of GAC and KM appear more discontinuous than the results of MEC and DSKM method. GAC and KM tend to confuse the vegetation with crop along the river, delineating the crop more than it should. However, MEC and DSKM tend to identify the vegetation in the bottom left as the river, due to the nature of the gray-level of the leads in that region. DSKM also tends to confuse the vegetation with crop in the region along the river and the bottom left of the image. Generally speaking, MEC does better than DSKM, GAC does better than KM, and MEC and DSKM do much better than GAC and KM, in partitioning this Ku-band SAR image.

3.4.5 Robustness and computing time

In order to compare the robustness of these methods, we follow the criteria used by [76]. In detail, the relative performance of the algorithm m on a particular data set is represented by the ratio b_m of its mean value of Adjusted Rand Index R_m and the highest mean value of Adjusted Rand Index among all the compared methods:

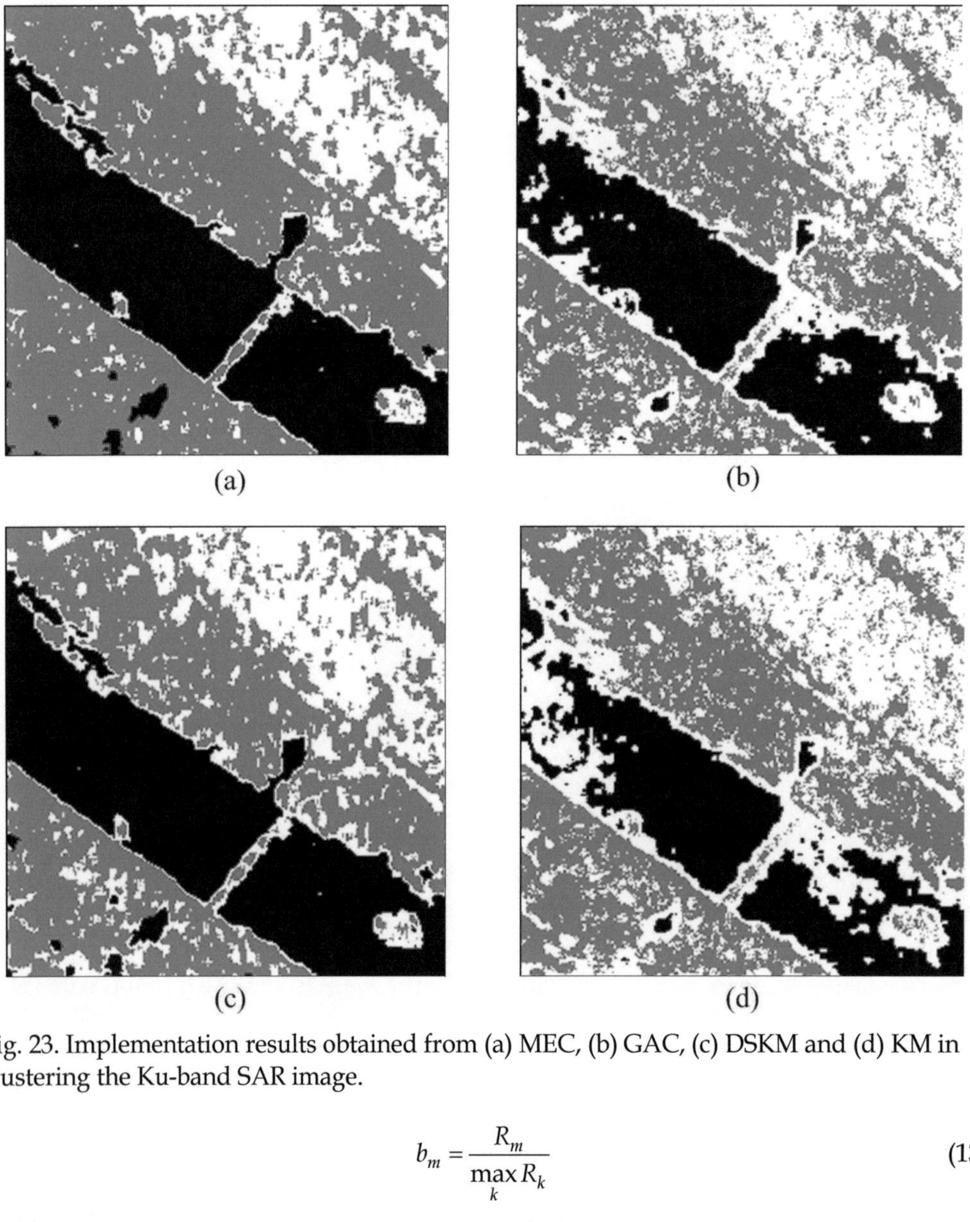

Fig. 23. Implementation results obtained from (a) MEC, (b) GAC, (c) DSKM and (d) KM in clustering the Ku-band SAR image.

$$b_m = \frac{R_m}{\max_k R_k} \qquad (13)$$

The best method m^* on that data set has $b_{m^*}=1$, and all the other methods have $b_m \leq 1$. The larger the value of b_m, the better the performance of the method m is in relation to the best performance on that data set. Thus the sum of b_m over all data sets provides a good measurement of the robustness of the method m. A large value of the sum indicates good robustness.

Fig. 24 shows the distribution of b_m of each method over the ten problems. For each method, the 10 values of b_m are stacked and the sum is given on top of the stack. Fig. 24 reveals that MEC has the highest sum value. In fact, the b_m values of MEC are equal or very close to 1 on all the test problems, which denotes MEC performs very well in different situations. Thus MEC is the most robust method among the compared methods.

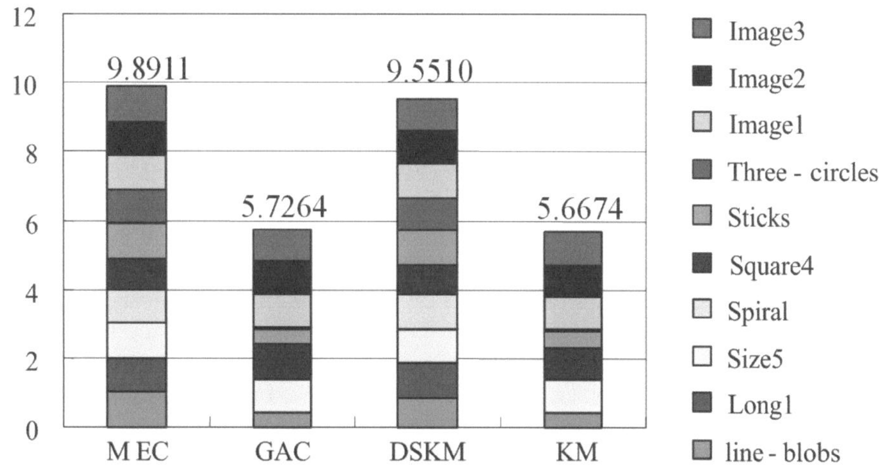

Fig. 24. Robustness of the compared algorithms

Fig. 25 illustrates the sum of the computing time of the four algorithms in solving the twelve problems at an IBM IntelliStation M Pro 6233. From Fig. 25, it can be seen that the computing time of MEC is obviously longer than the computing time of GAC and KM. The main computational cost of MEC lies in computing the manifold distance between each pair of data points.

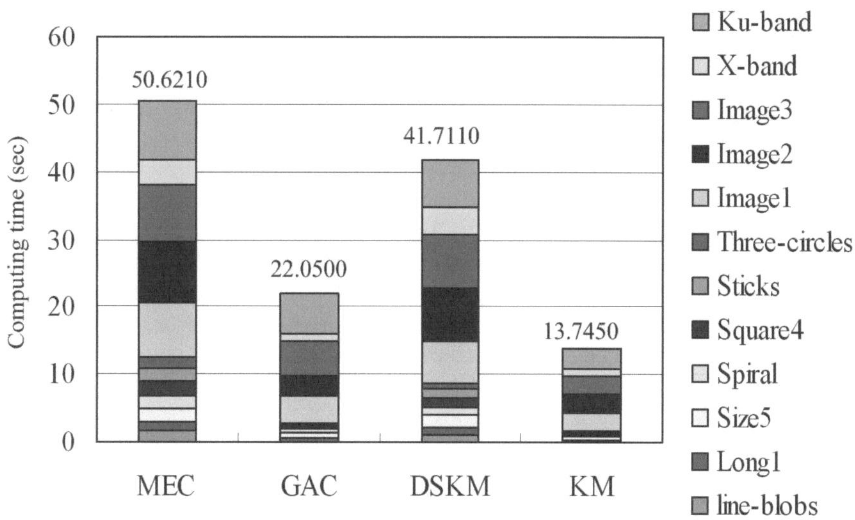

Fig. 25. Computing time of the compared algorithms.

4. Concluding remarks

In the first method, we proposed a novel image segmentation approach based on memetic algorithm called MISA. MISA applies the idea of clustering to achieve image segmentation task. In preprocessing phase, gray-level co-occurrence matrix and wavelet decomposition are used for feature extraction. The watershed segmentation is employed to segment images into non-overlap small regions. MISA tries to find the optimal combination of the watershed regions under the criteria of interclass variance in feature space by a memetic algorithm. In MISA, after implementing cluster-based crossover and mutation, the individual learning procedure moves exocentric regions in current cluster to the one they should belong to according to the distance between these regions and cluster centers in feature space. Then, tournament selection and elitism strategy are used for producing the next generation. If stop criterion is satisfied, the segmentation result is outputted directly using the best individual in population.

In order to evaluate the new algorithm, six artificial texture images, three remote sensing images and three natural images are employed in experiments. The EGSA, SCEA, GISA, FCM and KM are our compared algorithms. We exhibit typical segmentation results, convergence curves for all kinds of images, and numerical results on artificial texture images for which the true partitioning is known. Experimental results showed that MISA outperformed GISA on most of the tested images. The only difference between GISA and MISA lies in the individual learning strategy. Thus the new improvement of MISA could benefit from the learning operator. The comparisons between MISA and the compared algorithms showed that MISA was an effective image segmentation approach.

Image segmentation remains a challenging problem. The main contribution of this study is to make substantial progress through the introduction of memetic computing methods to solving this problem. This study also shows that MAs provide useful computational tools. However we only designed one local search technique for image segmentation problem in this method. We will try to design more individual learning methods to cooperate together as well as higher order learning strategy in our future work.

In this study, we have attempted to illustrate the power of MA for segmenting the three kinds of images, namely texture images, remote sensing images and natural images. In fact, it is difficult or impossible to design an always powerful general-purpose algorithm. Thus, applying the proposed algorithm for practical applications such as magnetic resonance imaging (MRI) image segmentation and synthetic aperture radar (SAR) image segmentation with domain-specific knowledge is also planned in our future work.

In the second method, we proposed the manifold evolutionary clustering using a novel representation method and a manifold distance-based dissimilarity measure to solve unsupervised image classification based on texture features. The experimental results on seven artificial data sets with different manifold structure, three artificial texture images and two SAR images showed that the novel manifold evolutionary clustering algorithm outperformed the KM, GAC and DSKM in terms of cluster quality and robustness. MEC made up the drawbacks of DSKM by evolutionary searching the cluster representatives from a combinatorial optimization viewpoint instead of recalculating the center of each cluster after cluster assignment.

The manifold evolutionary clustering algorithm is a trade-off of flexibility in clustering data with computational complexity. The main computational cost for the flexibility in detecting clusters lies in searching for the shortest path between each pair of data points which makes it much slower than GAC and KM. To find a fast or approximate computing method of the manifold distance is also our future work.

5. References

[1] M. Wertheimer, "Laws of Organization in Perceptual Forms(partial translation)," A Sourcebook of Gestalt Psycychology, W.B.Ellis, ed., pp 71-88, Harcourt, Brace, 1938.

[2] J. Shi, J. Malik. Normalized cuts and image segmentation.IEEE Transactions on Pattern Analysis and Machine Intelligence PAMI, vol. 22, no. 8, pp 888-905, 2000.

[3] L. G. Shapiro and G. C. Stockman. Computer Vision. New Jersey, Prentice-Hall, ISBN 0-13-030796-3, pp 279-325, 2001.
[4] K.V. Mardia and T.J. Hainsworth. A Spatial Thresholding Method for Image Segmentation. IEEE Transactions on Pattern Analysis and Machine Intelligence, vol. 10, no. 6, pp. 919-927, 1988.
[5] P. Perona and J. Malik. Scale-space and edge detection using anisotropic diffusion. IEEE Transactions on Pattern Analysis and Machine Intelligence, vol.12, no. 7, pp. 629-639, 1990.
[6] K. Haris, S. N. Efstratiadis, N. Maglaveras, and A. K. Katsaggelos. Hybrid Image Segmentation Using Watersheds and Fast Region Merging. IEEE Transactions on Image Processing, vol. 7, no. 12, pp. 1684-1699, 1998.
[7] P. F. Felzenszwalb and D. P. Huttenlocher. Efficient Graph-Based Image Segmentation. International Journal of Computer Vision, vol. 59, no. 2, pp. 167-181, 2004.
[8] J. A. Hartigan and M. A.Wong. A K-Means clustering algorithm. Applied Statistics, vol. 28, pp. 100-108, 1979.
[9] B. Bhanu, S. Lee, J. Ming. Adaptive image segmentation using a genetic algorithm. IEEE Transactions on Systems, Man and Cybernetics, vol. 25, no. 12, pp. 1543-1567, 1995.
[10] S. M. Bhandarkar, H. Zhang. Image segmentation using evolutionary computation. IEEE Transactions on Evolutionary Computation, vol. 3, no. 1, pp. 1-21, 1999.
[11] P. Andrey. Selectionist relaxation: Genetic algorithms applied to image segmentation. Image and Vision Computing, vol. 17, no. 3-4, pp. 175-187, 1999.
[12] C. J. Veenman, M. J. T. Reinders, E. Backer. A cellular coevolutionary algorithm for image segmentation. IEEE Transactions on Image Processing, vol. 12, no. 3, pp. 304-313, 2003.
[13] M. Koppen, K. Franke, R. Vicente-Garcia. Tiny GAs for image processing applications. IEEE Computational Intelligence Magazine, vol. 1, no. 2, pp. 17-26, May 2006.
[14] K. E. Melkemi, M. Batouche, and S. Foufou. A multiagent system approach for image segmentation using genetic algorithms and extremal optimization heuristics. Pattern Recognition Letters, vol. 27, no. 11, pp. 1230-1238, 2006.
[15] Maoguo Gong, Licheng Jiao, Liefeng Bo, Ling Wang, Xiangrong Zhang. Image Texture Classification Using a Manifold Distance based Evolutionary Clustering Method. Optical Engineering, vol. 47, no. 7, pp. 077201-1-10, 2008.
[16] U. Maulik. Medical Image Segmentation Using Genetic Algorithms. IEEE Transactions on Information Technology in Biomedicine, vol. 13, no. 2, pp. 166-173, 2009.
[17] Q. C. Nguyen, Y. S. Ong and M. H. Lim. A Probabilistic Memetic Framework. IEEE Transactions on Evolutionary Computation, vol. 13, no. 3, pp. 604-623, 2009.
[18] K. W. C. Ku, M. W. Mak, and W. C. Siu. A study of the Lamarckian evolution of recurrent neural networks. IEEE Transactions on Evolutionary Computation, vol. 4, no. 1, pp. 31-42, 2000.
[19] S. A. Kazarlis, S. E. Papadakis, J. B. Theocharis, V. Petridis. Microgenetic algorithms as generalized hill-climbing operators for GA optimization. IEEE Transactions on Evolutionary Computation, vol. 5, no. 3, pp. 204-217, 2001.
[20] Y. S. Ong and A. J. Keane. Meta-lamarckian learning in memetic algorithms. IEEE Transactions on Evolutionary Computation, vol. 8, no. 2, pp. 99-110, 2004.
[21] N. Krasnogor and J. Smith. A tutorial for competent memetic algorithms: model, taxonomy, and design issues. IEEE Transactions on Evolutionary Computation, vol. 9, no. 5, pp. 474–488, 2005.

[22] A. Caponio, G. L. Cascella, F. Neri, N. Salvatore, and M. Sumner. A fast adaptive memetic algorithm for online and offline control design of pmsm drives. IEEE Transactions on Systems, Man and Cybernetics - Part B, vol. 37, no. 1, pp. 28-41, 2007.
[23] M. Tang and X. Yao. A memetic algorithm for VLSI floorplanning. IEEE Transactions on Systems, Man and Cybernetics - Part B, vol. 37, no. 1, pp. 62–69, 2007.
[24] J. Tang, M. H. Lim, and Y. S. Ong. Diversity-adaptive parallel memetic algorithm for solving large scale combinatorial optimization problems. Soft Computation, vol. 11, no. 9, pp. 873-888, 2007.
[25] Z. Zhu, Y. S. Ong and M. Dash. Wrapper-Filter Feature Selection Algorithm Using A Memetic Framework. IEEE Transactions On Systems, Man and Cybernetics - Part B, vol. 37, no. 1, pp. 70-76, Feb 2007.
[26] S. Hasan, R. Sarker, D. Essam, and D. Cornforth. Memetic algorithms for solving job-shop scheduling problems. Memetic Computing, vol. 1, no. 1, pp. 69-83, 2009.
[27] Jong-Hwan Kim, Ye-Hoon Kim, Seung-Hwan Choi, In-Won Park. Evolutionary multi-objective optimization in robot soccer system for education. IEEE Computational Intelligence Magazine, vol. 4, no. 1, pp. 31-41, February 2009 .
[28] Shinkyu Jeong, S. Hasegawa, K. Shimoyama, S. Obayashi. Development and investigation of efficient GA/PSO-HYBRID algorithm applicable to real-world design optimization. IEEE Computational Intelligence Magazine, vol. 4, no. 3, pp. 36-44, Aug. 2009.
[29] S. C. Chiam, K. C. Tan, and A. Al. Mamun. A memetic model of evolutionary PSO for computational finance applications. Expert Systems With Applications, vol. 36, no. 2, pp. 3695-3711, March 2009.
[30] K. C. Tan, S. C. Chiam, et al. Balancing exploration and exploitation with adaptive variation for evolutionary multi-objective optimization. European Journal of Operational Research, vol. 197, no. 2, pp. 701-713, 2009.
[31] J. H. Ang, K. C. Tan, and A. A. Mamun. An evolutionary memetic algorithm for rule extraction. Expert Systems With Applications, vol. 37, no. 2, pp. 1302-1315, March 2010.
[32] Y. S. Ong, M. H. Lim, X Chen. Research Frontier: Towards Memetic Computing. Technical Report, School of Computer Engineering, Nanyang Technological University, Singapore, December 2009.
[33] E. Fernandez, M. Grana, J. Cabello. An instantaneous memetic algorithm for illumination correction. In: Proceedings of the IEEE Congress on Evolutionary Computation, vol. 1, pp 1105-1110, 2004.
[34] K. Batenburg. An evolutionary algorithm for discrete tomography. Discrete Applied Mathematics, vol. 151, no. 1-3, pp 36-54, 2005.
[35] V. Tirronen, F. Neri, T. Kärkkäinen, K. Majava, T. Rossi. An enhanced memetic differential evolution in filter design for defect detection in paper production. Evolutionary Computation, vol. 16, no. 4, pp 529-555, 2008.
[36] V. D. Gesù, G. L. Bosco, F. Millonzi, C. Valenti. A Memetic Algorithm for Binary Image Reconstruction. Lecture Notes in Computer Science, vol. 4958, Springer, pp 384-395, 2008.
[37] V. D. Gesù, G. L. Bosco, F. Millonzi, C. Valenti. Discrete tomography reconstruction through a new memetic algorithm. Lecture Notes in Computer Science, vol. 4974, Springer, pp 347-352, 2008.

[38] Qingzhou Zhang, Ziqiang Wang and Dexian Zhang. Memetic Algorithm-Based Image Watermarking Scheme. Lecture Notes in Computer Science, vol. 5263, Springer, pp 845-853, 2008.

[39] J. C. Bezdek. Pattern Recognition with Fuzzy Objective Function Algoritms. Plenum Press, New York, 1981.

[40] Xiangrong Zhang, Licheng Jiao, Fang Liu, Liefeng Bo, Maoguo Gong. Spectral Clustering Ensemble Applied to Texture Features for SAR Image Segmentation. IEEE Transactions on Geoscience and Remote Sensing, vol. 46, no. 7, pp 2126-2136, 2008.

[41] R. M. Haralick, K. Shanmugam and I. Dinstein. Textural features for images classification. IEEE Transactions on Systems, Man, and Cybernetics, vol. 3, no. 6, pp. 610-621, 1973.

[42] S. Fukuda and H. Hirosawa. A wavelet-based texture feature set applied to classification of multifrequency polarimetric SAR images. IEEE Transactions on Geoscience and Remote Sensing, vol. 37, no. 8, pp. 2282-2286, 1999.

[43] D. A. Clausi and B. Yue. Comparing Cooccurrence Probabilities and Markov Random Fields for Texture Analysis of SAR Sea Ice Imagery. IEEE Transactions on Geoscience and Remote Sensing, vol. 42, no. 1, pp. 215-228, 2004.

[44] D.A. Clausi. An analysis of co-occurrence texture statistics as a function of grey level quantization," Canadian Journal of Remote Sensing, vol. 28, no. 1, pp. 45-62, 2002.

[45] D. Wang. A Multiscale Gradient Algorithm for Image Segmentation Using Watersheds. Pattern Recognition, vol. 30, no. 12, pp. 2043-2052, 1997.

[46] A. Hoeffler, U. Leysner, and J. Weidermann. Optimization of the layout of trusses combining strategies based on Mitchel's theorem and on biological principles of evolution. In: Proceedings of the Second Symposium on Structural Optimization, Milan, Italy, 1973.

[47] P. Moscato. On Evolution, Search, Optimization Algorithms and Martial Arts: Towards Memetic Algorithms. Report 826, Caltech Concurrent Computation Program, California Institute of Technology, Pasadena, 1989.

[48] L. O. Hall, I. B. Ozyurt and J. C. Bezdek. Clustering with a genetically optimized approach. IEEE Transactions on Evolutionary Computation, vol. 3, no. 2, pp. 103-112, 1999.

[49] U. Maulik and S. Bandyopadhyay. Genetic algorithm-based clustering technique. Pattern Recognition, vol. 33, no. 9, pp. 1455-1465, 2000.

[50] H. Pan, J. Zhu and D. Han. Genetic algorithms applied to multiclass clustering for gene expression data. Genomics, Proteomics & Bioinformatics, vol. 1, no. 4, pp. 279-287, 2003.

[51] Maoguo Gong, Licheng Jiao, Ling Wang, Liefeng Bo. Density-Sensitive Evolutionary Clustering. In: Proceedings of the 11th Pacific-Asia Conference on Knowledge Discovery and Data Mining, PAKDD07. Springer-Verlag, Lecture Notes in Computer Science, LNAI, vol. 4426, pp. 507-514, 2007.

[52] P. Brodatz. Textures: A Photographic Album for Artists and Designers. Dover Publications, New York, 1966.

[53] M. Tuceryan and A. K. Jain, "Texture analysis," In *Handbook of Pattern Recognition and Computer Vision*, C. Chen, L. Pau and P. Wang, Eds., pp. 235-276, World Scientific, Singapore (1993).

[54] D. A. Clausi and B. Yue, "Comparing Cooccurrence Probabilities and Markov Random Fields for Texture Analysis of SAR Sea Ice Imagery," *IEEE Transactions on Geoscience and Remote Sensing*, 42(1), 215-228 (2004).

[55] R. M. Haralick, K. Shanmugam and I. Dinstein, "Textural features for images classification," *IEEE Transactions on Systems, Man, and Cybernetics*, 3(6), 610-621 (1973).
[56] H. Frigui and R. Krishnapuram, "A Robust Competitive Clustering Algorithm with Applications in Computer Vision," *IEEE Transactions on Pattern Analysis and Machine Intelligence*, 21(5), 450-465 (1999).
[57] Y. Leung, J. Zhang and Z. Xu, "Clustering by Space-Space Filtering," *IEEE Transactions on Pattern Analysis and Machine Intelligence*, 22(12), 1396-1410 (2000).
[58] J. A. Hartigan and M. A.Wong, "A K-Means clustering algorithm," *Applied Statistics*, 28, 100-108 (1979).
[59] L. O. Hall, I. B. Ozyurt and J. C. Bezdek, "Clustering with a genetically optimized approach, " *IEEE Transactions on Evolutionary Computation*, 3(2), 103-112 (1999).
[60] U. Maulik and S. Bandyopadhyay, "Genetic algorithm-based clustering technique, " *Pattern Recognition*, 33(9), 1455-1465 (2000).
[61] H. Pan, J. Zhu and D. Han, "Genetic algorithms applied to multiclass clustering for gene expression data," *Genomics, Proteomics & Bioinformatics*, 1(4), 279-287 (2003).
[62] J. Handl, J. Knowles, "An evolutionary approach to multiobjective clustering," *IEEE Transactions on Evolutionary Computation*, 11(1), 56-76 (2007).
[63] M.C. Su and C. H. Chou, "A modified version of the K-Means algorithm with a distance based on cluster symmetry," *IEEE Transactions on Pattern Analysis and Machine Intelligence*, 23(6), 674-680 (2001).
[64] D. Charalampidis, "A Modified K-Means Algorithm for Circular Invariant Clustering," *IEEE Transactions on Pattern Analysis and Machine Intelligence*, 27(12), 1856-1865 (2005).
[65] L. Wang, L. F. Bo and L. C. Jiao, "A modified K-Means clustering with a density-sensitive distance metric," *Lecture Notes in Computer Science*, 4062, 544-551 (2006).
[66] A. Blum and S. Chawla, "Learning from labeled and unlabeled data using graph mincuts," In *Proceedings of the Eighteenth International Conference on Machine Learning*, 19-26 (2001).
[67] O. Bousquet, O. Chapelle and M. Hein, "Measure based regularization," *Advances in Neural Information Processing Systems 16 (NIPS)*, MIT Press, Cambridge, MA (2004).
[68] G. Syswerda, "Uniform crossover in genetic algorithms," In *Proceedings of the Third International Conference on Genetic Algorithms*, pp2-9, Morgan Kaufmann Publishers, San Francisco, CA (1989).
[69] D. Whitley, "A genetic algorithm tutorial," *Statistics and Computing*, 4, 65-85 (1994).
[70] D. E. Goldberg, *Genetic Algorithms in Search, Optimization, and Machine Learning*, Addison-Wesley, Massachusetts (1989).
[71] D. A. Clausi, "An analysis of co-occurrence texture statistics as a function of grey level quantization," *Can. J. Remote Sens.*, 28(1), 45-62 (2002).
[72] L. Hubert and P. Arabie, "Comparing partitions," *Journal of Classification*, 193-218 (1985).
[73] K. Y. Yeung and W. L. Ruzzo, "Principal component analysis for clustering gene expression data," *Bioinformatics*, 17(9), 763-774 (2001).
[74] W. Rand, "Objective criteria for the evaluation of clustering methods," *Journal of the American Statistical Association*, 66(336), 846-850 (1971).
[75] P. Brodatz, *Textures: A Photographic Album for Artists and Designers*, Dover Publications, New York (1966).
[76] X. Geng, D. C. Zhan and Z. H. Zhou, "Supervised nonlinear dimensionality reduction for visualization and classification," *IEEE Transactions on Systems, Man, and Cybernetics - Part B: Cybernetics*, 35(6), 1098-1107 (2005).

11

Segmentation of Handwritten Document Images into Text Lines

Vassilis Katsouros and Vassilis Papavassiliou
Institute for Language and Speech Processing/R.C. "Athena"
Greece

1. Introduction

There are many governmental, cultural, commercial and educational organizations that manage large number of manuscript textual information. Since the management of information recorded on paper or scanned documents is a hard and time-consuming task, Document Image Analysis (DIA) aims to extract the intended information as a human would (Nagy, 2000). The main subtasks of DIA (Mao et al. 2003) are: i) the document layout analysis, which aims to locate the "physical" components of the document such as columns, paragraphs, text lines, words, tables and figures, ii) the document content analysis, for understanding/labelling these components as titles, legends, footnotes, etc. iii) the optical character recognition (OCR) and iv) the reconstruction of the corresponding electronic document.

The proposed algorithms that address the above-mentioned processing stages come mainly from the fields of image processing, computer vision, machine learning and pattern recognition. Actually, some of these algorithms are very effective in processing machine-printed document images and therefore they have been incorporated in the workflows of well-known OCR systems. On the contrary, no such efficient systems have been developed for handling handwritten documents. The main reason is that the format of a handwritten manuscript and the writing style depend solely on the author's choices. For example, one could consider that text lines in a machine-printed document are of the same skew, while handwritten text lines may be curvilinear.

Text line segmentation is a critical stage in layout analysis, upon which further tasks such as word segmentation, grouping of text lines into paragraphs, characterization of text lines as titles, headings, footnotes, etc. may be developed. For instance, a task for text-line segmentation is involved in the pipeline of the Handwritten Address Interpretation System (HWAIS), which takes a postal address image and determines a unique delivery point (Cohen et al., 1994). Another application, in which text line extraction is considered as a pre-processing step, is the indexing of George Washington papers at the Library of Congress as detailed by Manmatha & Rothfeder, 2005. A similar document analysis project, called the Bovary Project, includes a text-line segmentation stage towards the transcription of the manuscripts of Gustave Flaubert (Nicolas et al., 2004a). In addition, many recent projects, which focus on digitisation of archives, include activities for document image understanding in terms of automatic or semi-automatic extraction and indexing of metadata such as titles, subtitles, keywords, etc. (Antonacopoulos & Karatzas, 2004, Tomai et al., 2002). Obviously, these activities include text-line extraction.

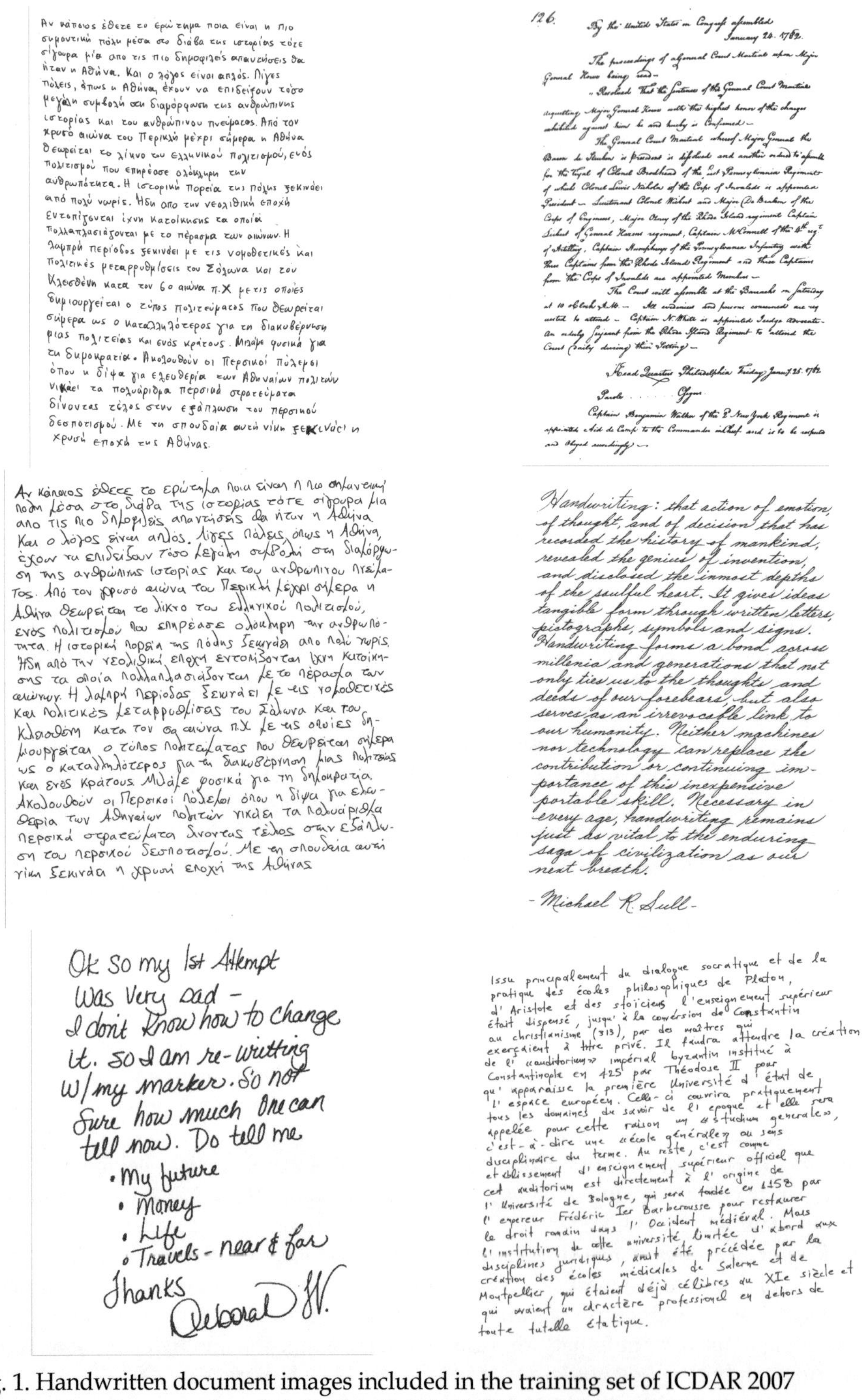

Fig. 1. Handwritten document images included in the training set of ICDAR 2007 Handwriting Segmentation: 024.tif, 016.tif, 010.tif, 044.tif, 068.tif and 026.tif

This chapter is a comprehensive survey of methods exploited to segment handwritten document images into text lines during the last two decades. The main underlying assumption is that the non-textual information has been removed and the document image comprises only plain text. Even though this hypothesis seems to simplify the task, text-line segmentation has to face many challenges, such as the touching or overlapping text lines and the variation of skew angles. Some typical examples of handwritten document images are illustrated in fig. 1. In the next sections, we will describe, in detail, how the proposed methods try to overcome these difficulties.

The main idea in text-line segmentation is to consider the foreground pixel density and employ one of the following three broad classes of techniques (Razak et al., 2008). The first includes traditional methods that have been applied to printed documents and is based on the analysis of projection profiles. The second class incorporates grouping techniques, also known as bottom-up strategies that attempt to build text lines by considering the alignments of foreground pixels or connected components. The third category includes smearing approaches that aim to enhance the text lines structure by applying linear or morphological filters and exploiting well-known image segmentation methods, such as level sets, scale-space analysis (Lindeberg, & Eklundh, 1992), etc. Moreover, there are some methods that exploit a combination of these techniques with the purpose to improve further the segmentation results.

In section 2, the problem definition and the main challenges of the task are described. Several techniques and the contributions of the most effective algorithms within each class are presented in section 3. The available recourses for validating relative methods and the comparative results of recent contests are reported in section 4. Finally, the chapter is concluded with a discussion of the main outcomes.

2. Background

When creating a manuscript, the author selects the writing instrument and the paper in such a way as to produce a readable document, namely a document with high contrast between the traces of the pen (foreground) and the paper (background). As a consequence, the digitisation of these documents in most of the cases generates binary images. In the case of grey-scale document images, most of the proposed methods for text-line extraction incorporate an initial processing stage of binarization by employing global (Otsu, 1979) or local thresholding (Niblack, 1986, Sauvola & Pietikäinen, 2000). However, some recent techniques combine the results of processing both the grey-scale and the binary versions of the document image.

In binary document images, the traces of the writing instrument are represented by pixels that have value one and constitute the text. The other pixels have value zero, corresponding to the background. The convention for using the values 1 and 0 for foreground and background pixels respectively is very common in studies related to the binary images.

2.1 Definitions

Considering that a two-dimensional binary image is defined on the discrete plane $\mathbb{Z}^2$ and by selecting a square grid and a certain type of connectivity (e.g. 8-n denotes all the neighbours of a pixel, while 4-n indicates only the cross neighbours), we could represent objects or shapes of the image as groups of neighbouring pixels with the same value. In the view of set theory, a binary image is modelled by the corresponding set S as follows:

$$S = \{\mathbf{x} \in \mathbb{Z}^2 : s(\mathbf{x}) = 1\} \quad (1)$$

where $\mathbf{x}$ denotes the coordinates of a pixel and s is a binary function $s : \mathbb{Z}^2 \rightarrow \{0,1\}$ (Soille, 2004). Then, the shapes in the binary image are defined as the maximal connected subsets of the image foreground pixels, called connected components (CCs). Therefore, the CCs in a document image could be noise specks, dots, single symbols, groups of touching characters, parts of a character that is broken, etc. The extraction of CCs is accomplished by applying a connected component operator that assigns the same value to every pixel of each distinct CC. A common algorithm for identifying CCs is outlined in (Haralick & Shapiro, 1992).

A text line could be considered as a group of CCs that are adjacent, relative close to each other and correspond to occurrences of text elements. By adopting this simple definition, text-line segmentation produces an image, in which each text pixel has a value that identifies the proper text-line (fig. 2, left). Alternatively, a text line could be represented by a large CC that covers the corresponding part of the image, or by a closed curve that represents the boundary of each text line (fig. 2, right).

Fig. 2. Representation of text lines as: groups of text pixels with the same value (left) and parts of the document image (right)

2.2 Challenges

The main challenges of text-line segmentation of handwritten documents arise from the variation of the skew angle between text lines or along the same text line, the existence of overlapping and/or touching lines, the variable character size, the variation of intra-line and inter-line gaps and the non-manhattan layout. To overcome these difficulties, an efficient text-line segmentation algorithm should represent the boundaries of each text line by a closed curve instead of enclosing a text line with a rectangular. In addition, such an algorithm should incorporate procedures for cutting CCs which running along two or more text lines. These are the major differences in handling manuscripts rather than machine-printed documents.

Actually, text line segmentation in printed documents could be seen as a solved problem (Plamondon & Srihari, 2000), which is equivalent with the estimation of the document's skew angle. A comprehensive survey and the annotated bibliography on skew detection of printed document images are presented in (Hull, 1998). To this point, it is supposed that text lines in a printed document have a unique skew angle. Thus, the proper rotation of the image will result to horizontal text lines that could be easily located. A well-known and efficient method for layout analysis of printed documents, called Docstrum, is outlined in (O'Gorman, 1993). The main assumption is that the distances between characters of the same text line are smaller than the distances between characters of successive text lines. The fact that this assumption does not hold for manuscripts, explains why Docstrum cannot handle handwritten documents successfully, as shown in fig. 3.
As mentioned above, this task focuses on text elements only. Therefore, noise removal is the first pre-processing step. In binary document images which incorporate merely textual information, noise removal is equivalent with the elimination of CCs that do not represent text elements but mainly occur due to misses at the digitisation phase. In document images which are considered as normally "clear", simple methods adopting median filters or heuristics based on geometrical and topological properties of the CCs are employed to remove the noisy data. For example, a large CC, which is lying on the edges of the image arises due to the inaccurate placement of the manuscript to the scanner and need to be removed. However, the extraction of actual text elements from digitised historical archives might be a significant issue. Actually, historical documents suffer from smudges, smears, faded print and bleed-through of writing from the opposite side of a page (Likforman-Sulem et al., 2007).
Document images are captured in high resolution (about 300dpi) in order to be suitable for OCR engines. However, text lines have an underlying texture that is manifest in printed documents at low resolutions about 40dpi (Bloomberg, 1996). Hence, subsampling methods that prevent aliasing are also applied in text-line segmentation.

3. Proposed methods

Handwritten documents are characterised by high variability of writing styles. Thus, most of the existing methods adapt to the properties of a document image and eliminate the use of prior knowledge. According to the adopted strategy, the existing methods are classified in three categories, which are discussed in this section. In general, text-line segmentation techniques are script independent. However, some special scripts such as Indian and Arabic incorporate many characters with diacritical points that require great care in CCs assignment.

3.1 Projection-based methods

Given that an image $\mathbf{A}$ with height M and width N could be considered as a matrix of the same dimensions, the projection profile of the image is defined as follows:

$$P(i) = \sum_{j=1}^{N} \mathbf{A}(i,j), \quad i = 1,\dots,M \tag{2}$$

Therefore, the projection is a one-dimensional signal that denotes the amount of text pixels per row. Consequently, the lobes (valleys) of the projection correspond to foreground

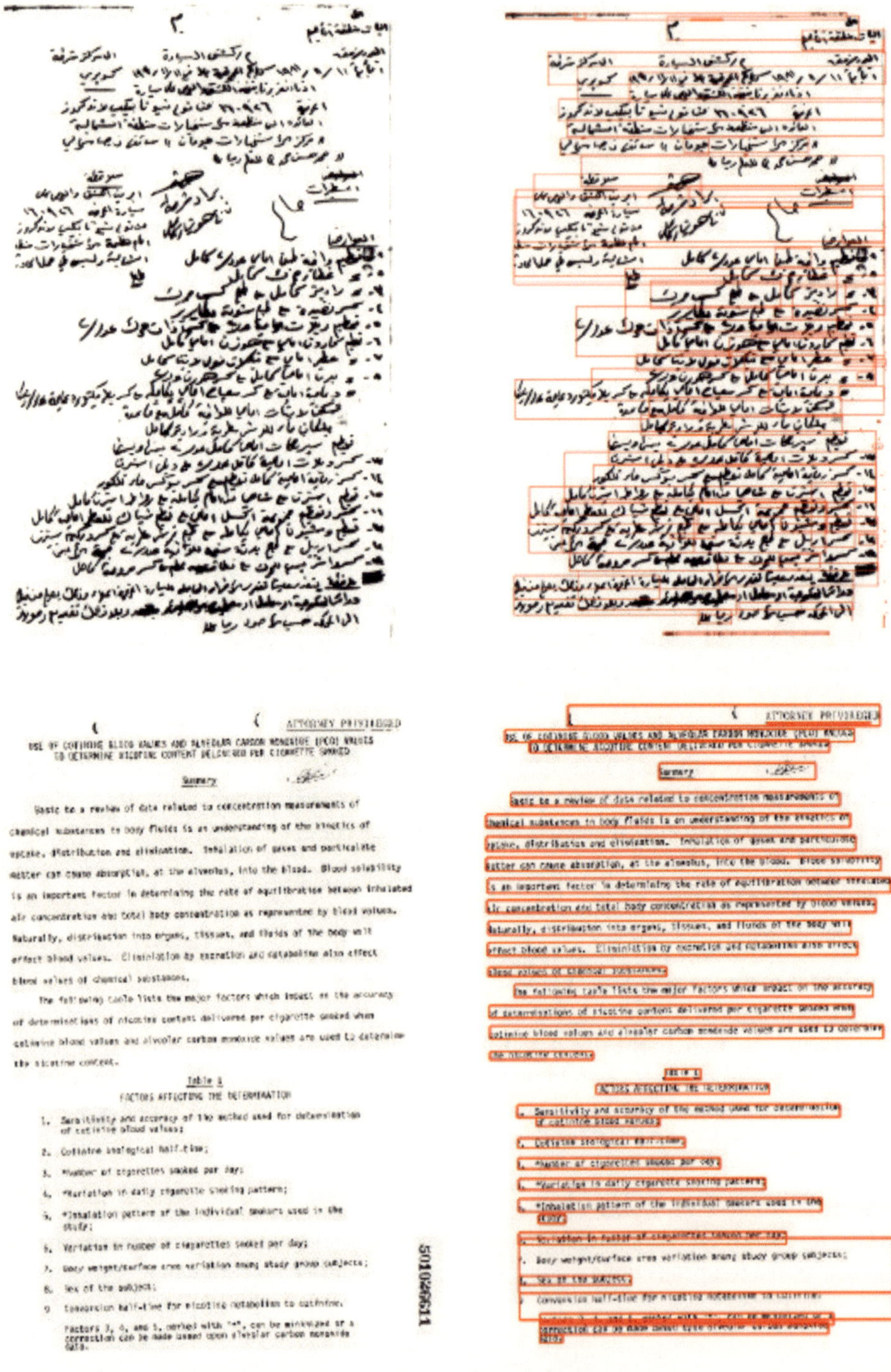

Fig. 3. Text-line segmentation of a machine-printed and a handwritten document image by exploiting the Docstrum method (O'Gorman, 1993). The figure is reprinted (Li et al., 2008) with permission from the author.

(background) areas of the image. Supposing that the text lines have the same skew angle, the amplitude and the frequency of the projection are maximized when the skew of the text is zero. Based on this characteristic, many proposed approaches rotate the image through a range of angles, calculate the projection for each angle and estimate the global skew angle according to a properly selected criterion. Such a criterion could be based on the variance of the projections (Bloomberg et al., 1993) and the sum of the coefficients of the power spectrum (Postl, 1988). After estimating the unique skew angle and rotating the image appropriately, the local minima of the projection allocate the positions of text-line separators.

In machine-printed documents, the separators will be horizontal lines lying within the space between adjacent text lines. Apparently, this might be occurred in some manuscripts written with great care and consistency. In fact, this technique is adopted for the process of 1000 sampled documents from the George Washington corpus at the Library of Congress (Manmatha & Rothfeder, 2005). The additional processing step is the smoothing of the projection by applying a Gaussian low pass filter in order to eliminate false alarms (i.e. insignificant minima) and reduce the noise. A similar method (Santos et al., 2009) includes a post-processing stage for labeling candidate text lines as false or actual, according to their geometrical features (i.e. lines, which correspond to very narrow lobes of the projection, should be removed). Although this approach has been tested in 150 images from the IAM off-line handwritten database (Marti & Bunke, 2002) and showed almost excellent results, it is worth to mention that the text-line segmentation in documents of this database seems to be a straightforward task.

A common feature of manuscripts is the overlapping of successive text lines due to the ascenders and/or descenders of some characters. Hence, the formulation of a horizontal line as a separator is often not feasible. With the purpose to overcome this difficulty, some researchers exploit the projections in order to locate the areas (i.e. the areas between two successive maxima) in which the separators should be allocated. Considering ascenders/descenders as obstacles, the algorithms try to find a path from the left to the right edge in each area, by attempting to move around the obstacles (fig. 4). If the deviation is too high, the algorithm intersects the character and continues forward. Such segmenters could be based on predefined constrains (Yanikoglu & Sandon, 1998) or on the minimization of a proper cost function (Weliwitage et al., 2005).

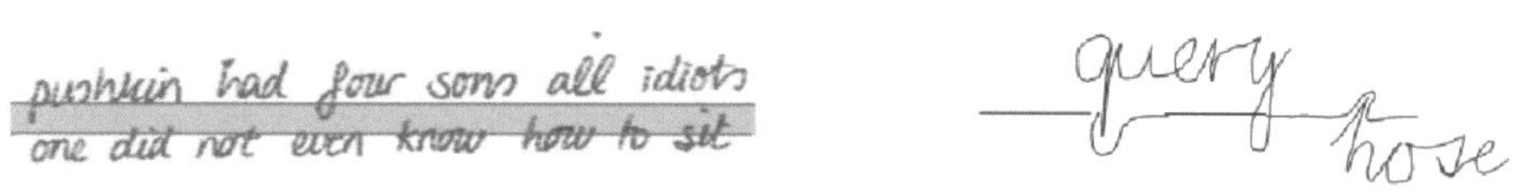

Fig. 4. The line separator should be lying in the gray area between the text lines (left, reprinted from Yanikoglu & Sandon, 1998). The final line separator (right, reprinted from Weliwitage et al., 2005).

Since variation of skew angles between text lines or along the same text line is common in manuscripts, the global projections based approaches cannot provide a general solution. Piece-wise projections can be seen as a modification of global projections to the properties of handwritten documents, by which the separators between text lines are drawn in staircase function fashion along the width of the document page. The main idea of piece-wise projections is to divide the document image in vertical non-overlapping equi-width zones and find the critical local minima of each projection. The selection of the width of the zones is a trade-off between the local skew and the text density. In other words, if the width was large enough, the skew should not be considered as constant. Furthermore, a narrow width would produce zones, which do not include adequate amount of text. Relative experiments showed that a zone width equal to 5% of the document image width seems to be an appropriate value.

However, the non-manhattan layout of manuscripts will result in vertical zones without enough foreground pixels for every text line. In such cases, some local minima may be lost and the results of two adjacent zones may be ambiguous. To deal with these problems, we calculate a smooth version of the projections influenced by the neighboring zones and introduce a separator-drawing algorithm that combines separators of consecutive zones according to their proximity and the local text density as shown in fig. 5 (Papavassiliou et al. 2010).

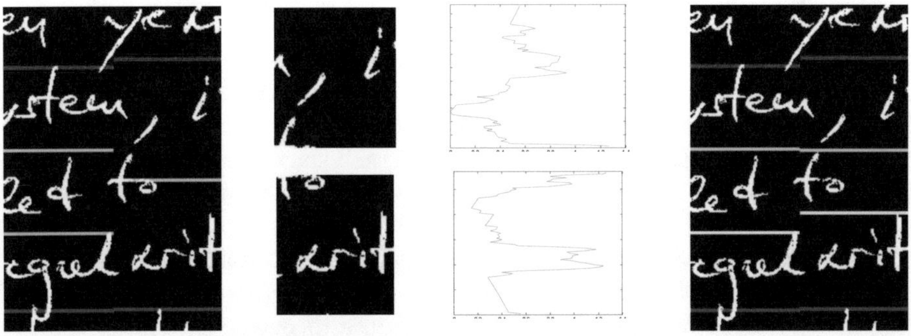

Fig. 5. The separator-drawing algorithm (reprinted from Papavassiliou et al., 2010). The separators in green are ambiguous (first column). New separators in these areas (second column) should be located at the global minima of the metric function (third column) influenced by the local foreground density and the proximity of the separators. The separators with the same colors are associated (fourth column).

The last challenge that projection-based methods have to face is the assignment of CCs to the proper text-lines. In most of the cases, this is a straightforward task since the majority of CCs lie between two line separators. However, some CCs either overlap with two text lines (i.e. characters with ascenders/descenders) or run along two text lines (touching lines). In order to preserve the ascending/descending symbols from been corrupted by arbitrary cuts, several heuristics based on the geometrical and topological properties such as the height, the length, the distance of neighboring CCs, etc. have been proposed. An interesting approach models the text lines by bivariate Gaussian densities considering the coordinates of the pixels of the CCs that have been already assigned. Then, the probabilities that the CC under consideration belongs to the upper or lower text lines are estimated and the decision is made by comparing the probabilities (Arivazhagan et al., 2007). This method has been tested on 720 documents including English, Arabic and children's handwriting and performed a detection rate of 97.31%. In the case that a character should be split, the segmentation occurs at a proper cross point of the skeleton (Lam et al., 1992) by taking account the distance from the separator (fig. 6) as well as the slope and curvature of the stroke (Kuzhinjedathu et al., 2008).

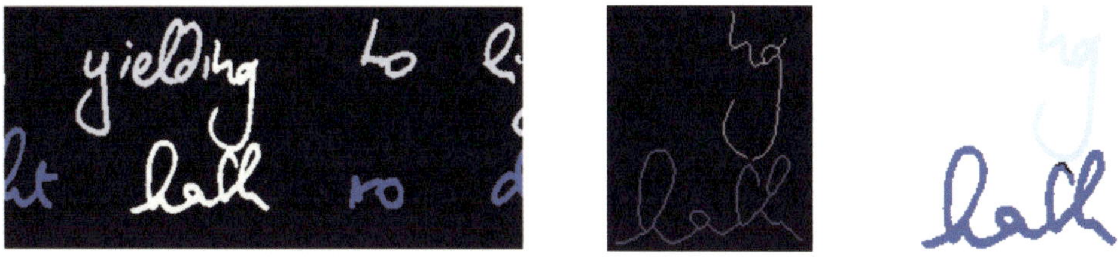

Fig. 6. Segmentation of a CC running along two text lines (reprinted from Papavassiliou et al., 2010).

3.2 Grouping methods

Grouping approaches, also known as bottom-up techniques, were very popular in text-line segmentation of handwritten documents due to their success in prior tasks concerning the process of machine-printed documents (Simon et al., 1997). These methods try to group CCs considering geometrical and topological characteristics of the CCs such as their distances, locations and orientation. The common strategy is to represent each CC with an appropriate vector (e.g. the coordinates of its gravity centre), calculate the distances between that point and the corresponding points of its neighbouring CCs and compare the distances with a proper predefined value. If the constrain is satisfied the CCs are grouped (Khandelwal et al., 2009). Since such methods strongly depend on the values of the thresholds, they cannot handle variation in writing styles. In fact, (Feldbach & Tonnies, 2001) report that a similar method tested on historical church registers achieved a 97% recall rate when the thresholds values are adjusted to specific authors but decreased to 90% when these parameters remained constant for various authors. As a result, many recent methods produce an adjacency graph constructed by linking the pairs of neighbouring CCs with edges. Then, they try recursively to find the minimum spanning tree, which likely crosses CCs of the same text line (Nicolas et al., 2004b).

Additionally, the orientations of the edges that connect these points are also examined. Supposing that CCs in the same text line could be represented by almost collinear points, Hough transform (Duda, & Hart, 1972) has been applied on handwritten documents. Although Hough-based approaches locate text lines with different skew angles correctly, they are not flexible to follow variation of skew along the same text line (fig. 7 left).

3.3 Smearing methods

In general, smearing approaches include two main processing steps. The first stage aims to enhance text areas by blurring the input image. The second step concerns the modification and use of well-known image segmentation methods in order to formulate the text lines. Li et al. (2008) apply an anisotropic Gaussian filter to smooth the image and provide a grey-scale "probabilistic" image that denotes the text line distribution. It is worth to mention that the horizontal dimension of the filter is greater than the vertical in order to advance the mainly horizontal text-line orientation. Then, they locate the initial boundaries of text lines or parts of them using Niblack's algorithm for binarization and finding the contours of the CCs in the produced binary image. Next, the level set method (Osher & Fedkiw, 2003) is adopted and the boundaries evolve concerning the local curvature and density with the purpose of moving fast along the horizontal direction and towards areas with high

Fig. 7. (left) Results of Hough-based transform (reprinted from Louloudis et al., 2008); (right) Segmentation of CCs based on min-cut/max-flow algorithm (reprinted from Kennard & Barret, 2006).

probability being text. This method has been tested on several manuscripts in different scripts and performed pixel-level hit rates varying from 92% to 98%. As expected, the proposed method fails when the gap between two neighbouring text lines is smaller than the vertical dimension of the Gaussian filter. A similar approach adopts the Mumford-Shah model to locate text lines and then applies morphological operations to either segment merged text lines or join parts of the same text line (Du et al., 2008). Instead of using erosions and dilations Yin & Liu (2009) apply a modification of the variational Bayes framework to the downsampled input image. The binary image (after down-sampling, smoothing and binarization) is considered as a mixture model in which each CC is a Gaussian component. Since, a CC may correspond to more than one text lines, a CC is split according to the second eigenvalue of the covariance (i.e. thick CCs are candidate to be segmented).

Other smearing strategies enhance the text areas by estimating an adaptive local connectivity map (ALCM). This map is actually a grey-scale image in which each pixel has a value that denotes the amount of text pixels in the proximity of the pixel under consideration. By converting this image to a binary one, the resulting CCs represent the text areas of the document image. In most cases, these CCs include many text lines and should be split. Considering such a CC as a graph with candidate source (sink) nodes the pixels in the upper (lower) part, the min-cut/max flow algorithm has been proposed for segmenting the CC to its main components (Kennard & Barret, 2006), as illustrated in fig. 7 right. Alternatively, the ALCM could be replaced by another image produced by applying the run length smoothing algorithm (RLSA). In this image, the value of a pixel is the distance of that pixel from the nearest text pixel. As previously, text areas are represented by pixels with small (dark) values while background corresponds to bright areas. Then, dark areas are grouped according to their orientation and proximity in order to formulate text lines (Shi & Govindaraju, 2004).

4. Evaluation

Research groups test their method either on their own collection of handwritten documents or on a public available database. As a result, many such test sets have been constructed. In this section, we refer to three well-known collections that could be used for evaluating various processing steps such as text-line segmentation, word segmentation and character recognition. The IAM handwriting database[1] consists of 1539 pages of scanned text containing 13353 and 115320 isolated and labelled text lines and words respectively. Although, this database is an excellent resource for validating word segmentation and character recognition algorithms, the text-line extraction seems not to be a complex task due to significant gaps between successive text lines in many images. Another famous database is the NIST Handprinted Forms and Characters Database[2], which includes handwritten sample forms from 3600 writers. This collection is mainly used for evaluating character recognition techniques but it could be also employed to assess text-line segmentation algorithms.

The other two benchmarking databases are the training and test sets constructed for the Handwriting Segmentation Contests in the context of ICDAR 2007[3] and 2009[4]. The first collection consists of 100 images (20 and 80 for training and test, respectively). The second database includes these images (as the training set) and 200 images that construct the test set. The documents are either modern manuscripts written by several writers in several languages (English, French, German and Greek) or historical handwritten archives, or document samples selected from the web. It is worth to mention that none of the documents includes any non-text elements (lines, drawings, etc.)

The comparative results of the algorithms, which participated in ICDAR 2007 Handwriting Segmentation Contest (Gatos et al., 2007) or have been tested on this dataset, are presented in Table 1. Detection Rate (DR) denotes the ratio between the number of text lines detected correctly and the number of ground-truth lines (1771). Similarly, Recognition Accuracy (RA) is calculated by dividing the number of correctly detected lines with the total number of detected text lines. FM denotes the harmonic mean of DR and RA.

	DR(%)	RA(%)	FM%
BESUS (Das et al., 1997)	86.6	79.7	83.0
DUTH-ARLSA	73.9	70.2	72.0
ILSP-LWSeg (Papavassiliou et al., 2010)	97.3	97.0	97.1
PARC	92.2	93.0	92.6
UoA-HT (Louloudis et al., 2008)	95.5	95.4	95.4
PROJECTIONS	68.8	63.2	65.9
Ridges-Snakes (Bukhari et al., 2009)	97.3	95.4	96.3
Shredding (Nikolaou & Gatos, 2009)	98.9	98.3	98.6

Table 1. Evaluation results of algorithms tested on the database of ICDAR2007 Handwriting Segmentation Contest.

[1] http://www.iam.unibe.ch/fki/databases/iam-handwriting-database

[2] http://www.nist.gov/srd/nistsd19.cfm

[3] http://users.iit.demokritos.gr/~bgat/HandSegmCont2007/resources.htm

[4] http://users.iit.demokritos.gr/~bgat/HandSegmCont2009/resources.html

The evaluation results of algorithms participated in ICDAR2009 Handwriting Segmentation Contest are presented in Table 2. We mention that the test set consists of 200 binary images and their dimensions vary from 650x825 to 2500x3500 pixels. The total number of text lines included in this dataset is 4034.

	DR(%)	RA(%)	FM(%)
CASIA-MSTSeg (Yin & Liu, 2008)	95.86	95.51	95.68
CMM	98.54	98.29	98.42
CUBS (Shi et al., 2009)	99.55	99.50	99.53
ETS	86.66	86.68	86.67
ILSP-LWSeg-09	99.16	98.94	99.05
Jadavpur Univ	87.78	86.90	87.34
LRDE	96.70	88.20	92.25
PAIS	98.49	98.56	98.52
AegeanUniv (Kavallieratou et al., 2003)	77.59	77.21	77.40
PortoUniv (Cardoso et al., 2008)	94.47	94.61	94.54
PPSL	94.00	92.85	93.42
REGIM	40.38	35.70	37.90

Table 2. Comparative results of ICDAR2009 Handwriting Segmentation Contest.

PAIS and ILSP are based on piece-wise projections and achieved high results. On the other hand, similar methods presented poor results because they either adopt global projections (PROJECTIONS) or divide the image into only three vertical zones (AegeanUniv).
Ten participating methods are classified as grouping approaches. In particular, five methods (Jadavpur Univ, CASIA-MSTSeg, CMM, PPSL and REGIM) introduce constrains on the topological and geometrical properties of the CCs in order to create groups of CCs that correspond to text lines. Since, these approaches require many predefined thresholds, the selection of appropriate (improper) values results in good (poor) results. Three approaches (BESUS, ETS and PARC) apply morphological operations to produce new CCs by merging the initial neighbouring CCs and then adopt similar constrains. Another grouping approach is UoA-HT, which exploits the Hough transform. As expected, the algorithm is not very effective when the skew of a text line varies along its width. Although, two methods (DUTH-ARLSA and CUBS) exploit the RLSA algorithm, their results differ significantly. The reason is that CUBS applies the RLSA algorithm in five directions (-20°, -10°, 0°, 10°, and 20°) and combines the results in order to calculate the local skew of each text line.
PortoUniv proposes a tracing algorithm that tries to find proper paths that connect the edges of the image without cutting the textual elements. A similar approach (Shredding) includes a pre-processing step for blurring and then exploits the tracing algorithm. LRDE is a fast algorithm that enhances the test areas by anisotropic Gaussian filtering, smoothes the image by applying morphological operations and segments it by using the watershed transform (Vincent & Soille, 1991). A recent method (Ridges-Snakes) uses a multi-oriented anisotropic Gaussian filter bank for smoothing, approximates the ridges as the central lines of the text parts and then the ridges evolve until they overlap the CCs of the manuscript.

5. Conclusions

After reviewing the existing methods for text-line segmentation we conclude that there are pros and cons for each approach. For example, piece-wise projection based methods can handle text lines with varying skew angles, but fail when the document includes high degree of curl text lines. In addition, the benefit of some grouping strategies is that they succeed to extract text lines from a complex layout but may fail to segment touching text lines. Regarding smearing approaches, some of them seem to be promising since they exploit image segmentation algorithms that have been already applied on other kinds of images. However, they may merge two successive text lines if the gap between them is not large enough. As a conclusion, we report that the existing methods do not generalize very well to all possible variations encountered in handwritten documents.

Thus, text-line segmentation of handwritten documents remains an open issue. This fact explains why the number of relative papers and contests is increasing. Since different methods can face different challenges of this task, we foresee that a combination of complementary techniques could result in a generalized solution.

6. References

Antonacopoulos A. & Karatzas D (2004), Document Image analysis for World War II personal records, *Proceedings of International Workshop on Document Image Analysis for Libraries DIAL'04*, pp. 336-341, ISBN 0-7695-2088-X, Palo Alto, USA, January 23-24, 2004

Arivazhagan, M.; Srinivasan, H. & Srihari, S. (2007). A statistical approach to line segmentation in handwritten documents, *Proceedings of Document Recognition and Retrieval XIV SPIE*, Vol.6500, No.1, ISSN 0277-786X, San Jose, CA, USA, January 30, 2007

Bloomberg, D.S. & Kopec, G. (1993). Method and apparatus for identification and correction of document skew. Xerox Corporation, U.S. Patent 5,563,403, October 8, 1996.

Bloomberg, D.S. (1996). Textured Reductions for Document Image Analysis, *Proceedings of IS&T/SPIE EI '96, Conference 2660: Document Recognition III*, pp. 160-174, ISBN: 9780819420343, San Jose, USA, March 7, 1996

Bukhari, S.S.; Shafait, F. & Bruel, T.M. (2009). Script-Independent Handwritten Textlines Segmentation using Active Contours, *Proceedings of International Conference on Document Analysis and Recognition*, pp. 446-450, ISSN 1520-5363, Barcelona, Spain, July 26-29, 2009

Cardoso, J.S.; Capela, A.; Rebelo, A. & Guedes, C. (2008). A Connected Path Approach for Staff Detection on a Music Score, *Proceedings of International Conference on Image Processing*, pp.1005-1008, ISSN 1522-4880, San Diego, CA, USA, October 2-15, 2008

Cohen, E.; Hull, J.J. & Srihari, S.N. (1994). Control Structure for Interpreting Handwritten Addresses. *IEEE Transactions on Pattern Analysis and Machine Intelligence*, Vol.16, No.10, (October 1994), pp. 1049- 1055, ISSN 0162-8828

Das, A.K.; Gupta, A. & Chanda, B. (1997). A Fast Algorithm for Text Line & Word Extraction from Handwritten Documents, *Image Processing & Communications*, Vol. 3, No. 1-2, pp. 85-94

Du, X.; Pan, W. & Bui, T.D. (2009). Text Line Segmentation in Handwritten Documents Using Mumford-Shah Model, *Pattern Recognition,* Vol. 42, No. 12, (December 2009), pp. 3136-3145, ISSN 0031-3203

Duda, R.O. & Hart, P. E. (1972). Use of the Hough Transformation to Detect Lines and Curves in Pictures, *Communications of the ACM,* Vol. 15, No. 1, (January 1972), pp. 11-15,

Feldbach M. & Tonnies, K.D. (2001) Line Detection and Segmentation in Historical Church Registers, Proceedings of International Conference on Document Analysis and Recognition, pp. 743-747, ISBN 0-7695-1263-1, Seattle, WA , USA, September 10-13, 2001

Gatos, B.; Antonacopoulos, A. & Stamatopoulos, N. (2007). ICDAR2007 Handwriting Segmentation Contest, *Proceedings of International Conference on Document Analysis and Recognition,* pp. 1284-1288, Curitiba, Brazil, September 23-26, 2007

Gatos, B.; Stamatopoulos, N. & Louloudis, G. (2009). ICDAR2009 Handwriting Segmentation Contest, *Proceedings of International Conference on Document Analysis and Recognition,* pp. 1393-1397, ISSN 1520-5363, Barcelona, Spain, July 26-29, 2009

Haralick, R.M. & Shapiro, L.G. (1992). Computer and Robot Vision, Addison-Wesley Longman Publishing Co., Inc. Boston, MA, USA, ISBN:0201569434

Hull, J.J. (1998). Document Image Skew Detection: Survey and Annotated Bibliography, In: Document Analysis Systems II, Hull, J.J. & Taylor, S.L. (Eds.), pp. 40-64, World Scientific Publishing Co. Pte. Ltd, ISBN 978-981-02-3103-3

Kavallieratou, E.; Dromazou, N.; Fakotakis, N. & Kokkinakis, G. (2003). An Integrated System for Handwritten Document Image Processing, *International Journal of Pattern Recognition and Artificial Intelligence,* Vol. 17, No. 4, pp. 101-120, DOI 10.1.1.107.7988

Khandelwal, A.; Choudhury, P.; Sarkar, R.; Basu, S.; Nasipuri, M. & Das, N. (2009). Text Line Segmentation for Unconstrained handwritten Document Images Using Neighborhood Connected Components Analysis, *Lecture Notes in Computer Science,* Vol. 5909/2009, pp. 369-374, DOI: 10.1007/978-3-642-11164-8_60

Kuzhinjedathu, K.; Srinivansan, H. & Srihari, S. (2008). Robust Line Segmentation for Handwritten Documents, *Proceedings of Document Recognition and Retrieval XV ST/SPIE Annual Symposium,* Vol. 6815, San Jose, CA, January 2008

Lam, L.; Lee, S.W. & Suen, C.Y. (1992). Thinning Methodologies-A Comprehensive Survey, *IEEE Transactions on Pattern Analysis and Machine Intelligence,* Vol 14, No. 9, (September 1992), pp. 869-885, ISSN 0162-8828

Li, Y.; Zheng, Y.; Doermann, D. & Jaeger, S. (2008). Script-Independent Text Line Segmentation in Freestyle Handwritten Documents, *IEEE Transactions on Pattern Analysis and Machine Intelligence,* Vol.30, No.8, (August 2008), pp. 1313-1329, ISSN 0162-8828

Likforman-Sulem, L.; Zahour, A. & Taconet, B. (2007). Text-line Segmentation of Historical Documents: a Survey, *International Journal on Document Analysis and Recognition,* Vol. 9, No. 2, (April 2007), pp. 123–138, ISSN:1433-2833

Lindeberg, T. & Eklundh, J.O. (1992). Scale-Space Primal Sketch: construction and experiments, *Image and Vision Computing,* Vol. 10, No.1, (January-February 1992), pp. 3–18, doi 10.1016/0262-8856(92)90079-I

Louloudis, G.; Gatos, B. & Halatsis, C. (2008). Text line detection in handwritten documents, *Pattern Recognition,* Vol.41, No.12, (December 2008), pp. 3758-3772, ISSN 0031-3203

Manmatha, R. & Rothfeder, J.L. (2005). A Scale Space Approach for Automatically Segmenting Words from Historical Handwritten Documents. *IEEE Transactions on Pattern Analysis and Machine Intelligence*, Vol. 27, No.8, (August 2005), pp. 1212-1225, ISSN 0162-8828

Mao, S.; Rosenfeld, A. & Kanungo, T. (2003). Document Structure Analysis Algorithms: A Literature Survey, *Proceedings of Document Recognition and Retrieval X SPIE*, Vol. 5010, pp. 197-207, ISBN 0-8194-4810-9, Santa Clara, California, USA, January 22-23, 2003

Marti, U.V. & Bunke, H. (2002). The IAM-Database: an English sentence database for off-line handwriting recognition, *International Journal on Document Analysis and Recognition*, Vol.5, No. 1, (), pp. 39-46, DOI: 10.1007/s100320200071

Nagy, G. (2000). Twenty Years of Document Image Analysis. *IEEE Transactions on Pattern Analysis and Machine Intelligence*, Vol. 22, No. 1, (January 2000), pp. 38–62, ISSN 0162-8828

Niblack, W. (1986). An Introduction to Digital Image Processing, pp. 115-116, Prentice Hall, ISBN-13: 978-0134806747

Nicolas, S.; Paquet, T. & Heutte, L. (2004a). Enriching Historical Manuscripts: The Bovary Project, In: Document Analysis Systems VI, LNCS 3163, pp. 135-146, Marinai, S. & Dengel, A. (Eds.) Springer-Vergal, ISBN 3-540-23060-2, Berlin/Heidelberg

Nicolas, S.; Paquet, T. & Heutte, L. (2004b). Text Line Segmentation in Handwritten Document Using a Production System, *Proceedings of International Workshop on Frontiers in Handwriting Recognition*, pp. 245–250, ISSN 1550-5235, Tokyo, Japan, October 26-29, 2004

Nikolaou, A. & Gatos, B. (2009). Handwritten Text Line Segmentation by Shredding Text into its Lines, *Proceedings of International Conference on Document Analysis and Recognition*, pp. 1393-1397, ISSN 1520-5363, Barcelona, Spain, July 26-29, 2009

O'Gorman, L. (1993). The document spectrum for page layout analysis. *IEEE Transactions on Pattern Analysis and Machine Intelligence*, Vol.15, No.11, (November 1993), pp. 1162–1173, ISSN 0162-8828

Osher, S. & Fedkiw, R. (2003). Level Set Methods and Dynamic Implicit Surfaces, Springer, ISBN 978-0-387-95482-0

Otsu, N. (1979). A Threshold Selection Method From Gray-Level Histograms. *IEEE Transactions on Systems, Man and Cybernetics*, Vol.9, No.1, (January 1979), pp. 62-66, ISSN 0018-9472

Papavassiliou, V.; Stafylakis, T.; Katsouros, V. & Carayannis, G. (2010). Handwritten Document Image Segmentation into Text Lines and Words, *Pattern Recognition*, Vol.43, No.1, (January 2010), pp. 369-377, ISSN 0031-3203

Plamondon, R. & Srihari, S.N. (2000). On-Line and Off-Line Handwriting Recognition: A Comprehensive Survey, *IEEE Transactions on Pattern Analysis Machine Intelligence*, Vol.22, No.1, (January 2000), pp. 63–84, ISSN 0162-8828

Postl, W. (1988). Method for automatic correction of character skew in the acquisition of a text original in the form of digital scan results. Siemens AG, U.S. Patent 4,723,297, February 2, 1988

Razak, Z.; Zulkifee, K.; Idris, M.Y.I.; Tamil, E.M.; Noor, M.N.M.; Salleh, M.; Yaakob, M.; Yusof, Z.M. & Yaacob, M. (2008). Off-line Handwriting Text Line Segmentation: A

Review, *International Journal of Computer Science and Network Security*, Vol. 8, No. 7, (July 2008), pp. 12-20, http://paper.ijcsns.org/07_book/200807/20080703.pdf

Santos, R.P.; Clemente, G.S.; Ren, T.I. & Calvalcanti, G.D.C. (2009). Text Line Segmentation Based on Morphology and Histogram Projection, *Proceedings of International Conference on Document Analysis and Recognition*, pp. 651-655, ISBN 978-1-4244-4500-4, Barcelona, Spain, July 26-29, 2009

Sauvola, J. & Pietikäinen, M. (2000). Adaptive document image binarization, *Pattern Recognition*, Vol. 33, No. 2, (February 2000), pp. 225-236, doi:10.1016/S0031-3203(99)00055-2

Shi, Z. & Govindaraju, V. (2004). Line Separation for Complex Document Images Using Fuzzy Runlength, Proceedings of International Workshop on Document Image Analysis for Libraries, pp. 306-312, ISBN : 0-7695-2088-X, Palo Alto, USA, January 23-24, 2004.

Shi, Z.; Seltur, S. & Govindaraju, V. (2009). A Steerable Directional Local Profile Technique for Extraction of Arabic Text Lines, *Proceedings of International Conference on Document Analysis and Recognition*, pp. 176-180, ISBN 978-1-4244-4500-4, Barcelona, Spain, July 26-29, 2009

Simon, A.; Pret, J.C. & Johnson, A.P. (1997). A Fast Algorithm for Bottom-Up Document Layout Analysis, *IEEE Transactions on Pattern Analysis and Machine Intelligence*, Vol. 19, No. 3, (March 1997) pp. 273-277, ISSN 0162-8828

Soille, P. (2004). Morphological Image Analysis Principles and Applications, (2nd ed.), Springer-Verlag New York, Inc. Secaucus, NJ, USA, ISBN:3540429883

Tomai C. I.; Zhang B. & Govindaraju V. (2002), Transcript Mapping for Historic Handwritten Document Images, *Proceedings of International Workshop on Frontiers in Handwriting Recognition IWFHR2002*, pp. 413 - 418, ISBN 0-7695-1692-0, Ontario, Canada, August 6-8, 2002.

Vincent, L. & Soille, P. (1991). Watershed in Digital Spaces: An Efficient Algorithm Based on Immersion Simulations, *IEEE Transactions on Pattern Analysis and Machine Intelligence*, Vol. 13, No. 6, (June 1991) pp. 583-598, ISSN 0162-8828

Weliwitage, C.; Harvey, A.L. & Jennings, A.B. (2005). Handwritten Document Offline Text Line Segmentation, *Proceedings of Digital Image Computing: Techniques and Applications Conference (DICTA2005)*, pp. 27, ISBN: 0-7695-2467-2, Cairns, Australia, December 6-8, 2005

Yanikoglu, B. & Sandon, P.A. (1998). Segmentation of Off-line Cursive Handwriting Using Linear Programming, *Pattern Recognition*, Vol.31, No.12, (December 1998), pp. 1825-1833, doi:10.1016/S0031-3203(98)00081-8

Yin, F. & Liu, C.L. (2008). Handwritten Text Line Segmentation by Clustering with Distance Metric Learning, *Proceedings of International Conference on Frontiers in Handwriting Recognition (ICFHR 2008)*, pp.229-234, Montreal, Quebec, Canada, August 19-21, 2008

Yin, F. & Liu, C.L. (2009). A Variational Bayes Method for Handwritten Text Line Segmentation, *Proceedings of International Conference on Document Analysis and Recognition*, pp. 436-440, ISSN: 1520-5363, Barcelona, Spain, July 26-29, 2009

12

IR Image Segmentation by Combining Genetic Algorithm and Multi-scale Edge Detection

Li Zhaohui[1,2] and Chen Ming[1]
[1]*Northwestern Polytechnical University;*
[2]*Chinese Flight Test Establishmen*
China

1. Introduction

The Canny operator applied in a multi-scale edge detection for images is the most optimal step edge detection operator. However the Canny edge detection operator is optimal only for the step edge detection influenced by white noises because the Canny operator utilizes the first order derivative of a Gauss function to get a better compromise between noises restraint and edges detection. The Canny operator based edge detection finishes the implementation per the three criteria, namely, detecting (no losing important edges and no false edges), locating (with the minimal deviation between the real edges and the edges detected) and responding singly (reduce multi-response into a single edge response).
Because the Canny operator is based on a derivative operator (the first order derivative) to seek for the derivatives in two directions and their directions about image grey scale, it determines the maximum gradient and local maximum by means of non-maximum restraint to the gradient. But the function with the maximum gradient and local maximum meeting with the above three standards limits is in fact the optimizing process of a multivariate function. Generally if an object function is continually differential, the space equation of a solution is simpler, and the general analysis is effective. However for the image segmentation with a complex configuration or sophisticated texture, it is very difficult to describe the multivariable object function satisfied with the above three standard limits by use of simple analysis functions because the image function itself is a multivariable nonlinear random function. So it has only an approximate and local sense to get the maximum gradient and local maximum of a function in traditional analysis methods. For multi-scale based Canny operator edge detection, Canny once presented the algorithm to get a multi-scale edge image based upon the above three standards for final edges composed, but it is related to the problem about the composition of different scale detections[1]. Jeong and Kim proposed a method for a single pixie to select local optimized scales by minimizing a scale-space energy function. Although this method is able to detect step edges exactly, delete false edges, restrain random noises relatively, and parry the problem mentioned above, the experiments showed that this method is not ideal compared with some fixed large scale methods. The reason is that the algorithm successive over relaxation (SOR) used for the solution of a minimizing energy function especially depends on initial given values resulting in not converging to the whole optimum solution[2,3]. Because there are some individual differences about homogenous properties and edges

vagueness between IR (infrared) images and general grey scale images, the former region segmentation mainly depends on the temperature field distribution of an equivalent black body for a target and the edge contour tends to blurring. It is more convenient to deal with the IR image edge detection by use of the individual fitness and mutation operation of the genetic algorithm. The individual fitness evaluation may be applied to the evaluation of a region segmentation with no segmentation reference. And the variation operation may be integrated with a kind of local contrast to design a dynamic variation operator as to measure the fuzziness of region edge information. This paper proposed a new multi-scale edge detection method based upon an optimized genetic searching algorithm, and put it into the image segmentation of IR target signature.

2. Optimized genetic searching algorithm

The genetic algorithm is introduced into an image segmentation based on edge detection. Firstly we determine the selection of a coding mode and a fitness function. Here according to the n cities' universal rank as a genetic coding, we take the inverse of Hamilton ring length, Td, as a fitness function because there are always legal restraints of a hidden TSP problem in the initialization for possible solutions, crossover operation and mutation operation.

$$f = 1/(T_{\mathrm{d}} + \alpha \cdot N_{\mathrm{t}}) \tag{1}$$

where Nt is the measurement for TSP route illegality, α is a penalty coefficient.
The application of crossover strategy: based upon the above TSP rank coding, the *OX* [4] method proposed by Davis is used in order to reduce the space searched. Firstly select a region to be matched:

$$\begin{aligned} A &= 9 \quad 8 \quad 4 \quad | \, 5 \quad 6 \quad 7 \, | \quad 1 \quad 3 \quad 2 \quad 0 \\ B &= 8 \quad 7 \quad 1 \quad | \, 2 \quad 3 \quad 0 \, | \quad 9 \quad 5 \quad 4 \quad 6 \end{aligned} \tag{2}$$

In accordance with the relation mapped of a region to be matched, H is signed at the relative position outside the region, thus

$$\begin{aligned} A' &= 9 \quad 8 \quad 4 \quad | \, 5 \quad 6 \quad 7 \, | \quad 1 \quad H \quad H \quad H \\ B' &= 8 \quad H \quad 1 \quad | \, 2 \quad 3 \quad 0 \, | \quad 9 \quad H \quad 4 \quad H \end{aligned} \tag{3}$$

Move the region matched to the initial position, pre-leave the space (H number) equal to the region matched afterwards, and then range other codes behind the region pre-left in accordance with their relative rank, thus

$$\begin{aligned} A'' &= 5 \quad 6 \quad 7 \quad H \quad H \quad H \quad 1 \quad 9 \quad 8 \quad 4 \\ B'' &= 2 \quad 3 \quad 0 \quad H \quad H \quad H \quad 9 \quad 4 \quad 8 \quad 1 \end{aligned} \tag{4}$$

Finally interchange the father's A, B regions, put them into A″, B″ regions pre-left, and then get two descendant generations:

$$\begin{aligned} A''' &= 5 \quad 6 \quad 7 \quad | \, 2 \quad 3 \quad 0 \, | \quad 1 \quad 9 \quad 8 \quad 4 \\ B''' &= 2 \quad 3 \quad 0 \quad | \, 5 \quad 6 \quad 7 \, | \quad 9 \quad 4 \quad 8 \quad 1 \end{aligned} \tag{5}$$

The mutation is an operation on backgrounds in the whole sense of genetic algorithms. For the TSP problem, the "Inverse mutation" operation is used in order to keep the individual of population varied so that there is a great change in possible solutions rank. Randomly select two points and inversely insert the subset between the points into the original positions.

Because the above mutation operation for the TSP problem made the TSP ring length changed around adjustments and this change led to the finest adjustments, the local accuracy arrive at a better level.

From the optimization of genetic algorithms the individual with a superior fitness has more opportunities to breed in a limited scale of population. The another feature of the genetic algorithm is not good enough to optimize locally. In practical applications GA generally converges to some possible solution which is not surely a optimized point as a whole or even not a local optimized point.

To improve the deficiency of a basic genetic algorithm in local optimization and upgrade the quality of a solution as a whole, this paper proposed an improved hybridized algorithm SGA (Simple genetic algorithm)+SA (Simulated anneal)+TABU, in which SGA is integrated with a heuristic searching algorithm. The alternative optimization strategy applied is as follows,

1. Utilize a stochastic method to produce many different possible solutions for an initial possible solution population.
2. For one half of the individuals of possible solutions, execute TABU searching to get a local optimization solution.
3. For the other half of the individuals of possible solutions, execute SA searching to get a local optimization solution.
4. For the local solution from 2) and 3) steps, execute genetic selection and crossover operations.
5. Repeat 2), 3) and 4) steps until the objective condition of an algorithm is finally satisfied.

Fig.1 shows the comparison between SGA+SA+TABU and SGA performances. Where the SGA optimization as a whole is better but poor at local. Relatively the SGA+SA+TABU algorithm intensifies the local ability of the simplex SGA. And compared with the simplex SA and simplex TABU, the SGA+SA+TABU algorithm extends the local optimization range of SA and TABU, and strengthens the whole optimization ability of simplex SA and simplex TABU.

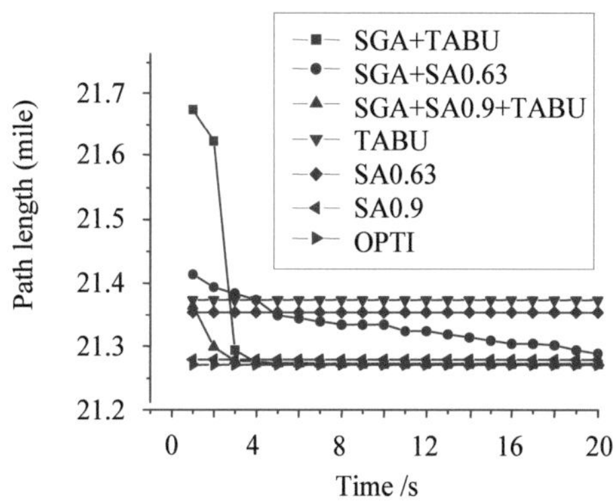

Fig. 1. Performances comparison of optimization algorithms

3. Genetic algorithm + Canny multi-scale edges detection

Because an image segmentation is different from the simple optimization on the shortest route of n cities, the latter is only the construction of a closed route. But the former is about a population optimization among route groups composed of many closed and open routes. So it is necessary to combine the radiation signature of IR images when the cleavage and mergence are used to segment an image into regions in accordance with the homogeneity firstly and then execute edges detection based upon the Canny multi-scale in each region, searching for the shortest route problem of n cities TSP composed of wavelet transformation module maximum values. The specific steps are as follows,

1. According to the equivalent black body temperature distribution of an IR radiation image, specify the initial regions conformed to homogeneity requirements. Supposing the maximum number of an image segmentation is n1, the individual chromosome coding is an integer sequence Ik={ri | i=1, 2, …, n1}. Where ri is a sub-region order number and k is an individual number.

   Crossover operation: it is completed by use of the improved PMX crossover method. Here the gene codes in sequence coding may be repeated after finishing a crossover operation. Just based upon gene codes generate repeatedly, an image region is able to execute the further cleavage and mergence. If the region ri is merged with an adjacent region rj , Ik[i]=I, Ik[j]=i , the region rl merged with the region rj is also combined with the region ri , Ik[l]=i . So the gene code of the region combined with the region ri is i .

   Mutation operation: it is the design of a dynamic mutation operator in conjunction with a local contrast. The operator is used to measure the information vagueness degree of the region borders. The distance between the rejoin ri and its adjacent region rj is

$$d_{ij} = \frac{1}{n_{ij}} \sum_{k=1}^{n_{ij}} \| x_{ijk} - x_{jik} \|^2 \tag{6}$$

   where xijk(j=1,2,…, ni; k=1,2,…,nij) is the k-th pixel on the border between the region ri and its adjacent region rj ; nij is the total pixels number of the border between the region ri and its adjacent region rj . The relative distance between the region ri and its adjacent region rj is

$$u_{ij} = d_{ij} / (\sum_{j=1}^{n_i} d_{ij}) \tag{7}$$

   Because uij is conformed to uij∈[0, 1], it may be used as a probability of the choice between the cleavage and mergence. According to the definition of a relative distance between regions, define the local contrast in any region,

$$C_i = \begin{cases} \min(\dfrac{\min_j(u_{ij})}{\max_j(u_{ij}) - \min_j(u_{ij})} , & \min_j \neq \max_j \\ 1 , & \min_j = \max_j \end{cases} \tag{8}$$

   Individual fitness estimation: the region segmentation estimation, with no a segmentation reference, includes the region homogeneity measurement and edge vagueness measurement.

- Region homogeneity measurement
  The region homogeneity measurement is defined as follows

$$AI_i \approx \frac{1}{n_k n_l} \sum_{k=1}^{n_k} \sum_{l=1}^{n_l} (g_{kl} - \mu_i)^2 \tag{9}$$

where gkl is the grey scale of the pixels in the region ri , μi is the average grey scale in the region ri . And the reason why the above equation is not an equality is that the region ri is not always a rectangle.

- Edge vagueness measurement
  The integrated measurement definition for all region edges vagueness is as follows,

$$E = \sum_{(i,j)} \frac{u_{ij}(|\nabla G|)}{u_{ij}(|\nabla G'|)} \tag{10}$$

where $|\nabla G|$ is the grey scale gradient of the pixels after cleavage and mergence. $|\nabla G'|$ is the grey scale at the pixels in an initial region division. Because there exists always $|\nabla G(i,j)| \le |\nabla G'(i,j)|$, so here is 0≤E≤1.

2. For each region above divided take a Canny multi-scale edge detection. Suppose the unit vectors $\mathbf{n}_j(u) =$ $(\cos Af(u, 2^j), \sin Af(u, 2^j))$ and $\nabla(f * \overline{\theta}_{2^j})(u)$ are linear each other. At a 2j scale, the Mf(u, 2j) in the direction of $u = v + \lambda \mathbf{n}_j(v)$ gets a local maximum at a point u=v , when |λ| becomes small enough. Such a point is the edge point in this region, and is also called the wavelet transformation module maximum point.
3. Take the wavelet module maximum point from 2) as the universal point for n cities and constitute a TSP problem. The GA+SA+TABU is applied to the solution of an optimal route curve and to the formation of an optimal edge curve.
4. Change the scale 2j and return to 2). Continue the edge detection and re-find the n wavelet module maximum points as the universal points for cities, and then go to the next optimization step.
5. Here is the measurement for a region uniformity computation. The uniformity measurement of an image segmentation denotes that the weighting sum for the uniformity measurement of all regions:

$$G = \frac{1}{n} \sum_{i=1}^{n} w_i(p_i) G_i \tag{11}$$

where n is the sum of segmented regions. wi(pi) is the weighting coefficient of a region area. pi is a region area. The computation of a weighting coefficient is in accordance with the following eq.

$$w_i(p_i) = \begin{cases} 2p_i^2 / \beta^2 , & \alpha \le p_i < 2/\beta \\ 1 - 2(p_i - \beta)^2 / \beta^2 , & 2/\beta \le p_i < \beta \\ 1 , & p_i \ge \beta \end{cases} \tag{12}$$

where α and β denote the minimum and maximum area respectively.

For image segmentation based on a genetic algorithm the multiplication of the equations (10) and (11) is applied to a composite individual fitness estimation.

$$F=E \cdot G \tag{13}$$

When the value got from eq. (13) is satisfied with the setting objective value the optimization searching ceases, otherwise returns to the 2) step for continuous optimization computations.

4. Experiment results and analysis

In the course of a FLIR target image detection, take a target point source as the initial information of a potential target and determine an initial growing point of signature regions according to the sequence images inputed.

The five threshold values of equal intervals[5] are employed in this paper, that is $tmax > t0 > t1 > t2 > tmin$. where tmax is towards the maximum equivalent black body radiance temperature of a target image, tmin towards the minimum grey temperature scale of a target image. The first level of isothermal region is determined by tmax-t0 interval, and the second isothermal region tmax-t1 is determined by tmax-t1 interval. For the division of isothermal regions by use of a genetic algorithm, any grey scale interval in the above regions may be used as a seeding region for a target pixel seed till one of the following two conditions is satisfied.

1. the region grows large enough to reach the edge;
2. the equivalent black body radiance temperature or radiance intensity of a searching region degrades too much.

The seed regions are defined as {tmax-t0, tmax-t1, tmax-t2, tmax-tmin} where {tmax, t0, t1, t2, tmin} is used, in a genetic algorithm, as five inner nodes of each segmentation region for construction of four layers of equivalent black body temperature differences. Fig.2(a) shows the original long wave FLIR image of a running truck, and Fig.2(b) and Fig.2(c) respectively illustrate the target IR image segmentation results by means of Laplace-Gauss edge detection or wavelet nerve-network algorithm[6]. Although the Laplace-Gauss edge detection algorithm is able to locate target contours, a great deal of target details are lost. For the PCA analysis about a target region the wavelet nerve-network algorithm embedded in a wavelet time-frequency analysis could keep the high frequency details of region contours. Fig.2(d) shows the image segmentation based on the genetic and wavelet multi-scale edge detection. Compared with the former segmentation algorithms this detection algorithm could not only extract edges of a target clearly but also the edges succession behaves better because of the "non-maximum restraint" for pixels gradient in course of optimization. From Fourier transformation frequency spectra Fig.3(a), Fig.3(b) and Fig.3(c) relative to Fig.2(b), Fig.2(c) and Fig.2(d) the effect of the Laplace-Gauss edge detection[7] could be evaluated. Their energy is basically along the main axis and lower inside quadrants with a great loss of details information. The high energy of an image processed by a wavelet nerve-network algorithm is distributed along the two axes from the original point, but the energy distribution inside each quadrant exists low state. So the number of little targets with bad pixels is available to be restrained. The energy spectrum gotten from the genetic and a wavelet multi-scale edge detection is focused around the spectrum center and basically exists low value distribution with no mixture of medium value energy. This signature of the frequency spectrum distribution has an instant relationship with the segmentation structure of an image because the latter algorithm pays more attention to the edges segmentation inside image textures. As is showed in Fig.4 the Pratt quality factor is used as the evaluation of edges detection. Under a low signal-noise ratio the Pratt quality factor of a genetic and wavelet multi-scale edge detection algorithm is much more superior than other two detection algorithms, and more suitable to an image with complex texture and fine construction.

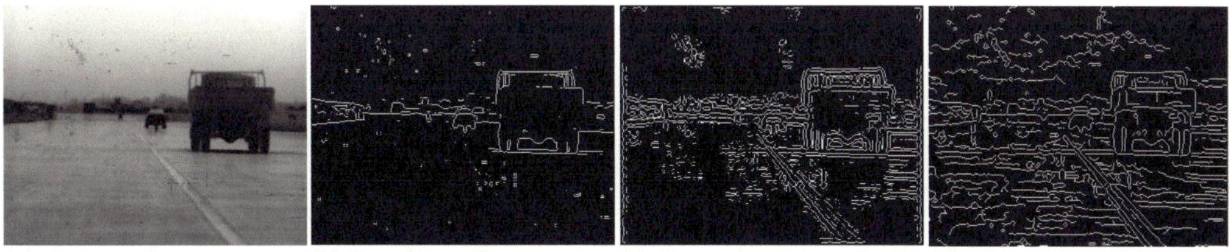

(a) Original image (b) Laplace-Gauss edge detection (c) Wavelet-Nero-NET (d) Genetic+multi-scale edge detection

Fig. 2. Experimental results

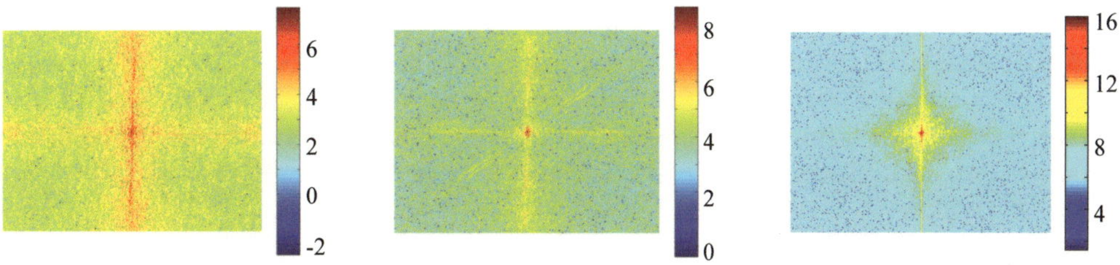

(a) Spectrum to Fig.2(b) (b) Spectrum to Fig.2(c) (c) Spectrum to Fig.2(d)

Fig. 3. Fourier transform spectrum

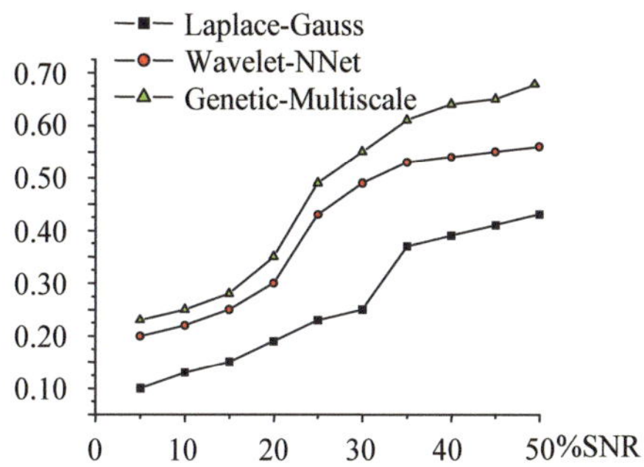

Fig. 4. Pratt qualities for different algorithms

5. Conclusions

The image segmentation based upon a genetic and wavelet multi-scale edge detection is very much suitable for the contour extraction of a dynamic IR target in clutters. It could restrain clutter background signals of a target image while reserving its high frequency signature. From the view of energy spectra the energy spectra of an IR target image after a genetic and wavelet multi-scale edge detection procession could be expressed according to the IR radiance energy levels of the target so as to avoid the loss of fine details (high frequency contents) inside the target image while its image edge is extracted.

6. References

[1] Tan H L, Gelfand S B. A cost minimization approach to edge detection using simulated annealing [J]. *IEEE Transaction on Pattern Analysis and Machine Intelligence* (S0162-8828), 1992, 14(1): 3-18.

[2] Jeong H, Kim C I. Adaptive determination of filter scales for edge detection [J]. *Pattern Analysis and Machine Intelligence* (S0162-8828), 1992, 14(5): 579-585.

[3] ZHONG Fan, ZHOU Ji-liu, LANG Fang-nian, et al. Adaptive Scale Filtering for Edge Detection [J]. *Acta Automatica Sinica,* 2007, 33(8): 867-870.

[4] WANG Xiao-tong, DAVIS Lawrence, FU Chun-sheng. Genetic Algorithms And Fine-grained Topologies For Optimization [C]// *Proceedings of the Genetic and Evolutionary Computation Conference,* New York, USA, July 9-13, 2002: 981-988.

[5] Correia B, Dinis J, Davies R. Automatic Detection and Recognition of Stationary Motorized Vehicles in Infrared Images [J]. *Proc. of SPIE*(S0277786X), 1999, 3718: 140-151.

[6] LI Zhao-hui, CHEN Ming. FLIR image segmentation based on wavelet neural networks with adaptive learning [J]. *Journal of Computer Applications,* 2005, 25(8): 1760-1763.

[7] Greenspan H, Anderson C H, Akber S. Image Enhancement by Nonlinear Extrapolation in Frequency Space [J]. *IEEE Transactions on Image Processing*(S1057-7149), 2000, 9(6): 1035-1048.

13

Segmentation of Remotely Sensed Imagery: Moving from Sharp Objects to Fuzzy Regions

Ivan Lizarazo[1] and Paul Elsner[2]
[1]*Universidad Distrital Francisco Jose de Caldas*
[2]*Birkbeck College, University of London*
[1]*Colombia*
[2]*United Kingdom*

1. Introduction

The increasing availability of remotely sensed imagery data with high spatial resolution is demanding more efficient, and more accurate methods for image analysis. Traditional per-pixel classifiers focus on analysing spectral characteristics of single pixels and ignore contextual properties from surrounding pixels (Townshend et al., 2000). This inability to integrate neighbourhood information triggered the need of developing image analysis algorithms able to go 'beyond pixels' and take also into account spatial information (Jensen, 2005).

New approaches for land cover characterization from high spatial resolution images include object-based image analysis (OBIA), also referred to as geospatial object based image analysis (GEOBIA) (Blaschke, 2010). OBIA uses segmentation techniques to group pixels into discrete image objects as a first stage of the image analysis process. By analysing image objects rather than individual pixels, it is then possible to include spatial and/or textural properties of image objects into the process (Blaschke et al., 2006). Recent research demonstrates that this segmentation based approach for image classification produces higher thematic accuracy than the traditional per-pixel methods (Blaschke et al., 2006; Lang et al., 2006; Platt & Rapoza, 2008; Thomas et al., 2003).

The OBIA approach is based on the assumption that image objects produced by segmentation can be unambiguously linked to the geographic objects of interest and has proven valuable in a number of applications, see, for example, Shackelford & Davis (2003); Wei et al. (2005); Zhou et al. (2007). However, it can not be considered to be a silver bullet: when classes overlap spectrally, high classification accuracy is still difficult to achieve (Platt & Rapoza, 2008). The aim of creating meaningful image objects may be affected by blurring and distortion problems inherent to the image acquisition process (Bezdek et al., 1999).

A central stage of OBIA is the segmentation stage. Standard image segmentation usually requires considerable parameterisation effort to find the right sizes and homogeneity criteria that produce meaningful image objects for a given scene and application. In many situations, image segmentation becomes a time consuming task which requires iterative processing, and may not always succeed (Lang et al., 2006; Schiewe et al., 2001a). Depending on the complexity of the landscape, the quality of the image and the parameterisation procedure, image segmentation may produce image objects that represent real-world objects, part of objects or just noise. Such image segmentation approach is a subjective and user driven task which esentially prevents automated processing of large data sets.

The traditional image segmentation looks for delineating discrete image objects with sharp boundaries. The underlying assumption of this hard segmentation is that it is always possible to determine spatial boundaries between land cover classes. However, many geographic objects, both natural and man made, may not appear clearly bounded in remotely sensed images. Therefore, a fuzzy segmentation approach which takes into account the fuzziness of the real world and the ambiguity of remote sensing imagery is potentially more appropriate than a hard segmentation to resolve the spectral and spatial confusion which characterizes urban landscapes.

Over the last decades, geographic information systems (GIS) researchers have applied fuzzy concepts to deal with the vagueness and imprecision widespread among geographic objects (Burrough, 1989; Burrough & Frank, 1996). Remote sensing researchers have applied per-pixel fuzzy classification to study geographic phenomena that are continuous and lack sharp boundaries (Fisher & Pathirana, 1990; Foody, 1992; Wang, 1990). However, fuzzy concepts have not been applied yet in the segmentation process for environmental remote sensing image analysis. As remote sensing applications include a wide spectrum of geographic phenomena ranging from discrete objects to continuous fields, a fuzzy segmentation approach can be potentially useful for land cover characterization on natural and man-made landscapes.

This chapter proposes a method for land cover characterization based on fuzzy image segmentation. It argues that, in order to handle uncertainty of real world landscapes, image segmentation should output fuzzy image regions rather than sharp image objects.

The chapter has been structured in two parts. In the first part, basic principles and assumptions of OBIA are explained. It is highlighted that a successful application of OBIA depends on the quality of the discrete image objects produced at the segmentation stage. In the second part, a fuzzy image segmentation approach is proposed in more detail.

2. Traditional Object-based image classification

A basic assumption underlying traditional object-based image classification is that it is always possible to identify groups of pixels that can be related to geographic objects. These groups of pixels with meaning in the real world are referred to as image objects (Schneider & Steinwender, 1999). Thus, image objects are basic entities, composed of similar digital values, and possessing intrinsic sizes,shapes and geographic relationships with the real-world scene they model (Hay et al., 2001).

The standard object-based image analysis (OBIA) approach for image classification can be represented as shown in Figure 1 using a three stage workflow (Benz, 2001):

1. image segmentation which creates *meaningful* image objects;
2. feature analysis which measures spectral, spatial, and contextual attributes of image objects; and
3. classification which allocates image objects to target classes

Image segmentation, the first stage, outputs image objects that hopefully represent, completely or partially, the structural properties of the geographic objects under study. Feature analysis, the second stage, aims to select a set of attributes (also referred to as a feature vector) able to differentiate the classes of interest (i.e. the target classes). This stage requires users to establish correspondence between the image objects and the real-world objects (classes), and also to determine which properties can be relevant for the problem under

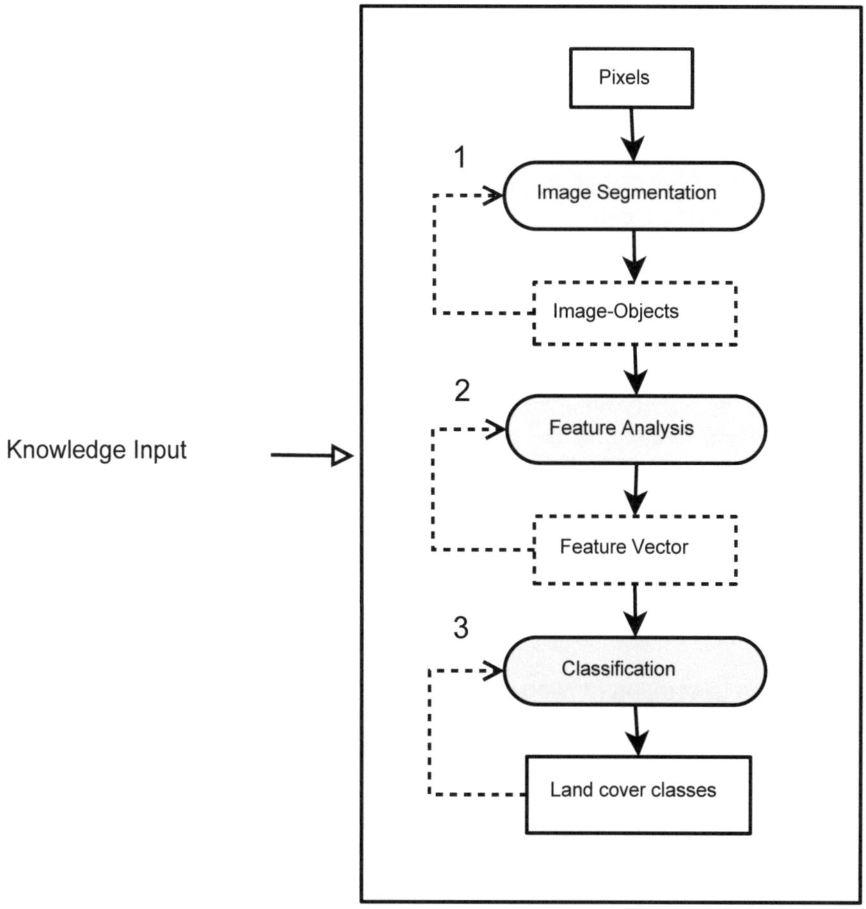

Fig. 1. Flowchart of the OBIA image classification process.

study. Classification, the last stage, assigns classes to image objects applying appropriate classification rules which can be set up automatically or manually. This classification may be conducted using conventional (e.g. maximum likelihood or minimum distance to mean) or non-conventional techniques (e.g. neural networks, fuzzy logic, nearest neighbor) (Gao, 2009; Jensen, 2005). The final outcome of the process are digital objects representing the categories of interest. The OBIA process is iterative rather than linear and strictly subsequent, and knowledge input may occur at any stage of the process (Lang, 2008).

2.1 Image segmentation

Image segmentation is recognized as the critical step of the OBIA approach because its results affect directly all the subsequent tasks (Carleer et al., 2005; Neubert et al., 2006; Rekik et al., 2007). Image segmentation aims to partition the image into a set of regions which are distinct and uniform with respect to some intrinsic property of the image, such as grey level, texture or color (Freixenet et al., 2002). The selection of an appropriate segmentation technique depends greatly on the type of data being analyzed and on the application area (Pal & Pal, 1993).
A successful segmentation produces image objects which can be unambiguously linked with ground objects. Typically, the segmentation stage is not concerned with the thematic identity

of the image objects as they are class labelled later in the classification stage (Rosenfeld & Kak, 1992).

The result of image segmentation is determined by the purpose of the study, the grouping strategy and specific decisions about the desired levels of homogeneity and (or) the expected size of the resulting segments (Pal & Pal, 1993). Image segmentation is therefore a highly subjective task which has to be adapted to the specific interest of users and the spatial and spectral constraints of the available images (Bock & Lessing, 2002). This poses significant problems for the transferability of image segmentation methods and the development of automated classification rules (Bock & Lessing, 2002).

Traditional image segmentation can be referred to as crisp or hard segmentation because it produces image objects with clearly defined boundaries. In a crisp segmentation, it is assumed that the image can be partitioned into spatially continuous, disjoint and homogeneous groups of pixels which represent the relative homogeneity of geographic phenomena (Blaschke et al., 2006). However, real-world landscapes are comprised by objects of different sizes which may exhibit internal heterogeneity (Herold et al., 2003). As single scale segmentations may not suffice to capture such complexity, it has been suggested that image segmentation be conducted in a nested hierarchy of scales modeling relationships between sub-objects, objects and super-objects (Burnett & Blaschke, 2003). While it is an appealing approach, it can bring further complications to the classification stage due to the additional need for user-driven individual parameterization.

2.1.1 Image segmentation in computer vision

Computer vision is concerned with the theory for building artificial systems that obtain information from images. The image data can take many forms, such as a video sequence, views from multiple cameras, or multi-dimensional data from medical scanners (Azad et al., 2008). As opposed to multispectral remote sensing, computer vision deals mainly with single band data sets, i.e. greyscale images.

Image segmentation is an active field of research in computer vision and 'hundreds of segmentation algorithms have been proposed in the last 30 years' (Freixenet et al., 2002) (p. 408). This proliferation of algorithms shows how elusive a satisfactory segmentation is. There is an almost infinite number of ways an image can be sub-divided, they are all technically correct, but most of them are not what users want (Shi & Malik, 2000).

Comprehensive reviews of image segmentation techniques have been published in the last two decades in the computer vision literature, including, for example Freixenet et al. (2002); Haralick & Schapiro (1992); Pal & Pal (1993).

In computer vision, image segmentation is the process of extracting objects from background or separating the image into several regions which are considered to be coherent and meaningful (Pal & Pal, 1993). Generally, image segmentation is a process of clustering pixels in an image based on some rules, e.g. pixels with similar attributes should be together (Pal & Pal, 1993).

In general terms, image segmentation techniques may be divided into two basic categories: edge-based and region-based (Pal & Pal, 1993). Edge-based segmentation methods look for detecting image discontinuities. In this category, the assumption is that boundaries of regions are sufficiently different from each other and from the background to allow boundary detection based on local discontinuities in grey level intensity. On the another hand, region-based segmentation methods are based on partitioning an image into regions that are similar according to a set of predefined criteria such as grey level, shape or texture.

Two common approaches for region-based segmentation are either merging individual image objects (bottom-up approach) or recursively splitting regions starting from the whole image (top-down approach) (Pal & Pal, 1993).

Although the edge and region approaches are considered to yield good results, some researchers have argued the impossibility of extracting complete information of either aspect of the image independent of the other and have proposed hybrid approaches which integrate boundary and region information (Moigne & Tilton, 1995; Pal & Pal, 1993). One example of these approaches is the watershed algorithm which sees an image as a topographic surface and, after identifying maxima (ridges) and minima (valleys), attempts 'flooding' the terrain to obtain catchment regions (Dam, 2000).

2.1.2 Image segmentation in remote sensing

Image segmentation is a relatively recent field of research in environmental remote sensing, despite the fact that it has been applied extensively in neighboring disciplines such as computer vision and medical imaging (Carleer et al., 2005) . The main problem was the inability of computer vision algorithms to process color or multiband image data sets. However, in the last decade, the remote sensing community has adapted and enhanced the computer vision segmentation approach for dealing with multispectral data sets. A number of operational software tools are now available to conduct segmentation-based image classification for remote sensing. This includes *Definiens Developer*, previously known as *eCognition*, ENVI's *Feature Analysis*, ERDAS's *Objective*, and IDRISI's *Segmentation*. Although all of these programs offer a number of similar functionalities, *Definiens Developer* implements the most advanced algorithms and is a popular choice in OBIA applications (Blaschke et al., 2006) and will therefore be reviewed as example for current standard 'crisp' OBIA implementations.

Definiens implements the *fractal net evolution* algorithm which provides multiresolution segmentation capabilities 'applicable and adaptable to many problems and data types' (Baatz & Schape, 2000) (p. 1). Multiresolution segmentation is a bottom up, region-merging technique which starts building one-pixel image objects which grow by merging adjacent objects based on heterogeneity criteria (Yan et al., 2006). These objects may be extracted from the image in a number of hierarchical levels and each subsequent level yields image objects of a larger size by combining objects from a level below, which represents information on different scales simultaneously (Baatz & Schape, 2000).

Image object heterogeneity can be spectral heterogeneity, $h_{spectral}$, or shape heterogeneity, h_{shape} (Baatz & Schape, 2000). Spectral heterogeneity is a function of user-assigned layer weights, number of pixels comprising the objects, and standard deviation of pixel values within each layer. Shape heterogeneity is based upon the change in object shape before and after an eventual merge. Object shape is described in two ways: (i) compactness and (ii) smoothness.

Compactness C is measured as indicated in Equation 1:

$$C = s_n * l_n / b_n \tag{1}$$

where s_n is the size of each image object, l_n is the perimeter of the image object and b_n is the perimeter of a minimum box bounding each image object.

Smoothness S is measured as indicated in Equation 2:

$$S = s_n * l_n / \sqrt{s_n} \tag{2}$$

Spectral and shape heterogeneity are summarized by a single *fusion value* (f), which indicates the potential merge between two image objects given by Equation 3 (Zhang, 2006):

$$f = (1 - w) * h_{spectral} - w * h_{shape} \quad (3)$$

where w is the weight associated with shape heterogeneity (Definiens, 2007).
Throughout a single segmentation step, the underlying optimization procedure minimizes the heterogeneity of resulting image objects weighted by their size. A segmentation step is finished when every original image object is assigned to the optimal higher level image object. To achieve adjacent image objects of similar size and thus of comparable quality, the procedure simulates the growth of objects over a scene in each step and also for the final result (Yan et al., 2006).
Other alternatives to multiresolution segmentation are provided by *Definiens*. The chessboard algorithm produces a regular grid of segments with a predefined size. The quadtree segmentation splits an image domain into squares, and then into smaller squares, until the spectral heterogeneity of every image object falls below a user-defined threshold. The spectral difference segmentation merges adjacent image objects that do no exceed a user-defined threshold for a weighted spectral difference (Esch et al., 2008).
An approach to address the problems associated with multi-level segmentation is the move from multi-level to single-level segmentation approaches (Corcoran & Winstanley, 2006). This approach is advantageous due to two main reasons. First, it looks for conducting segmentation in a way closer to human visual perception. Second, it helps to solve practical problems for evaluation of multi-level segmentation such as complex hierarchical classification schemas and complicated quality evaluation procedures. In fact, it has been argued that a robust set of intensity and texture features could be extracted and integrated to represent urban land cover in a "true form" with just one level segmentation (Corcoran & Winstanley, 2006).
In summary, the traditional approach for image segmentation is problematic due to the following reasons: (i) remotely sensed images portray an ambiguous representation of geographic objects which often prevents the formation of meaningful image objects; (ii) the current implementations of such segmentation are highly dependent on complicated parameterisation procedures which are both labour intensive and time consuming; (iii) linking image objects to real world classes, and identifying appropriate attributes, are not trivial tasks, and usually require a trial and error approach. This means that the effectiveness of crisp segmentation for land cover classification is at least partly depending on effort and skill of the individual user.

2.1.3 Segmentation quality

Image segmentation can be seen as an improvement of the analysis process of remotely sensed imagery. It provides an alternative means to conduct image classification. However, it has been observed that object-based image classification also has limitations (Song et al., 2005):

- classification accuracy depends on the quality of the image segmentation (i.e. if objects are extracted inaccurately, subsequent classification accuracy will not improve);
- classification error could be accumulated due to error in both image segmentation and classification process; and
- once an object is mis-segmented, all pixels in this object will be misclassified.

Image segmentation is therefore the critical stage in OBIA, but it is also viewed as an *ill-posed problem* in the sense that it has no unique solution: a minor change of the homogeneity measure leads to different segmentation outcome (Hay & Castilla, 2008).

However, not all segmentation methods are good enough for a particular type of images and users of each application have to evaluate the quality of the image output from a given segmentation algorithm. Thus, the problem is to ensure that the evaluation of the segmentation results is an objective process. A common approach, in computer vision applications, is to create a vector of comparison measures between the segmented image and a 'ground truth' segmentation (Pal & Pal, 1993).

A simple way to evaluate the quality of segmentation, provided that such ground truth segmentation is available, is to use an overlapping area matrix (OAM) and the following metrics (Ortiz & Oliver, 2006):

- percentage of correctly grouped pixels (CG);
- percentage of oversegmentation (OS); and
- percentage of undersegmentation (US).

In the field of environmental remote sensing, similar concepts have been proposed to evaluate segmentation quality. A good segmentation is achieved when the overall differences between the segmentation results and the associated reference objects are as low as possible (Meinel & Neubert, 2004; Neubert et al., 2006). In general, the quality of image segmentation may be evaluated using both qualitative and quantitative methods. Qualitative measures are visual evaluations of general criteria such as the delineation of varying land cover types, the segmentation of linear objects, or the ocurrence of faulty segmentation. Quantitative measures make a comparison between clearly defined reference areas (varying in location, form, texture, contrast, land cover type) and segmentation results using geometric properties such as area A_i, perimeter P_i, and shape index $S_i = P_i/4\sqrt{A_i}$ of the image object i (Meinel & Neubert, 2004; Neubert et al., 2006).

As presented, all of the methods proposed for quantitative evaluation of segmentation quality of remotely sensed images rely on a reference segmentation. A main issue is how to define such ground truth or reference segmentation. Some researchers have suggested adopting a library of reference images with their corresponding segmentation reference image, as computer vision community does, in order to evaluate different segmentation algorithms (Corcoran & Winstanley, 2006). Using that approach, a group of researchers have evaluated the performance of different segmentation algorithms using a common set of remotely sensed images and measures (Neubert et al., 2008). However, this initiative is just a first step on the path to well established criteria and methods for judging the quality of segmentation for remote sensing applications.

For practical purposes, users need to build the reference segmentation suitable for their own applications by visual interpretation. In this case, expert humans partition the image into spectrally homogeneous regions, adjust them to accommodate spatial or contextual characteristics and, then, use that ideal segmentation to evaluate segmentation results. A problem with this approach is that the whole process of image classification becomes more dependent on visual interpretation and harder to automate.

Segmentation evaluation becomes more complex with multiscale segmentation which produces a number of segments at different scales. It seems impractical to define an ideal reference segmentation for each scale. A sensible approach in this case would be a qualitative evaluation through visual inspection of each segmentation level. However, a subjectivity

problem may arise with visual evaluations. This problem suggests that, while multi-scale segmentation seems valuable to capture both the coarse and the fine scales of real world objects (Benz, 2001), it may demand intensive user interaction to validate the consistency of the different segmentation levels.
An additional issue could emerge as a by-product of changing the classification paradigm from pixels to image objects. Although quality assessment of pixel-based classes can be done without many problems using proven techniques based on the well known mis-classification or error matrix, it could be not entirely right for objects obtained using the object-based approach. It could be necessary to build a new framework for assessing the quality of ground objects derived from remotely sensed data. In that direction, Zhan et al. (2005) have proposed adopting a so-called per-object method of quality assessment able to measure spatial or contextual attributes of the object-classes not just the label assigned to each pixel.
In summary, the objective evaluation of segmentation quality remains problematic. As an example, a detailed evaluation of four different segmentation algorithms (i.e. optimal edge detector, watershed segmentation, multilevel thresholding, and fractal net evolution) concluded that the 'miraculous segmentation' method which segments in a correct way for all types of landscape does not exist (Carleer et al., 2005).

2.1.4 Uncertainty in image segmentation

A useful model for understanding uncertainty in image analysis is the *image chain approach* which considers the remote sensing process as a chain linking subsequent stages from image collection to the final thematic mapping (Schott, 1997). In such a view, image analysis is only as strong as the weakest link in the chain and limitations existing at each step affect the entire process (Woodcock, 2002).
In the case of object-based image analysis, image segmentation is not only the weakest link in the chain but also the earliest one. Understanding uncertainties associated with the image classification process may be useful to propose alternative ways for conducting image segmentation.
Atkinson & Foody (2002) suggested dividing uncertainty between ambiguity and vagueness. Ambiguity is the uncertainty associated with crisp sets, for example, when hard classification is conducted to allocate pixels to one of several possible land cover classes. Vagueness, on the other hand, is expressed by the degree of incompleteness of land cover classification schemas or the eventual fuzziness needed to deal with borderline cases (e.g. the dividing line between a sprawling shrub and a woody vine which is indefinite).
Such ambiguity intensifies in urban areas, where mixed pixels occur in images with different spatial resolution (Herold et al., 2003; Mesev, 2003). This ambiguity is due to the complex composition of urban landscapes where the same materials may be present in different land cover classes, as for example in roads and rooftops made of asphalt and concrete. In such cases, any attempt to produce crisp image objects representing one or another land cover class can fail easily. As a simple illustration, Figure 2 shows eight crisp segmentations obtained from a high spatial resolution image over an urban area. In this example, image segmentation was conducted using a watershed segmentation algorithm which needs three parameters as input: (i) denoising factor (conductance of an anisotropic diffusion filter), (ii) scale (size of the image objects), and (iii) dissimilarity criteria (threshold value to merge the image objects). A visual assessment of the resulting image segmentations suggests that none of these single level segmentations produces meaningful image objects. Morever, it demonstrates that parameterisation of a meaningful segmentation is really a complicated and hard task. This

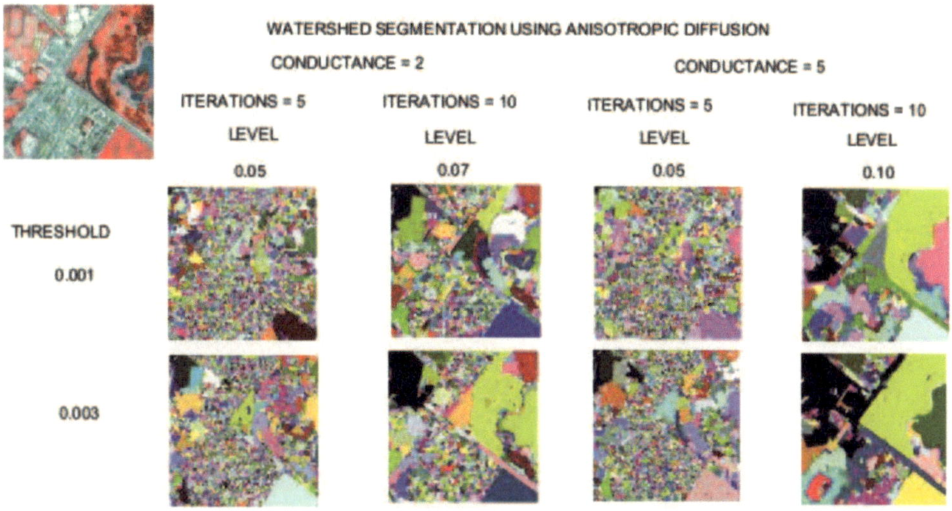

Fig. 2. Examples of crisp image objects produced by a hard image segmentation of a multispectral image using the watershed algorithm and different combinations of parameters

example illustrates that, very often, a discrete image segmentation does not help to resolve the ambiguity present in urban image data sets.

On the other side of uncertainty is vagueness, a component which refers to the application of fuzzy sets concepts, for example, when fuzzy classification is used to establish degrees of membership to natural land cover that varies continuously (Atkinson & Foody, 2002). This topic is reviewed in the next section.

2.2 Fuzzy sets and image classification

Fuzzy classification attempts to address the fact that geographic information is imprecise, meaning that the boundaries between different phenomena are fuzzy, or there is heterogeneity within a class, perhaps due to physical differences. A fuzzy classification takes into account that there are pixels of mixed composition, that is, a pixel cannot be definitively assigned to one or another category (Fisher & Pathirana, 1990; Wang, 1990).

A *hard* classification algorithm is based on classic set theory, which requires precisely defined set boundaries for which an element (i.e. a pixel) is either a member (true = 1) or not a member (false = 0) of a given class. In contrast, a *fuzzy* classification allows degrees of membership of image objects to each of the different classes. A main advantage of fuzzy classifiers is that they provide a more informative and potentially more accurate alternative to hard classification (Atkinson & Foody, 2002). Thus, a fuzzy classifier is a realistic way to take into account the ambiguity problem described in the previous section.

Fuzzy approaches for per-pixel image classification have been proposed since 1990 (Foody, 1996; Wang, 1990; Zhang & Foody, 1998). It has been argued that, because of mixed pixels, remotely sensed images provide an ambiguous representation of the landscape (Fisher, 1997). As a consequence, identification of thematic classes from images can not be achieved with a high level of certainty (Molenaar & Cheng, 2000). Hence, a hard classification of images into well-defined classes has been evaluated as inappropriate and inaccurate (Doan & Foody, 2007). A fuzzy or soft image classification can be obtained by using either a per-pixel or a per-field approach (i.e. using existing boundary data) (Aplin & Atkinson, 2001; Zhang &

Stuart, 2001). A fuzzy classification is especially useful for analyzing and detecting changes in complex landscapes (Burrough & Frank, 1996; Fisher et al., 2006).
Pixel-based fuzzy classification is typically conducted using three main stages:

1. *fuzzification*, in which membership functions to classes are established for a number of features,
2. *fuzzy rules definition*, in which different membership functions are combined into a rule set base and used for classification, and
3. *defuzzification*, in which the fuzzy classification result is discretized to produce the eventual crisp allocation/classsification.

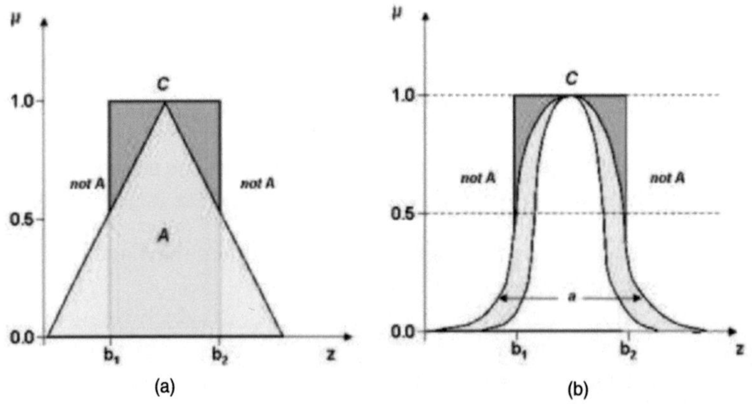

Fig. 3. Crisp (rectangular) and fuzzy (i.e. triangular and normal) membership functions for feature z.

Fuzzification is a term used to describe the transition from crisp (classic) sets to fuzzy sets. In a fuzzy system, every class is represented as a fuzzy set and memberships take values anywhere in the range $[0, 1]$ (Zadeh, 1965). Figure 3 shows that , for a particular feature z, the membership value μ to a given class can be defined by either a crisp membership function as the rectangular function or by a fuzzy membership function such as the triangular or the bell-shaped functions. In a crisp function, such as the rectangular one, the membership value μ is full (1.0) if $b_1 \leq z \leq b_2$, or null (0.0), otherwise. In a fuzzy function, such as the triangular in (a) or the normal in (b), the membership value μ can be any value between 1.0 and 0.0, depending on the value of z and the specific nature of the selected function.
The second stage is the definition of fuzzy rules, i.e. *if - then* rules in which, if a condition is fulfilled, an action takes place. Referring to Figure 4 the following rules apply: If the value of feature z is below 25, then the pixel has a full membership to a given land cover class (e.g. class A). If the value of feature z is 50, then the pixel has 0.5 membership to class A and 0.5 membership to class B. A fuzzy rule base produces a fuzzy classification which consists of discrete return values of membership of pixels for each of the output classes.
In *defuzzification*, the last stage of the process, every pixel is assigned to one of the classes of interest. A common way of defuzzification is to assign each pixel to the class with the highest membership degree value. If this value is below a certain threshold (e.g. less than 0.50), no classification is performed to ensure a minimum reliability of such allocation.

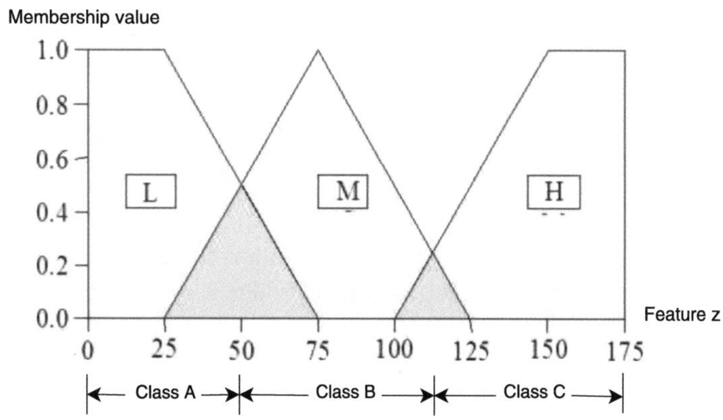

Fig. 4. The fuzzy membership functions for feature *z* define the fuzzy set *L* (low), *M* (medium), and *H* (high) of membership to classes A, B and C.

It should be noted that the use of fuzzy sets techniques in the context of conventional OBIA is not new. However, fuzziness has not been considered at the segmentation stage but later in the process chain, that is, at the classification stage. In this stage, the richness of fuzzy sets concepts is used to handle the uncertainty carried by sharp image objects and hopefully to increase the final thematic accuracy (Benz et al., 2004). Fuzzy classification is, however, the last stage of the process, and it may be too late to take into account uncertainty. As an example, *Definiens* software provides capabilities for fuzzy classification of image objects. However, in such implementation users need to manually select fuzzy membership functions and experiment with classification rules. This particular setup of the defuzzification step leads to time consuming trial and error experiments which add significant effort to the whole classification process.

Fuzzy sets concepts have been implemented in the segmentation stage of OBIA only very recently (Lizarazo & Elsner, 2009). This chapter links into this work and pursues the argument that a much more natural way for dealing with uncertainty is to apply fuzzy set concepts at the very beginning of the OBIA process, that is in the segmentation stage. By doing that, the earliest (and regularly weakest) link could be strengthened and therefore the entire classification process be improved.

In the next section , a general framework for object-based image classification based on fuzzy segmentation will be proposed.

3. Geographic objects and image objects

In the previous section, 'image objects' were introduced as the core spatial units for conducting object-based image analysis (OBIA). As segmentation, the OBIA's critical stage, produces such image objects which aim to identify real world objects, it is important to review how geographic objects are conceptualised in digital environments.

At its most basic level, geographic objects can be modeled as discrete objects or continuous fields, depending on a number of considerations, including purpose and scale of analysis (Couclelis, 1992; Goodchild, 1992; Goodchild et al., 2007).

Discrete objects are non-overlapping partitions of the geographic space which can be used to conceptualise sharply bounded objects like buildings, roads or real estate units. Continuous

fields are functions that map locations to a given property (attribute) which may serve to conceptualise spatially variant phenomena like elevation, soil type, agricultural suitability or flood risk. For some applications, a given geographic object can be modeled simultaneously as being a field and an object, e.g. an agricultural parcel can be conceptualised as an enclosed area of land whose soil acidity varies continuously (Bian, 2007; Goodchild et al., 2007).
Thus, geographic objects can be represented using three main categories: (i) geo-objects for discrete objects, (ii) geo-fields for continuous fields, and (iii) field-objects for spatial regions with internal heterogeneity (Goodchild et al., 2007). All categories can be derived from the concept of a geo-atom which associates a point location in space-time and a property. In formal language, a geo-atom is a tuple $\langle x, Z, z(x) \rangle$ where x defines a point in space-time, Z identifies a property and $z(x)$ defines the particular value of the property at that point.
A geo-object is therefore an aggregation of points in space-time whose geo-atoms have uniform values for certain properties. A geo-object can have either natural (also known as *bona fide*) boundaries or cognition-induced (also known as *fiat*) boundaries (Goodchild et al., 2007). Examples of bona fide boundaries are buildings, roads, or rivers. Examples of fiat boundaries are county borders or property-lines.
In geo-fields, the values for a particular property of geo-atoms are allowed to vary. A *scalar* geo-field describes a single property such as elevation; a *vector* geo-field describes both magnitude and orientation of continuous phenomena such as wind or temperature. A field-object is a mixed object which describes the variation of a continuous property across an areal geo-object such as changes on biomass in a forest. In current GIS practice, geo-objects can be represented in the two dimensional space using points, lines and polygons. Geo-fields are commonly represented by raster grid cells or triangular irregular networks (Goodchild et al., 2007). Field-objects, however, are not very well represented yet in GIS systems (Bian, 2007).
In the realm of OBIA, the segments output by standard 'hard' segmentation procedures can be related to geo objects. However, segmentation could be defined in a broader way to be compatible with other types of geographic objects as well. Such a more generic view of the image segmentation process would allow it to produce *image regions* able to resemble both discrete geo-objects and continuous geo-fields.
It is proposed here that image segmentation should be understood as the process of grouping pixels either spatially or thematically. In the first case, spatial segments can be identified as crisp *image objects* which are discrete groups of pixels with clearly delimited boundaries but no thematic description. These are the geo-object type segments that are produced by current standard OBIA approaches. In the second case, segments can be conceptualised as *image fields,* whose pixels store individual values to a given property. Image fields are not single layer output such as the spatial segments of standard OBIA approaches. Rather, image fields consist of as many layers as properties of interest, e.g. target land cover classes, exist. A set of image fields representing respective membership to a given set of thematic categories and individual image fields can be understood as continuous *image regions.*
Figure 5 illustrates both spatial and thematic image segmentation: (a) an example of spatial segmentation with four discrete image objects labelled as 1,2,3, and 4; (b) three layers of continuous image regions, identified as target land cover classes A, B, and C. In (c), the hypothetical thematic categories A, B, and C, are shown for reference. Typically, discrete image objects, or spatial segments, are crisply bounded, have individual identity but lack any thematic description. Crisp image objects are created using intrinsic homogeneity criteria which usually do not refer to thematic similarity. Thus, discrete image objects are simply *crisp*

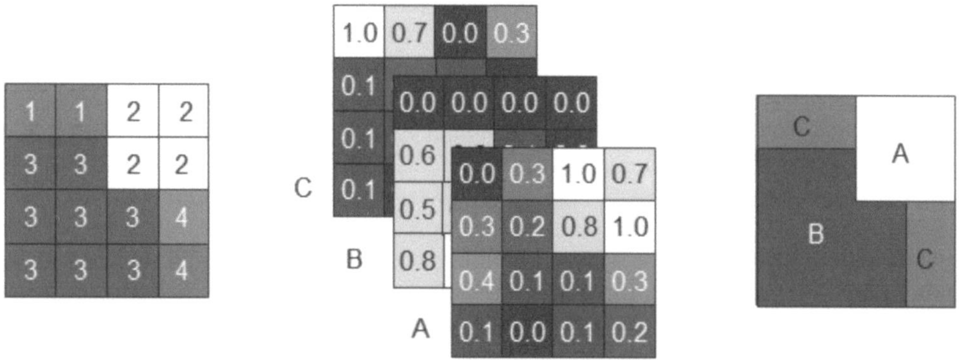

(a) (b) (c)

Fig. 5. Two different types of segments output by image segmentation: (a) discrete image objects with crisp boundaries but no thematic description; and (b) continuous image regions with indeterminate boundaries but thematic description. Three hypothetical thematic categories A, B and C are shown in (c) for reference.

regions whose spatial and spectral properties need to be analysed at a later stage of the OBIA process to produce an eventual thematic allocation.
Continuous image regions, or thematic segments, on the other hand, are a set of image fields with no spatial boundaries but holding a membership value to a given set of thematic categories. Thematic segments have no sharply defined boundaries, thus they can be considered as fuzzy or vague regions. As illustrated in (b), there are as many layers of image regions as target classes exist. Each pixel in a image region holds membership values to every one of target classes A, B and C. A given pixel, for example the one to the top right corner, holds the following membership values: 0.7 to class A, 0.0 to class B, and 0.3 to class C (in this example, it is assumed that membership values add up to 1.0 which is not always the case).

3.1 Spatial image segmentation and sharp image objects

Spatial or crisp image segmentation that is undertaken in traditional OBIA analysis can formally be described as follows. Let R represent the entire geographic region occupied by an image. Spatial segmentation can be seen as a process that partitions R into n homogeneous sub-regions $R_1, R_2, \ldots, R_n$ such that:

$$\bigcup_{i=1}^{n} R_i = R. \tag{4}$$

$$R \quad \text{is a connected set,} \quad i = 1, 2, \ldots, n. \tag{5}$$

$$R_i \cap R_j = \emptyset \text{ for all } i \text{ and } j, \quad i \neq j. \tag{6}$$

$$Pred(R_i) = TRUE \text{ for } \quad i = 1, 2, \ldots, n. \tag{7}$$

$$Pred(R_i \cup R_j) = FALSE \quad \text{for any adjacent regions } R_i \quad \text{and } R_j. \tag{8}$$

In equations 4 to 8, $Pred(R_k)$ is a logical predicate defined over the points in set R_k, and $\emptyset$ is the null set. The symbols $\cup$ and $\cap$ represent set union and intersection, respectively. A region is a connected set of pixels. Two regions R_i and R_j are considered adjacent if pixels lying on their boundaries are neighbours. A pixel may have either 4 neighbours (i.e. two *horizontal* and two *vertical*) or 8 neighbours (when the *four* diagonal neighbors are also considered). Equation 4 indicates that every pixel is allocated to a region. Equation 5 requires that pixels in a region be 4- or 8- connected. Equation 6 indicates that the regions must be disjoint (i.e. they have no pixel in common). Equation 7 indicates what properties must be satisfied by the pixels in a segmented region –for example, $Pred(R_i) = TRUE$ if all pixels in R_i have their intensity level within certain interval. Finally, equation 8 denotes that two adjacent regions R_i and R_j must be different in the sense of predicate P.

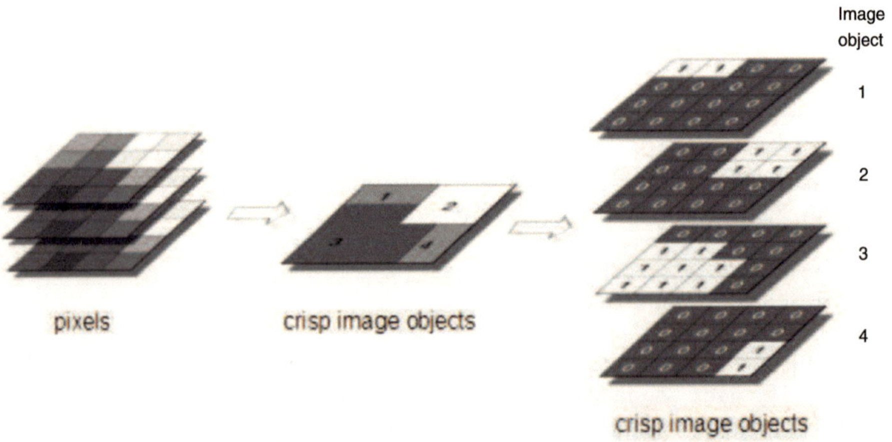

Fig. 6. Spatial or crisp image segmentation produces one single image composed of sharp image objects with clearly defined boundaries. In a field representation of sharp image objects, as the one depicted to the right, pixels hold full or null membership to image objects. In a *perfect* segmentation, discrete image objects can be unequivocally associated to target land cover classes.

Discrete image segmentation divides an image into a set of non-overlapping regions or image objects whose union is the entire image (Haralick & Schapiro, 1992). Figure 6 illustrates that crisp image objects are discrete structures with clearly defined boundaries which cover the totality of the imaged geographic area. Image objects are an aggregation of (raw or pre-processed) pixels whose digital values, located at one or several spectral bands, meet one or several homogeneity criteria defined by predicate P. Pixels aggregated as image objects satisfy predicate P –which usually involves properties of single pixels but may also include constraints related to the segment under construction like minimum or maximum size. As outlined earlier, the definition of predicate P is a subjective decision which usually entails a trial and error parameterisation procedure in established OBIA workflows.
However, Figure 6 demonstrates that such image objects can be expressed as well in the field view of thematic segmentation. This is done as three image regions in which the membership of pixels to image objects 1 to 4 is expressed in the binary 0/1 membership to each individual region. In a *perfect segmentation* each image object 1, 2, 3, and 4 can be unequivocally linked

to the target classes A, B, and C (as shown in Figure 5). This demonstrates that the spatial segments can also be conceptualised as extreme examples of thematic segmentation.

3.2 Fuzzy image segmentation and fuzzy image regions

Thematic segmentation offers the opportunity to widen the binary crisp membership attributes that are inherent in the spatial segmentation approach by allowing not just membership values of 0 or 1 but also any value in between, i.e. expressing fuzzy membership values. This is the central paradigm of the proposed *fuzzy* image segmentation approach. Figure 7 shows vague (or fuzzy) image regions output by a fuzzy segmentation. In this hypothetical example, the input image is a multispectral image composed of n spectral bands. The output of the fuzzy classification is a set X composed of m image regions, where m is defined by the number of target land cover classes of the OBIA process. In the example of Figure 7, X_m comprises of three land cover classes A, B, and C. Partial membership values $\mu(X_m)$ are represented by continuous values ranging from 0.0 (no membership) to 1.0 (full membership).

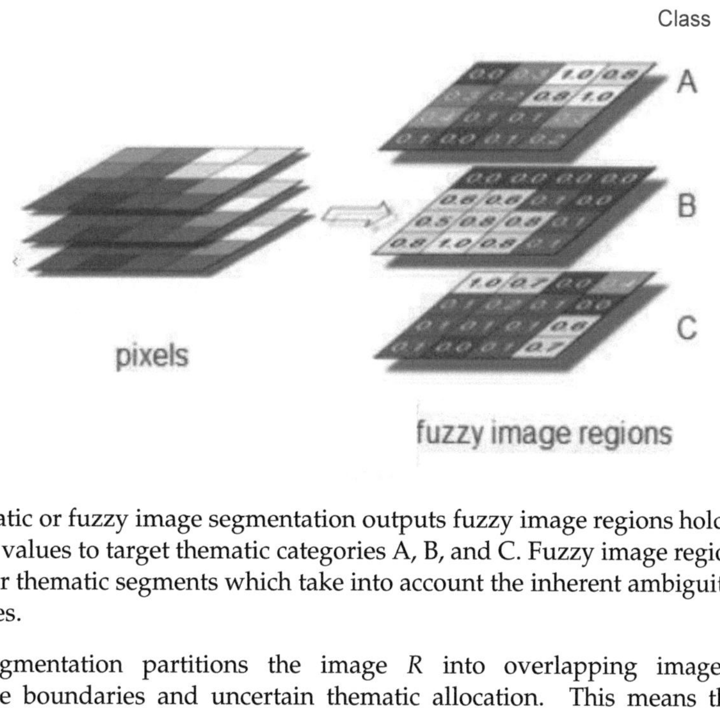

Fig. 7. Thematic or fuzzy image segmentation outputs fuzzy image regions holding multiple membership values to target thematic categories A, B, and C. Fuzzy image regions are continuous or thematic segments which take into account the inherent ambiguity of remotely sensed images.

A fuzzy segmentation partitions the image R into overlapping image fields with indeterminate boundaries and uncertain thematic allocation. This means that equations 5, 6 and 8 that apply to discrete segmentation do not hold for continuous or thematic segmentation. Instead, there is no condition of spatial connectedness (Equation 5); each pixel belongs to all m fuzzy image regions with varying degrees of membership (Equation 6); and there is no condition of dissimilarity between regions (Equation 8). In addition, membership values can be anywhere in the range from 0.0 to 1.0.

The concept of a fuzzy image region can be further extended in order to allow pixels to store not only a single membership value per class (a scalar) but a multi-valued membership per class (a vector). This extension may be useful to store, for example, minimum, mean and maximum estimated values of membership. This additional type of fuzzy image region can be referred to as a *composed* fuzzy image region. A composed image region can be seen as a

finite set of possible realizations of a fuzzy image-region where each realization is the value inferred using one specific processing technique.
Once fuzzy image regions have been established, there are two alternative approaches for conducting the subsequent OBIA classification process:

- *direct* discretization which transforms fuzzy image regions into discrete objects or classes skipping the feature analysis stage (i.e. using a similar approach to traditional pixel-wise fuzzy classification), or
- *object-oriented* discretization which introduces a feature analysis stage in which fuzzy image regions properties are measured before proceeding to the defuzzification/classification stage.

3.3 A general workflow for image classification

A general framework to conduct fuzzy segmentation-based image analysis is proposed in Figure 8. The image classification process can be understood as the sequential development of three distinct and interrelated stages: (i) *fuzzy segmentation* in which n spectral bands are transformed into m fuzzy image regions, (ii) *feature analysis* in which properties of fuzzy image regions are measured to build a set of relevant features, and (iii) *defuzzification* (or classification) in which fuzzy image regions are allocated to one of m land cover classes.

3.3.1 Fuzzy segmentation

In this stage, fuzzy image regions are created from raw or pre-processed pixels. As outlined in the previous section, fuzzy image-regions have membership values in the range $[0,1]$. Such values represent degrees of belongingness of every pixel to the classes under study. Fuzzy segmentation can be understood here as a supervised regression task in which, training samples are used to infer membership values to classes for the whole image. Thus, following such a concept, any statistical technique able to fit a supervised regression model may be used to produce fuzzy image regions. Once a set of membership grey-level images has been produced, there will be one fuzzy image region available for each target class.

3.3.2 Feature analysis

This stage aims to define, select and extract a relevant set of image regions' properties and relationships suitable to be used as a feature vector to infer appropriate decision rules to resolve the spectral ambiguity of land cover classes. An example metric is the absolute normalized difference index (ANDI) defined in Equation 9:

$$ANDI = |\mu iA - \mu iB| / (\mu iA + \mu iB) \tag{9}$$

where μiA and μiB are the membership values of the ith pixel to the classes A and B, respectively. The $ANDI$ value is an indicator of the overlap existing between two specific fuzzy image regions. ANDI values range in $[0,1]$. ANDI values close to 0 represent areas of thematic confusion.
Another metric is the sum of logarithms index (SOL) defined in Equation 10:

$$SOL = ln\mu iA + ln\mu iB \tag{10}$$

where ln is the natural logarithm. The SOL index measures the overlap between two fuzzy image regions A and B and highlights areas exhibiting high membership values to more than one target class.

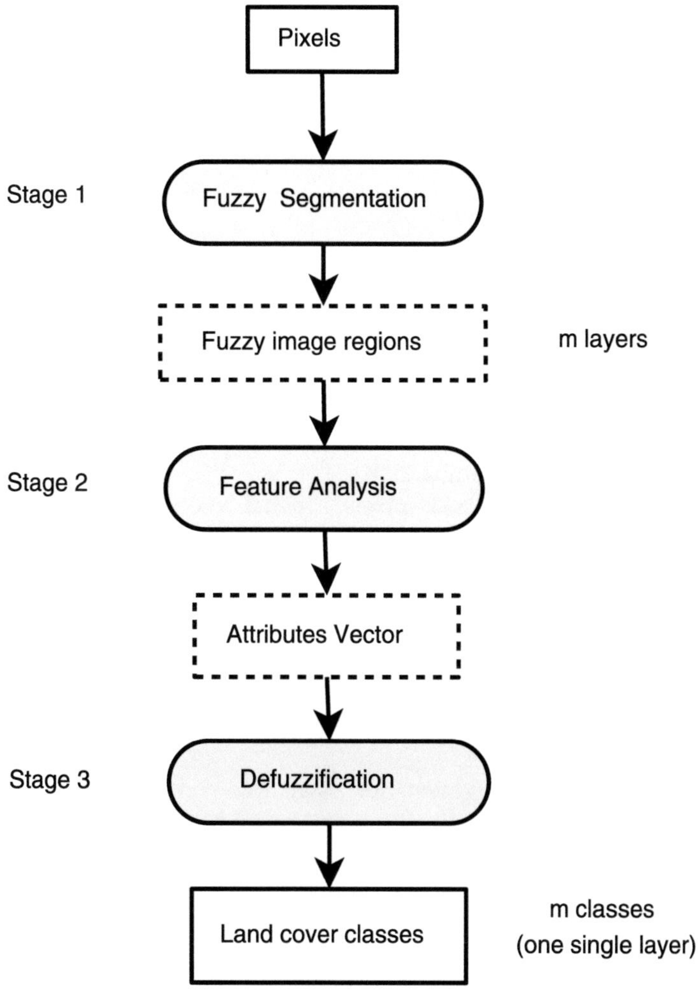

Fig. 8. A general workflow for image classification based on fuzzy segmentation.

3.3.3 Defuzzification

This stage aims to infer (and apply) appropriate decision rules to assign either full membership from the fuzzy image regions to the target land-cover classes (in the case of categorical qualitative analysis) or compositional values representing proportion of land cover classes at every pixel (in the case of quantitative analysis).

For *qualitative* analysis, a common defuzzification technique used in fuzzy applications is the allocation using the maximum membership values (Wang, 1990), which has been applied in per-pixel classification in the last two decades. Other approaches include the centroid method, the weighted average method and the mean max membership method (Ross, 2004). However, all these established techniques do not exploit the potential richness of information carried by fuzzy image regions (and quantified in the feature analysis stage). Thus, in the approach proposed here, the process of defuzzification is addressed as a problem of supervised learning in which a variety of non parametric classification algorithms could be applied.

For *quantitative* analysis, the defuzzification task can be understood as a supervised regression problem in which appropriate training samples are used to infer compositional land cover values for the whole image (in this case, fuzzy image regions need to add to 1.0). For solving such a problem, a double regression is conducted: one for the fuzzy segmentation, and the other one for the final classification.

3.4 Application of the proposed framework

The proposed framework has been applied to qualitative and quantitative land cover analysis. The following sections summarize main results of applying the fuzzy image segmentation approach for classification of a number of remotely sensed urban datasets.

3.4.1 Categorical land cover analysis

Lizarazo & Elsner (2009) applied the fuzzy segmentation method to classify the *University* image, a hyperspectral dataset of the University of Pavia (Italy) that was collected by the Hysens project on 8th July 2002 (Gamba, 2004).

The University data set size is 610x339 pixels. Spatial resolution is 1.2 m. There are 112 hyperspectral channels ranging from 400 to 1260 nm. This data set was chosen because it was used in a previous OBIA study using crisp image segmentation (Aksoy, 2006).

Seven spectral channels which roughly correspond to the center wavelength of Landsat Thematic Mapper (TM) channels were selected as input for the image classification experiment. The *University* data set includes training and testing samples for nine land cover classes: asphalt, meadows, gravel, trees, (painted) metal sheets, bare soil, bitumen, self-blocking bricks, and shadow. The training sample comprises 3921 pixels and the testing sample 42762 pixels.

For this experiment, the fuzzy segmentation stage was conducted using the generalized additive method (GAM) which output nine fuzzy image regions (i.e. one image region per target land cover class) from the seven spectral channels. For the feature analysis stage, the ANDI indices were calculated for the following pairs of classes as they were visually identified as potencial source of spectral confusion: asphalt and gravel, asphalt and bitumen, asphalt and bricks, meadows and trees, and meadows and bare soil. For the final defuzzification stage, a support vector machine (SVM) was used to output the intended land cover classification. The overall classification accuracy reported by Lizarazo & Elsner (2009) was a 0.95 confidence interval of KIA (Kappa Index of Agreement) equals to $[0.764, 0.784]$.

The performance of the proposed fuzzy segmentation method was evaluated by using an earlier classification of the *University* data set (Aksoy, 2006) as benchmark. In that work, a three stage crisp segmentation OBIA procedure was applied. Input to the crisp segmentation comprised of 24 bands as follows: 8 linear discriminant analysis (LDA) bands, 10 principal components analysis (PCA) bands, and 16 Gabor texture bands. The feature analysis step used a feature vector of 4 values for each image object by clustering spectral statistics from the 24 input bands and from 10 shape attributes. The final classification was based on Bayesian classifiers. The overall classification accuracy reported by Aksoy (2006) was a 0.95 confidence interval of KIA equals to $[0.788, 0.814]$.

It is apparent that the work of Aksoy (2006) achieved slightly higher accuracies. However, it also required significant user input and has very limited potential for automation. Fuzzy segmentation-based OBIA as implemented by Lizarazo & Elsner (2009) required very little user-input and could easily be automated for the analysis of large data sets.

3.4.2 Quantitative land cover analysis

The traditional OBIA methods, based on crisp segmentation, are mainly used to delineate and classify land cover efficiently (Duveiller et al., 2008). As crisp segmentation deals with the delineation of meaningful sharp image objects, it is clear that its main advantage relies on its ability to produce qualitative land cover units. The OBIA approach focuses on qualitative interpretation of remote sensing images. Often, however, it is preferable to use a continuous representation of land cover (i.e. a quantitative analysis) rather than a discrete classification (i.e. a qualitative classification). In a continuous representation of land cover, the different compositional classes vary continuously not only in space but also in time. By contrast, in the discrete representation of land cover, each spatial unit is represented by a single categorical value which is stable over time (Lambin, 2000). Quantitative land cover clasification is of particular relevance where a individual land surface characteristic is of interest, e.g. the fraction of impervious surface in each pixel, or the percentage of tree cover at each location.

Lizarazo (2010) applied the fuzzy segmentation method for estimation of impervious surface area (ISA) values in Montgomery County, Maryland, USA, from Landsat-TM ortorectified images. The Landsat images, collected in 1990 and 2000, comprised of seven spectral channels with pixel size of 28.5 m at 50 m root mean square error (RMSE) positional accuracy. As part of an extensive study on urbanization in the Chesapeake Bay Watershed, Jantz et al. (2005) obtained accurate ISA maps and qualitative land cover maps for the study area. These maps were used as ground reference for training sample collection and accuracy evaluation.

The estimation of quantitative land cover involved four main stages: (i) pre-processing for relative radiometric normalization of the two Landsat-TM scenes, (ii) fuzzy segmentation, (iii) feature analysis, and (iv) final regression. For the fuzzy segmentation stage, a supervised regression SVM model was fitted using land cover class memberships as a response variable and six independent analysis components (ICA) as predictor variables. Training sample comprised 1000 randomly selected pixels representing 0.27% of the study area. As a result of this stage, the following five fuzzy image regions were created: water, urban, grass, trees, and bare soil. For the feature analysis stage, ANDI indices were calculated for the following pair of fuzzy image regions: urban and water, urban and grass, urban and trees, and urban and bare soil. For the final regression stage, the SVM regression technique was used to predict ISA values from the five vague image regions and the four SOL indices.

As a final step, the accuracy of the fuzzy segmentation method was evaluated by comparing the predicted ISA values with the ground reference data using the standard correlation index (Jensen, 2005). The correlation index between the predicted ISA images and the ground reference images were 0.75 for the 1990 date, and 0.79 for the 2000 date. The fuzzy segmentation method overestimated ISA values by 10% and 8% respectively. This estimation level can be considered to be a good approximation to the real impervious surface area. Minor misprediction problems were detected only after a careful visual assessment.

Unlike traditional OBIA methods, the fuzzy segmentation approach can therefore be used for both qualitative and quantitative land cover analysis. This characteristic of the proposed approach is clearly one of its central advantages. This potential is very important for remote sensing image analysis, as there is an increasing need to estimate biophysical parameters to better understand the environmental dynamics at local and national scales (Camps-Valls et al., 2009). In this context, there seems to be an urgent need for robust and accurate regression methods in order to overcome the challenges posed by the inversion of analytical models which are often considered as too complex, computationally intensive, or sensitive to noise (Camps-Valls et al., 2009; Kimes et al., 2000).

Consequently, the fuzzy segmentation approach can be included in the list of emerging methods which use empirical models to learn the relationship between the acquired imagery and actual ground measurements. Furthermore, the fuzzy segmentation approach can act as an unifying framework which contributes to bridging the gap between the two traditional branches of remote sensing analysis, i.e. those methods that study categorical variables and those methods focused on estimating continuous variables, which are often considered as opposite, and independent worlds (Liang, 2007).

4. Conclusions

Fuzzy image regions can serve as a general conceptual framework for producing both accurate quantitative and qualitative characterizations of land cover. The application of the proposed method in several case studies illustrated that fuzzy image segmentation provides a robust, accessible and easy to use method for urban land cover analysis. The contribution of this chapter, which was discussed in last section, can be summarized as follows:

1. The potential of fuzzy sets concepts to extend the traditional perspective of image segmentation was evaluated.
2. The suitability of the fuzzy segmentation approach to produce both categorical and compositional characterization of land cover was tested.

The proposed method therefore enhances the range of OBIA alternatives and contributes to improving the remote sensing image analysis process. It addresses the concerns of Platt & Rapoza (2008) that traditional OBIA approaches commonly have difficulties dealing with spectrally overlapping classes. This is particularly true in urban landscapes which usually comprise objects of different sizes with high levels of within-class heterogeneity (Herold et al., 2007). In such landscapes, where spectral complexity is a common issue, the fuzzy segmentation approach represents a suitable alternative to the hard image segmentation approach, a trial and error process which may not always succeed (Frauman & Wolff, 2005; Lang et al., 2006; Robson et al., 2006; Schiewe et al., 2001b). In addition, in contrast to image classification based on hard segmentation, the proposed method is able to deal, throughout the whole process, with the inherent imperfections of remote sensing data such as sensor noise, local shading and highlights which often prevent the creation of meaningful image objects (Bezdek et al., 1999).

Lastly, standard *crisp* OBIA implementations require significant user input for the parameterization of segmentation models. This introduces significant subjectivity into the process and makes the eventual classification performance at least partly a function of individual user skill and effort. Fuzzy segmentation-based OBIA on the other hand requires very little user input. This makes the approach more robust, objective, and reproducible.

5. References

Aksoy, S. (2006). Spatial techniques for image classification, *in* C. C. H. (ed.), *Signal and Image Processing for Remote Sensing*, Taylor & Francis, pp. 491–514.

Aplin, P. & Atkinson, P. (2001). Sub-pixel land cover mapping for per-field classification, *International Journal of Remote Sensing* 22(14): 2853–2858.

Atkinson, P. M. & Foody, G. M. (2002). Uncertainty in remote sensing and GIS: Fundamentals, *in* G. M. Foody & P. M. Atkinson (eds), *Uncertainty in Remote Sensing and GIS*, Wiley, chapter 1, pp. 1–18.

Azad, P., Gockel, T. & Dillmann, R. (2008). *Computer Vision - Principles and Practice*, Elektor International Media BV.

Baatz, M. & Schape, A. (2000). Multiresolution segmentation: An optimization approach for high quality multi-scale image segmentation, *in* J. S. et al. (ed.), *Angewandte Geographische Informationsverarbeitung XII*, AGI Symposium, pp. 12–23.

Benz, U. (2001). Definiens imaging GmbH: Object oriented classification and feature detection, *IEEE Geoscience and Remote Sensing Society Newsletter* .

Benz, U., Hofmann, P., Willhauck, G., Lingenfelder, I. & Heynen, M. (2004). Multi-resolution, object-oriented fuzzy analysis of remote sensing data for GIS-ready information, *ISPRS Journal of Photogrammetry and Remote Sensing* 58(3–4): 239–258.

Bezdek, J., Pal, M., Keller, J. & Krisnauram, R. (1999). *Fuzzy Models and Algorithms for Pattern Recognition and Image Processing*, Springer.

Bian, L. (2007). Object-oriented representation of environmental phenomena: Is everything best represented as an object?, *Annals of the Association of American Geographers* 97(2): 267–281.

Blaschke, T. (2010). Object based image analysis for remote sensing, *ISPRS Journal of Photogrammetry and Remote Sensing* 65: 2–16.

Blaschke, T., Burnett, C. & Pekkarinen, A. (2006). Image segmentation methods for object-based analysis and classification, *in* S. de Jong & F. van der Meer (eds), *Remote Sensing Image Analysis: Including the Spatial Domain*, Springer, pp. 211–236.

Bock, M. & Lessing, R. (2002). Remote sensing, formation of objects and determination of quality, *Technical report*, DELPHI-IMM.

Burnett, C. & Blaschke, T. (2003). A multi-scale segmentation/object relationship modeling methodology for landscape analysis, *Ecological Modelling* 168: 233–249.

Burrough, P. A. (1989). Fuzzy mathematical methods for soil survey and land evaluation, *Journal of Soil Science* 40: 477–492.

Burrough, P. A. & Frank, A. U. (1996). *Geographic Objects with indeterminate boundaries*, Taylor and Francis.

Camps-Valls, G., Muñoz-Marí, J., Gómez-Chova, L., Richter, K. & Calpe-Maravilla, J. (2009). Biophysical parameter estimation with a semi-supervised support vector machine, *IEEE Geoscience and Remote Sensing Letters* .

Carleer, A., Debeir, O. & Wolff, E. (2005). Assessment of very high spatial resolution satellite image segmentations, *Photogrammetric Engineering and Remote Sensing* 71: 1285–1294.

Castilla, G. & Hay, G. J. (2008). Image objects and geographic objects, *Object-based Image Analysis*, Springer, pp. 91–110.

Corcoran, P. & Winstanley, A. (2006). Using texture to tackle the problem of scale in land-cover classification, *International conference on object based image analysis, Salzburg*.

Couclelis, H. (1992). *Theory and Methods of Spatial-Temporal Reasoning in Geographic Space*, Springer, chapter People manipulate objects (but cultivate fields): beyond the raster debate in GIS, pp. 65–77.

Dam, E. (2000). Evaluation of diffusion schemes for multi-scale watershed segmentation. MSc Thesis in Computer Science, University of Copenhagen, Denmark.

Definiens (2007). Developer 7 reference book.

Doan, H. T. X. & Foody, G. M. (2007). Increasing soft classification accuracy through the use of an ensemble of classifiers, *International Journal of Remote Sensing* 28(20): 4609–4623.

Duveiller, G., Defourny, P., Desclee, B. & Mayaux, P. (2008). Deforestation in central africa: Estimates at regional, national and landscape levels by advanced processing of systematically-distributed landsat extracts., *Remote Sensing of Environment* 112(5): 1969 – 1981.

Esch, T., Thiel, M., Bock, M., Roth, A. & Dech, S. (2008). Improvement of image segmentation accuracy based on multiscale optimization procedure, *IEEE Geosciences and Remote Sensing Letters* 5(3): 463–467.

Fisher, P. (1997). The pixel: a snare and a delusion., *International Journal of Remote Sensing* 18: 679–685.

Fisher, P., Arnot, C., Wadsworth, R. & Wellens, J. (2006). Detecting change in vague interpretations of landscapes, *Ecological Informatics* 1: 163–178.

Fisher, P. & Pathirana, S. (1990). The evaluation of fuzzy membership of land cover classes in the suburban zone, *Remote Sensing of Environment* 34: 121–132.

Foody, G. M. (1992). A fuzzy set approach to the representation of vegetation continua from remotely sensed data: an example from lowland heath, *Photogrammetric Engineering and Remote Sensing* 58: 221–225.

Foody, G. M. (1996). Approaches for the production and evaluation of fuzzy land cover classifications from remotely sensed data, *International Journal of Remote Sensing* 17: 1317–1340.

Frauman, E. & Wolff, E. (2005). Segmentation of very high spatial resolution satellite images in urban areas for segments-based classification, *International Archives of Photogrammetry, Remote Sensing and Spatial Information Sciences*.

Freixenet, J., Muñoz, X., Raba, D., Martí, J. & Cufí, X. (2002). Yet another survey on image segmentation: Region and boundary information integration, *Lecture Notes in Computer Science* 2352: 408–422.

Friedl, M. A., McGwire, K. C. & McIver, D. K. (2001). *An Overview of Uncertainty in Optical Remotely Sensed Data for Ecological Applications*, Springer, chapter 12, pp. 258–283.

Gamba, P. (2004). A collection of data for urban area characterization, *Geoscience and Remote Sensing Symposium*.

Gao, J. (2009). *Digital Analysis of Remotely Sensed Imagery*, Mc Graw Hill.

Goodchild, M. (1992). Geographical data modeling, *Computer and Geosciences* 18(4): 401–408.

Goodchild, M., Yuan, M. & Cova, T. (2007). Towards a general theory of geographic representation in GIS, *International Journal of Geographical Information Science* 21(3): 239–260.

Haralick, R. & Schapiro, L. (1992). *Computer and Robot Vision*, Addison-Wesley.

Hay, G. & Castilla, G. (2008). Geographic object-based image analysis (GEOBIA): A new name for a new discipline, *Object-based Image Analysis: Spatial Concepts for Knowledge-Driven Remote Sensing Applications*, Springer.

Herold, M., Gardner, M. & Roberts, D. (2003). Spectral resolution requirements for mapping urban areas, *IEEE Transactions on Geoscience and Remote Sensing* 41: 1907–1919.

Herold, M., Schiefer, S., Hostert, P. & Roberts, D. A. (2007). *Applying Imaging Spectrometry in Urban Areas*, CRC Press, chapter Chapter 7, pp. 137–161.

Jantz, P., Goetz, S. & Jantz, C. (2005). Urbanization and the loss of resource lands in the chesapeake bay watershed, *Environmental Management* 36(6): 808–825.

Jensen, J. (2005). *Introductory Image Processing: a Remote Sensing perspective*, Prentice Hall.

Kimes, D. S., Knyazikhin, Y., Privette, J. L., Abuelgasim, A. A. & Gao, F. (2000). Inversion methods for physically-based modelsŤ, *Remote Sensing of Environment* 18: 381 – 439.

Lambin, E. (2000). Land-cover categories versus biophysical attributes to monitor land-cover change by remote sensing, *Observing Land from Space: Science, Customers and Technology*, Kluwer Academic Publishers.
Lang, S. (2008). Object-based image analysis for remote sensing applications: modeling reality – dealing with complexity, *Object-based Image Analysis: Spatial Concepts for Knowledge-Driven Remote Sensing Applications*, Springer, chapter 1, pp. 3–27.
Lang, S., Albretch, F. & Blaschke, T. (2006). Tutorial: Introduction to object-based image analysis, Centre for Geoinformatics - Z-GIS.
Liang, S. (2007). Recent developments in estimating land surface biogeophysical variables from optical remote sensing, *Progress in Physical Geography* 31(5): 501 – 516.
Lizarazo, I. (2010). Fuzzy image regions for estimation of impervious surface areas, *Remote Sensing Letters* 1(1): 19–27.
Lizarazo, I. & Elsner, P. (2009). Fuzzy segmentation for object-based image classification, *International Journal of Remote Sensing* 30(6): 1643–1649.
Meinel, M. & Neubert, G. (2004). A comparison of segmentation programs for high resolution remote sensing data, *International Archives of Photogrammetry, Remote Sensing and Spatial Information Sciences*, ISPRS.
Mesev, V. (2003). *Remotely Sensed Cities*, Taylor & Francis.
Moigne, J. L. & Tilton, C. (1995). Refining image segmentation by integration of edge and region data, *IEEE Transactions on Geoscience and Remote Sensing* 33(3): 605Ű615.
Molenaar, M. & Cheng, T. (2000). Fuzzy spatial objects and their dynamics, *ISPRS Journal of Photogrammetry and Remote Sensing* 55(3): 164–175.
Neubert, G., Herold, M. & Meinel, M. (2006). Evaluation of remote sensing image segmentation quality - futher results and concepts, *First International Conference on Object-Based Image Analysis - Proceedings*, ISPRS.
Neubert, M., Herold, H. & Meinel, G. (2008). Assessing image segmentation quality - concepts, methods and application, *Object-Based Image Analysis - Spatial concepts for knowledge-driven remote sensing applications*, Springer, Berlin, pp. 769–784.
Ortiz, A. & Oliver, G. (2006). On the use of the overlapping area matrix for image segmentation algorithm: a survey and new perfomance measures, *Pattern Recognition Letters* 27: 1916–1926.
Pal, N. R. & Pal, S. K. (1993). A review of image segmentation techniques, *Pattern Recognition* 26(9): 1277–1294.
Platt, R. V. & Rapoza, L. (2008). An evaluation of an object-oriented paradigm for land use/land cover classification, *The Professional Geographer* 60(1): 87–100.
Rekik, A., Zribi, M., Hamida, A. B. & Benjellounl, M. (2007). Review of satellite image segmentation for an optimal fusion system based on the edge and region approaches, *International Journal of Computer Science and Network Security* 7(10): 242–250.
Robson, M., Vachon, P. W. & Seeker, J. (2006). Evaluation of ecognition for assisted target detection and recognition in sar imagery, *Geoscience and Remote Sensing Symposium, 2006. IGARSS 2006.* pp. 145–148.
Rosenfeld, A. & Kak, A. (1992). *Digital Picture Processing*, Academic Press.
Ross, T. (2004). *Fuzzy Logic with Engineering Applications*, Wiley.
Schiewe, J., Tufte, L. & Ehlers, M. (2001a). Potential and limitations of multiscale segmentation methods in remote sensing, *eCognition website* .
Schiewe, J., Tufte, L. & Ehlers, M. (2001b). Potential and problems of multi-scale segmentation methods in remote sensing, *GIS. Geo-Informations-Systeme* 6(9): 34–39.

Schneider, W. & Steinwender, J. (1999). Landcover mapping by interrelated segmentation and classification of satellite images, *International Archives of Photogrammetry & Remote Sensing, Vol. 32 Part 7-4-3*.

Schott, J. R. (1997). *Remote Sensing: The Image Chain Approach*, Oxford University Press.

Shackelford, A. & Davis, C. (2003). A combined fuzzy pixel-based and object-based approach for classification of high-resolution multispectral data over urban areas, *IEEE Transactions on Geoscience and Remote Sensing* 41(10): 2354–2363.

Shi, J. & Malik, J. (2000). Normalized Cuts and Image Segmentation, *IEEE Transactions on Pattern Analysis and Machine Intelligence* 22(8): 888–905.

Song, M., Civco, D. & Hurd, J. (2005). A competitive pixel-object approach for land cover classification, *International Journal of Remote Sensing* 26(22): 4981–4997.

Thomas, N., Hendrix, C. & Congalton, R. G. (2003). A comparison of urban mapping methods using high-resolution digital imagery, *Photogrammetric Engineering and Remote Sensing* 69(9): 963–972.

Townshend, J. R. G., Huang, C., Kalluri, S. N., DeFries, R. S., Liang, S. & Yang, K. (2000). Beware of per-pixel characterization of land cover, *International Journal of Remote Sensing* pp. 839–843.

Wang, F. (1990). Fuzzy supervised classification of remote sensing images, *IEEE Transactions on Geoscience and Remote Sensing* 28(2): 194–201.

Wei, W., Chen, X. & Ma, A. (2005). Object-oriented information extraction and application in high resolution remote sensing image, *International Geoscience and Remote Sensing Symposium (IGARSS)*, Vol. 6, pp. 3803–3806.

Woodcock, C. E. (2002). Uncertainty in remote sensing, *in* G. M. Foody & P. M. Atkinson (eds), *Uncertainty in Remote Sensing and GIS*, Wiley, chapter 2, pp. 19–24.

Yan, G., Mas, J. F., Maathuis, B. H. P., Zhang, X. & Van Dijk, P. M. (2006). Comparison of pixel-based and object-oriented image classification approaches Ű a case study in a coal fire area, Wuda, Inner Mongolia, China, *International Journal of Remote Sensing* 18(20): 4039–4055.

Zadeh, L. (1965). Fuzzy Sets, *Information and control* (8): 338–353.

Zhan, Q., Molenaar, M., Tempfli, K. & Shi, W. (2005). Quality assessment for geo-spatial objects derived from remotely sensed data, *International Journal of Remote Sensing* pp. 2953–2974.

Zhang, J. & Foody, G. (1998). A fuzzy classification of suburban land cover from remotely sensed imagery, *International Journal of Remote Sensing* 19: 2721–2738.

Zhang, J. & Stuart, N. (2001). Fuzzy methods for categorical mapping with image-based land cover data, *International Journal of Remote Sensing* 15(2): 175–195.

Zhang, Y. (2006). A fuzzy logic approach to supervised segmentation for object-oriented classification, *ASPRS 2006 Annual Conference*.

Zhang, Y. J. (1996). A survey on evaluation methods for image segmentation, *Pattern Recognition* 29(8): 1335–1346.

Zhou, C., Wang, Z., Zhang, C., Qi, C. & Wang, Y. (2007). Object-oriented information extraction technology from quickbird pan-sharpened images, *Proceedings of SPIE - The International Society for Optical Engineering*, Vol. 6279, p. 62793L.

14

Color-based Texture Image Segmentation for Vehicle Detection

Ricardo Mejía-Iñigo, María E. Barilla-Pérez and Héctor A. Montes-Venegas
Universidad Autónoma del Estado de México
México

1. Introduction

Traffic flow is the study of interactions between vehicles, drivers and related infrastructure with the goal of understanding and developing an efficient road network. A number of devices have been implemented for monitoring traffic flow such as magnetic strips and radar detectors (Haidarian-Shahri et al. (2007)). All these devices have served for a very specific purpose. However, they do not provide as much information of the scene as cameras may do. The resulting information acquired from cameras should be properly processed to monitor vehicles' behavior. Vision-based techniques have been increasingly used to extract useful traffic information from image sequences such as vehicle count, vehicle flow, vehicle speed, vehicle classification, and lane changes. All these tasks require an accurate vehicle tracking (Zhu et al. (2009)).

Vehicle tracking is a technique that generates the trajectory of the vehicle over time by locating its position in every frame of an image sequence (Yilmaz (2006)). Usually, vehicle tracking requires three initial steps, namely, (a) choosing a suitable object representation, (b) selection of image features used as an input for the tracker and (c) vehicle detection. Vehicle detection is considered a difficult task, as an appropriate feature selection is needed to deal with the visual complexity of the road scene that may include congestions, shadows, weather incidences, headlights, road conditions and other traffic participants (Coifman et al. (1998)).

Different approaches can be used to carry out the vehicle detection task, such as point detectors, background subtraction, segmentation or supervised learning methods. The selection of discriminative features plays a critical role because they should be so unique as to be easily distinguished in a feature space (Yilmaz (2006)).

Texture is considered to be a rich source of information about the nature and the three-dimensional shape of objects. It is defined by Petrou (2006) and Materka & Strzelecki (1998) as complex visual patterns and subpatterns with singular properties such as brightness, color and size. There exist different approaches for texture modeling, such as statistical models, structural models and models based on transforms. Nevertheless, texture by itself is not enough to differentiate among different objects because contrasting surfaces cause false positives detections (Sun et al. (2006)).

Color is considered a relevant feature when dealing with the perception of static and moving images. Visual contrast is useful to filter information present in each color component (Trémeau et al. (2008)) and to distinguish among similar gray-scale intensities (Barilla-Pérez & Spann (2008)).

The combination of color and texture have been proved to achieve better results and could be exploited more effectively when integrated than when treated in isolation (Barilla-Pérez & Spann (2008)). In this chapter we propose two segmentation methods based on color and texture to solve the problem of differentiating vehicles from the background. Both features were used under the following assumptions:

- Road color is considered homogeneous because the road surface is made of the same material.
- An abrupt difference between the color of the road and the color of the vehicles is useful to discriminate them from each other.
- Even if vehicles are similar in color to the road, car and road textures are different. Thus, texture may still be used to effectively discriminate between road and cars.

In this chapter two methods are described for vehicle detection by segmenting the regions they occupy, both methods use color and texture as main features. The first method uses L*u*v* color space and the Dual-Tree Complex Wavelet Transform (DTCWT) for texture modeling and a simple background identification to carry out the vehicle detection. The second method is based on a change detection technique that integrates the intensity and texture differences between the current frame and a previously modeled background. L*u*v* color space is also used in this method and texture differencing measure is based on a function between gradient vectors. In both methods, an additional process is also applied using morphological operations to improve the detection of the regions that describe the vehicles.
The chapter also includes an overview of related work and a detailed description of how color and texture features can be properly combined with both approaches to achieve accurate vehicle detection results. An experimental comparison of the two vehicle detection methods is performed both qualitatively and quantitatively. The Outex framework have been used in order to compare the accuracy of both methods (Ojala et al. (2002)). Finally, the work is summarized and results are discussed.

2. Overview of previous work

This section presents an overview of relevant vision-based vehicle detection systems. Vehicle detection using optical sensors is a very challenging task due to the various conditions found in any road scene. The variability of such conditions may be caused by the weather, by illumination changes, by the presence of shadows and by the numerous objects that are part of the scene. Additionally, vehicle features such as shape, size and color are not always sufficient for a reliable detection as the appearance of a vehicle also depends on its pose and its interaction with other traffic participants. In this section we identify several methods for vehicle detection, namely, background extraction methods, edges detection methods and statistical-based approaches. We also review previous works that deal with the occlusion problem as well as with the shadow removal problem.

2.1 Background subtraction

Background subtraction for vehicle detection methods compare each video frame against a reference background model. Assuming that all moving objects are vehicles, the elements in the current frame that are significantly different from the background model are considered the objects of interest. Methods for building a background model include estimates based on median filters (Cucchiara et al. (2003); Lo & Velastin (2001); Zhou & Aggarwal (2001)), Kalman filters (Halevy & Weinshall (1999); Wren et al. (1997)), Gaussian models (Cheng et al. (2007);

Lee et al. (2003); Stauffer & Grimson (2000)) or simple histograms and blob formation models (Elgammal et al. (1999); Sen-Ching et al. (2005)).

2.2 Edge detection

Edge detection methods have been used under the assumption that they are robust to illumination changes. In order to increase robustness of vehicle detection, edges have been used in conjunction with color information.

Tsai et al. (2007) proposed a color model to find candidate vehicles under the assumption that vehicles colors change with lightning conditions. Possible vehicles are then actually found by using local features such as corners, edge maps and wavelet coefficients. Eng et al. (2008) also use color and edge information to detect vehicles. They developed a vehicle detection method by subtracting objects from a background which is previously modeled by color and edges. Techawatcharapaikul et al. (2008) proposed a method for vehicles and shadows segmentation using temporal edge density information from adjacent frames. Mo & Zhang (2010) have detected vehicles by finding their voting center which is then used to implement a traffic analysis system. The vehicles voting centers are calculated by matching the results of a segmentation process with a previously learned spatial distribution of the objects of interest.

2.3 Statistical-based approaches

Wang & Lien (2008) proposed an statistical approach for vehicle detection based on the vector projection of three main local features of vehicles, namely the roof and the two headlights. Both *Principal Component Analysis* (PCA) and *Independent Component Analysis* (ICA) techniques are combined in order to improve the tolerance of the detection process under illumination variations and for vehicle position. Although the authors show very promising results, it is unclear if the method is robust under significant rotations of the main local features of the car. An additional work using a graph-based approach that considers the identity of neighboring vehicles has been proposed by Shahri et al. (2007). Their results showed that vehicle tracking is feasible, even for low quality and low frame rate traffic cameras.

2.4 Handling occlusions

Occlusion is one of the most difficult problems associated with vehicle detection. In order to address this problem Kamijo et al. (2000) proposed a method based on a *Spatio-Temporal Markov Random Field* model that considers the texture correlation between consecutive images and the correlation among neighbors within an image. This algorithm requires only gray scale images and does not assume any physical models of the vehicles. Even though occlusions in the scene happened in very complicated manners (vehicles appear in various shapes and they move in unpredictable ways), the method achieved a success rate as high as 95%.

Also to detect and handle vehicle occlusions, Zhang et al. (2008) presented a framework composed of three levels named *intraframe*, *interframe*, and *tracking*. On the intraframe level, occlusions are handled by evaluating the size of vehicles. On the interframe level, occlusions are detected by using the motion vectors of vehicles. On the tracking level, occlusions are handled while tracking the vehicle by performing a bidirectional occlusion reasoning algorithm. Most partial occlusions are handled on the intraframe and interframe levels, and full occlusions are handled on the tracking level. In addition to this work, Zhang & Yuan (2007) used low-resolution images for detecting and tracking vehicles as most of these images were captured far from the vehicles. The authors used borders to build a model to find outliers that can differentiate the vehicle from another object in the scene. Kalman Filters in combination with the body's radius allow handling total and partial occlusions when obstacles blocked the view of the vehicle. This method requires very low-resolution images to work correctly. Earlier research efforts for solving vehicle occlusions on monocular traffic-image sequences (Pang et al. (2004)) and for detecting and tracking vehicles by segmenting scenes with severe occlusions (Gentile et al. (2004)) have been published. However, based on their experimental results, Zhang et al. (2008) stated that "quantitative evaluation and comparison demonstrate that the proposed method outperforms state-of-the-art methods".

2.5 Shadows removal

Shadows interfere with moving vehicle detection because they cause erroneous segmentation of objects. For this reason, there is a recent interest on developing algorithms to deal with shadows of the vehicles present in the scene. Chen et al. (2010) have removed shadows from the luminance component of an image while keeping the chrominance components intact. Fang et al. (2008) have used spectral and geometrical properties of shadows to create a model to eliminate them from the scene. This method is considered a previous step before the actual vehicle detection.

2.6 Driver assistance

For traffic monitoring tasks it is crucial to detect the lane and other features of the road and then identify the presence of other vehicles. Kastrinaki et al. (2003) present a survey on video-based systems considering both areas of road traffic monitoring and automatic vehicle guidance. In their paper, the authors survey methods for the two main subtasks involved in traffic applications, i.e. the automatic lane finding and vehicle detection. Two particular cases are considered in this paper. The first one is the case in which a static camera (usually located in a high position) observes a road scene for the purpose of traffic surveillance. In the second case at least one camera is mounted on a vehicle that moves in a dynamic road scene. In a later work, Sun et al. (2006) present an extended review of systems for vehicle detection for on-board automotive driver assistance systems. For the methods summarized in this paper, the camera is mounted on the vehicle. Diaz-Alonso et al. (2008) have proposed an aid system to help the driver in overtaking and lane changing decisions. These tasks are addressed with an optic-flow-driven scheme, focusing on the visual field in the side mirror by placing a camera on top of it.

3. Color-based texture segmentation

Color-based texture segmentation is a process that divides an image into homogeneous regions using both color and textures features to distinguish from non-similar regions (Barilla-Pérez (2008)). Using more than one descriptor helps to improve the segmentation process when the descriptors are visually relevant and they can be integrated to obtain a single similarity measure.

In this section, a color-based texture segmentation algorithm originally proposed by Mejia-Iñigo et al. (2009) is described. The algorithm uses a feature vector based on color and texture to differentiate vehicles from the background. This selection of features is based on the assumptions listed in Section 1.

3.1 Texture and color

Texture is regarded as a rich source of information about the nature and three-dimensional shape of objects (Petrou (2006)). It consists of complex visual patterns and subpatterns with singular properties such as brightness, color and size (Materka & Strzelecki (1998)). There exist different approaches for texture modeling, such as statistical models, structural models and models based on transforms. Materka & Strzelecki (1998) suggested that transform methods permit the variation of spatial resolution to represent textures at different scales. In this sense, Wavelet Transform is a viable method to obtain time-frequency localization analysis and to identify stationary and non-stationary textures. As a framework, the Dual-Tree Complex Wavelet Transform (DTCWT) overcomes several difficulties present in other Wavelet Transform methods (Selesnick et al. (2005)) and offers the following advantages:

- Nearly shift invariance. When the transform is applied, the results seem to be mildly affected by translations in the original input.
- Directional selectivity. A resulting set of 6 different positive and negative directions: 15°, 45° , 75° , -15° , -45° and -75°.
- Moderate redundancy. The redundancy introduced by Complex Wavelets is 2^d:1 for d dimensions (Kingsbury (1999)).

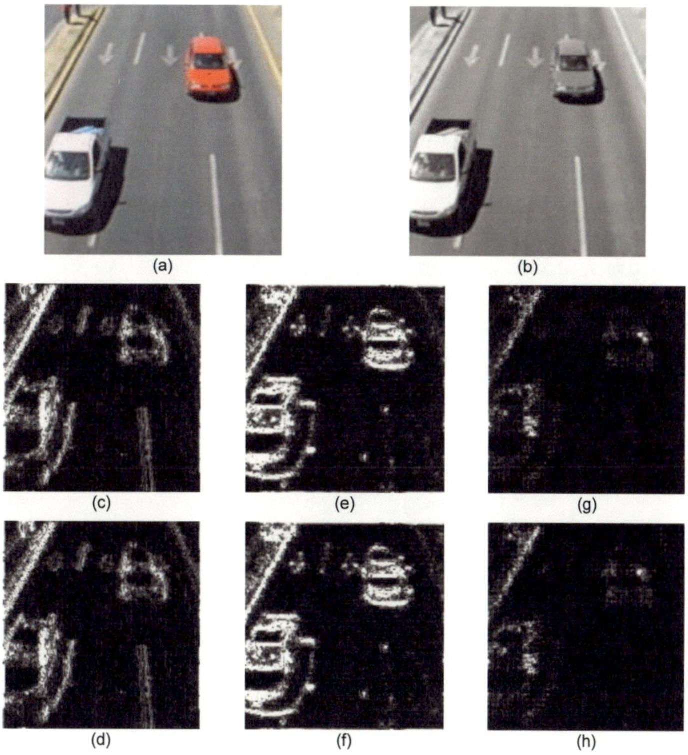

Fig. 1. Directional results of applying the Dual-Tree Complex Wavelet Transform to **L*** component (b) of a car image (a) for (c) 75°, (d) -75°, (e) 15°, (f) -15°, (g) 45° and (h) -45° directions

Color is perceived as a non-linear psycho-visual system too complex to be modeled by a simple function (Bovik & Bovik (2000)). The **L*u*v*** color space is considered one of the most suitable color spaces to represent human perception, as it is perceptually uniform (Malacara (2001)). Its **L*** component provides lightness information useful to describe texture by illumination changes on the surface of the object, whereas **u*** and **v*** provide chrominance information about the pixel values. Compared to other color spaces, **L*u*v*** has been proved to achieve high success rates for image segmentation when using texture and color features (Barilla-Pérez (2008)).

3.2 Feature extraction

Let be $I_{L^*u^*v^*}(x,y)$ a color image in the **L*u*v*** color space of size $M \times N$ where $\{x = 0, ..., M-1\}$ and $\{y = 0, ..., N-1\}$. For the color plane $I_{L^*}(x,y)$ of the image $I_{L^*u^*v^*}(x,y)$, we compute

$$W_{I_{L^*}}^{(s,b)}(i,j) = DTCWT\{I_{L^*}(x,y)\}. \tag{1}$$

where $W_{I_{L^*}}^{(s,b)}(i,j)$ are the wavelet coefficients as complex numbers, $\{s = 1, ..., S\}$ represents the levels of resolution from the highest to the lowest and $\{b = 1, ..., 6\}$ indicates the number of subbands produced by the wavelet transform at scale s. The size of the subbands b at scale s is $\frac{M}{2^s} \times \frac{N}{2^s}$ where $\{i = 0, ..., \frac{M}{2^s} - 1\}$ and $\{j = 0, ..., \frac{N}{2^s} - 1\}$. Computing the modulus of the wavelet coefficients yields its energy. The feature vectors are constructed from this energy combined with the chrominance components **u*** and **v***.

Vehicles traveling on a one-direction road have texture qualities in different directions, but if the vehicles are moving towards the capture device we only consider -75° and 75° given that these two components provide more information about the vertical displacement of the vehicles (see Fig. 1). Also, DTCWT can be applied successively until scale $s = S$ is achieved. Considering the resolution of the images, a $S = 3$ feature vector limit is employed.

L*u*v* color space components are separated in chrominance and lightness information (Sangwine et al. (1998)). DTCWT is applied on the **L*** component at different coarseness levels because texture features are considered to be more sensitive to lightness and scale changes. In contrast, color remains almost invariant to different textures variations. By reducing DTCWT components, the dimensional space of the feature vector is also reduced to decrease computational cost. The feature vector extraction process is depicted in Fig. 2.

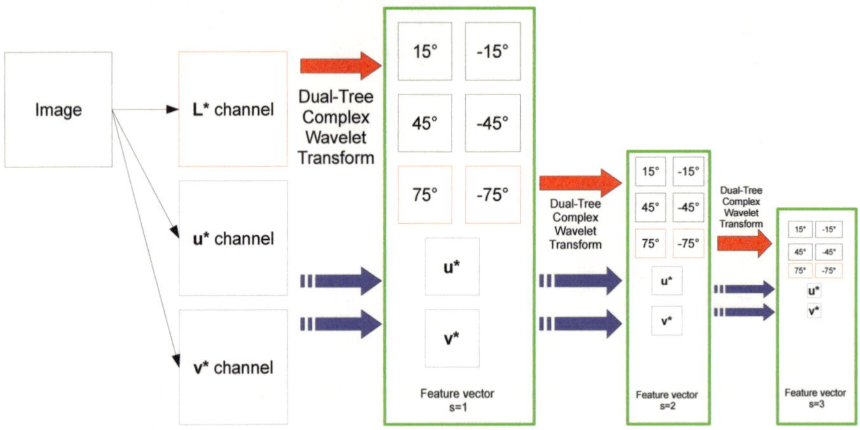

Fig. 2. Feature vector extraction and wavelet components.

3.2.1 Segmentation

Once the feature vectors have been calculated, the coarsest level at scale S is processed to obtain a global initialization that will be used to segment higher-resolution vectors. K-means clustering was used to provide this initial segmentation.

The reason for using K-means clustering is that can be easily implemented and provides a good reference to identify the most representative k macro-textures for the coarsest level $s = S$ (Barilla-Pérez (2008)). There are other segmentation methods that could be used to provide this initialization, such as statistical or graph-based methods (Felzenszwalb & Huttenlocher (2004)), but they require several parameters usually defined heuristically. In contrast, K-means clustering only requires a k parameter to indicate the most significant regions to be identified within the image.

Feature vectors are thought to have 2 representative regions: cars and road, so $k = 2$ seems to be a reasonable parameter value. The resulting classification at scale $s = S$ is used as an initialization for the Expectation-Maximization method at scale $s = S - 1$, and the result is used to process the feature vector at scale $s = S - 2$. This process is repeated until the same action is performed to the feature vector at scale $s = 1$ (See Fig. 3).

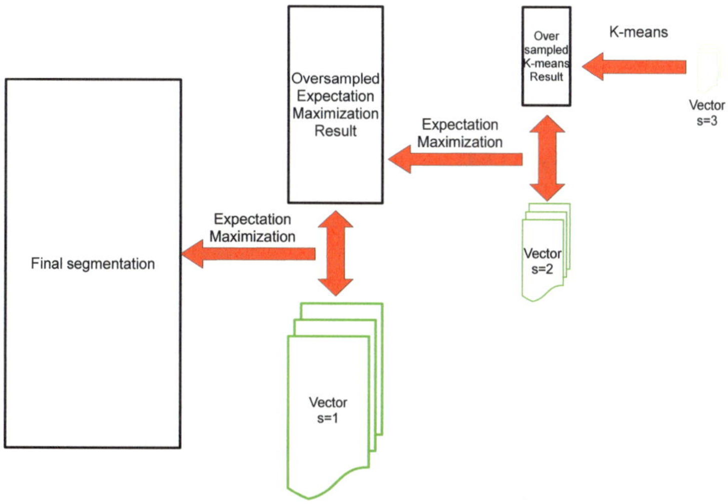

Fig. 3. Segmentation process of feature vectors at different scales.

Classification combines Multi Resolution Analysis (MRA) with a Gaussian Mixture Model to segment images at scale s based on the segmentation provided by scale $(s + 1)$. Segmentation results are in the form of a binary image as depicted in Fig. 4.

3.3 Vehicle motion detection

The analyzed scene is considered static, where only the vehicles are in constant change and the background always preserves the same texture and color. Modeling of the background is needed to separate vehicles from the road.

3.3.1 Background modeling

Considering a scene where images are taken at a time t and an interval between frames Δt, it is possible to build the background from the scene using binary images. Let *Frame(t)* be a frame taken at a time t; a pixel is part of the background if it keeps the same value from

Fig. 4. Binary image obtained by a 2-cluster segmentation. The white blob is the vehicle in motion and the white vertical stripes are divisions of the lanes.

$(t-1)$ to $(t-m)$ at interval Δt, where m can be as big as needed to classify the frame. For the experiments discussed in this chapter, the size of m is set to 9. Equation (2) represents the function that classifies pixels on an image at a given time.

$$Background(t,m) = \begin{cases} 0 & Frame(t-i) = Frame(t). \\ 1 & \text{otherwise.} \end{cases} \tag{2}$$

$$\forall i \in \{1, ..., m\},$$

An example of a classified background is shown in Fig.5.d.

3.3.2 Using logic operations for vehicle detection

The background model is represented by a binary value of 1 for all possible objects that can be described as a moving vehicle, and 0 for all objects that do not change in the images from $Frame(t-m)$ to $Frame(t)$. A possible vehicle, *PosVehicle*, is extracted by applying the logical AND operation between the modeled background *Background(t,m)* and frame *Frame(t)*. The resultant image contains the pixels that represent the vehicles (see Fig.5.e).

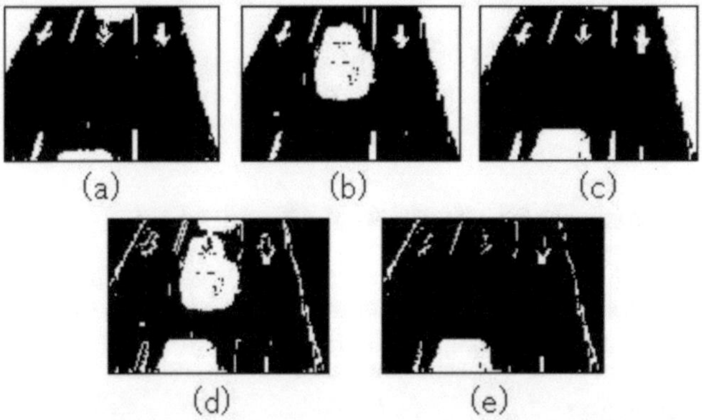

Fig. 5. Possible vehicle detection process. (a) *Frame(t-2)*, (b) *Frame(t-1)*, (c) current scene *Frame(t)*, (d) modeled background *Background(t)* and (e) possible vehicle.

A number of morphological operations are then used to reduce undesired elements present in the image where the possible vehicles have been detected.

3.3.3 Morphological processing

The resultant binary image contains the area of the vehicles along with several undesired elements as well as small holes inside those vehicles caused by illumination changes, background irregularities and vibrations of the capture device (Fig. 6 (a)). In order to remove these unwanted elements while distorting the shape of the objects as little as possible, erosion, opening, dilation and closing operations are applied (Fig. 6 (b)). These morphological operations are useful as describe above, but there are still elements that do not belong to the vehicle, seen as holes inside the objects of interest. Using region filling (González & Woods (2002)), these holes can be removed to produce a more precise shape of the vehicles detected (Fig. 6.c).

(a) (b) (c)

Fig. 6. Morphological processing. (a) Resultant binary image, (b) unwanted elements removal and (c) region filling.

4. Segmentation based on lightness and texture differences

Vehicle detection can be understood as a segmentation process, which allows us to separate the two most significative homogeneous regions in a traffic scene: (a) vehicles and (b) road. The method described in this Section attempts to deal with time-variant objects in the scene by differencing those regions in the current frame with a previously modeled background. The background and current frame difference is computed using features of texture and **L*** component intensities of the **L*u*v*** color space.

4.1 Background modeling

Vehicle detection can be achieved by building a background model and then identifying the pixels of every frame of the image sequence that vary significatively from that model (Yilmaz (2006)). Those pixels are assumed to be a moving vehicle.
Several techniques have been proposed to model background as they overcome different drawbacks usually related to the scene being examined (Cheung & Kamath (2004)). These techniques can be classified as follows:

- Recursive techniques: a single background model is updated on each input image. These techniques required less storage, but errors in the background model can persist over the time.
- Non-recursive methods: require an image buffer to estimate a background and variation is estimated for each pixel. Adaptability level is very high as they do not depend on previous background processing, but a large buffer is required to detect movement in congested roads.

In order to deal with noise and other objects that may appear in the scene, it is preferable to use non-recursive techniques to model the background, for instance, a *Median Filter*.

Let us consider an image buffer $B(x,y,t)$ that consist on a set of β images, where x and y are defined as spatial image coordinates at a given time t. Median filter background is defined as

$$Background(x,y,t) = Median(\ B(x,y,t-\beta),...,B(x,y,t-1)\ )\ \forall\, x,\ \forall\, y\,. \quad (3)$$

The median filter is very consistent even in the presence of outliers caused by noise or sudden object appearance. Correct background model is achieved only when the background is visible at least on 50% of the image buffer for each pixel (Gutchess et al. (2001)).
The background is modeled with a buffer using the **L*** component of the **L*u*v*** color space. This background model is updated every β frames and it is used as a reference to identify the most persistent pixels within an image. Vehicles are formed by the pixels of the current frame that have a significant deviation from the background.

4.2 Image difference

Image difference commonly use absolute value of two-frames intensities subtraction to identify moving objects. However, intensity subtraction is prone to errors because two different objects can have similar intensity. Adding an additional feature, such as texture, may help to effectively discriminate between different objects.
In line with Li and Leung's work (Li & Leung (2002)), texture and intensity information are used to detect changes between two images by using a gradient vector relationship that supports noise and illumination changes. Integrating intensity and texture differences for change detection works under the assumption that background texture remains relatively stable with respect to noise and illumination variations unless it is covered by moving objects or when abrupt lightness changes occur. When the background is covered by a moving object, even if intensities of foreground and background are similar, textures in both images are different. If texture difference is not sufficient to identify homogeneous regions, then intensities are considered more relevant to discriminate regions.

4.2.1 Texture difference

Li & Leung (2002) suggested gradients as a texture measure because neighborhood information is included and it is not easily affected by lightness conditions. Let I be an image, there exists an image $I' = (\ I^x,\ I^y\ )$, where I^x and I^y are results of Sobel gradient operators for its corresponding direction.
Image cross-correlation $C_{a,b}$ of gradient vectors for two frames a and b is defined as:

$$C_{a,b} = \ ||I_a'||\ ||I_b'||\ cos\theta \quad (4)$$

where θ is the angle between both vectors. Added to this measure, auto-correlation for a gradient vector frame is

$$C_{a,a} = \ ||I_a'||^2 \quad (5)$$

Vectorial correlation components satisfies triangle inequality

$$C_{a,a}\ +\ C_{b,b}\ \geq 2C_{a,b} \quad (6)$$

$$||I_a'||^2\ +\ ||I_b'||^2\ \geq 2||I_a'||\ ||I_b'||\ cos\theta \quad (7)$$

From equation 7, we can see that when $\theta \approx 0$ and when $||I_a'||^2 \ \approx\ ||I_b'||^2$, it means that a significative change inside the image does not exist. If there is a change in gradient image vectors directions of images **a** and **b**, the difference of both values will grow according to their magnitude and direction.

As mentioned above, auto-correlation and cross-correlation is applied to differentiate vector direction changes between the current frame **L*** component and the background model of the same component. Let $M_{x,y}$ be a 5x5 neighborhood centered at pixel (x, y), a gradient texture difference measure to discriminate objects between the background and the input frame is defined as follows:

$$R(x,y) = 1 - \frac{\sum\limits_{u,v \in M_{x,y}} 2C_{B,F}(u,v)}{\sum\limits_{u,v \in M_{x,y}} (C_{B,B}(u,v) + C_{F,F}(u,v))} \tag{8}$$

where B is the modeled background and F is the **L*** component of the current frame. The region $M_{x,y}$ is used to integrate gradient vector intensities of surrounding pixels that represent local texture features. A change is deemed *significant* when variations in direction are bigger than 90° in their orientation. Values of $R(x,y)$ are in the [0,1] interval; where lower values represent non significant changes in texture and if values approximate to 1 indicates a higher difference in gradient texture directions. This measure is valid as long as there exist noise and intensity variations in the pixels of the $M_{x,y}$ region; otherwise, texture becomes less relevant as there is not significant gradient change.

$R(x,y)$ is then adjusted through a series of validity weights $w_{texture}(x,y)$ using the definition given by Li & Leung (2002). To compute $w_{texture}(x,y)$, Li & Leung (2002) produced an image g (equation 9) that combines autocorrelations of two images to validate the pixel values of R. Information of autocorrelation is considered relevant as it contains significative intensity changes in both R and g images. Equation 9 uses a maximum function because texture information may exist in any images that have been compared.

$$g(x,y) = max_{i \in \{B,F\}} \sqrt{\frac{1}{|M_{x,y}|} \sum_{u,v \in M_{x,y}} C_{i,i}(u,v)} \tag{9}$$

The $g(x,y)$ values from equation 9 are coefficients used to detect all pixels with relevant gradient values whether those values belong to the background image or to the current frame. These coefficients are also used to estimate the validity weights $w_{texture}(x,y)$ in the $[0,1]$ interval. For the results reported in this chapter, it is not necessary to detect every change in texture because the images involved can have undesired textured regions not relevant in the current frame; i.e., when background is not modeled properly due to the existence of cluttered regions inside the image buffer, it then causes that the moving objects are considered part of the background. If so, texture detection is not precise because cluttered regions will cause high autocorrelation values, and consequently, high g values that promote a vehicle detection for as long as the same background model is used.

In order to address this issue, equation 9 has been modified as follows:

$$g(x,y) = \sqrt{\frac{1}{|M_{x,y}|} \sum_{u,v \in M_{x,y}} C_{F,F}(u,v)} \; \forall x, y \in F \tag{10}$$

$g(x,y)$ is used to estimate the validity weights $w_{texture}(x,y)$ as follows:

$$w_{texture}(x,y) = \begin{cases} 1, & if\ g(x,y) > 2T_w \\ g(x,y)/(2T_w) & otherwise \end{cases} \quad \forall x,y \tag{11}$$

From equation 11, T_w is a noise distribution parameter calculated from the image intensity difference. It is required that $T_w > 2\sqrt{2}\sigma_d$, however, a very large T_w would deem texture information less significant in R. For the experiments reported in this chapter, T_w has been set to a value of 50% larger than $2\sqrt{2}\sigma_d$; in turn, σ_d is defined in equation 16. Finally, the texture difference measure is computed as follows:

$$d_{texture}(x,y) = w_{texture}(x,y) \cdot R(x,y), \forall x, \forall y \tag{12}$$

4.2.2 Lightness difference

To compute lightness difference, first we perform an initial subtraction $d(x,y)$ defined as follows:

$$d(x,y) = L_F^*(x,y) - L_B^*(x,y) \tag{13}$$

where B is the modeled background and F is the current frame. $d(x,y)$ measures lightness variations that might be caused by the moving vehicles and other elements in the scene. These elements are removed by smoothing $d(x,y)$ using the following procedure:

$$\bar{d}(x,y) = \frac{1}{|M_{x,y}|} \sum_{u,v \in M_{x,y}} d(u,v) \tag{14}$$

Now we compute a difference image d' that contains only the lightness variations:

$$d'(x,y) = d(x,y) - \bar{d}(x,y) \tag{15}$$

It is assumed that the noise contained in image $d(x,y)$ (equation 13) follows a Gaussian distribution $N(0,\sigma_d)$. Consequently, σ_d is estimated from $d'(x,y)$ as it contains all the small lightness variations.

Outlier pixels with high lightness variation can cause a poor noise estimation when deviation needs to be calculated. To tackle this problem, the Least Median of Squares method (*LMedS*) (Rousseeuw & Leroy (1986)) is used on $d'(x,y)$ as it supports corruption of up to 50% of the input data. Following the definition given by Rosin (1988), the standard deviation of the noise is calculated as follows:

$$\sigma_d = \frac{LMedS}{0.33724} \tag{16}$$

Finally, $d(x,y)$ is used to estimate the lightness difference $d_{lightness}(x,y)$ as follows:

$$d_{lightness}(x,y) = \begin{cases} 1, & if\ |d(x,y)| > 2T \\ |d(x,y)|/(2T) & otherwise \end{cases} \tag{17}$$

The T parameter needs to be properly calculated to deal with Gaussian noise. Li & Leung (2002) sets the T parameter as:

$$T = |\bar{d}_s| + 3\sigma_d. \tag{18}$$

$\overline{d}_s$ in equation 18 describes lightness changes. It grows when global illumination changes occur, but shadows and local changes diminish this value. $\overline{d}_s$ is calculated as:

$$\overline{d}_s = \frac{1}{|N_s|} \sum_{u,v \in N_s} \overline{d}(u,v) \quad (19)$$

N_s is the set of pixels $\overline{d}(x,y)$ that satisfy equation 20.

$$N_s = \{x,y : (|d^{'}(x,y)| < 2\sigma_d) \wedge (|\overline{d}(x,y)| < T_{50\%})\} \quad (20)$$

where $T_{50\%}$ is the median value of $|\overline{d}(x,y)|$.

4.2.3 Texture and lightness differences integration

Assuming that texture and lightness differences complement each other in a [0,1] interval, $w_{lightness}(x,y) = 1 - w_{texture}(x,y)$, the integration of texture and lightness intensity differences with their corresponding validation weights is carried out by equation 21.

$$d_{texture,lightness}(x,y) = w_{lightness}(x,y) \cdot d_{lightness}(x,y) + w_{texture}(x,y) \cdot d_{texture}(x,y) \quad \forall x, \forall y \quad (21)$$

The final segmentation for vehicle detection is produced by thresholding the $d_{texture,lightness}(x,y)$ image with the median value of $[0,1] = 0.5$.

4.2.4 Morphological processing

The resultant binary image contains a number of the same unwanted elements that are present in the images produced by the *Color-based texture segmentation* method (Section 3). As a result, the morphological operations used in that method are also applied here in the same fashion.

5. Experimental results

In this section we present the results of applying both segmentation methods using natural scenes images. The image database used in our experiments is publicly available and it is described in Martel-Brisson & Zaccarin (2007). We have proceeded according to the supervised texture segmentation testing protocol of the Outex database (Ojala et al. (2002)). This framework involves the following components:

- **Image segmentation test suite.** The test sequence is called *Highway III* and it includes traffic flow scenes and ground truth images. Ground truth images show individual pixel group of vehicles and shadows. However, we have modified these images so both the vehicle and its shadow are within the same object.
- **Input data in an individual problem.** I is the image to be segmented with N_I pixels. R_I is the number of regions in I, each one with a distinct class label L_R.
- **Required output in an individual problem.** O is the output labeled image equal in size to I.
- **Performance metric in an individual problem.** Let I_{ij} and O_{ij} denote the class labels of pixel (i,j) in I and O, respectively. The score of an individual problem S_p is the proportion of all pixels that are correctly labelled:

$$S_p = \frac{100}{N_I} \sum_{ij}^{N_I} \delta(I_{ij}, O_{ij})\% \quad (22)$$

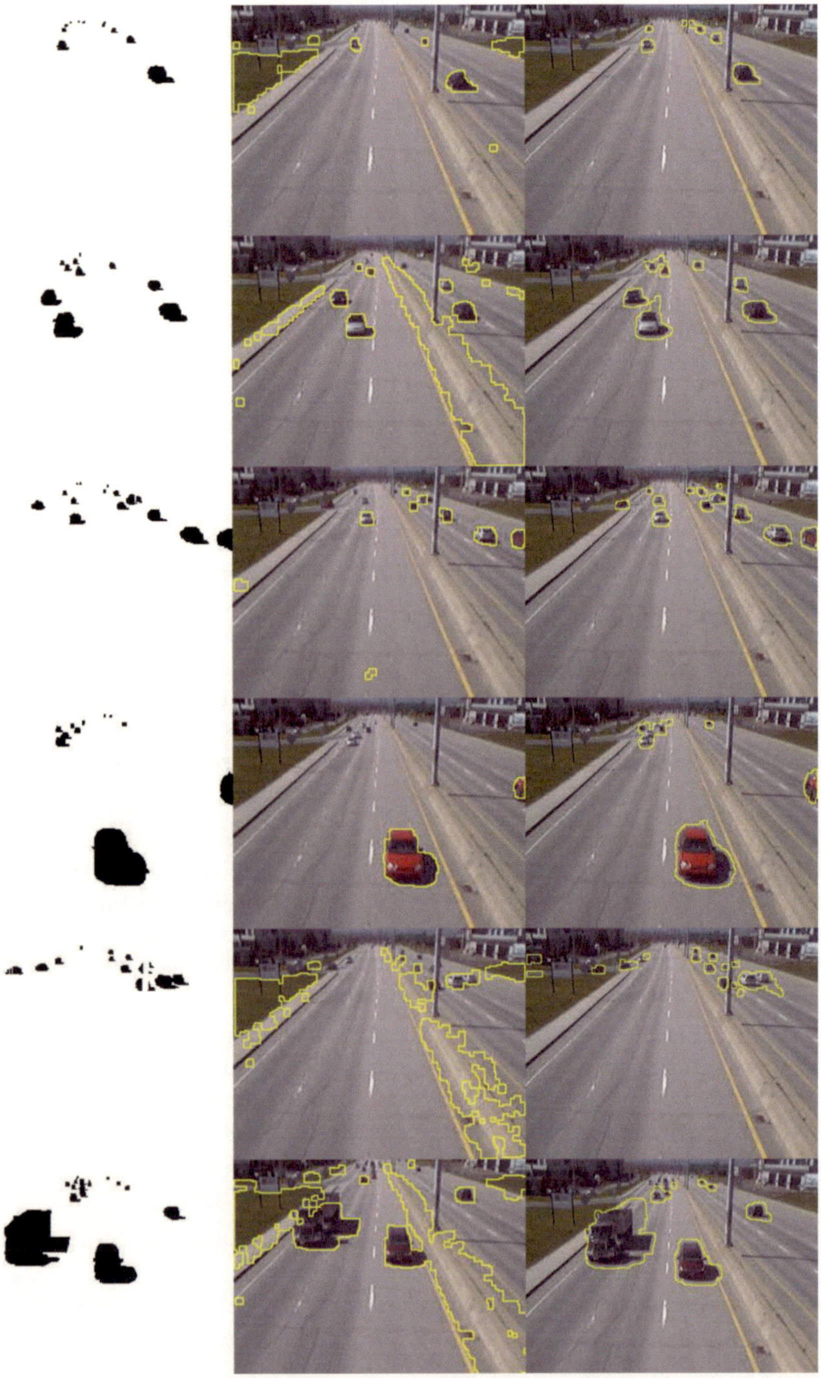

Fig. 7. First column shows the ground truth images. Second and third columns show the results of the methods described in Section 3 and Section 4, respectively.

where δ denotes the Kronecker delta function.

- **Test suite score.** Let P be the number of problems to be considered. If test suite contains $P > 1$ problems, then the scores from equations 23, 24, 25 and 26 are computed.

$$S_{mean} = \frac{1}{P}\sum_{p}^{P} S_p \tag{23}$$

$$S_{min} = \min(S_p) \quad \forall p \in \{1, ..., P\} \tag{24}$$

$$S_{max} = \max(S_p) \quad \forall p \in \{1, ..., P\} \tag{25}$$

$$S_{dev} = \sqrt{\frac{1}{P}\sum_{p}^{P}(S_p - S_{mean})^2} \tag{26}$$

We have measured the performance of the above values in both segmentation methods. Qualitative image results are shown in Figure 7 and quantitative measures over the image test suite are listed in Table 1.

Image ground truth	Color-based texture segmentation (Section 3)	Segmentation based on lightness and texture differences (Section 4)
S_{min}	78.5091%	97.2174%
S_{max}	99.1536%	99.4817%
S_{mean}	89.7853%	98.5516%
S_{dev}	8.0121%	0.6786%

Table 1. Performance scores of the two segmentation methods described in this chapter over the image test suite.

6. Discussion

Given the estimators shown in table 1, particularly the mean and standard deviation, it is evident, without any further analysis or evidence beyond themselves, that the *Segmentation based on lightness and texture differences* method (Section 4) has achieved a better performance than the *Color-based texture segmentation* method (Section 3).

The S_{mean} score measures how successful the segmentation rate is. This score is the average of the performance values of all the individual problems considered in our experiments expressed as a percentage. The *Segmentation based on lightness and texture differences* method achieved a $S_{mean} = 98.5516$, whereas the *Color-based texture segmentation* method achieved a $S_{mean} = 89.7853$.

Also, the S_{dev} score shows that the performance of the method is consistent under similar experimental conditions, as its value tends to be smaller when the dispersion from the mean (successful segmentation rate) is also small. For this score, the *Segmentation based on lightness and texture differences* method achieved a $S_{dev} = 0.6786$, whereas the *Color-based texture segmentation* method achieved a $S_{dev} = 8.0121$.

In the *Segmentation based on lightness and texture differences* method, the computed gradient vector's directions have a high tolerance to noisy images and illumination changes. This method builds a background model to detect the changes of the objects of interest with respect to that reference model. The method achieves a higher accuracy rate but the borders slightly exceed the region of interest because a number of filtering processes are used to make homogeneous the gradient textures.

On the other hand, the *Color-based texture segmentation* method is very discriminative when abrupt changes in color are present in the input images. Even though only two components are used in this method, namely 75° and −75°, calculating the DTCWT coefficients still involves multiple filtering of images at different coarseness levels, thus increasing the computational time cost.

The results derived from the experiments of the methods presented in this chapter can be useful in the preliminary phases of a vehicle tracking system. We will include these results in our future research efforts.

7. Acknowledgements

This work has been partially supported by the *Secretaría de Comunicaciones y Transportes del Gobierno del Estado de Tabasco* within the project *"UAEM 110171: Plan Integrado de Movilidad de Villahermosa y su zona metropolitana Fase II"* and the research grant *PROMEP/103.5/08/3016*.

8. References

Barilla-Pérez, M. E. (2008). *Colour-based Texture Image Segmentation*, PhD thesis, University of Birmingham.

Barilla-Pérez, M. E. & Spann, M. (2008). Colour-based texture image classification using the complex wavelet transform, *5th International Conference on Electrical Engineering, Computing Science and Automatic Control*.

Bovik, A. & Bovik, A. (2000). *Handbook of Image and Video Processing*, Academic Press.

Chen, C.-T., Su, C.-Y. & Kao, W.-C. (2010). An enhanced segmentation on vision-based shadow removal for vehicle detection, pp. 679 –682.

Cheng, S., Luo, X. & Bhandarkar, S. M. (2007). A multiscale parametric background model for stationary foreground object detection, *IEEE Workshop on Motion and Video Computing*.

Cheung, S.-C. S. & Kamath, C. (2004). Robust techniques for background subtraction in urban traffic video, *Visual Communications and Image Processing* 5308(1): 881–892.

Coifman, B., Beymer, D., McLauchlan, P., Malik, J. & Malik, H. (1998). A real-time computer vision system for vehicle tracking and traffic surveillance.

Cucchiara, R., Grana, C., Piccardi, M. & Prati, A. (2003). Detecting moving objects, ghosts, and shadows in video streams, *IEEE Transactions on Pattern Analisys and Machine Intelligence* 25(10): 1337–1342.

Diaz-Alonso, J., Ros-Vidal, E., Rotter, A. & Muhlenberg, M. (2008). Lane-change decision aid system based on motion-driven vehicle tracking, *IEEE Transactions on Vehicular Technology* 57(5): 2736–2746.

Elgammal, A., Harwood, D. & Davis, L. (1999). Non-parametric model for background subtraction, *Proc. IEEE ICCV '99 Frame-rate workshop*, Corfu, Greece.

Eng, H.-L., Thida, M., Chew, B.-F., Leman, K. & Anggrelly, S. (2008). Model-based detection and segmentation of vehicles for intelligent transportation system, pp. 2127 –2132.

Fang, L. Z., Qiong, W. Y. & Sheng, Y. Z. (2008). A method to segment moving vehicle cast shadow based on wavelet transform, *Pattern Recognition Letters* 29(16): 2182–2188.

Felzenszwalb, P. F. & Huttenlocher, D. P. (2004). Efficient graph-based image segmentation, *International Journal of Computer Vision* 59(2): 167–181.

Gentile, C., Camps, O. & Sznaier, M. (2004). Segmentation for robust tracking in the presence of severe occlusion, *IEEE Transactions on Image Processing* 13(2): 166Ű178.
González, R. C. & Woods, R. E. (2002). *Digital Image Processing*, 2nd edition edn, Prentice Hall.
Gutchess, D., Trajkovic, M., Cohen-Solal, E., Lyons, D. & Jain, A. K. (2001). A background model initialization algorithm for video surveillance, *in proc. International Conference on Computer Vision*, pp. 733–740.
Haidarian-Shahri, H., Namata, G., Navlakha, S., Deshpande, A. & Roussopoulos, N. (2007). A graph-based approach to vehicle tracking in traffic camera video streams, *Proceedings of the 4th International Workshop on Data Management for Sensor Networks*.
Halevy, G. & Weinshall, D. (1999). Motion of disturbances: detection and tracking of multi-body non-rigid motion, *Machine Vision and Applications* 11(3): 122Ű137.
Kamijo, S., Matsuchita, Y., Ikeuchi, K. & Sakauchi, M. (2000). Occlusion robust vehicle tracking utilizing spatio-temporal markov random field model, *Proc. IEEE Intelligent Trasportation Systems*, Dearborn, MI.
Kastrinaki, V., Zervakis, M. & Kalaitzakis, K. (2003). A survey of video processing techniques for traffic applications, *Image and Vision Computing* 21: 359Ű381.
Kingsbury, N. G. (1999). Shift invariant properties of the dual-tree complex wavelet transform, *International Conference on Acoustics, Speech and Signal Processing ICASSP99*, Phoenix, AZ. Paper SPTM 3.6.
URL: *citeseer.ist.psu.edu/kingsbury99shift.html*
Lee, D. S., Hull, J. & Erol, B. (2003). A bayesian framework for gaussian mixture background modeling, *Proc. IEEE International Confererence on Image Processing (ICIP Š03)*.
Li, L. & Leung, M. (2002). Integrating intensity and texture differences for robust change detection, *IEEE Transactions on Image Processing* 11: 105–112.
Lo, B. & Velastin, S. (2001). Automatic congestion detection system for underground platform, *Proc. International Symposium on Intelligent Multimedia*.
Malacara, D. (2001). *Color Vision and Colorimetry, Theory and Applications*, SPIE International Society for Optical Engineering, Bellingham, Washington USA.
Martel-Brisson, N. & Zaccarin, A. (2007). Learning and removing cast shadows through a multidistribution approach, *Pattern Analysis and Machine Intelligence, IEEE Transactions on* 29(7): 1133 –1146.
Materka, A. & Strzelecki, M. (1998). Texture analysis methods - a review, *Technical report*, University of Lodz.
Mejia-Iñigo, R., Barilla-Perez, M. E. & Montes-Venegas, H. (2009). Color-based texture image segmentation for vehicle detection, *6th International Conference on Electrical Engineering, Computing Science and Automatic Control*, pp. 1–6.
Mo, G. & Zhang, S. (2010). Vehicles detection in traffic flow, Vol. 2, pp. 751 –754.
Ojala, T., Mäenpää, T., Pietikäinen, M., Viertola, J., Kyllönen, J. & Huovinen, S. (2002). Outex - new framework for empirical evaluation of texture analysis algorithms. Proc. 16th International Conference on Pattern Recognition, Quebec, Canada, 1:701 - 706.
Pang, C. C. C., Lam, W. W. L. & Yung, N. H. C. (2004). A novel method for resolving vehicle occlusion in a monocular traffic-image sequence, *IEEE Transactions on Intelligent Transportation Systems* 5(33): 129Ű141.
Petrou, M. (2006). *Image Processing, Dealing With Texture*, John Wiley & Sons Ltd.
Rosin, P. (1988). Thresholding for Change Detection, *Brunel University*.
Rousseeuw, P. & Leroy, A. (1986). Least median of squares: A robust method for outlier and model error detection in regression and calibration, *Analytica Chimica Acta* 187: 171–179.

Sangwine, S. J. & Horne, R. E. N. (1998). *The Colour Image Processing Handbook*, Chapman and Hall.

Selesnick, I. W., Baraniuk, R. G. & Kingsbury, N. G. (2005). The dual-tree complex wavelet transform, *IEEE Signal Processing Magazine* pp. 123–151.

Sen-Ching, Cheung, S. & Kamath, C. (2005). Robust background subtraction with foreground validation for urban traffic video, *EURASIP Journal on Applied Signal Processing* 14: 2330–2340.

Shahri, H. H., Namata, G., Navlakha, S., Deshpande, A. & Roussopoulos, N. (2007). A graph-based approach to vehicle tracking in traffic camera video streams, *Proceedings of the 4th International Workshop on Data Management for Sensor Networks*.

Stauffer, C. & Grimson, W. (2000). Learning patterns of activity using real-time tracking, *IEEE Transactions on Pattern Analisys and Machine Intelligence* 22(8): 747Ű757.

Sun, Z., Bebis, G. & Miller, R. (2006). On-road vehicle detection: a review, *Pattern Analysis and Machine Intelligence, IEEE Transactions on* 28(5): 694 –711.

Techawatcharapaikul, C., Kaewtrakulpong, P. & Siddhichai, S. (2008). Outdoor vehicle and shadow segmentation by temporal edge density information of adjacent frames, Vol. 1, pp. 433 –436.

Trémeau, A., Tominaga, S. & Plataniotis, K. N. (2008). Color in image and video processing: most recent trends and future research directions, *J. Image Video Process.* 2008: 1–26.

Tsai, L.-W., Hsieh, J.-W. & Fan, K.-C. (2007). Vehicle detection using normalized color and edge map, *Image Processing, IEEE Transactions on* 16(3): 850 –864.

Wang, C.-C. R. & Lien, J.-J. (2008). Automatic vehicle detection using local features - a statistical approach, *Intelligent Transportation Systems, IEEE Transactions on* 9(1): 83 –96.

Wren, C., Azarbayejani, A., Darrell, T., & Pentland, A. (1997). Pfinder: real-time tracking of the human body, *IEEE Transactions on Pattern Analisys and Machine Intelligence* 19(7): 780Ű785.

Yilmaz, A. (2006). Object tracking: A survey, *ACM Computing Surveys* 38: 1–45.

Zhang, H. & Yuan, F. (2007). Vehicle tracking based on image alignment in aerial videos, *Energy Minimization Methods in Computer Vision and Pattern Recognition*.

Zhang, W., Wu, Q. M. J., Yang, X. & Fang, X. (2008). Multilevel framework to detect and handle vehicle occlusion, *IEEE Transactions On Intelligent Transportation Systems* 9(1): 161–174.

Zhou, Q. & Aggarwal, J. (2001). Tracking and classifying moving objects from videos, *Proc. 2nd IEEE Workshop on Performance Evaluation of Tracking and Surveillance (PETS Š01)*.

Zhu, H., Li, M., Zhu, Y. & Ni, L. M. (2009). Hero: Online real-time vehicle tracking, *IEEE Transactions on Parallel and Distributed Systems* 20: 740–752.

Part 3

Image Segmentation Applications

15

An Enhanced Level Set Algorithm for Wrist Bone Segmentation

Donatello Conte, Pasquale Foggia, Francesco Tufano and Mario Vento
Università degli Studi di Salerno
Italy

1. Introduction

In the last decades there was a growing interest in designing CAD devices for medical imaging: the main role of these system is to acquire the images, generally TAC or RMI, and to display the parts of interest of human body on suitable visual devices, after some pre-elaboration steps aimed to improve the quality of the obtained images. A TAC or a MRI sequence, obtained as a result of a scan process of the interested parts of the human body is a generally wide set of 2D gray-level images, seen as the projection of the body into three different coordinate planes. Starting from these sequences it is rather difficult, for the radiologist, to imagine the whole appearance of the body parts, since without a 3D model of each part it is only possible to browse the images in the three planes independently.

In this framework, the most challenging task remains that of extracting, from the whole images, a 3D model of the different parts; such a model would be important not only for visualization purposes, but also for obtaining quantitative measurements that could be used as an input to the diagnostic process.

Even if the pre-processing step of the acquired images plays a key role in the achievement of a good visualization quality, the literature is today so rich of papers describing procedures aimed to increase the signal/noise ratio that this problem can be now considered as definitely solved. So, the attention of researchers is nowadays concentrated on the definition of robust methods for the 3D segmentation. In the case of Magnetic Resonance Images (MRI), the segmentation is made complex by the unavoidable presence of inhomogeneity in the images, as well as the presence of image distortions.

Despite the research efforts and the significant advances achieved in recent years, the image segmentation problem still remains a notoriously known challenging problem, especially in the case of poor quality images. In particular, the segmentation of MR images is made even more complex, by the complexity of the shapes of the parts to be segmented, and by the lack of suitable anatomical models able to fully capture all the possible shape variations for each of them. These models can provide, if suitably exploited, important information: for bone tissues it is relevant the knowledge about the shape and the size of the synovial parts, devoted to connecting bones: their characterization allows the scientist to choose the most appropriate technique for a correct segmentation. Namely, synovia appears in the images as a darker surface surrounding the bones; its presence is fundamental for the correct segmentation, since often the bone tissues and the adjacent cartilagineous tissues have similar intensity levels, and would be indistinguishable without the synovia.

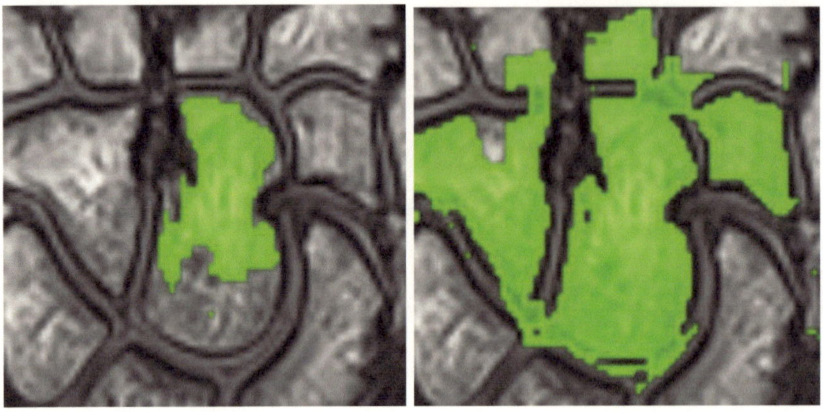

a) b)

Fig. 1. The effect of the similarity threshold on region growing segmentation. a) A threshold too low produces an over-segmentation. b) A threshold too high produces an under-segmentation.

The simplest segmentation approaches are those based on a thresholding applied to each pixel (or voxel) on its intensity values: they result to be generally uneffective in the case of an MR image: the segmentation results are in fact very poor, as the intensity levels of the pixels of bones and the synovia are quite similar, so causing the undersegmention of some regions contemporarily to oversegmented areas. A threshold, appropriate for reaching the solution all over the image is practically impossible to be determined. More complex solutions, based on partitioning of the image in different parts, on which different values of the thresholds, in the experience of the authors, can perform better but the results are far from satisfying the radiologist.

An other class of segmentation algorithms are those based on the well known region growing paradigm. A point, surely belonging to the area to be segmented, is given as input by the user, and considered as a seed: the pixels adjacents to the seed are considered as belonging to the region to be segmented, if their intensity values are similar to that of the seed: the similarity is suitably defined on the application domain and generally a threshold is applied to determine wether two pixels are similar or not. The process is iterated for the last added pixels until, at the given step, no further pixel is added to the region. Although different variants of this class of algorithms have been developed along the years, their rationale is that of expanding the regions on the basis of their homogeneity. Their application in all the cases in which foreground and background have little gray level differences can results in over-segmentation problems. Figure 1 highlights these effect on a wrist bone, with two different similarity thresholds, so demonstrating the difficulty of obtaining effective results in a practical case.

More recently, some approaches, based on the attempt of facing the segmentation approach by a classification system, have been proposed. The rationale of these methods is aimed to obtaining algorithms able to work without the interaction with the radiologist: they perform the training of the classifier on a suitably built training set of pixels and, once adequately trained, classify the pixels of the image as belonging to a foreground area or to the background. In this way, the interaction with the radiologist, if any, is required in the training phase. The simplest implementations of this class of methods is based on the k-nearest-neighbor, as

in Vrooman et al. (2007), where brain tissues are segmented; the k-NN classifier is trained automatically using an a priori model of the brain provided by a brain atlas. Another approach of this kind is based on Bayes classifiers Banga et al. (1992); in particular in the cited article the segmentation of the retina is performed using an unsupervised Bayesian classifier whose parameters have been estimated using the Expectation-Maximization algorithm. In spite of their simplicity and their low computational cost, their intrinsic nature does not allows them to take into account spatial information, so making them unprofitable in all those cases in which the latter information is crucial for the final result, as in the case of bone tissues.
A further class of segmentation algorithms are those based on (unsupervised) clustering techniques. The three most used clustering techniques are the K-means, the Fuzzy C-means and the Expectation-Maximization algorithm. An example of the use of K-means is Vemuri et al. (1995), that performs the segmentation of brain MR images by clustering the voxels on the basis of wavelet-derived features. Two papers using the Fuzzy C-means clustering are Ardizzone et al. (2007), that is also applied to brain MR images, and Foggia et al. (2006), that is applied to mammographic images. Finally, in Wang et al. (2005) a clustering method based on the Expectation-Maximization algorithm is used for segmenting brain images showing a greater robustness with respect to the noise due to field inhomogeneity.
The algorithms discussed so far assume that the intensities of each voxel class are stationary: this assumption does apply only on limited sets of images, due to the intrinsic heterogeneity of a class, the nonuniform illumination, or other imaging artifacts. So, to take into account spatial information, recently some approaches based on the use of the Markov Random Field (MRF) Models have been used, as in Ruan & Bloyet (2000) and Krause et al. (1997). The idea behind them is that, in the case of biomedical images, the probability of a pixel to belong to a class is strongly related to the values of the surrounding pixels, as rarely the anatomical parts are composed by just one pixel. Two critical points of MRF approach are the computational burden (due to the required iterative optimization schemes) and the sensitivity of the results to the model parameters.
The most used approach in segmentation of medical images is the level set (Cremers et al. (2005)), based on an optimization apprach. A segmentation of the image plane Ω is computed by locally minimizing an appropriate energy functional $E(C)$ by evolving the contour C of the region to be segmented starting from an initial contour. In general, method based on this approach may use either an explicit (parametric) or implicit representation of the contours. In explicit representations (Leitner & Cinquin (1991), McInerney & Terzopoulos (1995)) – such as splines or polygons – a contour is defined as a mapping from an interval to the image domain: $C : [0,1] \to \Omega$. In implicit contour representations (Dervieux & Thomasset (1979), Osher & Sethian (1988)), contours are represented as the (zero) level line of some embedding function $\phi : \Omega \to \Re$:

$$C = \{x \in \Omega | \phi(x) = 0\}.$$

In the original level set algorithm, only gradient information is taken into account in the energy term $E(C)$. Some authors (Osher & Santosa (2001), Chan & Vese (2001), Russon & Paragios (2002)) have proposed improvements of the classical algorithm by introducing some priors information (e.g. shape, color or motion information).
Level set algorithms are widely used in medical images segmentation because they are very effective. However they present some drawbacks:

- The segmentations obtained by a local optimization method are strongly dependent to the initialization. For many realistic images, the segmentation algorithm tends to get stuck in

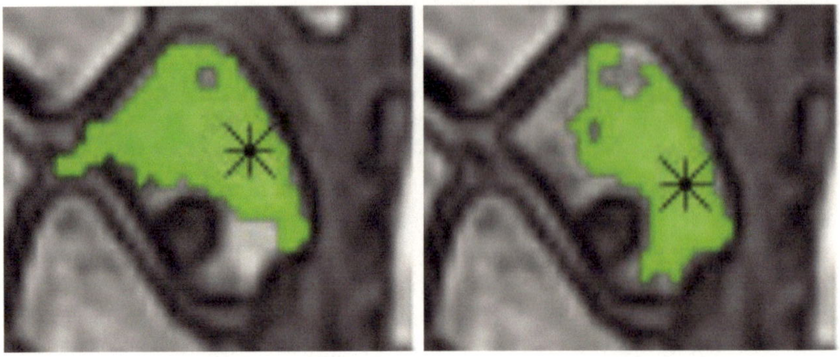

a) b)

Fig. 2. The effect of the seed point on Level Set segmentation. Between a) and b), a slight change of the seed point determines a different segmented region shape (the seed point in the image is indicated by the star-like cursor).

undesired local minima (especially in the presence of noise) forcing the user to try with several seed points before obtaining a satisfactory solution.

- This approach lacks a meaningful probabilistic interpretation. Extensions to other segmentation criteria Ű such as color, texture or motion Ű are not straight-forward.
- This algorithm has a problem in finding correct contours of the regions when the region boundaries have corners or other singularities.

In a recent paper (Conte et al. (2009)) we presented a new algorithm that overcomes the first of the considered problems. In this paper we propose a significant improvement, especially with respect to the last problem (that is still an open problem in the literature).
The paper is organized as follows: in section 2 a review of the most used approaches for segmenting MR images is shown; the proposed algorithm is presented in section 3 while in section 4 the experimental phase together with the analysis of the results are described. Section 5 summarizes the conclusions obtained from our work.

2. Important

Manuscript must contain clear answers to following questions: What is the problem / What has been done by other researchers and where you can contribute / What have you done / Which method or tools you used / What are your results / What is new and good, what is not good / Future research

3. The proposed method

As we have seen, every segmentation approach has its strenght and its weak points. Our proposal is to base the segmentation on the integration of two complementary approaches: region growing and level set segmentation.
Region growing has problems with local noise, especially on the boundary of the region to be segmented, and has a strong dependency on a similarity threshold, leading to either over-segmentation (if the threshold is chosen conservatively) or under-segmentation (if the threshold is chosen to capture as much as possible the shape of the region). But neither of those problems affect the level set algorithm.

On the other hand, level set has a strong dependency on the choice of the seed point, as shown in fig. 2, and also may have problems where the region boundary has some singularity (e.g. a sharp corner). Region growing instead is fairly immune to both those problems. So, region growing and level set segmentation appear to complement each other with respect to their strenght, and this is the reason why we have chosen to combine them into a technique that should overcome the limitations of both.
Basically, our method is composed of the following steps:

- first, a smoothing of the image is performed using a low pass filter; this step is related to the use of the Laplacian Level Set variant of the level set technique, as we will discuss later;
- then a pre-segmentation is realized using region growing, to obtain a rough, conservative estimate of the region;
- the result of the pre-segmentation is used to initialize the proper segmentation, performed by means of a level set algorithm; in this way the result of the level set algorithm is not dependent on the choice of the seed point;
- finally, a local contour refinement, based again on region growing, is applied in order to better fit the contour to sharp corners and other singularities.

Each of these steps will be described with more detail in the following subsections. As an illustration of the different steps, we will present their effect on an example image, shown in figure 3.

3.1 Smoothing filter

The region growing technique used for the pre-segmentation step is highly sensitive to pixel-level noise. So it is important to remove this kind of noise before the pre-segmentation. Moreover, for the proper segmentation step, we have used a variant of the level set technique called Laplacian Level Set (LLS), introduced in Conte et al. (2009). The LLS algorithm performs a Laplacian filter on the image to enhance the boundaries of the regions; but a side effect of the Laplacian filter is a magnification of the high-frequency noise components. Hence, the denoising is important also for the LLS segmentation.
In order to remove the noise we have used a Gaussian smoothing filter, which is a well known low-pass filter widely used in the image processing field.
The use of a low-pass filter may seem contradictory with the goals of a segmentation algorithm: if the algorithm has to determine the sharp edges that form the boundary of the regions, it may be thought that by smoothing those very edges should make the task of the algorithm more complicated. However, the following factors should be considered:

- by carefully choosing the filter cutoff frequency, the filter can cancel out only the intensity variations that are due to noise, while the ones due to the boundaries between regions will only be a little bit blurred
- the pre-segmentation process needs only to find a reasonable approximation of the region, so it can easily be tuned to be unaffected by the blurring of the region boundary; on the other hand it greatly benefits from the reduction of the pixel level noise achieved by the low-pass filter
- the proper segmentation process will apply a laplacian filter to the image; the net effect of the combination of the low-pass and laplacian filter is that of a band pass filter that, by virtue of the choosen cutoff frequency, will preserve exactly the variations whose spatial frequency correspond to the boundaries between the regions.

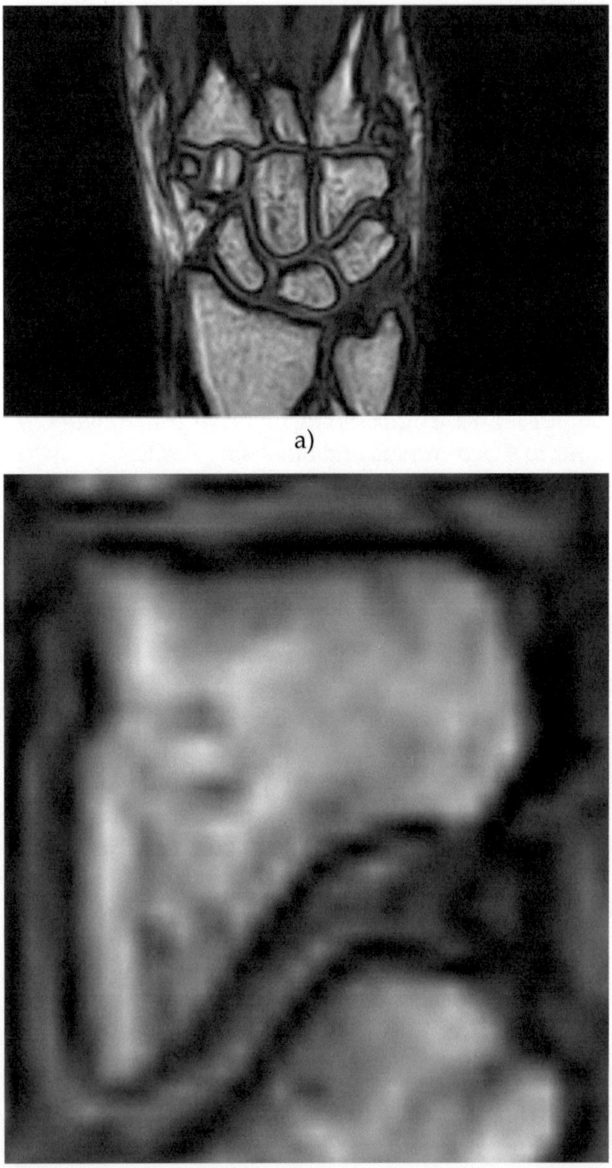

a)

b)

Fig. 3. An example image, that will be used to illustrate the different steps of the proposed algorithm. What is actually shown is a 2D slice of the 3D MR image. a) The original image. b) A zoomed image of the bone that will be the target for the segmentation.

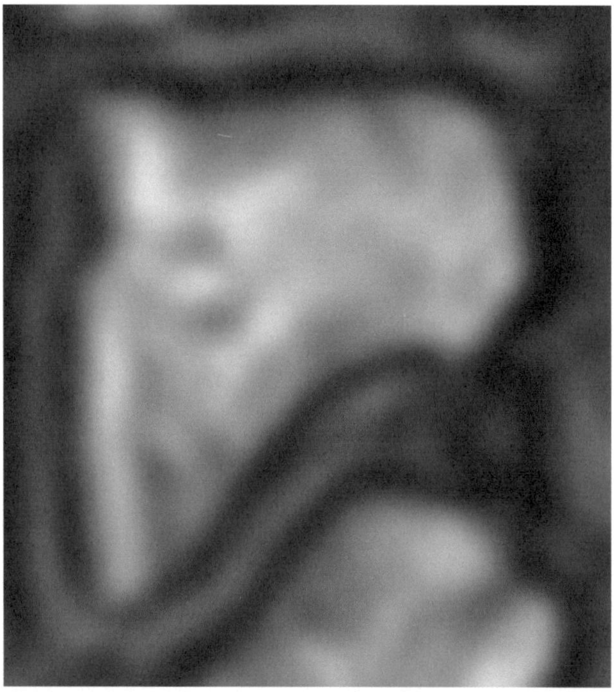

Fig. 4. The result of the application of the Gaussian filter to the image of fig. 3b.

The Gaussian filter introduces a parameter σ, related to the cutoff frequency, that needs to be tuned for obtaining an adequate performance. However the optimal value of σ depends only on the resolution of the image and the size of the smallest features of interest in the segmented region. Hence, for a given MRI machine and anatomical district, the tuning of σ has to be performed only once.
Figure 4 shows the effect of the gaussian filter on our example image.

3.2 Image pre-segmentation

The level set technique starts with a tentative contour of the region to be segmented, and makes this contour evolve so as to reach a (local) minimum of a suitably defined energy function. The usual approach for initializing the contour is to choose a small sphere around the user selected seed point.
However, especially if the shape of the target region is complex, starting with a contour that is so different from the desired one may easily lead the algorithm to a local minimum that does not correspond to the ideal segmentation. Furthermore, this local minimum strongly depends on the choice of the seed point, making it difficult to have a repeatable result for the segmentation process.
On the other hand, if the level set algorithm starts from a tentative contour that is reasonably close to the true boundary of the region, it usually converges without problems to the desired minimum of the energy function.
In order to provide such an initial contour, our method performs a pre-segmentation step. In this step, our system attempts to segment the region of interest using a region growing technique Adams & Bischof (1994). In region growing, basically, the algorithms starts with a

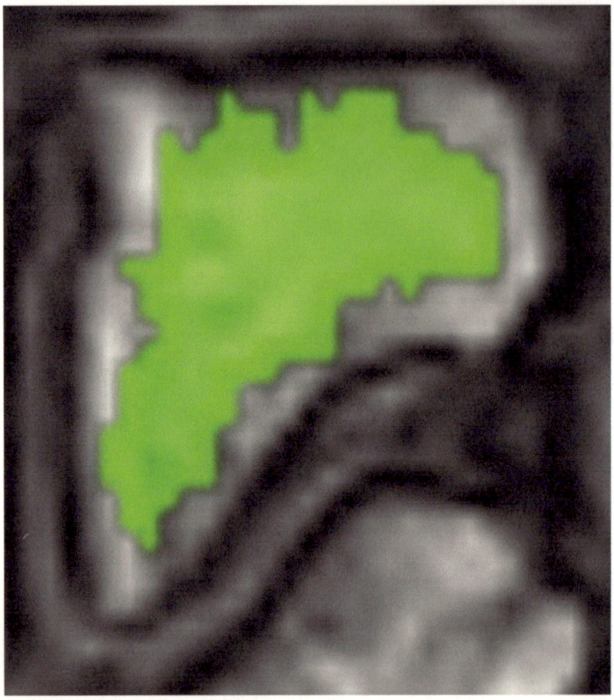

Fig. 5. The result of the pre-segmentation on the image of figure 3b

tentative region formed by the seed point alone; and then repeatedly add adjacent voxels as long as their intensity is within a threshold θ from the average intensity of the region built so far.

The tuning of θ is one of the most delicate aspects of region growing, since a value too tight will not make the algorithm cover the whole region (over-segmentation), while a value too loose would cause extra parts to be included in the region (under-segmentation).

However, since we are using region growing only as a pre-segmentation step, we do not need to find the optimal value for θ. We just need to be sure to "err on the safe side", in the sense that the algorithm should not produce an under-segmentation. This is necessary because the level set algorithm can expand the contour, but cannot contract it.

So, also the tuning of θ can be done once for a given MRI machine/anatomical district combination, instead of adjusting this parameter for each different image.

As an alternative to region growing we have also tried the fast marching technique Zhang et al. (2007) for pre-segmentation. The results of both algorithms are similar, but fast marching is slower than region growing, and has more parameters to be tuned. Hence, we have decided to adopt region growing.

The pre-segmentation of our example image is shown in figure 5.

3.3 Laplacian Level Set

The current trend in MR imaging is towards the reduction of the intensity of the magnetic field to which the patient is exposed, in order to obtain a reduction in the costs but also in the weight and and space occupied by the MRI machines. At the same time, the acquisition time

Fig. 6. The result of the Laplacian filter applied to the example image of figure 3b.

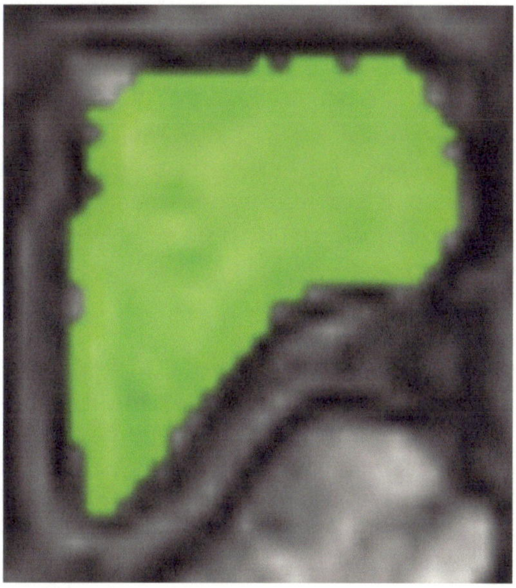

Fig. 7. The result of the Laplacian Level Set segmentation applied to the example image of figure 3b.

has to be kept short, since during the scan the patient has to remain still, and so the MRI exam would be too uncomfortable if it were too long.
As a result, the contrast between different tissues is often quite low, and this can cause problems to any segmentation algorithm. In order to overcome this issue, in Conte et al. (2009) the so called Laplacian Level Set (LLS) algorithm has been proposed. The LLS algorithm is based on the use of the Laplacian filter, defined as:

$$\nabla^2 f(x,y,z) = \frac{\delta^2 f(x,y,z)}{\delta x^2} + \frac{\delta^2 f(x,y,z)}{\delta y^2} + \frac{\delta^2 f(x,y,z)}{\delta z^2}$$

where $f(x,y,z)$ is the intensity of the voxel at position (x,y,z). Actually, a discrete approximation of the filter is used. The filtered image enhances the contours of the regions, as exemplified (on a 2D slice of the image) in Fig. 6.
The algorithm operates on the filtered image, starting with a contour surface C that is initialized as the contour of the region found in the pre-segmentation step, and evolving it in order to minimize an energy function $E(C)$ which is defined as:

$$\begin{aligned} E(C) = & \int_{V_{in}(C)} (u(x,y,z) - \mu_{in}(C))^2 dxdydz + \\ & + \int_{V_{out}(C)} (u(x,y,z) - \mu_{out}(C))^2 dxdydz + \\ & + k \frac{|C|}{|V_{in}(C)|} \end{aligned} \quad (1)$$

where

- $V_{in}(C)$ is the region inside C
- $V_{out}(C)$ is the region outside C
- $u(x,y,z)$ is the intensity of the filtered image
- $\mu_{in}(C)$ and $\mu_{out}(C)$ are the average value of $u(x,y,z)$ over $V_{in}(C)$ and $V_{out}(C)$ respectively
- $|C|/|V_{in}(C)|$ is the ratio between the area of C and the volume of $V_{in}(C)$, that acts as a regularization factor for the contour; this factor is weighted by the parameter k: a larger value for k makes the algorithm oriented towards smoother contours and more robust to noise, but also less able to follow sharp corners on the region boundary

The result of the LLS algorithm on our example image is presented in figure 7.

3.4 Local contour refinement

The last step of the algorithm starts with the contour C found by the Laplacian level set and tries to refine it to better fit the sharp corners that are usually smoothed out by the level set.
Namely, this refinement is performed using a limited form of region growing, that has no problem in following sharp corners. Since region growing is prone to under-segmentation, especially in low contrast images such as the ones produced by MRI, special care is taken in the definition of the stopping criterion to ensure that only small corrections to the contour C are performed.
More formally, the voxels adjacent to C are examined and are added to the contour iff:

$$|f(x,y,z) - f(n(x,y,z,C))| < \theta' / d(x,y,z,C) \quad (2)$$

where:

Fig. 8. The result of the local contour refinement applied to the segmentation shown in figure 7.

- $f(x, y, z)$ is the intensity value of the considered voxel of coordinates (x, y, z)
- $n(x, y, z, C)$ is the position of the voxel in C that is the nearest to (x, y, z); so $f(n(x, y, z, C))$ is the intensity of this voxel
- $d(x, y, z, C)$ is the Euclidean distance between (x, y, z) and $n(x, y, z, C)$
- θ' is a suitably defined threshold

The division of the threshold θ' by $d(x, y, z, C)$ ensures that this refinement step will never extend too much the initial contour C. In particular, this extension is performed on a local basis, only where the adjacent pixels are very similar to the ones already in C.
Figure 8 shows the effect of the local contour refinement algorithm on our example image, starting from the segmentation presented in figure 7.

4. Experimental results

The algorithm has been tested on 11 MRI sequences of wrist bones acquired at low magnetic field, for a total of 762 bi-dimensional slices. The ground truth has been manually traced by medical experts.
We compare the proposed enhanced laplacian level set algorithm (ELLS) with the following algorithms:

- our previous algorithm (Laplacian Level Set, LLS);
- the basic level set (BLS)
- the basic level set with pre-segmentation module (PLS)
- Geodesic Active Contours (see Caselles et al. (1997) and Yan & Kassim (2006)); Geodesic Active Contours (GAC) algorithms are similar to Level Set algorithms, but the first are motivated by a curve evolution approach and not by an energy minimization one;

- Geodesic Active Contours with pre-segmentation module (PGAC).

The choice of Geodesic Active Contours for the comparison is motivated by the fact that also this family of algorithms, like our method, is fairly robust with respect to the choice of the seed point.
To evaluate the results of the proposed algorithm we used the *precision, recall* and *f-index* indices so defined:

$$precision = \frac{TP}{TP+FP}$$
$$recall = \frac{TP}{TP+FN}$$
$$f\text{-}index = \frac{2 \cdot precision \cdot recall}{precision + recall}$$

where TP is the number of correctly detected objects of interest, FP is the number of wrongly detected objects of interest and FN is the number of missed objects of interest.
The most commonly used definition of these indexes is directly usable for applications where the objects of interest are either completely detected or completely missed. In our application, however, the objects of interest are not atomic regions, so we need to consider also partial recognition of the tissue of interest. For this reason we have redefined TP, FP and FN in a fuzzy sense as follows:

$$TP = \frac{|g \cap d|}{|g \cup d|}$$

$$FP = \frac{|d| - |d \cap g|}{|d|}$$

$$FN = \frac{|g| - |d \cap g|}{|g|}$$

where g is the set of voxels actually belonging to the region of interest (ground truth), d is the set of voxels detected by the algorithm and $|\cdot|$ denotes the cardinality of a set. It is simple to show that when the object of interest is perfectly detected (in the sense that all the voxels in the ground truth are detected, and no voxel outside of the ground truth is detected), then $precision = 1$ and $recall = 1$; on the other hand, if the algorithm detects voxels that do not belong to the ground truth, it will have $precision < 1$, and if the algorithm misses some of the voxels in the ground truth, it will have $recall < 1$.
In the following table we report the results, averaged over the 11 MRI sequences:

	Precision	*Recall*	*f-index*
BLS	0.81	0.89	0.85
PLS	0.92	0.94	0.93
GAC	0.95	0.89	0.92
PGAC	0.99	0.90	0.94
LLS	**0.99**	**0.94**	**0.96**
ELLS	**0.98**	**0.97**	**0.97**

Table 1. Experimental Results

Notice that for the BLS algorithm we had to perform the test changing both the seed point and the value of the parameter k of the Level Set energy function, since the algorithm did not provide adequate results for all the images with a single choice of these parameters. The other algorithms did not have this problem. It is important to remark that the idea of the pre-segmentation phase allows also the level set algorithm to overcome this problem.
Furthermore, the results presented in table 1 show that the Laplacian operator provides an important contribution to the improvement of the performance. Indeed, the two algorithms based on this operator (LLS and ELLS) achieve the best overall performance.
Algorithms that exhibit an under-segmenting behavior can be expected to obtain a low value of the precision index. This is indeed the case of the BLS algorithm, as it is evident from table 1.
On the other hand, algorithms with a tendence to over-segmentation attain a low value of the recall index. As shown in table 1, this happens for BLS, GAC and PGAC. Notice that the BLS algorithm can yield (depending on the input image) both an under-segmentation and an over-segmentation.
Table 1 shows that Geodesic Active Contours based approaches have a relatively low recall value. From a detailed analysis of the images it can be concluded that the while the boundary of the region is usually well approximated, the low recall is due to the fact that often these algorithms miss voxels that are internal to the region.
In conclusion, Table 1 shows that our approaches are more effective than all the others. In particular, the ELLS algorithm shows a significant improvement in the recall index. A good recall index (together with a good precision) is important for applications that use the segmentation as the basis for quantitative measurements, e.g. for diagnostic purposes.
To have a visual idea of the effectiveness of our proposed algorithm, in Fig. 9 the results of each segmentation algorithm are shown.
Note that the result of the PLS algorithm, even after a difficult calibration phase, is not able to avoid the under-segmentation problem. Also notice that the result of the PGAC algorithm presents some holes within the tissue.
The comparison between fig. 9f and fig. 9g, and between fig. 9f and fig. 9g, demonstrates how the new ELLS algorithm is able to segment correctly the sharp corners of the tissue, overcoming the problems of our previous method.

5. Conclusion

In this paper we propose a novel segmentation method for MRI images, that is based on the integration of two complementary techniques: region growing and level set segmentation. Each technique is used at a different stage of the segmentation process, and the results are combined in such a way as to obtain a final segmentation that is not affected by the problems and limitations of both techniques when used alone.
The new method is robust with respect to the choice of the initial seed and to the setup of the (few) parameters, yielding repeatable results; furthermore, its performance is high in terms of both the precision and recall indices, as we have demonstrated experimentally, resulting appropriate for Computer Aided Diagnosis applications that need accurate quantitative measurements.

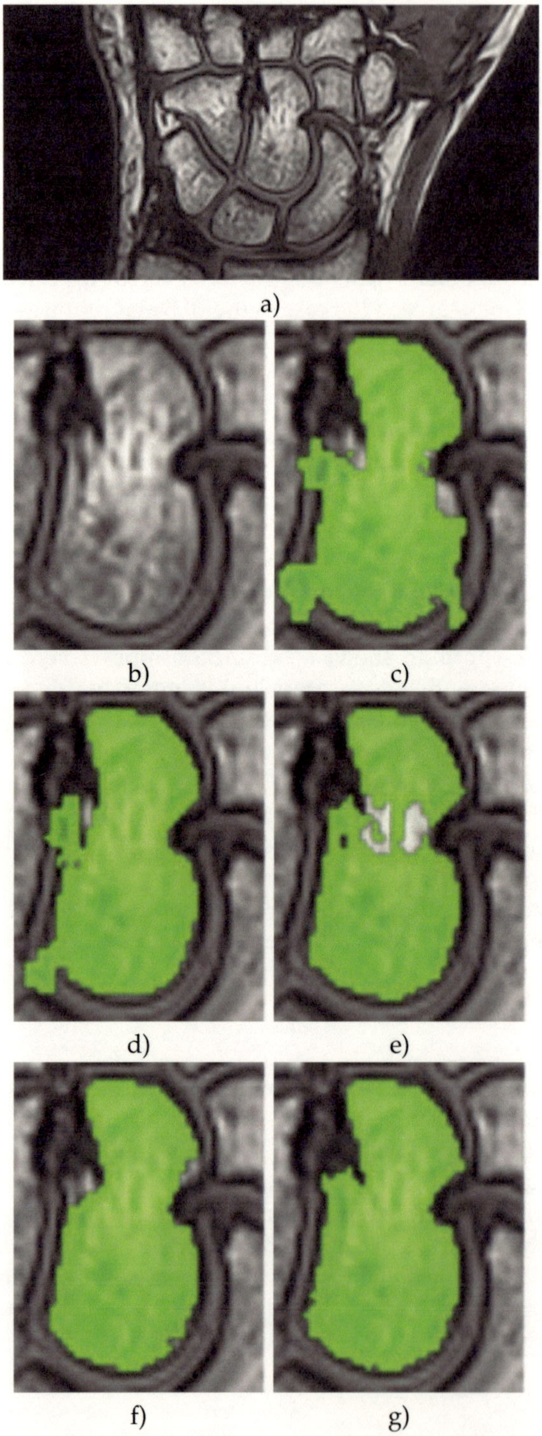

a) b) c) d) e) f) g)

Fig. 9. An example of the segmentation obtained by the tested algorithms (only a 2D slice is presented). a) Original image. b) A zoomed image of the region of interest. c) Basic Level Set segmentation (BLS). d) Level Set with Pre-segmentation (PLS). e) Geodesic Active Contours (GAC). f) Laplacian Level Set (LLS). g) Extended Laplacian Level Set (ELLS).

6. References

Adams, R. & Bischof, L. (1994). Seeded region growing, *IEEE Transaction on Pattern Analysis and Machine Learning* 16(6): 641–647.

Ardizzone, E., Pirrone, R. & Gambino, O. (2007). *Fuzzy C-Means Segmentation on Brain MR Slices Corrupted by RF-Inhomogeneity*, Springer-Verlag, chapter 48, pp. 378–384.

Banga, C., Ghorbel, F. & Pieczynski, W. (1992). Unsupervised bayesian classifier applied to the segmentation of retina image, *IEEE Proceedings of the Annual International Conference of the Engineering in Medicine and Biology Society* 5: 1847–1848.

Caselles, V., Kimmel, R. & Sapiro, G. (1997). Geodesic active contours, *International Journal of Computer Vision* 22-1: 61–79.

Chan, T. & Vese, L. (2001). Active contours without edge, *IEEE Transaction on Image Processing* 10(2): 266–277.

Conte, D., Foggia, P., Tufano, F. & Vento., M. (2009). Evaluation and improvement of the level set method for m images segmentation, *International conference on Computer Vision Theory and Application*.

Cremers, D., Rousson, M. & Deriche, R. (2005). Review of statistical approaches to level set segmentation: Integrating color, texture, motion and shape, *International Journal on Computer Vision* 19(10): 1–35.

Dervieux, A. & Thomasset, F. (1979). A finite element method for the simulation of raleigh-taylor instability, *Springer Lecture Notes in Mathematics* 771: 145–158.

Foggia, P., Guerriero, M., Percannella, G., Sansone, C., Tufano, F. & Vento., M. (2006). A graph-based method for detecting and classifying clusters in mammographic images, *in* D.-Y. Y. et al (ed.), *Lecture Notes in Computer Science*, Vol. 4109, Springer-Verlag, Berlin, pp. 484–493.

Krause, B., Wells, W., Kikinis, R., Held, K. & Kops, E. (1997). Markov random field segmentation of brain mr images, *IEEE Transaction on Medical Imaging* 16(6): 878–886.

Leitner, F. & Cinquin, P. (1991). Complex topology 3d objects segmentation, *SPIE Conference on Advances in Intelligent Robotics Systems*.

McInerney, T. & Terzopoulos, D. (1995). Topologically adaptable snakes, *5th International Conference on Computer Vision*, IEEE Comp. Soc. Press, pp. 840Ű–845.

Osher, S. J. & Sethian, J. A. (1988). Fronts propagation with curvature dependent speed: Algorithms based on hamiltonŰjacobi formulations, *Journal of Computational Physics* 79: 12Ű–49.

Osher, S. & Santosa, F. (2001). Level set medhods for optimization problems involving geomertry and constraints i. frequencies of a two-density inhomogeneous drum, *Journal of Computational Physics* 171: 272–288.

Ruan, S. & Bloyet, D. (2000). Mrf models and multifractal analysis for mri segmentation, *IEEE International Conferece on Signal Processing*.

Russon, M. & Paragios, N. (2002). Shape priors for level set representation, *Lecture Notes in Computer Science* 2351: 78–92.

Vemuri, B. C., Rahman, S. M. & Li, J. (1995). Multiresolution adaptive k-means algorithm for segmentation of brain mri, *ICSC '95: Proceedings of the Third International Computer Science Conference on Image Analysis Applications and Computer Graphics*, Springer-Verlag, pp. 347–354.

Vrooman, H. A., Cocosco, C. A., van der Lijn, F., Stokking, R., Ikram, M. A., Vernooij, M. W., Breteler, M. M. & Niessen, W. J. (2007). Multi-spectral brain tissue segmentation using automatically trained k-nearest-neighbor classification, *NeuroImage* 37(1): 71–81.

Wang, J., Qiu, M., Papademetris, X. & Constable, R. T. (2005). Brain tissue segmentation based on corrected gray-scale analysis, *Proceedings on Engineering in Medicine and Biology*.

Yan, P. & Kassim, A. A. (2006). Segmentation of volumetric mra images by using capillary active contour, *Medical Image Analysis* 10: 317–329.

Zhang, H., Zhang, J., Cao, J., Wang, W., Gong, J. & Wang, X. (2007). Robust fast marching method based on anisotropic diffusion, *Third International Conference on Natural Computation*, Vol. 3, pp. 159–162.

16

Mineral Grain Boundary Detection With Image Processing Method: From Edge Detection Operation To Level Set Technique

Bibo Lu , Weixing Wang
School of Computer Science and Technology, Henan Polytechnic University, Jiaozuo China

1. Introduction

The recognition of grain boundaries in deformed rocks from images of thin-sections or polished slabs is an essential step in describing and quantifying various features and analysis, which is usually achieved by image processing procedures. Recently, researchers from geoscience and computer science focused on this issue and many methods have been proposed.

We begin with an application of mineral grain boundary detection of thin section in geoscience: strain analysis[1]. Strain analysis plays an important role in the study of structural geology, especially when investigating the tectonic history of a region(see [2] and [3]). The following scheme illustrates main steps of strain analysis. The critical step in the above scheme

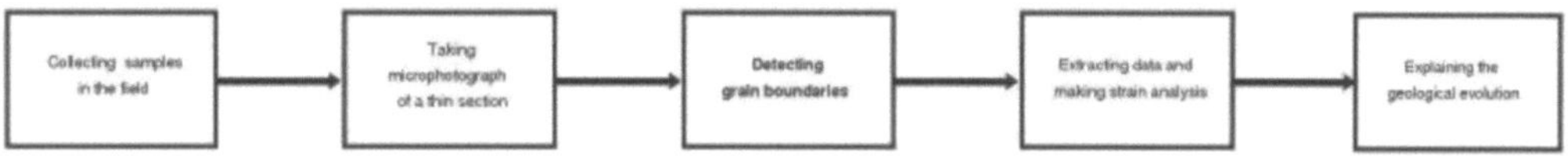

is identifying mineral with image segmentation techniques based on edges or regions. High sample intensity is required to provide adequate raw data for precious strain analysis. But in recent publications, the samples used for analysis seem to be insufficient. The primary reason maybe is the laborious and time-consuming methods to obtain the raw data required for strain analysis[4]. Though many methods based on the technology of image processing have been proposed, there is still much room for improving in efficiency and accuracy.

In image processing and computer version, segmentation or boundary detection is still a challenging problem and is motivated by some new certain applications. As a interdisciplinary problem, grain boundary detection provides much room to improve well established method to tackle with the special situations in geosciences. Three aspects should be paid more attention when designing the new approaches. The two of them are derived from image capture, and the other is the features of objects to be identified.

- Light phenomenon: under plane-polarised light, many mineral grains appear as colorless; under cross-polarised light, mineral grains show varying colors and intensities. In cross-polarized light the interference color displayed depends on the mineral type, the orientation of the indicatrix of the grain with respect to the polarizers and the thickness of the thin section.

- Rotating stage: grains may appear different light with different angels. To get a better visual effect, thin section must be rotated and several images are captured. Each of these image contains the important available for image segmentation. But how many images should be collected and how to fuse the information from these image have been completely answered yet.
- Grain features: every kind of grains has its own special shape features. However, in a thin section image, some grains are with a certain orientation, which is determined by the way how it is cut and polished. These features provide important cues for image segmentation and data match.

In the previous publications, various techniques have been reported for some certain grains identify. Threshold is used to identify grains of thin section image, while interview is often necessary to select different thresholds to separate several kinds of mineral. Edge detection has a simple control structure and provides more precise location of grain boundaries, but cannot guarantee closure of boundaries. If a boundary is discontinuous, pixels belonging to adjacent grains may be connected and therefore identified as belonging to a single mineral grain. Thus, grain identification will be finished completely. Several techniques, such as heuristic search and artificial neural net can be used to correct such edge detection errors. Instead of directly identifying the grain boundary, region based method is proposed to identify a region, i.e. a set of points that purportedly belong to the clast. Region-based segmentation uses image features to map individual pixels to sets of pixels that correspond to objects. Closed boundaries are always segmented but the positions of the boundaries may not be as accurate as those obtained from edge detection. Seeds are always selected by human interaction, which can be replaced by an automated complex algorithm. Holes may appear in the identified region, but for extracting features like major and minor axes, orientation, centroid, etc., the presence of these holes has a far diminished role to play than incorrectly identified edges. Watershed usually produce over-segmentation results for boundary detection. An important tool of post-processing, it is often used to separate touching grains in binary map created by other arithmetic.

In the past two decades, methods based on the partial differential equation (PDE) have been widely used in image segmentation and other image science fields recently. Impressive effects have been obtained with various PDE models. In [5] and [6] , Chan and Verse proposed a successful segmentation model (C-V model) using level set, which derived from the classical active contour(snake) model[7]. The essential idea of the snake model is to evolve an initial contour governed by a PDE until it stops on the edge of the objects. To represent the evolving curve, level set technique is adopted. Level set method is based on the description of the curve as the zero crossing of a higher-dimensional function and allows major simplifications. It offers a nature representation for the contour of the object, which can deal with complicated structures with many advantages, especially when the curve undergoes complex topological change. The key of level set method is to identify grain boundaries and to represent them as closed outlines. A framework of level set for mineral boundary detection was reported recently[8]. Level set method identifies all the objects simultaneity instead of identifying all the interesting objects chosen by clicking them using mouse one by one.

In this paper, we present a framework for boundary detection with level set for different kinds of input images. After reviewing related work, we first introduce the the level set for boundary detection with a single gray scale image as input. Then level set for color image is presented. For processing two color polarising images as input, a novel energy functional with a curve represented with level set is constructed and a new mathematical model for mineral identification is obtained. The curve evolves driven by the structures of two color polarising images and stops at the region edge of the grains.

2. Previous work: Brief view

Boundary detection of mineral from thin section image is not a trivial task. Various method, including threshold, gradient operator, region grow, watershed, level set, artificial neural network or a combination of them, have been proposed to address this problem. We give a detailed review of previous work in order of publication.

Lumbreras and Serrat considered the segmentation of grains in digital image of thin marble section[10]. An over-segmentation of the image with watershed method was performed and a region-merging procedure was carried out with some parameters determined by a sequence of images of the same sample with polarized light. In [11], polished rock samples were scanned by a color image scanner and an automatic mineral classification approach was presented. Fueten devised a computer-controlled rotating polarizer stage for the petrographic microscope. In this pioneer work, Fueten presented an important system allowed a thin section to remain fixed while the polarizing filters were rotated by stepper motors. This approach permitted a better integration between the processing software and the microscope and hence better data gathering possibilities. In 1998, Goodchild and Fueten proposed a boundary detection procedure which calculated closed boundary with a series of image processing routines[12]. A color RGB image was converted into a gray intensity image and seven steps were performed to produced accurate and closed edges for mineral grains. Whereas this algorithm was not perfect effective it presented a significant improvement over existing routines of that time. In fact, only intensity information was utilized in the original publication and some of color information was missed. The work of Nail and Murthy in [13], in which they constructed a standardization of edge magnitude in color image, may be helpful to improve the algorithm in [12]. To depict the geometrical structures of rock, boundary was defined as pixel with high gradient and fragmentation were rebuilt and reconnected ro form an uninterrupted boundary net[14]. Orientation contrast (OC) images represent a useful starting point to develop an automated technique able to assess grain boundaries in a completely objective and reproducible way. The method in [15] defined boundaries as high brightness gradient features on an OC image of a quartz mylonite through a specifically designed sequence of detection and filter algorithms that minimize the effect of local background noise. The initial boundaries produced by edge detection methods were with many imperfections. They employed a detection-filtering algorithm to automatically rebuild the real boundary net. When quantifying microstructures of fine grained carbonate mylonites, manually setting the threshold value was adopted to select as much of the dark grain-boundary area as possible without selecting the grey values of the grain interiors[16]. Heilbronner presented a simple procedure for creating grain boundary maps in a crystalline aggregate from multiple input images: for each image of a given input set, only the most significant grain boundaries were detected with gradient filtering and by combining those, a single grain boundary map was obtained[17]. Thompson, Fueten and Bockus used an artificial neural network(ANN) for the classification of minerals[18]. Based on a set of seven primary images during each sampling, a selected set of parameters were estimated and a three-layer feed forward neural network was trained on manually classified mineral samples. This is a beginning of ANN for mineral classification. Ross, Fueten and Yashkir proposed an automatic mineral identification with another important evolutionary computation: genetic algorithm[19]. Touching grains in digital images of thin sections is a hot potato when considering segmentation. Van den Berg and his collaborators tried to deal with it with a algorithm by separating touching grain sections in binary images of granular material[20]. The algorithm detected characteristic sharp contact wedges in the outline of touching grain sections and created an intersection after checking if the angle of the contact wedge was smaller than a user-defined threshold value. When making analysis of deformation of rock analogues, Fueten et.al applied gradient filtering for different types of movies with frames[21]. Zhou et al. proposed a segmentation method of petrographic images by integrating edge detection and region grow method[22]. They employed a boundary detection method to get the edge information, with which the seeds for region grow were selected automatically. Gradient filtering and threshold were also adopted step by step to pick several minerals in olivine–phyric basalts[23]. A similar method with multi-threshold was presented to extract several kinds of objects and to produce the corresponding binary images[24]. A recent method was presented by Roy Choudhury et al. , which they called CASRG, to identify a 'region', a set of points belonging to the grain[4]. The authors selected the seeds manually and chose the optimal threshold separately for each grain instead of using a single threshold for the whole image. The modification was very efficient and the accuracy has been validated for low and high strain samples in their contribution. The imperfections of this method was that all the seeds should be chosen by clicking the mouse. The working of choosing the seeds was also onerous for the large or high stress samples when the clats needed to be clicked are too much or the clasts were deformed badly. In fact, complex optical properties of plagioclase, such as twinning, present a particularly difficult challenge to thin section image processing. Gradient-based boundary detection method are likely to classify optical twin zones as different grains. Barraud shown an example of textural analysis of thin sections of rocks with a Geographic Information System (GIS) program, in which boundary was obtained by watershed segmentation on digital pictures of the thin section[25]. Region-grow method have also been improved to identify both twinned and un-twinned plagioclase areas as seeds[26]. To overcome this problem, a set of plane polarised light images, taken at 51 intervals with 18 polarizer rotations were used to create an average grey level image with high resolution. homogeneous zones were detected and they were classified manually as seeds to form the basis of further grain boundary recognition. Obara presented a registration algorithm for reversed transformation of rock structure images taken with polarizing microscope stage rotations[27]. The idea behind this algorithm was based on finding the optimal rotation angle and optimal translation vector, thus ensuring the best correspondence between analysed images. The criteria for optimization was formulated on the basis of the shapes of edges located on images, in which edges were detected with gradient filtering. To identify transcrystalline microcracks in microscope images of a dolomite structure, Obara devised a polarizing system using two nicols: one was fixed and the other could be rotated, while the thin section was kept fixed. 12 colour images were taken: 11 images with two crossed nicols and one with one nicol[28]. Based on the dolomite structure, CIELab color system was used and some image processing techniques, including gradient, threshold and mathematical morphology functions utilizing linear structuring elements, were performed for different components to detect transcrystalline microcracks. The maximum of standard deviation values of 11 α components were fused to be a single image for consequent operations. Obara also used a similar method to detection of the morphological anisotropy of calcite grains in marble[29]. Filtering with a rotated stencil consisting of two linear structuring elements preserved fine structure in thin section image. Fueten and Mason proposed to edit edges with an artificial neural net assisted approach[30]. The goal of this method was to produce close boundaries and enclose areas were considered to be grains. This method significantly improved the speed with which edges could be edited in preparation for other studies, although training of the neural network and manual correction of the results were still necessary.. Using GIS, Li, Onasch and Guo presented an automated method to detect grain boundaries and construct a boundary database in which the shape, orientation, and spatial distribution of grains could be quantified and analyzed in a reproducible manner[31]. In this procedure, they calculated the difference between the maximum and minimum value within a specified neighborhood, large values were recognized as grain boundaries.

In [8], level set method(LSM) was introduced to detect the grain boundary. The major advantage of the LSM is that the grain boundary detected by the LSM is a closed curve, which is preferred for features extraction and data analysis. To quantify microstructures of coarse-grained marbles, Ebert et al. presented a new approach based on the intensity of light reflectance in dependence of the crystallographic orientation of calcite grains[32]. As filters could not distinguish between twin boundaries and different phases (especially in the case of thin micas), and the grain boundaries were compiled from a stack of images (one image for each sample rotation increment), grain boundaries was traced with Photoshop manually. To determine crystal size distributions of olivine in kimberlite, scanned images of polished rock slab were analysed and region of interesting(ROI) was determined by combining texture, colour and grey intensity analysis outputs. Adjoined crystals were separated by adapting and extending the marker-based watershed algorithm. In a study in [33], the application of 2D and 3D textural analysis to the quantification of olivine populations in kimberlites was investigated. Olivine grains were segmented with a threshold filter selecting grey-values from 50 to 73 connected to grey-values from 50 to 66 (seeded threshold) after the data set was subjected to a median filter for noise reduction. Using ANN for image processing seemed to be more popular and is a highly researched area. Baykan proposed an ANN for the classification of minerals using color spaces without boundary detection[36]. A microscopic information system(MIS) for petrographic analysis was presented with GIS and applied to transmitted light images[37]. Two region functions were developed and embedded in the GIS environment. GIS software provided optimal management of the MIS database, allowing the cumulative measurement of more than 87,000 grains.

The methods mentioned above are mainly based on the traditional image segmentation and edge detection technology in image processing. The initial boundaries produced by edge detection methods have many imperfections. The boundary may be open, discontinuous, which do not coincide with the realistic boundary. Grain boundary, specifically a close one, provides fundamental information about material properties, such as area, orientation, percent, microstructural analyse [32] and crystal size distributions [33]. Such boundaries can not be used to feature extraction and other image processing tasks and a post processing arithmetic is needed to obtain more realistic boundaries. So post-processing is necessary to get a closed boundary. Some techniques, as suggested in [30], have been reported to link edges. Concomitantly, the subjectivity and the modification on raw data introduced by the post-processing make them unsuitable for data analysis. Region grow method tries to identify the region of the grain by 'absorbing' all the points similar with the 'seed' point. It's best advantage is that the boundary of the region is closed, which is preferred for measurements and analysis. A critical point in this method is to select the seeds, which often involves human interventions to avoid the seeds failing to grow according to the given rules. In CASGR[4], seed was selected by human interaction and the threshold was set adaptive to data automatically. Zhou et al. tried to overcome this problem by introducing a hybrid method that the results of edge-detection provided clues for automated seed select[22]. Apart from the human intervention in seeding, another defect is the occur of the holes within the region. The size of the hole depends on the noise distribution and the area of the heterogeneity of color information within the clasts. The small holes can be filled by employing simple morphological operations, but the larger ones remains almost unchanged. Such post-processing ineluctably affects the extracted boundaries as well as the extracted features, such as major and minor axes, orientation, centroid, etc[4].

3. Level set method for grain boundary detection

Methods based on the partial differential equation (PDE) have been widely used in image segmentation and other image science fields recently. Impressive effects have been obtained with various PDE models. In [6], Chan and Verse proposed a successful segmentation model (C-V model) using level set, which derived from the classical active contour (snake) model [7]. The essential idea of snake model is to evolve an initial contour governed by a PDE until it stops on the edge of the objects. For initial snake model, the edge is defined where have larger magnitude of gradient. As imposed with a second order derivative constraint, the curve have a good smoothing shape, which is contrast to the boundaries produced by edge-detection operator. Level set method is based on the description of the curve as the zero crossing of a higher-dimensional function and allows major simplifications[38]. In level set, a closed curve is seen as the zero level set of a function in high dimension. It offers a nature representation for the contour of the object, which can deal with complicated structures with many advantages, especially when the curve undergoes complex topological change. It is a thriving method in image science for its following advantages:

- easy to implement numerically;
- the outline of the object is closed;
- tackle with the topology change easily, such as merge and split.
- some geometric quantities can be expressed directly.

With this method, initial curve can be anywhere or with any shape in the image plane. In the following, we will give a framework of level set for grain boundary detection. First we introduce level set for gray scale image. Then, active contour for vector image is given. We end this section by consider a level set model with two polarising images as input.

3.1 Level set for gray scale image

For a garyscale image u, considering the following energy functional:

$$E(c_1, c_2, C) = \int_{inside(C)} |u_0(x,y) - c_1|^2 dxdy + \int_{outside(C)} |u_0(x,y) - c_2|^2 dxdy + \mu \cdot \text{Length}(C), \tag{1}$$

where c_1 and c_2 are constant unknowns representing the average value of u inside and outside the curve C.

For curve evolution, the level set has been used widely. It can deal with cusps, corners and automatic topological changes. Now, we rewrite the original model (1) in the level set formulation. The curve C is defined as the zero level set as follows: $C = \{(x,y) \in \Omega | \phi(x,y) = 0\}$. Assuming that ϕ has opposite signs on each side of C, the energy can be rewritten as:

$$E(c_1, c_2, \phi) = \int_{\Omega} ((u(x,y) - c_1)^2 H(\phi) + (u(x,y) - c_2)^2 (1 - H(\phi))) dxdy + \mu \int_{\Omega} |\nabla H(\phi)| dxdy, \tag{2}$$

where ϕ is level set function, ν is a positive coefficient, H denotes the Heaviside function:

$$H(z) = \begin{cases} 1, & z \geq 0; \\ 0, & z < 0. \end{cases}$$

In order to compute the associated Euler–Lagrange equation for the unknown function, we consider slightly regularized versions of the function H, denoted here by H_ϵ as $\epsilon \to 0$. One example of such approximations is given by

$$H_\epsilon(z) = \begin{cases} 1, & z > \epsilon, \\ 0, & z < \epsilon, \\ \frac{1}{2}\left[1 + \frac{z}{\epsilon} + \frac{1}{\pi} sin(\frac{\pi z}{\epsilon})\right], & |z| \leq \epsilon, \end{cases}$$

as proposed in [6].
For minimizing the functional defined in (2), fixing c_1 and c_2, we obtain the following Euler-Lagrange equation:

$$\delta_\epsilon(\phi)[\nu \mathrm{div}(\frac{\nabla\phi}{|\nabla\phi|}) - (u_0 - c_1)^2) + (u_0 - c_2)^2] = 0 \tag{3}$$

where δ is one-dimensional *Dirac* measure and $\delta_\epsilon = H'_\epsilon(z)$. Using gradient descent method by an artificial time t, we yield the following evolution equation:

$$\frac{\partial\phi}{\partial t} = \delta_\epsilon(\phi)[\nu \mathrm{div}(\frac{\nabla\phi}{|\nabla\phi|}) - (u_0 - c_1)^2) + (u_0 - c_2)^2] \tag{4}$$

An alternative way to improving the above model is to replace $\delta_\epsilon(\phi)$ by $|\nabla u|$ to extend the evolution to all level set of ϕ.
Keeping ϕ fixed and minimizing the energy yields the following expressions for c_1 and c_2:

$$c_1(\phi) = \frac{\int_\Omega u(x,y)H_\epsilon(\phi(x,y))dxdy}{\int_\Omega H_\epsilon(\phi(x,y))dxdy}, \tag{5}$$

$$c_2(\phi) = \frac{\int_\Omega u(x,y)(1 - H_\epsilon(\phi(x,y)))dxdy}{\int_\Omega (1 - H_\epsilon(\phi(x,y)))dxdy}. \tag{6}$$

To solve this evolution problem, we use a finite differences scheme, as suggested in [6].
As the thin section image contain abundant structure, the initial contour we obtain is so complex that it is almost impossible to make strain analysis directly, though all the valuable ones have been identified. The following we have to do is to select the useful grains suitable for analysis. It is a difficult task as the noise disturbs the segmented results, and the small objects are too much, so we should set constrains to discard the useless ones. The select depends on the grain to be identified and the question tackled with. Here we provide a simple way, which could be improved by the Recalling when the image is processed manually or using other automated methods, the intensity, area and shape of the grain are dominant factors for human inspection and segmentation criterion. Level set provides the boundaries of the objects by utilizing the intensity distribution, so area and shape criterions are adopted for a tough tentative strains to abandon the unsuitable objects. The theory of level set method shows that the contour is a closed curve, so the objects whose area is ranging between two

thresholds k_1 and k_2 are selected. As for the shape information, the ration of major axis and minor axis could be adopted as another important criterion for high formed minerals. It is a simple attempt to devise such constraints, more precious constraints, mainly decided by the previous knowledge of the the grains, will be proposed in future work.

3.2 Level set for color image

Color information is important factor for image segmentation and edge detection. Though luminance could be extracted from color image and processed as gray scale image, but it is still necessary to consider color components for grain boundary detection. In the following we will discuss the level set for color micrographic of thin section.

Let $u_{i,j}$ be the jth channel of an color image u on Ω, with $j = 1,2,3$ channels and C the evolving curve. Each channel would contain the same image with some differences. Let $c^+ = (c_1^+, c_2^+, c_3^+)$ be a unknown constant vector. The extension of the C-V model to vector images is

$$E(c^+, c^-, C) = \int_{inside(C)} \frac{1}{3}\sum_{j=1}^{3} \lambda_j^+ |u_j(x,y) - c_j^+|^2 dxdy + \int_{outside(C)} \frac{1}{3}\sum_{j=1}^{3} \lambda_j^- |u_j(x,y) - c_j^-|^2 dxdy + \mu \cdot \text{Length(C)}. \tag{7}$$

The curve C is defined as the zero level set as follows: $C = \{(x,y) \in \Omega | \phi(x,y) = 0\}$.

In this model, the active contour C is the boundary between two regions defined over all channels. Rewrite it in level set form, we obtain

$$E(c^+, c^-, \phi) = \int_\Omega \frac{1}{3}\sum_{j=1}^{3} \lambda_j^+ |u_j(x,y) - c_j^+|^2 H_\epsilon(\phi(x,y))dxdy + \int_\Omega \frac{1}{3}\sum_{j=1}^{3} \lambda_j^- |u_j(x,y) - c_j^-|^2 (1 - H_\epsilon(\phi(x,y)))dxdy + \mu \int_\Omega |\nabla H_\epsilon(\phi)| dxdy, \tag{8}$$

for $j = 1,2,3$. The parameters μ is the weight for the length term of the curve. $\lambda^{+,-} = (\lambda_j^{+,-})$ are the weights for the noise error. H denotes the Heaviside function, again.

Minimizing the energy with respect to the constant c_j^+, c_j^-, for $j = 1,2,3$, we obtain:

$$c_j^+ = \frac{\int_\Omega u_j H_\epsilon(\phi(x,y))dxdy}{\int_\Omega H_\epsilon(\phi(x,y))dxdy}, \quad \text{average}(\mathrm{u_j})\text{on}\text{Œ} \geq 0,$$

$$c_j^- = \frac{\int_\Omega u_j (1 - H_\epsilon(\phi(x,y)))dxdy}{\int_\Omega H_\epsilon(\phi(x,y))dxdy}, \quad \text{average}(\mathrm{u_j})\text{on}\text{Œ} < 0.$$

Assuming that c_j^+ are constant vectors, and minimizing the energy functional with respect to ϕ, we obtain the following Euler-lagrange equation for ϕ:

$$\delta_\epsilon(\phi)\left[-\frac{1}{3}\sum_{j=1}^{3} \lambda_j^+ (u_j - c_j^+)^2 + \frac{1}{3}\sum_{j=1}^{3} \lambda_j^- (u_j - c_j^+)^2 + \mu \cdot \text{div}\left(\frac{\nabla \text{Œ}}{|\nabla \text{Œ}|}\right)\right] = 0, \tag{9}$$

where δ is one-dimensional *Dirac* measure and $\delta_\epsilon = H'_\epsilon(z)$. To solve this PDE numerically, we introduce an artificial time as gradient descent method

$$\frac{\partial \phi}{\partial t} = \delta_\epsilon(\phi)\left[-\frac{1}{3}\sum_{j=1}^{3}\lambda_j^+(u_j - c_j^+)^2 + \frac{1}{3}\sum_{j=1}^{3}\lambda_j^-(u_j - c_j^+)^2 + \mu \cdot \text{div}\left(\frac{\nabla Œ}{|\nabla Œ|}\right)\right] = 0, \quad (10)$$

in Ω with the boundary condition

$$\frac{\delta_\epsilon(\phi)\partial\phi}{|\nabla u|\partial\overline{n}} = 0$$

on $\partial\Omega$, where $\partial\overline{n}$ denotes the unit normal at the boundary of Ω.

3.3 Level set for polarised images

Polarised images captured under different light contain important clues for mineral boundary detection. For a thin section, two images can be captured from plane- or cross-polarised light in microscopy. The main difference between polarizing images and ordinary images is polarised light phenomenon: under plane-polarised light, many mineral grain appear as colorless; under cross-polarised light, mineral grains show varying colors and intensities. The colors and intensity rely the mineral, the thickness of the grain and its crystallographic orientation. In the previous publications, gradient filtering has been proposed to deal with every image followed by a fuse procedure. We extend the level set method to segment multi images captured from different light. Figure 1 shows the two images of a thin section. Figure 1(a) is of a less contrast and the edges of Fig. 1(b) seems to be more legible. It is not proper to detect the grain boundary with any image. To segmentation the polarised images, we construct a new active contour model below. The energy as well as the evolving is similar with that of the equation above.

Let $u_{i,j}$ be the jth channel of an image u_i on Ω, with $j = 1,2,3$ channels, $i = 1,2$ images and C the evolving curve. Each channel would contain the same image with some differences. Let $c^+ = (c^+_{1,1}, c^+_{1,2}, c^+_{1,3})$ and $c^- = (c^-_{2,1}, c^-_{2,2}, c^-_{2,3})$ be two unknown constant vectors. The extension of the C-V model to polarised images is

$$\begin{aligned} E(c^+, c^-, C) = & \int_{inside(C)} \frac{1}{6}\sum_{i=1}^{2}\sum_{j=1}^{3}\lambda^+_{i,j}|u_{i,j}(x,y) - c^+_{i,j}|^2 dxdy \\ & + \int_{outside(C)} \frac{1}{6}\sum_{i=1}^{2}\sum_{j=1}^{3}\lambda^-_{i,j}|u_{i,j}(x,y) - c^-_{i,j}|^2 dxdy + \mu \cdot \text{Length}(C). \end{aligned} \quad (11)$$

In this model, the active contour C is the boundary between two regions defined over all channels. Rewrite it in level set form, we obtain

$$\begin{aligned} E(c^+, c^-, \phi) = & \int_\Omega \frac{1}{6}\sum_{i=1}^{2}\sum_{j=1}^{3}\lambda^+_{i,j}|u_{i,j}(x,y) - c^+_{ij}|^2 H_\epsilon(\phi(x,y))dxdy \\ + & \int_\Omega \frac{1}{6}\sum_{i=1}^{2}\sum_{j=1}^{3}\lambda^-_{i,j}|u_{i,j}(x,y) - c^-_{ij}|^2(1 - H_\epsilon(\phi(x,y)))dxdy + \mu\int_\Omega |\nabla H_\epsilon(\phi)|dxdy, \end{aligned} \quad (12)$$

for $i = 1,2$ and $j = 1,2,3$. The parameters μ is the weight for the length term of the curve. $\lambda^{+,-} = (\lambda^{+,-}_{i,j})$ are the weights for the noise error.

(a) Taken under plane-polised light

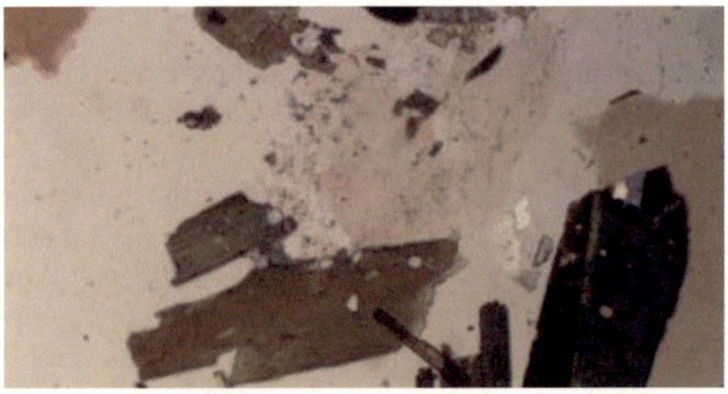

(b) Taken under cross-polised light

Fig. 1. Two polarizid thin section images.

Minimizing the energy with respect to the constant $c^+_{i,j}, c^-_{i,j}$, for $i = 1, 2, j = 1, 2, 3$, we obtain:

$$c^+_{i,j} = \frac{\int_\Omega u_{i,j} H_\epsilon(\phi(x,y))dxdy}{\int_\Omega H_\epsilon(\phi(x,y))dxdy}, \qquad \mathrm{average(u_{i,j})onŒ} \geq 0,$$

$$c^-_{i,j} = \frac{\int_\Omega u_{i,j}(1 - H_\epsilon(\phi(x,y)))dxdy}{\int_\Omega H_\epsilon(\phi(x,y))dxdy}, \quad \mathrm{average(u_{i,j})onŒ} < 0.$$

Assuming that $c^+_{i,j}$ are constant vectors, and minimizing the energy functional with respect to ϕ, we obtain the following Euler-lagrange equation for ϕ (introducing an artificial time as gradient descent method):

$$\frac{\partial \phi}{\partial t} = \delta(\phi)\left[-\frac{1}{6}\sum_{i=1}^{2}\sum_{j=1}^{3}\lambda^+_{i,j}(u_{i,j}(x,y)-c^+_{ij})^2+\frac{1}{6}\sum_{i=1}^{2}\sum_{j=1}^{3}\lambda^-_{i,j}(u_{i,j}(x,y)-c^+_{ij})^2+\mu\cdot\mathrm{div}\left(\frac{\nabla Œ}{|\nabla Œ|}\right)\right], \tag{13}$$

in Ω with the boundary condition

$$\frac{\delta_\epsilon(\phi)\partial\phi}{|\nabla u|\partial\overline{n}} = 0$$

on $\partial\Omega$, where $\partial\overline{n}$ denotes the unit normal at the boundary of Ω. To solve this evolution problem, we use a finite differences scheme, as suggested in [6].

The mail difference between the proposed model and the classical model in [6] is the income images. Our model is strongly inspired by the work of [6]. The three methods evolve the curve depending on the information with multichannel. The main difference is the number of the input image and channel. Our model deals with the two polarised images of a thin section of the same view. Under plane- and cross-polarised light, different color information is captured. Some grains can be observed in one image while they may have a unconspicuous edges or regions. In the new model, the active contour evolves according to the structure of the two polarised images instead of any single image. More information is concerned to locate a more reasonable and accurate edge position. Similarly, the contour produce by the above model need a post-processing to remove unmeaning objects.

4. Experimental results

We present in this section some numerical results obtained with the models from the previous section. For the details of the numerical schemes and for other numerical results, we refer the reader to [6],[8],[39]. As we will see in this section, these models have the abilities of automatic detection of grain boundaries. Every grain boundary is represented with a closed curve.
In Fig.2–Fig.4, we illustrator the whole procedures of low strain grain boundaries detection using level set with gray scale as input. We also compare the grains detected by level set with that of hand-drawn method. Comparisons of features and strain analysis results can be found in [8]. In Fig.5, an example of high strain sample boundary detection is given and the result is compared with that of a region growing method: CASGR[4]. A note to this example is that our detection is performed on gray scale image and CASGR is performed with color image. In Fig.6, we show the result of color grain boundary detection with equation (10). We skip the preprocessing of TV flow and the we refer to [40] for more details. In Fig.7 , we demonstrate the segmentation of polarising images of a thin section. The thin section contains some grains and other clasts. The red contours represent the edges of the identified grains. In Fig.7(a), segmentation of plane-polarising image with classical vector-valued image is shown. Some small clasts are identified as grains wrongly. Segmentation of cross-polarising image is shown in Fig.7(b). In the left of the image, a large part of ares is recognized as inner of a grain according to the structure of the cross-polarsing image, which is not coincide with the fact of plane-polarising image. The edges of grains detected with the proposed model is shown in Fig.7(c). The time space is 0.1 and the total iter number is set 200. The other parameter are set as follows: $\mu = 0.2, \lambda_{+,-}^{i,j} = 1, i, j = 1, 2, 3$. Some clasts are excluded from the identified grains. The reason for a new segmenting result is that the information in six channel is used to determine the regions of the grains. With more clues concerned, the disturb of the noise and false edges is suppressed.

5. Conclusion

We have presented in this paper a framework for grain boundary detection using level set with different input images: gray scale image, color image, plane-polarising and cross-polarising images. The obtained variational level set models yield closed grain boundary which is preferred for feature extraction and data analysis. Application to grain boundary detection have been illustrated. In future, we will focus on the grain identification and classification with multi-phase level set approach for thin section image of complex topologies.

6. Acknowledgements

The authors would like to thank editor for the invitation to contribute to this book. This work has been supported in part by grants NSFC 10926075 and The Doctor Grant of Henan Polytechnic University(B2009-41).

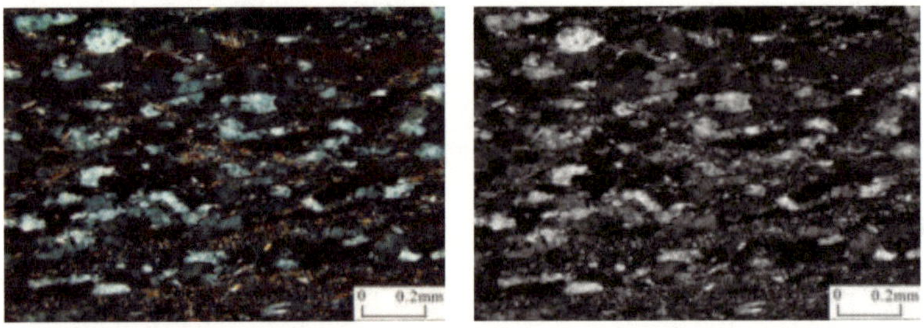

(a) Original color image. (b) Gray scale image.

Fig. 2. Thin section image of mylonite.

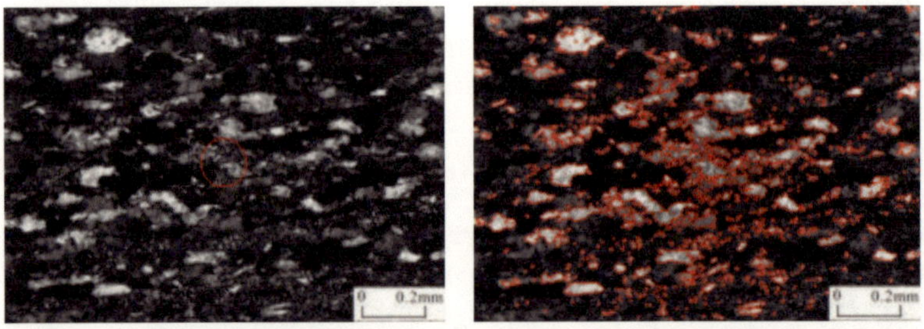

(a) iter=0 (b) iter=10

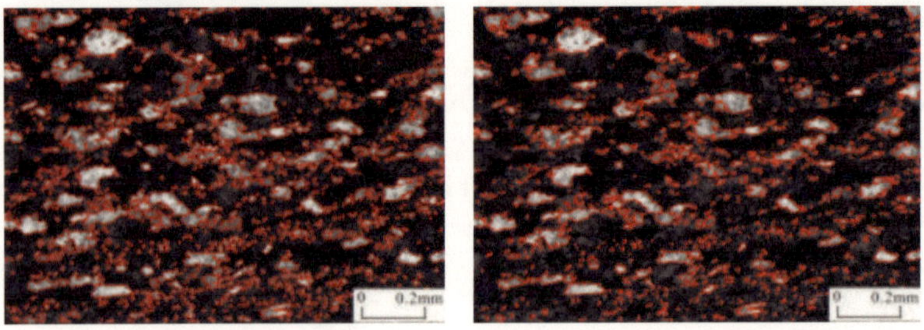

(c) iter=15 (d) iter=22

Fig. 3. Curve involving of thin section image.

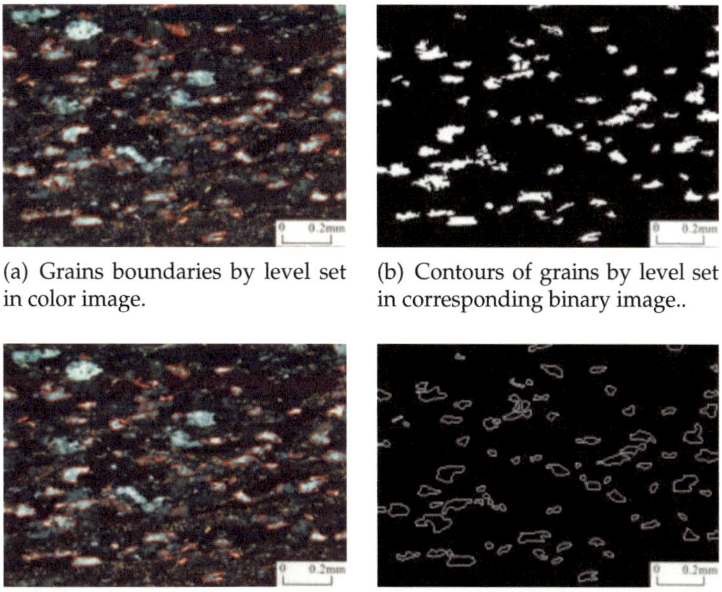

(a) Grains boundaries by level set in color image.

(b) Contours of grains by level set in corresponding binary image..

(c) Hand-drawn boundaries of grains in color image.

(d) Hand-drawn boundaries of grains in corresponding binary image.

Fig. 4. Grain boundaries: level set VS hand-drawn.

(a) Color image .

(b) Gray scale image .

(c) Grain boundaries by CASGR.

(d) Grain boundaries by level set.

Fig. 5. Grain boundaries detection of low strain sample.

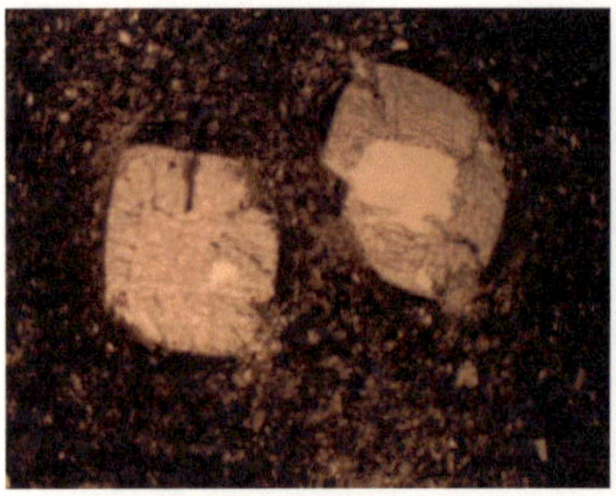

(a) Color thin section image

(b) Red channel

(c) Blue channel

(d) Green channel

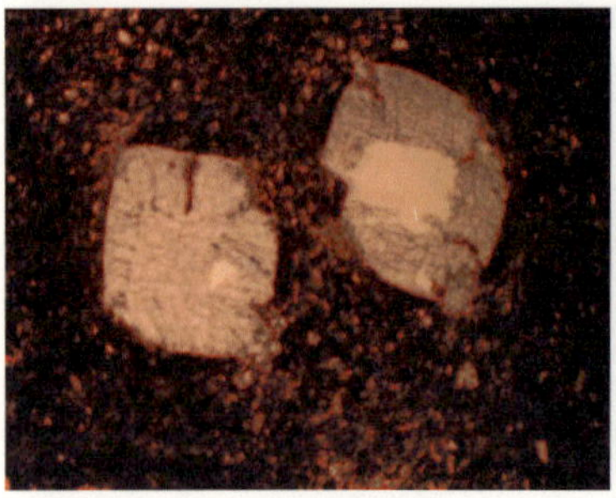

(e) Contour of segmenting result

(f) Boundary of identified andalusite

Fig. 6. Grain boundary detection of andalusite with color image.

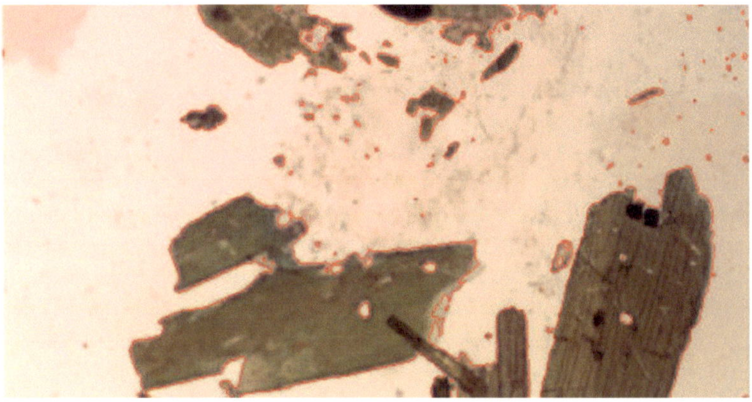

(a) Segmentation of plane-polarising image

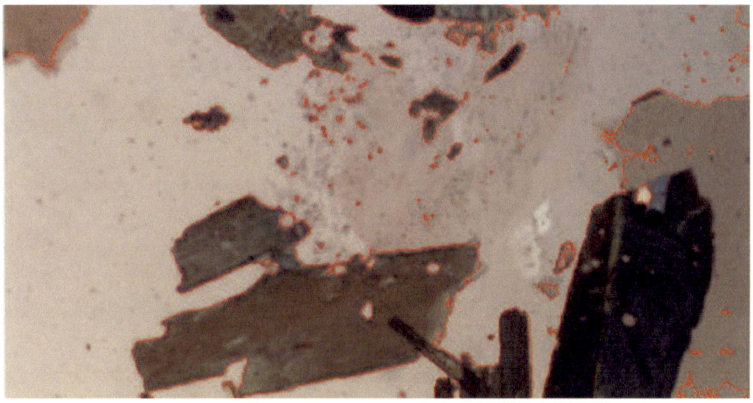

(b) Segmentation of cross-polarising image

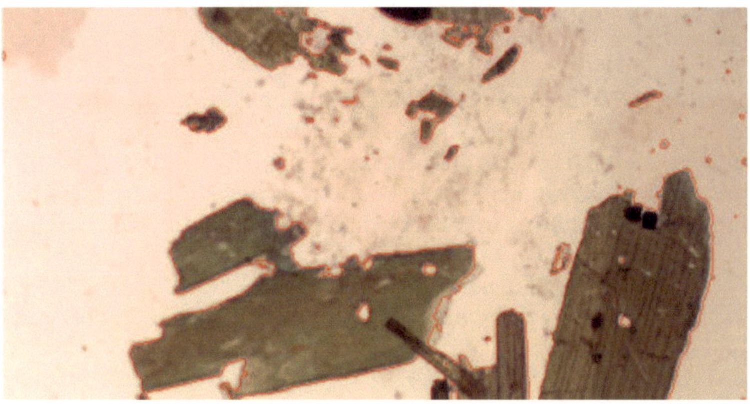

(c) Segmentation of two palarising images

Fig. 7. Grain boundary detection with different input images

7. References

[1] Ramsay, J. G., 1967. Folding and Fracturing of Rocks. McGraw Hill, New York.
[2] Ailleres, L., M. Champenois., 1994. Refinements to the Fry method (1979) using image processing. Journal of Structural Geology 16 (9), 1327-1330.
[3] Yu, H., Zheng, Y., 1984. A statistical analysis applied to the R_f/f method. Tectonophysics 110, 151-155.
[4] Roy Choudhury, K., Patrick A. M., Kieran, F. Mulchrone., 2006. Automated grain boundary detection by CASRG. Journal of Structural Geology 28(3), 363-375.
[5] T. F. CHAN, B. SANDBERG, and L. VESE, Active contours without edges for vector-valued images, J. Visual Comm. Image Rep. 11(2) (2000), 130-141.
[6] T. F., Chan, L. Vese, 2001. Active contours without edges. IEEE Transactions on Image Processing 10, 266-277.
[7] Kass, M., Witkin, A., Terzopoulos, D., 1988. Snakes: Active contour models. International Journal of Computer Vision 1, 321-331.
[8] Bibo Lu, Min Cui, Qiang liu, Yangang Wang, 2009, Automated grain boundary detection using the level set method, Computers and Geosciences, 35(2), 267-275.
[9] Starkey, J., Samantaray, A. K., 1993. Edge detection in petrographic images. Journal of Microscopy 172(3), 263-266.
[10] Lumbreras, F., Serrat, J., 1996. Segmentation of petrographical images of marbles. Computers and Geosciences 22, 547-558.
[11] Frank Fueten, 1997, A computer-controlled rotating polarizer stage for the petrographic microscope, Computers and Geosciences, 23(2), 203-208.
[12] Goodchild, J., Fueten, F., 1998. Edge detection in petrographic images using the rotation polarizer stage. Computers and Geosciences 24, 745-751.
[13] S.K. Naik and C.A. Murthy, 1999, Standardization of edge magnitude in color images, IEEE Transactions on Image Processing 5 , 1ÍC8.
[14] Mlynarczuk, M., 1999. Some remarks on the application of image analysis and image processing for the description of the geometrical structures of rock. Physicochemical problems of mineral processing 33, 107-116.
[15] Bartozzi, M., Boyle, A.P., Prior, D.J., 2000. Automated grain boundary detection and classification in orientation contrast images. Journal of Structural Geology 22(11), 1569-1579.
[16] Marco Herwegh, 2000, A new technique to automatically quantify microstructures of fine grained carbonate mylonites: two-step etching combined with SEM imaging and image analysis, Journal of Structural Geology, 22(4) 391-400.
[17] Heilbronner, R., 2000. Automatic grain boundary detection and grain size analysis using polarization micrographs or orientation images. Journal of Structural Geology 22(15), 969-981.
[18] Sean Thompson, Frank Fueten, 2001, David Bockus, Mineral identification using artificial neural networks and the rotating polarizer stage, Computers and Geosciences, 27(9), 1081-1089.
[19] Ross, B. J.; Fueten, F.; Yashkir, D. Y. ,2001, Automatic Mineral Identification Using Genetic Programming. Machine Vision and Applications 13, 61-69.
[20] E. H. van den Berg, A. G. C. A. Meesters, J. A. M. Kenter, W. Schlager, 2002, Automated separation of touching grains in digital images of thin sections, Computers and Geosciences, 28(2) 179-190.

[21] Frank Fueten, Kristen Hynes, Ryan L. Van Luttikhuisen, 2002, An experimental setup for the analysis of analogue deformation experiments using the rotating polariser stage, Journal of Structural Geology, 24(1), 241-245.
[22] Zhou,Y., Starkeyb, J, Mansinha, L, 2004. Segmentation of petrographic images by integrating edge detection and region growing. Computers and Geosciences 30, 817-831.
[23] C. S. Perring, S. J. Barnes, M. Verrall, R. E. T. Hill, 2004, Using automated digital image analysis to provide quantitative petrographic data on olivine-phyric basalts, Computers and Geosciences, 30(2), 183-195.
[24] Nicoletta Marinoni, Alessandro Pavese, Marco Foi, Luca Trombino, 2005, Characterisation of mortar morphology in thin sections by digital image processing, Cement and Concrete Research, 35(8), 1613-1619.
[25] Joseph Barraud, 2006, The use of watershed segmentation and GIS software for textural analysis of thin sections, Journal of Volcanology and Geothermal Research, Volume 154, Issues 1-2, Modern Trends in Petrography: - Textural and Microanalysis of Igneous Rocks, 1, 17-33.
[26] John V. Smith, Eberhard Beermann, 2007, Image analysis of plagioclase crystals in rock thin sections using grey level homogeneity recognition of discrete areas, Computers and Geosciences, 33(3), 335-356.
[27] Boguslaw Obara, 2007, An image processing algorithm for the reversed transformation of rotated microscope images, Computers and Geosciences, 33(7), 853-859.
[28] Obara, B., 2007, Identification of transcrystalline microcracks observed in microscope images of dolomite structure using image analysis methods based on linear structuring element processing. Comput. Geosci. 33(2), 151ÍC158.
[29] Obara, B., Kožušníková, A., 2007. Utilisation of the image analysis method for the detection of the morphological anisotropy of calcite grains in marble. Computational Geoscience. 11,275ÍC281.
[30] F. Fueten and J. Mason, 2007, An artificial neural net assisted approach to editing edges in petrographic images collected with the rotating polarizer stage, Computers and Geosciences 33, 1176ÍC1188.
[31] Yingkui Li, Charles M. Onasch, Yonggui Guo, 2008, GIS-based detection of grain boundaries, Journal of Structural Geology, 30(4), 431-443.
[32] A. Ebert, D. Rieke-Zapp, M. Herwegh, K. Ramseyer, E. Gnos, D. Decrouez, 2009, Microstructures of coarse-grained marbles, analyzed using a new technique based on the bireflectance of calcite, Tectonophysics, 463(1), 175-184.
[33] Dougal A. Jerram, Alex Mock, Graham R. Davis, Matthew Field, Richard J. Brown, 2009, 3D crystal size distributions: A case study on quantifying olivine populations in kimberlites, Lithos, Volume 112, Supplement 1, Proceedings of the 9th International Kimberlite Conference, 9th International Kimberlite Conference, November, 223-235.
[34] N.Singh, T.N.Singh, A. 2009, Tiwary and Kripamoy Sarkar,2009,Textural identification of basaltic rock mass using image processing and neural network,Computational Geosciences. 14(2), 301-310.
[35] Holden et al., E.J. Holden, S. Moss, J.K. Russell and M.C. Denith, 2009, An image analysis method to determine crystal size distributions of olivine in kimberlite, Computational Geosciences 13(3), 255-268.
[36] Nurdan Akhan Baykan, Nihat Yilmaz, 2010, Mineral identification using color spaces and artificial neural networks, Computers and Geosciences, 36(1), 91-97.
[37] Simone Tarquini, Massimiliano Favalli, 2010, A microscopic information system (MIS) for petrographic analysis, Computers and Geosciences, 36(5), 665-674.

[38] Osher, S., Sethian,J.A., 1988. Fronts Propagating with Curvature- Dependent Speed: Algorithms Based on Hamiton-Jacobi Formulations, J. Computational Physics 79, 12-49.
[39] Tony F. Chan, B. Yezrielev Sandberg, Luminita A. Vese, 2000, Active Contours without Edges for Vector-Valued Images, Journal of Visual Communication and Image Representation, 11(2), 130-141.
[40] Bibo Lu, Chao Ning, 2010, PDE-based Grain Boundary Detection, Procedding of Second IITA Conference on Geoscience and Remote Sensing (IITA- GRS 2010), China, 170-173.

17

Multiscale Segmentation Techniques for Textile Images

Xiqun Lu
College of Computer Science, Zhejiang University
Hangzhou, 310027,
China

1. Introduction

In this chapter we focus on image segmentation techniques for some very special images – textile images. They are generated from the color halftoning technique in textile and printing production lines. In contrast with natural color images, textile images have some very distinctive features: (1) generally there are a few dominant colors in a textile image, whereas there may exist hundreds of significant colors in a natural color image; (2) in the textile industry designers combine threads of different colors, thickness, and densities to produce the visual impression of other colors (the color halftoning technique in textile printing). The fabric texture structure – texture noise – has a great influence on the colors' appearance in textile images, which makes the color segmentation of textile images a very difficult problem [1].

A typical textile image is shown in Fig.1. According to human visual observation, there are about six dominant colors in the textile image, but when the image is enlarged to the pixel-level, we will find that there are many different colors in perceived uniform color regions as shown in Fig.1. (a) and (b). Four histograms of the spatial variation magnitudes of the four uniform and edge blocks (as shown in Fig.1 (a), (b), (c) and (d)) are illustrated in Fig.2 (Here the spatial variation magnitude is computed as the added value of the two absolute forward differences along the horizontal and vertical directions on the luminance component of each

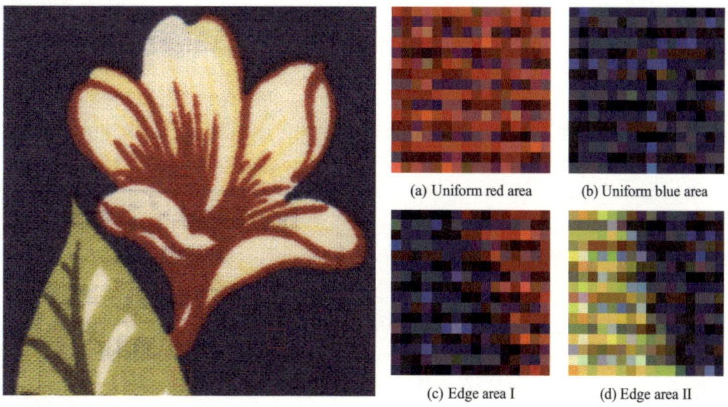

Fig. 1. A typical textile image

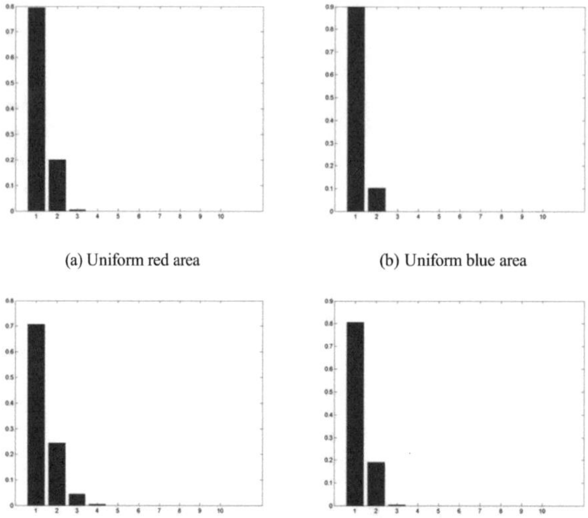

(a) Uniform red area (b) Uniform blue area

(c) Edge area I (d) Edge area II

Fig. 2. Histograms of the spatial variation magnitudes of uniform areas and edge areas in the textile image

block). From these histograms, we can see that it is very difficult to distinguish the variations caused by genuine spatial edges from those caused by texture noise.

Some distinctive properties of texture noise are compared with those of white Gaussian noise in [2]. Fig.3. (a) shows a 16×16 texture noise block extracted from the textile image as shown in Fig.1. Fig.3. (d) is a 16×16 white noise block generated by the "randn" function in Matlab™. Texture noise is clearly non-Gaussian distributed, and has highly correlative spatial structure.

Any image segmentation algorithm that independently classifies each pixel in the image plane is unlikely to perform well for textile images since there is insufficient information to make a good decision. So many segmentation algorithms divide the image into arbitrary blocks, and classify each block independently. However, if the block size is too small, discriminating among similar textures may be difficult. Alternatively, if the block size is too large, regions of differing textures may be lost. In either case, the resulting boundaries will not be accurate since there is no reason to believe that the actual boundaries occurred along the block boundaries [3].

Multiscale image segmentation approaches [1, 3-14] have been proven efficient to integrate both image features and contextual information to classify a region in an image differently from its surroundings if there is sufficient statistical evidence to justify a distinct region regardless of size, and refine the segmentation results recursively between different scales. The number of important contributions in this area is so great that just listing all of them would more than exhaust the page budget of this chapter (for example, the bibliography in [4] is 8 pages in a two-column format). So in Section 2 we review a few representative multiscale image segmentation techniques which developed over the past decades. In Section 3 we test some of the benchmark multiscale image segmentation techniques on textile images, and compare the experimental results analytically. We finally give some concluding remarks in Section 4.

In the following sections, we will follow the convection of using upper-case letters for random variables and lower-case letters for their realizations.

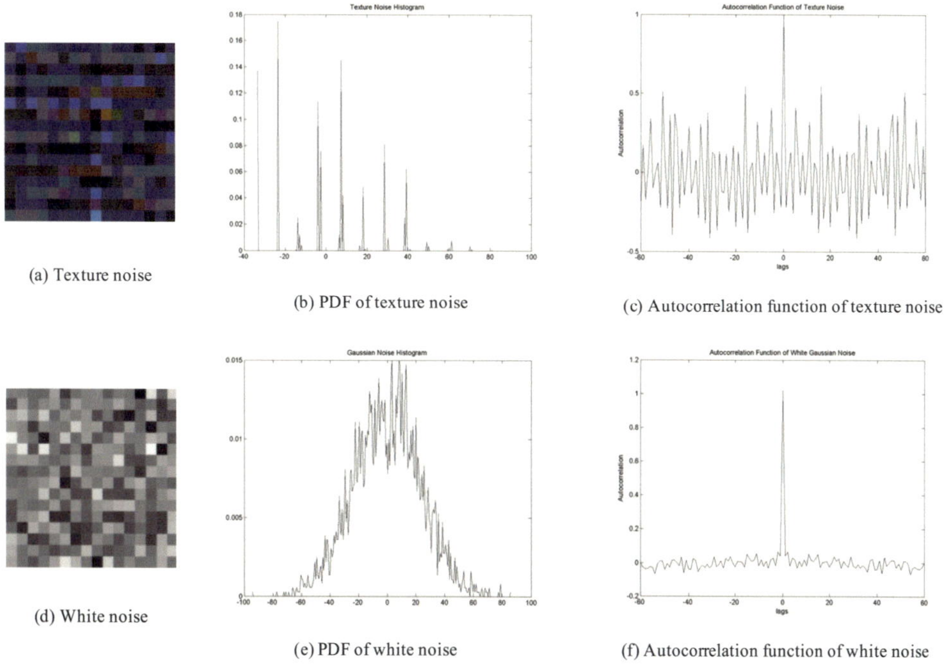

(a) Texture noise (b) PDF of texture noise (c) Autocorrelation function of texture noise

(d) White noise (e) PDF of white noise (f) Autocorrelation function of white noise

Fig. 3. Distinctive properties of texture noise

2. Multiscale image segmentation techniques

2.1 Problem statement and notations

The image segmentation problem can be considered as the process of inferring the "best" configuration of labelling X from the observed image data $Y = y$, and both random fields X and Y are defined on a rectangular gird S. Each random variable of X takes its values from a finite set of class labels $\Lambda = \{1 \ \cdots \ K\}$, where K is the total number of classes. The standard Bayesian formulation of this inference problem consists in minimizing the expectation of some cost function C, given the data

$$\hat{x} = \arg\min_{x} E(C(X,x) \mid Y = y) \tag{1}$$

Where $C(X,x)$ is the cost of estimating the true segmentation X by an approximate segmentation x.

The MAP (Maximum a Posteriori) estimator is an solution of (1) if we use the cost functional of $C(X,x) = 1$ whenever any pixel is incorrectly classified. The MAP estimator aims at maximizing the probability that all pixels will be correctly classified. It is well known that the MAP estimator is excessively conservative, and appear even more inappropriate for the estimation of multiscale Markov random fields [6].

An alternative criterion to the MAP estimation is to minimize the probability of classification error, the Maximization of the Posterior Marginals (MPM) estimator, which associates to each cite the most probable value given all the data

$$\forall s \in S, \quad \hat{x}_s = \arg\min_{x_s \in \Lambda} P(x_s \mid Y = y) \tag{2}$$

The MPM estimator results in high computational complexity since each of these functions should be obtained by simultaneously integrating out all $x_t (t \neq s)$ [5]. Usually in real situations, it is unfeasible to compute these posterior marginals $P(x_s \mid y)$ exactly since the original joint distribution $P(x,y)$ is unavailable or it is intractable to specify the joint distribution for each possibility.

2.2 Sequential MAP [6]

Although the MPM criterion seems to be more appropriate than the MAP criterion, both the MPM and MAP cost functions do not take into account the location of estimation errors in a hierarchical quadtree structure. Bouman and Shapiro introduced the following cost function in [6]

$$C_{SMAP}(X,x) = \sum_{n=0}^{L} 2^{n-1}\left(1 - \prod_{i=n}^{L} \delta(X^{(i)}, x^{(i)})\right) \tag{3}$$

At each scale n, the segmentation or labeling is denoted by the random field $X^{(n)}$, and the set of lattice points is denoted by $S^{(n)}$. This sequential MAP (SMAP) cost function is to sum up the segmentation errors from multiple scales together. The SMAP estimator aims at minimizing the spatial size of errors.

The multiscale image model proposed in [6] is composed of a series of random fields at multiple scales. Each scale has a random field of image feature vectors $Y^{(n)}$, and a random field of class labels $X^{(n)}$. We denote an individual sample at scale n by $y_s^{(n)}$ and $x_s^{(n)}$, where s is the position in the 2-D lattice $S^{(n)}$. Markovian dependencies are assumed across scales to capture interscale dependencies of multiscale class labels, and the SMAP recursion can be estimated in a fashion of coarse-to-fine

$$\hat{x}^{(n)} = \arg\max_{x^{(n)}} \left\{ \log p_{y^{(n)}|x^{(n)}}(y^{(n)} \mid x^{(n)}) + \log P_{x^{(n)}|x^{(n+1)}}(x^{(n)} \mid \hat{x}^{(n+1)}) \right\} \tag{4}$$

The two terms in (4) are the likelihood function of the image feature $y^{(n)}$ and the context-based prior knowledge from the next coarser scale, respectively. Specifically, the quadtree pyramid developed in [6] is to capture interscale dependencies of multiscale class labels regarding the latter part of (4). But a big problem with the quadtree pyramid is that spatially adjacent samples may not have a common parent sample at the next coarser scale which may result in discontinuous boundaries. Therefore a more generalized pyramid graph model was introduced in [6] where each sample has multiple parents at the next coarser scale. However, this pyramid graph also complicates the computation of likelihood functions, and the coarse-to-fine recursion of (4) has to be solved approximately.

Based on the same framework, a trainable context model for multiscale Bayesian segmentation was proposed in [7], where the contextual behavior can be trained off-line by providing image data the corresponding ground truth segmentations. Then the segmentation can be accomplished efficiently via a single fine-to-coarse-to-fine iteration through the pyramid.

2.3 Wavelet-domain HMT [8]

A distinct context-based Bayesian segmentation algorithm was proposed in [8] where the context model is characterized by a context vector $v^{(n)}$ derived from a set of neighboring samples (3×3) at the next coarse scale. It is assumed that, given $y_s^{(n)}$, its context vector $v_s^{(n)} = \left\{ x_{ps}^{(n)} \quad x_{ls}^{(n)} \right\}$ can provide supplement information regarding $x_s^{(n)}$, where $x_{ps}^{(n)}$ denotes the class label of its parent sample, and $x_{ls}^{(n)}$ denote the dominant class label of the 3×3 samples at the next coarser scale. Given $v_s^{(n)}$, $x_s^{(n)}$ is independent with all other class labels. In particular, the contextual prior $p_{x^{(n)}|v^{(n)}}(c \mid u)$ is involved in the SMAP estimation which has the same purpose as the second term in (4), and it can be estimated by maximizing the following context-based mixture model likelihood as

$$f(y^{(n)} \mid v^{(n)} = u) = \prod_{s \in S^{(n)}} \sum_{c=1}^{K} p_{x^{(n)}|v^{(n)}}(x_s^{(n)} = c \mid \hat{v}_s^{(n)} = u) f(y_s^{(n)} \mid c) \tag{5}$$

where the likelihood function $f(y^{(n)} \mid x^{(n)})$ is computed by using the wavelet-domain hidden Markov model (HMT) proposed in [9]. An iterative Expectation Maximization (EM) training algorithm was developed in [8] to approach the above problem.

The HMT is a tree-structure model in the wavelet-domain to characterize the joint statistics of wavelet coefficients across scales. In order to perform multiscale segmentation, an image is recursively divided into four sub-images of same size J times, and a pyramid is constructed with J scales. A block $y^{(n)}$ at scale n is associated with three wavelet subtrees in three subbands as, $\left\{ T_{LH}^{(n)} \quad T_{HL}^{(n)} \quad T_{HH}^{(n)} \right\}$. The computation of the model likelihood of $f(y^{(n)} \mid \theta)$ is a realization of the HMT model θ and is obtained by

$$f(y^{(n)} \mid \theta) = f(T_{LH}^{(n)} \mid \theta_{LH}) f(T_{HL}^{(n)} \mid \theta_{HL}) f(T_{HH}^{(n)} \mid \theta_{HH}) \tag{6}$$

Where it is assumed that the three DWT subbands are independent and each one in (6) can be estimated based on a close formula proposed in [9].

An improved wavelet-domain hidden Markov model, HMT-3S [10], was developed to capture the wavelet coefficients dependencies not just across scales, but across subbands as well, where the three DWT subbands are grouped into one quadtree structure. It is worth noting that two-state GMMs (Gaussian Mixture Model) in HMT [8] are still used to characterize the DWT marginal statistics, and there will be eight states in a node of HMT-3S. Thus, HMT-3S is parameterized by

$$\theta_{HMT-3S} = \left\{ p_J(u), \varepsilon_{j,j-1}^{u,v}, \sigma_{b,j,h}^2 \mid b \in B, j = 1, \cdots J; u, v = 0, \cdots, 7; h = 0, 1 \right\} \tag{7}$$

Where $B = \left\{ LH \quad HL \quad HH \right\}$, and $\varepsilon_{j,j-1}^{u,v}$ is the transition probability of the Markov chain from scale j to scale $j-1$. The EM training algorithm in [8] can be straightforwardly extended to the eight-state HMT-3S.

2.4 Joint multi-context and multiscale HMT-3S [12]

Most multiscale segmentation algorithms adopt SMAP estimator and mainly consider interscale dependencies of multiscale class labels by assuming Markovian dependencies across scales, and intrascale dependencies are not considered due to the fact that the non-causal structure usually requires extra iterative training process.

However, the characterization of intrascale dependencies is useful for boundary localization [11]. Based on three numerical segmentation criteria: 1) P_a the percentage of pixels which are correctly classified; 2) P_b the percentage of boundaries that are coincided with the true ones; 3) P_c the percentage of true boundaries that can be detected, Fan and Xia quantified the segmentation performances of five contextual models in [11]. And show that interscale context models (context-1 and context-2) may favor P_a by encouraging the homogeneity of texture classification across the scales of the pyramid, and the intrascale context model (context-5) may help P_c by being sensitive to texture boundaries within a scale. As hybrid context models (context-3 and context-4) may provide high P_b by appropriately balancing both interscale dependencies and intrascale dependencies of multiscale class labels into the MAP estimation. It is shown that none of the five context models can work well singly [11].

Since a single context model is unable to provide high accuracy for both texture classification and boundary localization, Fan and Xia proposed a joint multi-context and multiscale (JMCMS) approach to Bayesian segmentation in [12] which reformulates (1) as a multi-object optimization as

$$\begin{aligned} \hat{x} &= \arg\min_x E(C_{SMAP}(X,x) \mid Y = y_1) \\ &\vdots \\ \hat{x} &= \arg\min_x E(C_{SMAP}(X,x) \mid Y = y_z) \end{aligned} \tag{8}$$

Where an image y can be represented as multiple (Z) copies characterized by distinct context models, i.e., $\{y_z \mid z = 1,\cdots,Z\}$. Different context models provide different multiscale modeling, the multi-objective problem in (8) is roughly analogous to the multiple criteria: P_a, P_b and P_c. The above problem can be solved by a heuristic algorithm called the multistage problem-solving technique [11].

Both JMCMS [11] and HMT-3S [10] can improve segmentation results in terms of P_a, P_b and P_c by emphasizing the two terms in (4), respectively. It is shown in [12] that combination of them provides the best segmentation result regarding P_a and P_b.

2.5 Multiresolution Gaussian Autoregressive Models (MGAR) based on MMPM [13]

A double-stochastic model is proposed in [13] for multiresolution textured-image segmentation where the observed image is represented as a multiresolution Gaussian autoregressive (MGAR) model and class labels are assumed to be dependent on both the same scale and the adjacent finer and coarser scales as a 3-D MRF.

The optimization criterion used for segmentation is the minimization of the expected value of the number of misclassified nodes in a multiresolution lattice. The estimator that satisfies this criterion is referred to as the "multiresolution maximization of the posterior marginals" (MMPM) estimator, and is a natural extension of the single-resolution MPM estimate [13]. The cost function in (1) is given by

$$C(X,x)=\sum_{j=0}^{J-1}\sum_{s\in S^{(j)}}\delta(X_s^{(j)},x_s^{(j)}) \tag{9}$$

Where J denotes the total number of levels of the multiresolution lattice S, and the multiresolution representation of the observed image Y and the class label pyramid X are defined on the same lattice S. The segmentation x that minimizes the conditional expectation of this cost function will be denoted as x^*. Thus

$$\begin{aligned}
E[C(X,x^*)\,|\,Y=y] &= \min_x E[\sum_{s\in S}(1-\delta(X_s,x_s))\,|\,Y=y] \\
&= \min_x \sum_{s\in S} E[(1-\delta(X_s,x_s))\,|\,Y=y] \\
&= \min_x \sum_{s\in S} P(X_s \neq x_s\,|\,Y=y) \\
&= \min_x \sum_{s\in S} (1-P(X_s = x_s)\,|\,Y=y)) \\
&= \max_x \sum_{s\in S} P(X_s = x_s\,|\,Y=y)
\end{aligned} \tag{10}$$

where $\delta(X_s,x_s)=1$, if $X_s=x_s$; $\delta(X_s,x_s)=0$, otherwise.
It is assumed that the number of distinct textures in the observed image is known in this approach, but the parameters θ of the MGAR model – the means, prediction coefficients, and prediction error variances of different textures are unknown. A modified version of the EM algorithm is used to estimate the parameters [13].
The Gibbs sampler with constant temperature can be used to generate a Markov chain $X(t)$ which converges in distribution to a random field with probability mass function $p_{X|Y}(X\,|\,Y,\theta)$. The marginal conditional probabilities $p_{X_s|Y}(k\,|\,Y,\theta)$, which are to be maximized, are then approximated as the fraction of time the Markov chain spends in state k at node s, for each k and s [13]. If N_0 is the number of iterations (complete passes through the pyramid) of the Gibbs sampler, then the approximations

$$p_{X_s|Y}(k\,|\,Y,\theta)=\frac{1}{N_0}\sum_{t=1}^{N_0}\delta(X_s(t),k) \qquad \forall k,s \tag{11}$$

provide estimates of the value needed to obtain the MMPM estimate of X. Integrating the multiresolution EM with the approximated MMPM algorithm, image segmentation and parameters estimation can be obtained simultaneously [13].

2.6 Multi-grid Belief Propagation [14]

Markov random field models provide a robust and unified framework for image segmentation, but the MRF framework yields an optimization problem that is NP hard, and it is usually highly advantageous to use graphs as diagrammatic representations to facilitate analysis and manipulations. One of the feasible approximation solutions is belief propagation [14-16]. Belief Propagation (BP) algorithm utilizes the conditional independent properties in the network to derive efficient solutions. Corresponding to the MPM and the MAP estimators, there are two types of BP algorithms. One is belief update (BU) also known

as the sum-product algorithm for the MPM inferences, and another is belief revision (BR) a.k.a. the max-product algorithm for the MAP inferences [15].
The quality of image segmentation can be described in an energy function as following

$$E(x) = \sum_{s \in S} D_{x_s}(x_s) + \sum_{(s,p) \in N} W(x_s, x_p) \tag{12}$$

Where N are the (undirected) edges in the four-connected image grid graph. $D_{x_s}(x_s)$ is the cost of assigning label $x_s(x_s \in \{1, \cdots, K\})$ to pixel s in the lattice S, and is referred to as the data cost. $W(x_s, x_p)$ measures the cost of assigning different labels to two neighboring pixels s and p, and is generally referred to as the discontinuity cost. An intuitive measurement of the discontinuity cost is based on the degree of difference between the two neighboring labels, that is, $W(x_s, x_p) = V(x_s - x_p)$.
The BP algorithm works by passing messages around the graph defined by the four-connected image grid. The method is iterative, with messages from all nodes (pixels) being passed in parallel. At each iteration, in the max-product BP algorithm, new messages can be computed with negative log probabilities where the max-product becomes a min-sum:

$$m_{s \to p}^{t}(x_p) = \min_{x_s}(V(x_s - x_p) + D_{x_s}(x_s) + \sum_{q \in N(s) \backslash p} m_{q \to s}^{(t-1)}(x_s)) \tag{13}$$

In the sum-product BP algorithm, new messages are updated as

$$m_{s \to p}^{t}(x_p) = \min_{x_s}(V(x_s - x_p) \cdot D_{x_s}(x_s) \cdot \prod_{q \in N(s) \backslash p} m_{q \to s}^{(t-1)}(x_s)) \tag{14}$$

The standard implementation of max-product message passing algorithm on the grid graph runs in $O(nK^2T)$ time, where n is the number of pixels in the image, K is the number of possible labels for each pixel and T is the number of iterations. So the computation complexity is very high for images with large sizes.
Felzenszwalb and Huttenlocher [14] proposed an efficient multi-grid BP technique without changing the graph structure and the energy function: first the data costs are constructed from fine to coarse scales, where the data cost at coarse level can be calculated by summing over four data costs at the next finer level; then the message propagation process is started at the coarsest level, and the belief information is propagated from coarse to fine scales.
In contrast, the underlying graph in the example proposed in [16] is changed. First, a multiscale algebraic multigrid technique is used to select nodes that strongly influence others as the coarse nodes at the next coarser level, and an iterated weighted aggregation (IWA) process is followed to calculate the new edge weights among the selected coarse nodes. Second, given the belief propagation result at coarse level is interpolated as a start point for the next finer scale. Since the start point is believed to be close to the true solution, this BP is expected to converge rapidly.

2.7 Multiscale probabilistic reasoning model [1]

The quadtree structure induces causal properties that enable design of a non-iterative coarse-to-fine multiscale segmentation algorithm. However, an important disadvantage of the quadtree structure is that blocks that are spatial adjacent may not have common neighbors at the next coarser scale, and this may result in blocky artifacts in the final segmentation [1].

Fan and Xia listed five contextual models in [11], and proved that the context-4 model can provide a high percentage of boundaries that coincide with the true ones. A hierarchical probabilistic reasoning model is proposed in [1] to alleviate the problem of blocky artifacts by providing a quadtree structure which combined with a spatial lattice neighborhood at each scale.

This hierarchical probabilistic reasoning model [1] is very different from the multiscale models proposed in [6-13]. The concept of scale in [1] is related to the size of a block in the spatial domain. While the scale described in [6-13] is related to either the Gaussian pyramid or the wavelet decomposition of the observed image. The Gaussian low-pass filter can alleviate texture noise to some degree, but it can also blur edges at the same time, especially for those low-contrast edges. The wavelet transform is very useful to represent the singularities (edges and ridges) in an image at multiple scale and three different orientations [8]. However, for textile images, the singularities are corrupted by uniformly distributed texture structure (see Fig.2). So it is more appropriate to perform segmentation in the spatial domain directly than in the wavelet-domain, and the experimental results in Section 3 also prove this scheme is inappropriate for textile images.

As we know that a large block usually enhances the classification reliability (because the use of many pixels can lessen the disturbance caused by texture noise), but simultaneously risks having pixels of different classes inside the block; while a small block reduces the possibility of having multiple classes in the block, but sacrifices classification reliability due to the paucity of color information and texture noise. So both the large and small scale behavior should be utilized to properly segment both large homogeneous regions and detailed boundary regions.

In [1], no special prior distribution assumption is made about the size and shape of regions. At every increasing scale, each block is subdivided into four child blocks, forming a quadtree structure. By adopting the context-4 model proposed in [11] the correlations of spatial blocks across different scales and within the same spatial scale are integrated as shown in Fig.4

$$\hat{x}^{(n)} = \arg\max_{k} \left\{ p_{b^{(n)}|c_k}(b^{(n)} \mid c = c_k) \cdot p_{c_k|v_b}(c = c_k \mid v_b) \right\} \tag{15}$$

Where $p_{b^{(n)}|c_k}(b^{(n)} \mid c = c_k)$ is the likelihood of the block $b^{(n)}$ at scale n given the dominant color $c_k(k = 1,\cdots,K)$. Since textile images are corrupted by non-Gaussian texture noise, it is not appropriate to specify this conditional probability $p_{b^{(n)}|c_k}(b^{(n)} \mid c = c_k)$ as a multivariate Gaussian distribution as done in other multiscale models [6-13]. In [1], we calculated the ratio of how many pixels in the current block $b^{(n)}$ are within a sphere centered at the dominant color $c_k(k = 1,\cdots,K)$ with a radius of r_k in the color space as the likelihood:

$$p_{b^{(n)}|\mathbf{c}_k}(b^{(n)} \mid \mathbf{c} = \mathbf{c}_k) = \frac{\#(|c_{p_{ij}} - c_k| < r_k, p_{ij} \in b^{(n)})}{size(b^{(n)})} \tag{16}$$

Where # is the counting operator, and r_k is half of the minimum distance between the dominant color $c_k(k=1,\cdots,K)$ and the other dominant color $c_l(l\neq k, l=1,\cdots,K)$.

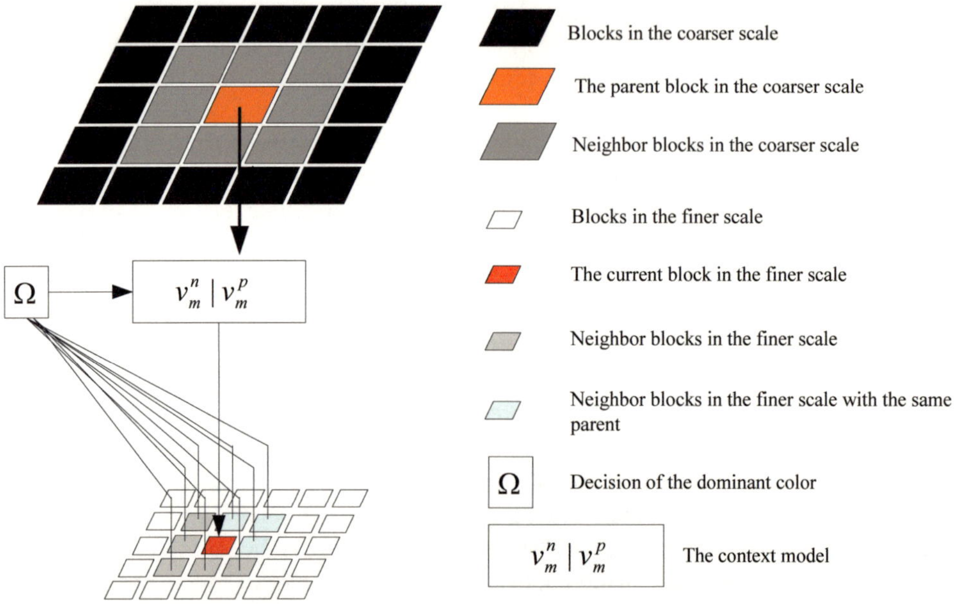

Fig. 4. Hierarchical probabilistic reasoning model [1]

The contextual information v_b in (15) contains the color information of its parent block at the next coarser scale and that of the eight neighbor blocks of the current block at the same scale. We assume that the dependence on its parent block's color information is totally uncorrelated with the dependencies on its eight neighbor blocks' color information at the same scale. Therefore we can write the contextual probability $p_{c_k|v_b}(c=c_k \mid v_b)$ as

$$p_{c_k|v_b}(c=c_k \mid v_b) = p(c=c_k \mid v_b^{parent}) \cdot p(c=c_k \mid v_b^{neighbor}) \tag{17}$$

where "parent" denotes the parent block at the next coarser scale, and "neighbor" denotes the eight neighboring blocks at the same scale of the current block. According to Bayes rule, the probability $p(c=c_k \mid v_b^{parent})$ or $p(c=c_k \mid v_b^{neighbor})$ can be computed as follows:

$$\begin{aligned} p(c=c_k \mid v_b^{\sim}) &= \frac{p(v=v_b^{\sim} \mid c=c_k)p(c=c_k)}{p(v=v_b^{\sim})} \\ &= \frac{p(v=v_b^{\sim} \mid c=c_k)p(c=c_k)}{\sum_{j=1}^{K} p(c=c_j)p(v=v_b^{\sim} \mid c=c_j)} \end{aligned} \tag{18}$$

where ~ indicates either "parent" or "neighbor". The prior distribution of the dominant color $p(c=c_k)$ $(k=1,\cdots,K)$ can be computed according to (16), where $b^{(n)}$ will be the size of the entire image. The likelihood $p(v = v_b^{parent} \mid c = c_k)$ of the parent block and the likelihood $p(v = v_b^{neighbor} \mid c = c_k)$ of the eight neighbor blocks, given the dominant colors $c_k(k = 1,\cdots,K)$, can be computed from coarse to fine scales according to (15) respectively.

3. Performances of multiscale image segmentation techniques on textile images

In this section we focus on textile image segmentation based on several representative multiscale image segmentation techniques, and test their performance analytically.

Texture noise – the texture appearance of the fabric in textile images makes bottom-up, solely image-driven segmentation techniques always prone to errors [1]. Most of textile images are taken directly from the production line in textile industries, there are no ground truth segmentation results for these textile images, and it is difficult for us to manually prepare training data for training-based supervised image segmentation [7, 8]. In this paper we mainly consider supervised multiscale image segmentation, that is, it is assumed the number of distinct colors in the input textile image is known, and the dominant colors and their corresponding features can be obtained earlier.

The texture statistical characteristics are very helpful for image segmentation when the given image contains different visual texture regions [3, 8, 10-13]. However textile images contain uniformly distributed texture structure (as shown in Fig.1), so the color information is the main feature can be handled with during segmentation with during segmentation. Since there are usually only a few dominant colors in textile images, we obtain dominant colors by picking and averaging homogeneous regions from the given image. We extract six dominant colors: blue, red, white, yellow, dark green and shallow green from textile image 1, and eleven dominant colors from textile image 2, and five dominant colors from textile image 3 and textile image 4, respectively.

In order to capture the cross-scale relationships of texture regions, prior to segmentation, learning-based supervised image segmentation techniques [7, 8] have to pick large enough homogeneous regions as training data from textile images. However, some of the dominant colors only occupied very small areas in textile images, such as black color in textile image 2 and textile image 3, so we only apply the HMTSeg algorithm [8] to textile image 1 and 4 because in these two images each dominant color occupies large enough area. In this paper we only examine supervised multiscale image segmentation techniques on textile images: the multiscale probabilistic reasoning model [1], sequential MAP [6], HMTSeg [8], belief propagation [14].

In the multiscale probabilistic reasoning model [1], no special prior distribution is assumed about the size and shape of regions, but in the SMAP [6] a multivariate Gaussian distribution is applied for that purpose, so in addition to inputting the number of dominant colors and corresponding RGB values, the SMAP algorithm requires inputting the covariance matrices of the three RGB channels of the dominant colors. The SMAP algorithm is good for textile images with fine texture structure and large homogeneous regions, such as textile image 4. Although the computation complexity of the SMAP algorithm is higher than that of the maximum likelihood algorithm, the performance of SMAP is comparable to that of ML for textile images with coarse fabric texture structure and delicate structures.

In order to apply the HMTSeg algorithm [8] to textile images, we have to pick several homogeneous blocks from the inputted image as training data. Both textile image 1 and textile image 4 have large homogeneous regions, and for each dominant color, we randomly pick ten 16×16 blocks. With this training data and interscale tying in the wavelet-domain HMT models [8], the EM training algorithm [9] is used to estimate the parameters of the HMT model for each dominant color. Since each HMT model is trained on 16×16 uniform blocks, the output segmentation results are very blocky (see Fig.5. (f) and Fig.8. (f)). Though the wavelet-domain HMT model is very helpful to images with edges and ridges, in textile images, edges and ridges are corrupted by uniformly distributed texture noise and the test image generally is much larger than the training images, so repeat the likelihood computations for image subblocks assuming that the blocks are independent. The wavelet-domain HMT model which designed for distinct visual texture statistics is not suitable for textile images, and from the segmentation results, we can see that the misclassified color areas are large. We don't apply the HMTSeg algorithm to textile image 2 and 3 because some of the dominant colors only occupied very small areas in these two images, and it is difficult for us to pick large enough training blocks from those images.

The belief propagation approach [14] can be used to approximate the MAP solutions to MRF problems. The local minima found by BP are minima over "large neighborhoods", so they can produce high accurate segmentation results in practice. In [14] they proposed three algorithmic schemes to improve the running time of the loopy belief propagation approach: the min-convolution algorithm, belief propagation on grid graphs and a multi-grid method which speed up and reduce the memory requirements of belief propagation. In order to allow for large discontinuities in the labelling, the cost function stops growing after the difference becomes large, and they introduced a data term d to $V(x)$ in eq. (13) to control the cost to stop increasing when the discontinuities are large. Another parameter λ is applied to balance between the fidelity of the data cost term $D(x)$ and the smoothness of the discontinuity cost $V(x)$. Both d and λ are selected heuristically. In all the experiments, d is set as 10^4, and λ is set as 15. The iteration number for each scale is set as 10, and the experimental results do not change too much as the iteration number increases above 10. The BP algorithm is good for large homogeneous regions but will simplify fine structures, and good examples are illustrated in Fig.6 and Fig.8.

4. Conclusions

In contrast with natural images, textile images have some very distinctive properties: 1) generally there are a few dominant colors in a textile image, whereas there may exist hundreds of significant colors in a natural image; 2) the fabric texture structure caused by the color halftoning technique in textile printing has a great influence on the colors' appearance in textile images.

The uniform fabric structure (texture noise) makes it a difficult problem for the existing automatic color segmentation methods to extract the dominant colors from textile images. In this chapter, we study various multiscale image segmentation techniques by considering image segmentation as inferring the "best" labeling configuration X from the observed image data Y. The causal properties induced by multiscale structure enable the design of exact, non-iterative inference algorithms. In most multiscale image segmentation techniques, the joint probability density of (X,Y) and the marginal density are modeled as multivariate Gaussian distributions or Gaussian mixtures. Whereas textile images are corrupted by non-

Gaussian texture noise, it is difficult to specify a prior distribution about the size and shape of regions, and this is an open problem of our future research work.

We analyze the performances of different multiscale image segmentation techniques on some representative textile images, and find that the spatial contextual model proposed in [1] can produce high visual quality segmentation results on average. Since these textile images have no ground truth segmentation results, it is difficult for us to evaluate the performances of different techniques quantitatively. So to evaluate the segmentation results quantitatively is also a problem of our future research works.

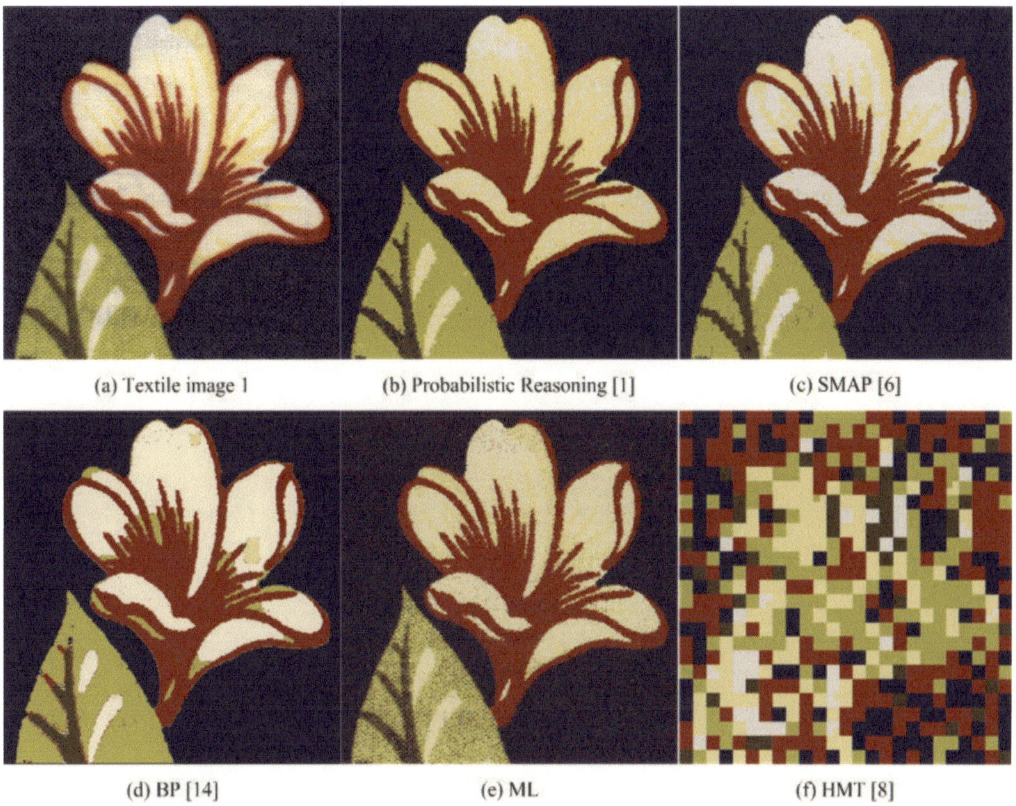

Fig. 5. Segmentation results of textile image 1

(a) Textile image 2 (b) Probabilistic Reasoning [1] (c) SMAP [6] (d) BP [14]

Fig. 6. Segmentation results of textile image 2

(a) Textile image 3 (b) Probabilistic Reasoning [1] (c) SMAP [6] (d) BP [14]

Fig. 7. Segmentation results of textile image 3

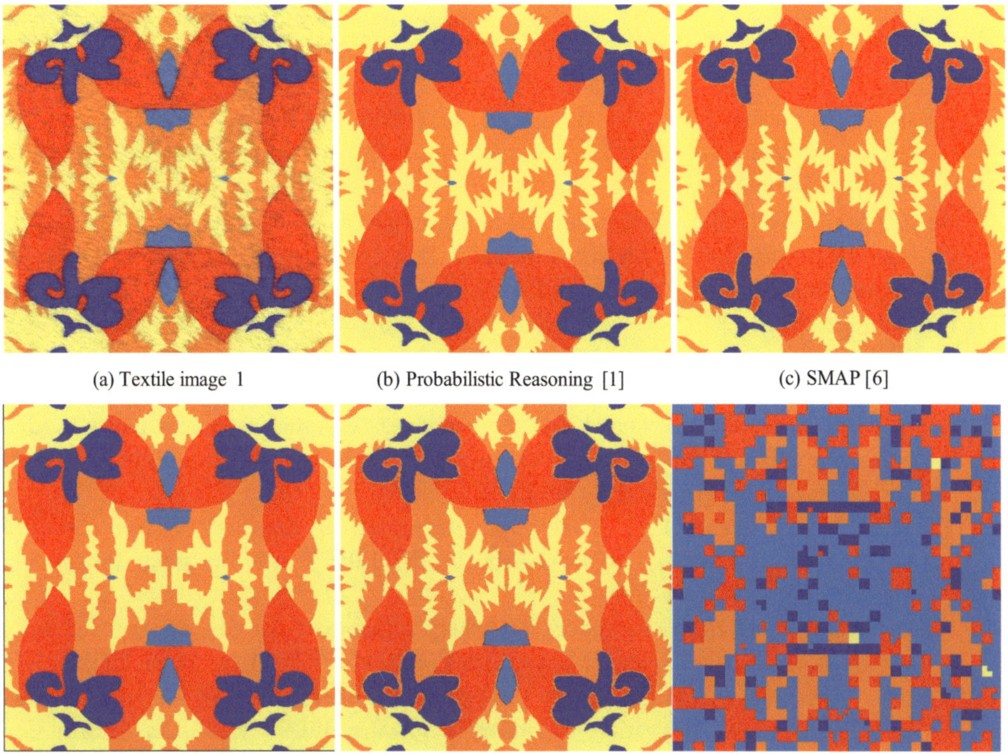

(a) Textile image 1 (b) Probabilistic Reasoning [1] (c) SMAP [6]

(d) BP [14] (e) ML (f) HMT [8]

Fig. 8. Segmentation results of textile image 4

5. References

[1] Lu, X.-Q. (2007). Color textile image segmentation based on multiscale probabilistic reasoning, Optical Engineering, 46(8), Article ID 087002

[2] Lu, X.-Q.; Sakaino, H. (2009). A spatial adaptive filter for smoothing of non-Gaussian texture noise, Proc. of IEEE ICASSP, pp.841-844, Taibei, Apr. 2009, IEEE

[3] Bouman, C.; Liu, B. (1991). Multiple resolution segmentation of textured images, IEEE Trans. On Pattern Analysis and Machine Intelligence, vol.13, no.2, pp.99-113, 1991

[4] Wilsky, A. S. (2002). Multiresolution Markov models for signal and image processing, Proc. of the IEEE, vol.90, no.8, pp.1396-1458, 2002

[5] Laferte, J.-M.; Heitz, F. (2000). Discrete Markov image modeling and inference on the quadtree, IEEE Trans. On Image Processing, vol.9, no.3, pp.390-404, 2000

[6] Bouman, C. A.; Shapiro, M. (1994). A multiscale random field model for Bayesian image segmentation, IEEE Trans. On Image Processing, vol.3, no.2, pp.162-177, 1994

[7] Cheng, H.; Bouman, C. A. (2001). Multiscale Bayesian segmentation using a trainable context model, IEEE Trans. On Image Processing, vol.10, no.4, pp.511-525, 2001

[8] Choi, H.; Baraniu, R. G. (2001). Multiscale image segmentation using wavelet-domain hidden Markov models, IEEE Trans. On Image Processing, vol.10, no.9, pp.1322-1331, 2001

[9] Crouse, M. S.; Nowak, R. D., and Baraniu, R. G. (1998). Wavelet-based statistical signal processing using hidden Markov models, IEEE Trans. On Signal Processing, vol.46, no.4, pp.886-902, 1998

[10] Fan, G.; Xia, X.-G. (2000). Maximum likelihood texture analysis and classification using wavelet-domain hidden Markov models, Proc. of 34th Asilomar Conference on Signals, Systems and Computers, Pacific Grove, CA, 2000

[11] Fan, G.; Xia, X.-G. (2001). A joint multicontext and multiscale approach to Bayesian Image segmentation, IEEE Trans. On Geoscience and Remote Sensing, vol.39, no.12, pp. 2680-2688, 2001

[12] Fan, G.; Xia, X.-G. (2003). Wavelet-based texture analysis and synthesis using hidden Markov models, IEEE Trans. On Circuits and Systems – I: Fundamental Theory and Applications, vol.50, no.1, pp. 106-120, 2003

[13] Cormer, M. L.; Delp, E. J. (1999). Segmentation of textured images using a multiresolution Gaussian autoregressive model, IEEE Trans. On Image Processing, vol.8, no.3, pp.408-420, 1999

[14] Felzenszwalb, P. F.; Huttenlocher, D. P. (2006). Efficient belief propagation for early vision, International Journal of Computer Vision, vol.70, no.1, pp.41-54, 2006

[15] Weiss, Y.; Freeman, W. T. (2001). On the optimality of solutions of the max-product belief-propagation algorithm in arbitrary graphs, IEEE Trans. On Information Theory, vol.47, no.2, pp.736-744, 2001

[16] Xiong, L; Wang, F. & Zhang, C. (2007). Multilevel belief propagation for fast inference on Markov random fields, Proc. of 7th IEEE International Conference on Data Mining, pp.371-380, 2007

18

JSEG Algorithm and Statistical ANN Image Segmentation Techniques for Natural Scenes

Luciano Cássio Lulio, Mário Luiz Tronco and Arthur José Vieira Porto
Engineering School of Sao Carlos, University of Sao Paulo (EESC/USP)
Sao Carlos, Sao Paulo
Brazil

1. Introduction

Computer vision, when used in open and unstructured environments as in the inspection of crops for natural scenes, demands and requires complex analysis of image processing and segmentation algorithms, since these computational methods evaluate and predict environment physical characteristics, such as color elements, complex objects composition, shadows, brightness and inhomogeneous region colors for texture.
Several segmentation algorithms proposed in literature were designed to process images originally characterized by the above-mentioned items. Additionally, agricultural automation may take advantage of computer vision resources, which can be applied to a number of different tasks, such as crops inspection, classification of fruits and plants, estimated production, automated collection and guidance of autonomous machines.
Bearing the afore-named in mind, the present chapter aims the use of JSEG unsupervised segmentation algorithm (Deng et al., 1999a), Statistical Pattern Recognition and Artificial Neural Networks (ANN) Multilayer Perceptron (MLP) topology (Haykin, 2008) as merging processing techniques in order to segment and therefore classify images into predetermined classes (e.g. navigable area, planting area, fruits, plants and general crops). The intended approach to segment classification deploys a customized MLP topology to classify and characterize the segments, which deals with a supervised learning by error correction - propagation of pattern inputs with changes in synaptic weights in a cyclic processing, with accurate recognition as well as easy parameter adjustment, as an enhancement of iRPROP algorithm (*improved resilient back-propagation*) (Igel and Hüsken, 2003) derived from *Back-propagation* algorithm, which has a faster identification mapping process, that verifies what region maps have similar matches through the explored environment.
To carry through this task, a feature vector is necessary for color channels histograms (layers of primary color in a digital image with a counting graph that measures how many pixels are at each level between black and white). After training process, the mean squared error (MSE), denotes the best results achieved by segment classification to create the image-class map, which represents the segments into distinct feature vectors. Several metrics (vector bundle) can be part of a feature vector, however, a subset of those which describes and evaluates appropriate classes of segments should be chosen.

2. JSEG image segmentation

Color images with homogeneous regions are segmented with an algorithm to generate clusters in the color space/class (different measures classes in spectral distribution, with distinct intensity of visible electro-magnetic radiation at many discrete wavelengths) (Cavani, 2007). One way to segment images with textures is to consider the spatial arrangement of pixels using a region-growing technique whereby a homogeneity mode is defined with pixels grouped in the segmented region. Furthermore, in order to segment texture images one must consider different scales of images.

An unsupervised color-texture regions segmentation algorithm is ideal for this purpose, since it tests the homogeneity of a given color-texture pattern, which is computationally more feasible than model parameter estimation. It deals with the following assumptions for the acquired image:

- Image containing homogeneous color-texture regions.
- Color information is represented by quantized colors.
- Colors between two neighboring regions are distinguishable.

The JSEG algorithm segments images of natural scenes properly, without manual parameter adjustment for each image and simplifies texture and color. Segmentation with this algorithm passes through two major stages, namely color space quantization (number reduction process of distinct colors in a given image), and hit rate regions with similar color regions merging, as secondary stage.

In the first stage, the color space is quantized with little perceptual degradation by using the quantization algorithm (Deng *et* al, 1999b; Deng and Manjunath, 2001) with minimum coloring. Each color is associated with a class. The original image pixels are replaced by classes to form the class maps (texture composition) for the next stage.

Before performing the hit rate regions, the J-image - a class map for each windowed color region, whose positive and negative values represent the edges and textures of the processing image - must be created with pixel values used as a similarity algorithm for the hit rate region. These values are called „J-values“ and are calculated from a window placed on the quantized image, where the J-value belongs. Therefore, the two-stage division is justified through the difficult analysis of the colors similarity whital their distributions.

The decoupling of these features (color similarity and spatial distribution) allows tractable algorithms development for each of the two processing stages.

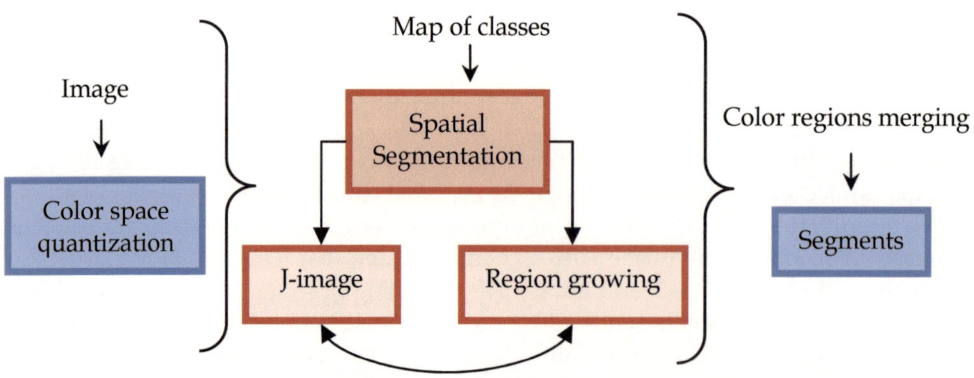

Fig. 1. JSEG image segmentation steps.

2.1 Segmentation algorithm evaluation

Natural scenes present a 24-bit chromatic resolution color image, which is coarsely quantized preserving its major quality. The main idea for a good segmentation criterion is to extract representative colors differentiating neighboring regions in the acquired image, as an unsupervised method.

Therewith, the color quantization using peer group filtering (Deng *et al.*, 199a) is applied through perceptual weighting on individual pixels, to smooth the image and remove the existing noise. Then, new values indicating the smoothness of the local areas are obtained, and a weight is assigned to each pixel, prioritizing textured areas to smooth areas. These areas are identified with a quantization vector to the pixel colors, based on General Lloyd Algorithm (GLA) (Gersho and Gray, 1999), which the perceptually uniform L*u*v color space is adopted, presenting the overall distortion D:

$$D = \sum_i D_i = \sum_i \sum_n v(n) \| x(n) - c_i \|^2 \rightarrow x(n) \in C_i \tag{1}$$

And it is derived for:

$$c_i = \frac{\sum v(n) x(n)}{\sum v(n)} \rightarrow x(n) \in C_i \tag{2}$$

The parameters: c_i is the centroid of cluster C_i, $x(n)$ and $v(n)$ are the color vector and the perceptual weight for pixel n. D_i is the total distortion for C_i.

With the centroid value, as denoted by Equation (2) - after the vector quantization and merged clusters, pixels with the same color have two or more clusters, affected by GLA global distortion. For merging close clusters with minimum distance between preset thresholds for two centroids, an agglomerative clustering algorithm is performed on c_i (Duda and Hart, 1970), as the quantization parameter needed for spatial distribution.

After clustering merging for color quantization, a label is assigned for each quantized color, representing a color class for image pixels quantized to the same color. The image pixel colors are replaced by their corresponding color class labels, creating a class-map.

segmented class-map 1	not segmented class-map 2
+ + + + + + + + +	+ # + # + # + # +
+ + + + + + + + +	- + - + - + - + -
+ + + + + + + + +	+ # + # + # + # +
- - - - - - - - -	- + - + - + - + -
- - - - - - - - -	+ # + # + # + # +
- - - - - - - - -	- + - + - + - + -
# # # # # # # # #	+ # + # + # + # +
# # # # # # # # #	- + - + - + - + -
# # # # # # # # #	+ # + # + # + # +

Fig. 2. Two different class-map representing three distinct classes of data points.

In Figure 2, class-map 1 indicates three regions containing a single class of data points for segmentation process, and class-map 2 is not segmented indicating a color uniformity.

The symbols (+, -, #) denotes the label values (*J-value*) for three distinct data points. All necessary segmentation information, after color quantization, is extracted and relocated to a class-map. A specific region contains pixels from a color class set, which is distributed in image regions. These regions, forming each one, a class-map, has distributed points in all spatial data segments, corresponding a two-dimensional plane, and represents the cartesian position vector *(x,y)*.
In order to calculate the J-value, Z is defined as the set of all points of quantized image, then $z = (x, y)$ with $z \in Z$ and being m the average in all Z elements. C is the number of classes obtained in the quantization. Then Z is classified into C classes, Z_i are the elements of Z belonging to class i, where $i=1,...,C$, and m_i are the element averages in Z_i.

$$m = \frac{1}{N}\sum_{z \in Z} z \tag{3}$$

$$m_i = \frac{1}{N_i}\sum_{z \in Z} z \tag{4}$$

The J-value is as follows:

$$J = \frac{S_B}{S_W} = \frac{(S_T - S_W)}{S_W} \tag{5}$$

$$\text{where: } S_T = \sum_{z \in Z} \|z - m\|^2 \tag{6}$$

$$S_W = \sum_{i=1}^{C}\sum_{z \in Z} \|z - m_i\|^2 \tag{7}$$

The parameter S_T represents the sum of quantized image points within the average in all Z elements. Thereby, the relation between S_B and S_W, denotes the measures of distances of this class relation, for arbitrary nonlinear class distributions. J for higher values indicates an increasing distance between the classes and points for each other, considering images with homogeneous color regions. The distance and consequently, the J value, decrease for images with uniformly color classes.
Each segmented region could be recalculated, instead of the entire class-map, with new parameters adjustment for $\bar{J}$ average. J_K represents J calculated over region k, M_k is the number of points in region k, N is the total number of points in the class-map, with all regions in class-map summation.

$$\bar{J} = \frac{1}{N}\sum_{k} M_k J_k \tag{8}$$

For a fixed number of regions, a criterion for $\bar{J}$ is intended for lower values.

2.2 Spatial segmentation technique

The global minimization of $\bar{J}$ is not practical, if not applied to a local area of the class-map. Therefore, the idea of *J-image* is the generation of a gray-scale image whose pixel values are

the J values calculated over local windows centered on these pixels. With a higher value for J-image, the pixel should be near region boundaries.
Expected local windows dimensions determines the size of image regions, for intensity and color edges in smaller sizes, and the opposite occurs detecting texture boundaries.

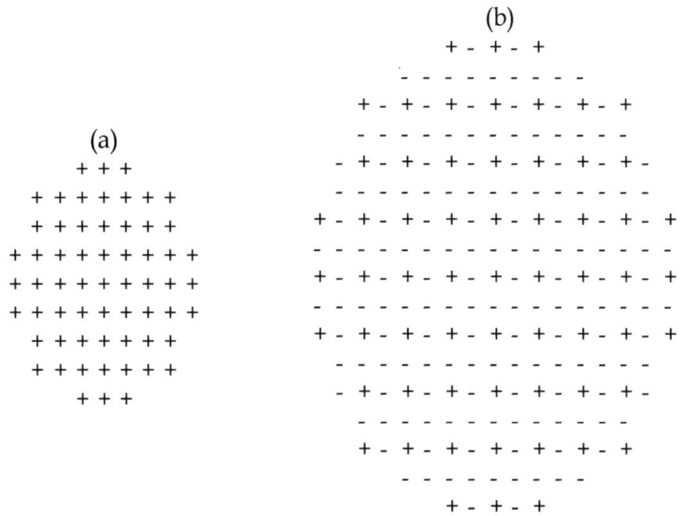

Fig. 3. (a) A 9x9 circular window to avoid rectangular objects bias for local J values; (b) A downsampling scale 2, for a 17x17 window.

Using a region-growing method to segment the image, this one is considered initially as one single region. The algorithm for spatial segmentation starts segment all the regions in the image at an initial large scale until the minimum specified scale is reached. This final scale is settled manually for the appropriate image size. The initial scale 1 corresponds to 64x64 image size, scale 2 to 128x128 image size, scale 3 to 256x256 image size, with due proportion for increasing scales and the double image size.
Below, in Figure 4, the spatial segmentation algorithm is structured in flow steps.

2.2.1 Valley determination

A heuristics for the valley determination, presupposes a condition for small initial regions to be determined as the pattern growing. These regions have the lowest J values (valleys). As follows:

a. Calculate the standard deviation and the average of the local J values in the region, denoted by σ_J and μ_J, respectively.
b. Threashold for parameters above:

$$T_J = \mu_J + a\sigma_J \tag{9}$$

The condition to consider candidate valley points for pixels with local J values is determined $T_J > J$. Connect the points based on the 4-connectivity and obtain the valleys.

a. For candidate valleys smaller than the spatial segmentation relation between scale and image size, they are denoted as valleys.

b. A preset parameter values [-0.6, -0.4, -0.2, 0, 0.2, 0.4] is given for variable *a*, which gives the most number of valleys.

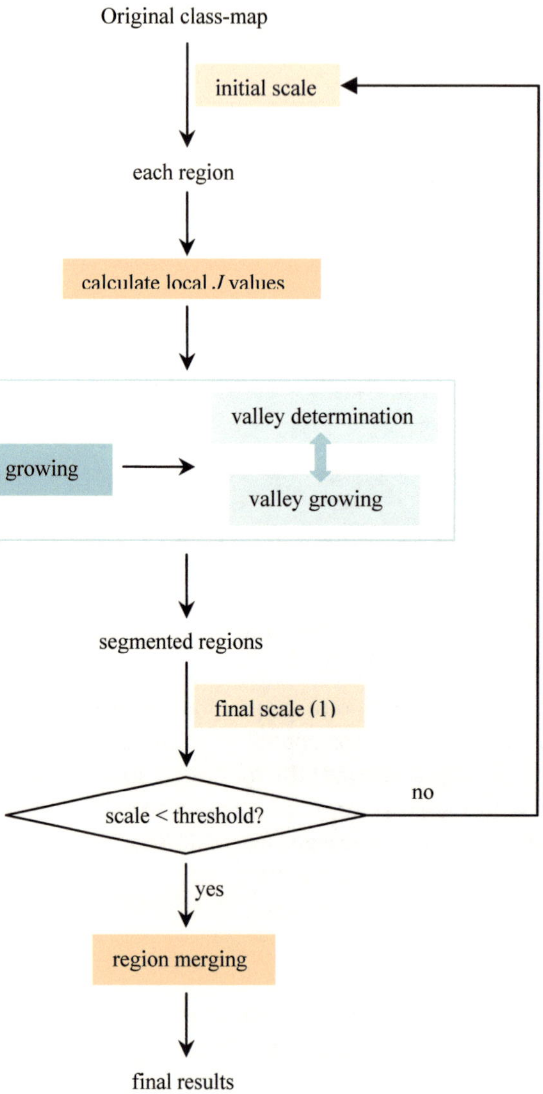

Fig. 4. Sequence for spatial segmentation algorithm.

2.2.2 Valley growing and region merge

After valley determination, the new regions grow from the valleys, which obey the following rules:

c. Non-determined pixels must be removed in the valleys, producing the local *J* values average in the remaining unsegmented regions. Then, pixels are connected below the average to form growing areas, and if these are adjacent to one and only one valley, they are assigned to that valley.

d. Calculate local *J* values for the remaining pixels at the corresponding scale to locate the boundaries regions.
e. Grow the remaining pixels at the final scale. Unclassified pixels at valley boundaries are stored in a buffer. The buffer is updated when all pixels are classified.

An initial segmentation of the image is obtained, after region growing, providing over-segmented regions, merged on their color similarity. The quantized colors represent color histogram bins and their distance features are calculated through the regions extraction. This distance means the Euclidean distance between two neighboring regions. The pair of regions with minimum distance is merged together. All distances are stored in a database and it is updated when an estimate for color feature vector and the corresponding region is calculated. The process continues until a maximum threshold for the distance is reached. After region merging, the final segmentation results are obtained.

3. Programming (Color quantization and spatial distribution)

The sequential images in Figure 5 evince not only the color quantization (spatial distributions forming a map of classes), but also the space segmentation (J-image representing edges and regions of textured side).

Several window sizes are used by J-values: the largest detects the region boundaries by referring to texture parameters; the lowest detects changes in color and/or intensity of light. Each window size is associated with a scale image analysis. The concept of J-image, together with different scales, allows the segmentation of regions by referring to texture parameters.

Regions with the lowest values of J-image are called valleys. The lowest values are applied with a heuristic algorithm. Thus, it is possible to determine the starting point of efficient growth, which depends on the addition of similar valleys. The algorithm ends when there are spare pixels to be added to those regions.

Figures 6 to 10 illustrate not only color quantization and spatial distributions of J-image in others natural scenes, but the flood fill implemented algorithm, for determining the boundaries edges connected on the region growing areas (using queue data structure provided from region valleys). All scenes were submitted to a gradient magnitude, as segmentation function rating (Sobel masks for higher values at the borders of navigation areas and lower values inside planting areas), then image is segmented with a watershed transform directly on the gradient magnitude. JSEG outperforms the evaluation for all images, with an effective spatial distribution on planting lines.

4. Artificial Neural Networks (ANN) and statistical pattern recognition

Due to the nature of nonlinear vectors, it is fundamental that an ANN-based classification method associated with a statistical pattern recognition be used. *Multi-Layer Perceptron* (MLP) is suitable for default ANN topology to be implemented through a customized *back-propagation* algorithm for complex patterns.

The most appropriate segment and topology classifications are those using vectors extracted from HSV color space (Hue, Saturation, Value), matching RGB color space (Red, Green, Blue) components. Also, the network with less MSE in the neurons to color space proportion is used to classify the entities.

Statistical methods are employed as a combination of results with ANN, showing how accuracy in non-linear features vectors can be best applied in a MLP algorithm with a

(a) (b) (c)

Fig. 5. (a) Original images; (b) Color quantization (map of classes); (c) J-image representing edges and regions of textured side (Spatial distributions).

Fig. 6. JSEG segmentation and watershed transform of gradient magnitude in flood fill class-map for scene 1.

Fig. 7. JSEG segmentation and watershed transform of gradient magnitude in flood fill class-map for scene 2.

Fig. 8. JSEG segmentation and watershed transform of gradient magnitude in flood fill class-map for scene 3.

Fig. 9. JSEG segmentation and watershed transform of gradient magnitude in flood fill class-map for scene 4.

Fig. 10. JSEG segmentation and watershed transform of gradient magnitude in flood fill class-map for scene 5.

statistical improvement, which processing speed is essentially important, for pattern classification. *Bayes Theorem* and *Naive Bayes* both use a technique for iterations inspection, namely MCA (*Main Component Analysis*), which uses a linear transformation that minimizes co-variance while it maximizes variance. Features found through this transformation are totally uncorrelated, so the redundancy between them is avoided. Thus, the components (features) represent the key information contained in data, reducing the number of dimensions. Therefore, RGB space color is used to compare the total number of dimensions in feature vectors with HSV. With a smaller dimension of iterations, HSV is chosen as the default space color in most applications.

Bayes Theorem introduces a modified mathematical equation for the Probability Density Function (PDF), which estimates the training set in a conditional statistics. Equation (4) denotes the solution for $p(C_i \mid y)$ relating the PDF to conditional class i (classes in natural scene), and y is a n-dimensional feature vector. *Naive Bayes* implies independence for vector features, what means that each class assumes the conditional parameter for the PDF, following Equation (5).

$$P(C_i \mid y) = \frac{p(y \mid C_i)P(C_i)}{\sum_{j=1}^{K} p(y \mid C_j)P(C_j)} \tag{10}$$

$$P(y \mid C_i) = \prod_{j=1}^{n} p(y_j \mid C_i) \tag{11}$$

Thus, the following items detail these merging techniques for image processing and pattern recognition as far as generated and customized segmenting algorithms are concerned withal. As a result, a modular strategy with JSEG algorithm, ANN and Bayes statistical theorem approach is essential for based applications on agricultural scenes.

4.1 Multilayer perceptron customized algorithm

Derived from back-propagation, the iRPROP algorithm (improved resilient back-propagation) (Cavani, 2007) is both fast and accurate, with easy parameter adjustment. It features an Octave (Eaton, 2006) module which was adopted for the purposes of this work

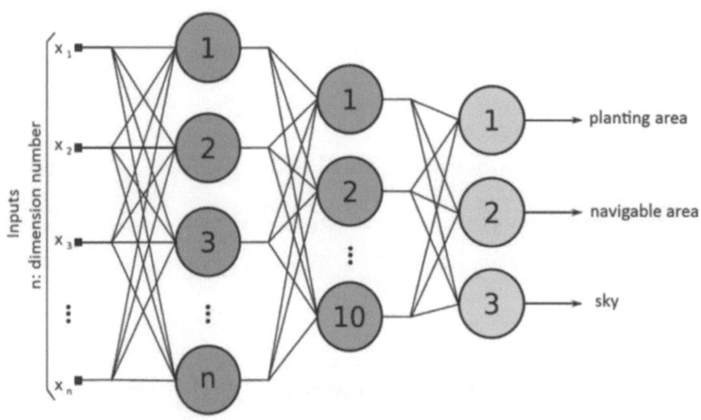

Fig. 11. ANN schematic topology for planting lines with three classes.

and it is classified with HSV (H - hue, S - saturation, V - value) color space channels histograms of 256 categories (32, 64,128 and 256 neurons in a hidden layer training for each color space channel: H, HS, and HSV). The output layer has three neurons, each of them having a predetermined class.

All ANN-based topologies are trained with a threshold lower than 0.0001 mean squared errors (MSE), the synaptic neurons weights are initiated with random values and the other algorithm parameters were set with Fast Artificial Neural Network (FANN) library (Nissen, 2006) for Matlab (Mathworks Inc.) platform, and also its Neural Network toolbox. The most appropriate segment and topology classifications are those using vectors extracted from HSV color space. Also, a network with less MSE in the H-64 was used so as to classify the planting area; for class navigable area (soil), HSV-256 was chosen; as for the class sky, the HS-32.

5. Normalization and feature extraction

This section tackles how statistical methods were employed as a combination of results with ANN, showing how accuracy in non-linear features vectors can be best applied in a MLP algorithm with a statistical improvement, which processing speed is essentially important, for patter classification. The MSE results for each topology, shown in Table 1, were partitioned to eliminate the feature vectors that are distant from the class centroids, so the classifier will deal in less dispersed vectors. Upon observing the following table, which shows the vector distribution in five training sets (20%, 30%, 50%, 70% and 100%), this work approached two probabilistic classification methods in order to match final pattern recognition results with ANN: Bayes theorem and Naive Bayes.

MSE	Neurons	Navigation area	Planting area	Sky
H	32	0,079117	0,098437	0,098574
	64	0,110642	0,098566	0,190555
	128	0,075546	0,079303	0,079874
	256	0,086501	0,023520	0,079111
HS	32	0,089143	0,094905	0,023409
	64	0,099398	0,045956	0,089776
	128	0,049100	0,095064	0,097455
	256	0,057136	0,099843	0,034532
HSV	32	0,089450	0,022453	0,067545
	64	0,059981	0,010384	0,082364
	128	0,049677	0,078453	0,043493
	256	0,038817	0,079856	0,045643

Table 1. MSE results for each topology.

RGB space color is used to compare the total number of dimensions in feature vectors with HSV. With a smaller dimension of iterations, HSV was chosen as the default space color. For such iterations inspection, a technique (main component analysis - MCA) uses a linear transformation that minimizes co-variance while it maximizes variance. Features found through this transformation are totally uncorrelated, so the redundancy between them is avoided. Thus, the components (features) represent the key information contained in data, reducing the number of dimensions (Costa and Cesar Jr, 2001; Haykin, 1999; Comaniciu and Meer, 1999).

In HSV space color, the Bayesian classifiers have produced results which are similar to RGB, where there is a hit rate when the number of dimensions increases in an accuracy average ranging from 20% to 50%. A maximum rate accuracy for HSV is 0.38817, which occurs for 30% and 6777 dimensions. In RGB space color, Bayesian conventional classifiers are identical to Naive results, because as the dispersion of classes increases, there is an average hit rate, which goes up to 50%. The classifiers concerning the number of dimensions are different from the previous ones, which range from 20% and 30%, where hit rates fall as the number of dimensions increases.

	RGB			HSV		
%	NA	PA	Sky	NA	PA	Sky
20	1029	5486	34	1024	5384	26
30	1345	5768	54	1342	5390	45
50	1390	6094	130	1390	6003	103
70	1409	6298	149	1402	6209	140
100	1503	6300	158	1402	6209	145

Table 2. Vector distribution for RGB and HSV space colors. (Navigation area = NA; Planting are = PA)

As a consequence, Bayesian classifiers in HSV space color, outperforms the other classifiers as shown in "Fig. 12". The average rate of achievement value, together with the number of dimensions *draw a linear convergence* for all vector distribution in the five training sets.

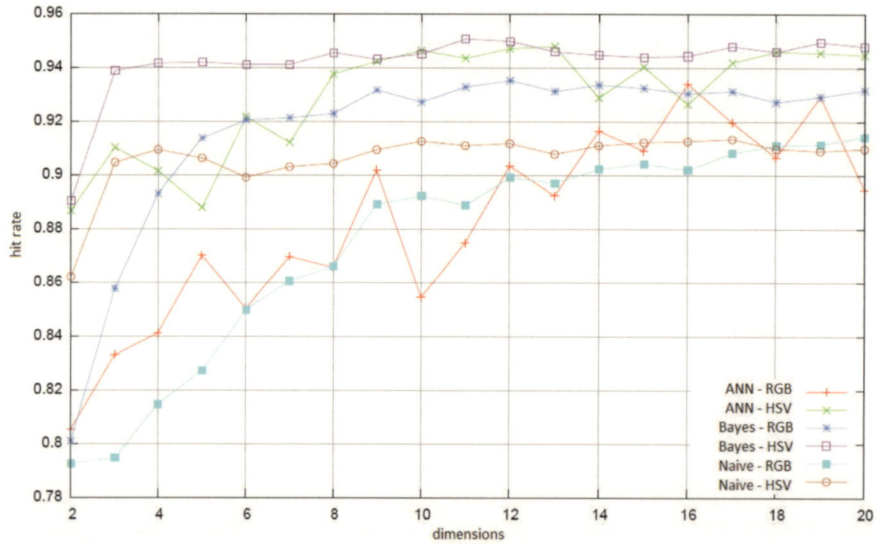

Fig. 12. Average hit rates for the three major training sets.

Although the three methods deliver different performances, yet similar behavior, because the hit rate of the class sky tends to improve owing to the increase in the number of dimensions. Navigation and planting area classes are listed as false feature vectors by the texture similarities in training, which means that ANN and Bayesian must be coupled for improved results.

The following graph about the first components shows that the RGB curves have a higher percentage than most HSV curves. Also, it can be observed that all curves present values lower than 90%.

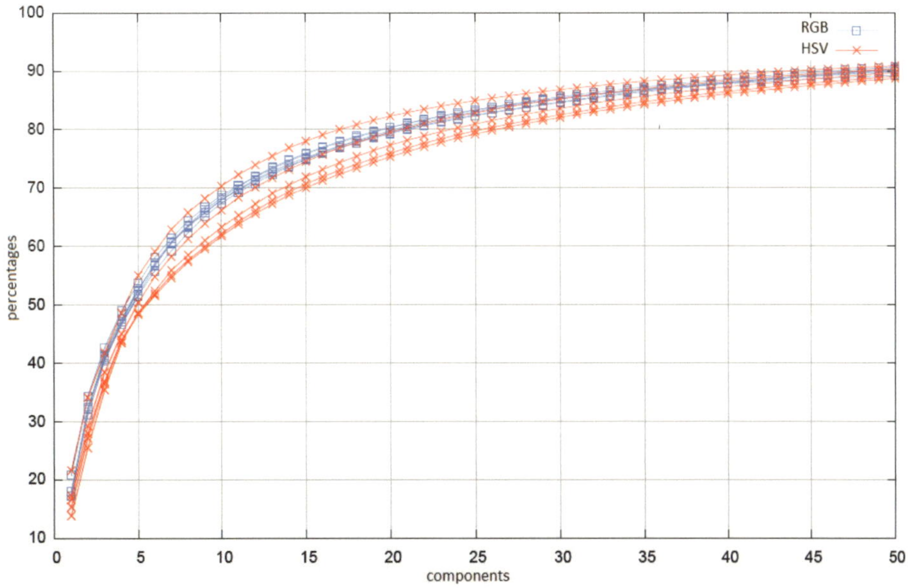

Fig. 13. RGB and HSV relation with amount of dimensions.

After the main component analysis (MCA), the following graph shows the HSV training sets for 100% feature vectors distribution.

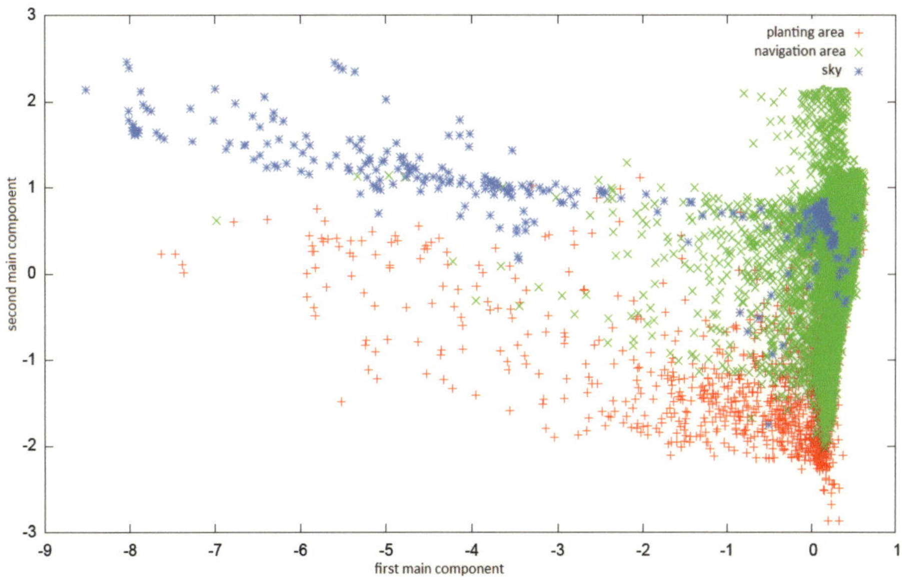

Fig. 14. HSV training set for 100% feature vectors distribution.

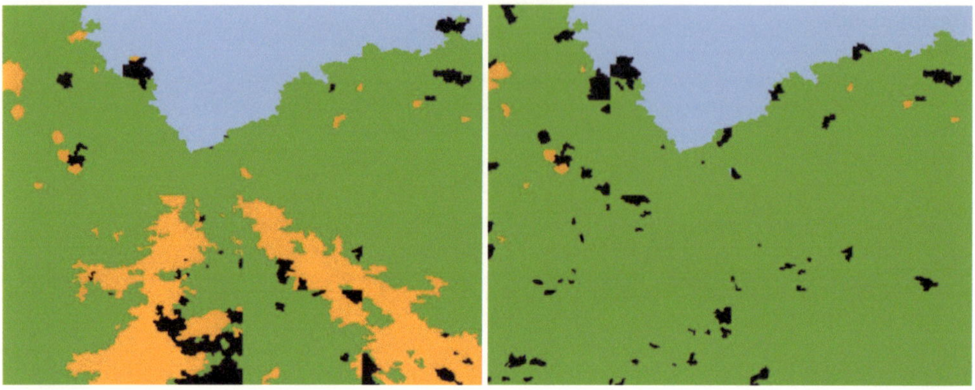

Fig. 15. Class-map 1 – Bayes/HSV and Bayes/RGB.

Fig. 16. Class-map 1 – Naïve Bayes/HSV and Naïve Bayes/RGB.

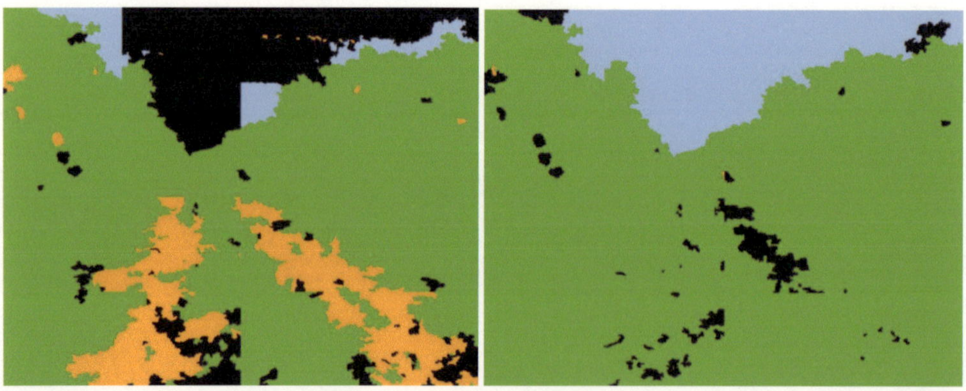

Fig. 17. Class-map 1 – ANN/HSV and ANN/RGB.

Fig. 18. Class-map 2 - Bayes/HSV and Bayes/RGB.

Fig. 19. Class-map 2 - Naïve Bayes/HSV and Naïve Bayes/RGB.

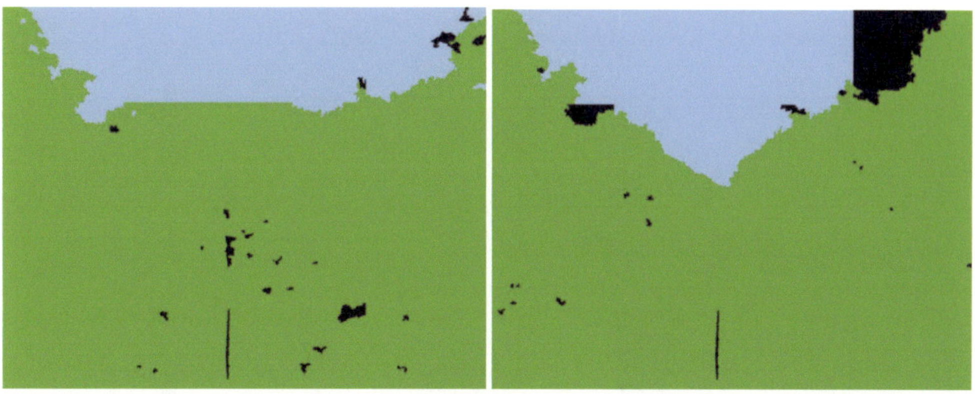

Fig. 20. Class-map 2 - ANN/HSV and ANN/RGB.

Fig. 21. Class-map 3 – Bayes/HSV and Bayes/RGB.

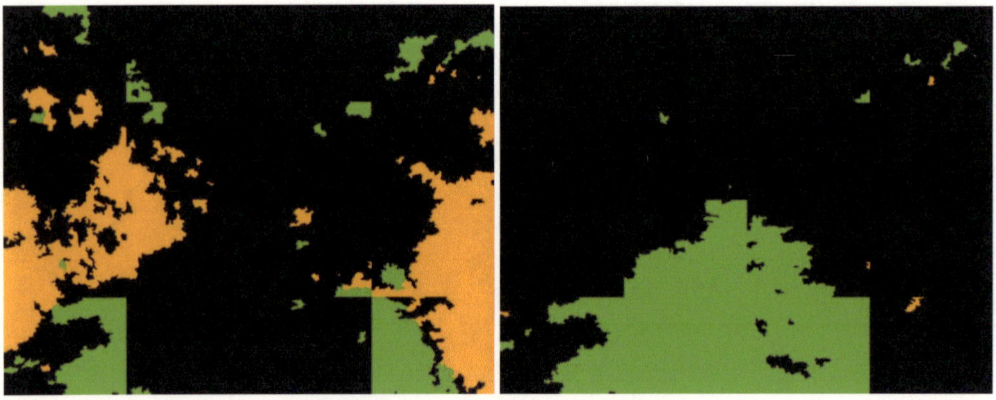

Fig. 22. Class-map 3 – Naïve Bayes/HSV and Naïve Bayes/RGB.

Fig. 23. Class-map 3 – ANN/HSV and ANN/RGB.

The corresponding class maps, the corresponding class-maps for the three first natural scenes in Figure 4, were shown above, for normalization merging techniques and space colors (Bayes/HSV), (Bayes/RGB), (Naive Bayes/HSV), (Naive Bayes/RGB), (ANN/HSV) and (ANN/RGB).

6. Conclusions

This chapter presented merging techniques for segmentation and ANN-statistical classification of navigation agricultural scenes, running multiple segmentation tests with JSEG algorithm possible. As the data provided evince, this generated algorithms fulfils the expectations as far as segmenting is concerned, so that it sorts the appropriate classes (navigation area, planting area and sky). As a result, a modular strategy with ANN and Bayes statistical theorem can be an option for the classification of segments.

Moreover, the classification using different types of feature vectors caused the classification metric to be more accurate and sophisticated with ANN, as well as the HSV color space to have lower MSE in test values. Both JSEG and MLP proved suitable for the construction of an image recognition system.

7. References

Cavani, F. A. Analysis of natural scenes through image segmentation and pattern recognition, (*Master Thesis*) University of Sao Paulo (EESC/USP), 2007.

Comaniciu, D. and Meer, P. Robust analysis of feature spaces: color image segmentation. In: *Conference on Computer Vision and Pattern Recognition*, IEEE Computer Society, 1997.

Costa, L. F. and Cesar Junior, R. M. Shape analysis and classification - Theory and Practice. *1. ed. Boca Raton, Florida, EUA: CRC Press LLC*. ISBN 0-8493-3493-4, 2001.

Deng, Y., Kennedy, C., Moore, M.S., Manjunath, B.S. Peer group filtering and perceptual color image quantization. *Proceedings of the 1999 IEEE International Symposium on Circuits and Systems*, 1999a. v. 4, p. 21-25.

Deng, Y., Manjunath, B.S., Shin, H. Color image segmentation. *Conference on Computer Vision and Pattern Recognition*, IEEE Computer Society, 1999b. p. 446-451, v. 2.

Deng, Y. and Manjunath, B.S. Unsupervised segmentation of color-texture regions in images and videos. *IEEE Transactions on Pattern Analysis and Machine Intelligence* (PAMI '01), vol. 23, no. 8, pp. 800-810, Aug. 2001.

Duda, R.O. and Hart, P.E. *Pattern Classification and Scene Analysis*, John Wiley & Sons, New York, 1970.

Eaton, J.W. *et* al. Octave. Avaliable at: http://www.octave.org. (02/12/2006).

Gersho, A. and Gray, R.M. *Vector quantization and signal compression*, Kluwer Academic, Norwell, MA, 1992.

Haykin, S. Neural networks: a comprehensive foundation. *2. ed. New Jersey, EUA: Prentice-Hall*. ISBN 0-13-273350-1, 1999.

Haykin, S. Neural Networks and Learning Machines. *3.ed. McMaster University, Canada: Prentice-Hall*. ISBN 0131471392, 2008.

Igel, C., Hüsken, M. Empirical evaluation of the improved Rprop learning algorithm. *Neurocomputing*, v. 50, p. 105-123, 2003.
Nissen, S. *et al.* Fann: fast artificial neural network library. Avaliable at: http://leenissen.dk/fann/ (02/12/2006).

19

Image Segmentation of Ziehl-Neelsen Sputum Slide Images for Tubercle Bacilli Detection

R. A. A. Raof[1], M. Y. Mashor[2], R. B. Ahmad[1] and S. S. M. Noor[3]
[1]*School of Computer and Communication Engineering, Universiti Malaysia Perlis*
[2]*School of Mechatronics Engineering, Universiti Malaysia Perlis*
[3]*School of Medical Science, Universiti Sains Malaysia*
Malaysia

1. Introduction

Tuberculosis (TB) remains one of the leading causes of death in developing countries and its recent resurgences in both developed and developing countries warrants global attention. Globally, there were an estimated of 9.27 million incident cases of TB in 2007. This is an increase from 9.24 million cases in 2006, 8.3 million cases in 2000 and 6.6 million cases in 1990. Most of the estimated numbers of cases in 2007 were in Asia (55%) and Africa (31%), with small proportions of cases in the Eastern Mediterranean Region (6%), the European Region (5%) and the Region of the Americas (3%). The five countries that rank first to fifth in terms of total numbers of cases in 2007 are India (2.0 million), China (1.3 million), Indonesia (0.53 million), Nigeria (0.46 million) and South Africa (0.46 million). Of the 9.27 million incident TB cases in 2007, an estimated 1.37 million (15%) were HIV-positive; 79% of these HIV-positive cases were in the African Region and 11% were in the South-East Asia Region (WHO, 2009).

Ziehl-Neelsen stain method is one of the common techniques that are being used to diagnose the TB infection. Smear microscopy with Ziehl-Neelsen technique has been the main means of diagnosing TB patients in developing countries. This is because the method is simple, rapid, reproducible, low cost and effective in detecting infectious disease such as TB (Luna, 2004). TB diagnosis is usually being done manually by microbiologist through microscopic examination of sputum specimen of TB patients for pulmonary TB diseases.

However, there are some problems that have been reported with manual screening process, such as time consuming and labor-intensive, especially for screening of the negative slides. (Veropoulus et al., 1998). When reporting the results of the microscopic examination, the microbiologist should provide the clinician with an estimation of the number of acid-fast bacilli detected. If the smear microscopy is clearly positive, very little observation time is needed to confirm the result. The slide is classified as TB positive if at least one tubercle bacilli is found in 300 microscopic fields. The case will then be classified into one of four severity category if the smear on the slide is found to be positive, according to the number of tubercle bacilli found in the slide. For a well-trained microbiologist, it takes 15 to 20 minutes to read and confirm one negative slide, with an average of 25 slides can be read per day. In addition, for some developing countries, there is also a lack of well-trained microbiologist, which may results in overload, fatigue and reduces the diagnostic performance (Khutlang et al., 2009). Therefore, an automated TB diagnosis is required so that large number of cases can be handled with the same accuracy and speeding up the process while improving the low sensitivity of manual TB diagnosis.

In this research, images of Ziehl-neelsen sputum slide are captured using a digital camera attached to a light microscope and displayed on a computer screen. In order to extract the TB bacilli pixels from the TB slide images, several image processing techniques are required. One of the image processing techniques is image segmentation, which is useful to classify the pixels in the image into two region, TB and background. The sputum specimen that has undergone the process of staining using Ziehl-Neelsen procedure will make the TB bacilli appear red and other cells and organisms in the sputum smear sample will retained blue background. Image segmentation is a part of image processing technique that will help to discriminate between the TB bacilli and background pixels in the digital image.

There are many attempts already been made to enable the image captured by a camera that is attached to the microscope to be viewed through the computer screen. Some image processing algorithms also have been developed in order to carry out automatic TB bacilli detection in the captured image. Forero applied adaptive color thresholding technique to the images that have been captured using fluorescence microscopy (Forero et al., 2003; Forero et al., 2004). Veropoulos used an identification method based on shape descriptors and neural network classifiers (Veropoulus et al., 1998; Veropoulus et al., 1999). Wilkinson proposed a rapid multi resolution segmentation technique based on computing thresholds for different areas in a monochromatic image (Wilkinson, 1996). The studies mentioned above used images captured from fluorescence microscope, which appear different from Ziehl-Neelsen sputum slide images captured under light microscope.

In this study, a method of grey thresholding technique is reviewed, and it is then being adapted to suit with color images. Thus the color thresholding algorithm is expected to be able to discriminate between the pixels that comprises the mycobacterium and sputum in the Ziehl-Neelsen slide images. The outcome of this study should be able to provide a way of getting the suitable threshold values for the images and using the values to achieve the main objective of color thresholding and image segmentation.

2. Image segmentation

Segmentation process subdivides an image into its constituent regions or objects. The level of subdivision depends on the problem being solved, where the segmentation should stop when the objects of interest in an application have been isolated. Image segmentation algorithms generally are based on one of the two basic properties of intensity values: discontinuity and similarity. Thresholding is a method of similarity category. It partitions an image into regions that are similar according to a set of predefined criteria. There are various thresholding techniques and it is also a fundamental approach to segmentation that enjoys a significant degree of popularity, especially in applications where speed is an important factor (Gonzalez & Woods, 2002).

Traditionally, one simple way to accomplish thresholding is by defining a range of brightness value in the original image, then selects the pixels within the range as belonging to the foreground and rejects all of other pixels to the background. Such an image is then usually displayed as a binary or two-level image (Sezgin & Sankur, 2004).

The general rule for grey level pixel thresholding is as in Equation (1).

$$g(x,y) = \begin{cases} 0, f(x,y) < T, \\ 1, f(x,y) \geq T, \end{cases} \tag{1}$$

where T is the threshold value, $f(x,y)$ is the original pixel value, and $g(x,y)$ is the resulted pixel value after thresholding has been done. Equation (1) specifies 0 and 1 as output values, which will give the result as a true binary image. Equation (1) can be further visualized by Figure 1 as mappings of input grey level to output grey level (Efford, 2000).

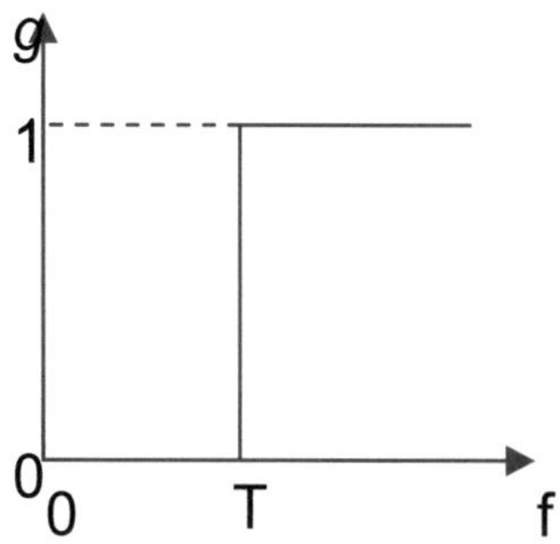

Fig. 1. Thresholding for a single threshold

There could be more than one thresholding value at a time, which change Equation (1), to

$$g(x,y) = \begin{cases} 0, f(x,y) < T_1, \\ 1, T_1 \leq f(x,y) \leq T_2, \\ 0, f(x,y) > T_2. \end{cases} \tag{2}$$

where $T1$ is the lower threshold value and $T2$ is the upper threshold value.

Figure 2 shows the visualization of how thresholding with a pair of threshold is being done (Efford, 2000).

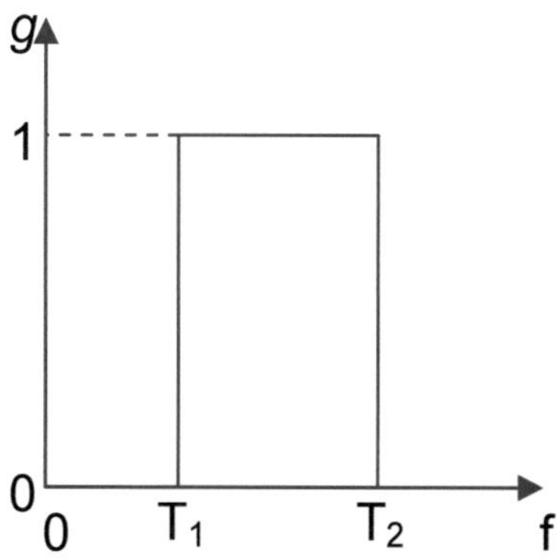

Fig. 2. Thresholding with a pair of threshold

For color images, more than one variable characterises each pixel in the image, which allows multi spectral thresholding (Otsu, 1979). In color imaging, each pixel is characterised by three red, green and blue (RGB) values. However, with multi spectral or multilayer images such as RGB model, it can be difficult to specify the selection criteria. The logical extension of thresholding is simply to place brightness thresholds on each image, for instance to specify the range of red, blue and green intensities.

These multiple criteria are then usually combined with an AND operation (i.e. the pixel is defined as part of the foreground if its three RGB components all lie within the selected range). This logically equivalent to segmenting each image plane individually, creating separate binary images and then combining them with a Boolean AND operator afterward. This color thresholding method is widely used in the image segmentation (Forero et al., 2003; Forero et al., 2004; Mancas-Thillou & Gosselin, 2005).

3. Methodology

In this study, a conventional thresholding method has been adopted to suit with color images of Ziehl-Neelsen sputum slide specimen for TB detection. The method is used to segment the image into two regions, which are TB and background (consists of sputum and other bacilli). Figure 3 demonstrates the steps involved in the proposed image segmentation process.

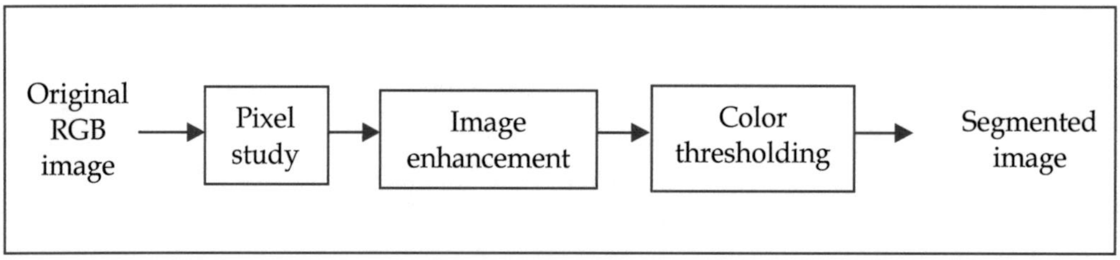

Fig. 3. Block diagram of proposed segmentation process

3.1 Image acquisition

The sputum specimens consist of TB bacilli were obtained from Department of Microbiology and Parasitology, School of Medical Science, Universiti Sains Malaysia, Kubang Kerian. The sputum specimens have been stained using Ziehl-Neelsen staining procedure. The sputum slides were analysed under 40x magnification using LEICA DM-LA microscope and the images were captured using Infinity-2 digital camera attached directly to the microscope. Figure 4 shows few samples of captured sputum slide images consist of TB bacilli. It can be seen that the TB bacilli appear to be red while the sputum background have bluish color.

The original images are images which are directly captured using the digital camera which is attached to the microscope. Since it is manually prepared by the technologist, the thickness of the specimen may vary from one end of the slide to the other end. That is why; it results in the variation in the quality of the images being captured.

3.2 Pixel study

A study on the color information on digital sputum slide images that consist of the tubercle bacilli and sputum was carried out to get the most suitable threshold values. The study was

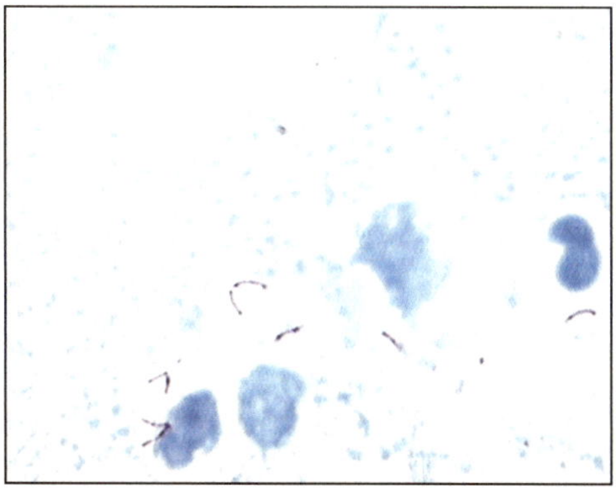

(a)

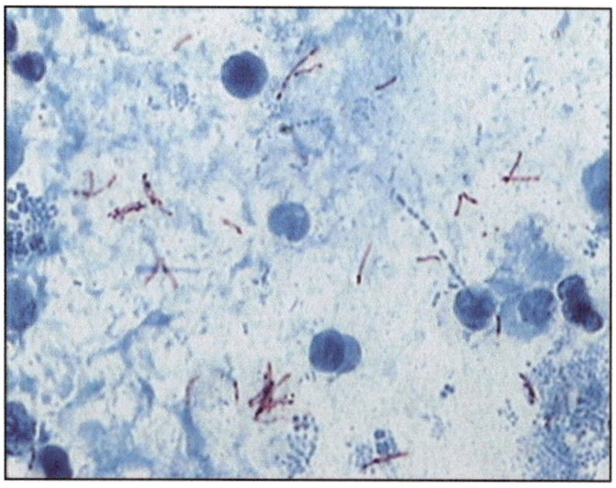

(b)

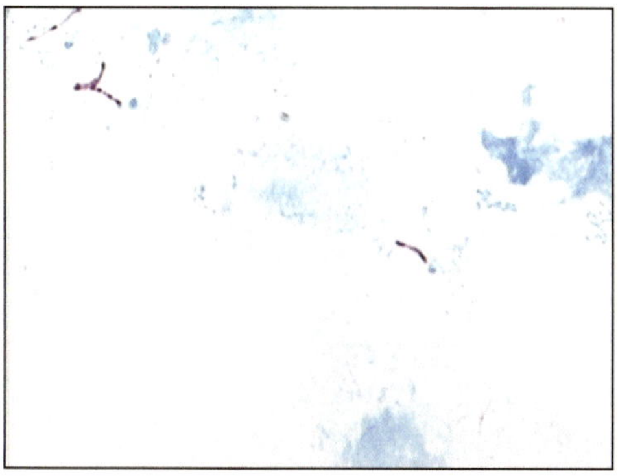

(c)

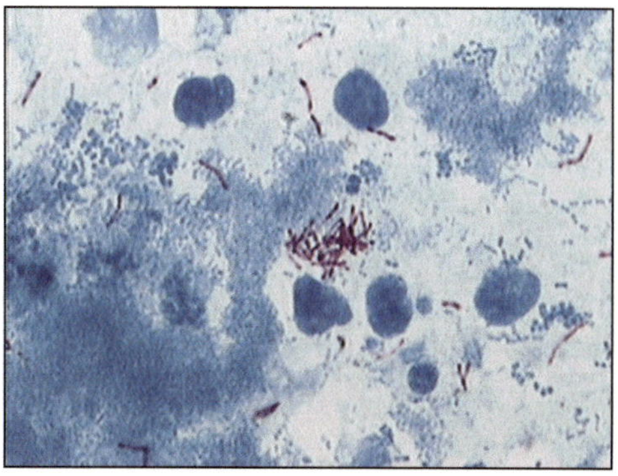

(d)

Fig. 4. Samples of sputum slide images consisting of TB bacilli

carried out on an amount of 244 TB bacilli with more than 2000 pixel samples together with more than 10000 background pixel samples. Sampling is done within five different category of images.

The properties of the RGB pixels are being studied to extract the important features from the image. Based on the color information, the color thresholding algorithm should be able to extract the pixels of tubercle bacilli and reject pixels of other objects. In order to view the important properties of each segment so that necessary features and accurate value of threshold can be obtained from the result, the information is being gathered in a table.

Among the features that are noted are the maximum, minimum and average values for each of the RGB components in tubercle bacilli and sputum respectively. It is found that the featured values are different from one category of images to another. Sample of featured values for normal and dark images are shown in Table 1 and Table 2.

	TB			Background		
	MIN	MAX	AVERAGE	MIN	MAX	AVERAGE
RED	14	255	175	14	255	230
GREEN	8	248	157	15	255	239
BLUE	45	255	196	61	255	252

Table 1. RGB information for images in normal category

From the data in Table 1, thresholding rules have been constructed based on average values. Rules for images from normal category are shown in Equation (3) – (5).

$$g(x,y)=\begin{cases} f(x,\ y), & red(x,y) < 230, \\ 255, & red(x,y) \geq 230. \end{cases} \tag{3}$$

$$g(x,y)=\begin{cases} f(x,y), green(x,y) < 239, \\ 255, green(x,y) \geq 239. \end{cases} \tag{4}$$

$$g(x,y)=\begin{cases} f(x,y), blue(x,y) < 252, \\ 255, blue(x,y) \geq 252. \end{cases} \tag{5}$$

where $red(x,y)$, $green(x,y)$ and $blue(x,y)$ are the pixel values for each of the red, green and blue components respectively.

	TB			Background		
	MIN	MAX	AVERAGE	MIN	MAX	AVERAGE
RED	5	252	155	0	255	160
GREEN	1	235	148	0	255	188
BLUE	38	255	183	33	255	217

Table 2. RGB information for images in dark category

Since the average values between RGB information for images in normal category and dark category are different, separate set of rules has to be constructed for dark images. Rules for images from dark category are shown in Equation (6) – (8).

$$g(x,y)=\begin{cases} f(x,\ y), & red(x,y) < 160, \\ 255, & red(x,y) \geq 160. \end{cases} \tag{6}$$

$$g(x,y)=\begin{cases} f(x,y), green(x,y) < 188, \\ 255, green(x,y) \geq 188. \end{cases} \tag{7}$$

$$g(x,y)=\begin{cases} f(x,y), blue(x,y) < 217, \\ 255, blue(x,y) \geq 217. \end{cases} \tag{8}$$

However, it is found that rules for one category of images are not universal and it can only be used within that particular image category. For example, rules for images in normal category will not give good result when it is applied to images in dark category. In order to overcome this problem, the images are brought through the image enhancement process so that the all the image from various categories are standardized into one same category.

3.3 Image enhancement

Image enhancement process are carried out to overcome the problem risen in the previous stage. This involves the adjustment of brightness, contrast and color in an image so that the pixel values fall into about the same range. Image enhancement technique that is used in

this study is partial contrast. Stretching method is done by requantizing each pixel value to a new value using pre-specified function. Linear stretching will generally improve the overall contrast of an image.
Contrast stretching is a process that applies auto-scaling method, which is a linear mapping function. It is usually used to enhance the brightness as well contrast level of the image. The general mapping function is shown in Equation (9) (Weeks, 1996).

$$p_k = \frac{(\max - \min)}{(f_{\max} - f_{\min})}(q_k - f_{\min}) + \min \tag{9}$$

Referring to Equation (9), $f_{\max}$ and $f_{\min}$ are the maximum and minimum color level in an input image. Variable max and min are the desired maximum and minimum color level in the output image. q_k is the color level of the input pixel while p_k is the color level of the output pixel. The combination of stretching and compressing process is called partial contrast. A part of the intensity level is being stretched to a new range, while other intensity levels left is being compressed to a different new range as well. The stretching and compressing processes are illustrated by Figure 5.

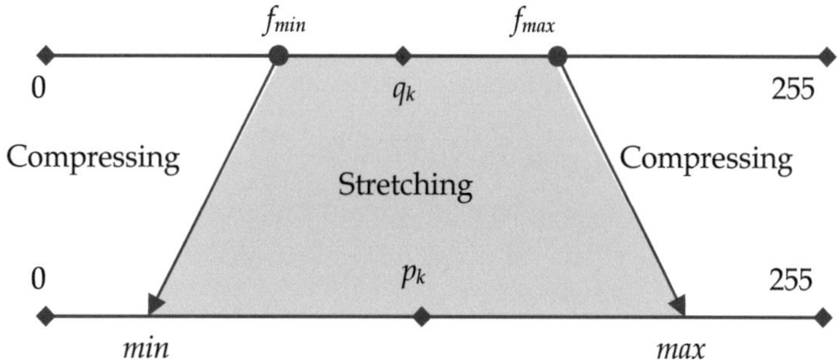

Fig. 5. Illustration of partial contrast process

The process illustrated by Figure 5 can be put into a mathematical function such as in Equation (10).

$$p_k = \begin{cases} \dfrac{\min}{f_{\min}}(q_k) & ;\ \mathit{for}\ q_k < f_{\min} \\[2ex] \dfrac{(\max - \min)}{(f_{\max} - f_{\min})}(q_k - f_{\min}) + \min & ;\ \mathit{for}\ f_{\min} \le q_k \le f_{\max} \\[2ex] \dfrac{(255 - \max)}{(255 - f_{\max})}(q_k - f_{\max}) + \max & ;\ \mathit{for}\ q_k \ge f_{\max} \end{cases} \tag{10}$$

3.4 Color thresholding

The color thresholding technique was carried out based on the color information of the bacterium to extract TB pixels from the sputum and other objects. This technique specifies the range of RGB intensities for thresholding. The objects that lie outside the selection range will be rejected. Therefore, it is very important to determine the selection range because if this threshold cannot acquire a suitable value, the thresholding algorithm will extract pixels other than the expected object.

After image enhancement is done, the process of pixel sampling is done once again using enhanced images and the information is gathered in a table to observe its properties. Table 3 reflect the featured values for all the images that have been enhanced.

	TB			Background		
	MIN	MAX	AVERAGE	MIN	MAX	AVERAGE
RED	0	255	185	0	255	235
GREEN	0	249	161	0	255	246
BLUE	24	255	206	27	255	254

Table 3. RGB information for enhanced images

This time a universal rule for segmentation is produced as in Equation (11) - (13).

$$g(x,y) = \begin{cases} g(x,\ y), & red(x,y) < 235, \\ 255, & red(x,y) \geq 235. \end{cases} \tag{11}$$

$$g(x,y) = \begin{cases} g(x,y), green(x,y) < 246, \\ 255, green(x,y) \geq 246. \end{cases} \tag{12}$$

$$g(x,y) = \begin{cases} 255, blue(x,y) \geq 252, \\ g(x,y), blue(x,y) < 252. \end{cases} \tag{13}$$

From Equations (11), (12), and (13), it can be seen that the original equation that has been mentioned in Equations (1) and (2) have been slightly modified to adopt the method of grey level thresholding to color thresholding. For the new equations, each RGB component is being treated independently. Since there are three components, the thresholding process is being done to one component at a time, and they are then combined into 1 rule using a Boolean AND operator. One more important feature that has been extracted from the information gathered from the study is that in sputum images, the values of green pixels are always greater than the values of red pixels. Therefore, this information also has been adopted as another rule for this thresholding algorithm as in Equation (14).

$$g(x,y) = \begin{cases} 0, green(x,y) < red(x,y), \\ 255, green(x,y) \geq red(x,y). \end{cases} \tag{14}$$

Another modification that has been made is that, the output value is not 0 or 1, but either 255 (white pixel) or retaining the old value of the pixel. This means that if the value of that particular pixel falls in the range of the rule whereby the output value is 255, the original pixel value will be automatically changed to 255, which indicates that it is the area of sputum. However, if it is not fall within that range the original value of the pixel is retained to enable it to go through the next filtering algorithm. Note that since Equation (14) is the last rule for the whole algorithm, then the final value is either 0 (red pixel) or 255 (white pixel).

4. Results

The rules that have been formulated are applied to the original raw image of Ziehl-Neelsen sputum slide. Rules for normal images as shown in Equation (3) - (5) have been applied to these images. The result is good for normal images. However, for other types of images, the result is not satisfactorily achieved. Some of the pixels are lost and in some images, too many noises exist. This is reflected in Figure 6.

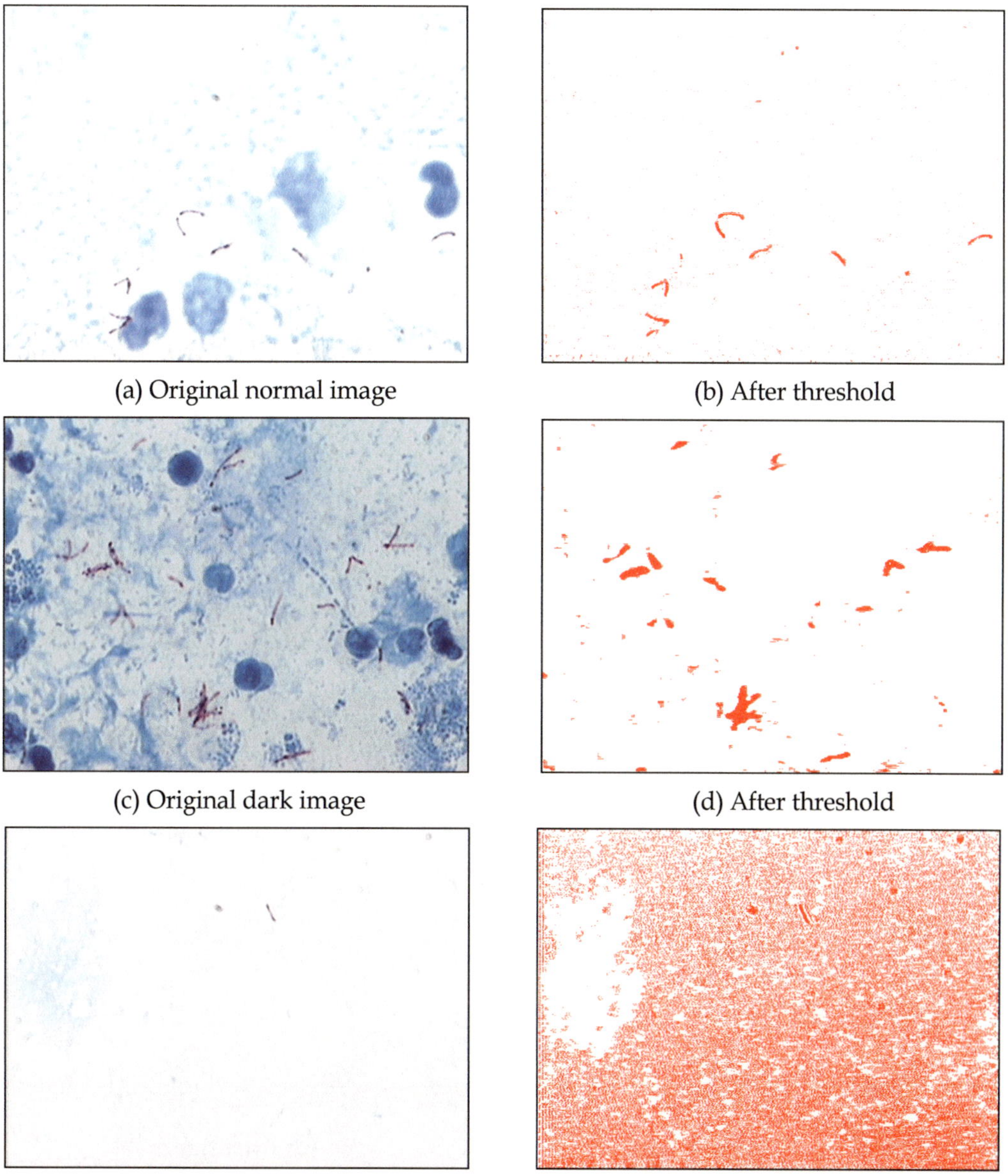

(a) Original normal image
(b) After threshold
(c) Original dark image
(d) After threshold
(e) Original bright image
(f) After threshold

Fig. 6. Original images from normal, dark and bright category with their respective result after applying rules for normal image

However, when the process of thresholding is done to the images with the rules formulated from its own category, the result is satisfying. In Figure 7, samples of dark images are thresholded using rules from dark category as shown in Equation (6) - (8).
In Figure 8, samples of bright images are thresholded using rules from bright category. This result proves that rules for one category of images are not universal and it can only be used within that particular image category. To overcome the poor result, the images are brought through the image enhancement process.
The results of thresholding to the image before the image enhancement process and the results of thresholding to the image after the image enhancement process are shown in Figure 9 to 11 .

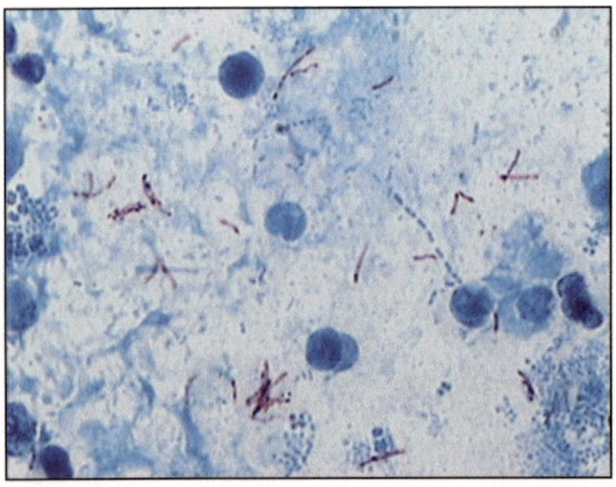

(a) Original dark image 1

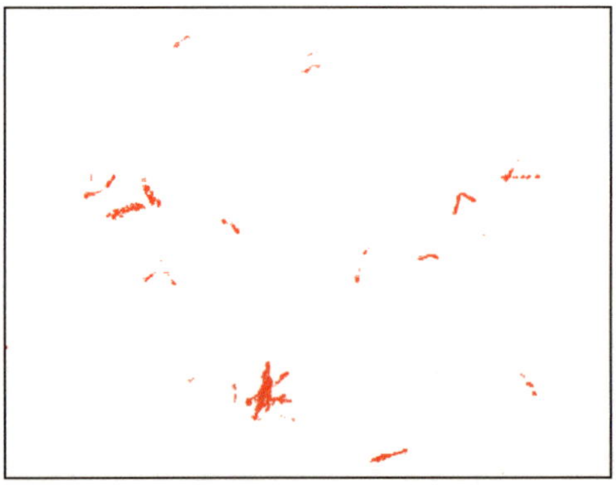

(b) After threshold

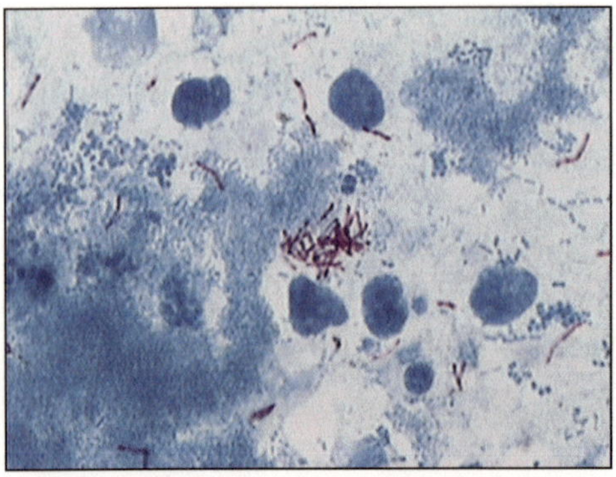

(c) Original dark image 2

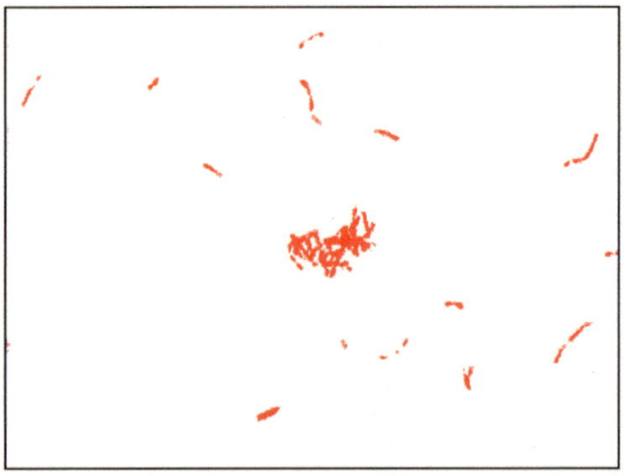

(d) After threshold

Fig. 7. Original images from dark category with the result after applying rules for dark image

(a) Original bright image 1

(b) After threshold

Fig. 8. Original images from bright category with the result after applying rules for bright image

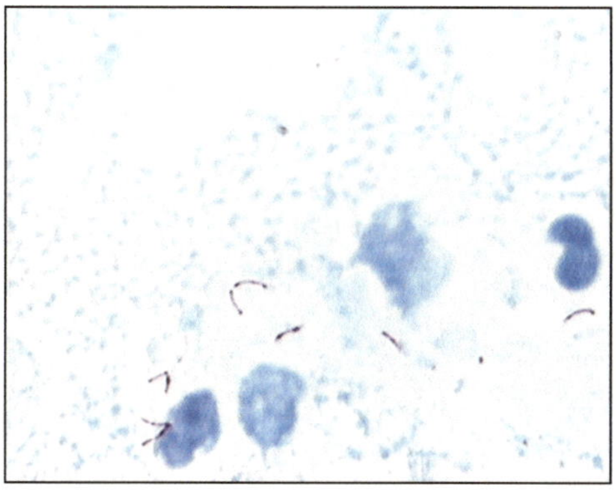

(a) Original Image

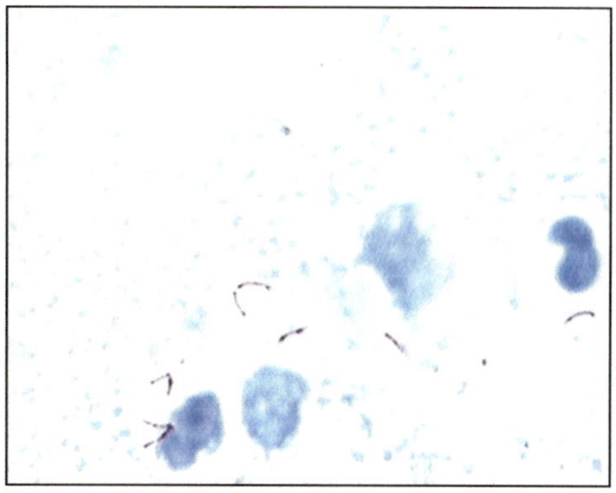

(b) Enhanced image

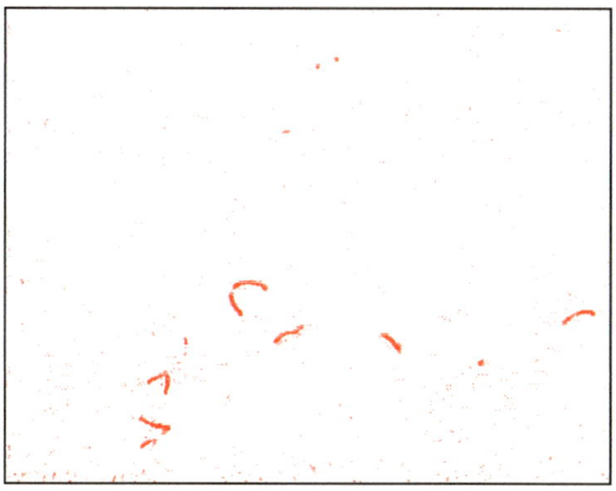

(c) Result of thresholding original image

(d) Result of thresholding enhanced image

Fig. 9. Segmentation result of normal image

In order to determine whether the thresholding method that has been carried out is successful or not, it relies solely on human intervention. Therefore, the threshold value need to be varied until acceptable results are achieved, based on the human observation. That is why, in carrying the color thresholding procedure, it may be necessary to do a few level of thresholding in order to get the best results.

The thresholding procedure must be done to the red, green and blue components. The thresholding on the three colors may be combined into one complete rule using the Boolean AND operator or it may also be separated into two or more rules. If more than one rule is being created, then it is considered to be done on a few level of thresholding. In this study, the process of thresholding is being done automatically based on the predetermined threshold value.

In the case of sputum slide images, it can be seen from the original images that most of the pixels appears to be blue in color. The main objective is to filter out those blue pixels and retain the reddish pixels, which are the tubercle bacilli. Therefore, the first level thresholding has been carried out, which involves pixels of RGB components which have been combined using Boolean AND operator, as mentioned earlier in the methodology part. The second level filtering which involves the difference between green and red pixel is carried out, resulting in a binary image, in which the tubercle bacilli finally appears red, while the background which are originally blue, turn out to be white.

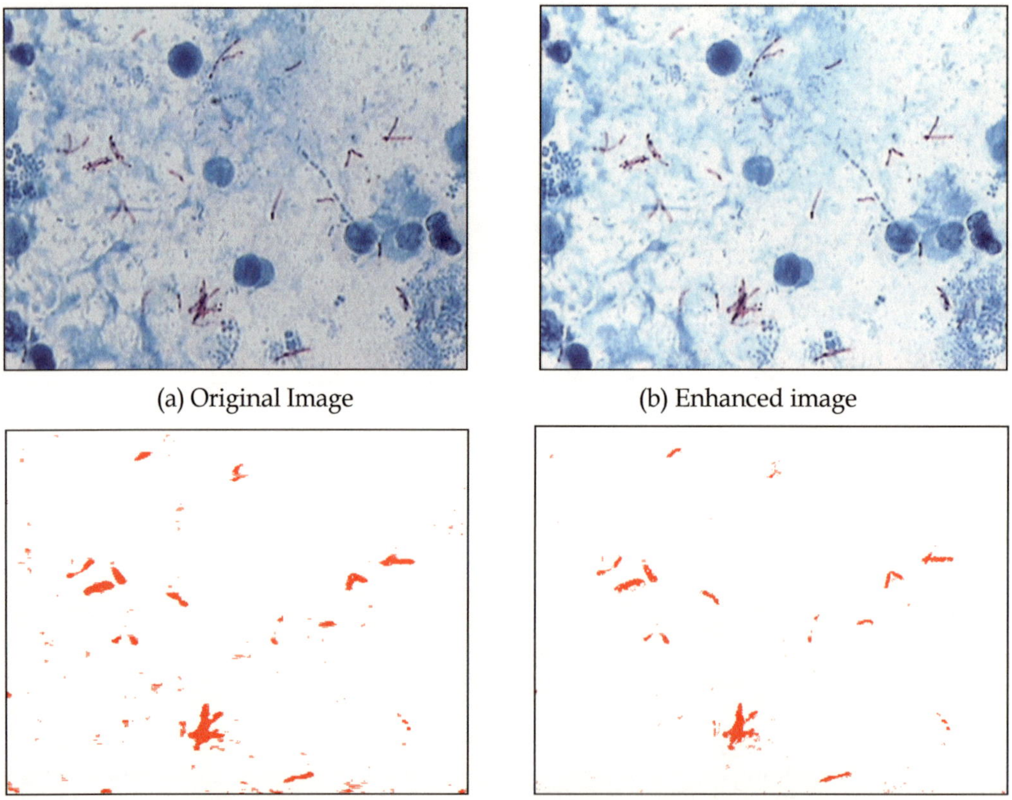

(a) Original Image

(b) Enhanced image

(c) Result of thresholding original image

(d) Result of thresholding enhanced image

Fig. 10. Segmentation result of dark image

From the resulted images that have been presented, it can be said that this technique could be an alternative solution for the image segmentation of TB bacilli, and to further helps the process of TB bacilli identification as well as classification in sputum samples. Most of the research that have been done previously used fluorescence images of sputum (Veropoulos et al., 1998; Veropoulos et al., 1999; Forero et al., 2003; Forero et al., 2004), whereby this research concentrates on the Ziehl-Neelsen stained images of sputum. Hence, it provides another option of TB bacilli identification especially for developing countries which are still sticking to this method for TB detection.

(a) Original Image

(b) Enhanced image

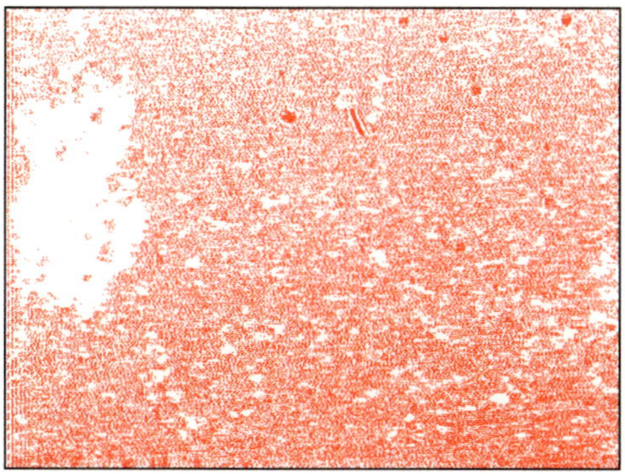

(c) Result of thresholding original image

(d) Result of thresholding enhanced image

Fig. 11. Segmentation result of bright image

5. Conclusion

A technique of image segmentation by conducting a thresholding method for sputum slide images has been presented. The segmentation allows the elimination of a great amount of unwanted pixels, and retained only those pixels characterised to have similar color to the TB bacilli. The key to this method is to conduct a study on the color attribute of the tubercle bacilli in order to get the basic rules of selecting the most accurate threshold value. The resulted images satisfactorily showed that after the image enhancement process, and by using the selected threshold values, the image segmentation method has been able to filter out the sputum images from the tubercle bacilli images.

6. References

Efford, N. (2000). Digital Image Processing: a practical introduction using Java, Pearson Education, ISBN 978-0201596236, USA

Forero, M. G.; Cristobal, G. & Borrego, J. A. (2003). Automatic identification techniques of tuberculosis bacteria, SPIE Proceedings Of The Applications Of Digital Image Processing XXVI, Vol. 5203, pp. 71-81, ISBN 0-8194-5076-6, San Diego, CA, Aug. 2003, SPIE, Bellingham WA

Forero, M. G.; Sroubek, F. & Cristobal, G. (2004). Identification of tuberculosis bacteria based on shape and color. Real-Time Imaging, Vol. 10, No. 4, (August 2004), pp. 251-262, ISSN 1077-2014

Gonzalez, R. C. & Woods, R. E. (2002). Digital Image Processing Second Edition, Pearson Education, ISBN 978-0201180756, New Jersey

Khutlang, R.; Krishnan, S.; Dendere, R.; Whitelaw, A.; Veropoulos, K.; Learmonth, G. & Douglas T. S. (2010). Classification of Mycobacterium tuberculosis in images of ZN-stained sputum smears. IEEE Transactions on Information Technology in Biomedicine, Vol. 14, No. 4, (July 2010), pp. 949-957, ISSN 1089-7771

Luna, J. A. C. (2004). A Tuberculosis Guide for Specialist Physicians, International Union against Tuberculosis and Lung Disease, Paris

Mancas-Thillou, C. & Gosselin, B. (2005). Color binarization for complex camera-based images, Proceedings of the Electronic Imaging Conference of the International Society for Optical Imaging (SPIE/IS & T), pp. 301-308, ISBN 0-8194-5640-3 , San Jose (California, USA), Jan. 2005, SPIE, Bellingham WA

Otsu, N. (1979). A threshold selection method from gray level histograms. IEEE Transactions on Systems, Man and Cybernetics, Vol. 9, No. 1, (Jan. 1979), pp. 62-66, ISSN 0018-9472

Sezgin, M. & Sankur, B. (2004). Survey over image thresholding techniques and quantitative performance evaluation. Journal of Electronic Imaging, Vol. 13, No. 1, (Jan. 2004), pp. 146-168, ISSN 1017-9909.

Veropoulos, K.; Campbell, C. & Learmonth, G. (1998). Image processing and neural computing used in the diagnosis of tuberculosis, Proc. IEE Colloquium on Intelligent Methods in Healthcare and Medical Applications (Digest No. 1998/514), pp. 8/1 - 8/4, York, UK

Veropoulos, K.; Learmonth, G.; Campbell, C. & Knight, B., Simpson, J. (1999). Automatic identification of tubercle bacilli in sputum. A preliminary investigation. Analytical and Quantitative Cytology and Histology, Vol. 21, No. 4, (Aug. 1999), pp. 277–81, ISSN 0884-6812

Weeks, J. R. (1996). *Fundamentals of Electronic Image Processing,* Wiley-IEEE Press, ISBN 978-0780334106

WHO Report 2009 (2009). *Global tuberculosis control 2009: Epidemiology, Strategy, Financing,* WHO Press, World Health Organization, ISBN 978 92 4 156380 2, Geneva, Siwtzerland

Wilkinson, M. (1996). Rapid automatic segmentation of fluorescent and phase-contrast images of bacteria, In: *Fluorescence Microscopy and Fluorescent Probes.* Slavik, J., pp. 261-266, NY: Plenum Press, ISBN 0-306-45392-4, New York

20

Image Segmentation Based on a Two-Dimensional Histogram

Masmoudi Lhoussaine[1], Zennouhi Rachid[1] and Mohamed EL Ansari[2]
[1]Mohammed V University (LETS Laboratory, Faculty of Science)
[2]Ibn Zohr University (LabSIV Laboratory, Faculty of Science)
Morocco

1. Introduction

Image segmentation refers to the partitioning of an image into non-overlapping different regions with similar attributes. For gray level images, the most basic attribute used is the luminance amplitude, and for color or multispectral images, color or information components are used. Various methods are found in the literature and are roughly classified into several categories according to the dominant features they employ. This includes edge-based methods (Zugaj & Lattuati, 1998), region growing methods (Tremeau & Borel, 1998; Schettini, 1993), neural networks methods, physics-based methods (Maxwell & Shafer, 1996; Bouda et al. 2008) and histogram thresholding methods (Sezgin & Sankur,2004).

It is demonstrated that in unsupervised classification cases the histogram threshold method is a good candidate for achieving segmentation for a wide class of gray level images with low computation complexity (Cheng et. al., 2001). This method ignores the spatial relationship information of the pixels that can give improper results. Abutaleb's work (Abutaleb, 1989) presents another type of 2D gray level histogram. It is formed by the Cartesian product of the original 1D gray level histogram and 1D local average gray level histogram generated by applying a local window to each pixel of the image and then calculating the average of the gray level within the window. Zhang and al. (Zhang & Zhang, 2006) proposed using a minimum gray value in the 4-neighbor and the maximum gray value in the 3×3 neighbor except pixels of the 4-neighbor. This method's main advantage is that it does not require prior knowledge regarding the number of objects in the image, and classical and fast gray level image processing algorithms can be used to cluster the 2D histogram (Clement, 2002).

For color or multispectral images, the one-dimensional (1D) histogram method detracts from the fact that a color cluster is not always present in each component and the combination of the different segmentations cannot catch this spatial property of colors (Clément & Vigouroux, 2001). It also does not take into account the correlation between components (Uchiyama & Arbib, 1994). Therefore multiple histogram-based thresholding is required. However, in a full multi-dimensional manner, the three-dimensional histogram (3D-histogram) method is handicapped by data sparseness, the complexity of the search algorithm (Lezoray & Cardot,2003) and a huge memory space (Clément & Vigouroux, 2001). An interesting alternative method lies with the use a partial histogram (2D-histogram)(

Kurugollu et al.,2001), obtained by projecting a 3D-histogram onto two color planes (Clément & Vigouroux, 2003). This has several advantages, including a lack of data encountered in the 3D case, such as RGB image color, that is partially overcome and the search complexity is drastically reduced (Lezoray & Cardot,2003). Another advantage is the fact that a 2D-histogram is nothing more than a gray level image. Therefore classical and fast gray level image processing algorithms can be used to cluster the 2D-histogram (Clément, 2002).

It is noted that the HSV color space is fundamentally different from the widely known RGB color space since it separates the intensity from the color information (chromaticity). HSV space was demonstrated to be a perceptual color space that consists of the three components H (hue), S (saturation) and V (value) and corresponds to the color attributes closely associated with the way human eyes perceive the colors. Many works related to the HSV color image have been developed and used (Qi et al., 2007; Sural et al, 2002 ; Zennouhi & Masmoudi, 2009).

The organization of this chapter is as follows: in section 2, the 2D-histogram strategy is presented. Section 3 details the segmentation algorithm based on a 2D-histogram using HSV space. The experimental results are presented and discussed in section 4. Section 5 concludes the chapter.

2. Two-dimensional histogram

The histogram threshold method is a good candidate for gray level image segmentation (Cheng et. al., 2001). It is based on the shape of the histogram properties, such as the peaks, valleys and curvatures of the smoothed histogram (Sezgin et Sankur, 2001). Abutaleb's work (Abutaleb, 1989) presents another type of 2D gray level histogram. It is formed by the Cartesian product of the original 1D gray level histogram and 1D local average gray level histogram generated by applying a local window to each pixel of the image and then calculating the average of the grey levels within the window. The change in the pixel value in the horizontal or vertical directions appears slow and the gradation change continuity appears strong compared to the change in the diagonal direction. Zhang and al. (Zhang & Zhang, 2006) proposed using a minimum gray value in the 4-neighbor and the maximum gray value in the 3×3 neighbor except pixels of the 4-neighbor. This method's main advantage is that it does not require prior knowledge about the number of objects in the image.

For RGB color or multispectral image, the one-dimensional (1D) histogram method detracts from the fact that a color cluster is not always present in each component and the combination of the different segmentations cannot catch this spatial property of colors (Clément & Vigouroux, 2001). It also does not take into account the correlation between components (Uchiyama & Arbib, 1994). Therefore multiple histogram-based thresholding is required. However, in a full multi-dimensional manner, the 3D-histogram method is handicapped by data sparseness, the complexity of the search algorithm (Lezoray & Cardot,2003) and a huge memory space (Clément & Vigouroux, 2001). An interesting alternative method lies with the use of 2D-histogram (Kurugollu et al.,2001), which selects two color bands together, namely RG, RB or GB in the RGB space color, obtained by projecting a 3D-histogram onto two color planes which can be constructed as follows.

A 2D-histogram p_n of a RGB color image I maps $p(x_1,x_2)$, the number of pixels in image I presenting the colorimetric components (x_1,x_2). Since each colorimetric axis of image I is quantified on 256 levels, the 2D-histogram p_n can be represented by an image J whose spatial resolution is equal to 256x256. The value $p_n(x_1, x_2)$ of the pixel of coordinates (x_1, x_2) in J is obtained by a linear dynamic contraction of the histogram between 1 and $M = \min(p_{max}, 255)$ (Clément & Vigouroux, 2003):

$$p_n(x_1, x_2) = \text{round}\left[\frac{(M-1)p(x_1, x_2) - Mp_{min} + p_{max}}{p_{max} - p_{min}}\right] \quad (1)$$

where p_{min} and p_{max} are respectively the minimum and maximum values of p.

3. Image segmentation algorithm

This section presents the segmentation algorithm based on 2D-dimensional histogram analysis using HSV space.

3.1 Two-dimensional histogram using HSV space

A three dimensional representation of the HSV color space is a hexacone that consists of three components: Hue, Saturation, and value. Hue is a color attribute that describes what a pure color (pure yellow, orange, or red) is. Hue refers to the perceived color (technically, the dominant wavelength). As hue varies from 0 to 1.0, the corresponding colors vary from red, through yellow, green, cyan, blue, and magenta, back to red, so that there are actually red values both at 0 and 1.0. Saturation is a measure of the degree to which a pure color is diluted by white light, giving rise to 'light purple', 'dark purple', etc. It can be loosely thought of as how pure the color is. Greater values in the saturation channel make the color appear stronger. Lower values (tending to black) make the color appear washed out. As saturation varies from 0 to 1.0, the corresponding colors (hues) vary from unsaturated (shades of gray) to fully saturated. As value, or brightness, varies from 0 to 1.0, the corresponding colors become increasingly brighter (Chen & Wu, 2005).

It is noted that the HSV color space is fundamentally different from the widely known RGB color space since it separates the intensity from the color information (chromaticity). And it was demonstrated that the HSV components correspond to the color attributes closely associated with the way human eyes perceive the colors. Many works related to the color image have been developed using this color space (Qi et al., 2007; Sural et al, 2002).

Sural et al. (Sural et al., 2002) analyzed the properties of the HSV color space with emphasis on the visual perception of the variation in hue, saturation and intensity values of an image pixel. For a given intensity and hue if the saturation is changed from 0 to 1, the perceived color changes from a shade of gray to the most pure form of the color represented by its hue. Looked at from a different angle, any color in the HSV space can be transformed to a shade of gray by sufficiently lowering the saturation. The saturation threshold that determines the transition, between the low and the higher values of the saturation, is once again dependent on the intensity. It is illustrated by Sural et al.(Sural et al., 2002) that for higher values of intensity, a saturation of 0.2 differentiates between hue and intensity dominance. Assuming the maximum intensity value to be 255, the threshold function to determine if a pixel should be represented by its hue or its intensity as its dominant feature is given by

$$Th_S(V) = 1 - \frac{0.8V}{255} \quad (2)$$

That can lead to a feature vector of two parts: the hue values between 0 and 2π quantized after a transformation and a quantized set of intensity values.
In this way we use the HSV color space to build the histogram where each pixel contributes to either its hue or its intensity. Based on the threshold function equation (2), we determine an intermediate image (Fig. 1a): for low values of saturation, a color can be approximated by a gray value specified by the intensity level, while for higher saturation; the color can be approximated by its hue value.

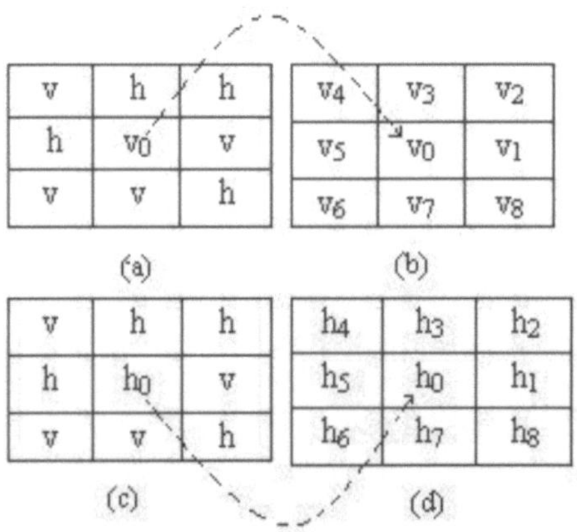

Fig. 1. 3x3 block : (a) and (c) intermediate image; (b) and (d) their component in the original image

Subsequently we can construct the 2D color histogram for the intermediate image as follow: for each block of 3x3 pixels of the intermediate image, we consider the central pixel which can be an intensity Component or a hue Component (Fig. 1a and c), according to the equation (2), and we calculate the maximum (Max) and the minimum (Min) in its corresponding component (H or V) in the original image (Fig. 1b and d) (zennouhi & Masmoudi, 2009). Where the Max is the maximum hue or intensity in the 3x3 neighbor except pixels of the four-neighbor and Min is the minimum hue or intensity in the four-neighbor

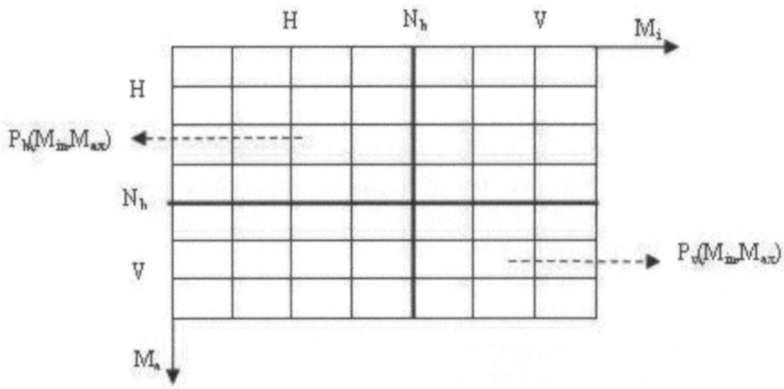

Fig. 2. 2D histogram

Max = maximum [(v_4, v_2, v_6, v_8) or (h_4, h_2, h_6, h_8)] and Min = minimum[(v_0,v_1,v_3,v_5,v_7) or (h_0,h_1,h_3,h_5, h_7)]
Then we build the 2D-histogram by mapping the number of pixels presenting the minimum and the maximum (Min, Max) in all 3x3 block of the image according to P_h(Min; Max) and P_v(Min; Max) for central pixel represented by H or V component respectively (Fig.2).

3.2 Segmentation algorithm

The segmentation algorithm is achieved in two main steps: one, building the 2D-histogram using HSV space according the approach developed before. Two, detecting the peaks representing classes using the classification algorithm proposed in Ref. (Clément & Vigouroux, 2003). A peak is labeled as significant if it represents a population greater than or equal to a threshold d_0 (expressed in per cent of the total population in image). The classification algorithm is performed by reclassification of the pixels not classified in the determined classes according to Euclidian distance.
In order to evaluate the segmentation algorithm, we use the Q function (Zhang et al., 2008; Borsotti et al. , 1998)

$$Q(Im) = \frac{1}{10000N}\sqrt{R} \times \sum_{i=1}^{R}\left(\frac{e_i^2}{1+\log N_i} + \frac{R(N_i)^2}{N_i^2}\right) \tag{3}$$

Im is the segmented image, N is the image size, R is the number of regions of the segmented image, N_i is the area of the ith region, $R(N_i)$ is the number of regions having an area equal to N_i, and e_i is the average color error of the ith region, which is defined as the sum of the Euclidean distances between the RGB color vectors of the pixels of the ith region and the color vector attributed to the ith region in the segmented image. The smaller the Q value, the better the image segmentation method.

4. Experimentation results

This section presents the experimentation results obtained on synthetic and real images.
Two color images are selected: the 465x386 synthetic Squares, which is comprised of four colors, the 709x608 real Mandrill image. Figure 3 shows the original images and the results of the proposed method. It can be seen that the performance is acceptable both for synthetic and real images.
In order to compare the performance of the segmentation method with other existing ones, two different images are used.
First, we consider a synthetic image (Gillet et al., 2002, Macaire et al., 2006) that contains four patterns with different shapes and different colors. The circular pattern contains two shapes that differ only by the variation of the saturation component. The image contains then, if we consider the background, six classes.
The difference between two regions due to the variation of saturation is still a difficult problem. Often, two distinct colors are merged together.
The 2D-histogram segmentation method using RGB space fails to separate the two shapes in the circular pattern. The same problem arises when we applied the 1D-histogram method using HSV space. It can be seen from experimentation results (Fig. 4) that the proposed

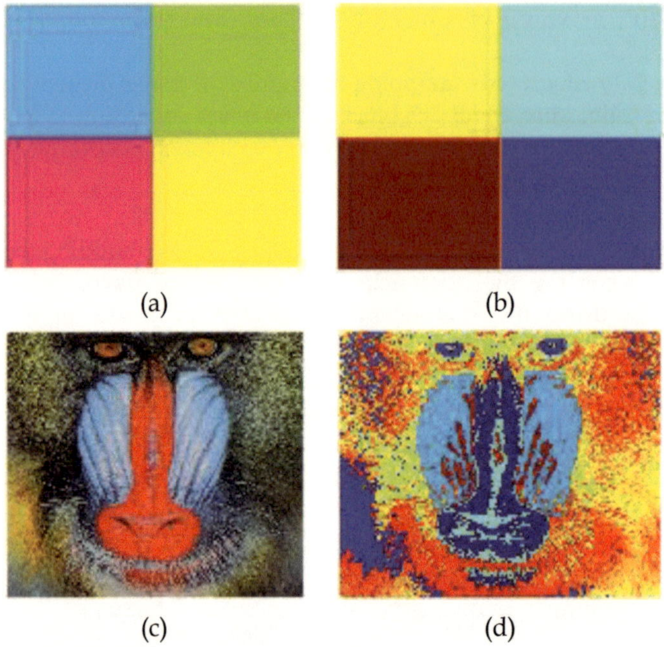

Fig. 3. (a,c) original images; (b,d) segmented images

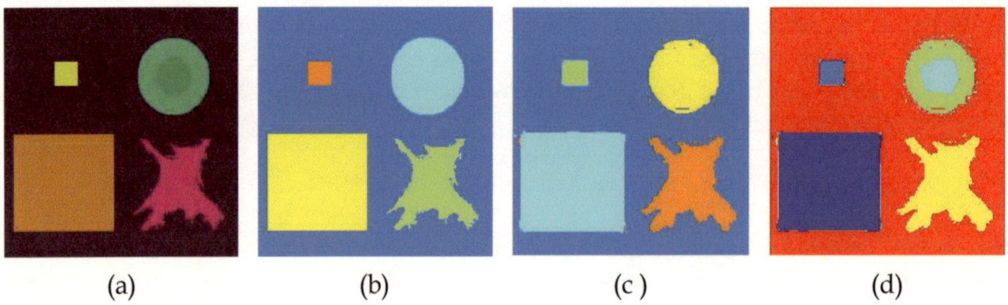

Fig. 4. (a) synthetic image; (b) RG-histogram; (c) 1D histogram using HSV space; (d) 2D histogram using HSV space.

approach gives better clustering and the problem of missing to separate the two shapes is alleviated.

From theses results, it can be deduced that RGB space is not able to separate the two shapes in the circular pattern. This is due to the high correlation among the R, G and B components and that the measurement of a color in RGB space does not represent color differences in a uniform scale; hence it is impossible to evaluate the similarity of two colors from their distance in RGB space. However, in the HSV space where the color and intensity information are separated, the segmentation of the two shapes can be achieved by the proposed method.

Second, we are interested in some agricultural applications. Plants are exposed to a multitude of natural biotic and abiotic stresses (Lichtenthaler,1996). Water availability is one of the most important limitations to photosynthesis and plant productivity (Tezara et al., 1999). The proper monitoring of plant water stress is essential for the development of appropriate, sustainable irrigation programs for crop production in semiarid areas (Penuelas & Filella, 1998). The use of non-destructive imaging methods, such as fluorescence imaging, thermal imaging and imaging using near infrared, holds great promise for early, efficient and objective detection of plant responses to various stresses (Govindjee and Nedbal, 2000; Chaerle & van der Straeten, 2001). However, these techniques provide less human intuition, are more difficult to assess during system integration and are the most costly and time consuming. So, the use of the imaging based on the electromagnetic radiation in the visible range would be of great interest.

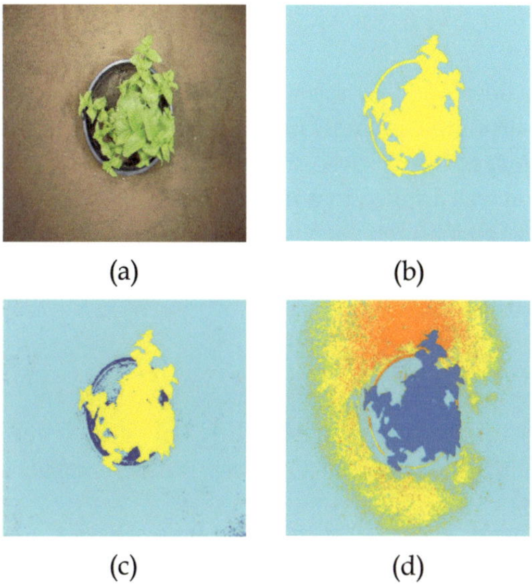

Fig. 5. (a) menthe image; (b) RG-histogram; (c) 1D histogram using HSV space; (d) 2D histogram using HSV space

In this study we have considered a medicinal plant. The first step in our procedure to detect early stress is to segment each image into two classes: vegetation and soil. The color RGB images of the plant are provided by a digital camera. Each color plane is quantized on 256 levels with a resolution of 640x480.

It was noted that the 2D histogram method using RGB space fails to determine the color and intensity variation presented in the image plant. It can be seen from the Fig. 5b that the RGB method could not separate the plant and pot. Figure 5c shows the obtained result of 1D histogram using HSV space. It is clear that the plant and pot are separated; however, this method could not separate the variation intensity presented in soil class which can be useful information for the study of the plant environment.

In contrast, it can be clearly seen from Fig. 5d that the performances of the proposed method are higher than those presented for comparison.

Finally, to evaluate the proposed technique, we have used the 'Q' evaluation function equation (3). From Table 1, it can be seen that the proposed method performs better than the analysis of 2D-histogram using RGB space.

	Square image	Mandrill image	Synthetic image (Fig 4)	Reel image (Fig.5)
2D-histogram using RGB space	35 ,5067	52128	8080,9	8765,8
2D-histogram using HSV space	33 ,0656	17367	721 ,7661	6466,8

Table 1. Values of evaluation function 'Q' for various images

5. Conclusion

In this chapter, we have developed an approach of color image segmentation which is based on the analysis of 2D-histogram using HSV space. The method was applied to various synthetic and real images to prove the performance of segmentation algorithm. Additionally, the method was applied to a particular agricultural application to separate the vegetation and soil. The obtained results have been compared to the methods of others, and shown to be more satisfactory than those obtained either by 1D-histogram using HSV or by 2D-histogram using RGB space.

6. References

Abutaleb, A. S.(1989). Automatic thresholding of gray-level pictures using two-dimensional entropy. *Journal of Computer Vision, Graphic and Image Process,* Vol. 47, (1989) 22–32

Borsotti, M.; Campadelli, P. & Schettini, R.(1998). Quantitative evaluation of color image segmentation results. *Patt. Recogn. Lett.,* Vol.19, (1998) 741–747

Bouda, B.; Masmoudi, L. & Aboutajdine, D (2008) . Cvvefm : Cubical voxels and virtual electric field model for detection in color images. *Signal Processing, Elsevier,* Vol. 88, No. 4, (2008) 905-915

Chaerle, L. & van der Straeten, D.(2001). Seeing is believing: imaging techniques to monitor plant health. *Biochim. Biophys. Acta,* Vol. 1519,(2001) 153–166

Chen, C. & Wu, W. (2005). Color pattern recognition with the multi-channel non-zero-order joint transform correlator based on the HSV color space. *Optics Communications, Vol.*244 (2005) 51–59

Cheng, H.D. ; Jiang, X.H.; Sun, Y.& Wang, J.(2001). Color image segmentation: advances and prospects. *Pattern Recognition,* Vol.34, No.6, (2001) 2259-2281

Clément, A. & Vigouroux, B. (2001). Un histogramme compact pour l'analyse d'images multi-composantes, *Actes du 18e Colloque sur le Traitement du Signal et des Images: GRETSI'01,* pp.305-307, Centre de congres Pierre Baudis,2001 Vol. 1, Toulouse, France

Clément, A. & Vigouroux, B.(2003). Unsupervised segmentation of scenes containing vegetation (Forsythia) and soil by hierarchical analysis of bi-dimensional histograms. *Patt. Recogn. Lett.,* Vol. 24,(2003) 1951–1957

Clément,A.(2002). Algorithmes et outils informatiques pour l'analyse d'images couleur. Application à l'étude de coupes histologiques de baies de raisin en microscopie optique, *PhD thesis*, Université d'Angers.

Gillet, A.; Macaire, L.; Botte-Lecocq, C. & Postaire, J. G.(2002). Color image segmentation by analysis of 3D histogram with fuzzy morphological filters, in: Springer-Verlag Editor, Fuzzy Filters for Image Processing-Studies in Fuzziness and Soft Computing, pp. 154-177, New York

Govindjee & Nedbal, G. L. (2000). Seeing is believing. *Photosynthetica*, Vol. 38, (2000) 481-482

Kurugollu, F.; Sankur, B. & Harmanci, A.(2001). Color image segmentation using histogram multithresholding and fusion. *Image and Vision Comput.*, Vol. 19, (2001) 915–928.

Lezoray, O. & Cardot, H. (2003). Hybrid color image segmentation using 2D histogram clustering and region merging, *Proc. Int. Conf. on Image and signal processing: ICISP'03*, pp. 22–29, Agadir, 2003, Maroc

Lichtenthaler, H. K.(1996). Vegetation stress: an introduction to the stress concept in plants. *J. Plant Physiol.*, Vol. 148,(1996) 4–14

Macaire, L.; Vandenbroucke, N. & Postaire, J. G.(2006). Color image segmentation by analysis of subset connectedness and color homogeneity properties. *Comput. Vision Image Understand.*, Vol.102, (2006) 105–116

Maxwell, B.A. & Shafer, S.A. (1996). Physics-based segmentation: looking beyond color, *Proceedings of Image Understanding Workshop*, pp. 867–878, Palm Springs, CA February 1996, ARPA, USA

Penuelas, J. & Filella, I.(1998). Visible and near-infrared reflectance techniques for diagnosing plant physiological status. *Trends Plant Sci.*, Vol.3, (1998)151 -156

Qi, X. J.; Qi, J. & Wu, Y. J. (2007). RootLM: a simple color image analysis program for length measurement of primary roots in Arabidopsis. *Plant Root*, Vol. 1, (2007) 10–16

Schettini, R. (1993). A segmentation algorithm for color images. *Pattern Recognition Letters*, Vol.14, (1993) 499–506

Sezgin, M. & Sankur, B. (2004). Survey over image thresholding techniques and quantitative performance evaluation. *Journal of Electronic Imaging*, Vol.13, No.1,(2004) 146-165

Sural, S.; Qian, G. & Pramanik, S.(2002). Segmentation and histogram eneration using the HSV color space for image retrieval, Proc. Int. Conf. on Image processing: ICIP'02, Rochester, NY, USA, IEEE, Vol. 2, pp. II589–II592

Tezara, W.; Mitchell, V. J.; Driscoll, S. D. & Lawlor, D. W. (1999). Water stress inhibits plant photosynthesis by decreasing coupling factor and ATP. *Nature*, Vol. 401, (1999) 914–917

Tremeau, A. & Borel, N. (1998). A region growing and merging algorithm to color segmentation, *Pattern Recognition*, Vol.30, No.7, (1998)1191-1203

Uchiyama, T. & Arbib, M.(1994). Color image segmentation using competitive learning. IEEE Trans. Pattern Anal. Mach. Intell., 16, (1994) 1197–1206

Zennouhi, R. & Masmoudi, LH. (2009). A new 2D histogram scheme for color image segmentation. *The Imaging Science Journal,* Vol. 57, (2009) 260-265

Zhang, H.; Fritts, J. E. & Goldman, S. A.(2008). Image segmentation evaluation: A survey of unsupervised methods. *Computer Vision and Image Understanding*, Vol. 110, (2008) 260–280

Zhang, Y. F. & Zhang, Y. (2006). Another Method of Building 2D Entropy to Realize Automatic Segmentation. *Journal of Physics Conference Series*, Vol. 48, (2006) 303–307

Zugaj, D. & Lattuati, V. (1998). A new approach of color images segmentation based on fusing region and edge segmentation outputs. *Pattern Recognition*, Vol. 31, No.2,(1998) 105–113

21

Segmentation Methods for Biomedical Images

Roberto Rodríguez Morales
Institute of Cybernetics, Mathematics & Physics (ICIMAF),
Digital Signal Processing Group
Cuba

1. Introduction

Nowadays biomedical imaging provides major aid in many branches of medicine; it enables and facilitates the capture, transmission and analysis of biomedical images as well as providing assistance towards medical diagnoses. Medical imaging is still on the rise with new imaging modalities being added and continuous improvements of devices' capabilities. Segmentation and contour extraction are important steps towards image analysis. Segmented images are now used routinely in a multitude of different applications, such as, diagnosis, treatment planning, localization of pathology, study of anatomical structure, computer-integrated surgery, among others. However, image segmentation remains a difficult task due to both the variability of object shapes and the variation in image quality. Particularly, biomedical images are often corrupted by noise and sampling artifacts, which can cause considerable difficulties when applying rigid methods.
In many occasions, segmentation is considered as a process of classification of objects in a scene, and also in certain measure, it is equivalent to its recognition (objects) since, as a consequence of segmentation the different objects (physical realizations of classes or abstract patterns), these stay perfectly located inside the digital image.
In a graphic way in Figure 1, it is represented the segmentation process of a simple image. It is appreciated in this Figure that as result of segmentation the image was transformed from a gross digital image with all their information in form of gray-levels to an image much more simplified, where the different objects are well distinguished.

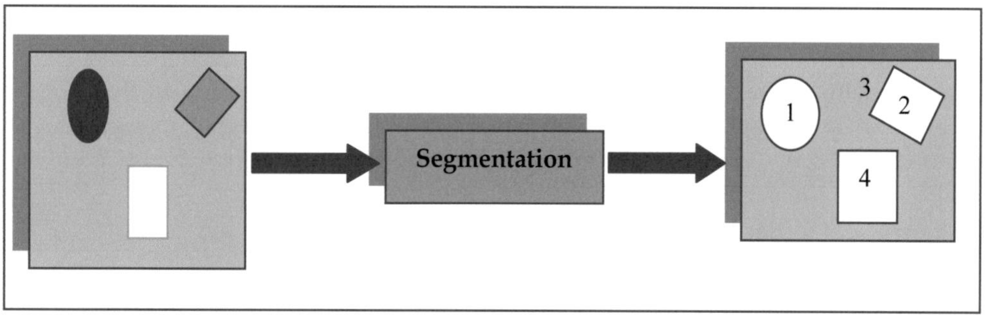

Fig. 1. Simple outline that represents the segmentation process

Many segmentation methods have been proposed for biomedical-image data [Chin-Hsing et al., 1998; Kenong & Levine, 1995; Koss et al., 1999; Rodríguez et al., 2002; Sijbers et al., 1997;

Schmid, 1999]. Unfortunately, segmentation using traditional low-level image processing techniques, such as thresholding, histogram and other classical operations, requires a considerable amount of interactive guidance in order to get satisfactory results. Automating these model-free approaches is difficult because of shape complexity, shadows, and variability within and across individual objects. Furthermore, noise and other image artifacts can cause incorrect regions or boundary discontinuities in objects recovered from these methods. However, it is accepted that despite the more complex algorithms developed so far, the segmentation of images remains highly dependent on the application and a single method has not yet been found that can solve all the problems in the universe.
In mathematical morphology (MM) important methods have been developed for image segmentation [Vicent & Soille, 1991; Vincent, 1993]. One of the most powerful tools developed in MM is the *Watersheds* transformation, which is classic in the field of topography and it has been used in many problems of image segmentation. However, the *Watersheds* transformation has the disadvantage of producing over-segmentation [Fuh et al., 1991; Najman & Schmitt, 1996]. For that reason, the correct way to use watersheds for grayscale image segmentation is to mark the regions we want to segment; that is, the objects, but also the background. One and only one marker must correspond to each region. The design of robust marker detection techniques involves the use of specific knowledge of the series of images under study.
Other technique very used in the last years for image segmentation is the mean shift, which is a non-parametric procedure for multimodal data analysis and has shown great superiority in many applications of high-level tasks [Comaniciu, 2000]. The mean shift was proposed in 1975 by Fukunaga et. al. [Fukunaga & Hostetler, 1975] and was largely forgotten until Cheng in 1995 rekindled interests in it [Cheng, 1995]. A computer model based on the mean shift procedure is an extremely versatile tool for feature analysis and can give a reliable solution for many tasks of computer vision [Comaniciu & Meer, 2002]. Segmentation by using the mean shift carries out a smoothing filter as a first step before segmentation is performed [Comaniciu, 2000].
The aim of this chapter is to present the advances that the author and their collaborators have obtained in the biomedical image segmentation. Also, some strategies that constitute appropriate tools are presented, which it can be used in many system of image analysis where methods of segmentation are required.
This chapter is structured as follows: In Section 2 the most significant theoretical aspects are detailed of each of the used methods in biomedical image segmentation. In Section 3 some of the characteristics of the studied images are described. In Section 4 the steps carried out in the experimentation are explained, and also an analysis and discussion of the proposed strategies is carried out. In this section two algorithms are presented to carry out the segmentation. Finally, in Section 5 the most important conclusions of this chapter are given.

2. Theoretical aspects

In mathematical morphology, it is usual to consider that grayscale images are often considered as topographic reliefs. In the topographic representation of a given image $\boldsymbol{I}$, the numerical value (that is, the gray tone) of each pixel stands for the elevation at this point. Such a representation is extremely useful, since it allows one to better appreciate the effect of the different transformations on the image under study.

2.1 Morphological grayscale reconstruction

Now, it is given a group of definitions and concepts which are important for a better understanding of the proposed strategies.
Let us consider a two-dimensional grayscale picture ***I*** whose definition domain is denoted $D_I \subset Z^2$. ***I*** is supposed to take discrete (gray) values in a given range *[0, L-1]*, *L* being an arbitrary positive integer

$$I\begin{pmatrix} D_I \subset Z^2 & \rightarrow \{0,1,2,\text{..........},L-1\} \\ p & \rightarrow I(p) \end{pmatrix} \tag{1}$$

Let ***J*** and ***I*** be two grayscale images defined on the same domain D_I, taking their values in the discrete set *{0, 1, ..., L-1}* and such that $J \leq I$ (i.e., for each pixel $p \in D_I$, $J(p) \leq I(p)$). In this way, it is useful to introduce the geodesic dilations according to the following definition [Vincent, 1993]:
Definition 2.1.1 (Geodesic dilation): The elementary geodesic dilation of $\delta_I^{(1)}(J)$ of grayscale image $J \leq I$, *J* "under" *I* (*J* is called the marker image and *I* is the mask) is defined as,

$$\delta_I^{(1)}(J) = (J \oplus B) \wedge I \tag{2}$$

where the symbol Λ stands for the pointwise minimum and $J \oplus B$ is the dilation of *J* by flat structuring element *B*. The grayscale geodesic dilation of size $n \geq 0$ is obtained by,

$$\delta_I^{(n)}(J) = \delta_I^{(1)} \circ \delta_I^{(1)} \circ \cdots \circ \delta_I^{(1)}(J),\ n\ times \tag{3}$$

Starting from the definition 2.1.1 and the expression (3) it can be derived an efficient definition for the morphological reconstruction of images in gray-levels.
Definition 2.1.2 (Grayscale reconstruction): The grayscale reconstruction $\rho_I^{(J)}$ of *I* from *J* is obtained by iterating grayscale dilations of *J* "under" *I* until stability is reached [Vincent, 1993], that is,

$$\rho_I(J) = \bigvee_{n \geq 1} \delta_I^{(n)}(J) \tag{4}$$

Definition 2.1.3 (Geodesic erosion): Similarly, the elementary geodesic erosion $\varepsilon_I^{(1)}(J)$ of grayscale image $J \geq I$, *J* "above" *I* is given by,

$$\varepsilon_I^{(1)}(J) = (J\, \theta\, B) \vee I \tag{5}$$

where $\vee$ stands for the pointwise maximum and $J\, \theta\, B$ is the erosion of *J* by flat structuring element *B*. The grayscale geodesic erosion of size $n \geq 0$ is then given by,

$$\varepsilon_I^{(n)}(J) = \varepsilon_I^{(1)} \circ \varepsilon_I^{(1)} \circ \cdots \circ \varepsilon_I^{(1)}(J),\ n\ times \tag{6}$$

Definition 2.1.4 (Dual reconstruction): The dual grayscale reconstruction $\rho_f^*(J)$ of mask *I* from marker *J* is obtained by iterating grayscale geodesic erosions of *J* "above" *I* until stability is reached; that is,

$$\rho_I^*(J) = \underset{n \geq 1}{\wedge} \varepsilon_I^{(n)}(J) \tag{7}$$

Reconstruction turns out to provide a very efficient method to extract regional maxima and minima from grayscale images. Furthermore, the technique extends to the determination of maximal structures, which will be call *h-domes* and *h-basins*. The *h-domes* transformation extracts light structure without involving any size or shape criteria. The only parameter *(h)* is related to the height of these structures. The mathematical background and other definitions can be found in [Vincent, 1993].

2.1.1 Dome extraction and regional maxima

We consider the successive thresholds $T_h(I)$ of I, for $h = 0$ to $L\text{-}1$ [Vincent, 1993],

$$T_h(I) = \{ p \in D_I \,/\, I(p) \leq h \} \tag{8}$$

They are said to constitute the threshold decomposition of I, where these sets satisfy the following inclusion relationship:

$$T_h(I) \subseteq T_{h-1}(I) \qquad \forall\ h \in [0, L\text{-}1] \tag{9}$$

Definition 2.1.1.1 (Regional Minimum): A regional minimum M at altitude h of grayscale image I is a connected component C of $T_h(I)$ such that $C \cap T_{h-1}(I) = \varphi$, T_h (I) being a threshold of I at level h and the symbol φ stands for empty set.
Definition 2.1.1.2 (Regional maximum): A regional maximum at altitude h of grayscale image I is a connected component C de T_h (I) such that $C \cap T_{h+1}(f) = \varphi$.
In Figure 2 one can observe a representation of regional maxima in a grayscale image.

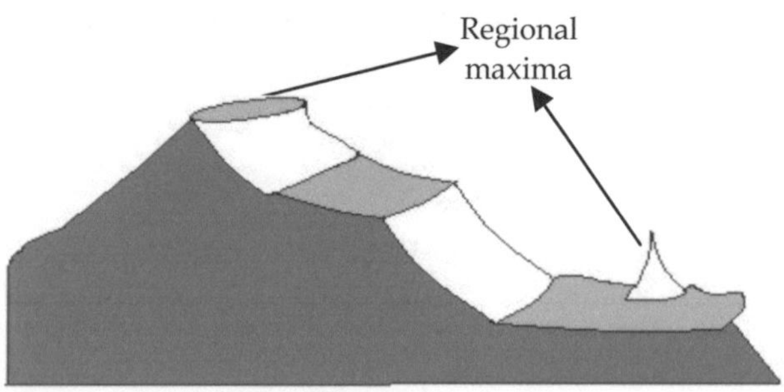

Fig. 2. Regional maxima in a grayscale image

Regional maxima should not be mistaken with local maxima. A pixel p of I is a local maximum for grid H if and only if its value $I(p)$ is greater or equal to that of any of its neighbours. All the pixels belonging to a regional maximum are local maxima, but the converse is not true. For example, a pixel p belonging to the inside of a plateau is a local maximum, but the plateau may have neighbouring pixels of higher altitude and thus not be a regional maximum.
One of the most efficient methods makes use of grayscale reconstruction and is based on the following proposition.
Proposition 2.1.1.1: The (binary) image $M(I)$ of the regional maxima of I is given by,

$$M(I) = f - \rho_I(I - 1)$$

where $\rho_I(I - 1)$, it is a morphological reconstruction (see definition 2.1.2, in this case $J = I\text{-}1$). The proof of this proposition can be seen in [Vincent, 1993].
For a better understanding of this proposition the same is illustrated in Figure 3.

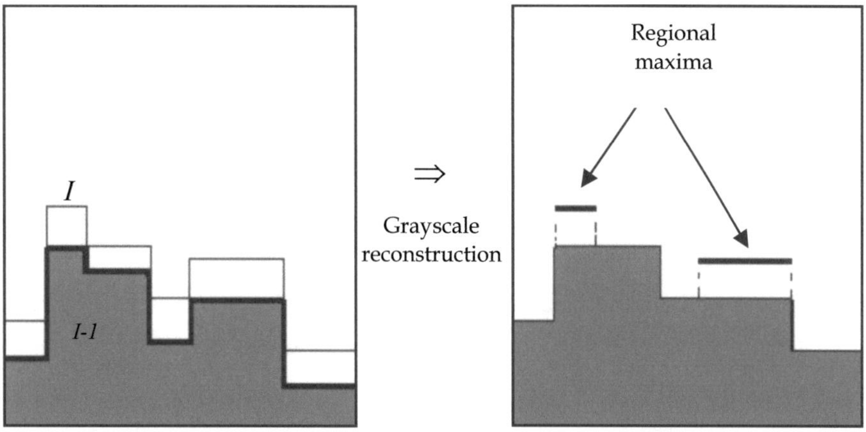

Fig. 3. Extracting the regional maxima of *I* by reconstruction of I from *I-1*

The proposition 2.1.1.1 can be generalized and instead of subtracting value *1*, an arbitrary gray-level constant *h* can be subtracted from *I*. This provides a useful technique for extracting domes of a given height, which is called h-domes. Then, be the following definition:
Definition 2.1.1.3: The *h-dome* image $D_h(I)$ of the *h-domes* of a grayscale image ***I*** is given by

$$D_h(I) = I - \rho_I(I - h)$$

The *h-dome* transformation is illustrated on Figure 4. Unlike the classical transformation *Top-Hat*, the *h-dome* transformation extracts light structures without involving any size or shape criterion. The only parameter *(h)* is related to the height of these structures [Vincent, 1993].

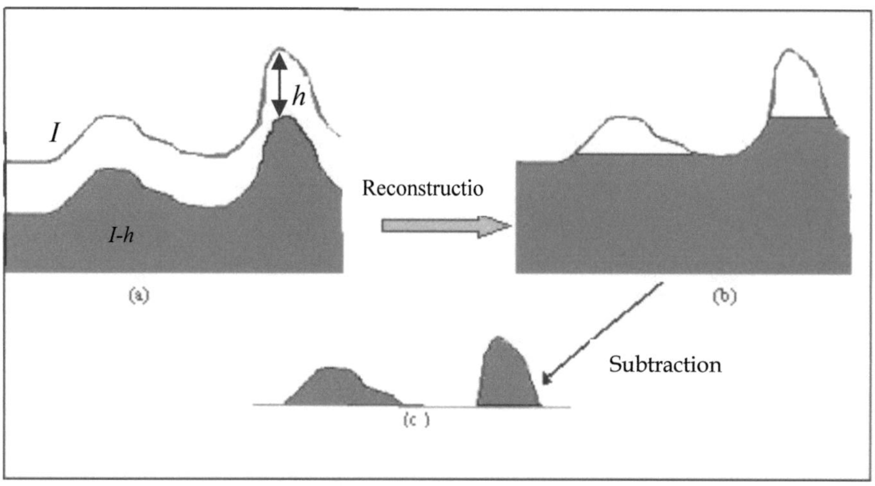

Fig. 4. Determination of the *h-domes* of grayscale image *I*

2.1.2 *Watershed* segmentation method

The *Watershed* segmentation consists in extracting objects from a gray-level image as precisely as possible [Vicent & Soille, 1991]. The advantage of this technique is that totally closed contours are obtained, and a complete partition of the domain of image is achieved. With this method is not necessary to carry out an additional connection of the edges. The disadvantage of this method resides in that it produces over-segmentation when the objects (to extract) are not appropriately marked. The following definitions and concepts are important for understanding better this method.

In the following, this work equally considers grayscale images as numerical functions or as topographic reliefs. Let H denote the underlying digital grid, which can be of any type: a square grid in four or eight connectivity, or a hexagonal grid in six connectivity. H is a subset of $Z^2 \times Z^2$.

Definition 2.1.2.1: A path P of length l between two pixels p and q in image I is a $(l+1)$-tuple of pixels $(p_0, p_1, \ldots\ldots, p_{l-1}, p_l)$ such that $p_0 = p$, $p_l = q$, and $\forall i \in [1,l], (p_{i-1}, p_i) \in H$

Given the previous definition, it will be denoted $l\ (P)$ as the length of a given path P. Also, it will be denoted $N_H\ (p)$ as the set of the neighbours of a pixel p, with respect to H; $N_H\ (p) = \{ p' \in Z^2, (p, p') \in H \}$.

Definition 2.1.2.2 (Catchment basin, first definition): Let I be a grayscale image. The catchment basin $C\ (M)$ associated with a minimum M is the set of pixels p of D_I such that a water drop falling at p flows down along the relief, following a certain descending path called the downstream of p, and eventually reaches M [Vicent & Soille, 1991]. The lines which separate different catchment basins build what is called the *watersheds* (or *dividing lines*) of I. (see Figure 5).

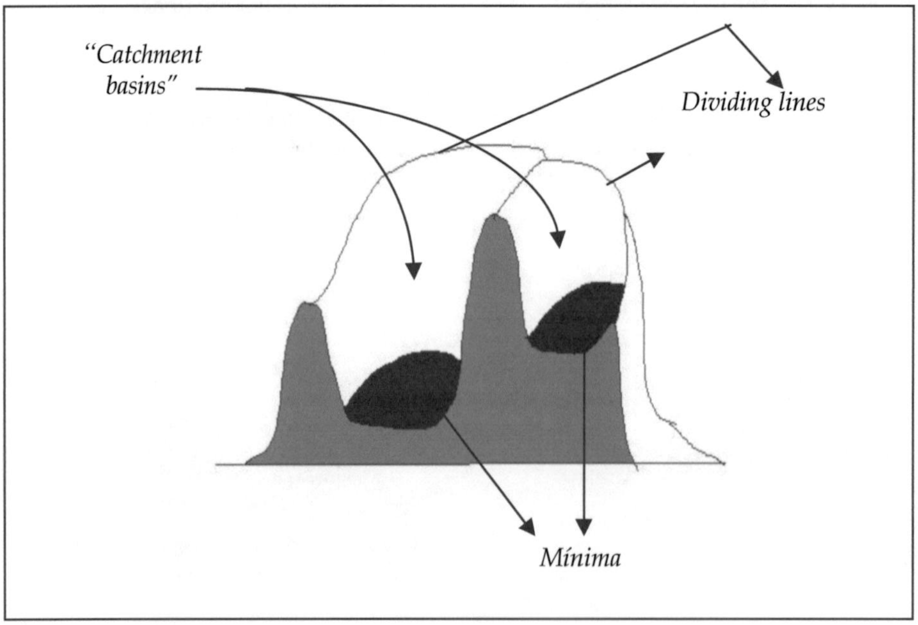

Fig. 5. Minima, catchment basins, and dividing lines

Note that the catchment basins of an image I correspond to the influence zones of its minima, also called areas of attraction of the drops of water. In this sense, it there is a close relation between the binary skeleton by influence zones and the watersheds. Therefore, this intuitive approach to watershed in not well suited to practical implementations [Vicent & Soille, 1991]. Then, the given definitions in the next section are more suited to the formalization of catchment basins and watersheds in digital space.

Definition 2.1.2.3 (Catchment basin by immersion): Suppose, that in each regional minimum of I is pierced a hole, this image being regarded as a topographic surface. Then, this image is slowly immersed into a lake. Starting from the minima of lowest altitude, the water will progressively fill up the different catchment basins of I. Now, at each pixel where the water coming from two different minima would merge, a "*dam*" is built (see Figure 6). At the end of this immersion procedure, each minimum is completely surrounded by dams, which delimit its associated catchment basin. The whole set of dams which has been built thus provides a tessellation of I in its different catchment basins. These correspond to the dividing lines of I.

It is possible to express the immersion procedure more formally [Vicent & Soille, 1991]: I being the grayscale image under study, denote h_{min} the smallest values taken by I on its domain D_I. Similarly, denote h_{max} the large value by I on D_I. In the following, $T_h(I)$ stands for the threshold of I at level h (see equation (8)). Denote $C(M)$ the catchment basin associated with a minimum M and $C_h(M)$ the subset of this catchment basin made of the points having an altitude smaller or equal to h:

$$C_h(M) = \{p \in C(M), f(p) \leq h\} = C(M) \cap T_h(f) \tag{10}$$

As concerns the minima of I, $min_h(I)$ refers to the set of points belonging to the minima at altitude h.

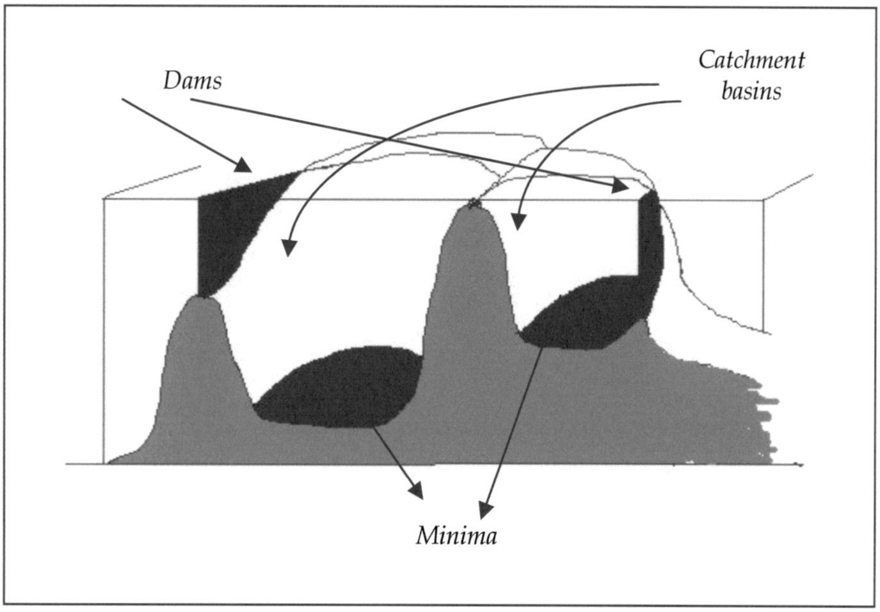

Fig. 6. Building dams at the places where the water coming from two different minima would merge

It is necessary for further understanding in what continues to introduce the definitions of *geodesic distance* and of the *geodesic influence zones*. Let X be a set which is first supposed to be simply connected.

Definition 2.1.2.4: The geodesic distance $d_X(p, q)$ between two pixels p and q in X is the infimum of the length of the paths which join p and q and are totally included in X (see Figure 7):

$$D_X(p, q) = \inf\{l(P), P \text{ path between } p \text{ and } q \text{ which is totally included in } X\}$$

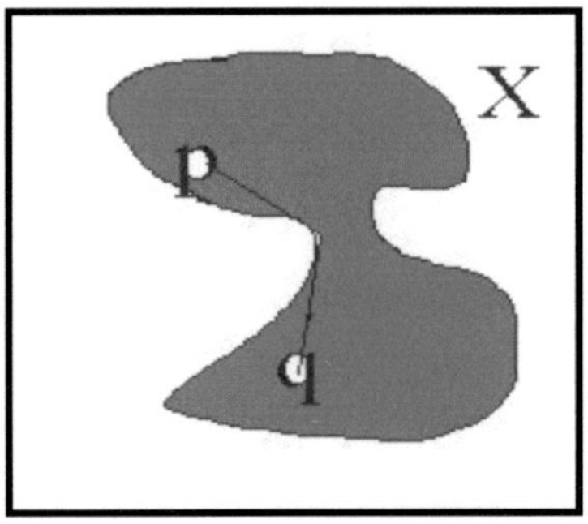

Fig. 7. Geodesic distance between p and q inside X

Suppose that X contains a set B made of several connected components $B_1, B_2, \ldots\ldots, B_k$.

Definition 2.1.2.5: The *geodesic influence zone* $iz_X(B_i)$ of a connected component B_i in X is the locus of the points of X whose geodesic distance to B_i is smaller than their geodesic distance to any other component of B (see Figure 8):

$$iz_X(B_i) = \{p \in X, \forall j \in [1, k]/\{i\}, d_X(p, B_i) < d_X(p, B_j)\} \tag{11}$$

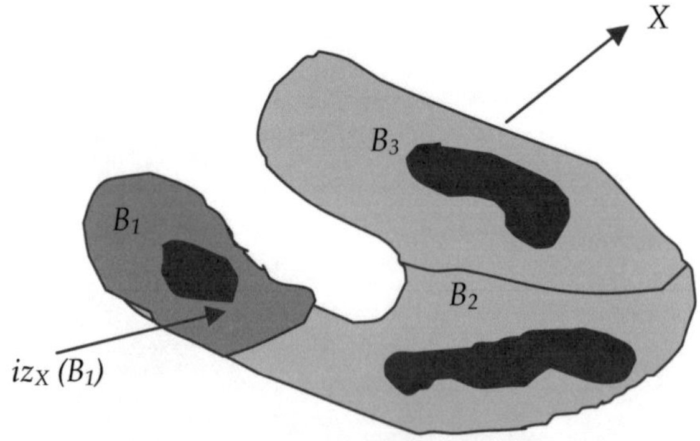

Fig. 8. *Geodesic influence zone* of connected component B_1 inside set X

Those points of X which do not belong to any geodesic influence zone constitute the *skeleton by influence zones, (SKIZ)* of B inside X, denoted $SKIZ_X(B)$:

$$SKIZ_X(B) = X / iz_X(B) \text{ with } iz_X(B) = \bigcup_{i \in [1;k]} iz_x(B_i) \tag{12}$$

In [Vicent & Soille, 1991], it is demonstrated that the previous definitions are easily extended to the case where X is not simply connected, nor even connected at all. Then, finally the following definition is presented.

In order to simulate the immersion procedure, one starts from the set $T_{h_{\min}}(I)$, the ponits of which being those first reached by the water. These points constityute the starting set of the recursion. So, of this way,

$$X_{h_{min}} = T_{h_{min}}(I),$$

$X_{h_{min}}$ is made of the points of I which belong to the minima of lowest altitude. For a bigger profundizaci6n of the theoretical aspects on this issue see [Vicent & Soille, 1991].

Definition 2.1.2.6 (Catchment basins and Watersheds by immersion): The set of the catchment basins of the grayscale image I is equal to the set $X_{h_{max}}$ obtained after the following recursion:

a) $X_{h_{min}} = T_{h_{min}}(I),$

b) $\forall h \in [h_{min}, h_{max} - 1], X_{h+1} = min_{h+1} \cup IZ_{T_{h+1}(I)}(X_h)$

The watersheds transformation of I correspond to the complement of this set in D_I; that is, to the set of the points of D_I which do not belong to any catchment basins. The recursion process between two successive levels is illustrated in Figure 9.

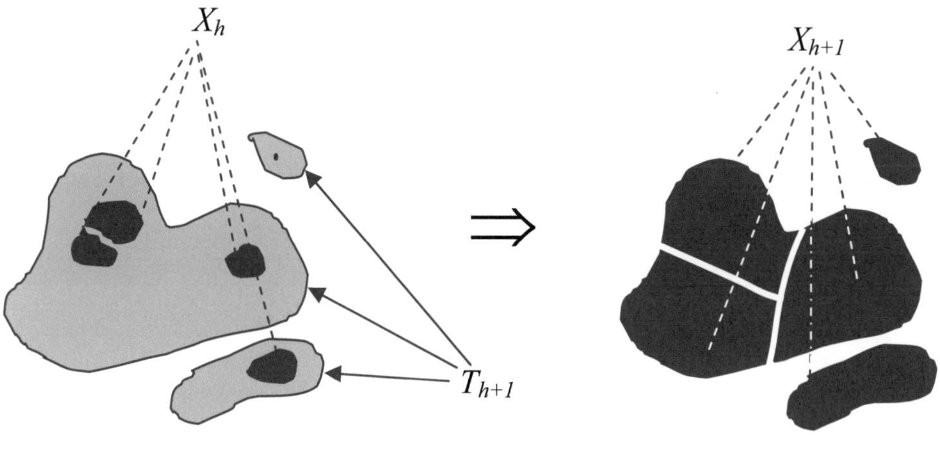

Fig. 9. Recursion process between X_h and X_{h+1}

In many practical cases, one of the principal problems is the obtaining of regional minima, due to the fact that, in general, digital images are corrupted by noise. Then, if one directly applies the watershed transformation to an image many dividing lines are obtained, which is known as over-segmentation.

Therefore, the first step consists in marking the objects we want to segment, and also the background. By marker of an object, it means a connected component of pixels located inside the object to be extracted. To each object one and only one marker must correspond.

The design of robust marker detection techniques involves the use of knowledge specific to the series of images under study. A marking function is then constructed, whose different catchment basins correspond to the desired objects. When one works in the other way, then the watershed transformation produces over-segmentation. The over-segmentation mainly comes from the fact that the markers are not perfectly appropriate to the objects to be contoured. In short, the quality of the segmentation is directly linked to the marking function. If this condition is attained, with the watershed method continuous edges are obtained. With the classical methods this is practically impossible. This statement will be verified in the section corresponding to the experimental results.
The proposed strategy in this work facilitates to obtain a marking function which is of great utility for the watershed segmentation. On one hand, the over-segmentation is avoided and on the other hand, a correct delimitation of contours of the objects of interest is achieved.

2.2 The mean shift and analysis

The iterative procedure to compute the mean shift is introduced as a normalized density estimate of the gradient. By employing a differentiable kernel, an estimate of the density can be defined as the gradient of the kernel density estimate; that is,

$$\hat{\nabla} f(x) = \nabla \hat{f}(x) = \frac{1}{nh^d} \sum_{i=1}^{n} \nabla K\left(\frac{x-x_i}{h}\right) \tag{13}$$

The function of the kernel *K (x)* is now a function defined by the vector $\boldsymbol{x}$, *d*-dimensional, which satisfies

$$\int_{R^d} K(x)dx = 1 \tag{14}$$

Conditions on the kernel *K(x)* and the window radius *h* are derived in [Fukunaga & Hostetler, 1975] to guarantee asymptotic unbiasedness, mean-square consistency, and uniform consistency of the estimate in the expression (13). For example, for *Epanechnikov* kernel:

$$K_E(x) = \begin{cases} 1/2c_d^{-1}\,(d+2)(1-\|x\|^2) & if\ \|x\| < 1 \\ 0 & otherwise \end{cases} \tag{15}$$

where c_d is the volume of the unit *d*-dimensional sphere, the density gradient estimate becomes

$$\hat{\nabla} f_E(x) = \frac{1}{n(h^d c_d)} \cdot \frac{d+2}{h^2} \sum_{x_i \in S_h(x)} (x_i - x) = \frac{n_x}{n\,(h^d c_d)} \cdot \frac{d+2}{h^2} \left(\frac{1}{n_x} \sum_{x_i \in S_h(x)} (x_i - x) \right) \tag{16}$$

where the region $S_h(x)$ is a hypersphere of radius *h* having volume $h^d c_d$, centered at $\boldsymbol{x}$, and containing n_x data points; that is, the uniform kernel. In addition, in this case $d = 3$, due to that the vector $\boldsymbol{x}$ has three dimensions, two for the spatial domain and one for the range domain (levels of gray).The last factor in expression (16) is called the *sample mean shift*,

$$M_{h,U}(x)=\frac{1}{n_x}\sum_{x_i\in S_h(x)}(x_i-x)=\frac{1}{n_x}\sum_{x_i\in S_h(x)}x_i-x \tag{17}$$

The quantity $\frac{n_x}{n\,(h^d c_d)}$ is the kernel density estimate $\hat{f}_U(x)$ (the uniform kernel) computed with the hypersphere $S_h(x)$, and thus we can write the expression (16) as:

$$\hat{\nabla} f_E(x)=\hat{f}_U(x)\cdot\frac{d+2}{h^2}M_{h,\,U}(x) \tag{18}$$

which yields,

$$M_{h,\,U}(x)=\frac{h^2}{d+2}\frac{\hat{\nabla} f_E(x)}{\hat{f}_U(x)} \tag{19}$$

Expression (19) shows that an estimate of the normalized gradient can be obtained by computing the sample mean shift in a uniform kernel centered on x. In addition, the mean shift has the direction of the gradient of the density estimate at x when this estimate is obtained with the *Epanechnikov* kernel. Since the mean shift vector always points towards the direction of the maximum increase in the density, it can define a path leading to a local density maximum; that is, to a mode of the density (see Figure 10).

In addition, expression (19) shows that the mean is shifted towards the region in which the majority of the points reside. Since the mean shift is proportional to the local gradient estimate, it can define a path leading to a stationary point of the estimated density, where these stationary points are the modes. Moreover, the normalized gradient in expression (19) introduces a desirable adaptive behavior, since the mean shift step is large for low density regions corresponding to valleys, and decreases as x approaches a mode.

Mathematically speaking, this is justified since $\frac{\hat{\nabla} f_E(x)}{\hat{f}_U(x)}>\hat{\nabla} f_E(x)$. Thus, the corresponding step size for the same gradient will be greater than the nearer mode. This will allow observations far from the mode or near a local minimum to move towards the mode faster than using $\hat{\nabla} f_E(x)$ alone.

In [Comaniciu, 2000], it was proven that the mean shift procedure obtained by successive:

- computation of the mean shift vector $M_h\,(x)$
- translation of the window $S_h\,(x)$ by $M_h\,(x)$,

is guaranteed to converge.

A digital image can be represented as a two-dimensional array of p-dimensional vectors (pixels), where $p = 1$ in the gray level case, $p = 3$ for color images, and $p > 3$ in the multispectral case.

As was pointed out in [Comaniciu, 2000] when the location and range vectors are concatenated in the joint spatial-range domain of dimension $d = p+2$, their different nature has to be compensated by proper normalization of parameters h_s and h_r. Thus, the multi-variable kernel is defined as the product of two radially symmetric kernels and the Euclidean metric allows a single bandwidth for each domain, that is:

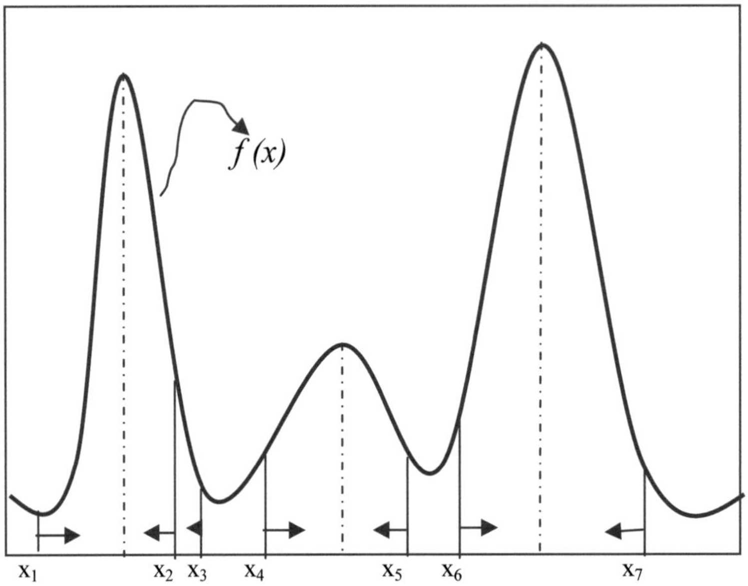

Fig. 10. Gradient mode clustering

$$K_{h_s,h_r}(x) = \frac{C}{h_s^2\, h_r^p} k\left(\left\|\frac{x^s}{h_s}\right\|^2\right) k\left(\left\|\frac{x^r}{h_r}\right\|^2\right)$$

where x^s is the spatial part, x^r is the range part of a feature vector, $k(x)$ the common profile used in both domains, h_s and h_r the employed kernel bandwidths, and C the corresponding normalization constant. The value hs is associated with spatial resolution of the analysis, while the value hr is associated with the resolution in the domain of range (levels of gray). More details related with the mean shift can be found in [Comaniciu, 2000; Comaniciu & Meer, 2002].

3. Some characteristics of the images under study

Studied images are of arteries, which have atherosclerotic lesions and these were obtained from different parts of the human body, from more of 80 autopsies. These arteries were contrasted with a special tint in order to accentuate the different lesions in arteries. Later, the lesions are manually classified by the pathologists according to World Health Organization. They classified the lesions in type I, II, III and IV. For example, the lesions I and II, these are the fatty streaks and fibrous plaques respectively, while the lesions III and IV are respectively the complicated and calcified plaques. The pathologists mark only the lesions; that is, they do not outline to them. For that reason, the edge automatically detection, it is very important, because these images will be subject to an additional morphometrical analysis in order to study the atherosclerosis and its organic-consequences.

The arteries were directly digitalized from the working desk by using a video camera and an A/D converter. In Figure 11(a) a typical image with lesions I and II can be seen, while in Figure 11(b) is shown its histogram. These images were captured via the MADIP system with a resolution of 512x512x8 bit/pixels. MADIP- Morphometrical Analysis by Digital Image Processing is a system created to help physicians in his research work using images. MADIP is a software for the morphometrical characterization of macro and micro lesions in biomedical images. In general, it may be used in any branch of science and technology, where not only quantitative techniques of high precision are required, but it is also necessary to do a big number of measurements with high accuracy and rapidly [Rodríguez et al., 2001].

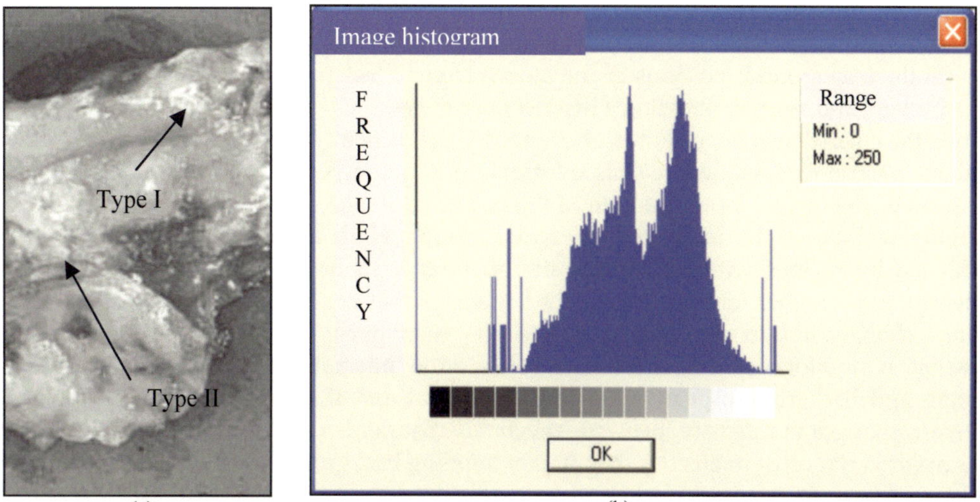

(a) (b)

Fig. 11. (a) Atherosclerosis image. (b) Histogram. It can be observed low contrast. The arrows show an example of structures that we attempt to segment.

Figure 12 shows other examples with other types of lesions.

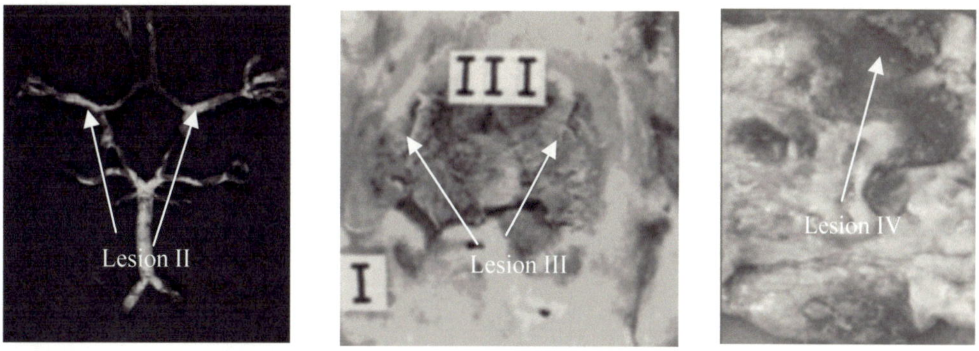

Fig. 12. Atherosclerosis images with different lesions, which are marked with arrows. The arrows show the lesions.

There are several remarkable characteristics of these images, which are common to typical images that we encounter in the atherosclerotic lesions:

1. High local variation of intensity is observed both, within the atherosclerotic lesions and the background. However, the local variation of intensities is higher within the lesions than in background regions.

2. The histogram of Fig. 11(b) shows that there is a low contrast in the images.
3. The lesions III and IV have better contrast than the lesions I and II (see Fig. 12). In addition, due to variations in the intensity of the background across the image and the low contrast between lesions and background intensities, principally for the lesions I and II, the atherosclerotic lesions in a region of the image may appear lighter than the background in a distant region.
4. It is common of these images the diversity in shape and size of the atherosclerotic lesions.
5. The boundaries of the atherosclerotic lesions, principally for the lesions I and II, may be extremely difficult to define. Due to variations in intensity, both within the lesions and in the background, portions of the atherosclerotic lesion may appear blended into the background, without creating a distinct boundary.

While the characteristics presented above testify the difficulty in identifying atherosclerotic lesions, a close examination reveals information that can be used. We observed that two features of the image, local variation of intensity and image intensity level, can be used to identify regions of the image that describe lesions. High local variation of intensity is exhibited by regions within and near the boundaries of lesions. Thus, local variation of intensity can roughly identify regions of the image that contain lesions. Across the entire image, changes in intensity level cannot reliably distinguish atherosclerotic lesions, due to possible nonuniformity of the average background intensity and low contrast between lesions and background; principally, in the lesions I and II. However, within a region of interest, changes in intensity level can effectively distinguish a lesion, since locally a lesion has major variation of intensities than its surrounding background. The exact shape and size of this region are not important, and hence the region is referred to as an approximate region. Other details on this study can be found in [Rodríguez & Pacheco, 2007].

For the study with images of blood vessels were used biopsies, which represent an angiogenesis process in malignant tumors. These were included in paraffin by using the inmunohistoquimic technique with the complex method of avidina biotina. Finally, monoclonal CD34 was contrasted with green methyl to accentuate formation of new blood vessels. These biopsies were obtained from soft parts of human bodies. This analysis was carried out for more than 100 patients. In Figure 13 can be seen typical images, which were captured via MADIP system with a resolution of 512x512x8 bit/pixels.

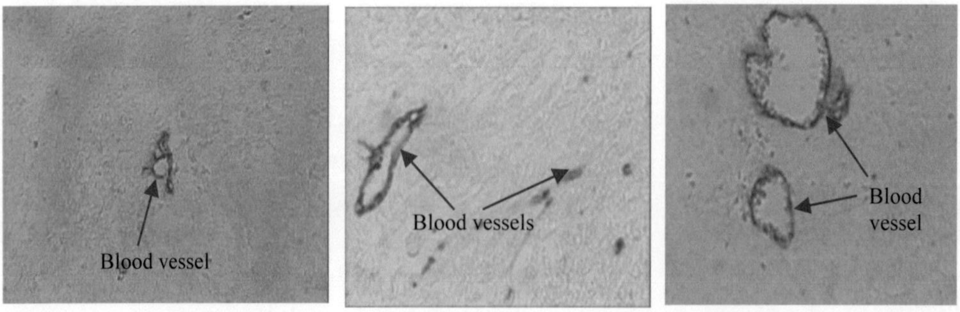

Fig. 13. These images represent the angiogenesis process. The blood vessels are marked with arrows

In Figure 14 a horizontal profile can be observed through the centre of a vessel; that is, a plot of the pixel intensities along a single row. In Figure 15 (b), the histogram of this image is represented.

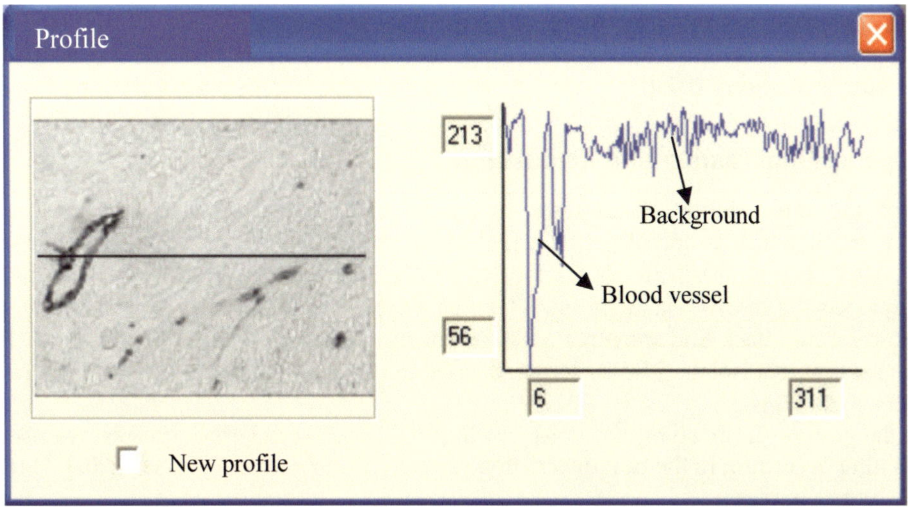

Fig. 14. An intensity profile through the centre of a vessel. Profile is indicated by a line

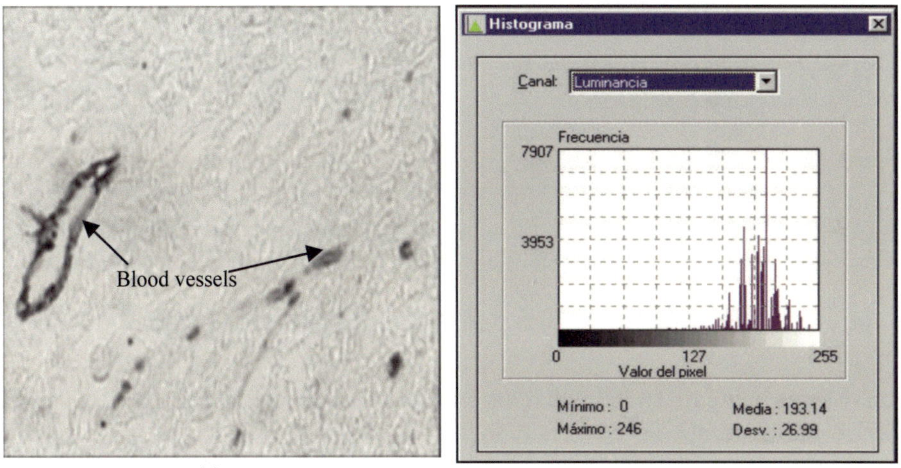

(a) (b)

Fig. 15. (a) Original image. (b) Histogram image

There are several notable characteristics of this image, which are common to typical images that we encounter in the tissues of biopsies:

1. The intensity is slightly darker within the blood vessel than in the local surrounding background. It is emphasized that this observation holds only within the local surroundings.
2. High local variation of intensity is observed both within the blood vessel and the background. However, the local variation of intensity is higher within the blood vessel than in background regions (see Fig. 14)
3. The variability of blood vessels both, in size and shape, it can be observed (see Fig. 13).
4. The contrast of intensities between the blood vessel (BV) and the background is low. This is evident from the intensity histogram (see Fig. 15 (b)). This histogram is uni-modal, reflecting the low separation in average intensity of the BV and background.

Due to acquisition protocol, the images are corrupted with a lot of noise. It can be observed the ripple of the histogram in Figure 15(b). Other details on this research can be found in [Rodríguez & Pacheco, 2005].

4. Experimental results and discussion

One of the most important diseases to study is the atherosclerosis and its organic-consequences, which is one of the principal causes of death in the world [Fernández-Britto et al., 1988; Fernández-Britto & Carlevaro, 1989]. The atherosclerosis produces as final consequence the loss of elasticity and increase of the wall of arteries. For example, heart attack, cerebral attack and ischemia are some of its principal consequences [Cotran, 2002]. Strategies that can isolate atherosclerotic lesions in an automatic way constitute important tools for pathologists.

With the goal of diminishing the noise existing in the atherosclerosis images, we used the Gauss filter according to the parameters described in [Rodríguez & Pacheco, 2007]. Figure 16 shows two examples.

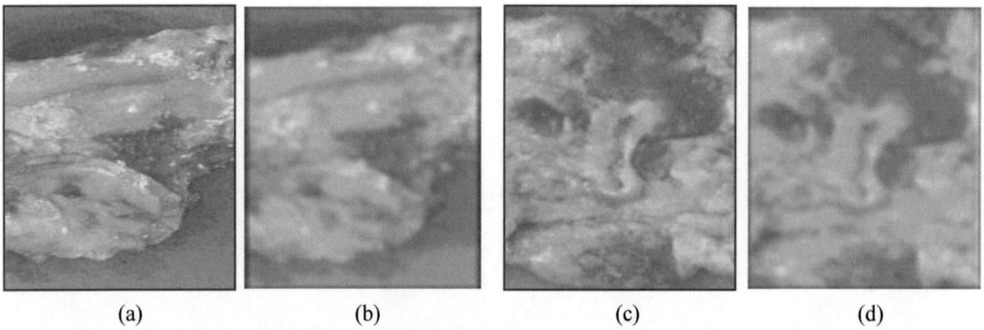

Fig. 16. (a) and (c) Original images, (b) and (d) Filtered images with Gauss ($\sigma = 3$, $5x5$ window size).

One can observe in Figure 16 (b, d) that the images are smoother. It is possible to see that the atherosclerotic lesions are more uniform, which is indicative that the noise was diminished.

In a second step, we carried out a modification of the histogram to these images, according to the algorithm presented in [Rodríguez & Pacheco, 2007]. This procedure was carried out in order to increase the contrast. We show in Figure 17 the obtained results.

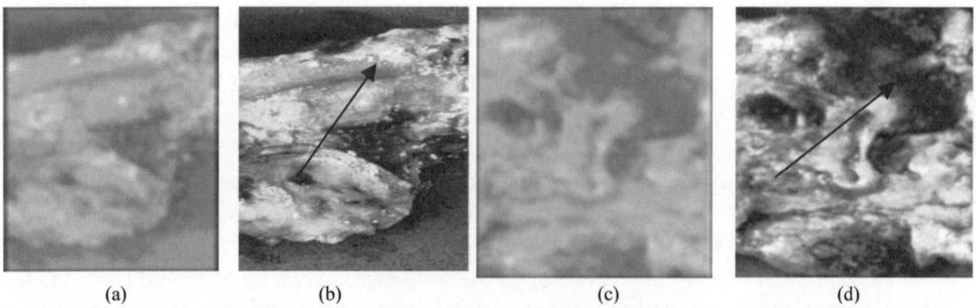

Fig. 17. (a) and (c) Filtered images with Gauss. Figures (b) and (d) contrasted images. It is evident the good obtained result with the enhancement.

We shall carry out a general description of the proposed method before going into the details of each one of the steps, which will allow having a panoramic vision of the proposed solution. In Figure 18 is depicted all steps of the proposed strategy to obtain robust markers for the atherosclerotic lesions.

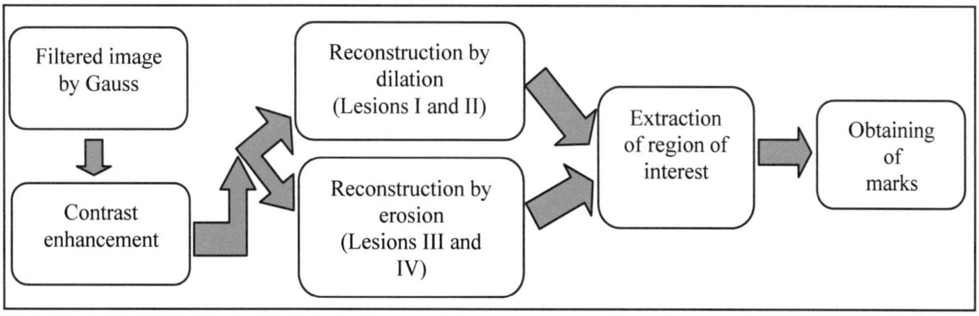

Fig. 18. Steps to obtain the markers of atherosclerotic lesions

It is very important to point out that the proposed strategy was obtained according to experimentation; that is, we carried out firstly a morphological reconstruction by erosion for all lesions (see definition 2.1.4), and secondly, we carried out a morphological reconstruction by dilation for all lesions (see definition 2.1.2). We verified that, in all cases for the lesions I and II, the best results by using a reconstruction by dilation were obtained; while for the lesions III and IV the best results were obtained carrying out a reconstruction by erosion. This affirmation will be appreciated in the next steps. We processed 100 images in total, but for space problem, we only reported 10 cases.

In order to cope with problems previously cited and with the goal of extracting the approximate regions of interest; after the histogram modification, we carried out a morphological reconstruction. The region of interest is a region that contains the lesion and its neighboring background, where the exact shape and size of this region are not important. This region of interest is referred to an approximate region. We verified that the reconstruction by erosion (for the lesions III and IV) led to an image where the dark zones correspond to these lesions. For example, in Figure 19 is shown the obtained result for a lesion of type IV.

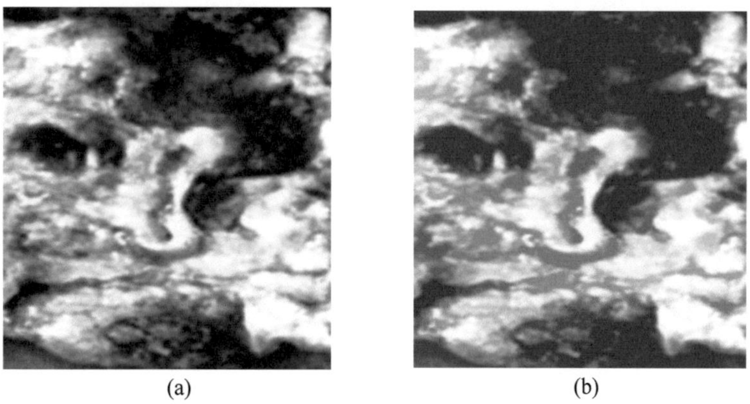

Fig. 19. (a) Resulting image of the histogram modification. (b) Image obtained by a reconstruction by erosion. The dark parts correspond to the lesion IV.

The result in Figure 19(b) was obtained by using a rhombus as structuring element of *5x5* pixels and a height equal to *60* (see definition 2.1.1.3). Basically, we used the *h*-domes, where the principle is to subtract an arbitrary constant *h* from the original image *I* and to perform a grayscale geodesic reconstruction of *I* from *I+h* (*J* = *I+h*). This provides a useful technique for extracting "*domes*" of a given height *h*. The choice of *h* turns out not to be a critical operation, since a range of values yield correct results, which we verified in the practice. In addition, the selection of this structuring element and its size was obtained via experimentation. It is important to point out that when one speaks of size of the structuring element its dimension is in pixels. In addition, the structuring element is plane. For an understanding better on this aspect, as an example, the form and size of four structuring elements are shown (see Figure 20).

In Figure 21, it is represented the obtained results (in the reconstruction) for other structuring elements. In all cases in order to carry out the geodesic reconstruction, the considered height was equal to *60*.

As can be appreciated in Figure 21(a), for a structuring element minor than *5x5* pixels, the area of the atherosclerotic lesions decreased. Comparing the image of Figure 19 (b) with those of Figures 21(b) and 21(c), one can see that for structuring elements (rhombus or circle) major than *5x5* pixels, the obtained results were very similar, but the computation time was increased. In Figures 21(d), 21(e) and 21(f), it can be observed that for diagonal segments as structuring elements, the obtained results were not good. The lesions were notably deformed. For these reasons, we considered that the rhombus of *5x5* pixels was the most suitable. This behaviour was similar for the 100 processed images.

		1		
	1	1	1	
1	1	1	1	1
	1	1	1	
		1		

Rhombus *5x5*

1				
	1			
		1		
			1	
				1

Segment of line 45^0

	1	1	1	
1	1	1	1	1
1	1	1	1	1
1	1	1	1	1
	1	1	1	

Circle *5x5*

	1	1	1	
	1	1	1	
1	1	1	1	1
	1	1	1	
	1	1	1	

Hexagon *5x5*

Fig. 20. Four structuring elements; superior left: rhombus of size *5x5* pixels, superior right: diagonal segment of *5* pixels, inferior left: circle of *5x5* pixels and inferior right: hexagon of *5x5* pixels.

With respect to the height for carrying out the geodesic reconstruction, we verified that for all our images the optimal values were in the range from *40* to *60*. In fact, in Figure 22 are depicted the obtained results considering a height out of this range.
In Figures 22 (b) and 22 (c), one can observe that for a large height the atherosclerotic lesions were very smoothed. Furthermore, the areas of the lesions also were increased. Some of them were fused (see arrows). For a height smaller than *40*, according to the criterion of pathologists, the area of the atherosclerotic lesions decreased (see Fig. 22(a)). Then, in these cases, an exact delimitation of the lesions is not obtained and the final results will be poor. This behavior was similar for all the processed images, which is not included here by space problem.

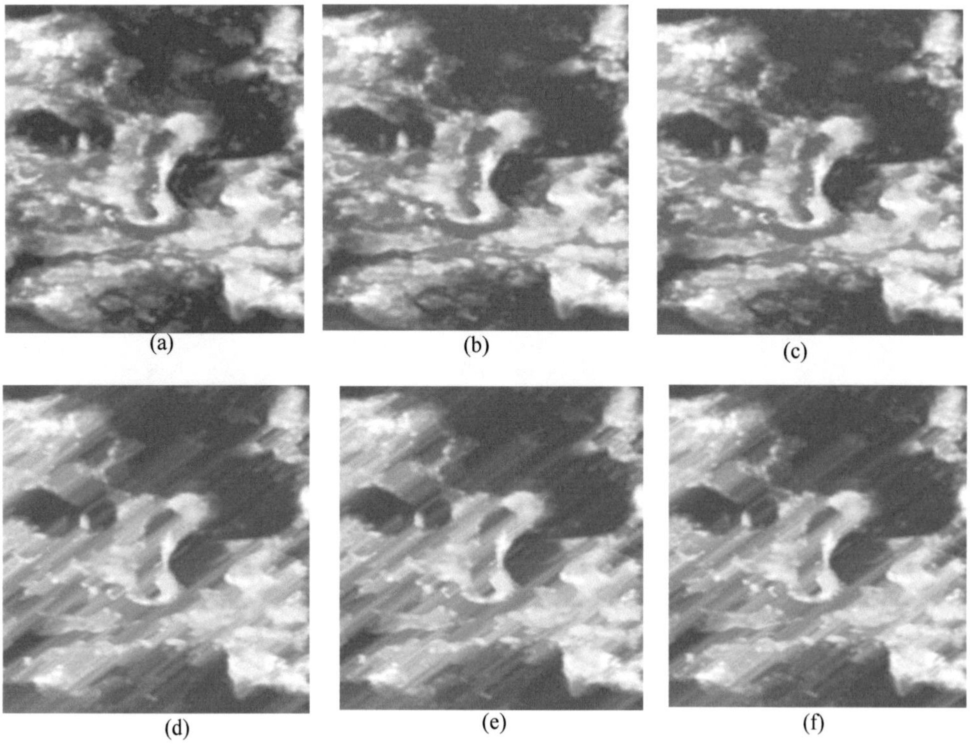

Fig. 21. (a) Reconstruction by a rhombus of *3x3* pixels. (b) Reconstruction by a rhombus of *7x7* pixels. (c) Reconstruction by a circle of *7x7* pixels. (d) Reconstruction by a diagonal segment (*45⁰*) of *3* pixels. (e) Reconstruction by a diagonal segment of *5* pixels *(45⁰)*. (f) Reconstruction by a diagonal segment of *7* pixels *(45⁰)*. The height was equal to *60*.

After obtaining both, the size of structuring element and the optimal height, the next step of our strategy was to segment the approximate region of interest. That is, as it was pointed out, a region that contains the atherosclerotic lesion and its neighbouring background. This step was carried out by applying a simple threshold through Otsu method [Otsu, 1978]. The thresholding value does not have much influence on the performance, because the exact shape and size of this region are not important. In this case, the region is referred to as an approximate region. In Figure 23(b) one can see the region of interest.

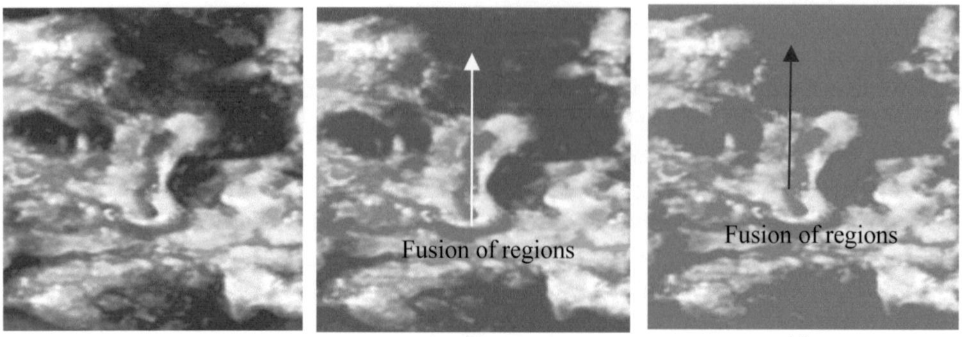

(a) (b) (c)

Fig. 22. (a) Reconstruction with a rhombus of *5x5* and height equal to *30*. (b) Reconstruction with a rhombus of *5x5* and height equal to *80*. (c) Reconstruction with a rhombus of *5x5* and height equal to *120*.

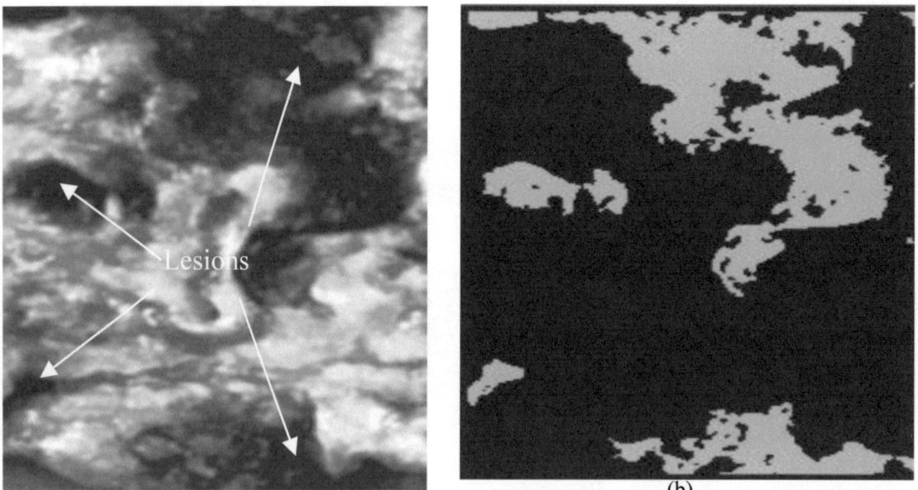

(a) (b)

Fig. 23. (a) Image of the reconstruction, where the arrows indicate the lesions. (b) Regions of interest

In Figure 23 (b), it is possible to observe that all the indicated lesions in Figure 23 (a) were detected. Furthermore, it can be seen that the regions of interest don't have the exact size of the lesions, since they simply are an approximation. We verified that the regions of interest, in general, were smaller than the atherosclerotic lesions. This result was the same one for all the processed images. Other regions of interest will be able to be observed in the next section. After this result, we developed an algorithm to obtain markers for the atherosclerotic lesion.

4.1 Algorithm to obtain markers

The steps of the algorithm are described below:

1. *Obtain the regions of interest, which as we pointed out, it are those regions belonging to the lesions and they are obtained through a thresholding procedure, after carrying out the*

geodesic reconstruction. To the resulting image of this procedure we will call IREZI.

2. Label the resulting image of the step 1. This step is as follows. Create an auxiliary image with all pixels in zero: Let IA1 be this image. Scan IREZI at iterative way, then in this image all the background is labeled with a value equal to 1.
3. With the goal of finding connected components, scan IREZI again from the top to the bottom and from the left to the right. If there is a pixel, which belongs to a connected component and in the image IA1 this pixel has zero value, then other iterative method begins to work. This new iterative method marks with a determined value within the image IA1 all pixels belonging to a connected component. In addition, pixels within the image IREZI are also marked with a value, which identifies the connected component to which they belong. This action is carried out in the whole image. As this step is finished, in the image IREZI all the connected components were filled and in the image IA1 all the connected components were labeled.
4. Create other auxiliary image (let IA2 be this image) with the same values of the image IA1. Also create an array, which controls if a connected component was reduced. In the image IA2 is where in each step the reduction of the connected components are obtained, the final result is represented in the image IA1.
5. Scan the labeled image (IA1). When in this image a pixel is found, which belongs to a connected component, through other iterative method, this component is reduced and in the image IA2 all the frontiers of the connected component are marked. If still there is some pixel within the connected component, which is no frontier, in the images IA2 and IA1, the mentioned pixel is eliminated and this function begins again until that all points are frontiers. In this case, the obtained result (reduction) is taken as the mark. In the array (see step 4) it is indicated that the labeled component with this value was processed and it is began to look for other component.
6. Finish when the image IA1 is completely scanned. When this step is concluded, in the image IA1 all marks of the atherosclerotic lesions are. These marks are collocated in the image IREZI. Here, after the step two, the connected components (in IREZI) were filled. The image IREZI is the resulting image.

All the functions in C of this algorithm appear in [Rodríguez & Pacheco, 2007]. The result of carrying out this algorithm to the image of Figure 23(b) is shown in Figure 24. In Figure 24(b) one can see that the mark is unique for each of the lesions, which is always inside the atherosclerotic lesion. In this case, we firstly applied this algorithm to the regions of interest of the lesions III and IV. In other words, to the contrasted images of this type of lesions (III and IV) a reconstruction by erosion is carried out, later we applied a thresholding in order to obtain the regions of interest; lastly the proposed algorithm is applied to the image of the regions of interest (see Fig. 24 (b)). This procedure is the same one for all the lesions III and IV. In total *40* lesions of type III and IV, it were processed.

Now, we shall explain the steps that we carried out to obtain the marks for the lesions I and II (see Fig. 18). In this case, the first step was to carry out a modification of histogram according to the algorithm that appears in [Rodríguez & Pacheco, 2007]. After this step, we carried out a reconstruction by dilation. This reconstruction improved, even more, the contrast of the lesions I and II. Figure 25 shows the obtained result of the reconstruction.

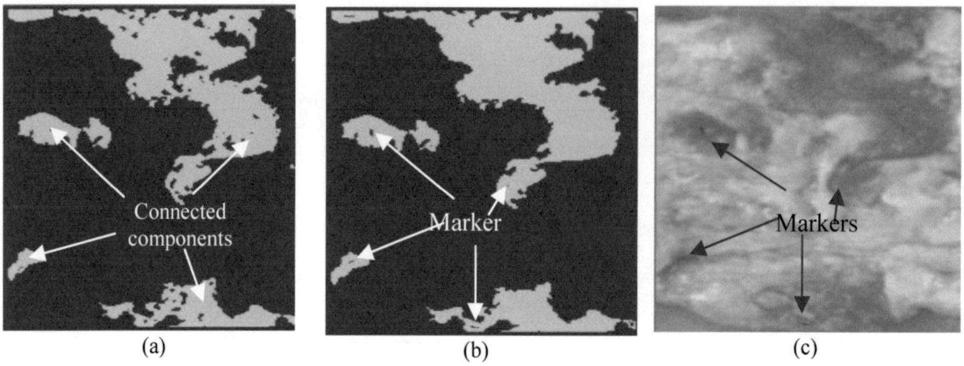

Fig. 24. (a). Image with regions of interest, (b) Marking image, (c) Marks superimposed on the original image

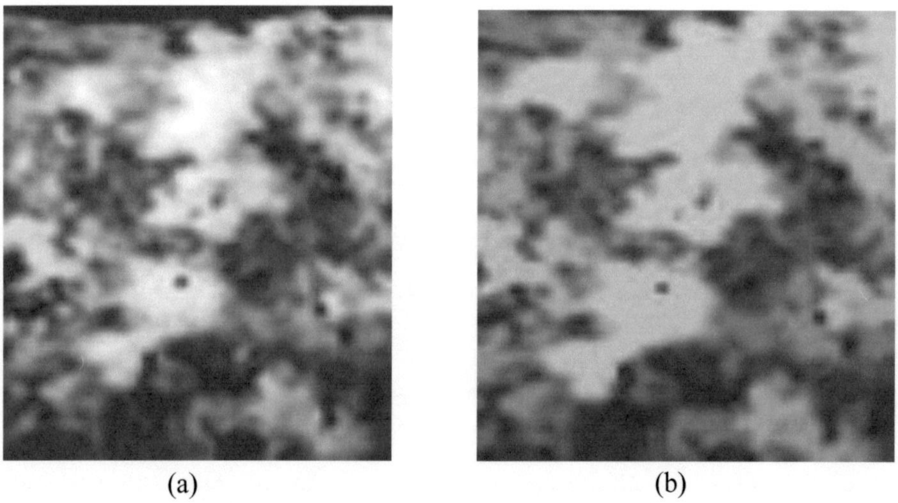

Fig. 25. (a) Initial image. (b) Reconstruction by dilation (lesion II)

The result in Figure 25(b) was obtained by using a structuring element type rhombus of *5x5* pixels, similar to the one used for the lesions III and IV. In this case, the used height in order to carry out a geodesic reconstruction by dilatation was equal to *40*. Also, for these lesions (I and II), several experiments with distinct structuring elements were carried out. The obtained results were very similar to those depicted in Figures 21 and 22. We verified that the structuring element type rhombus of *5x5* pixels was of the best performance. In addition, with respect to height for the reconstruction, we concluded that the optimal height was in the range from *40* to *60* too. Out of this range, similar results were obtained as in the lesions III and IV. This experiment was carried out for a total of 50 images (lesions I and II). All the obtained results were not shown here because they were very similar. Later, we obtained the approximate region of interest via a thresholding and lastly, the markers were obtained through the algorithm presented in section 4.1. The obtained result is shown in Figure 26. One can observe that the regions of interest are not exactly the atherosclerotic lesions, but simply an approximate region.

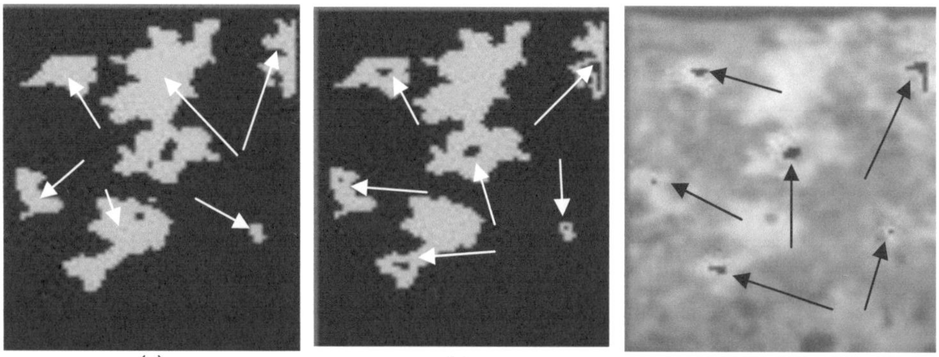

(a) (b) (c)

Fig. 26. (a) Regions of interest. The arrows indicate the connected components. (b) Image with marks. (c) The marks superimposed on the original image.

In Figure 26(b) it is possible to see that the marks are unique for each of the lesions, which are always inside the atherosclerotic lesion. This aspect is very important.

4.2 Application of the proposed strategy for atherosclerosis image segmentation by using the watershed method

As have been pointed out the watershed transformation has the drawback of producing over-segmentation. This is true even if one had taken the precaution of filtering the initial image or its gradient. In fact, Figure 27(b) shows the obtained result as we directly applied the watershed transformation to an atherosclerosis image without good markers for the lesions. It is evident as the contours of the atherosclerotic lesions were not well detected and it is observed a lot of noise. However, in Figure 27(c) is shown the excellent obtained result according to our strategy and the introduced algorithm in this work (see section 4.1). The contours of the atherosclerotic lesions were well defined.

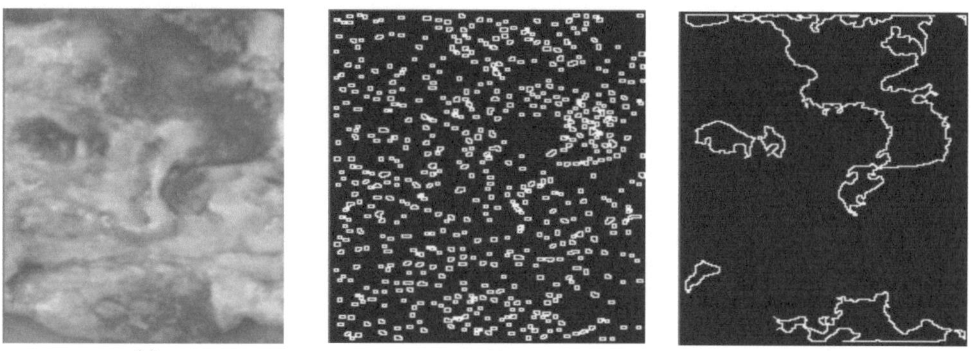

(a) (b) (c)

Fig. 27. (a) Original image. (b) The watershed segmentation without marks in the lesions. (c) The watershed segmentation according to our strategy.

In Figure 28, we show the contours superimposed on the original image in order to see the exact coincidence of the obtained contours. This result is evident.

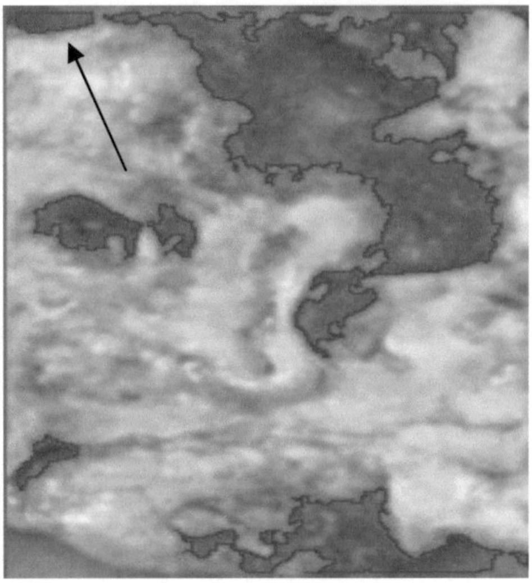

Fig. 28. The contours superimposed on the original image. It is possible to see the exact coincidence of the contours on the lesions. The arrow indicates an object, which does not correspond to an atherosclerotic lesion. In [Rodríguez & Pacheco, 2007], a quantitative evaluation of this algorithm was carried out.

In Figure 29, another example of the application of watershed method on other atherosclerosis image is shown. In Figure 29 (b), we applied watershed segmentation on the gradient of image. It is evident that, even though the watershed method was applied on the gradient of image, an over-segmentation was produced. In Figure 29 (c), one can observe the obtained result of carrying out our strategy. In Figure 30 is shown the obtained contours with our strategy superimposed on the original image. It is possible to observe the exact coincidence of the contours on the lesions.

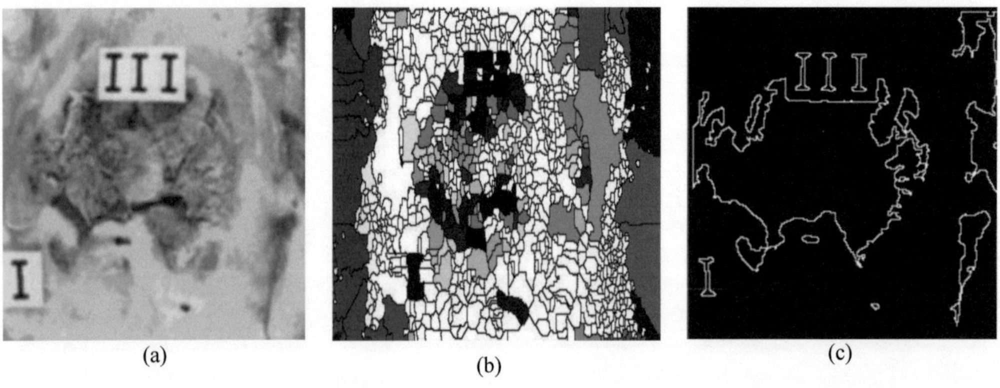

Fig. 29. (a) Original image. (b) Watershed transformation on the gradient of the original image (c) The watershed segmentation according to our strategy.

This same strategy was applied for image segmentation of blood vessels [Rodríguez et al., 2005], but here we will expose the obtained results on these images (blood vessels) by using the mean shift.

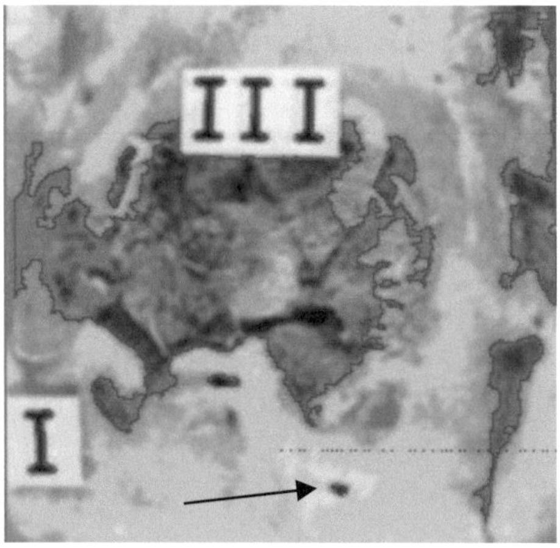

Fig. 30. The contours superimposed on the original image. The arrow indicates an object, which does not correspond to an atherosclerotic lesion (see reference [Rodríguez & Pacheco, 2007])

4.3 Obtained results in image segmentation of blood vessels by using the mean shift

The angiogenesis process is an important aspect in the histopathological research of diseases [Díaz-Flores et al., 1994]. This process is studied by pathological anatomy and it is characterised by a new formation of blood vessels in the tissue, which increases its growing. Angiogenesis is a normal process that occurs in all tissues, but it is known that in pathological cases the increase of blood vessels is abnormal. For example, in mammary, prostate, bladder and brain cancers the greater the number of blood vessels, the more developed the disease is [Díaz-Flores et al., 1994].

In the study of the angiogenesis process the pathologists analyse all information related with the blood vessels by using a microscope. This work is very tedious and time consuming and obviously, the automation of this analysis is highly desirable. In such a sense, a useful task for digital images processing should be the segmentation of blood vessels.

In this work we utilized the mean shift for segmentation of blood vessels. So, we proposed a segmentation algorithm, which will be exposed next.

In general, an image captured with a real physical device is contaminated with noise and in most cases a statistical model of white noise is assumed, mean zero and variance σ. For smoothing or elimination of this form of noise many types of filters have been published, the most classic being the low pass filter. This filter indiscriminately replaces the central pixel in a window by the average or the weighted average of pixels contained therein. The end result with this filtering is a blurred image; since this reduces the noise but also important information is taken away from the edges. However, there are low pass filtering techniques that preserve the discontinuities and reduce abrupt changes near local structures. A diverse number of approaches have been published taking into consideration the use of adaptive filtering. These range from an adaptive Wiener filter, local isotropic smoothing, to an anisotropic filtering. The mean shift works in the spatial-range domain, but differs from it (anisotropic filtering) in the use of local information.

The algorithm that was proposed in [Comaniciu & Meer, 2002] for filtering through mean shift is as follows:

Let $\{x_i\}_i$ and $\{z_i\}_i$, $i=1,\ldots,n$ be the input and filtered images in the joint spatial-range domain. For each pixel $p \in x_i, p=(x,y,z) \in \Re^3$, where $(x,y) \in \Re^2$ and $z \in \left[0,\, 2^B - 1\right]$, B being the quantity of bits/pixel in the image. The filtering algorithm comprises the following steps:

For each $i=1,\ldots,n$

1. *Initialize* $j=1$ *and* $y_{i,1} = p_i$.
2. *Compute the mean shift in order to obtain the mode where the pixel converges; that is, the calculation of the mean shift is carried out until convergence,* $y = y_{i,c}$.
3. *Store at* Z_i *the component of the gray level of calculated value:* $Z_i = \left(x_i^s, y_{i,c}^r\right)$, *where* x_i^s *is the spatial component and* $y_{i,c}^r$ *is the range component.*

4.3.1 Proposed segmentation algorithm via mean shift

1. *Run the mean shift filtering procedure for the image according to former steps, and store all the information about the d-dimensional convergence point in* ***Zi***.
2. *Define the regions, which are found in the spatial domain* (h_s) *with intensities smaller or equal than* $h_r/2$.
3. *For each region, which was defined in the step 2, look for all the pixels belonging to the region whose mean intensity values are assigned at* ***Zi***.
4. *Build the region graph through an adjacent list as follows: for each region, look for all adjacent regions to the right or under the region.*
5. *While there are nodes in the graph, which have been not visited, run a variant of the "Depth-First Search" (DFS), which allows concatenating adjacent regions; as parameter one has to provide a node which has been not yet visited. To do this the next steps are carried out:*
   - 5.1. *Mark the mentioned node as visited.*
   - 5.2. *While there is children not yet visited:*
     children = current child
     if $|Z_{parent} - Z_{child}| <= h_r$, *then,*
     The region of the child is fused with the region of the father, where the same label is assigned and it is marked as visited.
   - 5.3 *To the parent is assigned the children of the visited child from the first position and the children which have been not visited are remained.*
   - 5.4 *Look for the following child and come back to step 2 while stability it is not obtained (i.e., no more pixel values are modified).*
6. *Eliminate spatial regions containing less than M pixels, since those regions are considered irrelevant.*
7. *(Binary): To all the pixels belonging to background, assign the white color to the objects and the black color to the background.*

The effectiveness of this algorithm was recently proven in [Rodríguez et al., 2008]. In that paper was carried out a comparison of the obtained results with this algorithm and those attained by using the spectral methods.

Now, some of the obtained results will be exposed, in real images, using the proposed segmentation algorithm of the mean shift. In Figure 31 are presented a first example where one can appreciate the segmentation result.

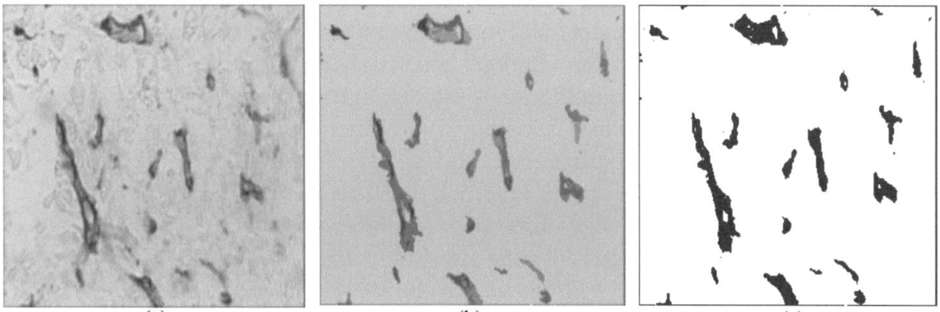

(a) (b) (c)

Fig. 31. (a) Original Image, (b) Image segmented with the proposed algorithm (*hs*=4, *hr*=15, *M* =20), (c) Binarized image.

In Figures 32 and 33, other two segmentation examples appear using the proposed algorithm.

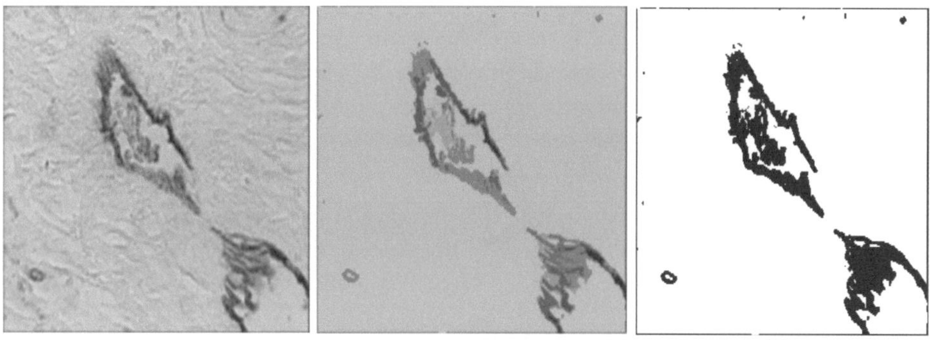

(a) (b) (c)

Fig. 32. (a) Original Image, (b) Image segmented with the proposed algorithm (*hs*=4, *hr*=15, *M* =20), (c) Binarized image.

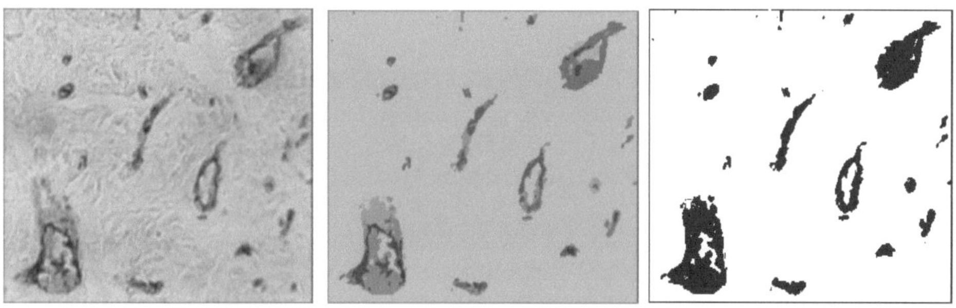

(a) (b) (c)

Fig. 33. (a) Original Image, (b) Image segmented with the proposed algorithm (*hs*=4, *hr*=15, *M* =20), (c) Binarized image.

One can see in Figures 31, 32 and 33 the robustness of the obtained results using the proposed segmentation algorithm. According to the opinion of specialists the method was able to discriminate all the objects of interest (blood vessels). This is of supreme importance from the point of view of the diagnosis. It is also observed that the obtained results are free of noise; in addition, for all the segmented images the same parameters h_r and h_s were used.
By the way of examples, two of the obtained results in [Rodriguez et al., 2008] it will be exposed. These results are shown in Figure 34 and 35. In the presented examples, the reader can appreciate that both methods were able to effectively well isolate the blood vessels. However, one also can see that the segmented images via the mean shift algorithm were less noisy than those obtained via the spectral method. Furthermore, the edges were more robust and better defined in the images segmented with the mean shift.
In order to obtain less noisy images with the spectral method it would be necessary to carry out an additional step of filtering with the aim of eliminating the noise that arises during the segmentation process. This procedure could be carried out through a morphological technique, which can be an opening or a majority filter. Another way could be to use the mean shift procedure as a pre-processing in order to improve performance of the spectral method. In [Rodriguez et al., 2008], it also can be seen a quantitative method of evaluation of these strategies.

(a) (b) (c)

Fig. 34. (a) Original image, (b) Segmentation via the mean shift, (c) Segmentation via the spectral method

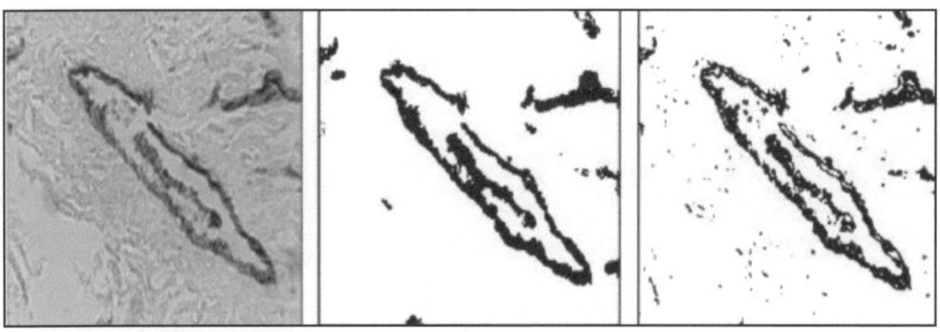

(a) (b) (c)

Fig. 35. (a) Original image, (b) Segmentation via the mean shift, (c) Segmentation via the spectral method

5. Conclusions

In this chapter was carried out a brief theoretical introduction of the *Watershed* transformation. Through the experimentation suitable markers were obtained for the atherosclerotic lesions (including to the background). In such a sense, a new algorithm was introduced, which was efficient in order to mark the atherosclerotic lesions and to eliminate all other spurious information. With the proposed strategy the application of the watershed segmentation gave good results, where the exact contours of the objects of interest were obtained (atherosclerotic lesions). Furthermore, over-segmentation never was obtained.

A theoretical introduction of the mean shift was carried out too. In such a sense, a new algorithm was proposed for image segmentation of blood vessels. The same was suitable for this application. In order to demonstrate its good performance, the same one was compared with another segmentation algorithm already established (the spectral method). Through several experiments with real images, we proven that the segmented images by using the mean shift were less noisy than those attained by means of the spectral method. In addition, the obtained edges were better defined by using the mean shift than those attained by the spectral method.

The strategies introduced in this chapter can be extended to other types of biomedical images and their application is valid for other tasks of image analysis where suitable methods of segmentation are required.

6. References

Cheng, Y. (1995). Mean Shift, Mode Seeking, and Clustering, IEEE Transactions on Pattern Analysis and Machine Intelligence, Vol. 17, No. 8, (August 1995), pp.(790-799), ISSN: 0162-8828

Chin-Hsing, C.; Lee, J.; Wang, J. & Mao, C. W. (1998). Colour image segmentation for bladder cancer diagnosis, Mathematical and Computer Modelling, Vol. 27, No. 2, (January 1998), pp (103-120), ISSN: 0895-7177

Comaniciu, D. I. (2000). Nonparametric Robust Method for Computer Vision, Ph.D. thesis, New Brunswick, Rutgers, The State University of New Jersey, January, 2000.

Comaniciu, D. & Meer, P. (2002). Mean Shift: A Robust Approach toward Feature Space Analysis, IEEE Transaction on Pattern Analysis and Machine Intelligence, Vol. 24, No. 5, (May 2002), ISSN: 0162-8828

Cotran, R. (2002). Patología Estructural y Funcional, Mc. Grow Hill, México, ISBN: 970-10-2787-6.

Díaz-Flores, L.; Guitiérrez, R. & Varela, H. (1994). Angiogenesis. An update, Histoogy and Histopathology, Vol. 9, (July 1994), pp (807-853), ISSN 0213-3911

Fukunaga, K. & Hostetler, L. D. (1975). The Estimation of the Gradient of a Density Function, IEEE Transactions on Information Theory, Vol. IT-21, No. 1, (January 1975), pp. (32-40), ISSN: 0018-9448

Fernández-Britto, J. E.; Carlevaro, P. V.; Bacallao, J.; Koch, A.S.; Guski, H. & Campos, R. (1988): "Coronary atherosclerotic lesion: its study applying an atherometric system using principal components analysis". Z. Klin. Med. 44: 291-294, 1988.

Fernández-Britto, J. E. & Carlevaro, P.V. (1989). Atherometric System: Morphometric standardized methodology to study atherosclerosis and its consequences, Gegenbaurs morphologisches Jahrbuch, Vol. 135, (November 1989), pp (1-12), ISSN: 0001-5180

Fuh, C-S.; Maragos, P. & Vincent, L. (1991). Region based approaches to visual motion correspondence, Technical Report 91-18, (November 1991), pp (1-29), Harvard

Robotics Laboratory, Harvard University, Division of Applied Sciences, Pierce Hall, Cambridge NA 02138

Grenier, T.; Revol-Muller, C.; Davignon, F. & Gimenez, G. (2006). Hybrid Approach for Multiparametric Mean Shift Filtering, Image Processing, IEEE, International Conference, Atlanta, GA, 8-11, (Oct. 2006), pp (1541-1544).

Kenong, W.; Gauthier, D. & Levine, M. D. (1995). Live Cell Image Segmentation, IEEE Transactions on Biomedical Engineering, Vol.42, No. 1, (January 1995), pp (1-11), ISSN: 0018-9294

Koss, J.; Newman, F.; Johnson, D. & Kirch, D. (1999). Abdominal organ segmentation using texture transforms and a hopfield neural network, IEEE Transactions Medical Imaging, Vol. 18, No. 7, (July, 1999), ISSN: 0278-0062

Najman, L. & Schmitt, M. (1996). Geodesic Saliency of Watershed Countours and Hierarchical Segmentation, IEEE Transactions on Pattern Analysis and Machine Intelligence, Vol. 18, No. 12, (December 1996), pp (1163-1173), ISSN: 0162-8828

Otsu, N. (1978). A threshold selection method from grey level histogram, IEEE Transactions on Systems, Man and Cybernetics, Vol. SMC-8, No. 1, (January 1978), pp (62-66), ISSN: 0018-9472

Rodríguez, R.; Alarcón, T. & Sánchez, L. (2001). MADIP: Morphometrical Analysis by Digital Image Processing, Proceedings of the IX Spanish Symposium on Pattern Recognition and Image Analysis, Vol. I, pp (291-298), ISBN 84-8021-349-3, Spain.

Rodríguez, R.; Alarcón, T.; Wong, R. & Sanchez, L. (2002). Color segmentation applied to study of the angiogenesis. Part I, Journal of Intelligent and Robotic System, Vol. 34, No. 1, (May 2002), pp (83-97), ISSN: 0921-0296

Rodríguez, R.; Alarcón, T. & Pacheco, O. (2005). A New Strategy to Obtain Robust Markers for Blood Vessels Segmentation by using the Watersheds Method, Journal of Computers in Biology and Medicine, Vol. 35, No. 8, (October 2005), pp (665-686), ISSN: 0010-4825

Rodríguez, R. & Pacheco, O. (2007). A Strategy for Atherosclerosis Image Segmentation by using Robust Markers, Journal Intelligent & Robotic System, Vol. 50, No. 2, (October 2007), pp (121 – 140), ISSN: 0921-0296.

Rodríguez, R.; Castillo, P. J.; Guerra, V., Sossa, J. H.; Suárez A. G. & Izquierdo, E. (2008). A comparison between two robust techniques for segmentation of blood vessels, Journal of Computers in Biology and Medicine, Vol. 38, No. Issue 8, (June 2008). pp (931 – 940), ISSN: 0010-4825

Sijbers, J.; Scheunders, P.; Verhoye, M.; Van der Linden, A.; Van Dyck, D. & Raman, E. (1997). Watershed-based segmentation of 3D MR data for volume quatization, Magnetic Resonance Imaging, Vol. 15, No. 6, (February 1997), pp (679-688), ISSN: 0730-725X

Schmid, P. (1999). Segmentation of digitized dermatoscopic images by two-dimensional color clustering, IEEE Transactions Medical Imaging, Vol. 18, No. 2, February 1999), pp (164-171), ISSN: 0278-0062

Vicent, L. & Soille, P. (1991). Watersheds in digital spaces: An efficient algorithm based on immersion simulations, IEEE Transactins on Pattern Analysis and Machine Intelligence, Vol. 13, No. 6, (June 1991), pp (583-593), ISSN: 0162-8828

Vincent, L. (1993). Morphological grayscale reconstruction in Image Analysis: Applications and Efficient Algorithms, IEEE Transactions on Image Processing, Vol.2, No. 2, (April, 1993), pp (176-201), ISSN: 1057-7149

Weidner N.; Carroll, P. R.; Flax, J.; Blumenfeld, W. & Folkman, J. (1993). Tumour angiogenesis correlates with metastasis in invasive prostate carcinoma, American Journal of Pathology, Vol. 143, No. 2, (October 1993). ISSN: 0002-9440

22

Algorithm Selection Based on a Region Similarity Metric for Intracellular Image Segmentation

Satoko Takemoto and Hideo Yokota
Bio-Research Infrastructure Construction Team, RIKEN
Japan

1. Introduction

Live-cell imaging using fluorescence microscopy has become popular in modern biology to analyze complex cellular events such as the dynamics of substances inside cells (Eils & Athale, 2003; Bhaskar & Singh, 2007). The next step in furthering this type of analysis is accumulating useful information from the observed images to quantify the dynamics (Cong & Parvin, 2000; Goldman & Spector, 2004; Harder et al., 2008, Waltera et al., 2010). However, quantification of intracellular images is a difficult process because microscopic images with ultra-high sensitivity have a low signal-to-noise ratio. In addition, the amount of data required for quantification has gradually increased as microscopy has developed. These obstacles make it more difficult for cell biologists to identify regions of interest and accumulate various types of quantitative information, such as the volume, shape, and dynamics of intracellular substances. Hence, it is important to develop computational methods for identifying objective targets, such as organelles labeled with, for example, a fluorescent protein.

Image segmentation, the process by which an image is divided into multiple regions corresponding to the components pictured in the image, plays a key role as one of the first steps in the quantification of objective targets from observed images. The use of segmented regions allows us to distinguish substances of interest from irrelevant regions, including background and noise. Numerous segmentation algorithms have been proposed (e.g., Haralick & Shapiro, 1985; Pal & Pal, 1993), but most approaches have been developed for a specific task and cannot be generalized for other segmentation tasks. As a result, researchers have had to face the difficult duty of choosing the most suitable algorithm for a given task while facing increasing numbers of images needing quantification. Moreover, recent notable improvements in live-cell imaging require that segmentation algorithms be flexible enough to accommodate time-variable changes in targets. No single algorithm performed with a fixed-parameter setting is considered to be sufficient for analyzing all time-lapse images, and optimizing algorithms for a variety of images is a tedious task for researchers.

Solutions to these problems have been proposed based on the idea of algorithm selection (e.g., Cardoso & Corte-Real, 2005; Zhang, 2006; Polak et al., 2009). An appropriate algorithm with an optimized parameter setting for each task is automatically selected according to unique evaluation metrics of algorithm performance. Evaluation can be roughly divided into two types: unsupervised evaluation and supervised evaluation. The former type can evaluate different algorithms only by simply computing some chosen evaluation metrics without requiring a prior knowledge about segmentation targets (Cardoso, 2005; Zhang et al., 2006). Statistical features, such as the grey-level standard deviation or homogeneity of pixel intensities in the segmented region, are generally computed. For example, a region contrast (Levine & Nazif, 1985) or region shape (Sahoo et al., 1988) have been proposed (see the comprehensive survey; Zhang et al., 2008). Although the advantage of unsupervised evaluation is that a large number of segmentation algorithms can be evaluated, if there is no guarantee that the pre-defined range for some statistical features will be satisfied, unsupervised evaluation should not be used. In addition, the range of features of intracellular substances cannot be pre-defined, and the diversity in features of intracellular substances may destabilize the result of evaluation.

The latter type can evaluate different algorithms by using some metrics based on similarity (or error) measurement between two regions: an automatically segmented region and a manually segmented region, called the reference region or the ground-truth (e.g., Zhang & Gerbrands, 1992; Martin et al., 2001; Jiang et al., 2006; Polak et al., 2009). For example, the number of mis-segmented pixels (Ysnoff et al., 1977), or the number of segmented targets (Zhang, 1996) is commonly used as an error measurement. Although metrics for supervised evaluation have been proposed so as to reflect the human perception, it is not clear whether the evaluation procedure has actually reflected the perception. That is, the region, which is segmented by using the selected algorithm, may not identify the objective targets to be quantified.

In this research, we propose a novel evaluation metric composed of similarity measurements of a combination of intensity-based and shape-based image features between a segmented region and the ground-truth. Our evaluation metric adopts the philosophy of supervised evaluation and expands it so as to reflect the human perception. We chose these two kinds of image features because cell biologists usually pay attention to them when identifying objective targets, and our proposed method is able to select an appropriate algorithm with optimal parameter settings so as to satisfy biologists' intentions.

The proposed method evaluates the performance of segmentation algorithms by comparing each segmentation result with the ground-truth specified by cell biologists, and it predicts which algorithm will provide the best performance on new images that have similar image features to the original ground-truth. We investigated the performance of two types of segmentation algorithms under our proposed evaluation metric for the identification of fluorescent labeled targets with granular shapes on real intracellular images. In addition to demonstrating the automatic selection of an appropriate algorithm suited to the segmentation task, we showed that our evaluation metric can rank different types of algorithms. We also tested to see whether the selected algorithm showed good segmentation results for other similar images.

The rest of the paper is structured as follows. In Section 2, we describe the algorithm selection framework and explain our proposed evaluation metric based on the region similarity. Experimental results and discussion including segmentation quality for intracellular images taken by a confocal microscope are presented in Section 3. Finally, a conclusion is offered in Section 4.

2. Algorithm selection framework

Many possible solutions must be considered when establishing a segmentation algorithm for a specific application that satisfies a user's intention. In many cases, a target intracellular substance can be represented by a homogeneous unique image feature and can be distinguished from other substances, even from background. Here, we focus on the segmentation techniques implemented by a pattern classification technique (Duda et al., 2007) that can classify image features into classes (or categories) associated with substances. When performing segmentation, the computer first calculates N-dimensional image features that are derived by pixel intensity and classifies them into multiple classes in the N-dimensional feature space. Ideally, each class is associated with one substance pictured in the image, such as an organelle in intracellular images. In the case of supervised classification, the distribution of image features of each class is initially specified by a user who has knowledge of the segmentation target. Then the classifier (i.e. classification rule), such as a discriminant function, is generated based on their distribution so as to assign the image features to a specified class. Manual segmentation is generally conducted for specifying classes. According to the generated classification rule, the computer is able to automatically classify the new inputs that are calculated from the still unsegmented images. As a result, target segmentation can be achieved by detecting only the pixels that have the feature classified as the target class (see Fig. 1).

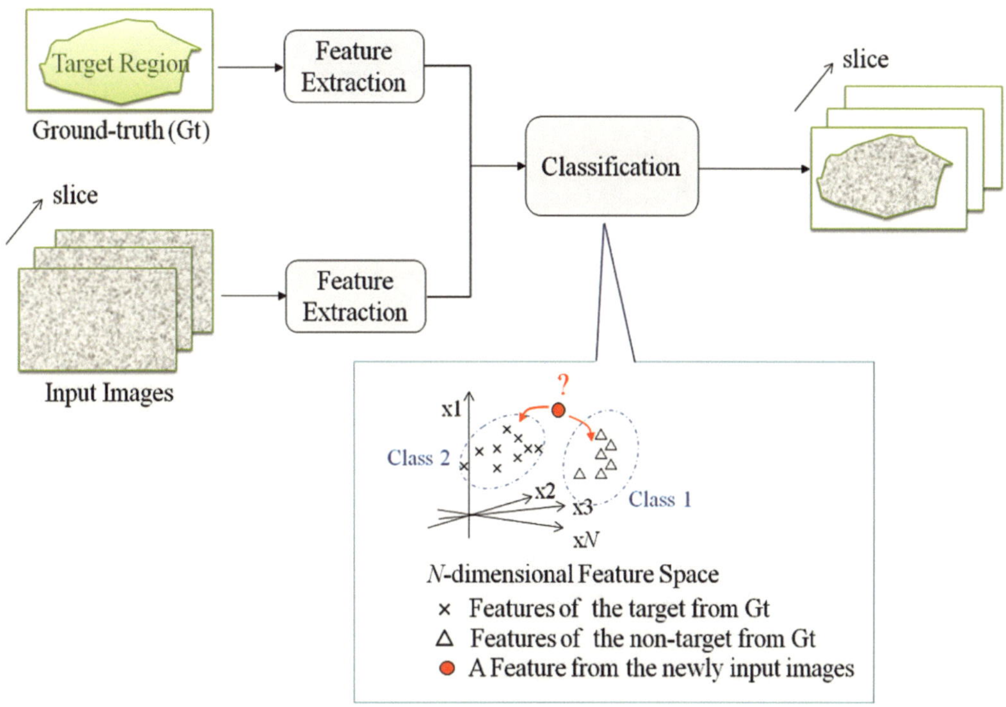

Fig. 1. A segmentation approach based on pattern classification theory. In this approach, the user specifies the region of the segmentation target.

However, the segmentation algorithm implemented by this classification technique is not general enough because there will be large differences in segmentation results depending on the algorithm used. That is, the segmentation results are greatly influenced by the type of features and classification rules adopted, and the optimal algorithm for one segmentation task may not be optimal for a different one. To solve these problems, we propose a new framework that can select an optimal algorithm that satisfies the user's intention in each segmentation task.

Here, "algorithm" means the set including the feature space constructed by the extracted image feature, the classification rule, and the parameter settings for generating the feature space and the classification rule. Our framework selects the algorithm that can extract the target region with the highest level of accuracy by means of our proposed evaluation metric, as long as the ground-truth is specified. As shown in Fig. 2, the algorithm that can segment the region most similarly to the ground-truth is automatically selected from a given set of algorithms.

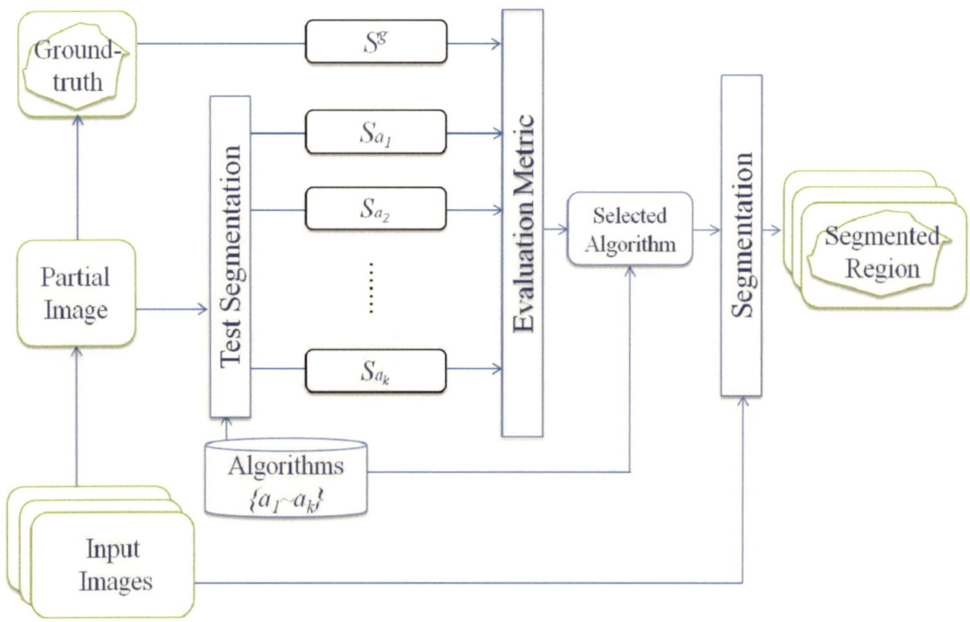

Fig. 2. A framework of algorithm selection.

2.1 Selection metric

The similarities between the ground-truth and the automatically segmented region produced by each given algorithm are used as an evaluation metric for selecting the proper algorithm in our framework. Previous researchers have used many evaluation metrics based on similarities with the ground-truth. For example, (Haindl & Mikes, 2008; Arbelaez, 2009) considered segmentations as a clustering of pixels, and used the Variation of Information (VI), which is based on the distance between two clusters in terms of their average conditional entropy, to measure similarity between two segmentations. Similarly, (Unnikrishnan et al., 2007) introduced the Rand Index (RI) for measuring the distance of two clusters by comparing the compatibility of assignments between pairs of elements in the clusters. Although it is possible to evaluate the performance of segmentation algorithms using the RI and VI and the number of segmented regions evaluated is not constrained with these indexes, their perceptual meaning (that is, an association between human judgement and these indexes) and applicability in the presence of the ground-truth reference (i.e., supervised evaluations) remains unclear.

Martin et al. (Martin et al., 2001) proposed the similarity indexes called Global Consistence Error (GCE) and Local Consistent Error (LCE), which are well-known as evaluation metrics for natural image segmentation. Although there are limitations in terms of the number of segmented regions that can be evaluated and computational cost, a notable advantage of these metrics is that supervised evaluation based on human perception can be conducted only from the viewpoint of region boundaries.

Our evaluation metric for intracellular image segmentation is composed of similarity measurements between the ground-truth and automatically segmented regions, not only from the viewpoint of region boundaries but also from the statistical features in the segmented region. The similarity is measured by the distance of the intensity-based and the shape-based image features between the two regions. The algorithm that produces the minimum distance is defined as the optimal one for a given segmentation task. That is, a user can obtain the most accurate segmentation result by using the selected algorithm to segment a target that has similar characteristics to the ground-truth. It is well known that, if a highly accurate identification is achieved for a feature distribution with a certain classification rule (e.g., a discriminant function), the rule is also applicable to a similar feature distribution and can lead to accurate classification results (Duda et al., 2007).

People generally focus on specific characteristics of a region when evaluating a segmented region. We consider that image features derived from the pixel intensity and boundary shape of the segmentation target are the most important characteristics. We defined S^g as the target region of the ground-truth that is supervised by a user and $S = \{S_a, a \in A\}$ as the automatically segmented regions by given algorithms in a plane (or a space). The similarity R_A between those two regions can be calculated as follows:

$$R_A = \frac{1}{dist(S^g, S)} = \frac{1}{dist(\mathbf{X}^g, \mathbf{X}_A) + dist(\mathbf{P}^g, \mathbf{P}_A)}, \quad (1)$$

where $\mathbf{X} = (x_1, x_2, ..., x_N)$ represents the N-dimensional image features and $\mathbf{P} = (p_1, p_2, ..., p_n)$, $(p_j \in C^N)$ represents the spatially discrete shape features of a region. The symbol $dist(\cdot)$ means the distance calculation of two elements. That is, R_A is defined as a linear combination of $dist(\mathbf{X}^g, \mathbf{X}_A)$ and $dist(\mathbf{P}^g, \mathbf{P}_A)$. We can select an optimal algorithm that can segment a similar region with the ground-truth as follows:

$$a_i = \arg \min_{0<i\le k} \frac{1}{R_{a_i}} \quad (2)$$

where k is the number of given algorithms. The feature derived from pixel intensity, such as texture, differential features, or local correlation, is set to $\mathbf{X}$. In our framework, we measure $dist(\mathbf{X}^g, \mathbf{X}_A)$ by using the Bhattacharyya distance, which is an approximate measurement between two statistical distributions.

2.2 Discrete description of boundary shape

To calculate the shape-based image feature $\mathbf{P}$, we use the set of boundary points (x_j, y_j) $(j = 0, 1, ..., M-1)$ obtained by sampling sequential boundary pixels to describe the shape of the target region. A complex autoregressive model is applied to these boundary points, and this leads to a stable shape description invariant to translation, rotation, and scale of patterns (Sekita et al., 1992). First, each boundary point is represented by a complex number $z_j = x_j + iy_j$ (see Fig. 3).

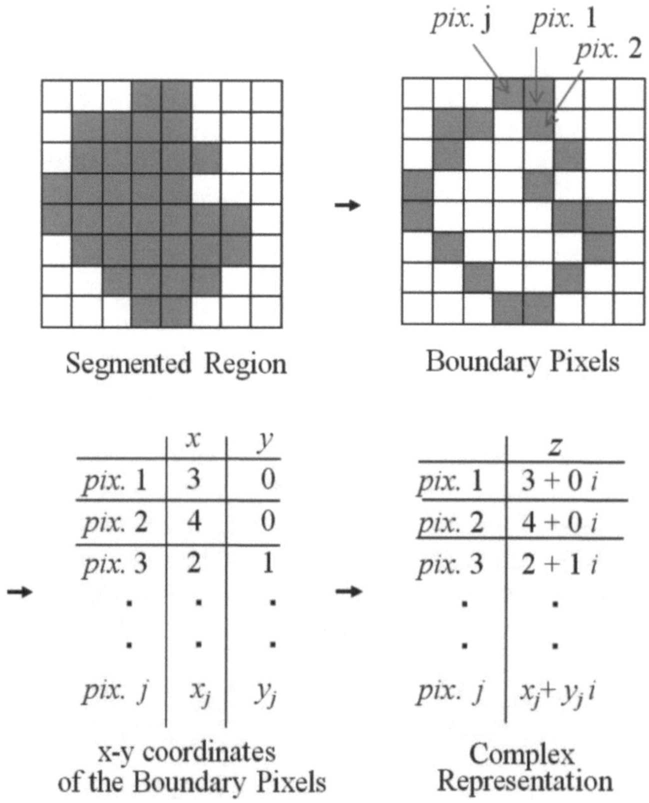

Fig. 3. Schematic diagram of the boundary shape description.

Next, the complex autoregressive model can be applied to each boundary point, which can be represented by a linear combination of the preceding m boundary points as follows:

$$\hat{z}_j = \sum_{k=1}^{m} b_k z_{j-k}, \tag{3}$$

where $\{b_k\}_{k=1}^{m}$ is defined by minimizing the mean squared error of $\varepsilon^2(m)$, which can be calculated as follows:

$$\varepsilon^2(m) = \frac{1}{M} \sum_{j=m}^{M-1} (\hat{z}_j - z_j)^2. \tag{4}$$

According to these definitions, the distance between the two boundaries $z^{(n)} \in C^N, (n \in \{1, 2\})$ can be defined as follows:

$$Db(1,2) \equiv \sqrt{\sum_{k=1}^{m} \left| b_k^{(1)} - b_k^{(2)} \right|^2} . \quad (5)$$

That is, the distances represented in Eq. (5) are defined as the Euclidean distance of each coefficient b_k represented in Eq. (3). For example, the distance between boundary shape S_0 and its deformed shape S_1 is 52.99 and that between S_0 and its deformed shape S_2 is 36.78 (see Fig. 4). The difference between S_0 and S_2 is less than that between S_0 and S_1, so the boundary shape of S_2 is more similar to the shape of S_0 than is the boundary shape of S_1. We use this similarity measure to evaluate whether the automatically segmented region is similar to the supervised region.

Fig. 4 Examples of a boundary shape (left, S_0) and two deformed shapes (centre, S_1; right, S_2).

3. Validation on confocal microscope images

Various types of organelles (e.g., nuclei and mitochondria) and cytoskeletons (e.g., actin and tubulin) exist in cells, and they can be roughly grouped as having granular shapes, fibrous structures, mesh structures, or other similar features. As a preliminary test of the algorithm selection for segmenting substances that have granular shapes, we used the Golgi apparatus region marked by a fluorescent protein from botanical yeast images as a segmentation target. Figure 5a shows the image taken under a confocal microscope, and Figure 5b shows the specified target region by a biologist, that is, the ground-truth. In this test, we evaluated

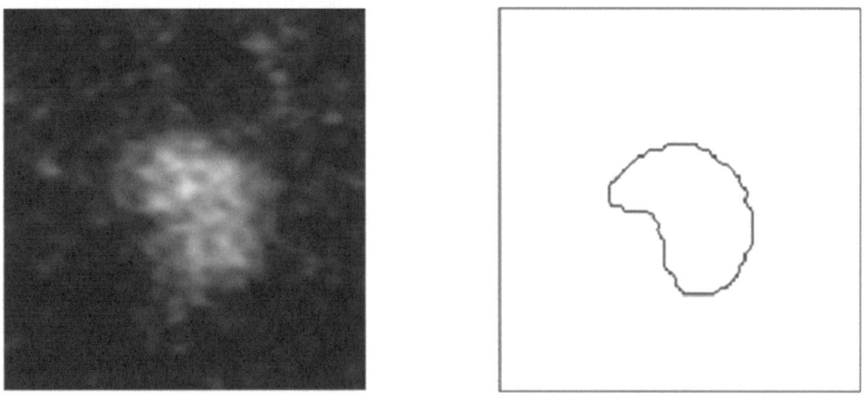

(a) Original Image (b) Ground-truth

Fig. 5. Experimental images. The line in (b) is the manually specified boundary of the segmentation target of the original image (a).

whether the given algorithms were able to extract the target region with a high degree of similarity to the ground-truth from the viewpoint of the previously discussed metric.

The test segmentation was first conducted for the entire group of multiple given algorithms; therefore, there was the same number of segmentation results as algorithms. Next, for all the segmentation results, we calculated the intensity-based image features inside the automatically segmented region and described the region's boundary shape numerically by the methods described in Section 2.2. At the same time, we calculated the intensity-based image features of the target region of the ground-truth and described its boundary shape numerically. Finally, we computed the similarity between the ground-truth and each automatically segmented region by Eq. (1).

Although numerous methods for extracting intensity-based image features can be applied in our framework, we used the two types of image features associated with each pixel as a prototype in this preliminary test: normalized pixel intensity and texture-based statistics inside the local region in which each pixel is centrally positioned. The latter is calculated as follows:

$$X_{pq} = \sum\sum m^p n^q f(m,n), \tag{6}$$

where m and n are the x-y coordinates inside the image, and $f(m,n)$ is the local region consisting of a 5×5 set of pixels. These calculated features are equivalent to moments, and in this test, we calculated the normalized moment of order 2 around (m,n) as the second image feature.

The Support Vector Machine (SVM) (Vapnik, 1995) and Approximate Nearest Neighbour (ANN) (Arya et al., 1994) were defined as classification rules in this test, and some parameters had to be set for each classification rule. We defined three types of parameter settings (P1–P3) related only to the kernel functions in SVM and two types of parameter settings (P4 and P5) related only to the number of nearest neighbours in ANN. The combination of features, classification rules, and parameters produced the 10 segmentation algorithms shown in Table 1. In this table, F1 shows the feature derived from pixel intensity, F2 shows the feature derived from texture-based statistics, M1 is SVM, and M2 is ANN.

Figure 6 shows the distance of intensity-based feature distribution between the ground-truth and each segmented region for each algorithm. Similarly, Figure 7 shows the shape

Algorithm Number	Feature	Classification Rule	Parameter-setting
A1	F1	M1	P1
A2	F1	M1	P2
A3	F1	M1	P3
A4	F2	M1	P1
A5	F2	M1	P2
A6	F2	M1	P3
A7	F1	M2	P4
A8	F1	M2	P5
A9	F2	M2	P4
A10	F2	M2	P5

Table 1. The 10 experimental algorithms.

distance between them. After normalizing each distance, the similarities were computed by Eq. (1), and the results indicate that the segmented region of A4 was most similar to the ground-truth (Table 2). Therefore, we regard A4 as the most proper segmentation algorithm, not only for this task but also for similar tasks, as long as the target has similar characteristics to the ground-truth.

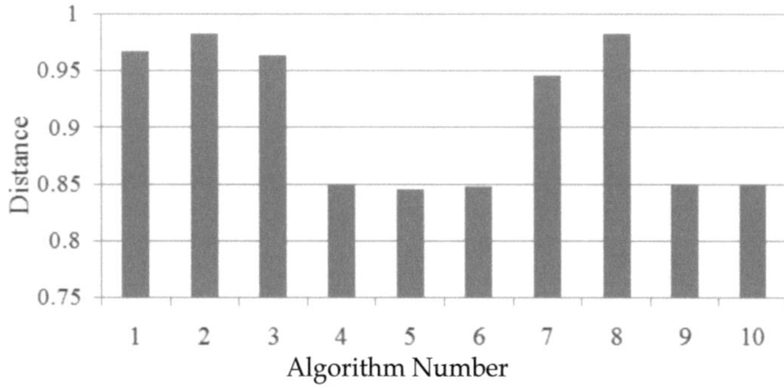

Fig. 6. Distance between the results of A*i* and the ground-truth for the intensity-based image features.

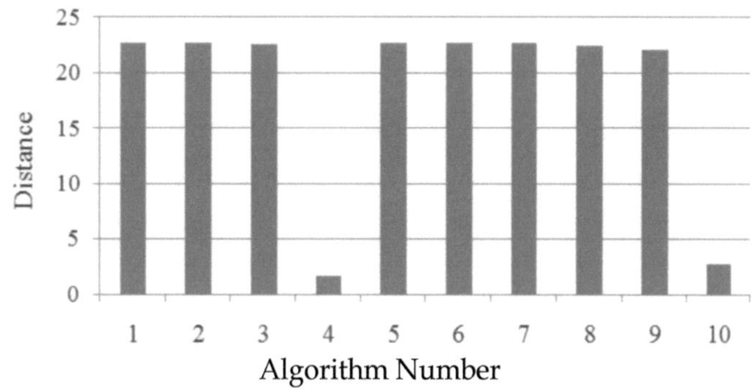

Fig. 7. Distance between the results of A*i* and the ground-truth for the shape-based image features.

Algorithm Number	Normalized Similarity	Performance Ranking
A1	1.48	8
A2	1.73	10
A3	1.41	7
A4	-3.05	1
A5	-0.52	3
A6	-0.49	5
A7	1.13	6
A8	1.70	9
A9	-0.50	4
A10	-2.91	2

Table 2. Performance ranking of the algorithms by our evaluation metric.

Figure 8 shows the target regions segmented automatically by using each algorithm; it is clear that several results include isolated regions other than the target region. In those cases, we calculated the distance on the basis of only the largest region. For comparison, we also show a binarization result provided by the Otsu method (Otsu, 1979) as A11. Because the original image was extremely noisy, the binarization result contained false positive errors. Algorithm A4, however, was not affected by the noise and achieved a highly accurate segmentation.

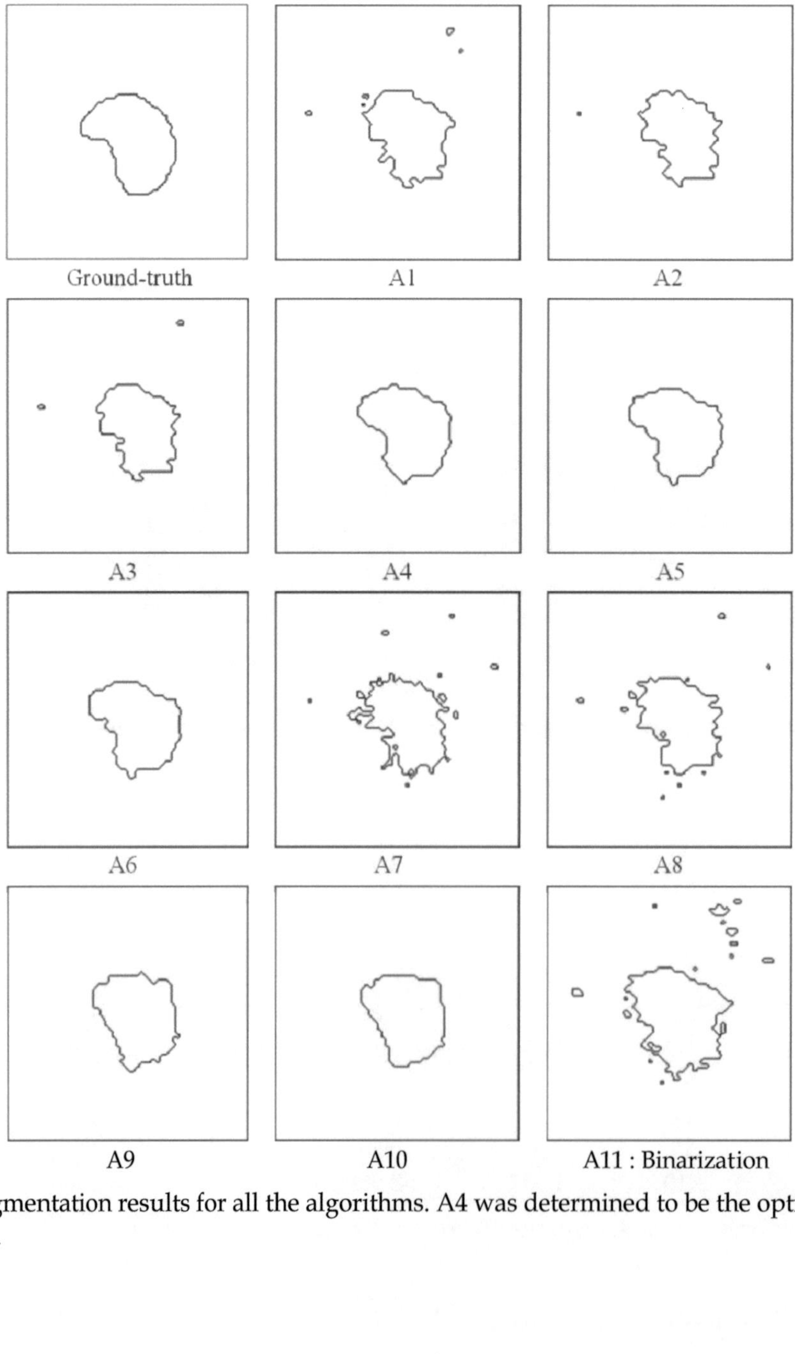

Fig. 8. Segmentation results for all the algorithms. A4 was determined to be the optimal algorithm

If we had used only the metric derived from the intensity-based image features, A4, A5, A6, A9, and A10 could have been selected as the proper algorithm. Similarly, if we had used only the metric derived from the shape-based image features, A4 or A10 could have been selected. However, as can clearly be seen in Fig. 8, over-segmentation occurs in A9 and A10. Because we used a combination of two metrics based on the image features in the evaluation function in Eq. (1), we avoided the risk of choosing a suboptimal algorithm.

In addition, although A4-A6 in Fig. 8 appear to be similar to each other, there is a large difference in the boundary shape when A4 is compared with A5 and A6 (see Fig. 7), especially for the biologists. In the segmented images of A4-A6, the centre-left of each segmented region clearly has a larger boundary change than the other regions. Although false-negative error occurs in that region in A5 and A6, A4 achieved an accurate segmentation reflecting the boundary of the ground-truth (see Fig. 8). Our evaluation function did not miss the difference between these results, which appears to be biologically important. Even if the differences were trivial, however, the evaluation framework was able to select the most proper algorithm to reflect the biologist's intention.

We conducted a similar test to validate the conventional evaluation metric. GCE proposed by Martin et al. (Martin et al., 2001) was used as an example of typically supervised evaluation metric. Evaluation for the same images shown in Fig. 8 according to GCE is summarized in Table 3. Although more data are required to validate the advantage of our proposed evaluation metric, GCE was not able to select A4 as the most proper algorithm for this segmentation task in this validation test.

Algorithm Number	Global Consistency Error	Performance Ranking
A1	0.01326	10
A2	0.01321	8
A3	0.01323	9
A4	0.01181	3
A5	0.01145	2
A6	0.01193	4
A7	0.01315	6
A8	0.01318	7
A9	0.01196	5
A10	0.01129	1

Table 3. Performance ranking of the algorithms by GCE (Martin et al., 2001).

Our segmentation framework assumes that images having similar characteristics will show similar segmentation results. To validate this concept, we conducted a follow-up experiment. Figure 9 shows six sequential images (in depth) taken by the confocal microscope of the marked Golgi apparatus. In fact, the image shown in Figure 5 was cropped from this set of images. Therefore, the segmentation target inside these six images should be similar to that of the previous experiment. We implemented an automatic segmentation of these six images by using the same 10 algorithms shown in Table 1. The target region (the Golgi apparatus) was clearly correctly segmented from these very noisy images in A4, A5, A6, A9, and A10 (Fig. 10). However, A9 and A10 made a crucial mistake in the number of segmented regions because target regions overlapped each other, whereas

A4, A5, and A6 achieved an accurate segmentation. The cell biologist who provided the ground-truth evaluated the result from A4 and determined that the selection result of this algorithm was correct.

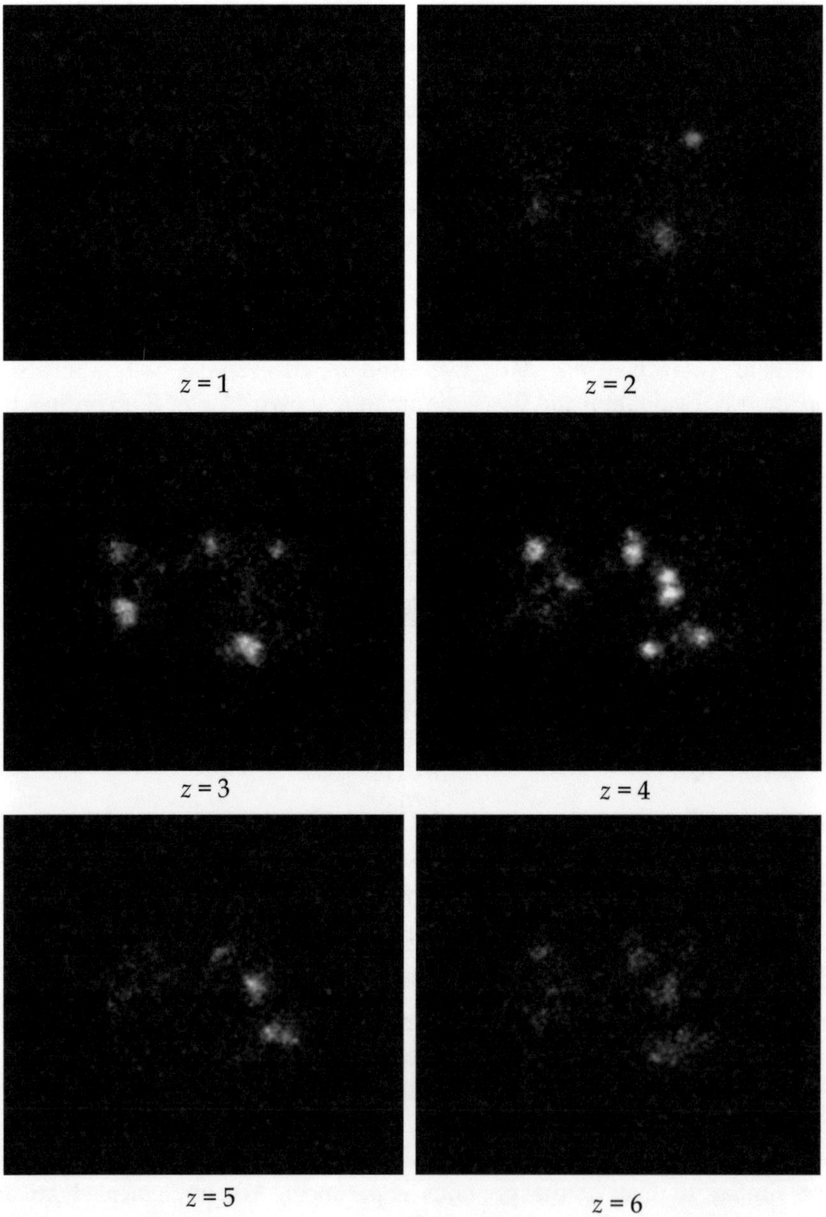

Fig. 9. Live-cell images of botanical yeast with marked regions of the Golgi apparatus. z indicates the depth position of each image.

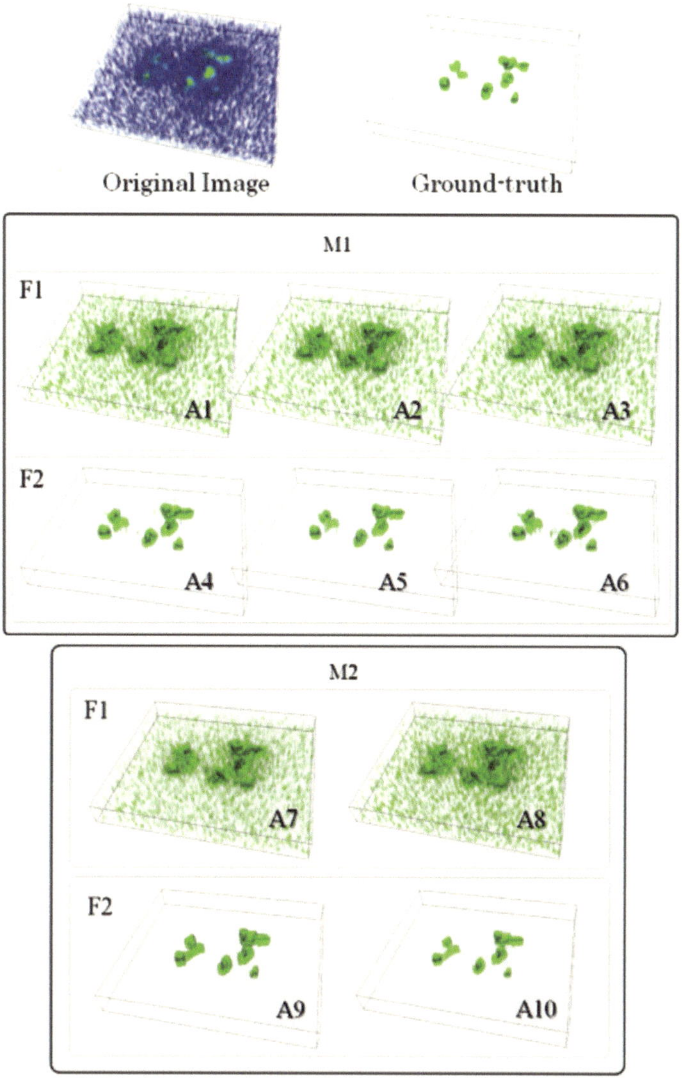

Fig. 10. Segmentation results of botanical yeast from multi-slice images. The green region in the ground-truth image shows the target region for segmentation.

4. Conclusion

We have proposed a novel framework for intracellular image segmentation based on effective algorithm selection. Selection is conducted by measurement both of similarities of intensity-based image features and of boundary shape between the user-supervised region and the automatically segmented regions generated by the given pattern classification techniques. Our framework assumes that the algorithm, which has powerful segmentation ability for a test image, will show good segmentation results for other similar images. That is, our framework can select an optimal algorithm to segment a region that has similar characteristics to the user-supervised region, even from many images. Furthermore, as shown in the experiment, our framework can rank different algorithms and define the parameters of each algorithm.

The evaluation function presented here is versatile, but further investigation may reveal other functions that are better able to reflect a user's intention. In addition, our framework needs to be expanded to be able to better represent image features and boundary shape, and it should include more classification rules and a greater variety of parameters. We tested only two types of features and two types of classification rules as a prototype framework. These types of improvements will lead to segmentation that will have the necessary generality to conduct the variety of segmentation tasks required by researchers. As a result, we believe that researchers will be released from a labour-intensive and troublesome task and able to concentrate on the accumulation of valuable data.

5. Acknowledgements

This work was supported in part by Strategic Programs for R&D (President's Discretionary Fund) of RIKEN and Grants-in-Aid for Scientific Research of Japan (19800062 and 20113007). The cell images were taken at the Molecular Membrane Biology Laboratory of RIKEN. Part of the results of the calculations was performed by using the RIKEN Super Combined Cluster (RSCC) system and the RIKEN Integrated Cluster of Clusters (RICC) system.

6. References

Arbelaez, P.; Maire, M.; Fowlkes, C. & Malik, J. (2009). From contours to regions: An empirical evaluation. *Proceedings of IEEE Computer Society Conference on Computer Vision and Pattern Recognition*, pp. 2294-2301, ISBN: 978-1-4244-3992-8, Miami, USA, June 2009.

Arya, S.; Mount, D.M.; Netanyahu, N.S.; Silverman, R. & Wu, A.Y. (1998). An optimal algorithm for approximate nearest neighbor searching in fixed dimensions. *Journal of the ACM*, 34, 6, pp. 891-923.

Bhaskar, H. & Singh, S. (2007). Live cell imaging: a computational perspective. *Journal of Real-Time Image Processing*, 1, pp. 195–212.

Cardoso, J.S. & Corte-Real, L. (2005). Toward a generic evaluation of image segmentation. *IEEE Transactions on Image Processing*, 14, 11, pp. 1773–1782, ISSN: 1057-7149.

Cong, G. & Parvin, B. (2000). Model-based segmentation of nuclei. *Pattern Recognition*, 33, 8, pp. 1383-1393.

Duda, R. O.; Stork, D. G. & Hart, P. E. (2000). *Pattern Classification (2nd edition)*, Wiley-Interscience, ISBN: 978-047105669-0, New York.

Eils, R. & Athale, C. (2003). Computational imaging in cell biology. *The Journal of Cell Biology*, 161, 3, May 2003, pp. 477-481.

Goldman, R.D. & Spector, D. L. (2004). Live Cell Imaging: A Laboratory Manual, *Cold Spring Harbor Laboratory Press*, ISBN: 978-087969683-2.

Haindl, M. & Mikes, S. (2008). Texture segmentation benchmark. *Proceedings of the 19th International Conference on Pattern Recognition*, Los Alamitos, December 2008, pp. 1-4.

Haralick. R.M. & Shapiro, L.G. (1985). Survey: Image segmentation techniques. *Computer Vision, Graphics, and Image Processing*, 29, pp. 100–132.

Harder, N.; Eils, R. & Rohr, K. (2008). Automated classification of mitotic phenotypes of human cells using fluorescent proteins. *Methods in Cell Biology*, 85, pp. 539–554.

Jiang, X.; Marti, C.; Irniger, C. & Bunke, H. (2006). Distance measures for image segmentation evaluation. *EURASIP Journal on Applied Signal Processing*, 35909, pp. 1-10, ISSN:1110-8657.

Levine, M.D. & Nazif, A.M. (1985). Dynamic measurement of computer generated image segmentation. *IEEE Transaction on Pattern Analysis and Machine Intelligence*, 7, 2, pp. 155-164, ISSN: 0162-8828

Martin, D.; Fowlkes, C.; Tal, D. & Malik, J. (2001). A database of human segmented natural images and its application to evaluating segmentation algorithms and measuring ecological statistics. *Proceedings of IEEE International Conference on Computer Vision*, 2, pp. 416–423, ISBN: 0-7695-1143-0, Vancouver, July 2001.

Otsu, N. (1979). A threshold selection method from gray-level histograms. *IEEE Transaction on Systems, Man and Cybernetics*, 9, pp. 62–66.

Pal, N.R. & Pal, S.K. (1993). A review on image segmentation techniques. *Pattern Recognition*, 26, 9, pp. 1277–1294.

Polak, M.; Zhang, H. & Pi, M. (2009). An evaluation metric for image segmentation of multiple objects. *Image and Vision Computing*, 27, 8, pp. 1223-1227.

Sahoo, P.K.; Soltani, S. & Wang, A.K.C. (1988). A survey of thresholding techniques. *Computer Vision, Graphics, and Image Processing*, 41, 2, pp. 233-260, ISSN:0734-189X.

Sekita, I.; Kurita, T. & Otsu, N. (1992). Complex autoregressive model for shape recognition. *IEEE Transactions on Pattern Analysis and Machine Intelligence*, 14, 4, pp. 489–496.

Vapnik, V.N. (1995). The Nature of Statistical Learning Theory, Springer Verlag, ISBN: 978-038794559-0, New York.

Unnikrishnan, R.; Pantofaru, C. & Hebert, M. (2007). Toward objective evaluation of image segmentation algorithms. *IEEE Transaction on Pattern Analysis and Machine Intelligence*, 29, 6, pp. 929-944.

Waltera, T.; Helda, M.; Neumanna, B.; Hérichéb, J.K.; Conrada, C.; Pepperkoka, R. & Ellenberga, J. (2010). Automatic identification and clustering of chromosome phenotypes in a genome wide RNAi screen by time-lapse imaging, *Journal of Structural Biology*, 170, 1, pp. 1-9.

Yasnoff, W.A.; Mui, J.K. & Bacus, J.W. (1977). Error measures for scene segmentation, *Pattern Recognition*, 9, 4, pp. 217-231.

Zhang, H.; Cholleti, S.R.; Goldman, S.A. & Fritts, J.E. (2006). Meta-Evaluation of Image Segmentation Using Machine Learning. *Proceedings of IEEE Computer Society Conference on Computer Vision and Pattern Recognition*, 1, pp. 1138-1145, New York, June 2006.

Zhang, H.; Fritts, J.E. & Goldman, S.A. (2008). Image segmentation evaluation: A survey of unsupervised methods. *Computer Vision and Image Understanding*, 110, 2, pp. 260-280, ISSN:1077-3142.

Zhang, Y.J. & Gerbrands, J.J. (1992). Segmentation evaluation using ultimate measurement accuracy. *Proceedings of SPIE*, 1657, pp. 449–460, Image Processing Algorithms and Techniques III, ISBN: 9780819408112 , May 1992.

Zhang, Y.J. (1996). A survey on evaluation methods for image segmentation. *Pattern Recognition,* 29, 8, pp. 1335–1346.

Zhang, Y.J. (2006). *Advances in Image and Video Segmentation,* IRM Press, ISBN: 978-159140753-9, USA.

23

Extraction of Estuarine/Coastal Environmental Bodies from Satellite Data through Image Segmentation Techniques

Ana Teodoro and Hernâni Gonçalves
Geo-Space Sciences Research Centre - Faculdade de Ciências, Universidade do Porto
Portugal

1. Introduction

The analysis of satellite imagery of natural scenes presents many unique problems, and it differs from the analysis and segmentation of urban, commercial, or agricultural areas. Natural scenes are not structured and cannot be represented easily by regular rules or grammars. The appearance of natural objects can vary greatly based on the geographic area, the season, the current weather conditions, or the past weather conditions (Soh & Tsatsoulis, 1999).

Segmentation is defined as the process that partitions an image into regions that are homogeneous according to given criteria (Gonzalez & Woods, 2008). Image segmentation is typically used to locate objects and identify boundaries. A number of problems in remote sensing require the segmentation of natural spectral classes such as water bodies, clouds or forested areas (Lira, 2006).

A wide variety of image segmentation methods may be found in the literature (Cheng et al., 2001; Pal & Pal, 1993). The most popular techniques are those based on gray level thresholding, including global thresholding (e.g. Otsu's method) or using local information (e.g. co-occurrence matrix). Another class of methods comprise segmentation obtained through the detection of edges, including those based on parallel differential operators (e.g. Sobel gradient) and the Canny's method (Canny, 1986). There are also methods that are based on finding the regions directly on the image domain (pixel values), where the region growing and region split-and-merge approaches are some of the available procedures (Gonzalez & Woods, 2008). The segmentation using morphological watershed is another approach, based on the feature space (the watershed transform of the image), and it is particularly attractive because it combine positive attributes of the methods previous referred (Gonzalez & Woods, 2008).

The coastal areas are zones of primary importance from human and ecological points of view. More than half of the world population lives at less than 100 km from a coast, which express the importance of coastal areas from the human point of view. The same occurs from the ecological point of view, since coastal zones are areas of strong interactions between the biosphere, atmosphere, and hydrosphere. An estuary is a partially enclosed body of water, where freshwater from rivers and streams flows into the oceans, mixing with the seawater. Estuaries and the lands surrounding them are places of transition from land to sea, and from fresh to saltwater. Estuarine outflow plumes are important coastal processes whose variable nature can make it difficult to monitor using traditional ship-based surveys. Plumes are a mixture of fresh water and river sediment load, with some dilution caused by currents. The river plumes are turbid and carry a high load of suspended sediments. Since these suspended sediments can be associated with nutrients, pollutants and other materials, it is of crucial importance to remotely survey their dispersal in order to assess the environmental quality of the regions surrounding river mouths.

The main idea of this chapter is to describe and evaluate different segmentation methods, in order to accurately extract two different estuarine/coastal features: river plumes and sand spits.

Several studies typically use a threshold value for determining the plume boundaries (e.g. Otero & Siegel, 2004). Dzwonkowski & Yan (2005) employed a gradient approach (MODIS and SeaWiFS data) on account of previous observations of physical differences (e.g. salinity) between the estuarine outflow and the ambient water. Valente & Silva (2009) used three years of MODIS-Aqua normalized water-leaving radiance to study Tagus estuary turbid plume. In the previous examples, the turbid plume was detected only by the backscattering characteristics of the surface waters in the vicinity of the estuary mouth. Nezlin et al. (2005) used SeaWiFS images to analyze the spatial-temporal dynamics of plumes in the San Pedro Shelf (California) and identified the factors that influence the incidence and dispersal patterns of plumes. Lira et al. (1997) developed a methodology to characterize the spatial distribution of suspended sediments in Pánuco river plume (Gulf of Mexico) employing remote sensing and pattern recognition techniques. Several attempts to segment specific spectral classes, as open water bodies, have been reported in the literature (Lira, 2006; McFeeters, 1996; Daya-Sabar et al., 1995).

A spit is a ridge or embankment of sediments attached to the land at one end, with the other ending in open waters, being younger than the land to which it is attached. The body of the spit extends from the land outward for some distance above the water. The size and shape of recurves depends on the space available on the inner side of a growing spit (Bird, 2008). The evolution of many spits has been modified by the addition of artificial structures. Sand spits are ecosystems of great biological interest. Therefore, environmental monitoring using remote sensing data and image processing algorithms is essential for assessing the local changes in this area.

A water body is a region (or area) limited by a well-defined topographic boundary. A sand spit does not present a well-defined topographic boundary. Moreover, the boundary is not static in time, as the majority of the water bodies. Therefore, the extraction of a sand feature from a water environment (e.g. an estuary) is a complex task and the segmentation techniques developed should be different in several aspects that those applied and optimized for the river plumes extraction.

This chapter aims to address the problem of segmentation of water bodies and sandy bodies in an estuarine/coastal environment, in order to accurately extract them through satellite data, allowing for further boundaries delineation. Different segmentation algorithms were applied and developed/optimized in order to correctly determine the features boundaries and accurately estimate the river plume size and sand spit area. Although the only considered attribute as output was the dimension, other attributes may be obtained from the segmentation result. The use of different types of satellite data (raw images and satellite products) is also a challenge and an important contribution of this work.

2. Methodology

The selection of the segmentation approach used to extract an estuarine/coastal environmental body, from remote sensing images, should account for the type of feature to be extracted. A flowchart which illustrates the proposed approaches is provided in Fig. 1. A concise characterization of the study area and the satellite data used in this work is given in section 2.1 and corresponding subsections. The procedures applied for the extraction of river plumes and sand spits dimensions are briefly described in the section 2.2 and section 2.3, respectively.

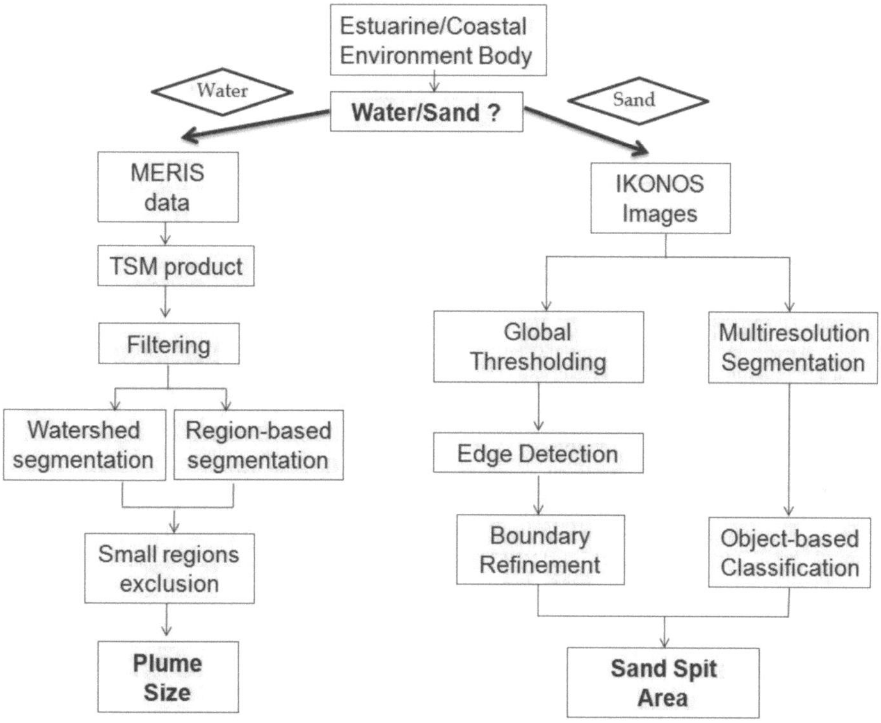

Fig. 1. Flowchart of the developed segmentation approaches for the extraction of river plumes and sand spits.

2.1 Study area and satellite data

The study area chosen in this work was the Douro River Estuary (Fig. 2). Douro is a granitic drowned valley river (927 km), draining to the N-W shore of Portugal. The Douro river basin is the largest hydrographical basin in the Iberian Peninsula (97,682 km^2). Its estuary is located in the Western Portuguese coast, subject to the North Atlantic meteorological and hydrodynamic conditions.

Two thirds of the river mouth are protected by a very dynamic sand spit (Cabedelo), creating a micro-ecosystem of great biological interest. Cabedelo sand spit is a very dynamic morphologic structure. This sand spit has an average length of 800 m, an average width of 300 m and an area that usually range between 220 000 and 270 000 m^2. The Cabedelo acts as a barrier, protecting the estuary banks from waves, especially during storms. In the last decades, the protection function of the sand spit has been reduced, especially due to the retreatment to the interior of the estuary. Therefore, two breakwaters were constructed (between 2004 and 2007) to stabilize the river mouth.

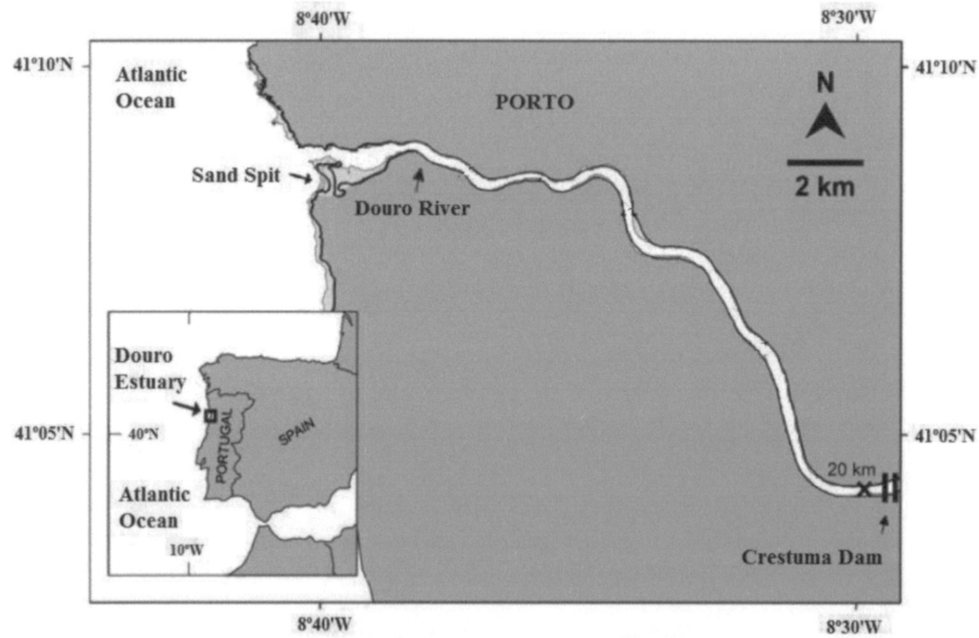

Fig. 2. Study area location in the Portuguese west coast (adapted from Portela (2008))

As previously mentioned and illustrated in Fig. 1, the considered type of satellite data depends on the features to be extracted. Accordingly, MERIS data and IKONOS-2 images are briefly addressed in the following (2.1.1 and 2.1.2, respectively).

2.1.1 MERIS data

In mid-2002 the European Space Agency (ESA) launched the MERIS (MEdium Resolution Imaging Spectrometer) hosting satellite ENVISAT. MERIS is an imaging spectrometer that measures the solar radiation reflected by the Earth, at a ground spatial resolution of 300 m, in 15 spectral bands (390 - 1040 nm), programmable in width and position, in the visible and near infrared. The primary mission of MERIS is the measurement of sea color in oceans and coastal areas. Knowledge of the sea color can be converted, for instance, into a measurement of total suspended matter (TSM) concentration. The algorithm of the ground segment of MERIS, used to retrieve the TSM concentration from spectra of radiances and reflectance of coastal waters, is an inverse modeling technique, carried out by an artificial neural network (Doerffer et al., 1999; Schiller & Doerffer, 2005). The TSM concentration is expressed as a concentration in g/m^3 or Log10 (g/m^3) with a valid range between 0.01-50.00 g/m^3.
The particulate backscatter at 442 nm is deduced from the water-leaving reflectance spectrum and converted from optical units (backscatter in m^{-1}) to geophysical units (concentration in g/m^3), using a fixed conversion factor (equation 1), derived for measurements on water samples using a GF/F filter. The TSM concentration for all the scenes is given by the following equation (1):

$$\text{Log}_{10}(\text{TSM})=\text{Scale}*\text{DV}+\text{Offset} \quad (1)$$

where DV is the digital value (no physical significance) for each pixel, the scale value is 0.015748031437397003 and the offset value is -2.01574802398681 (European Space Agency, 2007). The TSM concentration retrieved from one MERIS scene considered in this study is illustrated in Fig. 3.

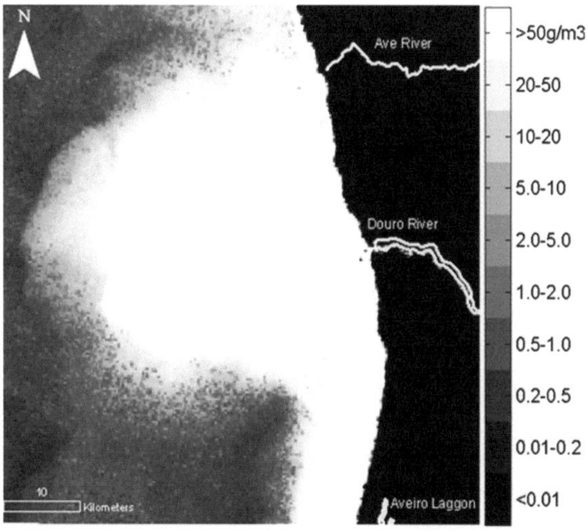

Fig. 3. TSM concentration retrieved from one of the considered MERIS scenes (08/03/2003).

In this study, a first dataset (assigned hereafter as "Dataset A") composed by 21 MERIS Full Resolution scenes (level 2 data) from March 2003 to January 2005 was considered (data provided by ESA), after the rejection of MERIS scenes that present: more than 10% cloud cover or invalid TSM quality flag; errors in the acquisition process (data corruption); or incoherent related river flow data. The number of scenes in each individual month is highly variable, from zero (e.g. August 2003) to 4 (June 2003). The most represented months in the considered three years (2003-2005) are May, June and September. Concerning the year distribution, the coverage in 2003 and 2004 was almost uniform, but in 2005 only one scene was available (Teodoro et al., 2008).
In the work developed by Teodoro et al. (2009), it was suggested that the accuracy could be improved by increasing the dataset. Additionally, a complete seasonal study of the Douro river plume would be interesting, for which a one year window of MERIS data is required. Therefore, a project was submitted to ESA in order to acquire a one year window (one hydrologic year) of MERIS data. A total of 107 MERIS scenes were considered, between August 2008 and October 2009 ("Dataset B"). No previous selection was performed. All the MERIS scenes available for this period were considered. The future data exclusion criteria will be based in the atmospheric conditions and in problems associated to the segmentation stage, as described in the section 4.1.2. Due to the fact that breakwaters were constructed between March 2004-2007 in the study area, these two datasets (A and B) were analyzed separately.

2.1.2 IKONOS-2 images

As already referred, one of the main objectives of this study was to extract the boundaries between Douro river and Cabedelo sand spit, and consequently estimate the sand spit area.

Therefore, the use of high spatial resolution satellite data is required. Six IKONOS-2 images were used in this study, acquired between 2001 and 2007, under the scope of the ESA project Earth Observation Program, Category 1 (ID#5899). IKONOS-2 is able to collect black-and-white (panchromatic) images with approximately 1-meter resolution and multispectral imagery with 4-meter resolution. The IKONOS-2 orbit altitude is approximately 681 km and inclined 98.1° to the equator, providing sun-synchronous operation. The main IKONOS-2 data specifications are given in Table 1.

Band	Spectral Range (μm)	Spatial resolution (m)	Swath width (km)
Panchromatic	0.45-0.90	1	11.3
Band 1 (blue)	0.45-0.53	4	
Band 2 (green)	0.52-0.61		
Band 3 (red)	0.64-0.72		
Band 4 (near infrared)	0.77-0.88		

Table 1. IKONOS- 2 data specifications: spectral range, spatial resolution and swath width.

The data were full 11-bit radiometric resolution and were geo-referenced to the Universal Transverse Mercator (UTM) coordinate system, Zone 29 North, World Geodetic System 1984 (WGS84). Information about the time of acquisition, cloud cover, sun angle elevation and nominal collection elevation, is given in Table 2.

Date (yyyy/mm/dd)	Acquisition time (GMT)	Cloud cover (%)	Sun angle Elevation (°)	Nominal collection elevation (°)
2001/12/24	11:44	0	24.54	69.58
2004/06/03	11:43	0	68.66	72.90
2004/07/31	11:55	6	64.61	61.97
2005/06/03	11:39	0	68.36	84.51
2005/09/18	11:36	0	49.01	71.7
2007/06/06	11:39	0	68.42	78.56

Table 2. Information related to the 6 IKONOS-2 images: date and time of acquisition, cloud cover, sun angle elevation and nominal collection elevation.

According to Helder et al., (2003), it appears to be a relationship between satellite elevation angle and geometric accuracy. It was found that higher elevation angles tend to result in lower root mean square error (RMSE). The relationship suggests that satellite elevation angles above 75° tend to maximize the geometric accuracy of the IKONOS-2 product. Terrain correction, even for a relatively 'flat' site (as the sand spit), improved RMSE values at lower satellite elevation angles (Helder et al., 2003). Since the nominal collection elevation values are mostly near or above 75°, there was no need to perform any terrain correction.

2.2 River plumes

As referred before, the MERIS product used in this research provides a suspended sediments concentration image, which allows for the extraction of objects corresponding to river plumes. A saturation of the TSM concentration values (50 g/m^3) is verified for most of the MERIS scenes, in the coastal waters (Case 2 waters). Figure 3 provides a selected window from MERIS data where the Douro river plume is visible. The proposed segmentation approach for the extraction of river plumes is based on an initial filtering, followed by one of the two addressed segmentation methods: region-based and watershed. The methodology will be briefly described in the following, and further details may be found in (Teodoro et al., 2009).

2.2.1 Initial filtering and segmentation

An initial filtering step is required in order to avoid noise and to smooth the image (and consequently the plume), which is based on a median filter with a 10x10 pixel window. The next and crucial step of the methodology is the segmentation stage. Two different segmentation methods were applied: watershed segmentation using gradients and region-based (region growing) segmentation.

2.2.1.1 Region-based segmentation

Region-based methods assume that neighboring pixels within the same region should have similar values, e.g. intensity, color and texture (Tremeau & Bolel, 1997; Hojjatoleslami & Kittler, 1998). Region growing is a procedure that groups pixels or subregions into larger regions based on predefined criteria for growth. The basic approach is to start with a set of "seed" points, and these regions grow by appending to each seed those neighboring pixels that have predefined properties similiar to the seed (specific ranges of intensity or color). The selection of similarity criteria depends not only on the problem under consideration, but also on the type of image data available (e.g. color, texture). The stopping criteria for this procedure is when no more pixels satisfy the criteria for inclusion in that region. Additional criteria that increase the power of region growing algorithm utilize the concept of size and the shape of the region being grown (Gonzalez & Woods, 2008).

2.2.1.2 Watershed-based segmentation

The major idea of watershed segmentation is based on the concept of topographic representation of image intensity. The gradient magnitude of an image is considered as a topographic surface for the watershed transformation. Watershed segmentation also embodies other principal image segmentation methods including discontinuity detection, thresholding and region processing (Gonzalez & Woods, 2008). Because of these factors, watershed segmentation displays more effectiveness and stableness than other segmentation algorithms. As already referred, the basic concept of watershed is based on visualizing a gray level image into its topographic representation, which includes three basic notions: minima, catchment basins and watershed lines. The objective of watershed segmentation is to find all of the watershed lines (the highest gray level). The most intuitive way to explain watershed segmentation is the *Immersion Approach* (Chen et al., 2004). An efficient algorithm to implement this approach proposed by Vincent & Soille (1991) involves two steps: the first one is called "sorting step" and the other is called "flooding step". Watershed segmentation produces good results for gray level images with different minima and catchment basins. For binary images, however, there are only two gray levels 0 and 1 standing for black and white. If two black blobs are connected together in a binary image, only one minimum and catchment basin will be formed in the topographic surface. The direct application of the watershed segmentation algorithm generally leads to over-segmentation of an image due to noise and other local irregularities of the gradient.

Therefore, it is recommended to smooth the image before starting the watershed segmentation, which is performed through the initial filtering step previously described.

2.2.2 Comparison of the region-based and watershed-based methods

The considered segmentation methods differ in the sense that region-based segmentation is based on the image domain (pixel values), whereas watershed segmentation is based on the feature space (the watershed transform of the image). An example of a segmentation result using these two approaches for the same MERIS scene is given in Fig. 4.

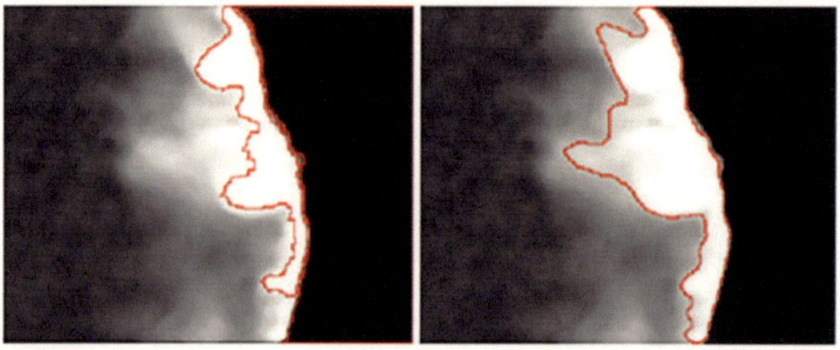

Fig. 4. Plume identification using image segmentation: watershed using gradients obtained through Sobel operator (left); region-based segmentation using a seed value of 225 and a threshold of 30 (right).

Although the segmentation results obtained from the application of these two approaches is different, they should be (linearly) related in some manner, since the segmentation is related to the same object. Fig. 5 illustrates a linear dependence between these two approaches,

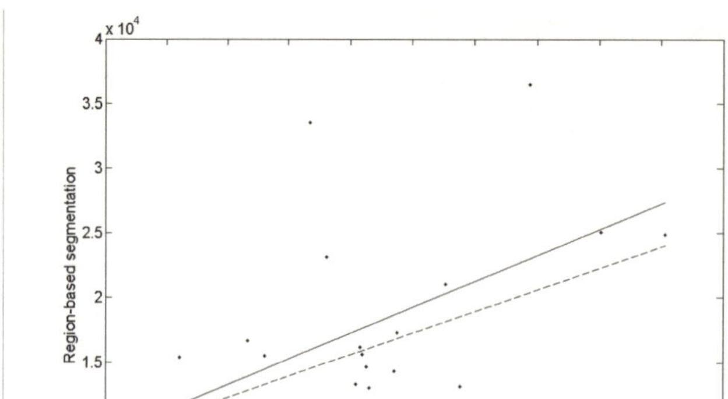

Fig. 5. Scatterplot of the region- and watershed-based segmentation values presented in Table 3. The solid regression line is defined as y=9241.77+1.00x (r=0.57 with p-value=0.007), and is associated to the 21 points. The dashed regression line is defined as y=8930.85+0.83x (r=0.71 with p-value=0.001), and is associated to the remaining 19 points obtained after excluding the two higher values of region-based segmentation (images of 18-06-2003 and 14-05-2003).

supported by a positive and significant correlation of 0.71 between them, where the slope of the regression line is 0.83. This reinforces that, although the shape of the plume is different when using these two segmentation approaches, they produce similar plume sizes related by a scale ratio (0.83 in this example).

This procedure of extracting the river plume object through image segmentation techniques has important practical applications. For instance, the reduction of the river sediment supply may be one of the main causes of the erosion process that has been affecting the Portuguese Northwest coast. The relationship between the river plume size and Cabedelo sand spit area is another challenge of this analysis.

2.3 Sand spits

Two segmentation approaches are addressed for the extraction of sand spits from high spatial resolution images, which are different from those previously described for river plumes extraction. The first is a new proposed methodology and is based on global thresholding refined through detected edges, whereas the second approach consists in a multiresolution segmentation (object-based). The segmentation approaches are applicable to a single band image, for which the NIR or panchromatic bands of the IKONOS-2 images are the most adequate. The NIR is the spectral band which provides better contrast between water and land, whereas the panchromatic band has the advantage of providing a better spatial resolution, and consequently a more accurate delineation of the sand spit. Several aspects regarding the application of these techniques should be taken into account, which are addressed in detail in the following.

2.3.1 Global thesholding refined through detected edges

The proposed approach for the extraction of sand spits is a new methodology, which presents considerable potential for later automation in the future. It consists on histogram global thresholding of the original image through the Otsu method (Otsu, 1979), followed by a refinement through detected edges. Different approaches for edge detection were tested and are addressed in the following.

2.3.1.1 Global thresholding

The histograms of IKONOS-2 images, representing a sand spit and a small neighborhood, are typically associated to a mode on a histogram with bimodal distribution (an example is illustrated in Fig. 6a and Fig. 6b). The Otsu's method is a nonparametric and unsupervised method of automatic threshold selection for image segmentation, having particular importance under the scope of bimodal histograms (Otsu, 1979). It assumes that only the gray-level histogram of the image is available, without other a priori knowledge, allowing for an unsupervised segmentation of an image. It is based on dichotomizing the pixels of the image, transforming the original image to a binary image. The determination of the optimal threshold k^* is performed through an approach based on probabilities computation. It is followed by the computation of discriminant criterion measures (or measures of class separability), generally consisting on finding the gray level k^* for which a discriminant function $\eta(k)$ corresponds to its maximum. It is equivalent to maximize the separability of the resultant classes in the binary image. This method is widely known, and further details may be found in (Otsu, 1979). An example of global thresholding is illustrated in Fig. 7a, regarding the image in Fig. 6a.

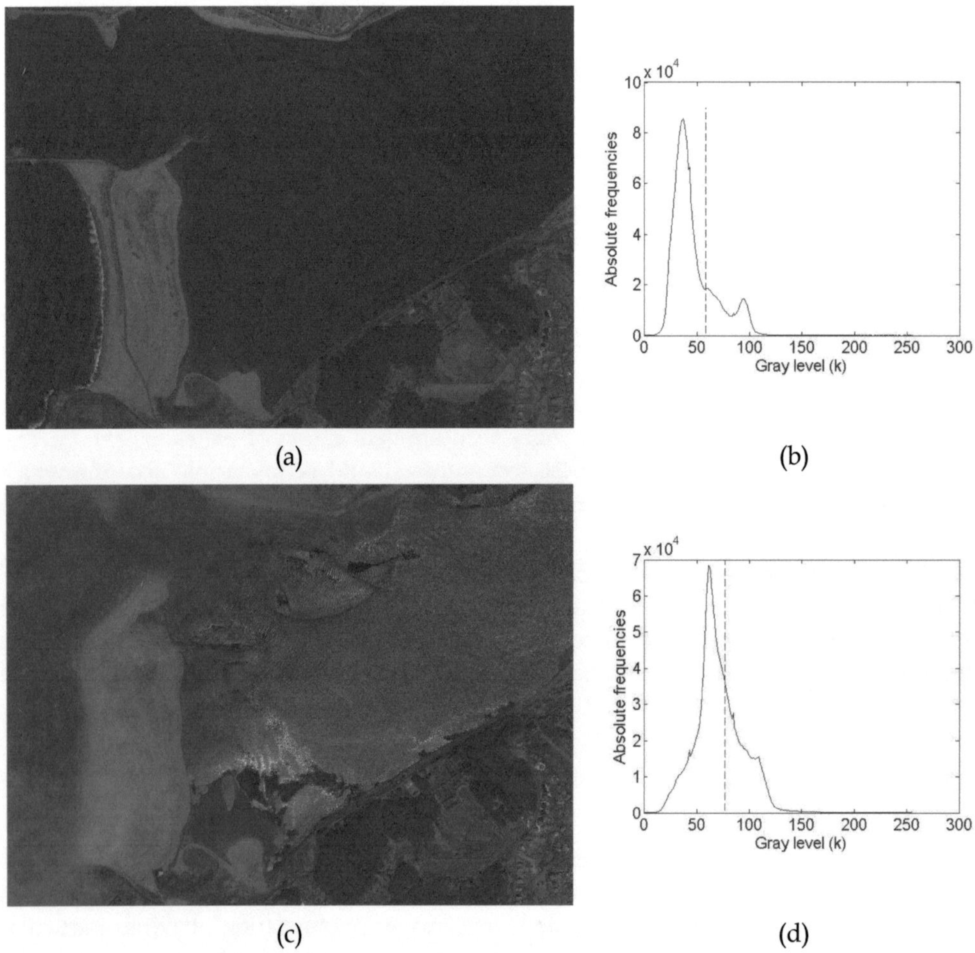

Fig. 6. (a) Panchromatic band of the IKONOS-2 image from 2005/06/03; (b) Histogram of the image in (a), with k*= 58 and $\eta(k^*)$= 0.735; (c) Panchromatic band of the IKONOS-2 image from 2004/06/03; (d) Histogram of the image in (c), with k*= 77 and $\eta(k^*)$= 0.605.

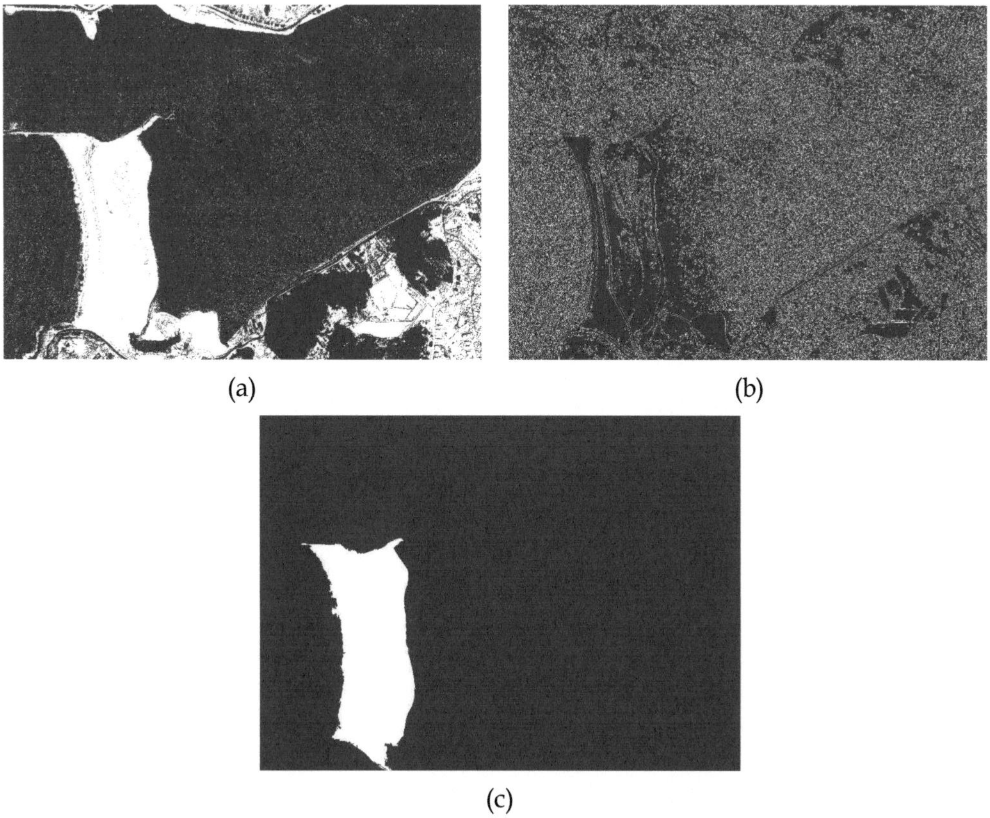

Fig. 7. (a) Global thresholding of the image in Fig. 6a through the Otsu's method; (b) Edges of the image in Fig. 6a obtained through the Canny edge detector; (c) Final extraction of the sand spit in Fig. 6a, through the refinement of the global thresholding in (a) through the edges represented in (b).

2.3.1.2 Edges detection and segmentation refinement

The previous step of global thresholding allows for an initial segmentation of the image. However, the sand spit is frequently still linked to other regions of the image, or to spurious pixels. Therefore, there is the need to perform a refinement on the result of the global thresholding, separating the sand spit from other parts of the image. A refinement of the sand spit delineation is proposed, performed through the application of a binary image obtained from detected edges. Several edge detection methods may be found in the literature, where the Sobel and Canny methods are among the most known (Gonzalez & Woods, 2008). The Sobel is mainly based on computing the partial derivatives $\partial f/\partial x$ and $\partial f/\partial y$ of the image, through the application of filter masks, returning edges at those points where the gradient of the image is maximum. The Canny edge detector is a more complex algorithm, and is based on three basic objectives: low error rate; edge points should be well localized; and single edge point response. Further details of this algorithm may be found in Canny (1986). Based on our experiments, the Canny edge detector, with a standard-deviation of the Gaussian filter equal to 0.5, presented better performance. Therefore, the edges used for further segmentation refinement are obtained in this manner. The edges computed by the Canny edge detector are then used on a clipping operation of the segmentation previously obtained on global thresholding. In the case that more than one region is produced, and accepting the initial assumption that the considered scene only covers the sand spit and a small neighborhood, the object with largest area is assumed to correspond to the sand spit. As a final segmentation step, the segmentation is improved through a morphological operation, consisting on filling the holes of the segmented object. An application example of the Canny edge detector is provided in Fig. 7b, and the final result is illustrated in Fig. 7c.

2.3.1.3 Evaluation of the global thresholding quality

The global thresholding becomes a simple and useful approach for extracting sand spits, in the case that the histogram of the image presents a bimodal shape. The adequacy of the image to global thresholding using the Otsu's method may be evaluated through the effectiveness metric $\eta(k)$ proposed in (Otsu, 1979), where k is the gray level. The measure $\eta(k)$ is always smooth and unimodal, assumes values between 0 and 1, and the optimal gray level k^* for thresholding the image corresponds to the maximum of $\eta(k)$. The segmentation will be more meaningful as long as $\eta(k^*)$ is near from 1. In Fig. 6 two panchromatic bands of different IKONOS-2 images are illustrated, together with their corresponding histograms and values of $\eta(k^*)$.
An example of 15 combinations of the sand spit area estimation error and their corresponding values of $\eta(k^*)$ is illustrated in Fig. 8. This example also provides an example of a possible criterion to be defined (dashed lines representing an acceptance region), which allows for automatically reject those segmentations which may lead to errors higher than 10%. Further research on this topic may allow for defining objective criteria, in order to evaluate whether an IKONOS-2 image is or not adequate for global thresholding, prior to its application.

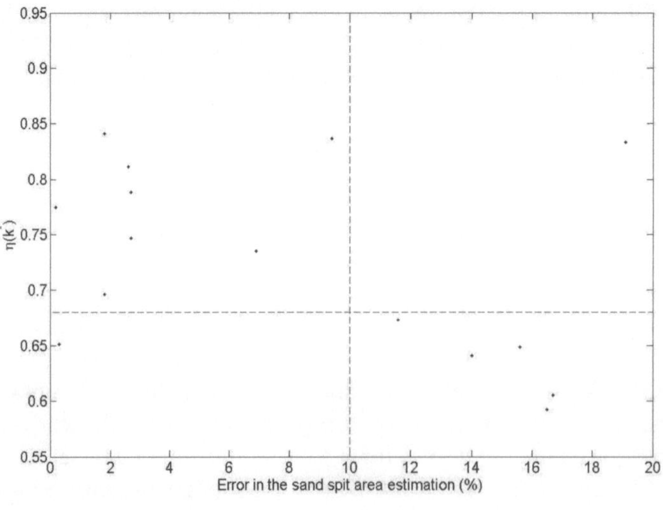

Fig. 8. Effectiveness metric $\eta(k^*)$ of Otsu's method as a function of the error obtained in the sand spit area estimation, considering the four bands of the 6 IKONOS-2 images described in Table 2, which led to sand spit area estimates with an error below 20% (n=15). The dashed lines represent a possible validation threshold based on $\eta(k^*)$ values higher than 0.68, regarding the achievement of errors below 10%.

2.3.2 Multiresolution segmentation

The second approach was based in the multiresolution segmentation method (followed by image-based classification in eCognition® software). The multiresolution segmentation groups areas of similar pixel values into objects. Consequently homogeneous areas result in larger objects, heterogeneous areas in smaller ones. In multiresolution segmentation, the homogeneity criterion is used to determine which heterogeneity attributes of image objects are to be minimized as a result of a segmentation run. Three criteria are used to describe image object heterogeneities: color, smoothness and compactness (Baatz et al., 2001). The smoothness and the compactness criteria are additionally summarized to the shape criterion. The composition of the entire homogeneity criterion based on the specific criteria can easily be defined by assigning weights to each of the specific criteria. The multiresolution segmentation algorithm consecutively merges pixels or existing image objects. Thus it is a bottom-up segmentation algorithm based on a pairwise region merging technique. Multiresolution segmentation is an optimization procedure which, for a given number of image objects, minimizes the average heterogeneity and maximizes their respective homogeneity. Scale parameter determines the average image object size and is an important parameter of this algorithm. The scale parameter is used to determine the upper limit for a permitted change of heterogeneity throughout the segmentation process (Rahman & Saha, 2008). By applying different scale parameter and color/shape combinations, the user is able to create a hierarchical network of image objects (Baatz et al., 2001). After segmentation, all image objects are automatically linked to a network in which each image object knows its neighbors, thus affording important context information for the classification step. In the second step the image segments are classified by generating class hierarchy, which is based on fuzzy logic (Rahman & Saha, 2008).

3. Results and discussion

The previously mentioned image segmentation techniques were applied to extract the Douro river plume and Cabedelo sand spit, both located in the Douro river, city of Porto, Portugal.

3.1 Douro river plume

With respect to the extraction of the Douro river plume, as previously mentioned in 2.1.1, two datasets presenting different characteristics were considered. Between March 2004-2007, two breakwaters were constructed in the Douro river estuary. Therefore, since this is associated to considerable changes in the river estuary dynamics, these two datasets were firstly analysed separately in 3.1.1 and 3.1.2. The comparison of the results obtained with the datasets A and B is given in 3.1.3. The relationship between the river plume size and the water volume, through models previously established in (Teodoro et al., 2009), is explored in 3.1.4.

3.1.1 Dataset A

As previously described in 2.1.1, the dataset A is composed by twenty-one MERIS scenes of the study area, covering 20 months from 2003 to 2005. The methodology used in the determination of the Douro river plume (DRP) size was implemented in Matlab® (Gonzalez et al., 2004). The watershed segmentation was applied using the Sobel filter in the gradient computation before the watershed transform (Gonzalez & Woods, 2008). The region growing segmentation was applied considering as region seeds (S) pixels with DN value of

225, and a threshold (T) of 30. These parameters were obtained on the basis of an iterative process (Teodoro et al., 2009).
After the two segmentation methods described were applied to the MERIS scenes, the small meaningless regions are further excluded, as well as those regions which correspond to rivers and water bodies, leading to the final segmentation result of the river plume. The number of pixels of the remaining regions were summed, resulting in the plume size (Teodoro et al., 2009). An example of a segmented image using both methods is presented in Fig. 4. The values of the plume size obtained through watershed and region-based image segmentation for the 21 MERIS processed scenes, are presented in Table 3.

Date (dd-mm-yyyy)	Plume size		Date (dd-mm-yyyy)	Plume size	
	Watershed	Region-based		Watershed	Region - based
08-03-2003	16 040	25 040	20-01-2004	8 604	13 012
14-05-2003	13 753	36 493	11-02-2004	5 197	15 461
26-05-2003	9 419	14 324	09-04-2004	7 238	23 144
05-06-2003	1 971	7 965	12-04-2004	2 423	15 361
18-06-2003	6 708	33 519	17-05-2004	9 510	17 321
04-07-2003	11 537	13 126	14-08-2004	5 192	7 090
10-07-2003	8 515	14 617	15-09-2004	4 641	16 677
12-09-2003	11 069	21 017	27-09-2004	18 141	24 893
18-09-2003	8 190	13 271	05-11-2004	8 386	15 595
07-10-2003	1 486	11 734	20-01-2005	8 330	16 168
10-12-2003	4 655	9 115			

Table 3. The Douro river plume size values (in number of pixels), obtained through watershed and region-based image segmentation methods, applied to dataset A.

The DRP size obtained through the region-based segmentation (image domain method) led to better results, since its nature allows for a more realistic delineation of the plume (Fig. 4). Since watershed only identifies sharper transitions on the image (it is a feature domain method), the plume is not entirely delineated. The considered segmentation methods retrieved significantly different values, as can be seen in Table 3. For instance, the plume estimation for 07-10-2003 image was 1 486 pixels for the watershed approach and 11 734 pixels for region-based approach. Although the values obtained through these two approaches are linearly related (as previously analyzed in 2.2.2), the differences found between the two segmentation methods are further explored in 3.1.3 and 3.1.4.

3.1.2 Dataset B: one hydrologic year

With the aim of a complete seasonal study of the DRP morphology, one hydrologic year (between August 2008 and October 2009) composed by 107 MERIS scenes (dataset B) were acquired through an ESA funded project. The previous segmentation methods applied to dataset A were firstly applied for the MERIS scenes. In a deeper analysis, it was verified that some MERIS scenes were not adequate for the segmentation purposes. The main reason is related to the presence of clouds or other atmospherics effects that could interfere with the plume extraction. The identification of the images presenting some of these problems was manually performed, resulting in 82 images. According to the work of Teodoro et al., (2009), the region-based approach is preferable against the watershed segmentation, as the later provides a less accurate delineation of the plume. Therefore, the focus of the segmentation methods applied to dataset B relied on the region growing segmentation.

In the previous analysis, the TSM values in the range 0–50 g/m^3 were rescaled to 8-bit (0-255). However, the region seed (S) and threshold (T) considered in the analysis of dataset A were not adequate for dataset B, due to slight changes on the content of the MERIS scenes. Therefore, in this approach, it was decided to use the TSM concentration values, which required an adaptation of the region seed (S) and threshold (T) considered in the previous work.

The adopted methodology consisted in the development and implementation of an algorithm to automatically select the region seed (S) and the threshold (T) values for each image. In this algorithm two options may be used to select the region seed (S) and the threshold (T) values. The first option consisted in assuming S as the centroid value and T as S/2, whereas the second option is based on assuming S as the mean value of the plume region and T as half the maximum. The second option led to better results, since its nature allows for a more realistic and accurate delineation of the plume (Fig. 9). The average, maximum, minimum and standard deviation values (in number of pixels) of the plume size, obtained through region-based image segmentation method (options 1 and 2) applied to dataset B, are presented in Table 4.

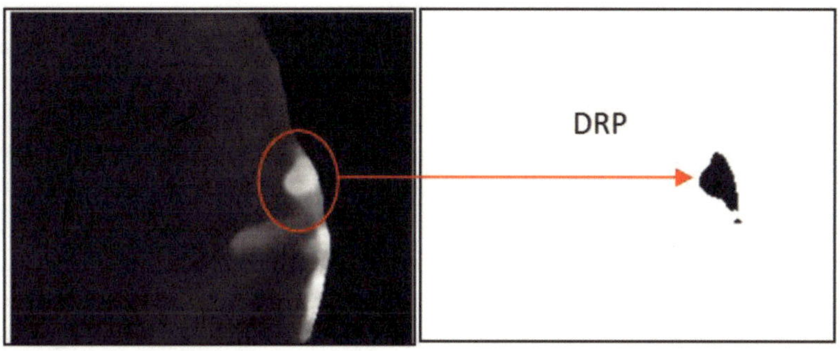

Fig. 9. Example of the segmentation with the developed region growing method (second option).

	Region-based Option 1	Region-based Option 2
Average	391	183
Maximum	997	715
Minimum	27	3
Stdv	250	123

Table 4. Average, maximum, minimum and standard deviation (Stdv) values obtained through the option 1 and option 2 region-based segmentation methods for one hydrologic year of MERIS scenes.

The two segmentation options applied led to different results in terms of the size of the plume. The estimation of the plume size through option 1 led to highest values when compared to the option 2, for all the processed MERIS images.

3.1.3 Comparison of segmentation results obtained from datasets A and B

Despite the slight changes on the selection of the region-growing parameters S and T, it was observed that the river plume size values obtained for dataset B (Table 4) were considerable lower than the values estimated for dataset A scenes (Table 3). This fact can be justified by the construction of two breakwaters between 2004 and 2007, in order to stabilize the Douro river mouth, and with the reduction of water flows and consequently the reduction of the amount of sediments injected into the sea (plume). This may lead in the future to an increase of the sand spit, and deserve further research on this topic.

3.1.4 Relation of river plume size with the water volume

The plume size had been modeled by several authors through satellite data by comparing the quantitative relations between rainstorm and plume size (Nezlin et al., 2005). Others had analyzed the effect of local wind and water discharge on the river plume (Choi & Wilkin, 2007). In this stage of the work, a simple linear regression model of the river plume (RP) on the water volume (Eq. 2) was firstly considered:

$$RP\ (t_i) = a_0 + a_1 * V(t_i) + \varepsilon \qquad (2)$$

where ε is the error associated to the proposed model, t_i is the present time of the considered image, a_0 and a_1 are the linear regression coefficients and V is the water volume. The water volume corresponds to the discharged water flow for the last downstream hydroelectric power plant of the Douro river (Crestuma) for each MERIS scene acquisition date. Given the lower river discharges in the summer, a refined analysis was performed considering separately the summer period (comprising 8 and 24 scenes regarding datasets A and B, respectively) associated to lower river discharges, and the rest of the year (the remaining 13 and 58 scenes for datasets A and B, respectively).

With respect to the time period of dataset A, a significant seasonal effect was verified on the relation between the RP and the water volume. Therefore, considering the model presented in Eq. 2 and excluding the summer period, a significant and positive correlation of 0.664 (p−value=0.013) was found between the RP obtained from watershed segmentation and water volume. For region-based segmentation, the correlation coefficient was 0.524 (p−value=0.066) for the same period. No significant correlations (α=5%) were found regarding the summer period. The lack of significant correlation in the summer period may be justified by the lower and time inconstant discharges at Crestuma dam, as illustrated in Fig. 10. The accuracy of this model was quantified by the mean percentage variation (MPV) of each estimated value (e_i, obtained through the model in (2)) to the correspondent computed value (c_i, obtained from segmentation), as presented in Eq. (3):

$$MVP = \frac{1}{N}\sum_{i=1}^{N}\frac{|e_i - c_i|}{c_i} \times 100\% \qquad (3)$$

The MPV for watershed was 67.4% and for region-based segmentation was 28.5%. This suggests that the plume size obtained from the region-based segmentation may be more appropriate than the watershed-based segmentation, when modeling the size of the plume as being linearly related to the water volume.

The second proposed model consists in the incorporation of several variables (last available plume, water volume, tide height, and wind speed), presumed to be related to the plume

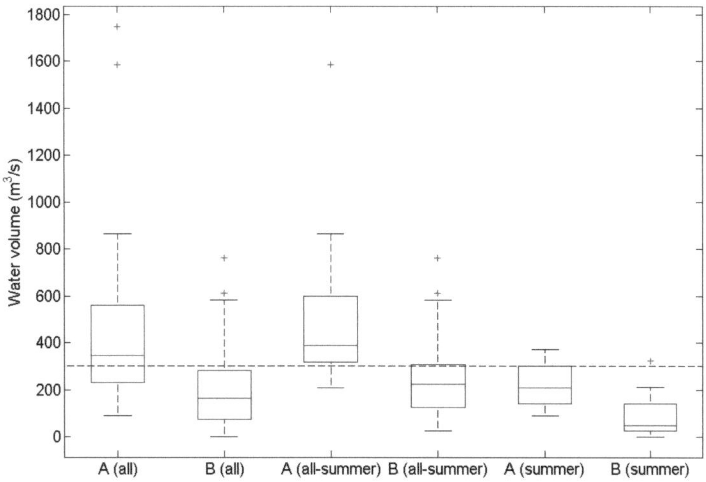

Fig. 10. Water volume (m^3/s) regarding the datasets A and B, considering all dates together ("All"), all year excluding the summer period ("All-Summer") and the Summer period ("Summer").

size. More details about this model may be found in Teodoro et al., (2009). Ignoring the seasonal effects the MPV for watershed was 65.4% and for region-based segmentation was 34.9%. The results of the two models proposed attest the best performance of the region-based segmentation method in the extraction of the Douro river plume size (Teodoro et al., 2009).

A better temporal resolution could increase significantly the performance of the two proposed models, considering and ignoring the seasonal effects. Therefore, the same procedure was applied to the dataset B (one hydrologic year of MERIS scenes). It was verified a significant seasonal effect on the relation between the RP and the water volume. Considering the model presented in Eq. 2 and excluding the summer period, a moderate and positive correlation of 0.45 (p−value=0.019) was found between the RP obtained from region-based segmentation (option 2) and water volume. No significant correlations (α=5%) were found regarding the summer period. Considering all the data, the best result were found for region-based segmentation (option 2) with a positive correlation of 0.37 (p−value=0.003). A more robust model incorporating other variables, as last available plume, water volume, tide height, and wind speed, will be established in order to improve the results. Moreover, a detection of outlying estimations will be performed. An outlier is a value in a dataset which appears to be inconsistent with the remainder of that set of data.

The plume derived from MERIS data represents river Douro plume only when the river flow exceeds a certain threshold. During low discharge, the remotely sensed plume results from other factors, namely, the flow of small rivers, the flow from a big wastewater treatment plant discharge near the river mouth and sediment resuspension resulting from waves, tides, and currents. The threshold between the river flow producing plume and the flow when the plume cannot be estimated from MERIS scenes is about 300 or 500 m^3/s (Teodoro et al., 2009). As illustrated in Fig. 10, the water volumes for the time period of dataset are mostly below 300 m^3/s. Therefore, this explains why lower correlation coefficient values were found for dataset B. Nevertheless, the segmentation approach applied in this work seems to be a valid method to estimate the plume size. The second option of the proposed region-based method (option 2) appears to be the more accurate alternative.

3.2 Cabedelo sand spit

The segmentation approaches previously mentioned in section 2.3 were applied to 6 IKONOS-2 images (Table 2), and the results are provided in 3.2.1 and 3.2.2. Some experiments considering local filtering methods are addressed in 3.2.3. The evaluation of the performance of global thresholding and multiresolution approaches are given in 3.2.4.

3.2.1 Global thresholding refined by detected edges

As previously mentioned in 2.3, the first segmentation approach mainly consists on histogram thresholding of the original IKONOS-2 image through the Otsu method, followed by a boundary refinement through detected edges. The area estimated for the sand spit through this approach is given in Table 5, regarding the 6 IKONOS-2 images mentioned in Table 2. With respect to the image from 03-06-2004, as already illustrated in Fig. 6, the panchromatic band is not the most suitable band to perform the segmentation. Therefore, the NIR band was used for this image. The disadvantage of using the NIR band instead of the panchromatic band is its lower spatial resolution, which leads to less accurate results, as will be further addressed in 3.2.4.

Date	Area (m^2)			
(dd-mm-yyyy)	2.3.1	2.3.2	Manual reference	DGPS reference
24-12-2001	188 123	198 000	191 056	n.a.
03-06-2004*	260 448	282 000	275 761	265 200
31-07-2004	258 973	250 000	260 095	259 864
03-06-2005	207 214	212 000	212 819	222 636
18-09-2005	229 186	223 000	228 092	228 688
06-06-2007	256 747	261 000	267 208	225 237

* The NIR band was considered instead of the panchromatic band.

Table 5. Sand spit area (m^2) estimated through the segmentation approaches described in 2.3.1 and 2.3.2, applied to the panchromatic bands of the IKONOS-2 images. The last two columns correspond to the reference areas manually obtained (on a GIS environment) and by DGPS field surveys. Further details regarding the reference areas may be found in 3.2.4.

Although the Otsu's method presents a good performance in several cases at the initial stage of global thresholding, it sometimes presents questionable thresholds. In the example provided in Fig. 6, it appears that the most adequate threshold should be slightly shifted. Therefore, other segmentation approaches based on the delineation of the modes in the histogram will deserve further research in the future.

3.2.2 Multiresolution segmentation

In the multiresolution segmentation method, the parameters used for the IKONOS-2 images were (10, 0.5, 0.5, 0.5, 0.5) for (scale, color, shape, smoothness, compactness), respectively. As already mentioned in 2.3.2, after segmentation, all image objects are classified by generating class hierarchy, based on fuzzy logic (Wang, 1990). The accuracy assessment of the classification process was performed analyzing the confusion matrix (overall accuracy- OA) and Kappa statistics (Smits et al., 1999; Stehman, 1996). The Kappa gives a measure that indicates if the confusion matrix is significantly different from a random result. The performance of the classification of the object-based method was evaluated through the error matrix based on the TTA Mask (Training or Test Areas). The OA varied between 96% (24-12-2001) and 100% (03-06-2005). The Kappa statistics varies between 0.92 and 1.0, for the same image dates. These values demonstrate the good performance of the segmentation and classification methods applied. An example of a sand spit extraction through this approach is illustrated in Fig. 11. The sand spit areas obtained through this segmentation method (described in 2.3) are provided in Table 5.

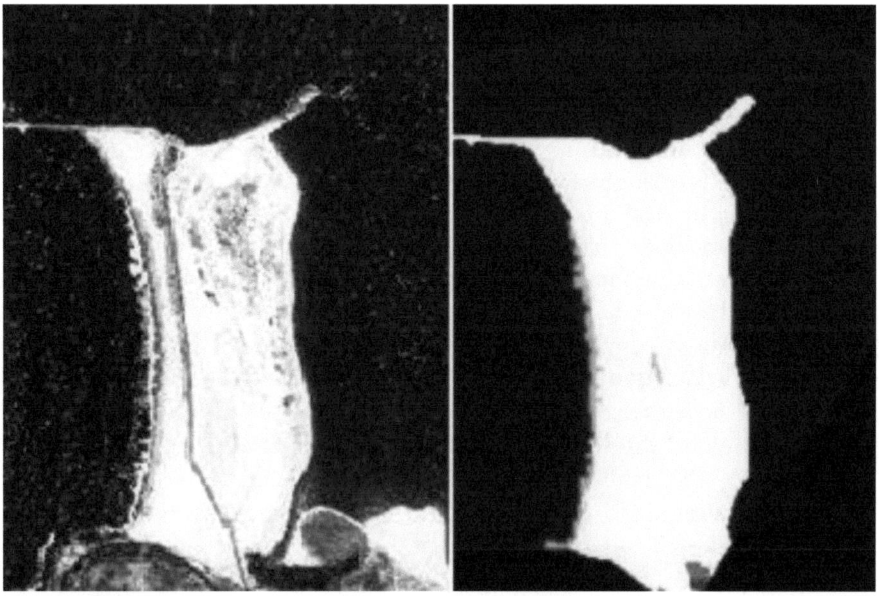

Fig. 11. An original IKONOS-2 image of June 2005 (left) and the sand spit extraction with multiresolution segmentation method - object based classification (right).

3.2.3 Local filtering methods

Other segmentation methods based on local filtering could have been used, such as entropy filtering, range filtering or standard deviation filtering. However, these methods decrease the contrast between the sand spit and the remaining parts of the image, leading to some linkage of the sand spit to other regions of the image. The segmentation of the images produced by entropy, standard deviation and range filtering was also tested, applying the Otsu's method to the filtered images. However, these filtering procedures lead to a lack of accuracy in the sand spit delineation, since it smoothes the transition from sand spit to water, and consequently introducing a connection between the sand spit and water in posterior segmentation. Taking this into account, an edge sensitive version of the low-pass Wiener filtering was also tested, aiming to achieve a more uniform sand spit for later segmentation. However, this also presented considerably lower performance than the proposed global thresholding, followed by refinement through detected edges.

3.2.4 Evaluation of the methods performance

In order to evaluate the performance of the two segmentation methods, used in the estimation of the sand spit area, two sets of reference values were used (Table 5). The first was based on a manual digitalization on a GIS environment of the sand spit on the IKONOS-2 image, followed by the computation of the resultant area. The second approach was based on regular trimesteral surveys conducted since 2002 through Diferencial Global Positioning System (DGPS) processing techniques (Baptista et al., 2008). According to Baptista et al., (2008), the ground point positioning of the sand spit boundary was done through a system comprising two kinematic antennas installed on an articulate arm fixed to a four-wheel motor quad. Because the positioning precision of the kinematic DGPS processing techniques around 0.02 and 0.04 m in planimmetric and altimetric measurements respectively, the overall precision of the determined ground point coordinates were near these values with this DGPS system (Baptista et al., 2008). The values were later processed in a GIS environment and linearly interpolated for different tide levels (z=0, z=1 and z=2 m). These values were used to estimate the correspondent sand spit area, for each analyzed IKONOS-2 image. It is important to refer that the DGPS values do not correspond to the IKONOS-2 acquisition date, but to the closest date (the maximum diference is about 45 days). The reference results obtained through this second approach are given in Table 5. Although a field survey would be the most accurate reference to evaluate the performance of the segmentation methods, the time difference between the field survey and the IKONOS-2 acquisition date for some images was considerably high. This justifies some differences observed in Table 5 between the manual and DGPS reference values.

The average and standard-deviation of the errors (in %), regarding the two segmentation methods described in 2.3.1 and 2.3.2, considering the manual and DGPS reference values are provided in Table 6. It can be observed that the proposed unsupervised segmentation method, based on global thresholding refined through detected edges, presented slightly better results than the multiresolution segmentation, with a clear advantage of a considerable faster performance, beyond requiring a small human intervention.

	Manual reference		DGPS reference	
	Average	Stdv	Average	Stdv
2.3.1	2.4	2.0	4.2	5.0
2.3.2	2.5	1.2	6.7	5.3

Table 6. Average and standard-deviation (Stdv) of the errors (in %), regarding the two segmentation methods described in 2.3.1 and 2.3.2, considering the manual and DGPS reference values (further details in 3.2.4).

In the analysis of the effectiveness metric of the Otsu's method, as a function of the error in the sand spit area estimation, a sketch of a possible threshold of acceptance was illustrated in Fig. 8. However, in the presence of larger datasets, it may become possible to define objective criteria of the appropriateness in using the proposed segmentation methodology. Such criteria may correspond to simple linear discriminants, or to other more complex nonlinear classification approaches, combining information of more than one spectral band.

4. Conclusions

A water body and a sand spit do not present a similar topographic boundary. Therefore, the extraction of a river plume and the extraction of a sand feature from a water environment are different in terms of the segmentation techniques employed. With this work, we have showed that the same segmentation techniques could not be applied directly in both cases.
The reduction of the river sediment supply may be one of the main causes of the erosion process that has been affecting the Portuguese Northwest coast. The Douro river is one of the major sources of beach sediments of the Portuguese Northwest coast. Therefore, the estimation of the river plume size from satellite images is an aspect of crucial importance, since there is no alternative for performing in situ measurements. The applied segmentation methods allowed for estimating the plume size. The plume size obtained through the region-based segmentation led to better results, since its nature allows for a more realistic delineation of the plume.
The reduction of the plume size is probably related to reduction of water flows and consequently the decreasing of river sediment supply. Associated to the breakwaters construction are the changes in the Cadedelo sand spit dynamics. From a regional point of view, this research allows for obtaining data in a simple way, currently nonexistent for the Cabedelo sand spit. Furthermore, it provides significant contributions to evaluate the behaviour of Douro river mouth breakwaters, related with coastal defence and sand spit stabilization, offering an effective and accurate methodology for monitoring the sand spit size. Moreover, it is a valid alternative for the delineation of sand spits, which allows for avoiding expensive DGPS field campaigns.
The use of different satellite data (MERIS products calibrated for TSM concentration and IKONOS raw data) was also a challenge. The considered satellite data showed to be adequate for the established purposes. The medium spatial resolution of MERIS data is enough to estimate the river plume size. Moreover, the high temporal resolution of MERIS data seems to be essential in monitoring the river plume, subject to rapid changes due to extreme situations (e.g. precipitation, floods). The high spatial resolution of IKONOS-2 data also seems to be a crucial factor in the sand spit area estimation.
The proposed unsupervised segmentation strategy for the extraction of the sand spit, presented slightly better performance than the multiresolution segmentation. Moreover, it presents the advantage of being a fast procedure and with a high potential for a fully automation. This would allow for a more consistent analysis of the sand spit behavior and evolution across the time. This approach has also the advantage of avoiding in situ surveys, and allows for assessment of historical records through archived satellite data. Other attributes beyond the area may be easily computed from the result of the sand spit segmentation, allowing for more complex analysis of the sand spit dynamics.
The estuarine environment, particularly the size and temporal and spatial variations of river plumes and sand spits, is an issue of great importance. Furthermore, very few studies have addressed this issue in the past as there are obvious difficulties in establishing an efficient and accurate methodology to extract the features boundaries. This work aspires to cover this gap.

5. Acknowledgements

The authors would like to thank to the European Space Agency (ESA) for providing the MERIS data (Earth Observation Program, Category 1, ID#5899) and the IKONOS images (Earth Observation Program, Category 1, ID# 6495).

The authors would also like to express their acknowledgment to Prof. Veloso-Gomes, Dr. Joaquim Pais-Barbosa and Hélder Almeida for their contributions in some work tasks.

6. References

Baptista, P.; Bastos, L.; Bernardes, C.; Cunha, T. & Dias, J. (2008). Monitoring sandy shores morphologies by DGPS - a practical tool to generate digital elevation models. *Journal of Coastal Research*, Vol. 24, No. 6, pp. 1516-1528.

Baatz, M.; Benz, U.; Dehghani, S.; Heynen, M.; Holtje, A.; Hofmann, P.; Lingenfelder, I.; Mimler, M.; Sohlbach, M.; Weber. M. & Willhauck, G. (2001), eCognition Object-oriented Image Analysis, V.2.2 User Guide. Definiens Imaging, Munchen, Germany.

Bird, E. (2008). *Coastal Geomorphology: An Introduction, second ed.*, John Wiley & Sons, ISBN 978-0470517307, England.

Canny, J. (1986). A computational approach to edge-detection. *IEEE Transactions on Pattern Analysis and Machine Intelligence*, Vol. 8, No. 6, pp. 679-698.

Chen, Q., Yang, X., & Petriu, E. M. (2004). Watershed segmentation for binary images with different distance transforms. *Proceedings of HAVE 2004-IEEE International Workshop on Haptic, Audio and Visual Environments and their Applications*, pp.111-116, Ottawa, Ontario, Canada, Oct. 2004.

Cheng, H. D.; Jiang, X. H.; Sun, Y. & Wang, J. (2001). Color image segmentation: advances and prospects. *Pattern Recognition*, Vol. 34, pp. 2259-2281.

Choi, B. & Wilkin, J. L. (2007). The effect of wind on the dispersal of the Hudson river plume. *J. Phys. Oceanogr.*, Vol. 37, No. 7, pp. 1878–1879.

Daya-Sabar, B. S.; Ghandi, G. & Prakasa-Rao, B. S. (1995). Applications of mathematical morphology in surface water body studies. *International Journal of Remote Sensing*, Vol. 16, pp. 1495-1502.

Doerffer, R.; Sorensen, K. & Aiken, H. J. (1999). MERIS potential for coastal zone applications. *International Journal of Remote Sensing*, Vol. 20, pp. 1809–1818.

Dzwonkowski, B. & Yan, X. H. (2005). Tracking of a Chesapeake Bay estuarine outflow plume with satellite-based ocean color data. *Continental Shelf Research*, Vol. 25, pp. 1942–1958.

European Space Agency. 2007. MERIS Product Handbook, Issue 2.1.

Gonzalez, R. C.; Woods, R. E. & Eddins, S. L. (2004). *Digital Image Processing Using MATLAB*, Prentice Hall, ISBN 978-0130085191, Upper Saddle River, NJ.

Gonzalez, R. C. & Woods, R. E. (2008). *Digital Image Processing*, 3nd ed., Prentice Hall, ISBN 978-0131687288, Upper Saddle River, NJ.

Helder, D.; Coan, M.; Patrick, K. & Gaska, P. (2003). IKONOS geometric characterization. *Remote Sensing of Environment*, Vol. 88, pp. 69–79.

Hojjatoleslami, S. A. & Kittler, J. (1998). Region growing: a new approach. *IEEE Transactions on Image Processing*, Vol. 7, No. 7, pp. 1079-1084.

Lira, J. (2006). Segmentation and morphology of open water bodies from multispectral images. *International Journal of Remote Sensing*, Vol. 27, pp. 4015-4038.

Lira, J.; Morales, A. & Zamora, F. (1997). Study of sediment distribution in the area of the Pánuco river plume by means of remote sensing. *International Journal of Remote Sensing*, Vol. 18, pp. 171-182.

McFeeters, S. K. (1996). The use of the Normalized Difference Water Index (NDWI) in the delineation of open water features. *International Journal of Remote Sensing*, Vol. 7, pp. 1425-1432.

Nezlin, N. P.; DiGiacomo, P. M.; Stein, E. D. & Ackerman, D. (2005). Storm water runoff plumes observed by SeaWiFS radiometer in the Southern California Bight. *Remote Sensing of Environment*, Vol. 98, pp. 494-510.

Otero, M. P. & Siegel, D. A. (2004). Spatial and temporal characteristics of sediment plumes and phytoplankton blooms in the Santa Barbara Channel. *Deep-Sea Research II*, Vol. 51, pp. 1129-1149.

Otsu, N. (1979). A threshold selection method from gray-level histogram. *IEEE Trans. Syst. Man Cybern.*, Vol. 9, pp. 62-66.

Pal, N. R. & Pal, S. K. (1993). A review on image segmentation techniques. *Pattern Recognition*. Vol. 26, No. 9, pp 1277-1294.

Portela, L. I. (2008). Sediment transport and morphodynamics of the Douro River estuary. *Geo-Marine Letters*, Vol. 28, pp. 77-86.

Rahman, M. R. & Saha, S. K. (2008). Multi-resolution segmentation for object-based classification and accuracy assessment of land use/land cover classification using remotely sensed data, *Journal of the Indian Society of Remote Sensing*, Vol. 36, No. 2, pp. 189-201.

Schiller, H. & Doerffer, R. (2005). Improved determination of coastal water constituent concentrations from MERIS data. *IEEE Transactions on Geoscience and Remote Sensing*, Vol. 43, No. 7, pp. 1585-1591.

Smits, P. C.; Dellepiane, S. G. & Schowengerdt, R. A. (1999). Quality assessment of image classification algorithms for land-cover mapping: a review and a proposal for a cost-based approach. *International Journal of Remote Sensing*, Vol. 20, No. 8, pp. 1461-1486.

Stehman, S. V. (1996). Estimating the Kappa coefficient and its variance under stratified random sampling. *Photogrammetric Engineering and Remote Sensing*, Vol. 62, pp. 401-407.

Soh, L. K. & Tsatsoulis, C. (1999). Segmentation of Satellite Imagery of Natural Scenes Using Data Mining. *IEEE Transactions on Geoscience and Remote Sensing*, Vol. 37, No. 2, pp. 1086-1099.

Teodoro, A.; Gonçalves, H.; Veloso-Gomes, F. & Gonçalves, J. A. (2008). Estimation of the Douro River plume dimension based on image segmentation of MERIS scenes. *Proceedings of SPIE, Remote Sensing for Agriculture, Ecosystems, and Hydrology X*, Vol. 7104, pp. , Cardiff, UK, September 2008, Christopher M. U. Neale; Manfred Owe; Guido D'Urso, Editors, 71040F.

Teodoro, A.; Gonçalves, H.; Veloso-Gomes, F. & Gonçalves, J. A. (2009). Modelling of the Douro river plume size, obtained through image segmentation of MERIS data. *IEEE Geoscience and Remote Sensing Letters*, Vol. 6, No. 1, pp. 87-91.

Tremeau, A. & Bolel, N. (1997). A region growing and merging algorithm to color segmentation. *Pattern Recognition*, Vol. 30, No. 7,pp. 1191-1203.

Valente, A. S. & Silva, J. C. B. (2009). On the observability of the fortnightly cycle of the Tagus estuary turbid plume using MODIS ocean colour images. *Journal of Marine Systems*, Vol. 75, pp. 131-137.

Vincent, L. & Soille, P. (1991). Watershed in Digital Spaces: An Efficient Algorithm Based on Immersion Simulations. *IEEE Transactions on Pattern Analysis and Machine Intelligence*, Vol. 13, pp. 583-598.

Wang, F. (1990). Fuzzy supervised classification of remote sensing images. *IEEE Transactions on Geoscience and Remote Sensing*, Vol. 28, No. 2, pp. 194-201.

24

Rock Fracture Image Segmentation Algorithms

Weixing Wang
School of Information Engineering, Chang'an University, Xi'an
China

1. Introduction

Since rock fracture is a key property for different rock engineering applications, rock fracture measurement is often carried out in classifying the rock mass. Most geo-mechanics models (e.g. finite element) are of the equivalent continuum type in which fractures are represented not individually, but by their influence on a large element of the rock mass. Elastic modulus, for example, is obtained either by large-scale testing of rock containing many joints, or, at less expense, by applying a reduction factor to the modulus obtained from small-scale tests on intact rock. Other models (e.g. those based on the key block concept) are capable of taking into account the position and mechanical characteristics of individual fracture. The shear strength of a fracture can be estimated from its roughness together with strength and thickness of filling materials, using a variety of empirical or semi-empirical methods. The techniques of image processing and segmentation can be applied as a power tool for obtaining more detailed information and analysis of rock fractures.

In this chapter, we firstly to give an overview of the current status of the rock fracture processing research, then, give a brief description of visual rock fracture properties and classify the types of rock fractures, finally, we summarize the work we have done in last year.

1.1 Overview of image processing literature on rock fractures

A series of the previous research work is related to the program for storage of high level radioactive waste. A repository represents changes of numerical, thermal, hydraulic and chemical conditions, which are studied by using numerical models. The models are based on the geological conditions of the site, especially characteristics of the fracture network and properties of single fracture, since these parameters control the flow through the rock mass.

Let us now turn to image processing and measurements of rock fractures/1-24/. Maria Johansson (1999) in her Lic. Thesis, presented three different algorithms for single rock fracture or crack detection. Quanhong Feng (1996) in his master thesis presented the BIP system for acquiring borehole images, and studied the measurement of the orientation of a single joint in a borehole, and other fracture properties. Masahiro Iwano (1995) in his doctoral thesis reviewed the research history of hydro-mechanical characteristics of a single rock joint, and studied a series of lab test and theatrical analysis. For the single joint measurement by using image technique, Eva Hakami (1995) in her doctoral thesis presented a method to measure aperture and roughness, and analyzed the relationship between aperture (and roughness) and hydro-mechanical characteristics.

For multiple fractures on an image, Reid and Harrison (2000) presented a semi-auto tracing method for rock fractures. Lemy and Hadjigeorgiou (2003) developed a auto-tracing method for rock fractures based on edge detection and neural network. Parviz Soroushian (2003) proposed an algorithm for fracture image binarization on theirlaboratory SEM images. Similar work have been done by John Kemeny, Randy Post, 2003, Wang, W.X. & Stephansson, O., 1997, Lee SW, Kim YJ. , 1995, Wang L, Pavlidis T., 1993, Harrison JP, 1993, G. X. Sun, D. J. Reddish and B. N. Whittaker, 1992, Hu J, Sakoda B, Pavlidis T., 1992, Whittaker RN, Singh RN, Sun G., 1992, Finn Ouchterlony, 1990, Tanimoto C, Murai S, Kiyama Joshi AK.,1989, John A. Franklin, Norberth H. Maerz and Caralyn P. Bennett, 1988. For the three-dimensional estimation, the previous work has been done by John Kemeny, Randy Post, 2003, Zou Dingxiang, Weixing Wang and Ma Bailing, 1986. Lyman (2003) has used neural network technique to detect fractures.

In the well-known BIPS system, rock fractures (curves) are traced based on input points (the more points, the more accurate is the tracing), to fit curves on theoretical sinusoidal shape (distribution). It is not an image processing or matching algorithm, the color or grey information is not needed.

In order to make measurements of rock fractures (or spacing, discontinuities) easy and sufficiently for the accurate analysis of rock mechanics and engineering geology, we combined all the knowledge we have, to establish a programming library for rock fracture measurement and analysis, and developed several rock fracture measurement algorithms on the rock mechanics and geology applications. Now I have setup an algorithm library, which includes a number of algorithms for rock fracture analysis and classification.

1.2 Visual rock fracture properties and classification for image segmentation

In most cases, rock surface is rough, except for the variations of colors and gray- scales, three dimensional surface roughness is the another property comparing to other applications. For image processing and analysis, fractures or cracks belong to linear curved objects; the length of an object is much longer than width. Inside the object, it may be empty or filled by different materials. The filling materials are with different colors. Since the large width and color variation, it is usual that there are many gaps on one object. Another property is that some fault object appears on an image due to rough and noised surface. Random and multiple fractures may form a complicated network where fractures cross each other. All the properties make image processing and segmentation harder than other applications. The following are reprehensive examples for different types of fractures or cracks.

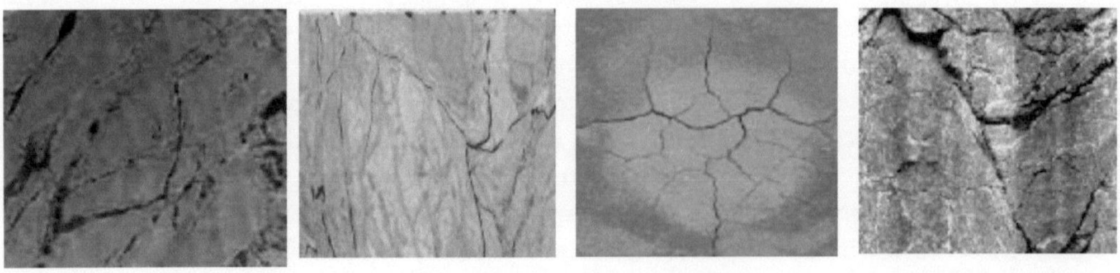

(a) (b) (c) (d)

Fig. 1. Four different types of rock fractures: (a) fractures are not continuous, (b) fractures have different gray-scales, (c) fractures form a network, and (d) very rough surface.

1.3 Summary of our work

In image processing, as a normal work sequence, we first used global filters and local filters to remove the noise and make gray variation correction, which is called image preprocessing. After image preprocessing, the image quality is increased, the remaining work is to abstract rock fractures from background, so-called image segmentation. In image segmentation part, we compared and used thresholding algorithms to binarize the rock fracture images for a rough analysis, in addition to this, both edge based algorithms and region similarity algorithms are tested and studied. Since the edge based algorithm can detect fracture boundary location accurately, and region similarity algorithms are better to alleviate producing extra noise, however, which type of algorithms, is selected to use, depending on the image properties. In the study, we found that the combination (or fusion) of the two or three types of image segmentation algorithms is a best way for segment our rock fracture images, but we have not fully used this procedure (it is still under development) yet in this work period. Since our image is resin injection fracture image, the simplest algorithm is image binarization, therefore we tested five different auto-thresholding algorithms which are widely used in the world. As the comparing result, we selected two binarization algorithms for our images; the one is Optimal binarization algorithm, and the other is Between class variance binarization algorithms. In edge based segmentation algorithm study, we tested popularly used edge detectors such as Canny edge detector and Robert edge detector etc. We found out that week and thin fractures cannot be detected y using these algorithms, since fractures are ridge objects, as an alternative, we developed a new edge detection algorithm for these kinds of edges. For high resolution images, the fractures are relatively thick: on the surface, a lot of white noise appears. To overcome this problem, we tried multi-scale technique for both region similarity and edge based algorithms. In conclusion, we tested 10 different preprocessing algorithms, five image binarization algorithms, and five edge detection algorithms. We developed and modified five different algorithms for image enhancement and segmentation. For our rock fracture images, we mainly used the modified image binarization algorithms.

2. Image preprocessing

The aim of image preprocessing is to enhance images for better visualization and processing. Image preprocessing techniques can be classified into global operators and local operators/25/. Linear contrast stretch and histogram equalization are two of the most widely used global operators. Adaptive histogram-equalization, contrast-limited adaptive histogram equalization, kernel filters, morphological functions and multi-scale enhancement belong to the local operators. While the global methods use a transformation applied to all the pixels of the image, the later methods use input-output transformation that varies adaptively with the local characteristics of the image. The typical types of image preprocessing can be expressed as:

Global operators: $f_{new}(x,y) = Trans\left(f_{original}(x,y)\right)$

Local operators: $f_{new}(x,y) = f_{original}(x,y) - Filter(x,y) + Const.$

Image enhancement algorithms have been designed to process a given image so the results are better than the original image for their applications or objectives. When the objective is to improve perceptual aspects, desirable image preprocessing can be performed by the contrast and dynamic range modification.

In this study, to enhance the fracture image for further processing and segmentation, we tried the both methods. To make comprehensively understanding the testing methods, we, first, briefly introduce some basic idea of digital images in separated sub-sections.

2.1 Image converting from color to gray scale

Notation: image converting from color to gray scale:

A grey scale image: $f(x,y)$ has $L(i=1,2,..,l \le 256)$ gray levels for each of image pixels, x, y are image sizes in horizontal and vertical directions respectively.

A color image (RGB) is a combination of three images: $F\{f_r(x,y), f_g(x,y), f_b(x,y)\}$.

If one converts a color image to a grey scale image, an general converting equation can be presented as:

$$F \Rightarrow f(x,y) = \alpha \cdot f_r(x,y) + \beta \cdot f_g(x,y) + \gamma \cdot f_b(x,y), \ (\alpha + \beta + \gamma = 1)$$

As an example in Fig. 2, we split a color image into R.G..B three images, the three images are different (the worst one may be the blue image), the differentiation is image dependent. In the Fig.3, the color image is split into R.G. ($\alpha + \beta + \gamma = 0.5 + 0.5 + 0.0 = 1$), R.B.

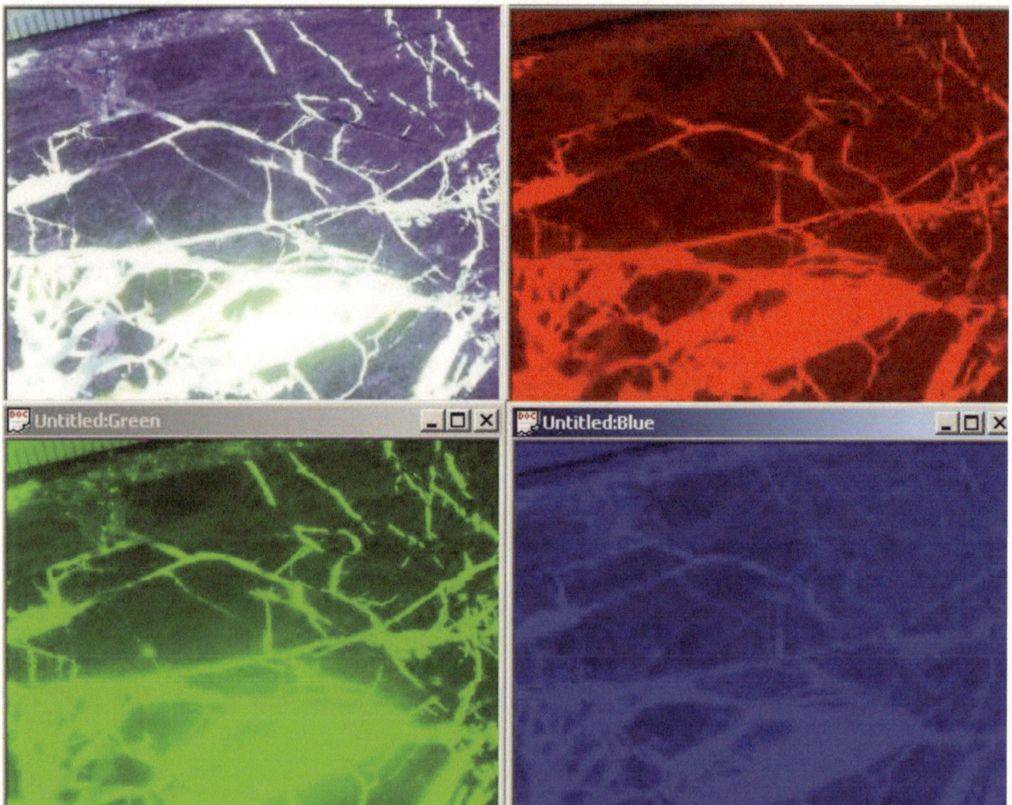

Fig. 2. A color fracture image is split into R.G..B. three images

($\alpha+\beta+\gamma=0.5+0.0+0.5=1$), and G.B ($\alpha+\beta+\gamma=0.0+0.5+0.5=1$) images. The each of the new images is a combination of two channel images, which make some new presentations for the original image. In the example, the yellow image may show fracture clearer than others.

Except for R.G..B, a color pixel can also be divided into the three values of intensity (I), hue (H) and saturation (S), which is another way to represent a color image. An example is shown in Fig. 4. For fractures, the best image may be the combination of light intensity (I) and color hue (H).

When a color image is to be converted to a gray scale image, the new image pixel value can also be calculated based on the R.G..B values or I.H.S. values in different ways. Fig. 5 shows that the above color image is converted to a gray scale image by using minimum or maximum R.G..B.values, which means that for each of the image pixels, checking its R.G..B. values, and choosing the minimum or maximum value of the three values, as input for the new image. In our application image, it is obviously that the minimum converting is better.

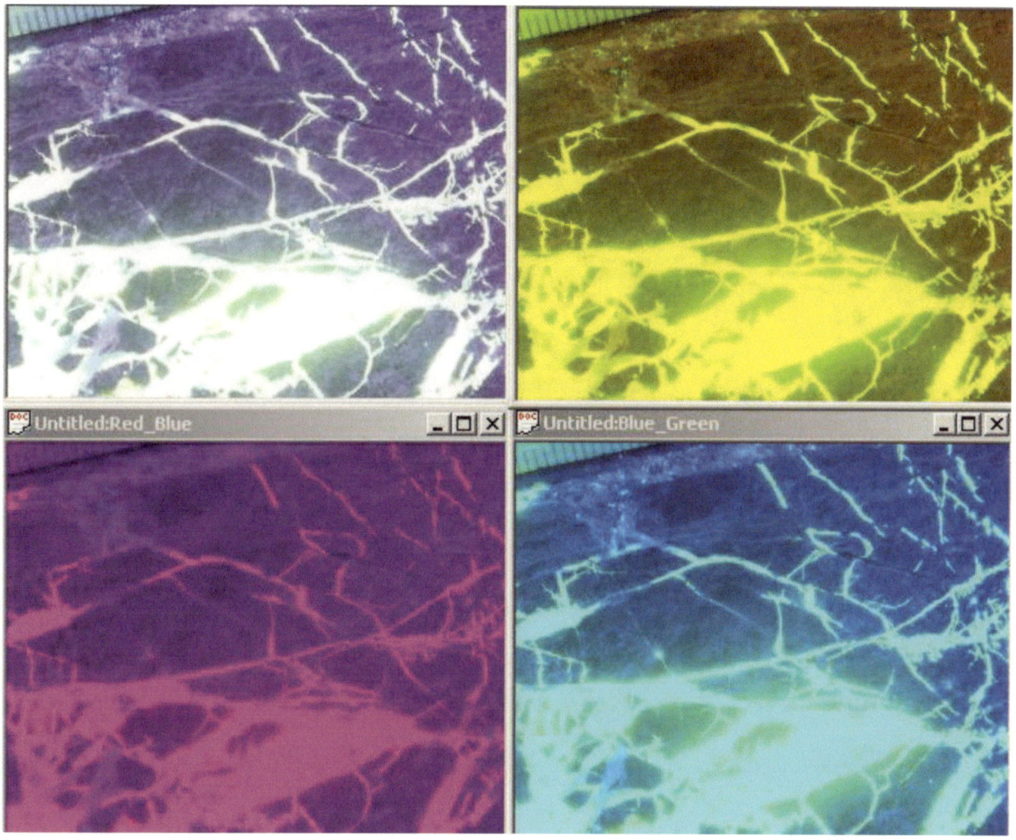

Fig. 3. A color fracture image is split into RG..RB.GB. three images.

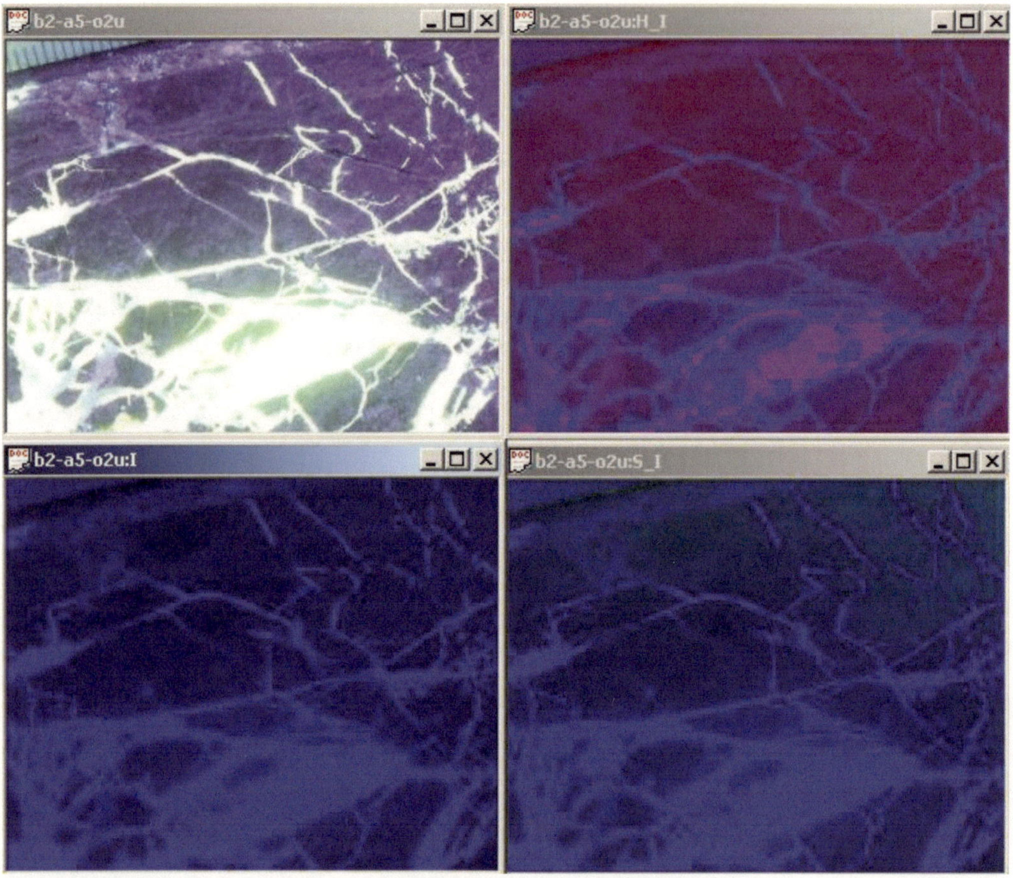

Fig. 4. A color fracture image is split into HI, I and SI three images

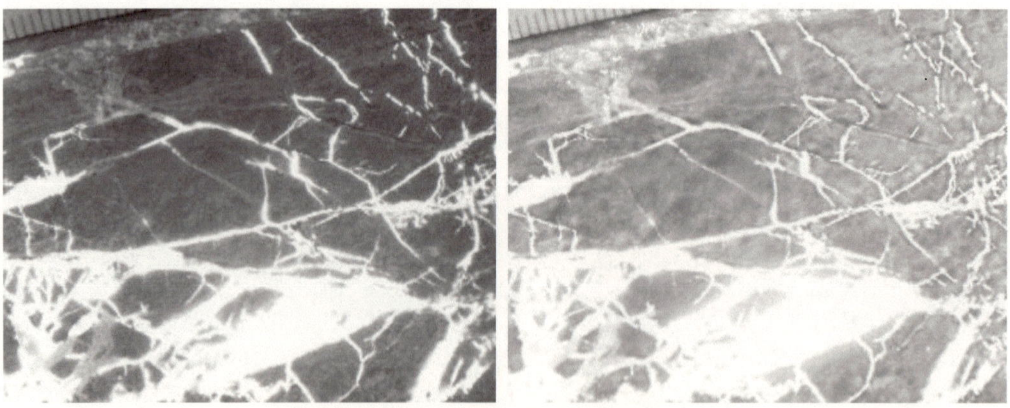

Fig. 5. The color fracture image is converted into a gray image. (a) Converted by using minimum R.G..B.values, and (b) Converted by using maximum R.G..B.values.

Anyhow, a color image includes a lot of information, some information is useful, and some cannot be used, which depends on the requirements for image processing and analysis. All the image converting methods belong to global operators. In our study, since we only consider the gray scale image segmentation, we have not used the color information yet, we normally directly convert a color image by using Minimum or Middle operators, in a few cases, and we also used the combination of GB image to obtain a gray scale image. To fully use the available color information, we may need more tests and studies.

2.2 Comparison of image preprocessing operators

No matter a color image or a gray scale image, a number of image preprocessing operators can be used for image enhancement. For a gray scale image, an operator acts on one image, and for a color image, an operator acts on three images (R.G.B.) respectively. Based on our rock fracture characteristics, we tested several widely used operators on the images. Based on our utilities, we classify all the tested operators into two types: the one is for image noise removal, and the other is for rock fracture sharpening on images.

In Fig. 6, we compared five different operators for a color rock fracture image. In Fig. 6(b), the operator is a 3x3 kernel with a Median filter operation (local operator) on the image, on the new image, the noise points and lines are removed, but the image is blurred; (c) Morphological operation (local operator): simple opening and closing, the operation result is similar to the median filter, it maybe more better for removing noise lines or curves; (d) Linear stretch (global operator): stretching the range of gray scales, it make intensity contrast more better.; (e) Sharpening (local operator): make fracture more shaper, but noise arising; and (f) Exponent transformation (global operator): decrease the gray values of the non-fracture regions.

For our images, we often used the operators of Exponent transformation, Linear stretch and Median filters. Since this is a testing stage, we have no an automatic procedure for enhancement of the rock fracture images currently, we may need to develop that in the next step of work. The auto-procedure development will be based on the further processing-image segmentation (fracture delineation or tracing) requirements.

3. Fracture delineation or tracing

After image preprocessing, the next is image segmentation-fracture tracing. The image segmentation is an old and topic subject of image analysis and pattern recognition. The current tendency is to combine different image segmentation algorithms for special application domain/. Our domain is rock fractures or fracture network.

3.1 Image thretholding

The scope of the present part is thresholding algorithms applied to a specific DOMAIN, that of rock fractures, in rock engineering. Fractures can be natural or man-made, where the former is of substantial interest in rock engineering applications. We stresses that the study deals with thresholding applied to a special domain rather than thresholding in general, because (a) the general problem is rather unspecified, (b) there is a greater chance of evaluating thresholding algorithms, if limiting the domain of possible images, and (c) there is the application of interest to us.

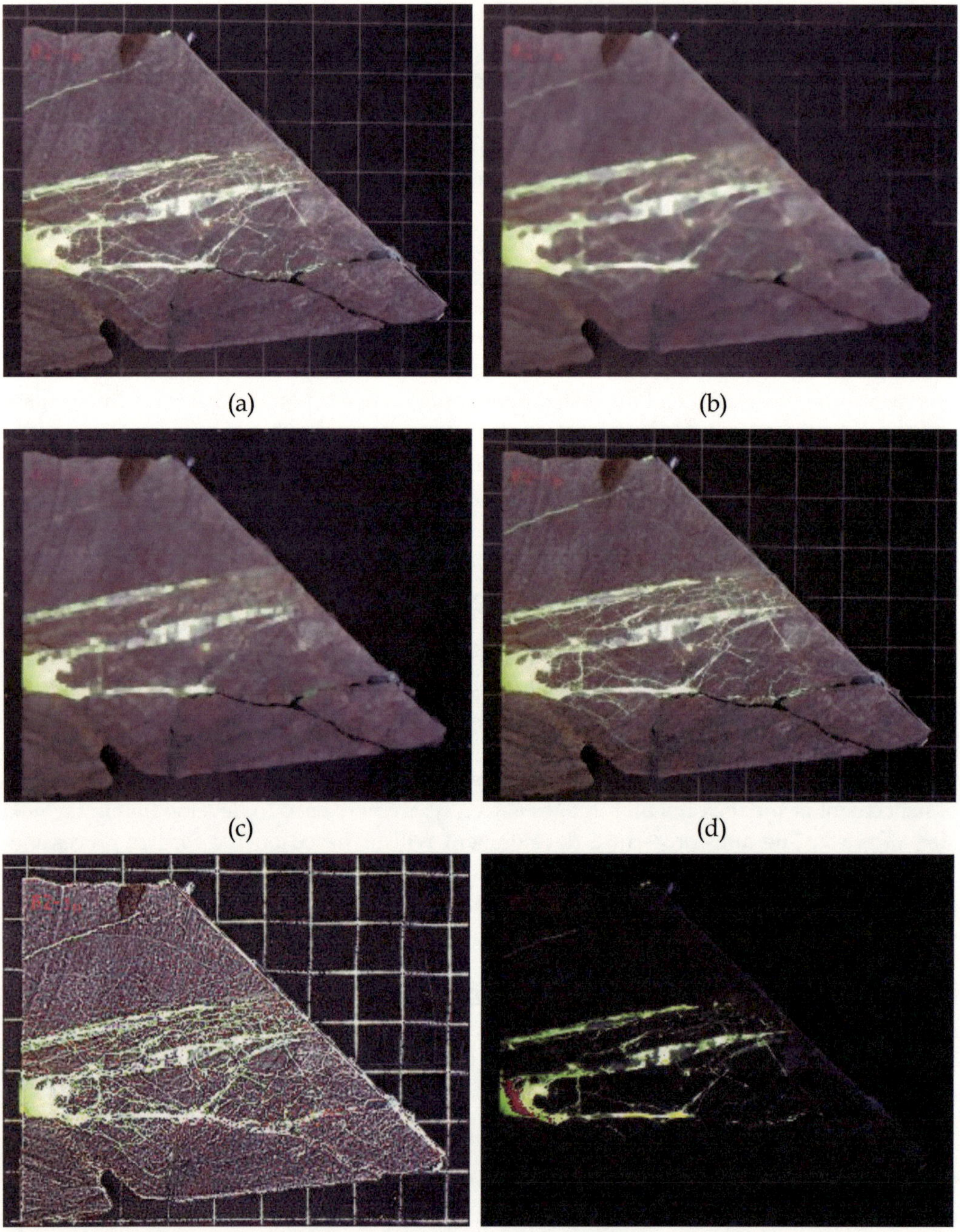

(a) (b) (c) (d) (e) (f)

Fig. 6. Comparison of image preprocessing operators: (a) Original image; (b) Median filter; (c) Morphological operation; (d) Linear stretch; (e) Sharpening; and (f) Exponent transformation.

The content of this part is (1) to compare the selected four of widely used global thresholding algorithms for four typical fracture images; (2) based on the comparison, to see how they work for rock fracture images, and (3) how to choose a global thresholding algorithm to segment the rock fracture images with a small variable background (the background is not completely uniform).

3.1.1 Thresholding algorithms selection and implementation

Thresholding is one of the old, simple, popular and most important approaches to image segmentation. From literature review, the thresholding algorithms can be classified thresholding algorithms into two groups /26-33/. One is based on the characteristic feature (e.g. gray level) histogram. Another is based on gradient (or Laplacian) of an image. The main global thresholding algorithms they summarized include: Optimal thresholding (OPT), Between class variance (BCV), Entropy, Moment preserving, Bi-modes (the threshold is a valley point between main two peaks) - we called it as BIM, Edge based thresholding (DIFF), dynamic edge based thresholding (DYN. Lee and Chung 1989 /28/, evaluated five of the global thresholding algorithms, the five algorithms are OPT, BCV, Entropy, Moment preserving and Quadtree. They gave a conclusion that Entropy and Quadtree are sensitive to image characteristics such as contrast and histogram distribution.

In order to evaluate these global algorithms (abbreviated OPT, BCV, BIM, DYN, and DIFF), how available they are for rock fracture images, the algorithms have been implemented into a PC computer. As a sever to readers comprehensively understanding the comparison between the algorithms, a brief description of these algorithms are listed as the follows.

Notation: an image $f(x,y)$ has gradient magnitude image $g(x,y)=\left|\nabla^2 f(x,y)\right|$, and the histograms $hisf(i)$ and $hisg(i)$ are corresponding to $f(x,y)$ and $g(x,y)$ respectively.

(1) OPT [30]: Suppose that an image contains two values combined with additive Gaussian noise. In addition of knowing the area percentage of objects, the mean values and their standard deviations are also known, the thresholding value can be obtained through an optimizing way. The implemented algorithm is iterative (optimal) threshold selection, which can be found in [30].

The details can be summarized as:

Pre-set a threshold T, separate an image into objects and background, then use Eq.(1) to obtain a threshold. Repeat the steps until $T^{t+1}=T^t$, T^t is the threshold.

$$u_B^t = \frac{\sum_{(i,j\in Backgound)} f(i,j)}{TNBP}, \quad u_O^t = \frac{\sum_{(i,j\in Object)} f(i,j)}{TNOP}$$

where , TNBP is the total number of background pixels, and TNOP is the total number of object pixels.

$$T^{t+1} = \frac{u_B^t + u_O^t}{2}$$

In our case: $T^{t+1} = 0.4u_B^t + 0.6u_O^t$.

(2) BCV[31]: The method supposes that the probability for each gray-level is $p_{i,}$ mean value $\mu = \sum_{i=1}^{m} ip_i$. The image is divided into two parts (i.e. background and objects foreground),

one has gray-levels from 1 to *k*, probability $\omega_0 = \sum_{i=1}^{k} p_i = \omega(k)$, mean gray value $\mu_0 = \sum_{i=1}^{k} ip_i = \mu(k)/\omega(k)$, the another from *k+1* to m, probability $\omega_1 = \sum_{i=k+1}^{m} p_i = 1 - \omega(k)$, mean gray value $\mu_1 = \sum_{i=k+1}^{m} ip_i = (\mu - \mu(k))/(1 - \omega(k))$, and $\omega_0\mu_0 + \omega_1\mu_1 = \mu$. Try to find maximum variance which is a function of variable *k*:

$$\sigma^2(k) = \omega_0(\mu_0 - \mu)^2 + \omega_1(\mu_1 - \mu)^2 = \omega_0\omega_1(\mu_1 - \mu_0)^2 = \frac{[\mu\omega(k) - \mu(k)]^2}{\omega(k)[1 - \omega(k)]} \quad (1)$$

obtain corresponding *k* as thresholding value.

(3) DIFF[33]: Define that *S* is the set of pixels having gray level *i*, find maximum value

$$d = \sum_{(x,y)\in S} g(x,y) \quad (2)$$

and obtain the corresponding *i* is the threshold.

(4) DYN: It is the similar to the above algorithm, the difference is that the threshold value is not constant on the whole image; it varies from place to place. In this algorithm implementation, we used Canny edge detector first, then, divide the image into a number windows, the thresholds are obtained on the information of windows.

(5) BIM [26-27, 30]: After calculating the histogram of gray-level image, the lowest valley point between two major peaks is found as the thresholding value. The program implemented is: firstly smooth the histogram by using Guassian smoothing function (1,2,3,2,1), then detect the two main peaks by using gradient at each point of gray level histogram, finally search the valley point between two main peaks. The valley point can be detected as

$$G_l^k = hisf(k) - hisf(k - m), \quad G_r^k = hisf(k) - hisf(k + m)$$

$$G^k = G_l^k + G_r^k \quad (G_l^k \rangle 0, \ G_r^k \rangle 0), \ T = MAX(G^k) \quad (3)$$

where, k=1,..., 256, threshold is corresponding to T. m is chosen by an operator, in the follows, we use m = 40.

3.1.2 Comparison between different global thresholding algorithms

In order to evaluate the performance of these five thresholding algorithms for rock fracture images, the test images were chosen based on (a) the images are the represents of fracture applications, and (2) fractures and background can be roughly distinguished by human vision (e.g. background is darker than fractures). Test images are of the size 320 by 240 uniformly quantified to 24 bits. Four typical images are shown in Fig. 7 and their histograms are shown in Fig.8 respectively. The image in Fig. 7a was taken from a slice, with two long fractures; its histogram is of a shape of a normal distribution. In Fig. 7b, the image is a microscope image with one fracture in details, and there are no two obvious peaks in the histogram. In Fig. 7c, the image is a slice image, the background is rough; the many fractures form a network. The images in Fig. 7d is a round surface image, there is much noise on the image, and the fracture network is complicated. Figs. 8a-d show the histograms of the corresponding images in Figs. 7a-d. Most of the histograms seem to be ones of two modes, with two main peaks, but their shapes are very different.

One of the most difficult problems in comparing and evaluating the performance of thresholding algorithm is choosing a meaningful object performance criterion. The problem is that a criterion suitable for one application may not be suitable for a different application of thresholding techniques. However, the most important concern is the accuracy in segmentation of fracture images. In evaluation of the performance, the probability of error (or maximum shape) and uniformity, which are often observed by human vision, could be set as criteria.

In this study, it is not supposed to threshold each of the test images perfectly, the evaluation is based on comparing to human vision. The test results could be used for the fracture analysis in this work stage.

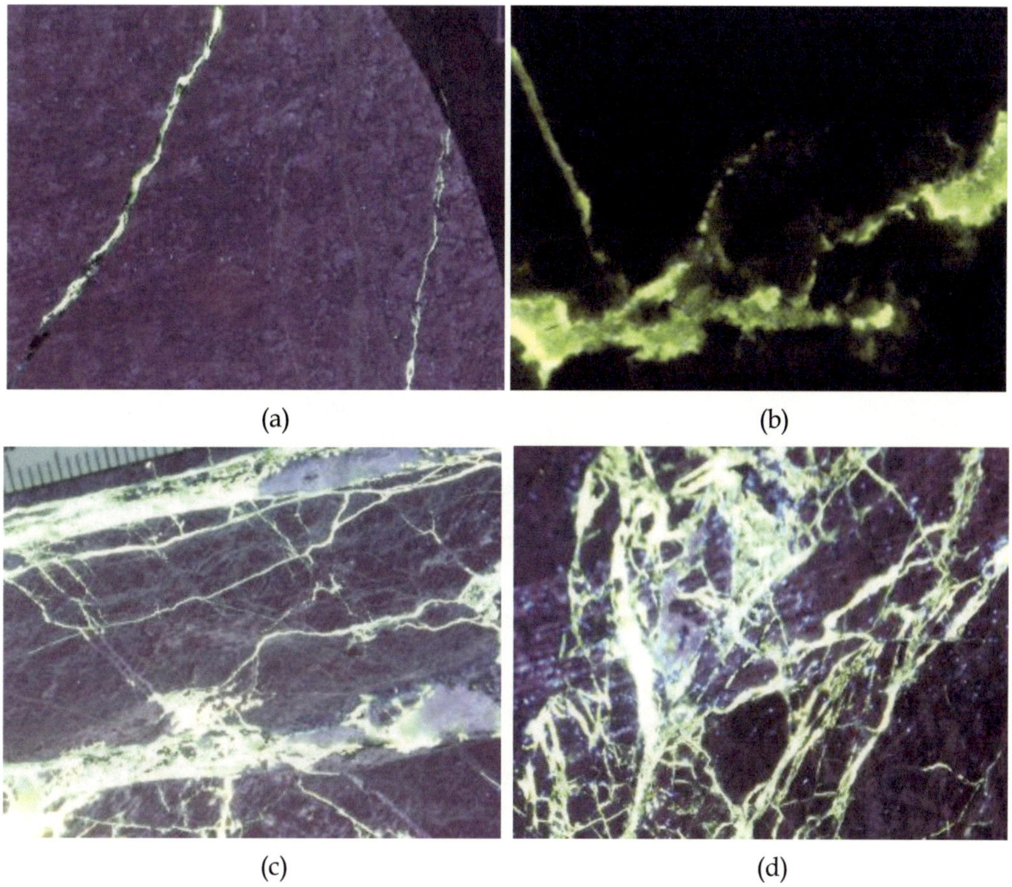

Fig. 7. Four typical rock fracture images.

As tested many times, OPT and BVC operations will give a similar result on any of our rock fracture images, therefore, in the figures 9-12, we just give OPT, BIM, DIFF and DYN operation results on each image in Fig. 7 for comparison. The testing results show (Fig. 9-Fig. 12) that OPT works on all the four images, BIM works on the image of a two modes (peaks) histogram, DYN may work for the images with complicated fracture network, and DIFF is sensitive to the information variation of rock fracture images.
Based on this testing result, we used OPT or BVC for all the rock fractures. The figure 13 demonstrates other four typical image thresholding results by using BVC thresholding algorithm. It is satisfied for our rock fracture images binarization, by using BVC or OPT.

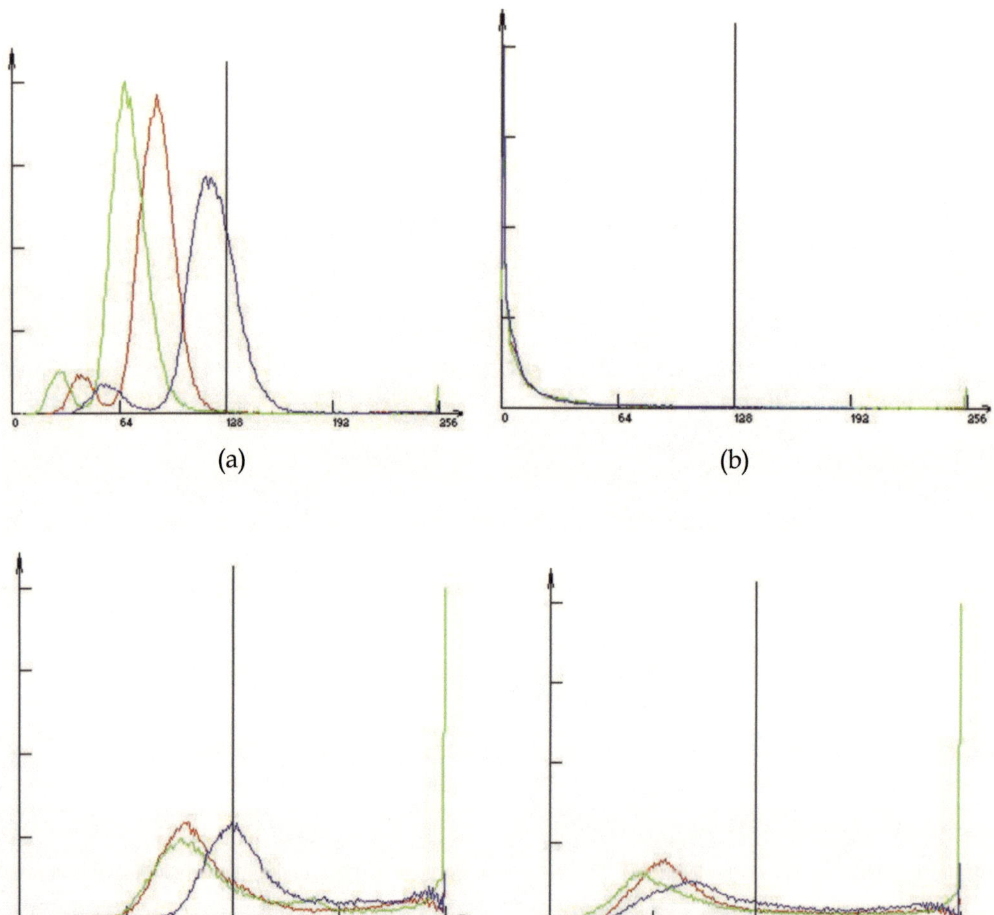

Fig. 8. Histograms for the images in Fig. 7 respectively.

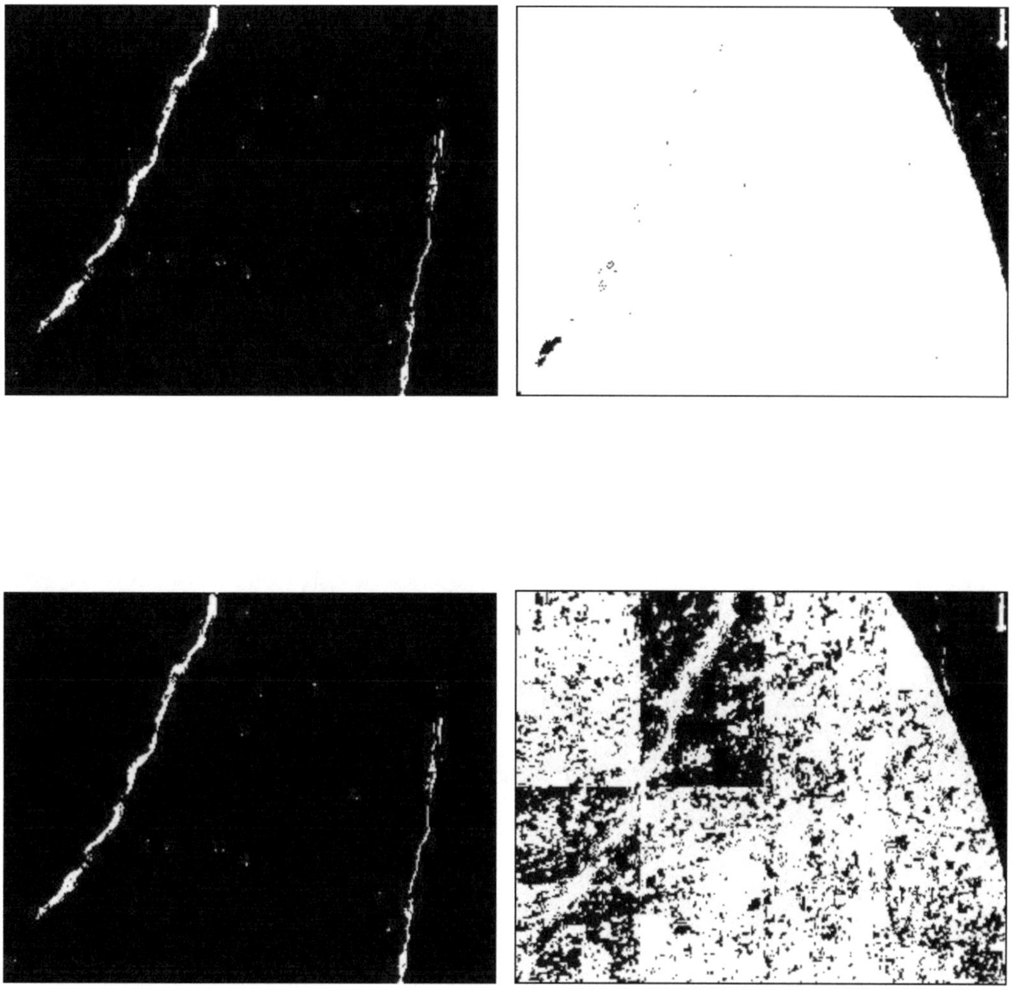

Fig. 9. Four threholding algorithms on the image in Fig. 7a: BIM and DYN are failed.

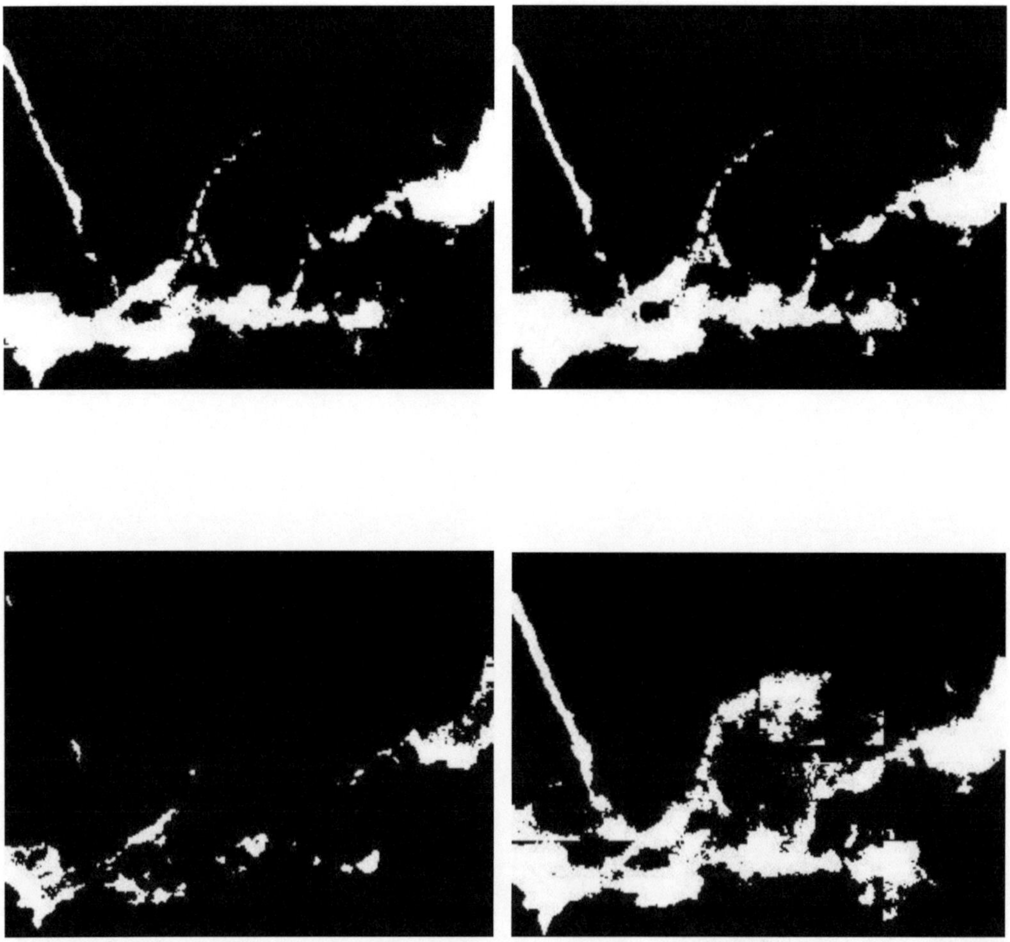

Fig. 10. Four threholding algorithms on the image in Fig. 7b: DIFF is failed, and DYN gives a larger fracture area than human vision detection.

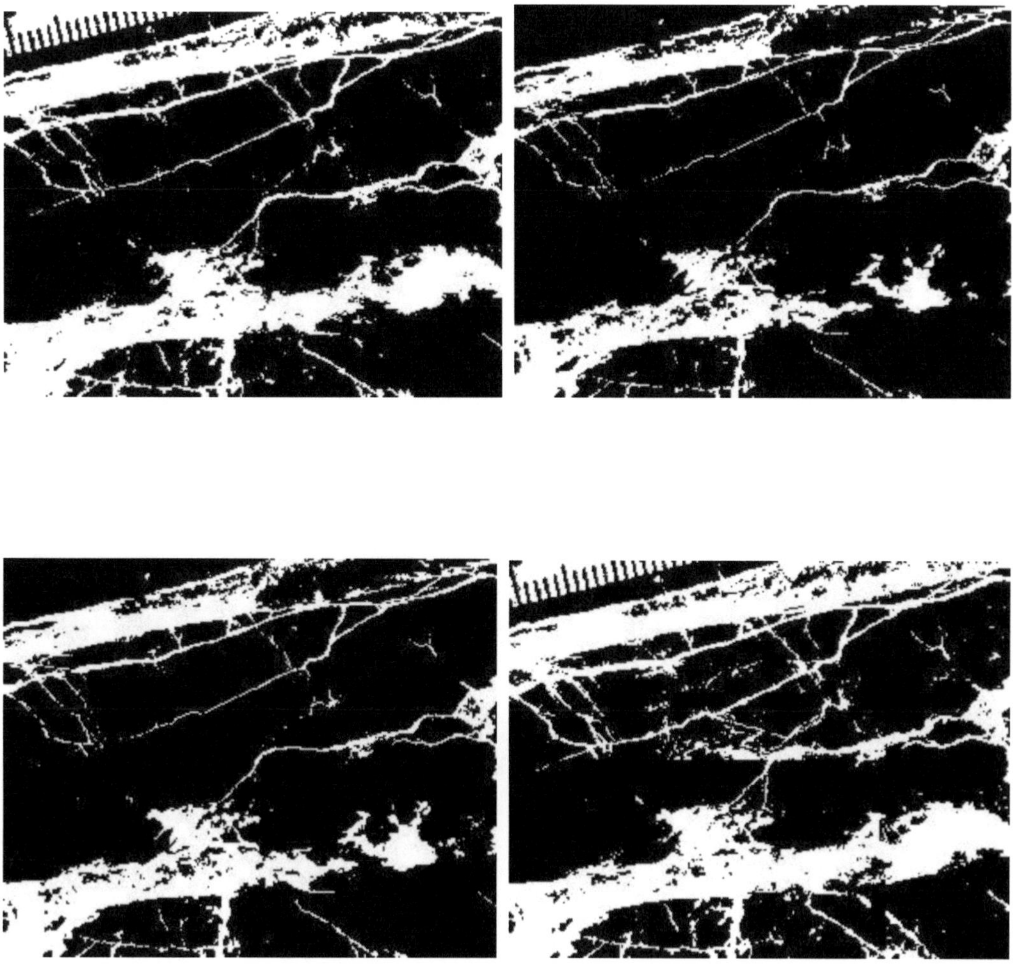

Fig. 11. Four threholding algorithms on the image in Fig. 7c: All the operations are seemed to be fair except for the scale ruler affection.

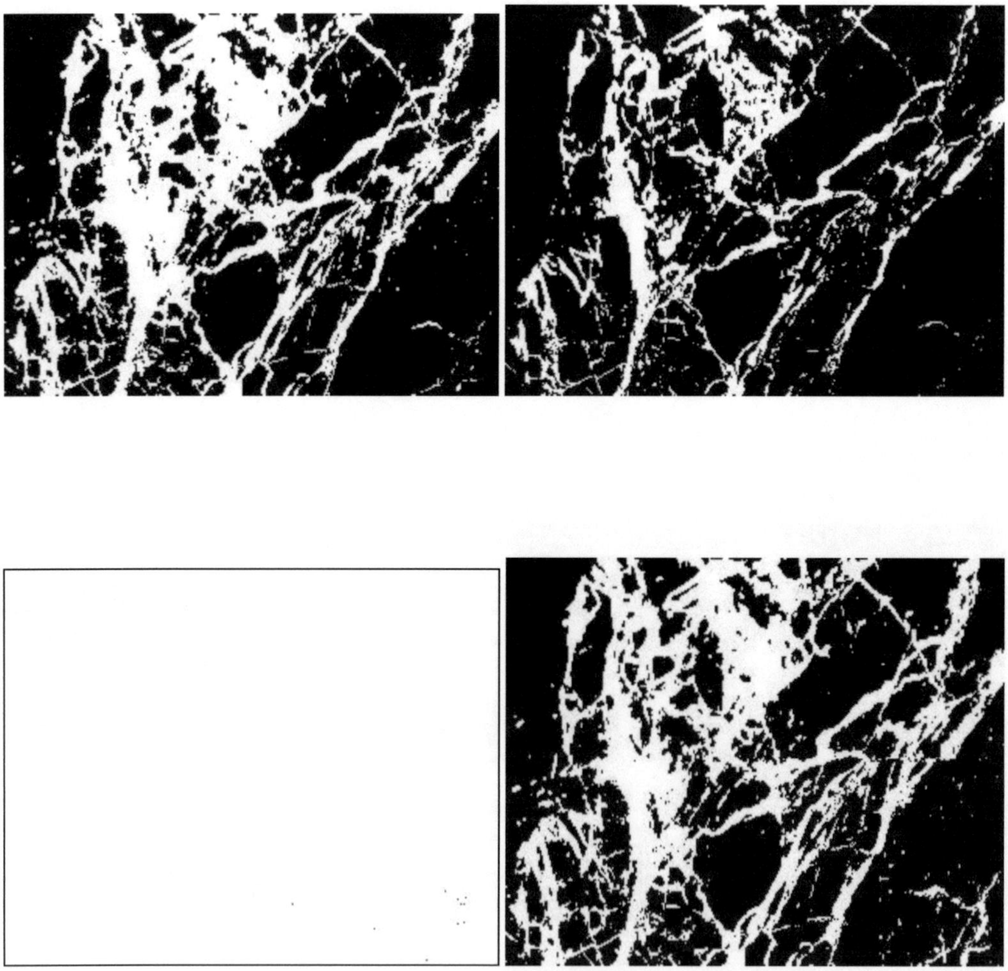

Fig. 12. Four threholding algorithms on the image in Fig. 7d: DIFF fails completely.

(a)

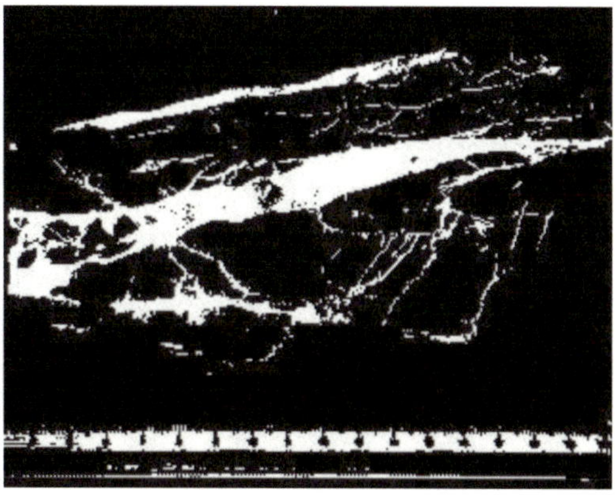

(b)

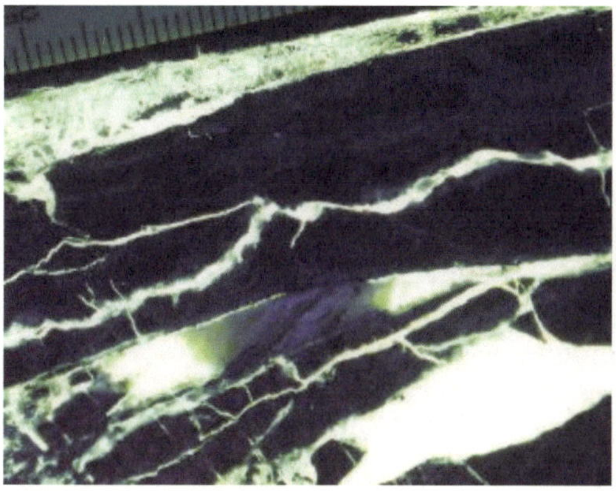

(c)

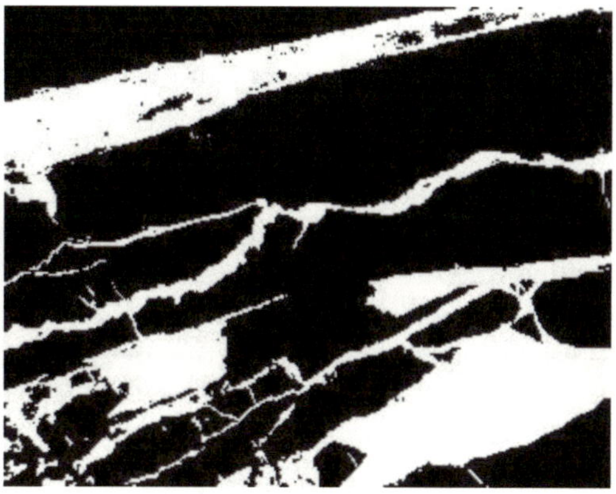

(d)

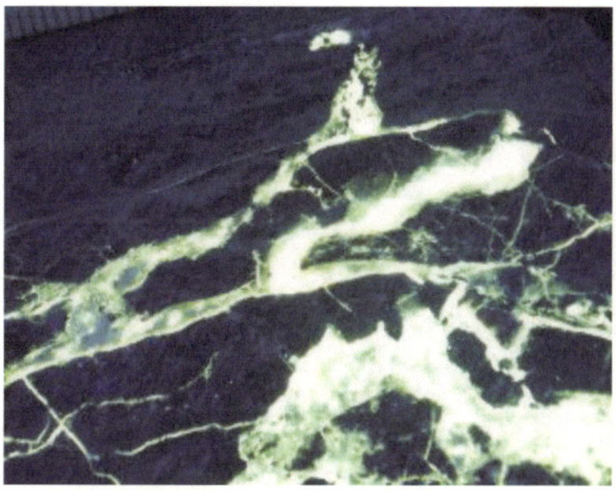

(e)

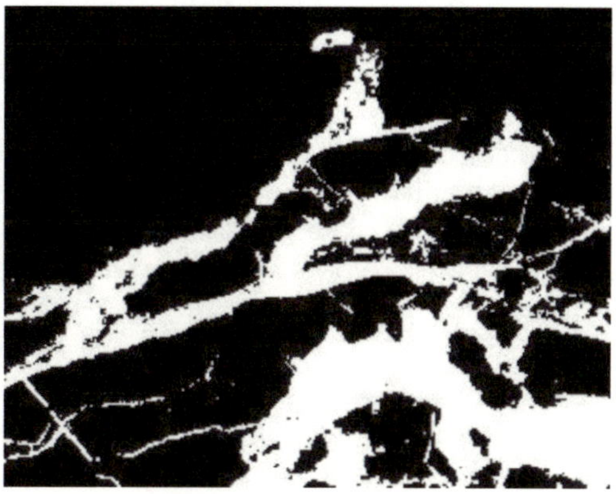

(f)

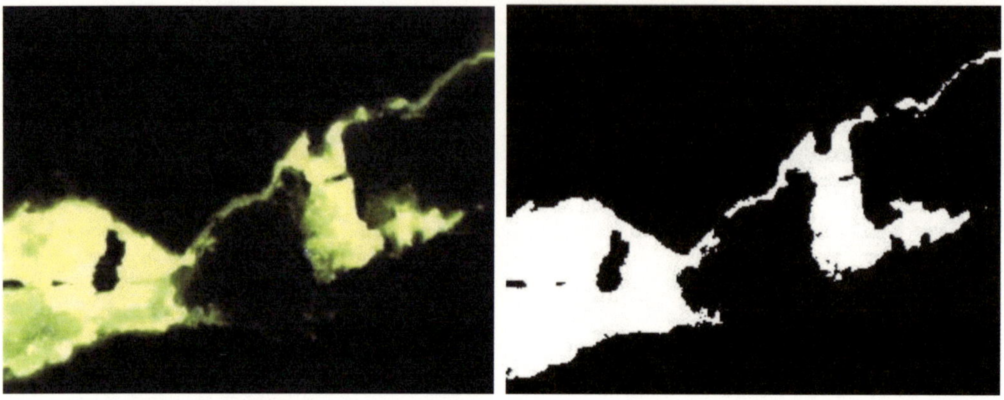

(a) (b)

Fig. 13. BVC algorithm on the four typical rock fracture images.

3.1.3 In conclusion

For a rock fracture image with a rather uniform background, and the range of the grey levels of fractures being not too large, the algorithms OPT and BCV are good choices for performing global thresholding.

In this study, a simple BIM algorithm is given, the test results show that it works for some kinds of images (the histogram consists of two main peaks); the algorithm design depends strongly on the types of histograms of fracture images.

For the fracture images, it is not suggested to use the thresholding algorithms based on gradient magnitude. The textured surfaces of the fractures will strongly affect the thresholding results although the background of images is rather uniform.

In general speaking, thresholding algorithms can be classified into manual, semi-automatic and automatic thresholdings. The automatic thresholding algorithms can be sub-classified into (1) the grey level histogram based and (2) based on the histogram of gradient magnitude. In the application of fracture recognition, if the images can be binarized satisfactorily by human vision, OPT and BCV are suggested to use for automatically thresholding. For the complex fracture images, adaptive thresholding algorithms maybe applied, in which, OPT and BCV are also suggested to use as a basis if needed.

To more accurately binarize the rock fracture images, adaptive thresholding, edge based or region based algorithms maybe needed to study. As a literature review, in recent years, many researchers recognized that it is difficult to use a single image segmentation algorithm to segment images in most of applications; the new focus topic is the fusion of different image segmentation techniques or algorithms. To do this kind of tests, we have developed some algorithms based on edge detection and region based (Fig. 14), the developed algorithms are useful for fracture tracing in some cases, the fusion procedure maybe next step development. In the next section, we will introduce our edge based segmentation idea.

3.2 Edge based segmentation algorithm

We here use gray-scale information (a color band) to trace the fracture curves. To develop the algorithm, several aspects must, generally speaking, be considered: (a) gray flatness or smoothness; (b) curvature variation; (c) magnitude strength; (d) computational searching costs; and (e) distance linking etc.

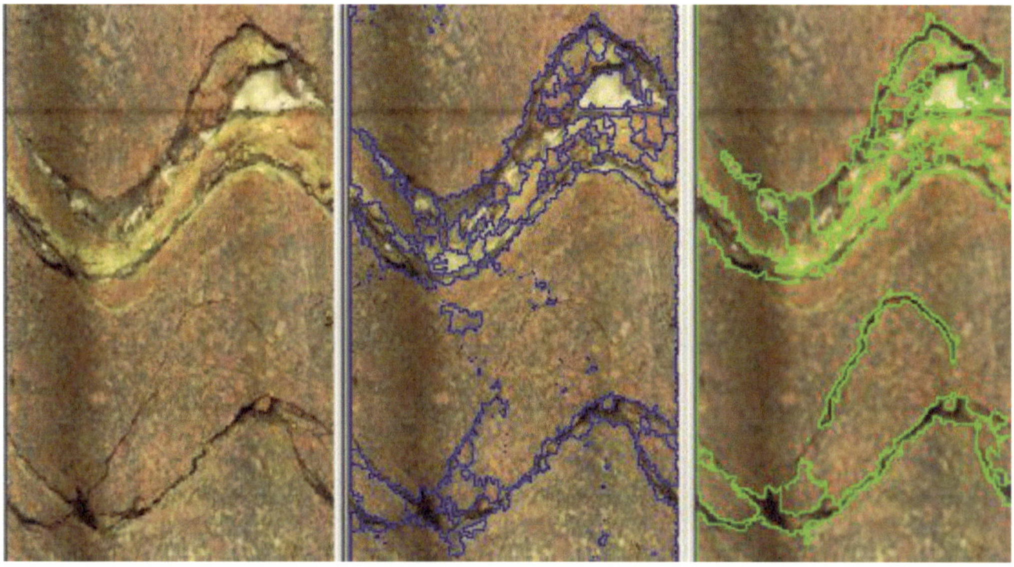

Fig. 14. Example of region based algorithm. Fracture tracing possibility for BIP images: Blue One is segmented based on image shrink, similarity (12, 80), and green one is segmented based on smoothing and similarity (7, 80). These are examples, for real segmentation, it need to modify the segmented fracture curves, e.g. to use triangle signal information, curve smoothing, small region merge and gap links. All these are post-processing, if the primary segmentation results can be like in the images, remaining tasks will be fixed anyway.

On the surface of rock mass, the objects of fracture often appear as step edges or ridge edges. The aim of image processing and image segmentation is to auto-tracing rock fractures, which is one of the most difficult tasks in image processing and image segmentation, due to the complicated properties on the rock surface.

Segmentation algorithms for monochrome images are generally based on one of two basic properties of gray-level values: discontinuity and similarity. In the first category, the approach is to partition an image based on abrupt changes in gray level.

An edge, in the image analysis literature, is a jump in intensity. The cross section of a so-called ideal edge has the shape of a ramp: infinite slope and flat portions on either side of the discontinuity. In smoother versions of the ideal edges, the first derivative (in appropriate direction) assumes a local maximum at a so-called edge point or edge pixel. A well-known edge detector of this type is the Canny edge detector, locating local maxima in gradient magnitude (=steepest slope). However, in our case we are more interested in another class of detectors, for example, those known as *ridge detectors* in the image analysis literature. A ridge can be simply thought of as a double edge (a bar edge). Between the step parts there is a narrow plateau or peak.

Sometimes, ridge detectors are expressed as follows: a bright (dark) ridge point is defined a point for which the intensity assumes a local maximum in the main principal curvature direction.

3.2.1 Ridge detection

The reported valley-edge detection algorithm in Wang and Bergholm (2003)/34/, may be used as a ridge detector. A valley-edge detector tries to detect the lowest valley point in a certain direction. If it is, the pixel is used as the valley-edge candidate, and its direction and location are marked, for further processing to form a valley-edge, by thinning and tracing procedures.

In Fig. 15a-b, when examining a pixel *p*, check the four different directions shown in the figure, to determine whether *p* is the valley-edge point or not. As an example, a small kernel valley-edge detection function runs as follows:

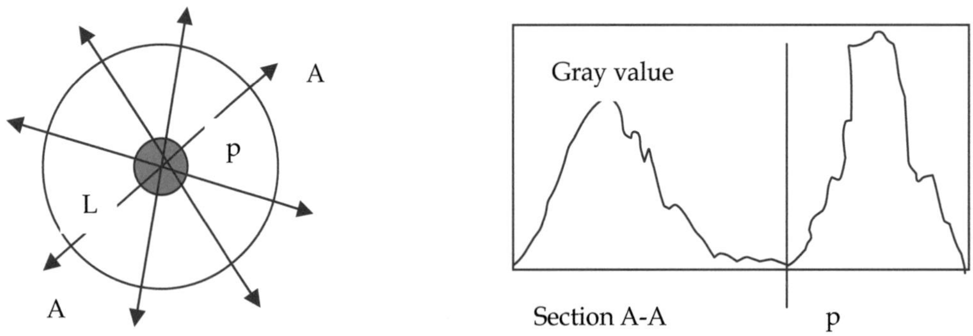

Fig. 15. The diagram for valley-edge detection algorithm, Wang and Bergholm (2003).

In the 0° direction:

If $f(x,y) < f(x-1,y)$, then $F_1^0 = f(x-1,y) - f(x,y)$,

If $f(x,y) < f(x+1,y)$, then $F_2^0 = f(x+1,y) - f(x,y)$,

If $f(x-1,y) < \alpha f(x-2,y-1) + \beta f(x-2,y) + \gamma f(x-2,y+1)$, then

$F_3^0 = \alpha f(x-2,y-1) + \beta f(x-2,y) + \gamma f(x-2,y+1) - f(x-1,y)$,

If $f(x+1,y) < \alpha f(x+2,y-1) + \beta f(x+2,y) + \gamma f(x+2,y+1)$, then

$F_4^0 = \alpha f(x+2,y-1) + \beta f(x+2,y) + \gamma f(x+2,y+1) - f(x+1,y)$;

And similar expressions in the 45^0, 90^0 and 135^0 directions.

In the directionθ, calculate the following sum:

$$T_\vartheta = w_1 F_1^\vartheta + w_2 F_2^\vartheta + w_3 F_3^\vartheta + w_4 F_4^\vartheta$$

$\theta = 0^0, 45^0, 90^0$ and 135^0 ; $w_i (i=1,2,3,4)$ are weights, e.g. $w_1 = w_2 = 1.2$, $w_3 = w_4 = 0.8$.

$T_{max} = \max(T_O, T_{45}, T_{90}, T_{135})$. If T_{max} is greater than a threshold T, the detected point will be marked as a valley-edge candidate.

The distance *L* (in the above formula, *L* = (i+1)-i = (j+1)-j=1)) is pre-determined based on image resolution and quality, and smoothing is done prior to valley-edge detection.

The details of the algorithm can be found in Wang et al. (2003)/34/, here we merely stress that for each direction two values are calculated, and two values are obtained, f1 and f2 (=two 2nd differences at two scales). A weighted sum of these (in e.g. the 135 degree direction) is:

After valley-edge detection, a post-processing subroutine must be added. In the post-processing subroutine, several functions are used, such as thinning, bridging of small gaps, and removal of short curves or lines (refer to Figs. 16-17).

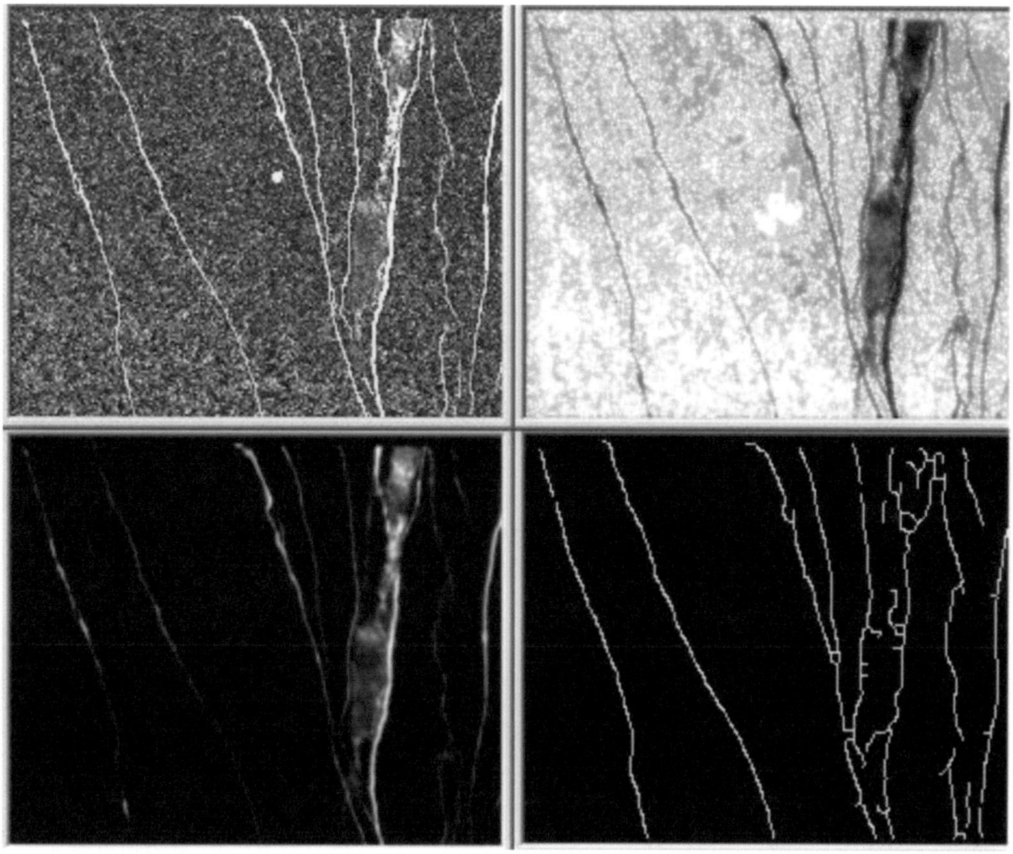

Fig. 16. Example 1 of fracture tracing by the new algorithm. The top-left image is original image, the top-right image is inverted and enhanced image, the bottom-left image is a magnitude image by Robert edge detector, and the bottom-right image is the result image.

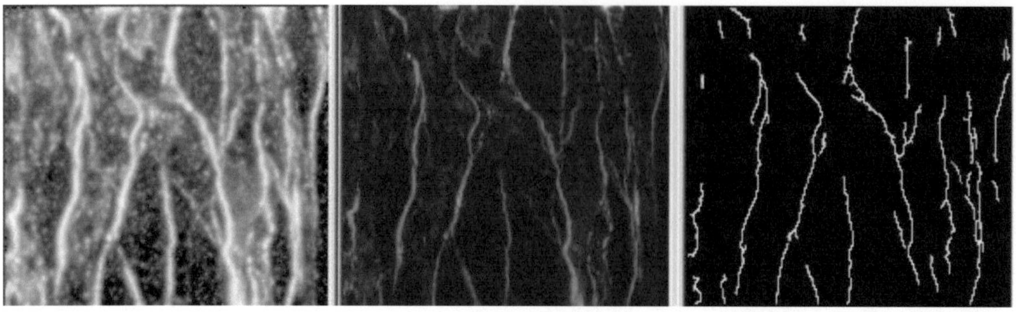

Fig. 17. Example 2 of fracture tracing by the new algorithm. The left image is original image, the middle image is a magnitude image, and the right image is the result image.

3.2.2 Multiple scales

Multi-scale representations are more or less related to scale-space theory, notably the theories of *pyramids*, *wavelets* and *multi-grid methods*. We will not describe and discuss the theory, the detailed information can be found in /35-37/. For the complicated rock fracture images, the methodology is very useful as we tested.

If most fractures in an image are very thin, the fine-detail information in the image is very important for fracture tracing, and the algorithm must avoid destroying the information. On the contrary, if fractures are thick, it is necessary to remove the detailed information on the rock surface, because it may produce a lot of fault fractures. In general, it is an image processing tool that the multiple scale technique makes image structures at coarse scales corresponding to simplifications of corresponding structures at fine scales.

By using the knowledge of multiple scales, we combine the valley edge detection results of different scale images, and have a promising fracture tracing result which is difficult to be obtained by using other methods. A gray scale fracture image of 734x596 pixels is presented in Fig. 18(a); its fracture tracing result is in Fig. 18(b). In Fig. 18(a), the noise edges randomly distributed on the whole image surface, and thick fracture cannot be detected properly by

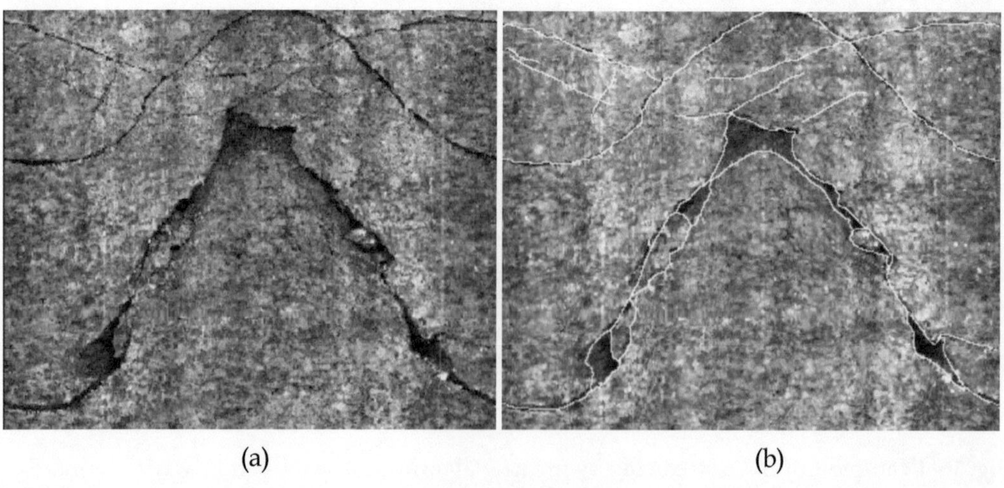

(a) (b)

Fig. 18. One example of rock fracture images: (a) Original image of resolution 734x596; and (b) Fracture tracing result.

using just valley edge detection. The fracture mapping result is processed based on the combination of multiple scales and our valley edge detection methods. The question is how to scale the image into different scale levels here, in the following; we will give a brief description of the question.
The image scale is reduced. Let $x = 1,...,n$, $y = 1,...,m$, and $f(x,y)$ is the original image. Then

$f(x_k, y_k)$, $x_k = 1,...,n/2^k$, $y_k = 1,...,m/2^k$, k = 1, 2, 3, 4,...

where, $k \le K$, $m \ge 2^K$, $n \ge 2^K$

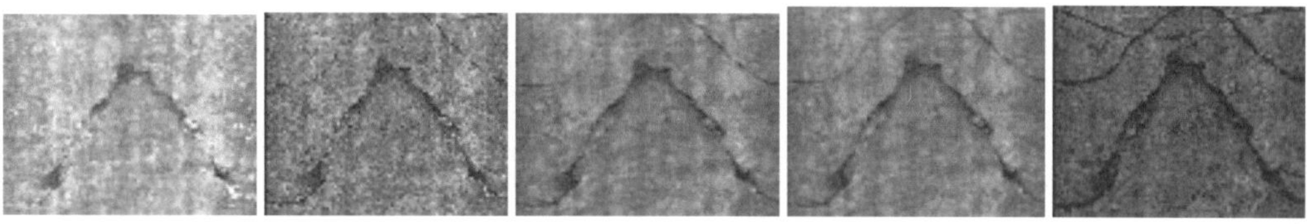

(a) (b) (c) (d) (e)

Fig. 19. Shrink image three times on the image in Fig. 18(a): (a) Maximum filter; (b) Odd lines; (c) Average filter; (d) Middle filter; and (e) Minimum filter.

To obtain valuable scaled $f(x_k, y_k)$, we tried several image shrink methods (e.g. used Gaussian, average, medium, adaptive, maximum and minimum etc. filters). The figure 6 is one of the examples to show the differences among the rock fracture image shrink methods. In figure 19, since fractures in Fig. 18(a) have low gray values, Maximum filter (in original image, choose maximum gray value pixel, of four neighboring pixels, as a new pixel in the shrink image) eras thin fractures, on the contrast, Minimum filter make fractures sharpen, but the noise are sharp too. In our case, we use Minimum filter to shrink image for three times, then smooth the scaled image by a Gaussian filter.
One of typical examples is shown in Fig. 20. The original image has a rough surface with thick fractures, if the developed ridge detection and fracture tracing algorithms are directly used without image scale operations, the detection result will include a lot of fault fractures. When we shrink the original image one time, the detection result will be better. The best detection result is in Fig. 20(d), where, we shrink the image for three times before ridge detection and fracture tracing.

3.2.3 In conclusion

For this study, we have developed a number of algorithms for image processing and segmentation, especially for rock fracture images. The presented fracture detection algorithm is the robust for ridge edge detection and fracture tracing, but for the rough surface with thick cracks or fractures, using multi-scale technology can allevate producing noise fractures. The next step of work is to use nural network and statistics /38-41/ to calssify images into different classes, then use pyramid methods to divide original image into several scale levels, to use the detection algorithm with different parameters to detect fractures.

3.3 Fractional differential algorithms

It is a new research topic that fractional differential theory is used into image processing. We a new type of algdeveloped new algorithms to improve the fractional differential Tiansi

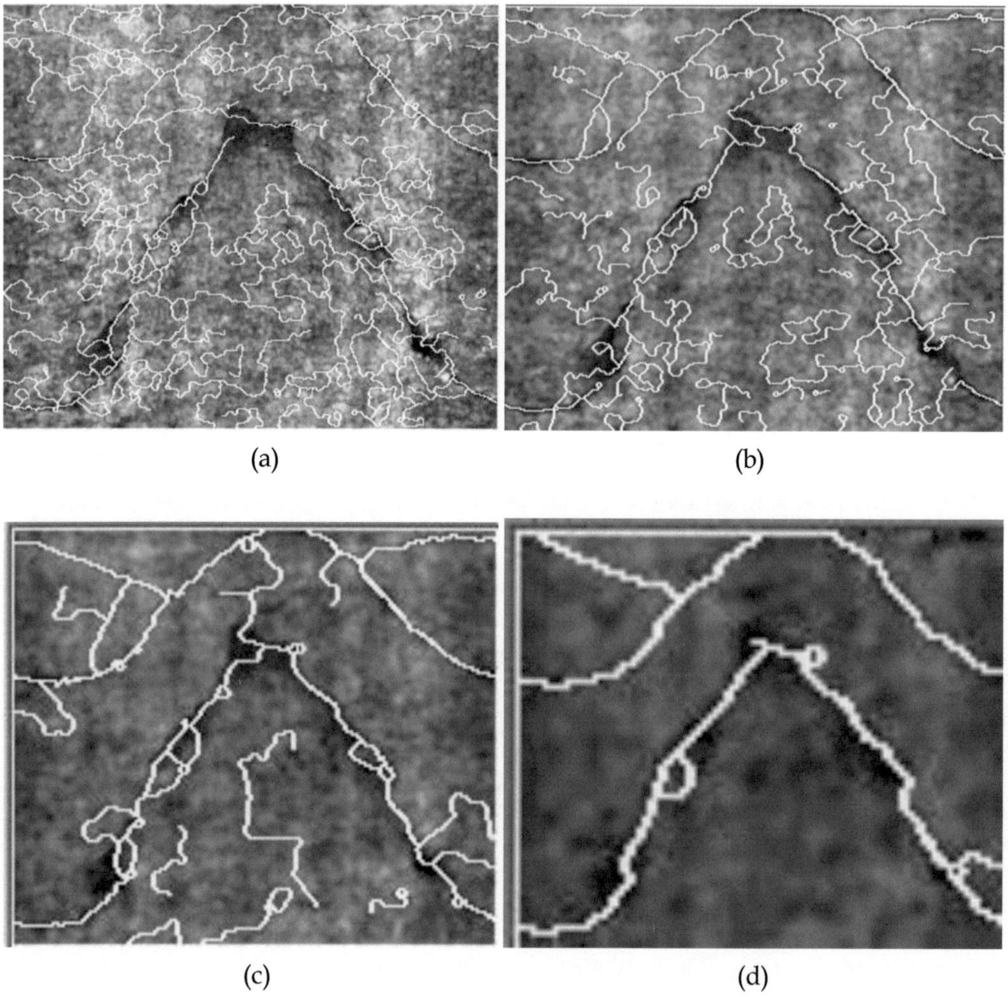

Fig. 20. Valley edge detection result: (a) Image of resolution 734x596; (b) Image of resolution 367x298; (c) Image of resolution 183x149; and (d) Image of resolution 91x74.

operator, which can significantly enhance the edge information. The studied algorithms are based on the enhancement ability of fractional differential to rock fracture image details, and they can be used to analyze the mechanism of fractional differential. The general procedure of the algorithms is as follows: Firstly, Tiansi template is divided into eight sub-templates with different directions around the detecting pixel, and then eight weight sum values for the eight sub-templates are obtained. Furthermore, those eight weights are classified into different groups. In this way, the three improved algorithms with different enhancing ranges are obtained. Finally, the experiments of edge enhancement show that the improve algorithms can enhance edge information more effectively and can show much more detailed information than traditional edge detection operators especially for the image segmentation of complicated rock fracture images. The detailed information can be found in reference [42].

3.4 Rock fracture detection based on quaternion convolution by scale multiplication

In order to suppress the noise, the dot product is computed at adjacent scales. At the same time, we apply gray-level difference to obtain the monochromatic edges. To merge the merits of the quaternion convolution and the gray-level difference, the two results are used at the same time. Finally, the thinned edges can be obtained by using modulus maximum suppression. Experimental results show that the algorithm is efficient and robust for rock fracture edge detection.

In this study, we firstly presented the rock fracture image acquisition method. Since the width and color of the fracture vary much, it is usual that there are many gaps on one crack or fracture. This study use quaternion convolution for rock fracture edge detection. When the pixels are chromatic, the quaternion convolution is more efficient than other methods. At the same time, we use the gray-level image to obtain the monochromatic edge points. Then thinned edges can be obtained by using modulus maximum suppression. Experiment results show that the method is both efficient and robust. The detailed information is in reference [43].

3.5 Rock fracture edge detection based on Wavelet Analysis

Wavelet analysis is internationally recognized up to minute tool for analyzing time frequency. This study discusses the technique of image processing based on wavelet transform.

There are many methods to obtain the rock fracture images. The inner fractures image can be obtain using ultraviolet and the external fractures image can be obtain using visible light. The methods are efficient and low cost.

To detect the ultraviolet image fractures, we presented an algorithm based on multiscale wavelet transform. After obtain the gray scale images, the image can be split to three types of area: the black, the white and the transitional area. The edge detection can be enhanced and the noise can be reduced by scale multiplication. The method is useful not only for rock fractures detection but for other images edge detection.

The color images are acquired using visible light and the fractures are more complicated. This paper presents the fracture detection algorithm based on quaternion convolution. After the color image is convoluted using different scale quaternion operators, the dot product is applied. At last, the edge map is obtained using modulus maxima suppressed.

Because of the color image is noisy and the ultraviolet image is clear edge, the better idea is fuse the two types of images. After the color image is transformed to IHS color space, the edge information is fused in different areas. The fused image is more using for image processing. The interested readers can refer to [44].

3.6 Rock fracture tracing based on image processing and SVM

This study presented a new methodology for automated rock fracture trace detection, description and classification based on automated image processing techniques and support vector machine (SVM). The developed procedure uses a series of photographs of a rock face which were taken by sophisticated CCD cameras. All digital image are be processing by the developed algorithm, and fracture traces extracted from the processed image are then identified and categorized by SVM. The proposed procedure has been tested by detecting fracture and classifying the fracture traces. Results show that the approach is useful and robust...

The aim of this study is to present a novel, automated and robust methods for rock fracture tracing. Image processing technology is used to get high quality of image segments for recognition. Support vector machine is introduced into the rock fracture classification for the first time in this field. Although the methods didn't achieve the expect performances, there are a lot of advantages compared with the current technology.

SVM is very promising to tackle complicated problems in rock fracture trace recognition and it could be enlarged to more complex structures in future research. As a reliable technique to identify fracture traces in practice, this method should be tested in more real measurement cases. And for further work, a SVM image segment and recognition system can be constructed. The detailed description for this study can be found in reference [45].

4. Conclusions and suggestions

1. For this study, we have developed and collected a number of algorithms for rock fracture image processing and segmentation.
2. A number image preprocessing algorithms have been discussed and compared.
3. Several auto-thresholding algorithms have been studied and compared, and the BCV or OPT algorithms are considered satisfactory for the rock fracture images in this testing stage roughly analysis of rock fracture network properties).
4. Except for the thresholding algorithms, a region based segmentation algorithm is also tested for BIPS images.
5. The developed edge detection algorithms are robust for ridge edge detection and fracture tracing. It has been tested for the images of single fracture and fracture network, it is promising, and it may need more tests further.
6. For difficult images (where cracks and fractures are difficult to distinguish due to either minerals or shadows etc.) and images with wide fracture apertures, using multi-scale technology can alleviate producing noise fractures.
7. The next step of work needs to create an auto preprocessing procedure to all the rock fracture images first, then, to modify the developed threhsolding, region based and edge based image segmentation algorithms, make them to fit for our rock fracture images respectively.
8. Finally to use neural network, fuzzy logic, wavelet/38-41/ and artificial intelligence technologies to classify images into different classes, then use pyramid methods to divide original image into several scale levels, to use the fusion of the different detection algorithms to setup a fracture image segmentation procedure, and to auto-detect rock fractures.

Anyhow, the different rock fracture images need different image segmentation algorithms. Since rock fracture images are so different that they cannot be segmented by only one image segmentation algorithm. In this chapter, eight different image segmentation algorithms are studied and developed for rock fracture images, one of the algorithms is suitable for one or several types of rock fracture images, but not for all the types of images. In the future work, the algorithms will be further studied and tested, then, one image segmentation system will be constructed by several image segmentation algorithms that are selected based on a neural network system, for a processing image of rock fractures.

5. Acknowledgements

This research is supported by the Special Fund for Basic Scientific Research of Central Colleges, Chang'an University in China with number: CHD2010JC004.

6. References

[1] Liu H. et al., 2004, Characterization of rock heterogeneity and numerical verification, Engineering Geology, Volume 72, Issues 1-2 , March 2004, Pages 89-119.

[2] Laubach S. et al.,2004, Coevolution of crack-seal texture and fracture porosity in sedimentary rocks: cathodoluminescence observations of regional fractures, Journal of Structural Geology Volume 26, Issue 5 , May 2004, Pages 967-982.

[3] Chen S. et al., 2004, Digital image-based numerical modeling method for prediction of inhomogeneous rock failure Int. J. Rock Mech. & Min. Sci., 41, 939-957. Chen, S., et al. (2004).

[4] Zhou Y. et al., 2004, Segmentation of petrographic images by integrating edge detection and region growing, Computer & Geosciences 30 (2004) 817-831.

[5] Final report of the TRUE Block Scale project, 4. 2003, Synthesis of flow, transport and retention in the block scale, March 2003, Swedish Nuclear Fuel and Waste Management Co. (SKB, Technical Report, TR-02-16).

[6] Lemy F., Hadjigeorgiou J., 2003, Discontinuity trace map construction using photographs of rock exposures, International Journal of Rock Mechanics and Mining Sciences, Volume 40, Issue 6 , September 2003, Pages 903-917.

[7] Lyman, G. J., 2003, Rock fracture mean trace length estimation and confidence interval calculation using maximum likelihood methods, International Journal of Rock Mechanics and Mining Sciences, Volume 40, Issue 6, September 2003, Pages 825-832.

[8] Kemeny, J., Randy Post, 2003. Estimating three-dimensional rock discontinuity orientation from digital images of fracture traces, Computer & Geosciences, v. 29 n. 1, p.65-77 February.

[9] Parviz S. et al., 2003, Specimen preparation and image processing and analysis techniques for automated quantification of concrete microcracks and voids Cement and Concrete Research, Volume 33, Issue 12, December 2003, Pages 1949-1962.

[10] Jorge A., Lambros J., 2002, Investigation of crack growth in functionally graded materials using digital image correlation, Engineering Fracture Mechanics Volume 69, Issues 14-16 , September 2002, Pages 1695-1711.

[11] Reid T., Harrison J., 2000, A semi-automated methodology for discontinuity trace detection in digital images of rock mass exposures, International Journal of Rock Mechanics and Mining Sciences, Volume 37, Issue 7, October 2000, Pages 1073-1089.

[12] Johansson M., 1999, Digital image processing of borehole images for determination of rock fracture orientation and aperture, Licentiate thesis, at Division of Engineering Geology, Department of Civil and Environmental Engineering, KTH, 1999, TRITA-AMI LIC 2041.

[13] Trevor Raymond Reid, A methodology for the detection of discontinuity traces in digital images of rock mass exposures, Doctoral thesis, in the University of London (Imperial College of Science Technology & Medicine), 1998.

[14] Power W,. Durham W., 1997, Topography of Natural and Artificial Fractures in Granitic Rocks: Implications for Studies of Rock Friction and Fluid Migration, Int. J. Rock Mech. Min. Sci. Vol. 34, No. 6. pp.979-989, 1997.

[15] Feng Quanhong, Application of Image processing to borehole logging, master thesis, at Division of Engineering Geology, Department of Civil and Environmental Engineering, KTH, 1996.

[16] Hakami, E., 1995, Aperture Distribution of Rock Fractures, Doctoral thesis, at Division of Engineering Geology, Department of Civil and Environmental Engineering, KTH, 1995, TRITA-AMI PHD 1003.

[17] Masahiro Iwano, 1995, Hydromechanical Characteristics of a Single Rock Joint, Doctoral thesis, in Massachusetts Institute of Technology, 1995.

[18] Harrison JP, 1993. Improved analysis of rock mass geometry using mathematical and photogrammetric methods. Ph.D. thesis, Imperial College, London, UK.

[19] Hu J, Sakoda B, Pavlidis T., 1992. Interactive road finding for aerial images. IEEE Workshop on Applications of Computer Vision.

[20] Franklin, John A., Norberth H. Maerz and Caralyn P. Bennett, 1988. Rock mass characterization using photoanalysis, International Journal of Mining and Geological Engineering, pp. 97-112.

[21] Takahashi M. , Takemura T., 2004，Microscopic visualization in rocks under confining pressure by means of micro focus X-ray CT, Proceedings of the ISRM International Symposium 3rd ARMS, Ohnishi & Aoki (eds) 2004 Millpress, Rotterdam, ISBN 90 5966 020 X, pp. 139-142.

[22] Sun, G. X., D. J. Reddish and B. N. Whittaker, 1992, Image analysis technique for rock fracture pattern studies around longwall excavations, Trans. Instr Min. Metall, Sect. A: Min. industry, v. 101, A127-204, London.

[23] Tanimoto C, Murai S, Kiyama Joshi AK. , 1989. Automatic detection of lineaments from Landsat data. Proceedings of the IGARSS'89, Vancouver, Canada.

[24] Zou Dingxiang, Weixing Wang and Ma Bailing, 1986. Computer simulation of spatial distribution of weakness planes and its influence on rock blasting, Proc. of the Int. Sym. on intense dynamic loading and its effects, in Beijing of China, pp. 1056-1062.

[25] Huang Kaiqi, Wu Zhenyang, Wang Qiao, Image enhancement based on the statistics of visual representation, Image and Vision Computing 23 (2005) 51-57.

[26] N. Otsu, A threshold selection method from gray-level histogram, *IEEE Trans. Systems Man Cybernet*, 1979, SMC-9, pp. 62-66.
[27] K.S. Fu and J.K. Mu, A survey on image segmentation, *Pattern recognition*, 1981, Vol. 13, pp. 3-16.
[28] N.R. Pal and S.K. Pal, A review of image segmentation techniques, *Pattern recognition*, 1993, Vol. 26, No. 9, pp. 1277-1294.
[29] K. Lee and S.Y. Chung, A comparative performance study of several global thresholding techniques for segmentation, *Computer Vision, Graphics, And Image Processing*, 1990, 2, pp. 171-190.
[30] A.M. Groenewald, E. Barnard and E.C. Botha, Related approaches to gradient-based thresholding, *Pattern recognition Letters*, 1993, Vo. l4, pp. 567-572.
[31] M. Sonka, V. Hlavac and R. Boyle, *Image processing, analysis and machine vision*, 1995, Champion & Hall, 2-6 , Boundary Row, London SEI 8HN, UK.
[32] W.H. Tsai, Moment-preserving thresholding: A new approach, *Computer Vision, graphics, And Image Processing*, 1985, 29, pp. 377-393.
[33] J.N. Kapur, P.K. Sahoo and A.K.C. Wong, A new method for grey-level picture thresholding using the entropy of the histogram, *Computer Vision, Graphics and Image processing*, 1985, 29, pp. 273-285.
[34] Wang, W.X. , Froth delineation based on image classification, International Journal of Mineral Engineering, Volume 16, Issue 11 , November 2003, Pages 1183-1192.
[35] Benoit Tremblais, Bertrand Augereau, 2004, A fast multi-scale edge detection algorithm, Pattern Regognition Letters 25 (2004) 603-618.
[36] Lindeberg, T., Detecting Salient Blob-Like Image Structures and Their Scales with a Scale-Space Primal Sketch: A Method for Focus-of-Attention, *International Journal of Computer Vision, 11(3), 283--318, 1993.*
[37] Sergios P., Stavros J., 2004, On the relation between discriminant analysis and mutual information for supervised linear feature extraction, Pattern Recognition 37(2004) 857-874.
[38] Manesh K. et al., 2004, Cosine-modulated wavelet based texture features for content-based image retrieval, Pattern Recognition Letters 25 (2004) 391-398.
[39] Munoz X. et al., 2003, Strategies for image segmentation combining region and boundary information, Pattern Recognition Letters 24(2003) 375-392.
[40] Egmont-Petersen M., de Ridder D., 2002, Image processing with networks- a review, Pattern Recognition 35(2002) 2279-2310.
[41] Anil K. et al., 2000, Statistical Patter Recognition: A Rview, IEEE Trans Pattern And Machine Intelligence, Vol. 22, No. 1, January, 2000, 4-37.
[42] Weixing Wang, Juan Wan and Yang Zhao, 2010, Rock Fracture Extracting on Fractional Differential, The 2nd International Workshop on Intelligent Systems and Applications (ISA 2010).
[43] Jiangyan Xu, Weixing Wang, Linning Ye, 2009, Rock fracture edge detection based on quaternion convolution by scale multiplication, Optical Engineering, 48(9), pp. 097001-(1-7) .
[44] Jiangyan Xu, Weixing Wang and Liwan Chen, 2007, An image fusion algorithm for rock fracture detection using wavelet transform, AOMATT 2007, Chengdu, August.

[45] Weixing Wang, Haijun. Liao and Ying Huang, 2007, Rock fracture tracing based on image processing and SVM, ICNC-FSKD 2007, Hainan, July 2007.

25

Image Segmentation Integrating Generative and Discriminative Methods

Yuee Wu and Houqin Bian
Computer & Information Engineering Dept.
ShangHai University of Electric Power, ShangHai
China

1. Introduction

Image segmentation is a long standing problem in computer vision, and it is found to be difficult and challenging for two reasons.

The first challenge is the difficulty of modeling the vast amount of visual patterns that appear in generic images. The second challenge is the intrinsic ambiguities in image perception, especially when there is no specific task to guide the attention. Furthermore, an image often demonstrates details at multiple scales. Therefore, it must be wrong to think that a segmentation algorithm outputs only one result. It should output multiple distinct solutions dynamically so that solutions "best preserve" the intrinsic ambiguity. In our opinion, image segmentation should be considered a computing process not a vision task.

Motivated by the above two observations, we present a stochastic computing method for image segmentation. We define image partition to be the task of decomposing an image I into its constituent visual patterns. The output is represented by a hierarchical graph. Firstly, we formulate the problem as Bayesian inference, and the solution space is decomposed into union of many subspaces of varying dimensions. The goal is to optimize the Bayesian posterior probability. Secondly, top-down generative models are used to describe how objects and generic region models (e.g. texture and shading) generate the image intensities. The goal of image partition is to invert this process and represent an input image by the parameters of the generative models that best describe it together with the boundaries of the regions and objects. Thirdly, in order to estimate these parameters we use bottom-up proposals, based on low-level cues, to guide the search through the parameter space.

We test the algorithm on a wide variety of grey level and color images, and some results are shown in the paper.

2. The Bayesian formulation for segmentation

Let $\Lambda = \{(i,j): 1 \le i \le L, 1 \le j \le H\}$ be an image lattice, and I_Λ an image defined on Λ. For any point $v \in \Lambda, I_v \in \{0,\cdots,G\}$ is the pixel intensity for a grey level image, or $I_v = \{L_v, U_v, V_v\}$ for a color image. The problem of image segmentation refers to partitioning the lattice into an unknown number of K disjoint regions.

$$\Lambda = \cup_{i=1}^{K} R_i, \quad R_i \cap R_j = \varnothing, \quad i \neq j \tag{2.1}$$

Each image region I_R is assumed to be coherent in the sense that I_R is a realization from a probabilistic model $p(I_R;\Theta)$. Θ represents a stochastic process whose model type is indexed by ℓ_i.

Thus segmentation is denoted by a vector of hidden variables *W*, which describes the world state for generating the image *I*.

$$W = \left(K, \{(R_i, \ell_i, \Theta_i); i = 1, 2, \cdots K\}\right) \tag{2.2}$$

In a Bayesian framework, we make the inference about *W* from *I* over a solution space Ω.

$$W \sim p(W|I) \propto p(I|W)p(W), W \in \Omega \tag{2.3}$$

The likelihood $p(I|W)$ specifies the image generating processes from *W* to *I*, and the prior probability $p(W)$ represents our prior knowledge of the world. The goal is to estimate the most probable interpretation of an input image *I*. This require computing the W^* that maximized a posteriori probability over Ω, the solution space of *W*,

$$\begin{aligned} W^* &= \arg\max_{W\in\Omega} p(W|I) \\ &= \arg\max_{W\in\Omega} p(I|W)p(W) \end{aligned} \tag{2.4}$$

3. Stochastic grammar of image

One fundamental difficulty that we encounter in vision is to represent the enormous amount of visual knowledge needed for making robust inference from real world images. The origin of image grammar is that certain elements of the image tend to occur together more frequently than by chance. These elements are then composed recursively to form increasingly larger units which can share some "reusable" parts.

Our production rules are graph operators and thus the image grammar is an attributed graph grammar. The graph grammar can be embedded in an And-Or graph representation ,where each Or-mode points to alternative choices of sub-configuration, and an And-node is decomposed into a number of parts. Each non-terminal node generates child nodes starting with the scene label at the root and proceeds to objects, object parts, and ends with pixels as the leaves (terminal nodes). This hierarchical representation includes a dictionary Δ_{gen} of generative image features used in the generative models. A special choice of the Or-nodes produces a configuration. The virtue of the grammar lies in its expressive power of generating a very large set of configurations through a relatively much smaller vocabulary.

Figure 1 shows the grammar graph for an input image. Each node of the graph has an attribute variable for the labels and model parameters. The top node 0 is the scene label, and the nodes at the bottom are the image pixels. Three types of objects with different entropies are shown in nodes 1, 2, and 3.

To formulate this representation, we denote the graph by $G = \langle V_N \cup V_T, E \rangle$. The scene descriptions (attributes) *W* are defined on the non-terminal nodes V_N, and the image I is defined on the terminal nodes V_T (pixels).

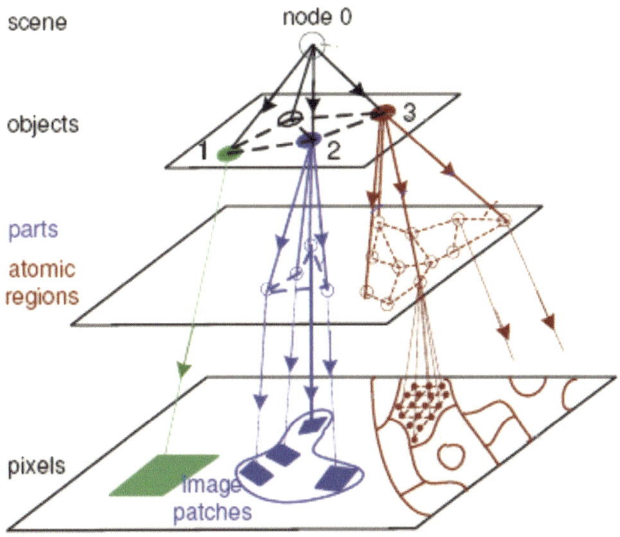

Fig. 1. The stochastic grammar for an input image

On each non-terminal node $v \in V_N$, we define attribute variables $w(v) \in W$ for the labels and model parameters. Each non-terminal node v contains a list of children nodes $child(v) = (u_1^v, \cdots, u_{k_v}^v)$ which can be expanded for more specific representations of the object. These children nodes form a subgraph G_v. The leaf nodes at the bottom are the image pixels which form a lattice Λ. The attributes defined on the leaf nodes (lattice) are the image intensity values J. Depending on the visual patterns, J can be determined by W either deterministically $J = g(W)$ or probabilistically $J \sim p(J|W)$. The correctness of a scene description W will depend on how well the synthesized image J matches the input image I. The full generative model allows the 30 different visual patterns to compete to explain the input intensity. The generative model is expressed as:

$$p(W;\Delta_{gen}) = \\ p(w) \prod_{v \in V_N} p(w(u_1^v), \cdots, w(u_{k_v}^v | w(v); \Delta(v)), \\ J = g(W) or J \sim p(J|W) \tag{2.5}$$

Where the conditional probability at v is a MRF defined on the graph G_v and captures the spatial relationship between the parts. Δ_v is a generative image dictionary for $w(v)$, such as PCA, image patches, or textons. We will have a collection of generative image vocabularies for the 30 types of objects ℓ over scale σ

$$\Delta_{gen} = \{\Delta_{\ell,\sigma} : \ell = 1,2,\cdots 30, \sigma = 1,2,3\cdots\} \tag{2.6}$$

Then we formulate image partition as Bayesian inference where the goal is to compute the partition graph W from the input image I and, or verification, to synthesize J sampled from the likelihood,

$$W \sim p\left(W \middle| I;\Delta_{gen}\right) \propto p\left(I \middle| W\right) p\left(W;\Delta_{gen}\right),\ W \in \Omega, J \sim p(J|W) \tag{2.7}$$

Our algorithm must achieve the difficult task of (1). constructing the stochastic grammar, whose structure, like parse trees in natural language, is not pre-determined but depend on the input image; (2). estimating the attributes of graph nodes (labels and model parameters); and (3). computing the spatial relations between sibling nodes.
The framework in the paper integrates two computing paradigms in vision -discriminative methods for fast speed and generative methods for generality and robustness.

4. Generative and discriminative methods

Generative methods specify how the image I is generated from the scene representation . it combines a prior $p(W;\Delta_{gen})$ and a likelihood function $p\left(I \middle| W\right)$ to give a joint posterior probability $p\left(W \middle| I;\Delta_{gen}\right)$. To perform inference using generative methods requires estimating $W^* = \arg\max p\left(W \middle| I;\Delta_{gen}\right)$. This is often computationally demanding because there are usually no know efficient inference algorithm.
By contrast, discriminative methods are very fast to compute. They do not specify models for how the image is generated. Instead they give discriminative probabilities $q(w_j|Tst_j(I))$ for components (w_j) of W based on a sequence of bottom-up tests $Tst_j(I)$ performed on the image. The tests are based on local image features $\{F_{j,n}(I)\}$ which can be computed from the image in a cascade manner,

$$Tst_j(I)) = \left(F_{j,1}(I), F_{j,2}(I), \cdots F_{j,n}(I)\right),\quad j = 1,2,\cdots K \tag{2.8}$$

These tests are selected from a dictionary of discriminative features Ψ_{dis}. In correspondence to the generative dictionary Δ_{gen} in eqn.(2.7), we denote it by

$$\Psi_{dis} = \left\{\Psi_{\ell,\sigma} : \ell = 1,2,\cdots,30, \sigma = 1,2,\cdots\right\} \tag{2.9}$$

The bottom-up tests generate two types of hypotheses.

i. The *what-is-what* hypothesis for some node v in the partition graph W, which are marginal posterior probabilities $q_v = q(w(v)|F_v(I))$ for the attributes $w(v)$ (object label and model parameters) of v. $F_v(I)$ denote the features used (in this paper we use Adaboost).
ii. The *what-go-with-what* hypotheses for some horizontal edge $e = <s,t>$ in the partition graph, which are posterior probabilities $q_e = q(e = off|f_e(I))$ for whether the two elements s, t belong to the same pattern. Equivalently it is the probability ratio $\frac{q(e = on|I)}{q(e = off|I)}$•$f_e(I)$ denotes the feature for measuring the dis-similarity between s, t. It has been proved that with sufficient number of tests $q(w(v)|F_v(I))$ can approach $p(w(v)|I)$ asymptotically, and so $\frac{q(e = on|f_e(I))}{q(e = off|f_e(I))}$ will approach $\frac{p(e = on|I)}{p(e = off|I)}$.

These two set of discriminative probabilities are then composed on-the-fly to generate hypotheses which are represented by importance proposal kernel, $Q_a(W,W'|Tst_t(I)) = q(W'|W,Tst_t(I))$ Generative methods optimizes the joint Bayesian posterior $p(W|I;\Delta_{gen})$ by a set A of reversible jumps, such as death-birth, spit-merge, model switching, etc. these jumps construct the partition graph and in combination they simulate an ergodic Markov chain search in the solution space of W. each type of jump $a \in A$ is represented by a Markov kernel $\kappa_a(W,W')$, which is a conditional probability for moving from partition graph W to a new partition graph W'.

The kernels are "informed" by proposal kernels computed by discriminative method, and are realized by the Metropolis-Hastings method,

$$\kappa_a(W,W'|Tst_t(I)) = Q_a(W,W'|Tst_t(I))\min\left(1,\frac{Q_a(W',W|Tst_t(I))}{Q_a(W,W'|Tst_t(I))}\bullet\frac{p(W'|I)}{p(W|I)},\right) \quad for \quad W \neq W', a \in A \tag{2.10}$$

The metropolis-Hastings step compares the discriminative probability ratio with the true Bayesian posterior probability ratio, and can be considered as a probabilistic version of hypothesis-and-test.

5. Experiments

The image segmentation algorithm is applied on a number of outdoor/indoor images. The speed in PCs is comparable to segmentation methods such as normalized cuts. It typically runs around 10-20 min. the main portion of the computing time is spent in segmenting the generic patterns and by boundary diffusion. Figure 3 and 4 show some example. We present the results in two parts. One shows the segmentation boundaries for generic region and objects, and the other shows the labelmap for generic region and objects to indicate objects recognition. From the segmentation results we can see high-level knowledge helps segmentation to overcome problem of oversegmentation.

(a) Input image (b) segmentation (c) labelmap of segmentation

Fig. 2. Results of segmentation on an outdoor image

(a) Input image (b) segmentation (c) labelmap of segmentation

Fig. 3. Results of segmentation on an indoor image

6. Acknowledgments

This work is supported by the Project of ShangHai Key Disciplines Construction (p1303) and Special Foundation for Outstanding Young Teachers in Colleges and Universities of ShangHai (z-2009-03).

7. References

[1] S.C. Zhu and D. Mumford, " A Stochastic Grammar of Images ", Foundations and Trends in Computer Graphics and Vision, 2007.

[2] T.F. Wu, G.S. Xia, and S.C. Zhu , "Compositional Boosting for Computing Hierarchical Image Structures" CVPR , 2007.

[3] S. Agarwal and D. Roth, "Learning a sparse representation for object detection", Proc. ECCV, 2002.

[4] J. Friedman, T. Hastie, and R. Tibshirani, "Additive logistic regression: a statistical view of boosting", The Annals of Statistics, 38(2):337-374, Oct. 2001.

[5] H. Chen and S.C. Zhu, "A generative model of human hair for hair sketching", Proc. IEEE Conf. on Computer Vision and Pattern Recognition, San Diego, 2005.

[6] Shiliang Sun, Changshui Zhang and Guoqiang Yu. "A Bayesian Network Approach to Traffic Flow Forecasting." IEEE Transactions on Intelligent Transportation Systems. March 2006. Volume 7, issue 1. pp. 124- 132.

[7] Z.Y. Yao, X. Yang, and S.C. Zhu, "Introduction to a large scale general purpose groundtruth dataset: methodology, annotation tool, and benchmarks", 6th Int'l Conf on EMMCVPR, August 2007.

26

Pixon-Based Image Segmentation

Hamid Hassanpour[1], Hadi Yousefian[2] and Amin Zehtabian[3]
[1]Shahrood University of Technology
[2]Iran University of Science & Technology (IUST)
[3]Noshirvani University of Technology (NIT)
Iran

1. Introduction

The pixon concept was introduced by Pina and Puetter in 1993. The pixon they introduced was a set of disjoint regions with constant shapes and variable sizes. Their pixon definition scheme was a local convolution between a kernel function and a pseudo image. The drawback of this scheme was that after selecting the kernel function, the shape of the pixons could not vary. Yang and Jiang presented a new pixon definition scheme, whose shape and size can vary simultaneously. They also used the anisotropic diffusion equation to form the pixons and finally they have combined the pixon concept and MRF for segmentation of the images. Recently, another well-behaved pixon-based image representation is proposed [Lei Lin et al., 2008]. In their presented scheme the pixons combined with their attributes and adjacencies construct a graph, which represents the observed image. They used a Fast QuadTree Combination (FQTC) algorithm to extract the good pixon-representation. These techniques integrated into MRF model. The main disadvantage of MRF-based methods is that in these algorithms the minimization problem of objective function is very time consuming. The most novel method which uses pixon concept to segment the images is introduced by Hassanpour et al. In this method, first a pre-processing step is performed which applies the wavelet thresholding technique. This step is suitable for image smoothing due to the noise reduction property of wavelet thresholding. To avoid over-smoothed problem, the value of the threshold must be assigned properly. Then, the pixon-based algorithm is used to form and extract the pixons. Finally, the Fuzzy C-Means (FCM) algorithm is applied to segment the image. The advantage of using pixons is that after forming the pixons the decision level changes from pixels to pixons and this decreases the computational time, because of the fewer number of pixons compared to number of pixels. This is the key aspect of pixon-based algorithms in image segmentation.

2. Pixon-based methods

2.1 Traditional Pixon-Based method (TPB)

The TPB method is known as one of the simplest pixon-based approaches applied for image segmentation. The method is mainly composed of two following steps: (1) form the pixons, and (2) segment the image.

2.1.1 Description of pixon model

In any pixon definition scheme, the ability to control the number of degrees of freedom used to model the image is the key aspect. In other word, the pixon definition scheme should yield an optimum scale description of the observed image. The pixon definition scheme which is used in this method can be described as follows:

$$IP = \bigcup_{j=1}^{m} P_j \tag{1}$$

where IP is the pixon-based image model; m is the number of pixons; P_j is a given pixon, which is made up of a set of connected pixels, a single pixel or even a sub-pixel. The mean value of the connected pixels making up of the pixon is defined as the pixon intensity. Both the shape and size of each pixon vary according to the observed image. After the pixon-based image model is defined, the image segmentation problem is transformed into a problem of labeling pixons. The procedure to determine the set of pixons, i. e. their shape and size, can be divided into three steps: 1) obtain a pseudo image, which has at least the same resolution as the observed image; 2) use an anisotropic diffusion filter to form the pixons; and 3) use a simple hierarchical clustering algorithm to extract the pixons.

Obtaining the Pseudo Image; The pseudo image is a basic image to form the pixons and to obtain a segmented image, which is derived from the observed image. Suppose the dimension of the observed image is $D_M \times D_N$, then the dimension of the pseudo image can be $lD_M \times lD_N$, where $l = 2^n$. When n = 0, the pseudo image is the observed image itself. When $n \geq 1$, the pseudo image can be obtained by the following iterative process

$$i_{2^n}(i,j) = \begin{cases} I_{2^{n-1}}\left(\frac{i}{2},\frac{j}{2}\right) & i,j \text{ is even} \\ \frac{1}{2}\left[I_{2^{n-1}}\left(\frac{i}{2},\frac{j-1}{2}\right) + I_{2^{n-1}}\left(\frac{i}{2},\frac{j+1}{2}\right)\right] & i \text{ is even}, j \text{ is odd} \\ \frac{1}{2}\left[I_{2^{n-1}}\left(\frac{i-1}{2},\frac{j}{2}\right) + I_{2^{n-1}}\left(\frac{i+1}{2},\frac{j}{2}\right)\right] & i \text{ is odd}, j \text{ is even} \\ \frac{1}{4}\left[\left(\frac{i-1}{2},\frac{j}{2}\right) + I_{2^{n-1}}\left(\frac{i-1}{2},\frac{j}{2}\right) + I_{2^{n-1}}\left(\frac{i-1}{2I_{2^{n-1}}},\frac{j}{2}\right) + I_{2^{n-1}}\left(\frac{i-1}{2},\frac{j}{2}\right)\right] & i,j \text{ are odd} \end{cases} \tag{2}$$

Where $i = 0,1,\ldots,2^M \times D_M - 1$ and $j = 0,1,\ldots,2^N \times D_N - 1$.

In the above iterative process, I_1 corresponds to the observed image. The essence of the process is increasing the resolution through interpolation to describe the image parts, which have a lot of details.

Parameter n is of great importance. If $n \geq 1$, then the resolution of the pseudo image is larger than the original image and the finally pixons formed are probable to be a sub-pixel. So, it determines the smallest size of the pixons. In the image parts, where the intensities of nearing pixels are similar, which means having little information, the intensity of newly inserted pixels will be similar with the intensities of the pixels in the observed image, from which the new pixels are obtained through interpolation.

So there is a little difference whether the pixons are derived from the original observed image or interpolated pseudo image. However, in the image parts, where have a lot of details, it will be better to derive the pixons from the interpolated pseudo image than from the original observed image. So, it is probable that a pixon is a sub-pixel to fully model the corresponding image parts. Therefore, if the image has many details, it should be large, otherwise it should be small. In current implementation, we let $n = 0$.

Formulation of Pixon; To form the pixons based on the pseudo image, let us consider the following anisotropic diffusion equation [Perona & Malik, 1990]:

$$\frac{\partial I(x,y,t)}{\partial t} = C(x,y,t)(\frac{\partial^2 I(x,y,t)}{\partial x^2} + \frac{\partial^2 I(x,y,t)}{\partial y^2}) + \frac{\partial I(x,y,t)}{\partial x} \cdot \frac{\partial C(x,y,t)}{\partial x} + \frac{\partial I(x,y,t)}{\partial y} \cdot \frac{\partial C(x,y,t)}{\partial y} \tag{3}$$

where C(x,y,t)is the diffusion coefficient, which controls the diffusion strength.

The partial differential equation is used to model the heat diffusion process. In regions with a large diffusion coefficient, the temperature tends to be uniform. While temperature differences will be retained in regions with small diffusion coefficients. We can view the pseudo image intensity as the temperature of the temperature field and the transformation of the gradient as the diffusion coefficient. The transformation function is

$$c(x,y,t) = \frac{1}{(1 + \frac{|\nabla I|^2}{k^2})} \tag{4}$$

where K is a constant.

To be convenient, the solution of the diffusion equation is called solution image. In the solution image, the intensity of the regions having less information (having fewer edges) will tend to be uniform and vice versa. So, the "regions" having similar intensity in the solution image can be regarded as the pixons in our image model. The diffusion equation can be approximately solved by the following discrete formulation:

$$(I(x,y,t+\Delta t) = I(x,y,t) + \Delta t(d_n c_n + d_s c_s + d_e c_e + d_w c_w) \tag{5}$$

where

$$\begin{aligned}
d_n &= I(x,y-1,t) - I(x,y,t) \quad c_n = \frac{1}{1+(\frac{d_n}{k})^2} \\
d_s &= I(x,y+1,t) - I(x,y,t) \quad c_s = \frac{1}{1+(\frac{d_s}{k})^2} \\
d_e &= I(x+1,y,t) - I(x,y,t) \quad c_e = \frac{1}{1+(\frac{d_e}{k})^2} \\
d_w &= I(x-1,y,t) - I(x,y,t) \quad c_w = \frac{1}{1+(\frac{d_w}{k})^2}
\end{aligned} \tag{5}$$

To ensure the convergence of the above iteration process, the parameter Δt should not be too large (here, $\Delta t = 0.25$). Larger values of K increase the pixon size. To describe the details of the image, K could not be too large (here $K = 5$)

Extraction of the Pixons; After forming the pixons according to the pseudo image, a segmentation method is applied based on hierarchical clustering to extract them. For this purpose, initially each pixel represents a cluster. Then the clusters are merged according to their intensities and made greater pixons. The mean value of the connected pixels making up of the pixon is defined as the pixon intensity. Both the shape and size of each pixon can vary according to the observed image.

To stop the algorithm, a threshold value, T, is assigned and the mergence process iterates until the difference between intensities of two adjacent pixons would be smaller than the threshold value (here, T = 10).

The pixon-based image model is represented by a graph structure G = (Q,E) , where Q is the finite set of vertices of the graph and E is the set of edges of the graph (Figure 1).

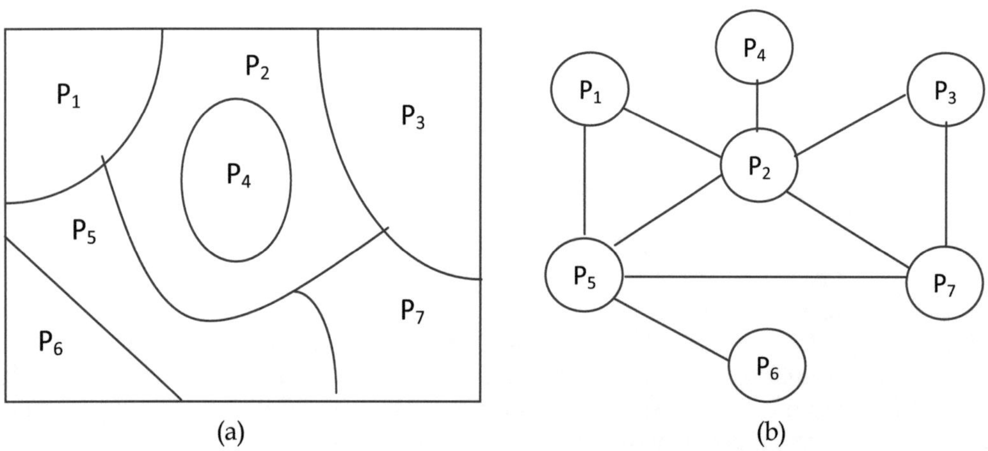

Fig. 1. (a) Pixon model of image, and (b) the corresponding graph structure

After the pixon-based image model is defined, the image segmentation problem is transformed into a problem of labeling pixons.

While the pixons are extracted, the image is divided into a set of disjoint regions. The extraction of pixons can be considered as a primary segmentation. In TPB method, to obtain the final segmented image, the combination of pixons is continued until the end condition of process occurs. This condition is the number of segments in final segmentation purpose.

2.2 MPB method

Pixon-based image segmentation using Markov Random Field (MRF) model is presented by (Lei Lin, et al 2008). In this method, first an image is expressed as a pixon-based model. As we said before, pixons are a set of disjoint regions with variable shape and size. These pixons are combined with their attributes and adjacencies construct a graph which represents the observed images. Then using this pixon-representation, a Markov Random Field (MRF) model is presented to segment the images.

In current procedure, a set of significant attributes of pixons and edges are introduced into the pixon-representation. These attributes are integrated into the MRF model and the

Bayesian framework to obtain a weighted pixon-based algorithm. Also, a Fast Quad Tree Combination (FQTC) algorithm is used to extract the good pixon representation.

2.2.1 Definition of pixon representation

Definition 1. Let $X = \{X_i\}_{i=1}^{M}$ be the set of all the image pixels. A subset of X is a pixon if and only if all the pixels in it are connected. A pixon is then denoted by $P_i = \{X_{ij}\}_{j=1}^{n_i}$.

An attribute vector of the pixon is extracted from the observed image

$$\vec{P_i} = (n_i, b_i, max_i, min_i, \mu_i, \sigma_i^2) \tag{6}$$

where n_i is the number of pixels in P_i, b_i is the perimeter of P_i, namely the length of the boundary between P_i and the other part of the observed image, max_i, min_i, μ_i and σ_i^2 are the maximum, minimum, mean and variance of the observed image intensities in P_i, respectively. Let $I(x_{ij})$ denotes the image intensity on the pixel x_{ij}. The attributes of the pixon intensity can be obtained by

$$\begin{aligned} max_i &= \max\left(I(X_{ij}) | X_{ij} \epsilon P_i\right) \\ min_i &= \min\left(I(X_{ij}) | X_{ij} \epsilon P_i\right) \\ \mu_i &= \sum_{j=1}^{n_i} I(X_{ij}) / n_i \\ \sigma_i &= \sum_{j=1}^{n_i} (I(X_{ij}))^2 / n_i - \mu_i^2 \end{aligned} \tag{7}$$

Definition 2. A set of pixons, $= \{P_i\}_{i=1}^{N}$, is a pixon-representation if and only if

$$\begin{aligned} &P_i \neq \varnothing \\ &P_i \cap P_j = \varnothing, if\ i \neq j \\ &\cup_{i=1}^{N} P_i = X \end{aligned} \tag{8}$$

The above definition shows that the pixon-representation segments the image into a set of disjoint regions. A set of edges, E, can be acquired from these regions,

$$E = \left\{E_{ij} \mid P_i, P_j \in P\, and\, P_i, P_j\, are\, adjacent\right\} \tag{9}$$

where P_i and P_j are adjacent if $\exists X_{ik} \in P_i$ and $X_{ji} \in P_j$, which are neighboring pixels to each other in the image.

The strength of an edge can be defined as the length of the boundary between the two adjacent pixons, which is denoted by b_{ij}, so $b_i = \sum_j b_{ij}$. An attribute vector, $\vec{e_{ij}}$, is used to denote all the attributes of an edge.

The pixons and edges, combined with their attribute vectors, construct a graph, $G = \{P, E\}$, which represents the observed image, as shown in Fig. 2.

2.2.2 Shortest pixon-representation with respect to a discriminant

There are two trivial pixon-representations, $P_0 = \{X\}$ and $P_1 = \{\{x_i\} \mid x_i \in X\}$. The former takes all the image pixels as one pixon; the latter takes each pixel as a pixon, which is a lossless representation. In order to represent the image using as few pixons as possible while limiting the representation error, the shortest pixon-representation with respect to a discriminant is defined.

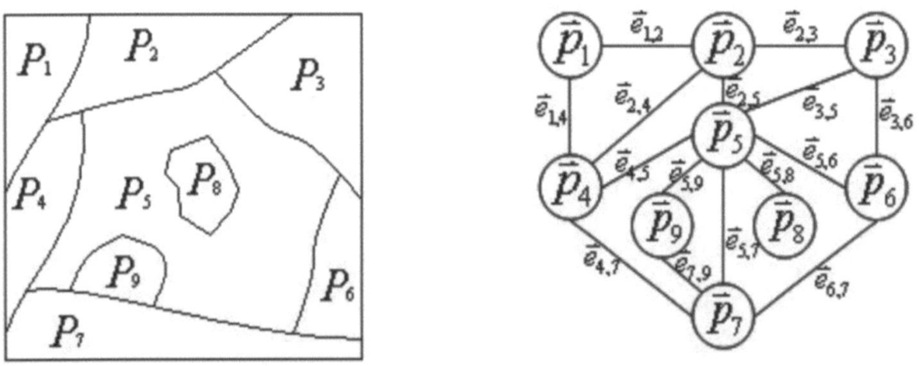

(a) (b)

Fig. 2. An example of Pixon-Representation. (a) The Pixon map, in which the boundaries between adjacent Pixons are shown; and (b) The corresponding graph, which combines the attribute vectors of Pixons and edges to represent the observed image.

Definition 3. A function $f(p) \geq 0$ of pixons is a pixon error function if and only if

$$\begin{aligned} &f(p) = 0 \text{ ,} if\ P = \{x_i\}, \\ &f(P_i) \geq f(P_j) \text{ ,} if\ P_i \supseteq P_j \end{aligned} \tag{10}$$

Definition 4. For a given pixon error function, $f(.)$, and a non-negative constant, T, the inequality, $f(.) \leq T$, defines a pixon discriminant.

Definition 5. A pixon-representation is called the shortest pixon representation with respect to a given discriminant, $f(.) \leq T$, if its number of pixons is least among all the pixon-representation satisfying $\forall P_i \in P,\ f(P_i) \leq T$.

In general, using the pixon attribute vector to describe the region of the observed image will loss some information, so a pixon error function is used to denote the error between the pixon and the region of the observed image. In this method error function is defined as $f(P_i) = \max_i - \min_i$. With a given discriminant $f(.) \leq T$ the shortest pixon-representation use the least number of pixons to represent the image, so we consider it the best pixon-representation whose pixons' errors do not exceed the threshold, T.

2.2.3 Extraction of pixon-representation

The shortest pixon-representation with respect to a discriminant is not unique, as shown in Fig. 3. And it is hard to extract the shortest one from a large and complex image. In this section, an approach to extract a GOOD pixon-representation is presented, which combines the adjacent pixons of the lossless pixon-representation, $P_1 = \{\{x_i\} \mid x_i \in X\}$, iteratively, until no pixons can be combined considering the given discriminant. The obtained good pixon-representation is dependent on the order of combination besides the discriminant.

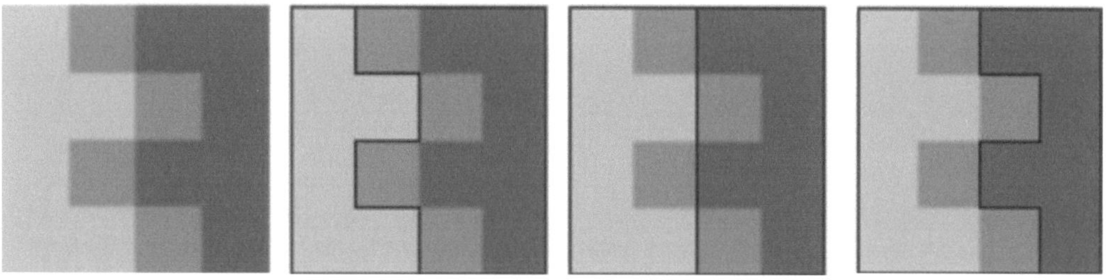

(a) (b) (c) (d)

Fig. 3. The non-uniqueness of the Shortest Pixon-Representation. (a) Observed image, whose pixel intensities are among 100, 150, and 200; (b), (c) and (d) are three of its shortest Pixon-Representations when $f(P_i) = max_i - min_i \le 50$ is given as a discriminant. The black lines overlapping on the image are the boundaries of Pixons.

2.2.3.1 Combination of adjacent pixons

The adjacent pixons in a pixon-representation, $G = \{P, E\}$, can be combined to form a new pixon, denoted by $P_{new} = P_i \oplus P_j$, whose attribute vector, $\vec{P}_{new}$, can be obtained from $\vec{P}_i$ and $\vec{P}_j$,

$$
\begin{aligned}
n_{new} &= n_i + n_j \\
b_{new} &= b_i + b_j - 2b_{ij} \\
max_{new} &= \max(max_i , max_j) \\
min_{new} &= \max(min_i , min_j) \\
\mu_{new} &= (n_i \mu_i + n_j \mu_j) / n_{new} \\
\sigma^2_{new} &= \left[n_i(\sigma_i^2 + \mu_i^2) + n_j(\sigma_j^2 + \mu_j^2) / n_{new} - \mu_{new}^2 \right]
\end{aligned} \tag{11}
$$

where b_{ij} is the edge strength, i.e. the length of the boundary between P_i and P_j.
It can be proved that $P - \{P_i, P_j\} + \{P_{new}\}$ is still a pixon-representation. And the edge set of the new pixon-representation can be obtained from E by combining the edges connecting the same two pixons after the pixon combination.

2.2.3.2 Combination-based extraction of pixon-representation

Given a discriminant, $f(.) \le T$, the edge error function is defined as $f_E(E_{ij}) = f(P_i \oplus P_j)$. Since $P_1 = \{\{x_i\} \mid x_i \in X\}$ satisfies all the discriminants, the shortest pixon-representation

with respect to $f(.) \leq T$ can be extracted by combining the pixons of P_1, the lossless representation, until all error function values of the edges are larger than T.
In fact, the pixon-representation obtained by combination scheme may not always be the shortest, which is dependent on the order of combinations. However, it is a substitute to the shortest, for the number of pixons has been sharply cut down.

2.2.3.3 Fast Quad Tree Combination algorithm

A fast Quad Tree combination algorithm is used to extract the shortest pixon-representation here. Firstly, a QuadTree-based multi-resolution pixon-representation is constructed, as shown in Fig. 4.

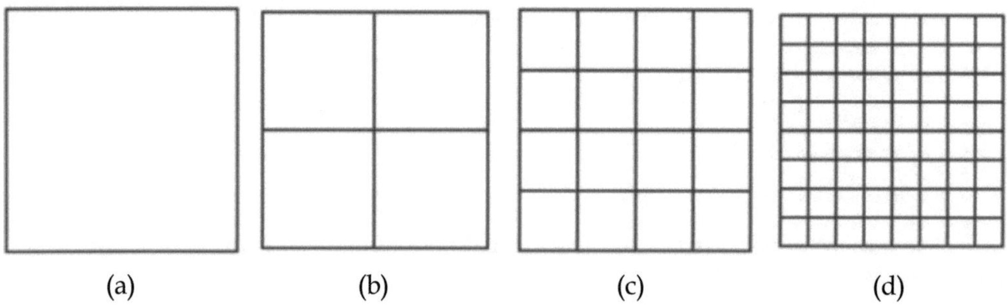

Fig. 4. The QuadTree-based multi-resolution Pixon-Representation. (a) Coarsest scale Pixon-Representation which uses the whole image as one Pixon; (b), (c), (d) is the followed scale pixon-Representation, which are obtained by subdividing each square of the coarser scale into four equal squares. The square in the finest scale only includes one pixel.

Then a initial pixon-representation with respect to $f(.) \leq T_{qt}$, $T_{qt} \in [0,T]$, is extracted by coarse-to-fine selecting a set of disjoint squares from the multi-resolution pixon-representation, which satisfy $f(.) \leq T_{qt}$. Finally, the pixons connected by the edge with the minimal edge error are combined iteratively, until the minimal edge error is larger than T.
If the image region is not a square whose edge length is the power of 2, the multi-resolution pixon-representation can be constructed as follows. Firstly, the image is put into a large enough square like (a) in Fig. 4. For each scale, the pixon is then defined as the set of pixels falling into a square of this scale; the squares including no pixel are ignored. An example using the fast Quad Tree combination algorithm is given in Fig. 5, where the error function is defined as

$$f(P_i) = max_i - min_i \tag{12}$$

2.2.4 Image segmentation based on pixon-representation

In this method, a Markov random field model-based image segmentation approach under Bayesian framework is used based on pixon-representation. The noise model of the Bayesian framework in this approach is based on the pixel intensity.

2.2.4.1 Bayesian framework

Let *I* be the observed image and *S* be the segmented image. In the Bayesian segmentation framework, the segmented image is obtained by maximizing the posterior probability,

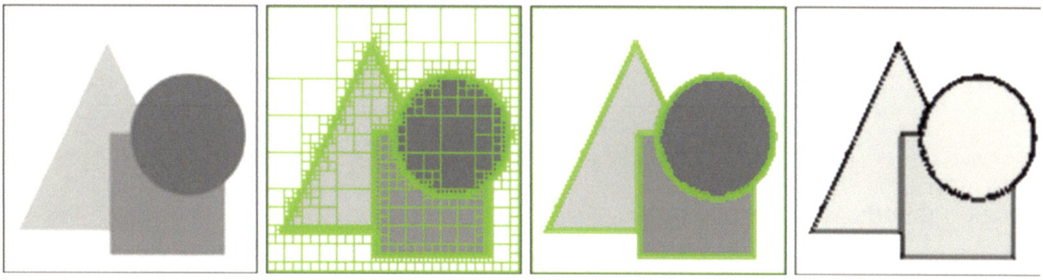

(a) (b) (c) (d)

Fig. 5. The fast QuadTree Combination Algorithm. (a) Observed image (13689 Pixels); (b) Initial Pixon-Representation (2115 Pixons). (c) Final Pixon-Representation (493 Pixons) after iterative Pixon combination; (d) The Pixon size map of the final Pixon-Representation, where the image intensity denotes the local Pixon size. The green lines in (b) and (c) are the boundaries between adjacent Pixons

$$S^{*} = \arg\max_{S} P(S|I) \tag{13}$$

where

$$P(S|I) \propto (PI|S)P(S). \tag{14}$$

We assume $I = S + N$, where N is independent Gaussian white noise. Then the conditional probability is

$$P(I|S) = \prod_{k=1}^{K} \prod_{x_i \in \Gamma_K} \frac{1}{\sqrt{2\pi}\sigma_K} \exp(-\frac{(I(x_i)-u_k)^2}{2\sigma_K{}^2}) \tag{15}$$

where K is the number of classes, Γ_K is the set of pixels segmented into the Kth class, and u_k is the intensity mean of pixels in Γ_K. Let $G = \{P, E\}$ be a pixon-representation of I. Since the characteristics of pixels in each pixon are similar, we assume that the pixels in one pixon will be segmented into the same class. So using (7) and (15), we get

$$\begin{aligned} P(I|S) &= \prod_{k=1}^{K} \prod_{P_i \subset \Gamma_K} \prod_{x_{ij} \in P_i} \frac{1}{\sqrt{2\pi}\sigma_K} \exp\left(-\frac{\left(I(x_{ij})-u_k\right)^2}{2\sigma_K{}^2} \right) \\ &= \prod_{k=1}^{K} \prod_{P_i \subset \Gamma_K} (2\pi)^{-n_i/2} \sigma_K{}^{-n_i} \exp(-\frac{n_i[(\mu_i-u_K)^2+\sigma_i{}^2]}{2\sigma_K{}^2}) \end{aligned} \tag{16}$$

The computation of $P(I|S)$ is simplified since the number of pixons is far less than that of pixels. $P(S)$ is the prior probability. In this method, the MRF model based on the pixon-representation is adopted to define the prior probability distribution as follows.

2.2.4.2 MRF model based on pixon-representation

A neighborhood system of the graph, $G = \{P, E\}$, is defined as

$$N(P) = \{N(P_i) \mid P_i \in P\} \tag{17}$$

where

$$N(P_i) = \{P_j \mid \exists e_{ij} \in E\}, 1 \le i \le N \tag{18}$$

is the neighborhood of each pixon.

Let $\Lambda = \{\lambda_1, \ldots, \lambda_K\}$ be the set of possible labels denoting the classes in the segmented image and $L = \{l_1, \ldots, l_K\}$ be a family of random variables where $l_1 \in \Lambda$ denotes the label of ith pixon and N is the number of pixons. The segmented image S can then be described by the event, $L = \omega$, since we assume that the pixels in one pixon will be segmented into the same class.

Let Ω be the set of all possible configurations, $\Omega = \{\omega = (\omega_1, \ldots, \omega_N) \mid \omega_i \in \Lambda\}$. L is a MRF with respect to the neighborhood, $N(P)$, if

$$P(L = \omega) > 0, \forall \omega \in \Omega \tag{19}$$

$$P(l_i = \omega_i \mid l_j = \omega_j, P_i \ne P_j) = P(l_i = \omega_i \mid l_j = \omega_j, P_j \in N(P_i)), \quad \forall P_i \in P \text{ and } \omega \in \Omega \tag{20}$$

where $P(.)$ and $P(.|.)$ are the joint and conditional probability density functions, respectively.

The configurations of MRF obey a Gibbs distribution [Hammersley & Clifford, 1971]

$$P(\omega) = 1 / Z.\exp(-U(\omega) / T) \tag{21}$$

where Z is a normalizing constant and T is a constant called temperature. $U(\omega)$ is the energy function, which is a sum of clique potentials $V_c(\omega)$ on all possible cliques, i.e.

$$U(\omega) = \sum_{c \in C} V_c(\omega) \tag{22}$$

In this method, the set of cliques is defined as

$$C = \{c_i \mid c_i = \{P_i\} \cup N(P_i), P_i \in P\} \tag{23}$$

where each pixon in $G = \{P, E\}$ defines one clique. And the clique potential is defined by

$$V_{c_i}(\omega) = w_c\left(\vec{P_i}\right) \sum_{P_{ij} \in N(P_i)} w_e\left(b_{ij}, b_i, b_j\right) w_p\left(\vec{P_i}, \vec{P_j}\right) \eta_{ij} \tag{24}$$

where η_{ij} is a binary variable which has the value 1 if P_i and P_j have the same label and the value 0 otherwise; $w_c\left(\vec{P_i}\right) = n_i$ is the clique weight; $w_e\left(b_{ij}, b_i, b_j\right) = b_{ij} / b_i$ is the normalized edge weight; and $w_p\left(\vec{P_i}, \vec{P_j}\right) = 1 / |\mu_i - \mu_j|$ is the pixon distance weight that denotes the difference of image characteristics between two pixons.

In all, the prior probability is defined as

$$P(S)=P(\omega)=\frac{1}{Z}\exp(-\frac{1}{T}\sum_{P_i\in P}n_i\sum_{P_{ij}\in N(P_i)}\frac{b_{ij}}{b_i}\frac{\eta_{ij}}{|\mu_i-\mu_j|}) \tag{25}$$

2.2.4.3 Optimization

From (13) and (14), the optimal segmented image can be written as

$$S^* = \arg\min_s(-\ln P(I|S)-\ln P(S)). \tag{26}$$

Using (16) and (25), the objective function is then obtained,

$$F(S)=F(\omega)=\sum_{k=1}^{K}\sum_{P_i\subseteq\Gamma_K}[n_i(\frac{[(\mu_i-u_K)^2+\sigma_i^2]}{2\sigma_K^2}+\ln\sigma_k)+\alpha n_i\sum_{P_{ij}\in N(P_i)}\frac{b_{ij}}{b_i}\frac{\eta_{ij}}{|\mu_i-\mu_j|}] \tag{27}$$

where $\alpha = 1/T$ is a weight of MRF model, which denotes the tradeoff between the fidelity to the observed image and the smoothness of the segmented image. The constant term has been removed from the objective function.

The class number K and the weight α are given before optimization. The initial segmented image is obtained using Fuzzy C-Means (FCM) clustering, and the initial parameters of each class are estimated from the initial segmented image, i.e. the means u_k and variances σ_k. Then the threshold T is computed, the value of T should not be too large, otherwise the pixon will contain many pixels which actually belong to two different classes. So we using follow empirical function:

$$T=\min_{0<i,k\le K,i\ne j}(|u_i-u_j|-\sigma_i-\sigma_j) \tag{28}$$

Finally, the segmented image and the parameters are optimized, simultaneously.

Let $F(\omega, I_{i,new})$ denote the objective function value when the ith label of ω is changed into $I_{i,new}$ and $\Delta F(\omega, I_{i,new})$ denote $F(\omega, I_{i,new})-F(\omega)$. The optimization is described as follows

1. Initialize the number of classes K; the total number of iteration NUM; $u_1, \ldots, u_k$ and $\sigma_1, \ldots, \sigma_k$ according to an initial segmentation, which is obtained using FCM method; compute the threshold T; and the iteration index $j = 0$;
2. Extraction of pixon-representation, then initialize the pixon-based image model: assign a label λ_k to each pixon P, which minimizes the expression $|\mu_P - u_{k_l}|$
3. Find the best label for each pixon, $l_{i,best}, 1 \le i \le N$, which minimizes $\Delta F(\omega, I_{i,new})$.
4. Find the $\Delta F(\omega, I_{min,best})$, satisfying $\Delta F(\omega, I_{min,best}) \le \Delta F(\omega, I_{i,best}), 1 \le i \le N$
5. If $\Delta F(\omega, I_{min,best}) < 0$ and $j < NUM$, go to step 4, otherwise stop iteration.
6. Update the best label of each pixon and re-estimate u_k, σ_k using new ω.
7. $j = j + 1$, Go to step 3.

In fact, $\Delta F(\omega, I_{i,best})$ can be calculated using the correlative terms with the ith label in $F(x)$, i.e.

$$F_i(\omega, I_{i,new}) = n_i \left(\frac{\left(\mu_i - u_{l_{i,new}}\right)^2 + \sigma_i^2}{2\sigma_{l_{i,new}}^2} + \ln \sigma_{l_{i,new}} \right) + \alpha \sum_{P_{ij} \in N(P_i)} \left(\frac{n_i b_{ij}}{b_i} + \frac{n_j b_{ij}}{b_j} \right) \frac{\eta_{ij,new}}{|\mu_i - \mu_j|} \tag{29}$$

2.3 WPB method

Pixon-based approach using wavelet thresholding is a recently developed image segmentation method [Hassanpour et al, 2009]. In this method, a wavelet thresholding technique is initially applied on the image to reduce noise and to slightly smooth the image. This technique causes an image not to be oversegmented when the pixon-based method is used. Indeed, the wavelet thresholding, as a pre-processing step, eliminates the unnecessary details of the image and results in a fewer pixon number, faster performance and more robustness against unwanted environmental noises. The image is then considered as a pixonal model with a new structure. The obtained image is segmented using the hierarchical clustering method (Fuzzy C-Means algorithm).

2.3.1 Pre-Processing step

As mentioned above, the wavelet thresholding technique is used as a pre-processing step in order to smooth the image. For this purpose, by choosing an optimal wavelet level and an appropriate mother wavelet, the image is decomposed into different channels, namely low-low, low-high, high-low and high-high (LL, LH, HL, HH respectively) channels and their coefficients are extracted in each level. The decomposition process can be recursively applied to the low frequency channel (LL) to generate decomposition at the next level. The suitable threshold is achieved using one of the different thresholding methods and then details coefficients cut with this threshold. Then, inverse wavelet transform is performed and smoothed image is reconstructed.

2.3.1.1 Wavelet thresholding technique

Thresholding is a simple non-linear technique which operates on the wavelet coefficients. In this technique, each coefficient is cut by comparing to a value as the threshold. The coefficients which are smaller than the threshold are set to zero and the others are kept or modified by considering the thresholding method. Whereas the wavelet transform is good for energy compaction, the small coefficients are considered as noise and large coefficients indicate important signal features [Gupta & kaur, 2002]. Therefore, these small coefficients can be cut with no effect on the significant features of the image.

Let $X = \{X_{i,j}, \ i, j = 1, 2 \ldots M\}$ denotes the $M \times M$ matrix of the original image. The two dimensional orthogonal Discrete Wavelet Transform (DWT) matrix and its inverse are implied by W and W^{-1}, respectively. After applying the wavelet transform to the image matrix X, this matrix is subdivided into four sub-bands namely LL, HL, LH and HH [Burrus et al., 1998].

Whereas the LL channel possesses the main information of the image signal, we apply the hard or soft thresholding technique to the other three sub-bands which contain the details coefficients. The outcome matrix which is produced after utilizing the thresholding level is denoted as $\hat{L}$ matrix. Finally, the smoothed image matrix can be obtained as follows:

$$\hat{X} = W^{-1}\hat{L} \tag{30}$$

The brief description of the hard thresholding is as follows:

$$\gamma(Y) = \begin{cases} Y & \text{if } |Y| > T \\ 0 & \text{otherrwise} \end{cases} \tag{31}$$

where Y is an arbitrary input matrix, $\gamma(Y)$ is the hard thresholding function which is applied on Y, and T indicates the threshold value. Using this function, all coefficients less than the threshold are replaced with zero and other coefficients are kept unchanged.

The soft thresholding acts similar to the hard one, except that in this method the values above the threshold are reduced by the amount of the threshold. The following equation implies the soft thresholding function:

$$\eta(Y) = \begin{cases} sign(Y)(|Y| - T) & \text{if } |Y| > T \\ 0 & \text{otherrwise} \end{cases} \tag{32}$$

where Y is the arbitrary input matrix, $\eta(Y)$ is the soft thresholding function and T indicates the threshold value. The researchs indicates that the soft thresholding method is more desirable in comparison with the hard one because of its better visual performance. The hard thresholding method may cause some discontinuous points in the image and this event may be a discouraging factor for the performance of our segmentation.

Three methods are presented to calculate the threshold value, namely Visushrink, Bayesshrink and Sureshrink. The method Visushrink is based on applying the universal threshold [Donoho & Johnstone, 1994]. This thresholding is given by $\sigma\sqrt{2\log M}$ where σ is standard deviation of noise and M is the number of pixels in the image. This threshold does not adapt well with discontinuities in the image. Sureshrink is also a practical wavelet procedure, but it uses a local threshold estimated adaptively for each level [Jansen, 2001]. The Bayesshrink rule uses a Bayesian mathematical framework for images to derive subband-dependent thresholds. These thresholds are nearly optimal for soft thresholding, because the wavelet coefficients in each subband of a natural image can be summarized adequately by a Generalized Gaussian Distribution (GGD) [Chang et al., 2000].

2.3.1.2 Algorithm and results

Our implementations on several different types of images show that "*Daubechies*" is one of the most suitable wavelet filters for this purpose. An image is decomposed, in our case, up to 2 levels using *8-tap Daubechies* wavelet filter. The amount of the threshold is assigned by the *Bayesshrink* rule and this value may be different for each image. This algorithm can be expressed as follows. First image is decomposed into four different channels, namely LL, LH, HL and HH. Then the soft thresholding function is applied on these channels, except on LL. Finally the smoothed image is reconstructed by inverse wavelet transform. Figure 6 shows the result of applying wavelet thresholding on the Baboon image. It can be inferred from this figure that the resulted image has fewer discontinuities than the original image and its smoothing degree increased and will be resulted in a fewer number of pixons.

In order to obtain a better view about pixonal image, we indicate the effect of pixon forming stage on an arbitrary image. As illustrated in Fig. 7, the boundaries between the adjacent pixons are sketched so that the image segments are more proper.

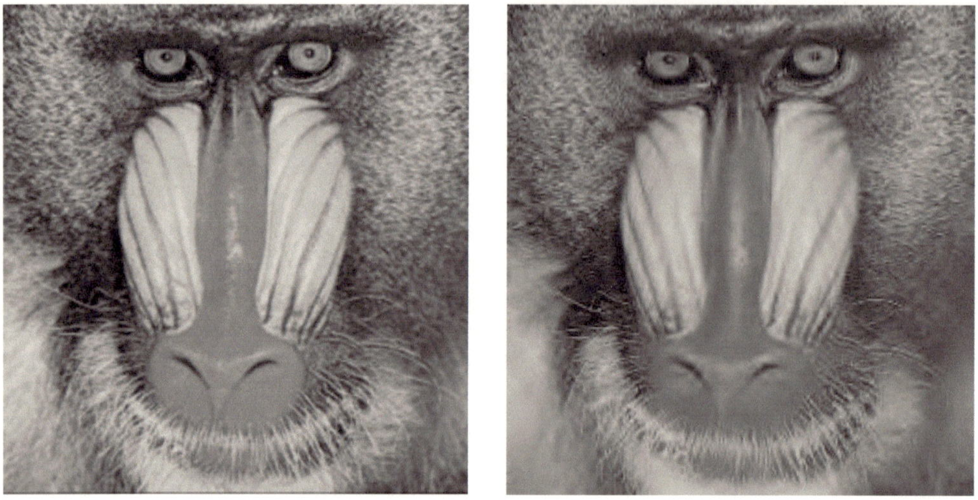

(a) (b)

Fig. 6. Result of applying wavelet thresholding technique on Baboon image: (a) Original image, and (b) smoothed image

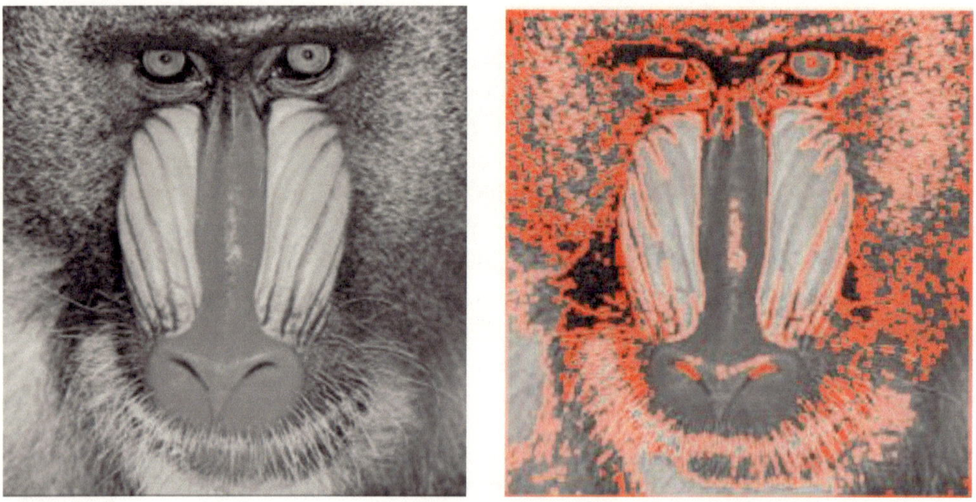

(a) (b)

Fig. 7. The effect of applying the pixon forming algorithm to the baboon image: (a) The original image, (b) the output image with boundaries between pixons

2.3.2 Image Segmentation using pixon method

In this approach the wavelet thresholding technique is used as a pre-processing step to make the image smoothed. This technique is applied on the wavelet transform coefficients of image using the soft thresholding function. The output of pre-processing step is then used in the pixon formulation stage. In TPB algorithm, after obtaining the pseudo image, the anisotropic diffusion equation was used to form the pixons. In WPB algorithm, utilizing the wavelet thresholding method as a pre-processing stage eliminates the necessity of using the diffusion equations. After forming and extracting the pixons, the Fuzzy C-Means (FCM) algorithm is used to segment the image. The FCM algorithm is an iterative procedure described in the following [Fauzi & Lewis, 2003].

Given M input data $\{x_m; m = 1,...,M\}$, the number of clusters $C(2 \le C < M)$, and the fuzzy weighting exponent $w, 1 < w < \infty$, initialize the fuzzy membership functions $u^{(0)}_{c,m}$ with $c = 1,...,C$ and $m = 1,...,M$ which are the entry of a $C \times M$ matrix $U^{(0)}$. The following procedure is performed for iteration $l = 1,2,...$:

1. Calculate the fuzzy cluster centers $v_c^{\,l}$ with $v_c = \sum_{m=1}^{M} (u_{c,m})^w x_m \,/\, \sum_{m=1}^{M} (u_{c,m})^w$
2. Update $U^{(l)}$ with $u_{c,m} = 1 / \sum_{i=1}^{C} (\frac{d_{c,m}}{d_{i,m}})^{\frac{2}{w-1}}$ where $(d_{i,m})^2 = x_m - v_i^{\,2}$ and . is any inner product induced norm.
3. Compare $U^{(l)}$ with $U^{(l+1)}$ in a convenient matrix norm. If $U^{(l+1)} - U^{(l)} \le \varepsilon$ stop; otherwise return to step 1.

The value of the weighting exponent, w determines the fuzziness of the clustering decision. A smaller value of w, i.e. w is close to unity, will give the zero/one hard decision membership function, and a larger w corresponds to a fuzzier output. Our experimental results suggest that w = 2 is a good choice.

Figure 8 illustrates this method block diagram.

3. Evaluation of the pixon-based methods

In this section the pixon-based image segmentation methods are applied on several standard images and the results of these implementations are extracted. For this purpose, commonly used images such as baboon, pepper and cortex are selected and the performance of applying the mentioned methods on them is compared. In order to evaluate these methods numerically, several experiments have been carried out on different standard images and some criteria such as number of the pixons in image, pixon to pixel ratio, normalized variance and computational time are used which are introduced in following.

3.1 Measurements

Computational time; In most applications, the time which is consumed to perform algorithms is an important parameter to evaluate them. So, researchers always seek to decrease the computational time.

Number of pixons and pixon to pixel ratio; As expressed previously, after forming the pixons, the image segmentation problem transformed to labeling the pixons. So, decrement in the number of pixons and related pixon to pixel ratio results in a decrement in computational time. Certainly it should be noted that the details of the image do not eliminate in this way.

Variance and Normalized Variance; One of the most important parameters used to evaluate the performance of image segmentation methods is the variance of each segment. The smaller value of this parameter implies the more homogeneity of the region and consequently the better segmentation results. Assume that after the segmentation process,

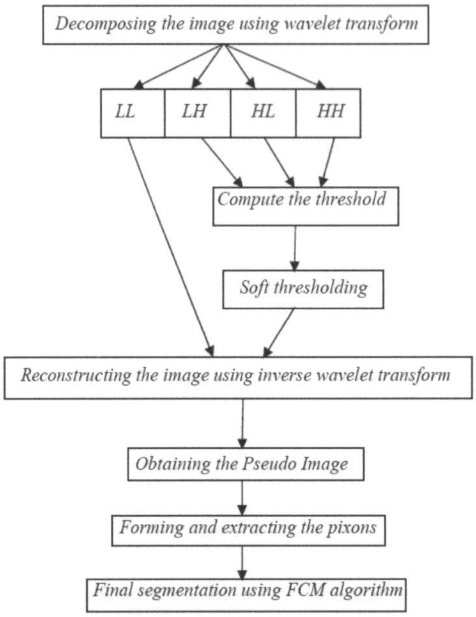

Fig. 8. The block diagram of the proposed method

the images are divided into K segments with different average values which we have called these segments as "Classes". In addition to the typical variance, the normalized variance of each image can be calculated. If N_k and $V(k)$ denotes the number of the pixels and the variance of each class respectively, the normalized variance of each image can be determined as below:

$$V^* = \frac{V_1}{V_2} \tag{33}$$

where

$$V_1 = \sum_{k=1}^{K} \frac{N_k V(k)}{N} \tag{34}$$

and

$$V_2 = \sum_{k=1}^{K} \frac{(I(x,y) - M)^2}{N} \tag{35}$$

In the above equations, k denotes the number of classes, $I(x,y)$ is the gray level intensity, M and N are the averaged value and the number of pixels in each image respectively.

3.2 Experimental results

In this section, results of applying the TPB, MPB and WPB methods on several standard images are considered. Figs. 9(a), 10(a) and 11(a) are the Baboon, Pepper and Cortex images used in this experiment. Figs. 9(b), 10(b), 11(b) and 9(c), 10(c), 11(c) show the segmentation results of TPB and PMB methods, respectively. The segmentation results of WPB method are illustrated in Figs. 9(d), 10(d) and 11(d). As shown in these figures, the homogeneity of regions and the discontinuity between adjacent regions, which are two main criteria in image segmentation, are enhanced in WPB method.

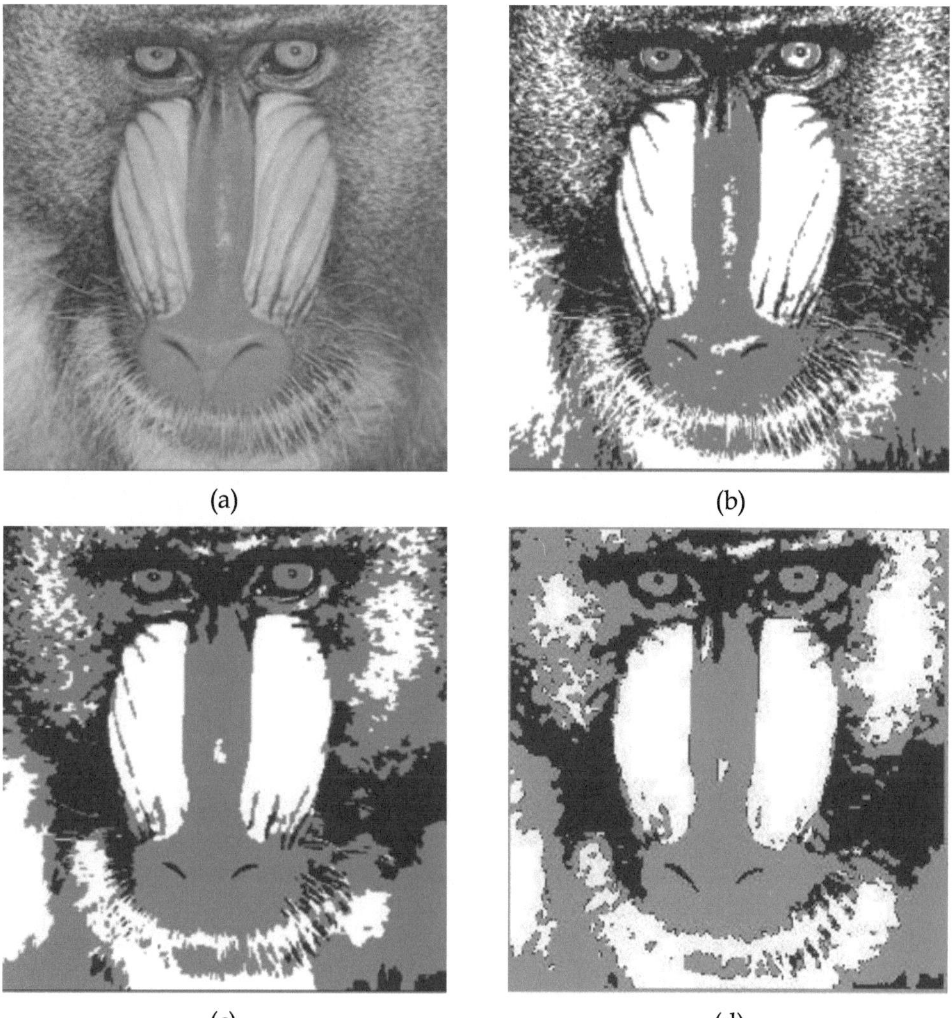

Fig. 9. Segmentation results of the Baboon image: (a) Original image, (b) TPB's method, (c) WPB's method, and (d) WPB's method

In addition, several experiments have been carried out on the different images and the average results are drawn in several tables. In Table 1, the number of pixons and the ratio of Pixon-Pixel in the three methods are shown. As can be seen from this table we can find that these parameters are decreased significantly in WPB method in comparison with two other methods which resulted from applying wavelet thresholding technique before forming pixons. Table 2 shows the computational time required of the three methods (Intel(R) Core(TM)2 Duo CPU 2.20 GHz processor, with MATLAB 7.4). By using pixon concept with

wavelet thresholding technique in the WPB method, the computational cost is sharply reduced. Since the MRF technique, because of its complicated mathematical equations, is a time consuming process, the MPB method expends much time compared to TPB method.
In this experience, after the segmentation process, the images are divided into three segments or Classes. The variance and average of each class are listed in Tables 3-5, for mentioned images. In most cases, the variance values of the classes of different images in WPB method are smaller in comparison with the other methods. In order to investigate the performance of methods more exact, the normalized variance of each image after applying the

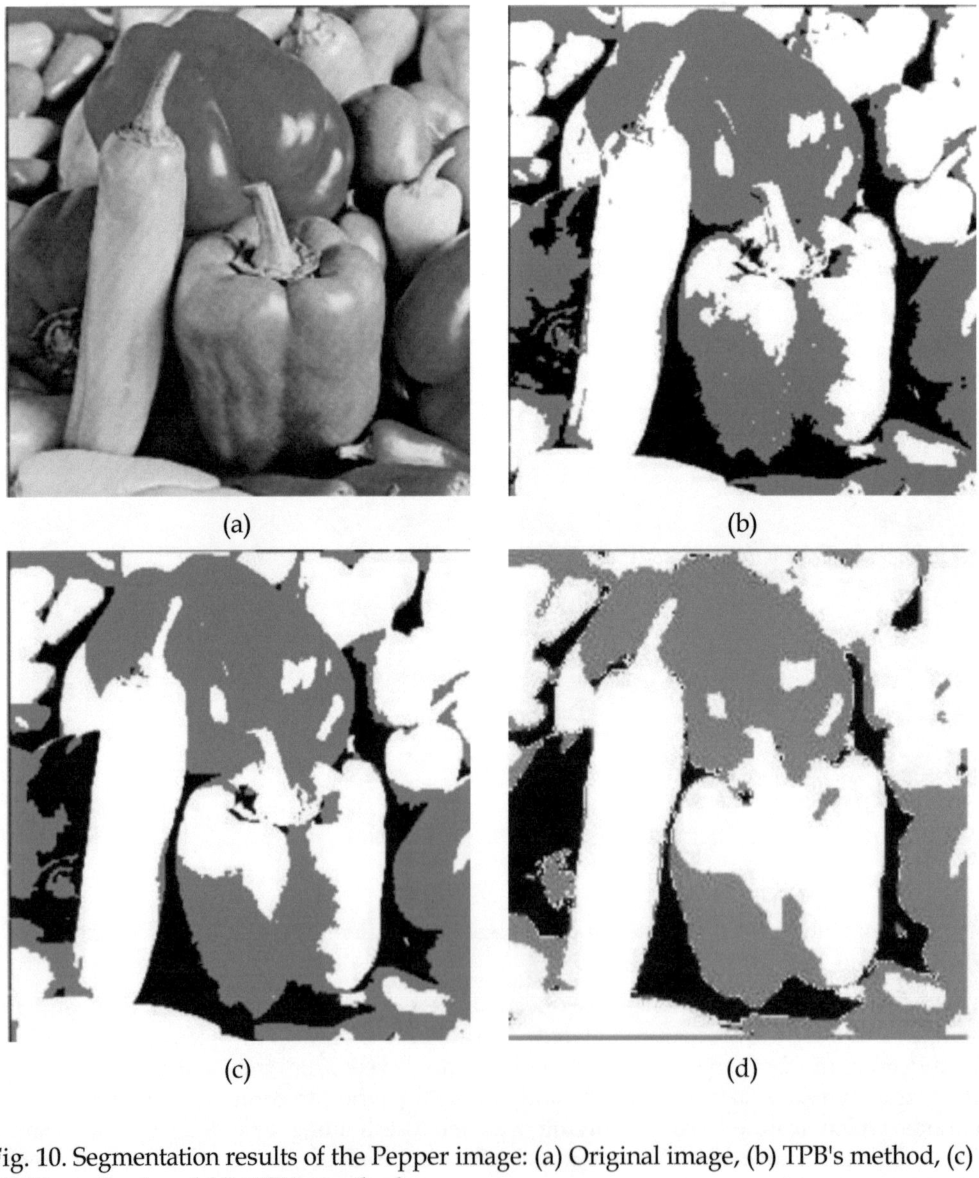

Fig. 10. Segmentation results of the Pepper image: (a) Original image, (b) TPB's method, (c) MPB's method, and (d) WPB's method

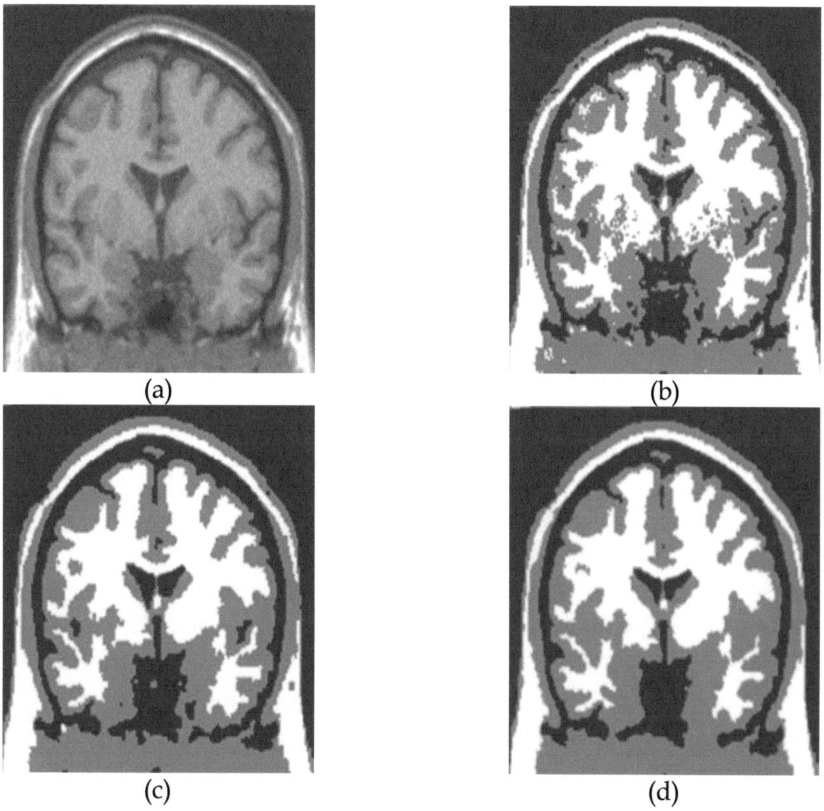

Fig. 11. Segmentation results of the Cortex image: (a) Original image, (b) TPB's method, (c) MPB's method, and (d) WPB's method

three methods are calculated too. The normalized variance results illustrated in the tables demonstrate that in the pixon-based approach which used wavelet (WPB method), the amount of pixels in each cluster is closer to each other and the areas of images are more homogenous.

Images (Size)	The number of pixels	The number of pixons			The ratio between the number of pixons and pixels		
		TPB's method	MPB's method	WPB's method	TPB's method	MPB's method	WPB's method
Baboon (256×256)	262144	83362	61341	25652	31.8 %	23.4 %	9.79 %
Pepper (256×256)	262144	31981	24720	13221	12.2 %	9.43 %	5.04 %
Cortex (128×128)	16384	1819	1687	1523	11.1 %	10.2 %	9.3 %

Table 1. Comparison of the number of pixons and the ratio between the number of pixons and pixels, among the three methods

Images	TPB's method (ms)	MPB's method (ms)	WPB's method(ms)
Baboon	18549	19431	15316
Pepper	15143	17034	13066
Cortex	702	697	633

Table 2. Comparison of the computational time, between the three methods

Method	Parameter	class 1	class 2	class 3
TPB's method	average	168.06	127.28	84.25
	variance	12.18	11.06	17.36
	Normalized Variance	**0.0279**		
MPB's method	average	167.86	126.45	82.18
	variance	12.05	11.55	16.67
	Normalized Variance	**0.0259**		
WPB method	average	170.40	128.36	83.95
	variance	11.34	11.46	16.96
	Normalized Variance	**0.0212**		

Table 3. Comparison of variance values of each class, for the three algorithms (Baboon).

Method	Parameter	class 1	class 2	class 3
TPB's method	average	190.59	123.29	35.47
	variance	16.64	21.89	21.79
	Normalized Variance	**0.0263**		
MPB's method	average	191.68	125.27	34.39
	variance	16.28	22.66	22.30
	Normalized Variance	**0.0251**		
WPB's method	average	189.75	122.56	37.17
	variance	15.87	22.86	20.30
	Normalized Variance	**0.0217**		

Table 4. Comparison of variance values of each class, for the three algorithms (Pepper).

Method	Parameter	class 1	class 2	class 3
TPB's method	average	22.44	93.71	197.23
	variance	12.59	11.67	14.11
	Normalized Variance	**0.0131**		
MPB's method	average	21.34	91.65	199.50
	variance	12.75	10.33	13.93
	Normalized Variance	**0.0119**		
WPB's method	average	24.25	92.49	196.72
	variance	11.37	10.51	12.81
	Normalized Variance	**0.0101**		

Table 5. Comparison of variance values of each class, for the three algorithms (Cortex).

4. Conclusion

This chapter provided an introduction to the pixon-based image segmentation methods. The pixon is a set of disjoint regions with variable shapes and sizes. Different algorithms were introduced to form and extract the pixons. Pixon-based methods were divided into three classes: TPB method, which used from the traditional pixon definition to segment the image; MPB method, which combined the pixon concept and MRF to obtain the segmented image; and WPB method, which segmented the image by a pixon-based approach utilizing the wavelet thresholding algorithm. The chapter was concluded with illustration of experimental results of applying these methods on different standard images.

5. References

Andrey P. & Tarroux, P. (1998). Unsupervised segmentation of Markov random field modeled textured images using selectionist relaxation, IEEE Trans. Pattern Anal. Machine Intell., vol. 20, pp. 252–262.

Bonnet, N. ; Cutrona, J. & Herbin, M. (2002). A 'no-threshold' histogram-based image segmentation method, *Pattern Recognition,* Volume 35, Issue 10, pp. 2319-2322.

Burrus, C. S. ; Gopinath, R. A. & Guo, H. (1998). Introduction to Wavelets and Wavelet Transforms, Prentice Hall,New Jersey.

Comaniciu, D. & Meer, P. (2002). Mean shift: a robust approach toward feature space analysis, *IEEE Trans. Pattern Anal.* Mach. Intell. 24 (5), pp. 1–18.

Donoho, D. L. &. Johnstone, I.M. (1994). Ideal spatial adaptation via wavelet shrinkage, *Biometrica,* Vol. 81, pp. 425-455.

Elfadel I. M. & Picard, R. W. (1994). Gibbs random fields, cooccurrences, and texture modeling, *IEEE Trans. Pattern Anal.* Machine Intell., vol. 16, pp. 24–37.

Fauzi M. F. A. & Lewis, P. H. (2003). A Fully Unsupervised Texture Segmentation Algorithm, *British Machine Vision Conference 2003,* Norwich, UK. pp.1201-1206

Francisco de A.T. de Carvalho, (2007). Fuzzy c-means clustering methods for symbolic interval data, *PatternRecognition Letters,* Volume 28, Issue 4, pp. 423-437.

Gonzalez, R. C. & Woods, R.E. (2004). *Digital Image Processing,* Prentice Hall,

Gupta,S. & kaur, L. (2002). Wavelet Based Image Compression using Daubechies Filters, *8th National conference on communications,* I.I.T. Bombay, pp. 88-92.

Hassanpour, H & Yousefian, H. (2010). A Pixon-Based Approach for Image Segmentation Using Wavelet Thresholding Method, *International Journal of Engineering(IJE),* Vol. 23, pp. 257-268.

Jansen, M. (2001). Noise Reduction by Wavelet Thresholding, Springer Verlag New York Inc., Pages. 875-879.

Chang, S. G. ; Yu, B. & Vetterli, M. (2000). Adaptive Wavelet Thresholding for image Denoising and compression, *IEEE Trans. Image Processing,* Vol.9, pp.1532-1545.

Kato, Z. ; Zerubia, J. & Berthod, M. (1999). Unsupervised parallel image classification using Markovian models, *Pattern Recognit.,* vol. 32, pp. 591–604.

Kim, I.Y. & Yang, H.S. (1996). An integration scheme for image segmentation and labeling based on Markov random field model, *IEEE Trans. Pattern Anal. Mach. intell.* Vol.18 No.1. pp. 69–73.

Lakshmanan, S. & Derin, H. (1989). Simultaneous parameter estimation and segmentation of Gibbs random fields using simulated annealing, *IEEE Trans. Pattern Anal.* Machine Intell., vol. 11, no. 8, pp. 799–813.

Lin, L. ; Zhu, L. & Yang, F. & Jiang, T. (2008). A novel pixon-representation for image segmentation based on

Markov random field, *Image and Vision Computing journal of ELSEVIER*, Vol.26, pp. 1507–1514.

Papamichail, G.P. & Papamichail, D.P. (2007). The k-means range algorithm for personalized data clustering in e-commerce, *European Journal of Operational Research*, Volume 177, Issue 3, pp. 1400-1408.

Piña, R. K. & Pueter, R. C. (1993). Bayesian image reconstruction: The pixon and optimal image modeling, *P. A. S. P.*, vol. 105, pp. 630–637.

Perona P. & Malik, J. (1990). Scale-space filtering and edge detection using anisotropic diffusion, *IEEE Trans. Pattern Anal.* Machine Intell., Vol.12, No. 7, pp. 629–639.

Puetter, R. C. (1995). Pixon-based multiresolution image reconstruction and the quantification of picture information content, *Int. J. Imag. Syst. Technol.*, vol. 6, pp. 314–331.

Shi, J. & Malik, J. (2000). Normalized cuts and image segmentation, *IEEE Trans. Pattern Anal.* Mach. Intell. 22 (8) pp. 888–905.

Yang, F. & Jiang, T. (2003). Pixon-based image segmentation with Markov random fields, *IEEE Trans. Image Process.* 12 (12) , pp. 1552–1559.

Zhu, S.C. & Yuille, A. (1996). Region competition: unifying snakes, region growing, and byes/mdl for multi-band image segmentation, *IEEE Trans. Pattern Anal.* Mach. Intell. 18 (9) ,pp. 884–900.

Part 4

Hardware Implementation

27

Hardware Implementation of a Real-Time Image Segmentation Circuit based on Fuzzy Logic for Edge Detection Application

Angel Barriga
Instituto de Microelectrónica de Sevilla (CNM/CSIC)/Univ. Sevilla
Spain

1. Introduction

Edge detection algorithms in images make it possible to extract information from the image and reduce the amount of required stored information. An edge is defined as a sharp change in luminosity intensity between two adjacent pixels. Most edge detection techniques can be grouped into two categories: gradient based techniques and Laplacian based methods. Techniques based on gradient use the first derivative of the image and look for the maximum and the minimum of this derivative. Examples of this type of strategies are: the Canny method (Canny, 1986), Sobel method, Roberts method (Roberts, 1965), Prewitt method (Prewitt, 1970), etc. On the other hand the techniques based on Laplacian look for the cross by zero of the second derivative of the image. An example of this type of techniques is the zero-crossing method (Marr & Hildreth, 1980).

Normally edge extraction mechanisms are implemented by executing the corresponding software realisation on a processor. Nevertheless in applications that demand constrained response times (real time applications) the specific hardware implementation is required. The main drawback of implementing edge detection techniques in hardware is the high complexity of the existing algorithms. The process of edge detection in an image consists of a sequence of stages. Image segmentation is one step in the edge detection process. By means of the segmentation the image is divided in parts or objects that constitutes it. In the case of considering only one region the image is divided in object and background. The level at which this subdivision is made depends on the application. The segmentation will finish when all the objects of interest for the application have been detected.

The image segmentation algorithms are based generally on two basic properties of the image grey levels: discontinuity and similarity. Inside the first category the techniques tries to divide the image by means of the sharp changes on the grey level. In the second category there are applied thresholds techniques, growth of regions, and division and fusion techniques.

The simplest segmentation problem appears when the image is formed by only one object that has homogenous light intensity on a background with a different level of luminosity. In this case the image can be segmented in two regions using a technique based on a threshold parameter. Thresholding then becomes a simple but effective tool to separate objects from the background. Most of thresholding algorithms are initially meant for binary thresholding. This binary thresholding procedure may be extended to a multi-level one with the help of

multiple thresholds $T_1, T_2,\dots,T_n$ to segment the image into n+1 regions (Liao et al., 2001), (Cao et al., 2002), (Oh & Kim, 2006). Multi-level thresholding based on a multi-dimensional histogram resembles the image segmentation algorithms based on pattern clustering.
Binary thresholding techniques classify the pixels of the image into two categories (black and white). This transformation is made to establish a distinction between the objects of the image and the background. This binary image is generated by comparing the values of the pixels with a threshold T. That is to say, any value lower than the threshold value is considered to be an object whereas values greater than the threshold belong to the background.

$$y_{ij} = \begin{cases} 0 & if \quad x_{ij} < T \\ L-1 & if \quad x_{ij} > T \end{cases} \tag{1}$$

where x_{ij} is a pixel of the original image and y_{ij} is the pixel corresponding to the binary image. In the case of a monochrome image in which the pixels are encoded with 8 bits the range of values adopted by the pixels corresponds to the range between 0 and 255 (L=256). It is usual to express the above mentioned range with normalized values between 0 and 1.

2. Thresholding techniques

A basic technique for threshold calculation is based on the frequency of grey level. In this case the threshold T is calculated by means of the following expression:

$$T = \sum_{i=1}^{L} p_i i \tag{2}$$

where i is the grey level, p_i represents the grey level frequency (also known as the probability of the grey level). For an image with n pixels and n_i pixels with the grey level i:

$$p_i = n_i / n \quad and \quad \sum_{i=1}^{L} p_i = 1 \tag{3}$$

Otsu's technique (Otsu, 1978) calculates the optimal threshold maximizing the variance between classes. For that it realizes an exhaustive search to evaluate the criterion of maximizing the variance between classes. One drawback of Otsu's method is the time required to select the value of the threshold.
In the case of two-level thresholding the pixels are classified into two classes: C_1, with gray levels [1, ..., t], and C_2, with gray levels [t+1, ..., L]. The distributions of probability of gray levels for the two classes are:

$$C_1 : \frac{p_1}{w_1(t)}, \dots\dots\dots\dots, \frac{p_t}{w_1(t)} \tag{4}$$

$$C_2 : \frac{p_{t+1}}{w_2(t)}, \frac{p_{t+2}}{w_2(t)}, \dots\dots\dots\dots, \frac{p_l}{w_2(t)} \tag{5}$$

where

$$w_1(t) = \sum_{i=1}^{t} p_i \quad \text{and} \quad w_2(t) = \sum_{i=t+1}^{L} p_i \tag{6}$$

The mean values for C_1 and C_2 classes are

$$\mu_1 = \sum_{i=1}^{t} \frac{ip_i}{w_1(t)} \quad \text{and} \quad \mu_2 = \sum_{i=t+1}^{l} \frac{ip_i}{w_2(t)} \tag{7}$$

Let μ_T be the average intensity of whole image, so that:

$$w_1\mu_1 + w_2\mu_2 = \mu_T \quad \text{and} \quad w_1 + w_2 = 1 \tag{8}$$

Using discriminant analysis the variance between classes can be defined as

$$\sigma^2{}_B = w_1(\mu_1 - \mu_T)^2 + w_2(\mu_2 - \mu_T)^2 \tag{9}$$

For a two-level thresholding the optimal threshold t^* is chosen so that $\sigma^2{}_B$ is maximum, ie

$$t^* = \max_t\{\sigma^2{}_B(t)\} \qquad 1 \le t \le L \tag{10}$$

Otsu's method can be easily applied to multiple thresholds. Assuming there are M-1 thresholds $\{t_1, t_2, \ldots, t_{M-1}\}$, which divide the image into M classes:

$$C_1 \; for \; [1,\ldots,t_1], C_2 \; for \; [t_1+1,\ldots,t_2], \; \ldots \; ,C_i \; for \; [t_{i-1}+1,\ldots,t_i], \; \ldots \; and \; C_M \; for \; [t_{M-1},\ldots,L], \tag{11}$$

The optimal thresholds t_1^*, t_2^*, ..., t_{M-1}^* are chosen to maximize $\sigma^2{}_B$:

$$\{t_1^*, t_2^*, \ldots, t_{M-1}^*\} = \max_{t_1, t_2, \ldots, t_{M-1}} \{\sigma^2{}_B(t_1, t_2, \ldots, t_{M-1})\} \qquad 1 \le t_1 < \ldots. < t_{M-1} < L \tag{12}$$

$$\text{where } \sigma_B{}^2 = \sum_{k=1}^{M} w_k(\mu_k - \mu_T)^2 \tag{13}$$

$$\text{with } w_k = \sum_{i=C_k} p_i \text{ and } \mu_k = \sum_{i=C_k} \frac{ip_i}{w_k} \tag{14}$$

ω_k is known as zero-order cumulative moment of the k-th class C_k, and the numerator of the last expression is known as first-order cumulative moment of the k-th class C_k, ie

$$\mu(k) = \sum_{i=C_k} ip_i \tag{15}$$

Regardless of the number of classes that are considered during the thresholding process the sum of the cumulative probability functions of the M classes are equal to 1 and the mean of the image is equal to the sum of the means of the M classes weighted by their corresponding cumulative probabilities, ie

$$\sum_{k=1}^{M} w_k = 1 \quad \text{and} \quad \mu_T = \sum_{k=1}^{M} w_k\mu_k \tag{16}$$

Using (16) the variance between classes in equation (13) can be rewritten as follows

$$\sigma_B^2(t_1, t_2, ..., t_{M-1}) = \sum_{k=1}^{M} w_k \mu^2_k - \mu_T^2 \quad (17)$$

Since the second term in equation (17) depends on the choice of thresholds $\{t_1, t_2, ..., t_{M-1}\}$, the optimal thresholds $\{t_1^*, t_2^*, ..., t_{M-1}^*\}$ can be chosen maximizing a modified variance between classes $(\sigma_B')^2$, defined as the sum of the terms of the right side of equation (17). That is, the optimal threshold values $\{t_1^*, t_2^*, ..., t_{M-1}^*\}$ are chosen by

$$\{t_1^*, t_2^*, ..., t_{M-1}^*\} = \max_{t_1, t_2, ..., t_{M-1}} \{\sigma^2{}_B(t_1, t_2, t_{M-1})\} \quad (18)$$

$$\text{where } (\sigma_B')^2 = \sum_{k=1}^{M} w_k \mu_k^2 \quad (19)$$

According to the criterion of expression (12) for σ_B^2 and equation (18) for $(\sigma_B')^2$, in order to find optimal thresholds, the search region for the maximum σ_B^2 and for the maximum $(\sigma_B')^2$ is $1<t_1<L-M+1$, $t_1+1<t_2<L-M+2$, …, $t_{M-1}+1< t_{M-1}<L-1$.

This exhaustive search involves $(L-M+1)^{M-1}$ possible combinations. Furthermore, equation (19) is simpler than (13) because it don't requires the subtractions.

In 1965 Zadeh proposed fuzzy logic as a reasoning mechanism that uses linguistic terms (Zadeh, 1965). Fuzzy logic is based on the fuzzy set theory in which an element can belong to several sets with different degrees of membership. This contrasts with the classic set theory in which an element either belongs or does not belong to a certain set. Thus a fuzzy set A is defined as

$$A = \{(x, \mu(x)) | x \in X\} \quad (20)$$

where x is an object of the set of objects X and $\mu(x)$ is the membership degree of element x to set A. In the classic set theory $\mu(x)$ takes values 0 or 1 whereas in the fuzzy set theory $\mu(x)$ belongs to the range of values between 0 and 1.

Techniques that apply fuzzy logic to threshold calculation are based mainly on three types of measures of fuzziness (Forero-Vargas & Rojas-Camacho, 2000): entropy, Kaufmann`s measure, and Yager's measure.

The technique based on entropy consists of minimizing the dispersion of the system. This way the pixels of the image are grouped into two classes corresponding to the objects and to the background. Huang and Wang (Huang & Wang, 1995) consider that the averages of the data corresponding to each class are μ_0 and μ_1. The membership function of each class is defined as:

$$u_x(x) = \begin{cases} \dfrac{1}{1 + \dfrac{|x - \mu_0|}{x_{\max} - x_{\min}}} & if \quad x < T \\ \dfrac{1}{1 + \dfrac{|x - \mu_1|}{x_{\max} - x_{\min}}} & if \quad x > T \end{cases} \quad (21)$$

The calculation of the threshold T is based on the entropy of a fuzzy set that is calculated using the function of Shannon:

$$H_f(x) = -x \log x - (1-x)\log(1-x) \tag{22}$$

The threshold will be that which minimizes the entropy of the data:

$$E(T) = \frac{1}{M}\sum_i H_f(\mu_x(i))h(i) \tag{23}$$

Kaufmann's measure of fuzziness is defined as (Kaufmann, 1975):

$$D(A) = \left[\sum_{x \in X} \left|\mu_A(x) - \mu_C(x)\right|^w\right]^{\frac{1}{w}} \tag{24}$$

This method is based on using the distance metric to set A. When w=1 Hamming's distance is used whereas if w=2 it is the Euclidean distance.
Yager's method (Yager, 1979) is based on the distance between a fuzzy set and its complementary, and basically entails minimizing the following function:

$$D_2(T) = \sqrt{\sum_i \left|\mu_x(i) - \mu_{\bar{x}}(i)\right|^2} \tag{25}$$

where $\mu_{\bar{x}}(i) = 1 - \mu_x(i)$.
(Barriga & Hussein, 2008) proposed a technique that, from a formal point of view, is based on calculating the average of the histogram of the image. One advantage of this technique is that the calculation mechanism improves the processing time since the image only needs to be processed once and the value of the threshold can be calculated directly. From the point of view of hardware implementation that enables low-cost circuit for fuzzy processing module as discussed in a later section
The fuzzy system receives the input pixel and generates an output that corresponds to the result of the fuzzy inference. Once the image has been read the output shows the value of threshold T. Basically the operation carried out by the fuzzy system is that of calculating the centre of gravity of the image histogram with the following expression:

$$T = \sum_{i=1}^{M}\sum_{j=1}^{R} \alpha_{ij}c_{ij} \Bigg/ \sum_{i=1}^{M}\sum_{j=1}^{R} \alpha_{ij} \tag{26}$$

where T is the threshold, M is the number of pixels of the image, R is the number of rules of the fuzzy system, c is the consequent of each rule and α is the activation degree of the rule.
In order to produce the fuzzy inference the universe of discourse of the histogram is divided into a set of N equally distributed membership functions. Figure 1 shows a partition example for N=9. Triangular membership functions have been used since they are easier for hardware implementation. These functions have an overlapping degree of 2 in order to limit the number of active rules. The membership functions of the consequent are singletons equally distributed in the universe of discourse of the histogram. The use of singleton-type membership functions for the consequent allows the application of simplified defuzzification methods such as the Fuzzy Mean. This defuzzification method can be interpreted as one in which each rule proposes a conclusion with a "strength" defined by its grade of activation. The overall action of several rules is obtained by calculating the average of the different conclusions weighted by their grades of activation. This type of processing,

based on active rules and a simplified defuzzification method, allows low cost and high speed hardware implementation.

Fig. 1. Membership functions for *N*=9, a) antecedent, b) consequent.

The rule base of the system in figure 2 use the membership functions defined in figure 1. The knowledge base (membership functions and rule base) is common for any images, and the values can therefore be stored in a ROM memory.

if x is L1 then c is C1;
if x is L2 then c is C2;
if x is L3 then c is C3;
if x is L4 then c is C4;
if x is L5 then c is C5;
if x is L6 then c is C6;
if x is L7 then c is C7;
if x is L8 then c is C8;
if x is L9 then c is C9;

Fig. 2. Rulebase for *N*=9.

It is possible to optimize the expression shown in equation (26) if the system is normalized. In this case the sum extending to the rule base of the grades of activation of the consequent takes value 1:

$$\sum_{i=1}^{R} \alpha_{ij} = 1 \tag{27}$$

Then (26) transforms in:

$$T = \frac{1}{M} \sum_{i=1}^{M} \sum_{j=1}^{R} \alpha_{ij} c_{ij} \tag{28}$$

For each pixel the system makes the inference in agreement with the rule base of figure 2. The output of the system accumulates the result corresponding to the numerator of (28). The final output is generated with the last pixel of the image after division by *M*.

3. Image segmentation

The technique presented in (Barriga & Hussein, 2008) has the disadvantage that the rule base is predetermined and therefore the threshold does not fit to the characteristics of the image. It is a linear approximation. A mechanism to adjust the threshold to the

characteristics of the image is to perform a nonlinear approximation. Figure 3 shows some examples of knowledge bases that give place to non-linear approximations. The figure shows five fuzzy systems (figure 3a to figure 3e). For each system there have been represented the membership functions for antecedents, the output function and the result of segmentation using the threshold generated in each case. In all cases the membership functions of antecedents constitute a family of functions. This family consists of triangular functions with an overlapping degree of two. This structure is determined by the hardware implementation requirements of the system as we will discuss in a later section. It may be noted that the base and the position of the membership functions change from one system to another giving rise to a nonlinear behavior.
This approach allows to obtain thresholds adapted to the characteristics of the image or the requirements of the application. Table 1 shows the thresholds obtained in different images using the Otsu method, the grey level frequency method and usign the fuzzy systems of figures 3a to 3e.

4. Hardware implementation

4.1 Architecture description

The design goals of the fuzzy inference module (FIM) for calculating the threshold are: a low cost system and high processing speed. The architecture of the FIM circuit is based on the proposal described in (Baturone et al., 2000) shown in Figure 4. The module consists of three stages: fuzzifier, inference and defuzzifier. The inference mechanism is based on active rules. This allows to process only those rules that are active and avoids to analyze the whole rulebase. This way the processing time is reduced. For it the overlapping degree of the membership functions is limited. Another architecture feature is the use of singleton consequents. This allows to apply simplified defuzzification methods which supposes a reduction of hardware resources.
The first stage of the architecture corresponds to the fuzzificación stage. This stage receives the input data and generates for each input the pair (Label, membership degree) = (L, μ). MFC blocks (Membership Function Circuit) perform this task. There are several alternatives to the design of MFC blocks (Baturone et al., 2000). One solution is to design the block as an arithmetic circuit that interpolates the right output for each input. This solution gives place to a simple and fast circuit. However it has as counterpart that limits the type of membership functions to triangular and trapezoidal functions. A more flexible solution is based on the use of a memory. In this case the input acts as a pointer to a memory location. This memory location stores the output values. This allows to have membership functions of any form. The shape of the membership function has no restrictions other than the selected precision and has no influence on the computational load. As opposed to this advantage, in situations of high resolution, memory requirements can become very large since the number of rows in the antecedents memory depends exponentially on the number of bits of the input. In the case of N membership functions, with P bits of precision for the input, and J bits of precision for the membership degree, the size of the required memory is given by the equation (29).

$$T = N \cdot J \cdot 2^{P} \tag{29}$$

Since the overlapping degree of the membership functions is fixed, the number of output values of the fuzzification stage is limited. For example, in the case of limiting the

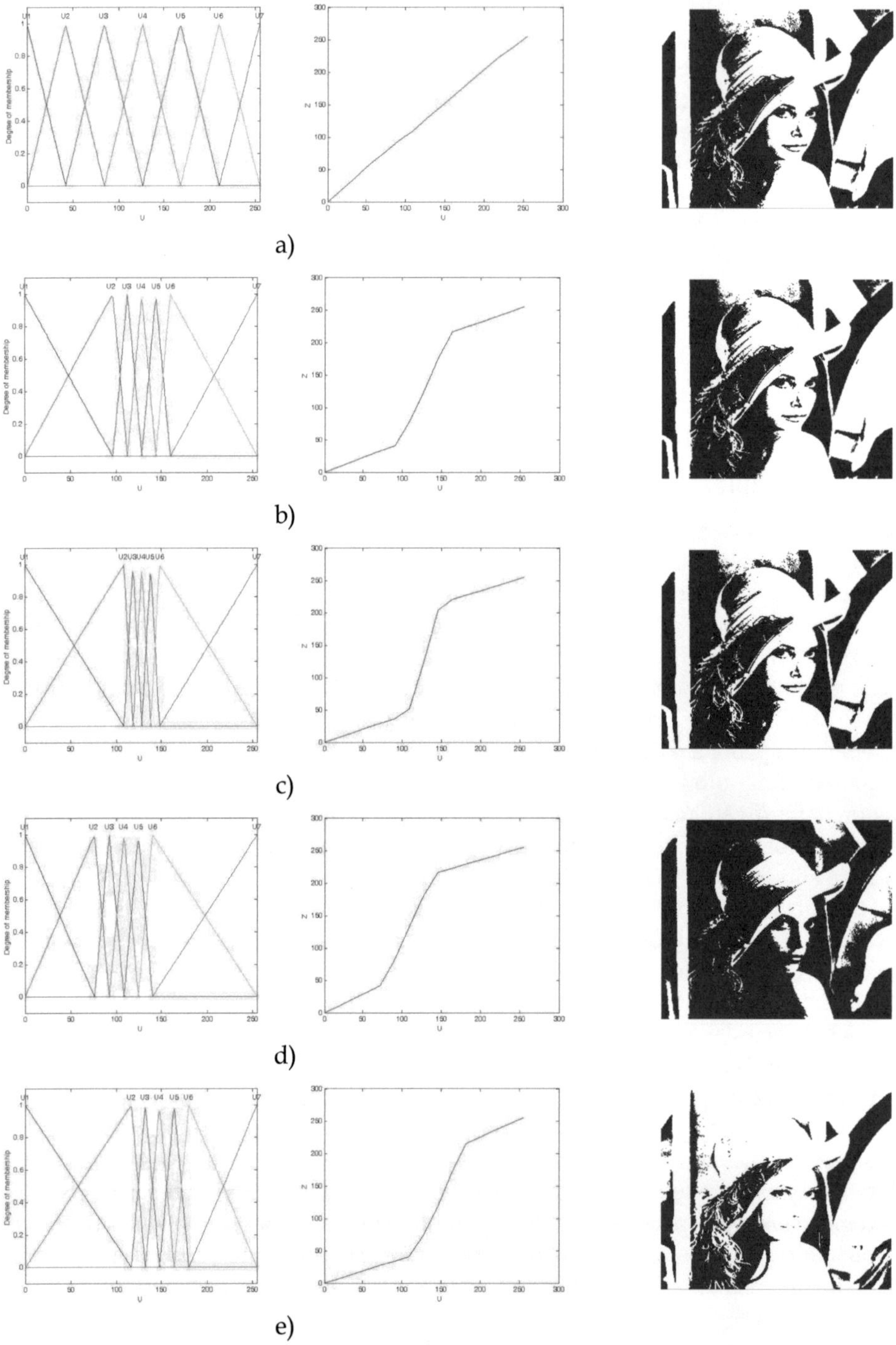

Fig. 3. Examples of fuzzy systems for image thresholding. For each subfigure there are: i) Membership functions for antecedent. ii) Output of the fuzzy system. iii) image segmentation sample.

	Otsu	Freq	Fuzz-a	Fuzz-b	Fuzz-c	Fuzz-d	Fuzz-e
Lena	116	123	126	124	126	152	96
Barbara	112	112	114	105	105	134	78
Cameraman	87	118	120	135	138	154	106
Peppers	101	104	106	103	105	123	80

Table 1. Thresholds obtained using different methods on sample images

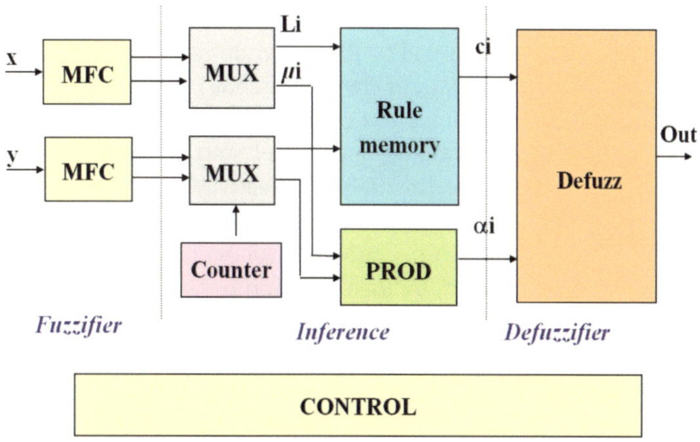

Fig. 4. Architecture of fuzzy inference module (FIM).

overlapping degree of the membership functions to 2, and in the case of a system of 2 inputs, only 4 couples of values (Label, degree) exist, i.e. only 4 rules are activated. Therefore the inference stage is constituted by the block that selects each one of the antecedents of the active rules. A set of multiplexers controlled by a counter allows to select sequentially the different combinations of antecedents of the active rules. In each counter cycle the membership degrees are processed through the conjunction operator to calculate the rule activation degree, while the labels of the antecedents address the memory position that contains its corresponding consequent. The output of the inference stage corresponds to the pair of values (Consequent, activation degree) = (c, α). for each rule.

The last stage performs the defuzzification. On having used singleton consequents, the defuzzification algorithm only requires operations on the rules. The hardware resources required for implementing the Fuzzy Mean defuzzification method are: a multiplier, two accumulators and a divisor. This defuzzification method corresponds to the following operation:

$$Out = \sum_r \alpha_i c_i \, / \sum_r \alpha_i \tag{30}$$

where the summations are extended to active rules, c_i is the consequent of each rule and α_i is the rule activation degree.

In the case of having normalized membership functions and applying the product as T-norm the denominator of the previous equation is 1. This means that a divisor is not needed and defuzzification operation is simplified according to the following expression:

$$Out = \sum_{r} \alpha_i c_i \tag{31}$$

4.2 Design and implementation

From the general characteristics of the FIM architecture it is possible to specify a set of simplification options that allow a reduction of hardware resources and increased parallelism (and thus the processing speed). Regarding the design of the different blocks of figure 4 and according to the knowledge base of the threshold system the memory requirements are: a) the MFC memory requires 256x10 bits; b) the rule memory requires 7x8 bits.

Figure 5 shows the system architecture. The FIM module receives input x corresponding to one pixel. MFC memory stores the data of the antecedent membership functions according to the scheme shown in figure 6a. Since the overlapping degree is fixed to 2, each row of memory only stores the value of a linguistic label and a membership degree (Label, degree)=(L, μ). The other label can be calculated increasing in a unit the stored value, since always the linguistic labels of both membership functions that are active are consecutive ($L_2=L_1+1$). While the other membership degree is calculated taking into account that the membership functions are normalized, by the operation $\mu_2=1-\mu_1$.

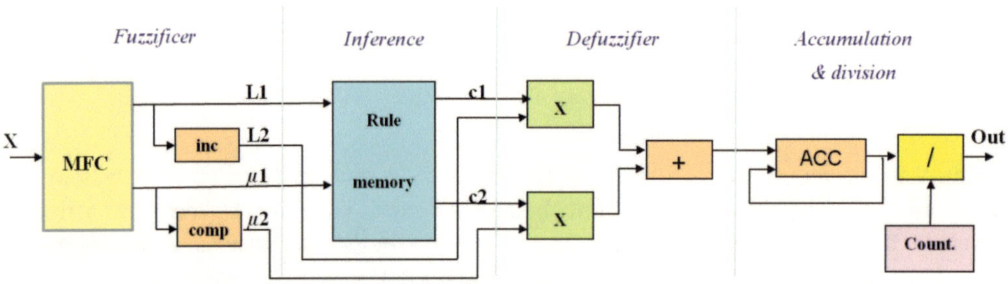

Fig. 5. FIM circuit for calculating the threshold

The rule memory is a dual-port memory. This way it is possible to access simultaneously to two active rules. This memory is addressed by the linguistic label that provides the MFC. This allows to eliminate the multiplexers and the counter of figure 4.

The defuzzification stage receives both the consequents (c_1 and c_2) and the activation degrees of the active rules (μ_1 and μ_2). The last stage makes the accumulation of the result generated by each pixel and the division by the number of pixels of the image. In agreement with the described FIM scheme it is possible to make an inference in each clock cycle.

In order to increase the operation speed of the system it is possible to process two pixels in parallel as shown in Figure 7. For it the blocks of higher cost (the MFC memory and the divisor) are shared by both inputs. The MFC memory is a dual-port memory. This allows to reduce by the half the time required to calculate the threshold.

The circuit of figure 7 has been implemented on a low cost FPGA Spartan3 device XC3S200 of Xilinx. The results of the required hardware resources on the Spartan3 FPGA circuit are shown in Table 2. The table shows the resources needed in the case of the circuit with and without the divisor. This division block is that of major cost of the system.

The circuit implemented on the Spartan3 FPGA operates at a frequency of 50MHz. In each clock cycle it allows to process two pixels. Thus the processing time of an SVGA image of

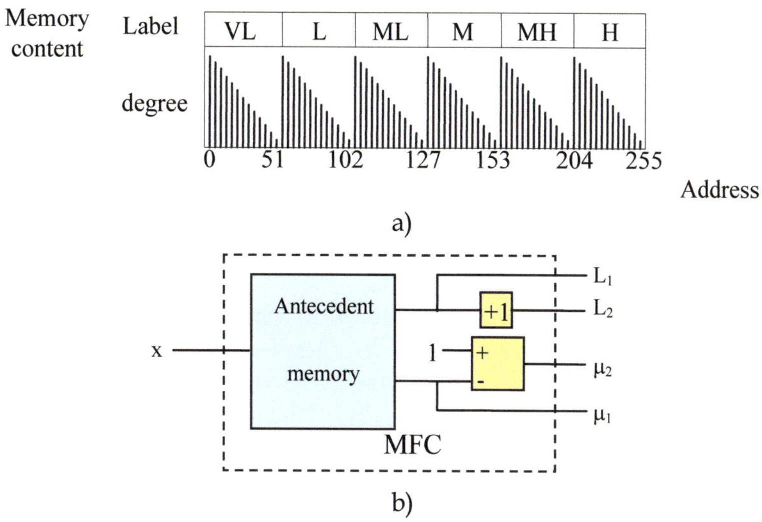

Fig. 6. a) Storage scheme in the antecedent memory. b) MFC circuit based on memory

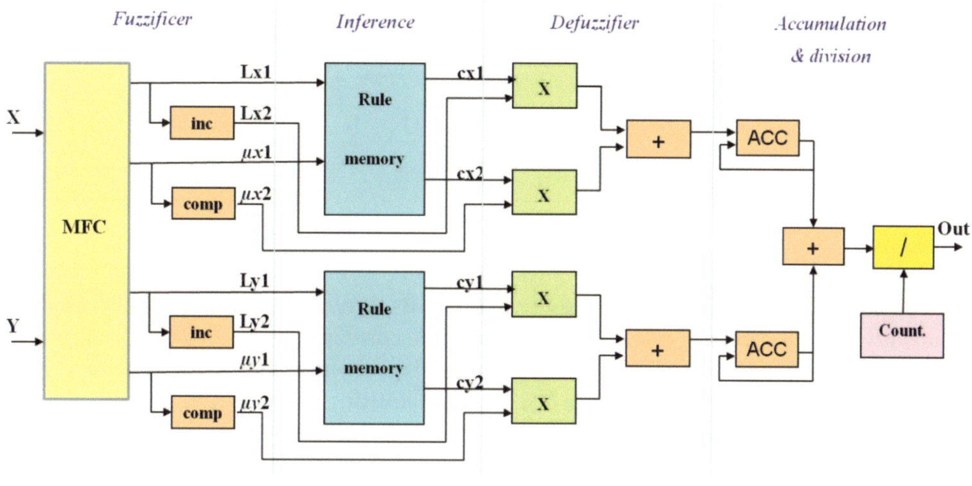

Fig. 7. Circuit that allows to process two pixels in parallel

Resources	without DIV	with DIV
slices	82	407
8x8 bit multiplier	4	4
Flip-flops	84	654
256x10 bit dual-port RAM	1	1
7x8 bit dual-port RAM	2	2

Table 2. Hardware resources on XC3S200 FPGA

800x600 pixels is 4.8 msec. This allows to make a processing of 208 frames per second. In the case of an HD image (1920x1080 pixels) it is possible to process 48 frames per second.

5. Edge detection

This section presents an application of image segmentation to edge detection. The method is applied to the luminosity of the image. An image is a bidimensional matrix of pixels whose values belong to certain range of values. In this section each pixel is codified with 8 bits, which gives rise to 256 possible values of grey tones. An image is therefore a function of two variables (dimensions) in the range from 0 to 255.
The process of edge detection in an image consists of the sequence of stages shown in figure 8. The first stage receives the input image and applies a filter to eliminate noise. The second step applies a threshold in order to classify the pixels of the image under two categories, black and white. The resulting image is a binary image. Finally, in the last stage the edges are detected.

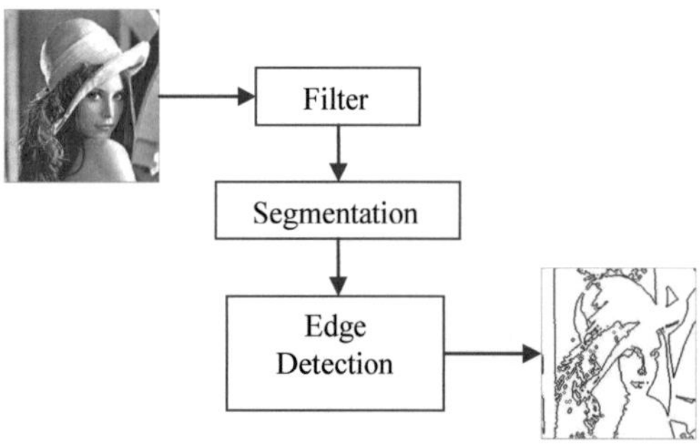

Fig. 8. Diagram flow for edge detection.

5.1 The filter stage

The filter stage makes it possible to improve details of edges in images and reduce or eliminate noise patterns. The aim of the filter step is to eliminate all those points that do not provide any type of information of interest. The noise corresponds to undesired information appearing in the image. It comes principally from the capture sensor (quantisation noise) and from the transmission of the image (fault in transmitting the information bits). Basically we consider two types of noise: Gaussian and impulsive (salt&peppers). Gaussian noise has its origin in differences of gains in the sensor, noise in digitalization, etc. Impulsive noise is characterized by arbitrary pixel values that are detectable because they are very different from their neighbours. A way to eliminate these types of noise is by means of a low pass filter, a filter which smoothens out the image replacing high and low values by average values.
The filter used in the proposed edge detection system is based on the bounded sum Lukasiewicz operator which is defined as:

$$BoundedSum(x,y) = \min(1, x + y) \quad (32)$$

The behaviour of the bounded-sum is shown in figure 9. It consists of a normalized function in the [0,1] range. An advantage of applying this operator lies in the simplicity of the hardware realisation.

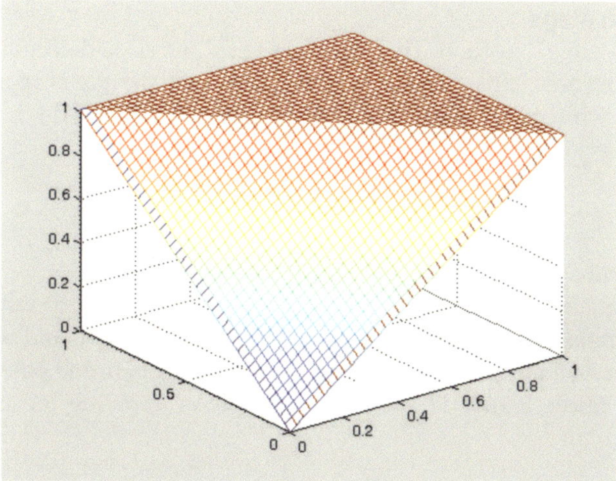

Fig. 9. Bounded sum graphical representation.

The Lukasiewicz bounded sum filter smoothens out the image and is suitable for both salt&peppers and Gaussian noise. Figure 10 shows the effect of applying this type of filter.

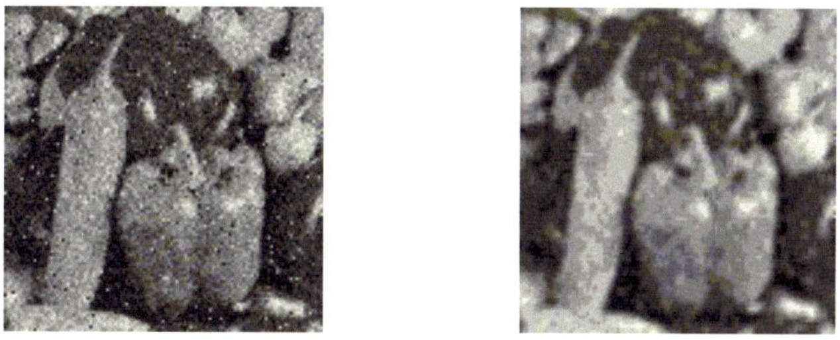

a) b)

Fig. 10. a) Input image with salt&peppers noise, b) Lukasiewicz's bounded sum filter output.

The filter has been applied using a mask based on a 3x3 array. For pixel x_{ij} the weighted mask is applied to obtain the new value y_{ij}, as is shown in the following expression:

$$y_{ij} = \min(1, \frac{1}{8} \sum_{k=-1}^{1} \sum_{l=-1}^{1} x_{i+k,j+l}) \quad (33)$$

5.2 The segmentation stage

Techniques based on thresholding an image allow pixels to de divided into two categories (black and white). This transformation is made to establish a distinction between the objects of the image and the background. This binary image is generated by comparing the values of the pixels with a threshold T. That is to say, any value lower than the threshold value is considered to be an object whereas values greater than the threshold belong to the background. In this stage there is applied the previously calculated threshold T in order to obtain the binary image.

5.3 Edge detection stage

The next step is the edge detection. The input image for the edge detection is a binary image in which pixels take value 0 (black) or 1 (white). In this case the edges appear when a change between black and white takes place between two consecutive pixels.

$$x_{edge} = \begin{cases} 0 & if\ x - y \neq 0 \\ 1 & if\ x - y = 0 \end{cases} \tag{34}$$

where x and y are consecutive pixels, and x_{edge} is the resulting pixel.
Edge generation consists of determining if each pixel has neighbours with different values. Since the image is binary every pixel is encoded with a bit (black=0 and white=1). This edge detection operation is obtained by calculating the *xor* logic operation between neighbouring pixels using a 3x3 mask. Figure 11 shows an example of applying the *xor* operator on the binary image.

a) b) c)

Fig. 11. a) Lena`s image, b) binary image, c) edge detection.

Using the 3x3 mask it is possible to refine the edge generation by detecting the orientation of the edges. To this end the four orientations shown in figure 12 can be considered. This enables calculation of the *xor* operation on 3 pixels. For a horizontal orientation we will therefore have

$$y_{i,j} = x_{i,j-1} \oplus x_{i,j} \oplus x_{i,j+1} \tag{35}$$

Whereas for an orientation of 45° it will be

$$y_{i,j} = x_{i+1,j-1} \oplus x_{i,j} \oplus x_{i-1,j+1} \tag{36}$$

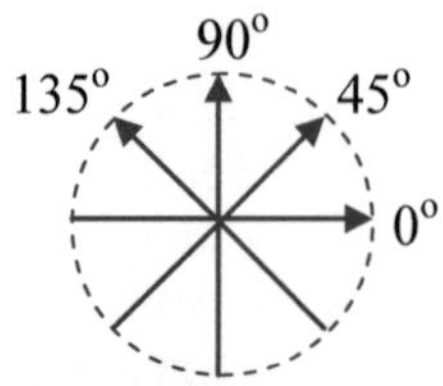

Fig. 12. Orientations for the edges generation

Figure 13 shows the results obtained when edge detection was carried out on a set of test images.

Fig. 13. Test images and edge detection results.

5.4 Hardware implementation

The edge detection circuit has been implemented on a low cost FPGA device of the Xilinx Spartan3 family. Figure 14 shows the block diagram for the system. The image is stored in a double port RAM memory. The data memory width is 32 bits. This makes it possible to read two words simultaneously.

In the first phase there is realized the calculation of the value of the threshold T. Later the edge detection circuit initiates its operation reading eight pixels from the memory in each clock cycle (2 words of 32 bits). The edge detection circuit is thus able to provide four parallel output data which are stored in the external memory. Each data corresponds to a pixel of the edge image. This image is binary, and only one bit is therefore needed to represent the value of the pixel (0 if edge or 1 if background). The new image of the edges is stored in the above mentioned memory.

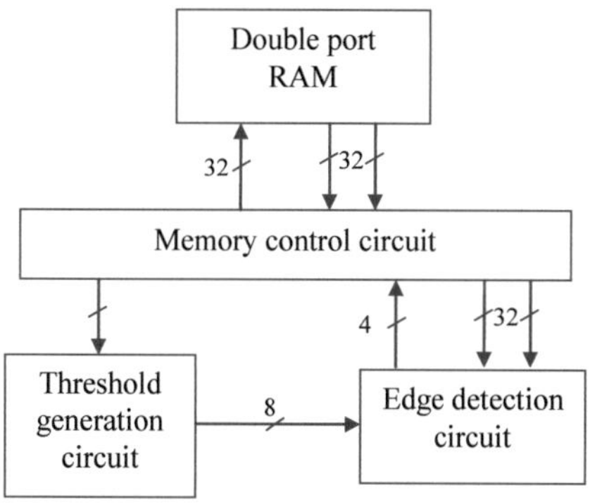

Fig. 14. Block diagram of the system.

The edge detection algorithm basically comprises three stages as shown in figure 8 (Hussein & Barriga, 2008, 2009). In the first stage the Lukasiewicz bounded-sum is performed. After

the filter stage a thresholding step is applied producing a black and white monochrome image. The value of the threshold is obtained by means of a fuzzy system that calculates the threshold related to the image.
In the third stage the edges of the image are obtained. For it the final value of each pixel is evaluated. Only those pixels that are around the target pixel are of interest (a 3x3 mask). Therefore if in the surroundings of a pixel the value is the same (all white or all black) this indicates no edge and the output value associates the above mentioned pixel with the background of the image. If a change is detected in any value of the surroundings of the pixel this indicates that the pixel at issue is in an edge, and it is therefore assigned the black value.
Figure 15 shows the system processing scheme. Pixels 1 to 9 correspond to the 3x3 mask that moves through the image. The Functional Unit (FU) processes the data stored in the mask registers.

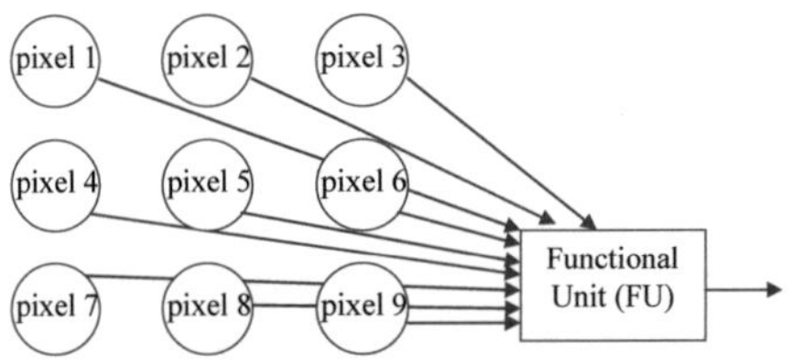

Fig. 15. System schema.

To improve image processing time the mask was spread to an 8x3 matrix as shown in figure 16a. Each Functional Unit (FU) operates on a 3x3 mask in agreement with the scheme shown in figure 15. The data are stored in the input registers (R3, R6, R9, ...) and in each clock cycle they move to their interconnected neighbours registers. In the third clock cycle the mask registers contain the data of the corresponding image pixels. The functional units then operate with the mask data and generate the outputs. In each clock cycle the mask advances one column in the image. Pixels enter on the right and shift from one stage to another outgoing on the left hand side. It is a systolic architecture with linear topology and it allows several pixels to be processed in parallel.
Figure 16b shows the input/output ports in the symbol of the system. The system receives two input data of 32 bits (*D1* and *D2*). These data come from a double port memory that stores the image. The memory access time makes it possible to read 8 pixels (each of 8 bits) in a clock cycle. The circuit also receives the previously calculated threshold (*T*) as input data. The input control signals are the following: the clock (*CLK*), the synchronous clear (*Clear*), and chip select signal (*CS*). The circuit generates as output the 4 bits (*Dout*) corresponding to the output values of the processed pixels stored in R5, R8, R11 and R14. The address of the pixel stored in R5 is also generated by means of the buses *Row* and *Column*. The output control signals *Dvalid* and *EndImage* respectively indicate the validity of the outputs and the completion of the image processing.
The functional unit operates on the 3x3 mask and generates the output value corresponding to the centered element of the mask (pixel 5 in figure 15). A block diagram of a functional unit is shown in figure 17. The circuit consists of two pipeline stages so that the data has a latency of two clock cycles. The first stage is the image filter. Then threshold *T* is applied. The edge detector, in the output stage, operates on the binary mask (black and white image).

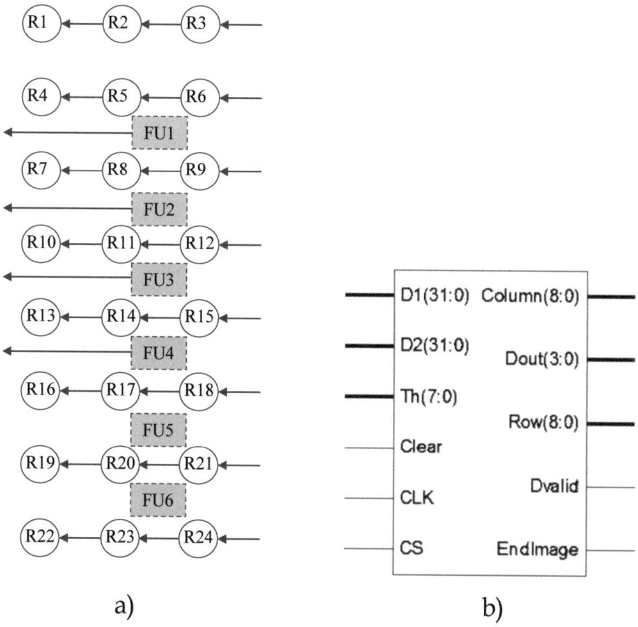

Fig. 16. a) 8x3 architecture, b) symbol of the system.

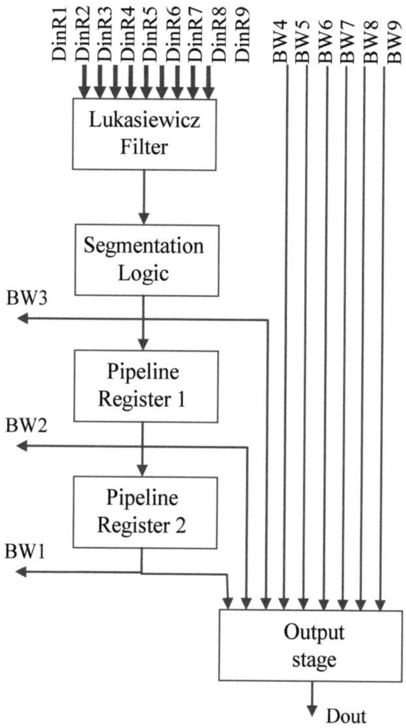

Fig. 17. Functional Unit (FU) circuit schematic.

Figure 18 shows the circuits corresponding to the different blocks of the functional unit (FU). As we can observe in figure 18a the filter based on Lukasiewicz's bounded sum receives the data stored in registers R1 to R9. These data are scaled by the factor 0,125 entailing division by 8, which signify a displacement of three places to the left. The sum of the data is compared (using the carry as control signal) with value 1. The segmentation circuit (figure 18b) compares the pixel with the threshold value. The output is a binary image (black and white) and only therefore requires one bit. Finally, the output stage receives a 3x3 binary image. It carries out the *xor* operation of the bits. If all the bits of the mask are equal the output pixel is in the background, whereas if some bit is different the output is an edge pixel.
The state machine that controls the system is shown in figure 19. This machine has four states. The mask moves through the image by columns. Whenever a row begins two clock

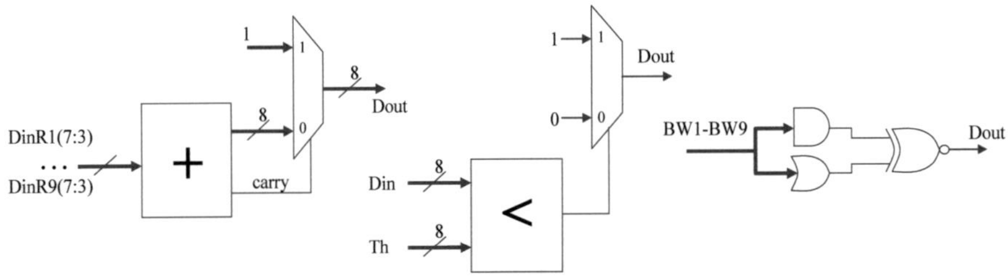

a) b) c)

Fig. 18. Lukasiewicz filter, b) Segmentation circuit, c) output stage.

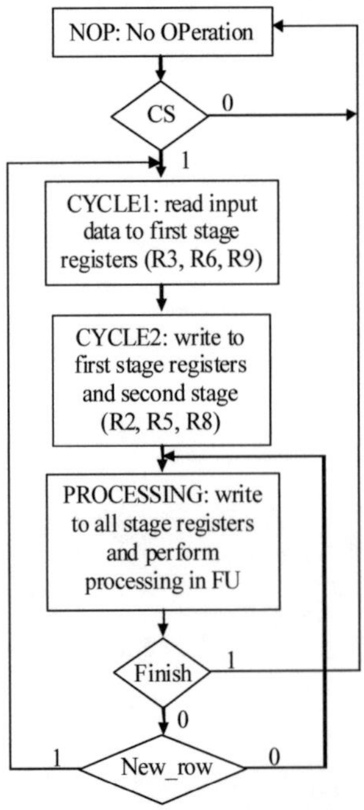

Fig. 19. FSM of the control unit of the edge detection system

cycles are needed to initialize the mask registers (CYCLE1 and CYCLE2 states). In the next cycle (PROCESSING state) the data is processed and the data of the following columns being processed in successive cycles.

Figure 20 shows the chronogram of the circuit. It can be observed that the operation of the system begins with the falling edge of signal *CS*. In the third clock cycle *Dvalid* signal take value 1, indicating a valid output. Input data are provided in each clock cycle. Once *Dvalid* has been activated the output data in the following cycles is also valid (since *Dvalid*=1).

The system has been implemented on an FPGA of the Spartan3 Xilinx family. The circuit for edge detection occupies an area of 318 slices. The resources needed for the full system (which includes the thresholding circuit and the edge detection circuit) occupies 735 slides which mean a 38% of the selected FPGA device. Regarding processing speed, the system required 7.2 msec to generate the edge image of a SVGA (800x600 pixels) using a 50 MHz clock cycle. This mean it is possible to process 132 frames per second. For a HD image (1920x1080 pixels) it is possible to process 32 frames per second.

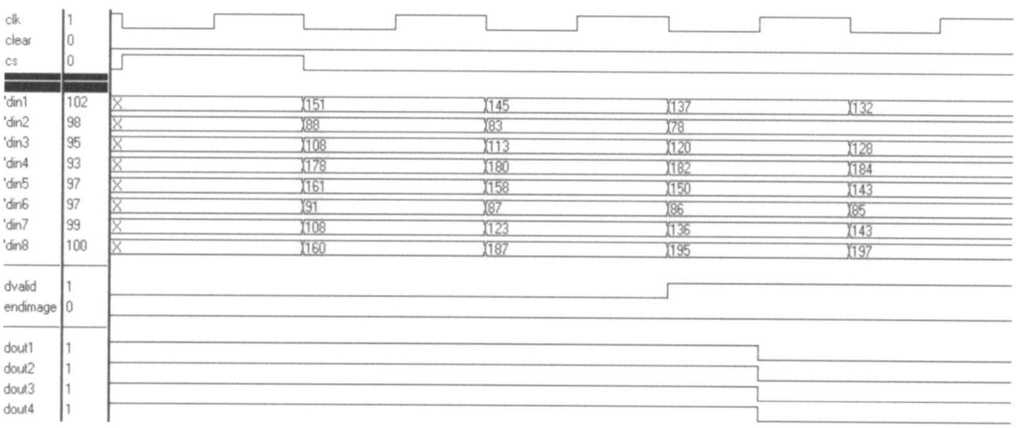

Fig. 20. Chronogram of the edge detection circuit

6. Acknowledgments

This work was supported in part by the European Community under the MOBY-DIC Project FP7-IST-248858 (www.mobydic-project.eu), by Spanish Ministerio de Ciencia y Tecnología under the Project TEC2008-04920, and by Junta de Andalucía under the Project P08-TIC-03674.

7. Conclusion

In this chapter there has been described a mechanism for binary image segmentation based on the application of fuzzy logic to calculate the threshold. The described thresholding method allows to adjust the threshold value to the characteristics of the image. The main advantage of this technique is that it allows very efficient hardware implementation in terms of cost and speed. This makes it especially suitable for applications which require real time processing. This technique has been applied for edge detection in images. The designed circuit has been implemented on an FPGA device.

8. References

Barriga, A. & Hussein, N.M. (2008). A Fuzzy Thresholding Circuit for Image Segmentation. International Conference on Knowledge-Based and Intelligent Information & Engineering Systems.

Baturone, I.; Barriga, A.; Sánchez-Solano, S.; Jiménez, C. J. & López, D. R. (2000). Microelectronic Design of Fuzzy Logic-Based Systems, CRC Press.

Canny, J. F. (1986). A computational approach to edge detection. IEEE Transaction of Pattern Analysis and Machine Intelligence, 679-698.

Cao, L.; Shi, Z.K. & Chenp E.K.W. (2002). Fast automatic multilevel thresholding method. In: Electronics Letters, 38 (16), 868-870.

Forero-Vargas, M.G. & Rojas-Camacho, O. (2000). New formulation in image thresholding using fuzzy logic. Portuguese Conference on Pattern Recognition, 117-124.

Huang, L.K. & Wang, M.J. (1995). Image thresholding by minimizing the measure of fuzziness. Pattern Recognition, 28, 41-51.

Hussein, N.M. & Barriga, A. (2008). Hardware Implementation of a Soft Computing Technique for Edge Detection. International Conference of Signal and Image Engineering (ICSIE 08), London (UK).

Hussein, N.M. & Barriga, A. (2009). High Speed Soft Computing based Circuit for Edges Detection in Images. In: Advances in Electrical Engineering and Computational Science. Gelman, L.; Balkan, N. & Ao, S.I., (Ed.). Springer.

Kaufmann, A. (1975). Introduction to the theory of fuzzy subsets. Academic Press.

Liao, P.S.; Chen, T.S. & Chung P.C. (2001). A Fast Algorithm for Multilevel Thresholding. In: Journal of Information Science and Engineering, 17, 713-727.

Marr, D. & Hildreth, E. (1980). Theory of Edge Detection. Proceedings of the Royal Society, London. 207, 187-217.

Oh, J.T. & Kim, W.H. (2006). EWFCM Algorithm and Region-Based Multi-level Thresholding, In: Lecture Notes in Artificial Intelligence, 4223, 864-873.

Otsu, N. (1978). A Threshold Selection Method from Gray Level Histogram. IEEE Trans. on Systems, Man and Cybernetics, 8, 62-66.

Prewitt, J.M.S. (1970). Object enhancement and extraction. In: Picture Processing and Psychophysics, A. Rosenfeld and B. S. Lipkin, (Ed.), Academic Press, New York, 75-149.

Roberts, L. G. (1965). Machine perception of three-dimensional solids. In: Optical and Electro-Optical Information Processing, J. T. Tippet et al., (Ed.), MIT Press, Cambridge, Massachusetts, 159-197.

Yager, R.R. (1979). On the measure of fuzziness and negation. Part 1: membership in the unit interval. Int. Journal of Genet. Syst., 5, 221-229.

Zadeh, L. A. (1965). Fuzzy sets, Information and Control, 8, 338-353.